GIANTS,
MONSTERS,
AND
DRAGONS

GIANTS, MONSTERS, AND DRAGONS

AN ENCYCLOPEDIA OF FOLKLORE, LEGEND, AND MYTH

Carol Rose

ABC-CLIO

Santa Barbara, California
Denver, Colorado
Oxford, England

Library of Congress Cataloging-in-Publication Data
Rose, Carol, 1943–
    Giants, monsters, and dragons : an encyclopedia of folklore, legend,
and myth / Carol Rose.
        p.   cm.
Includes bibliographical references.
    ISBN 0-87436-988-6 (hard : alk. paper)
    1. Monsters—Encyclopedias.   2. Giants—Encyclopedias.
3. Dragons—Encyclopedias.   I. Title.
GR825.R67   2000
398.2'03—dc21   00-009117
                                                                         CIP

05   04   03   02   01   00   10   9   8   7   6   5   4   3   2   1

ABC-CLIO, Inc.
130 Cremona Drive, P.O. Box 1911
Santa Barbara, California 93116-1911

This book is printed on acid-free paper ∞.
Manufactured in the United States of America.

For my father, Leslie Allen,
who taught me to love the world of enquiry,
and to love enquiring about the world

CONTENTS

GIANTS, MONSTERS, AND DRAGONS

AN ENCYCLOPEDIA OF FOLKLORE, LEGEND, AND MYTH

1

ENTRIES

Entries

xiv

Entries

Entries

xxii

Entries

xxiii

INTRODUCTION

Few people could fail to have been fascinated by the story of some gigantic or monstrous being at some point in their lives. Whether that being was part of some biblical text, ancient myth, or a childhood fairy tale, the frisson of fear and excitement in the human experience of an enormous, terrifying menace remains the same.

Many will also be familiar with the ancient cartographer's description of unexplored regions as "Here there be Dragons." Those *dragons* were a common feature of legends and folklore from ancient times in virtually every culture of the world. However, the word referred not only to creatures identified as *dragons* but also to those unnamed *monsters* thought to be lurking in wait for their human victims. What lay within the bounds of human knowledge and was relatively familiar could be reasonably and comfortably accommodated, no matter what its size. But that which lay outside the bounds of human knowledge was monstrous and awesome. Explanations for the chaotic, precreation nature of the world and the universe, the vast fissures, the threatening geographical features of the earth, the unexplored regions, and the disappearance or transformation of those who ventured into the unknown were accommodated in the concepts of the monstrous. Those beings that existed beyond the human realms of order were the constant threat that challenged the human world and had to be appeased, controlled, banished, or defeated.

Many of these gross destructive entities, such as *Tiamat* in Babylonian mythology, the *Leviathan* of biblical texts, or *Dalgeth* of the Navajo Native American peoples, were deemed to have preexisted the creation of the world as destructive forces and were therefore incorporated into the religious structures of those cultures. But because these beings could not have created the world and therefore had no powers, they were neither deities nor lesser spirits, even though their origins and existence had been supernatural. For the order of the world to be established, they therefore had to be destroyed or controlled through some divine power or divinely

inspired hero such as Marduk, Gilgamesh, or Nangenatzari and Tjhobadestchin.

In some early beliefs there were vast *giants* such as *Kua Fu* and *Pangu* of China, *Manzaširi* of the Kalmyk people of Mongolia, *Puntan* of Micronesia, *Purusha* of India, *sGrolma* of Tibet, and *Ymir* in the Norse mythology of Scandinavia, whose bodies either formed or provided the very earth and its vegetation.

Other primordial *giants* were incorporated into the mythological structures of the early cultures such as the *Titans* and *Gigantes* of classical Greek and Roman mythology and the *Hrimthurses* and the *Jotuns* of Norse mythology, all of whom were defeated or controlled by the emerging gods. Similarly, the *Anakim* and the *Nephilim* of Hebraic texts, which were later incorporated into the Christian biblical texts, accounted for the pre-Judaic period of the monstrous and chaotic that was destroyed in the Flood.

For ancient humans the existence of these immense beings was evidenced in the physical characteristics of the world, and their activities caused earthquakes, eclipses of the sun, rainbows, and floods; their vast skeletons were to be found in the very structure of the earth itself (these were, of course, unrecognized dinosaurs). Descriptions of these beings could be envisaged only by reference to those known already to humans. Consequently, they were often conceived of as terrifying hybrids and hideous mutations with the proportions of one being, the limbs of another, and the torso and head of others. Most frequently the *monsters* were deemed to be from the darkness of the cosmos or the bowels of the earth and were therefore envisaged as vast hybrids of human and reptilian forms.

Although the ancient religions were overtaken by others and transformed, the concept of the monstrous continued to influence beliefs and legends in all cultures. *Giants, monsters,* and *dragons* were conceived to represent the fearful elements of the regions unknown to humans. Subsequently, the *Lung* dragons of Chinese mythology controlled the waters of the earth; the eel *Jinshin Uwo* and the beetle *Jishin-Mushi* accounted for the earthquakes of Japan; and the serpents *Yurlunngur* and *Da* were responsible for the rains, floods, and rainbows of Australia and Dahomey in West Africa respectively.

In western Europe, with the advent of Christianity the *giants, monsters,* and *dragons* of mythology were assigned to the agency of the Devil, and it was only where some ancient beliefs prevailed, such as those of the Celts, that some were still regarded as benevolent. Curiously, through a semantic error following a mistranslation of the Latin, one of the most influential of the Christian saints, Saint Christopher, was not only deemed to have the head of a dog but also to have been a *giant.* However, for the most part, those beings beyond the realms of human control were, as ever, monstrous and to be combated through the Church. *Dragons* were especially the preserve of saintly combat, such as that of Saint George; the *Tarasque* and *Gargouille* of France were similarly defeated by saints.

One very early dialogue concerning the monstrous portrayed within the Church was written by Bernard of Clairvaux (1090–1153; see *Apologia* XII:29, translated by C. Rudolph, in *Things of Greater Importance, Bernard of Clairvaux, Apologia, and the Medieval Attitude Towards Art*, University of Pennsylvania, 1990), who related:

> In the cloisters, before the eyes of the brothers while they read—what is this ridiculous monstrosity doing, an amazing kind of deformed beauty and yet a beautiful deformity? What are the filthy apes doing there? The monstrous centaurs? The creatures part man part beast? You may see many bodies under one head, and conversely many heads on one body. On one side the tail of a *serpent* is seen on a quadruped, on the other side the head of a quadruped is on the body of a fish. Over there an animal has a horse for the front half and a goat for the back; here a creature which is horned in front is equine behind. In short everywhere so plentiful and astonishing a variety of contradictory forms is seen that one would rather read in the marble than in books, and spend the whole day wondering at every single one of them than in meditating on the law of God.

From the preserve of orthodox religions, *dragons* and *giants* entered the realms of legend. Many of the *monsters* of ancient mythologies, such as the *Unicorn,* which had been aggressive and frightening, were "highjacked" by the religious clerics for Christian moral teaching, as a result of which they entered legends and folklore in their transformed character as both beautiful and benevolent. Likewise, the benign and often beautiful *dragons* were similarly metamorphosed and became the villainous *monsters* of folk beliefs. Heroes and other patriots rid the lands of these threats to the community. Their tales are told in such epics as the Anglo-Saxon *Beowulf,* and, especially with the age of chivalry, the Arthurian legends, among others, featured them in abundance.

The many travelers, both secular and religious, in crossing the vast regions of the earth from Europe to the Far East and back, took with them tales of monstrous beings and races. These were recorded in such works as the *Great Imperial Encyclopedia* of China and the *Physiologus* of Alexandria, from which were derived the *bestiaries* of Christian monastic houses and other works such as the *Travels of Sir John Mandeville.* All of these incorporated many of the beings that had long before been part of the ancient religions, such as the *Sirens* of classical mythology. However, they also started to describe other *monsters* that clearly had some factual basis, such as the *Ypotamis,* which was a conglomerate or distortion of the hippopotamus. The inclusion of descriptions such as that of the *Basilisk* and *Wyvern* were made not only for moralizing religious reasons but also to give some interest for the emerging bibliophile and educated lay reader of the medieval period onward. Indeed, it was the invention of printing that gave the promulgation of such tales of *giants, monsters,* and *dragons* a new energy and audience. One such book, *On Monsters and Marvels,* by Ambroise Paré (1517–1590), was so successful that it is still being reprinted to this day. The European explorations of the "New World" of the Americas also brought an influx of monstrous descriptions from Native American sources of both creatures and races, all of which seem to have been reported by the Europeans with reference to ancient *monsters* such as the *Centaurs* or the *Cyclopes.* It would not be until some centuries later that these descriptions would be corrected.

The reconciliation between the religious texts and the everyday world in Europe became more and more difficult, and many clerics spent a considerable time pondering how the *giants* of chaos could possibly have survived the biblical Flood. *Giants* were mentioned in the Hebraic religious texts after the time of *Noah* as inhabiting the Promised Land when Moses took the Israelites out of Egypt. Some, such as Annius of Viturbo, accounted for this by considering *Noah* and his family to have been *giants,* while others invented a surviving *giant* who rode the roof of the Ark. Indeed, there was a fashion in the late medieval period for royalty and nobility to validate their line by tracing their ancestry to such *giants* or to some mythical hybrid such as *Melusine* in France. (Similarly in Burma, the royal family traced their ancestry to the *Nagini Besandi.*)

These deliberations and legends concerning *giants* also engendered the satirical literature of authors such as François Rabelais (c. 1494–1553), whose works *Pantagruel* (1532) and *Gargantua* (1534) became classic

French literature. Literature has since played a prominent role in the dissemination of tales of monstrous beings from the time of the Renaissance, with such works as *Baldus* by the Benedictine Teofilo Folengo (1491–1554), *Micromégas* by François Marie Arouet de Voltaire (1694–1778), *Pilgrim's Progress* by John Milton (1608–1674), *Gulliver's Travels* by Jonathan Swift (1667–1745), and *Through the Looking Glass and What Alice Found There* by Lewis Carroll (Charles Lutwidge Dodgson, 1832–1898).

However, not yet mentioned is another vast source of *giants, monsters,* and *dragons,* which is the folklore of every culture of the world. The folkloric versions have in part derived from the religions and mythologies of ancient times and the metamorphoses that these undertook over the millennia. However, the folkloric beings were the preserve of the common people, whose simple beliefs and folktales accounted for awesome features, terrors of the elements, and horrors endured in their lives. The floods of Australia were the result of upsetting a *Bunyip* and in Wales of annoying the *Afanc.* In northern England, whole regions were ravaged by the *Lambton Worm,* and in France it was the *Tarasque.* The terrors of child abduction were accounted for in Russia by the *Baba Yaga* and in the folk belief of Chile by the *Encerrados.* Difficult crossings of water had to be made with the propitiation of the water *Trolls* in Scandinavia and of the *Mishipizhiw, Misiganebic,* and *Miskena* in Native American beliefs. Further horrors included *Vampires* such as the *Vulkodlac* of the Slavs, the *Ivunche* of Chile, the *Skatene* of the Choctaw Native American people of the United States, the *Pontianak* of Malaysia, and the *Vis* of Melanesia. Yet another of the human horrors was the *Werewolf* and other *were-creature* variations, such as the *Azeman* of Surinam; the *Loup garou* of France, French Canada, and Haiti; and the *Macan Gadungan* of Java.

Many of these folkloric beings also became the subjects of literature, such as the classic novel *Dracula* by the Irish author Bram Stoker, and a whole genre of horror folktales emerged, especially during the nineteenth century. Other folktales, such as the *Beauty and the Beast,* which is to be found in many other cultures, had also been included in the literature of France. Collections of tales, such as the German *Grimms' Fairy Tales,* which included folkloric *giants* and *monsters,* became established traditional tales for children, although they were often moralizing in the Nursery bogie tradition. The taste for horror in association with children was further exploited in the tales of *cannibals* and *ogres* from folklore, such as *Jenny Greenteeth* and *Black Annis* of England through to the Native American *Owner-of-a-Bag* and the French *Père Fouettard.* Moralizing and satirical *monsters* were also "invented" by lumberjacks, especially in Wisconsin and Minnesota in the United States, where the *Guyascutus* and *Sliver Cat* belonged to a group of *Fearsome Critters* that explained the strange noises and frightening events derived from their fears of the wilderness.

Monsters still are very much a part of our cultures, from the early film portrayal of *King Kong* to the crypto-zoological explanations of the Native American *Sasquatch,* the Tibetan *Yet-teh,* the *Yowie* of the Native Australians, the *Mountain Man* of Japan, and the *Almas* of Siberia. Other species that have been investigated as having some possible reality are the *Seljordsorm* of Scandinavia, the *Ogopogo* and *Monster of Lake Champlain* of the United States and Canada, and the ever-elusive *Loch Ness Monster* of Scotland. The most recent *monster* to emerge, however, must be the *Great Galactic Ghoul* of the NASA space center, which apparently was the explanation proposed, somewhat satirically, for the unexplained disappearance of Russian spacecraft. And so the mythology and folklore of *monsters* have come full circle with the explanation of some monstrous entity outside the very boundaries of human knowledge proposed as responsible for the otherwise inexplicable disappearance and chaotic horrors of the unknown.

My own background, as a Yorkshire person, is deeply rooted in local culture and traditional tales. My academic research for qualifications in the fine arts, history, and psychology brought an awareness of the difficulties of finding comprehensive references for the lesser spirits and supernatural beings. Consequently, I built up an extensive library, which included many antiquarian books, to accommodate my interest. This was supplemented with information and knowledge of the folklore and cultural traditions gained whilst living and working in the Far East and, since then, in my research at the University of Kent.

When I undertook the research for my previous book, *Spirits, Fairies, Gnomes, and Goblins: An Encyclopedia of the Little People* (1996), following my recognition of the dearth of a comprehensive work of this kind for reference, I realized that there was still a large group of monstrous supernatural entities as yet unaccounted for in a similar work. These beings were not the gods, about whom numerous comprehensive works exist, nor the lesser spirits, whose powers also influence humans, but the monstrous manifestations of powerless supernatural creatures and beings in the mythology, legends, and folklore of human cultures throughout the world.

The criteria for inclusion in this book are that the supernatural being must be a creature that is not divine, but it may have been derived from, or later transformed into, a spirit or deity, such as *Hecate,* who was originally a *Titan* in the classical mythology of Greece and Rome. The being has no divine powers but may metamorphose supernaturally from one form to another, one of which must be monstrous, such as the *Werewolf* of Europe and the *Witico* of Native American legends, which transform from human to *monster*. Although these beings may metamorphose, in general they have little control over that metamorphosis. Other beings included are *giants,* not in the normal human sense of being oversized, but vast, primordial beings and enormous humanoids of supernatural strength having little intellect. Many of these beings, such as the *ogres* of European folklore and the *Buso* of Malaysian folklore, are so notoriously stupid that even children or animals may defeat them. The monstrous creatures to be included, must be from mythology, legend, folklore, or classic literature and be derived from some supernatural or semisupernatural origin. The supernatural origin would be such as that created by a deity, as in the instance of *Talos* in Greek mythology, or a semisupernatural origin, such as the *Golem* of Jewish legend and the *Wulgaru* of Native Australian legend, created by a human and activated by magical incantations. Other monstrous creatures, such as the many *dragons, serpents,* and *worms,* are of supernatural origin (rather than the real creatures such as the Komodo dragon and the earth's serpent species); and still other *monsters* may be from some distorted description of a reported "real" creature, such as those reported by the medieval and later travelers, which may have some crypto-zoological foundation. A final and very interesting group, which as far as I know has never been incorporated into a work such as this and yet deserves to have a recognizable placing, is the many symbolic beings such as the *Heraldic Beasts* and the *Town Giants,* which have a historical and folkloric derivation and still play a very important representative role in cultures today.

The material for this work has been drawn from many diverse reference areas. The sources consulted for research into these monstrous beings were encyclopedias and dictionaries of classical and nonclassical mythology for the major groups of religions from antiquity to the present day; ancient and medieval texts, such as the *Physiologus* and bestiaries, concerning the natural history of many nations; classic literature from different cultures; volumes of folktales and folklore for different periods of different cultures; sources of traditional tales and local legends; chronicles and annals of historical events; genealogical, heraldic, anthropological, and topographical surveys; and ancient fables, chapbooks, and nursery rhymes for children.

Each entry gives first the most common name by which the being is known, followed by variant spellings. If this is the same name with the addition of another letter, then this is shown as *Colbrand/e.*

Singular names that may most frequently be used in the plural are given as *Titan/s.* Within the text, and also cross-referenced, will be alternative names by which this being is known. Where names of other characters referred to in the text are known by alternatives in different cultures, these are shown together, such as in the case of the Greek and Roman names Heracles/Hercules or Dionysus/Bacchus.

The main entry gives the description of the being, the region, culture, and period during which it was known, and a description of its activities. This may also be followed by an illustrative anecdote where possible. Finally, the entry directs the reader, by way of numerical items, to the reference works listed in the Select Bibliography, from which the information was derived. This is followed by a cross-referenced list (*See also*) of similar or related beings that may give additional information for the researcher.

A further source of information for the reader is in the twenty-nine Appendixes, which list the beings by different categories, such as those associated with natural phenomena; those of hybrid animals or humanoids; and those from literature, mythology, or heraldry, including beings by different countries of origin.

For the most part, the entries are given in a mixture of grammatical tenses as follows: The descriptions are given in the present tense if the being is still thought to exist or to be described in some written version. If the being has been described as destroyed, then it may be described in the past tense. The anecdotes are given in the past tense if they are of a single occurrence; if, however, the anecdote is from a traditional tale that may have been related in dramatic form, then the original present tense may be retained.

The information has been derived from many different languages of many different periods. Where possible, the names have been rendered as consistently as possible into an acceptable English transcription. Inevitably, since spelling has only very recently been standardized for English, there are many regional and national variants, and some decisions have had to be made as to the most acceptable. One such decision involved the retention of the Wade-Giles format of the Chinese rather than the more modern Pinyin spellings. This decision was based on the fact that most of the names were derived from very ancient source materials transcribed in the Wade-Giles spelling, and very few were given in the modern format.

The very nature of these myths, legends, and folkloric tales has meant that they were derived originally from oral accounts from generation to generation prior to the eventual written version. The names and versions have, over the millennia, become distorted and embellished to such an extent that some may have been derived from others but now have a different context, such as the *Simargl* and *Simurgh* of Eastern Europe and Persia, respectively, or the *Tarasque* and *Tarasca* of France and Spain. Where this has happened, each is given under a separate entry but cross-referenced to the other version. Even with the eventual version being written down, the regional dialect may have given rise to a completely different spelling as the phonetic transcription was made. A further problem was the misspellings through subsequent handwritten copies of early manuscripts made by less well educated persons. As with the transcription of *Saint Christopher's* tale, these account for other interpretations, in different countries and religious sects, of the same being.

With the invention of printing, many versions were made more widely available, but spelling was still not standard until well into the twentieth century. Thus when some stories were printed from the original in one country and transcribed into the language and culture of another, as with *Strewwelpeter* and *der Kinderfresser*, or the *Yeteh* and the *Abominable Snowman*, the characters were again open to reinterpretation. Where this has happened, each has been given a separate entry, cross-referenced to the other. Sometimes, however, a few entries had little by way of reference material at all, but the fact that they have belonged to some culture must also be recorded and find a place within this work. Inevitably, choices have had to be made, and this has been done as sensitively as possible so that the reader may have as full a version of each entry.

Names of countries, regions, and cultures have been given for the period during which the being was popular; consequently these may not have modern borders. Where this occurs, the nearest equivalent modern name is frequently given, such as "Persia (now Iran)." However, the retention of the original name is to give the reader a greater grasp of the period context for the entry. In some cases this is quite clearly indicated by reference to some primary text such as the *Physiologus*, but this does not necessarily indicate the original source of the information, which can never really be known for mythological, legendary, or folkloric material (other than literary-derived beings, such as the *Ents* of J. R. R. Tolkien's work).

In creating this work I have been fascinated by the complexities, beauty, majesty, and grotesque terror of the *monsters* that human beings have feared to be lurking on the boundaries of their world. The awe-inspiring, gigantic, primeval beings and *serpents*, those *monsters* responsible for chaos and cosmic phenomena, to the horrors to be encountered by the traveler, the religious cleric, or the soldier, graphically related to the "home audience," who revered the storyteller for his bravery in enduring or overcoming those ordeals. Some terrors have been used as moralizing exemplars for sinful adults, while others were used to control adventurous and wayward children. Some *dragons* and *serpents* were protectors and guardians, while others were the symbols of evil and greed or represented the dangers of the unexplored wildernesses of both land and sea. Some *monsters* guarded the treasures that humans sought, while others brought death and destruction. From the earliest to the most recent, from the most remote to the most familiar, all cultures have expressed a fascination with the monstrous. It is in the exploration of these *giants, monsters,* and *dragons* that we may explore the various fears and difficulties with which humans have been confronted over the millennia, and understand how they have been accommodated or overcome, often with a wry sense of humor, in every culture of our world.

GIANTS, MONSTERS, AND DRAGONS

A

A BAO A QU

This creature is described in an erudite work on Malay witchcraft by Iturvuru (1937). It commences as an invisible, almost benign entity that lies menacingly yet impotently at the base of a pilgrim tower where it has existed for centuries. It is described as having numerous tentacles and a skin that feels like a peach. It is a curious creature that at the approach of a pilgrim to the bottom step of the tower is sensitized and draws life as it moves alongside the unwary pilgrim step by step. As the pilgrim climbs, with each level gained the A Bao A Qu becomes more and more visible, changing colors like a chameleon until it emits an iridescent bluish glow close behind the unsuspecting visitor. However, this creature can become absolutely complete only when a perfect victim is followed, and since all who have attempted to climb the tower so far have been imperfect pilgrims seeking the way, they inevitably return without accomplishing their fulfillment. As the pilgrim turns to descend, the A Bao A Qu emits a groan and fades with each level of descent to the bottom, where it must await the next pilgrim to attempt the tower.
References 18

AAPEP, APEP, APOP, APOPHIS, APOPIS

These are variations on the name of the "moon-serpent" in ancient Egyptian mythology that emerged from the great void at the beginning of the world, emitting a terrifying roar from the great abyss. Aapep is depicted in various ways in Egyptian art, each hideous and terrifying: depicted, for example, as a snake with a human head, as a contorted crocodile, or in the more familiar form as the vast cosmic reptile. Living deep in the Nile and symbolizing all the dark features of existence such as storms, night, and death, he became a co-conspirator of Set, the god of evil. The body of this vast serpent, instead of being coiled, undulated in pleats like a concertina (like the motion of a caterpillar), so it could shoot out and engulf its prey. The hapless souls of mortals on their journey between this life and the next were its usual victims. If they were engulfed by Aapep, their fate was nonexistence, unless they were pitied and rescued by one of the gods.

The gods themselves were not safe from the predations of this cosmic serpent. Each day Aapep lay in wait for the sun-god, Ra, to make his celestial journey, gaping wide the monstrous jaws to engulf the sun-disc and deprive the world of light at the Western Mountains. But, protected by the guardian serpent Mehen, Ra always escaped, reemerging in his sun-ship in the east to bring light to the world again. Sometimes Aapep was almost successful and an eclipse would occur, but Aapep was always forced to regurgitate the celestial boat containing Ra. A hymn to Osiris tells the story of how eventually the monster was bound by the god Horus and chopped to pieces by the god Osiris. Aapep was probably derived from the Babylonians' myths of Belmarduk and Tiamat.
References 7, 24, 38, 49, 89, 132, 138, 159, 165, 168
See also Mehen, Nagas, Rahu, Tiamat

AAVAK

The alternative spelling of the name Arvak, one of the giant horses that pulled the chariot of the sun-maiden Sol (or Sunna) in Norse mythology. The name means "Early Waker" and thus symbolizes the dawn.
References 20, 24, 89
See also Alsvid, Horses of the Sun

ABAC

This is an alternative name for the monstrous Addanc in the legends of Wales.
References 64, 159
See also Addanc, Afanc

ABADA

This is the name of a type of unicorn to be found in the legends of the peoples of the Congo region of Africa.
See also unicorn

ABAIA

This is a gigantic eel that features prominently in the mythology of Melanesia. Abaia exists in a vast lake and provides protection for its fish against predators. Should any humans be so foolish as to fish there, he causes a deluge that engulfs them and their people.
References 7, 89
See also Jinshin Uwo

ABATH

This is the name of a beast said by European travelers of the sixteenth century to live in the forests of the Malay Peninsula. It was also said to be the female form of the unicorn, having a single horn in the middle of its head. This horn was highly prized both as an aphrodisiac and as an antidote for poisons. The trade in unicorn horns with the Arabic peoples of the period was a royal monopoly. It is believed that this fabulous account actually describes the present-day Malaysian rhinoceros.
References 7, 89
See also Alicorn, Amduscias, Ass (Three-Legged), Biasd Na Srognig, Chio-Tuan, Karkadan, Ki-Lin, Kirin, Koresck, Licorn, Mi'raj (Al), Onyx Monoceros, Scythian Ass, unicorn

ABERE

This is the name of an evil being in the folk beliefs and legends of Melanesia. She is a female cannibal taking the shape of a "wild" woman, with young female attendants. Abere entices men to come willingly to her in the waters of a lake or swamp. Then she commands rushes and reeds to grow around and conceal her. Hidden by the reeds, she entraps the gullible men who search for her, then murders and devours them.
References 38, 159
See also cannibal

ABGAL

This is the name of a group of water creatures in the mythology of the ancient Sumerians in lower Mesopotamia. The seven spirits in the group are also known as Apkallu or Amphitrites. Portrayed as part man and part fish (like mermen), the Abgal are protective guardians of the realm. They derive from the earlier Apsu or Abzu in the entourage of Enki, the god of wisdom. Their role was that of tutor to the nation, teaching the sciences and arts while fasting during the day, then returning to the waters at nightfall.
References 63, 125
See also merman

ABHAC

This is an alternative name for the monstrous Addanc in the legends of Wales.

Abgal, a water creature in the mythology of the ancient Sumerians (Rose Photo Archive, UK)

References 64, 159
See also Addanc, Afanc

ABOMINABLE SNOWMAN

This is the popular European name for the Yeti, or Abominable Snowman, of the Himalayan mountain region of Tibet and Nepal. The concept of this elusive giant hairy humanoid existing in the mountains was first made popular in Europe by members of Shipton's Everest expedition of 1951; the later Hillary-Tensing conquest party also reported evidence. The name Abominable Snowman implies a humanoid shape, and, indeed, enormous tracks resembling those of a giant anthropoid have been photographed by Europeans climbing in the region. While others are skeptical about the authenticity of such evidence, there exists a definite mythology of the indigenous people for the more bearlike Yeti.
References 20, 61, 78, 94
See also Bigfoot, Sasquatch, Yeti

ACAMAS

This is the name of one of the Cyclopes in the classical mythology of Greece and Rome.
References 24, 94, 168, 177, 181
See also Cyclops

ACEPHALOS (sing.), ACEPHALI (pl.), ACEPHALITES (pl.)

These are variations on the name of a legendary, supernatural race of beings in the mythology of ancient Greece. Also known as Acephali, Akephale, or Aképhalos, they were said to inhabit Libya. The Acephalos is described in ancient Egyptian, Greek, and Roman mythology, by Herodotus and Josephus, as well as in medieval religion and folklore. According to these accounts, it has the shape of a headless human being, with eyes and a huge gaping mouth in its chest, causing terror and panic in those before whom it appears.

In the folklore of modern Greece there is a spirit named Phonos (the Greek word for "death") with the same physical description and ability to incite terror. This spirit is probably descended from the ancient monstrous humans.

References 20, 24, 62, 159
See also Coluinn Gun Cheann, Hsing-T'ien

ACHIYALABOPA

This is the fabled celestial bird-monster of the Pueblo Native American people. It is described as having feathers that resemble knives.

References 7

ACHLIS

This extraordinary European beast, resembling an elk, was described in *Natural History* by the Roman writer Pliny the Elder during the first century A.D. Though a grazing herbivore, the animal was hampered by several features of its anatomy, including an upper lip so extensive that the animal had to graze by moving backward in order to prevent the lip from folding across its mouth. It was also inconvenienced by the lack of joints in its hind legs, and was obliged to rest at night by leaning against a tree for support. This was the means by which hunters could trap the fleet-footed beast: by sawing partly through a favored tree, they were able to ensure that when the Achlis came to rest there, both the animal and the tree would fall to the ground. Unable to rise because of its stiff back legs, the Achlis could then be captured at the hunters' leisure.

References 7, 20

ACIPENSER

The name of a monstrous fish fabled by European travelers of the fifteenth and sixteenth centuries to exist in the northern seas of Europe. The Acipenser was said to be unable to swim as other fish do because its scales were reversed, the open end toward its head instead of toward its tail. However, this may have been a highly exaggerated description of the sturgeon from which caviar is derived.

References 7
See also Goofang

ACMONIDES

This is the name of one of the Cyclopes of classical Greek mythology. He is known also by the names Pyracmon and Arges according to whichever poet is describing his role in the myth.

References 168, 177
See also Cyclops

ACTAEON

This is the name of a horse in the classical mythology of Greece. Actaeon, whose name means "Effulgence," is one of the team of Horses of the Sun that pulled the golden chariot that Hephaestus had made for the sun-god Helios. Like the other horses, Actaeon is described as the purest white with flaring, fire-breathing nostrils. Each morning the nymphs of time, the Horae, harnessed Actaeon and the eight other Horses of the Sun to the chariot for their journey across the sky. When the journey was finished at dusk, they browsed on magical herbs in the Islands of the Blessed, until harnessed again on the next day.

References 89, 138
See also Horses of the Sun

ACTHON

The name of one of the great winged Horses of the Sun in classical Greek and Roman mythology. Ovid (43 B.C.–A.D. 17) describes how Acthon along with Eous, Phlegon, and Pyrois were harnessed to the sun's chariot to be driven daily across the heavens.

References 89, 132
See also Horses of the Sun

ACTORIDÆ, ACTORIONE

These are variations on the collective name of monstrous twins in the classical mythology of Greece and Rome. The Actoridæ, also known as the Molionids, were said to be the sons of Molione by her husband, Actor.

References 177
See also Molionids

ADAR LLWCH GWIN

This is the name of monstrous mythical birds, which resembled the Griffin, in the Arthurian legends of Wales. The name is derived from the Welsh *llwch*, meaning "dust" or "powder," and *gwin*, meaning "wine." These birds, which could understand human speech, were a gift to Drudwas ap Tryffin from his fairy wife. They were commanded to perform tasks for their master in the form of magical combat or protection. During one conflict with King Arthur and his knights, Drudwas, expecting the king to lead into the fray, instructed his birds to kill the first knight to enter the field of battle. Arriving at the appointed place, Drudwas found that the other army had been delayed; but as the first on the field, he was torn to death by his obedient birds.

References 128
See also Griffin

ADARO

This is a being in the myths and legends of the Solomon Islands. The Adaro is described as a "fish-

man" or type of merman, but unlike his European counterpart, this creature has legs and feet from which tail fins extend. On his head he has another huge fin like that of a shark, fish gills behind humanoid ears, and a long pointed extension where his nose might have been, resembling that of the narwhal. Along with his army of poisonous flying fish, the Adaro can travel through the air on rainbows after storms at sea. His troops of flying fish are the weapons with which he kills any humans in his watery domain.
References 113
See also merman, Triton

ADDANC, ADANC
This is the name of a water monster in the folklore of Wales in the British Isles. It was also called Abac, Afanc, or Avanc, depending on the area in which it was being described. It was said to inhabit, at one point of the tales' development, Lake Llyon Llion, where it caused terrible flooding by thrashing water over the banks and onto the surrounding countryside. Everyone in the region lived in terror of its activities until it was eventually dragged by the oxen of Hugh Gadarn from its abode and disposed of, some say, by Peredur.
References 64, 159
See also Afanc

ADLET
This is the name of a group of blood-drinking monsters in the mythology and folklore of the Inuit of the Labrador and west Hudson Bay coasts, also known by the people of Greenland and Baffin Island as the Erqigdlit. These monsters were the children of an Inuit woman who married a red dog. Five of her ten children were dogs that were set adrift in a boat to cross the seas to Europe, where they were responsible for engendering the European races. The other five monstrous children engendered worse monsters, the Adlet whose victims were the Inuit.
References 24, 77
See also Erqigdlit, monster

ÆGÆON, AEGAEON
In classical Greek and Roman mythology, these are variations on the name of one of the Hundred-Handed Giants, the sons of Uranus and Gaia. Ægæon was also referred to as Egeon and Briareus, and his brothers were called Cottys (or Cottus) and Gyges (or Gyes). These enormous beings had multiple limbs but, like most traditional giants, were not blessed with intelligence.

When the wars with the Titans were ended with their defeat by the new gods, Zeus/Jupiter charged the Hundred-Handed Giants with the responsibility of guarding the Titans in Tartarus. However, the Hundred-Handed Giants in turn rebelled against the Olympians. In the *Aeneid,* Virgil tells how the conquered Ægæon was bound to a huge rock face in the Aegean Sea by the triumphant Poseidon/Neptune.
References 20, 168, 177
See also Briareus, Cottus, Gaia, Gyges, Hundred-Handed Giants, Titan, Uranus

AEGIR
In Norse mythology this is the name of a giant of the sea who was the husband of Ran. During a feast for the Aesir, he lit up the hall of the gods by filling it with the glowing light from the gold he had brought there. He was on friendly terms with the Norse gods, who welcomed him to their feasts and visited his golden palace under the sea.
References 125, 138, 165
See also giant

AELLO, AËLLO, AELLOPUS
The name of one of the Harpies of classical Greek and Roman mythology. They were the hideous birdlike female tormentors of the blinded Phineus. Whatever was prepared for him to eat they either desecrated with their vile stench and droppings or devoured before he could feel his way to the food.
References 89, 138, 159
See also Harpy

ÆNOTHERUS
In French medieval folklore, this is the name of the bodyguard of the Emperor Charlemagne. So vast was his size and strength that he was said to be capable of destroying whole armies as simply as if mowing grass.
References 63
See also Balan, Charlemagne, Cheval Bayard, Fierabras

AETERNAE, ÆTERNÆ
These are variations on the collective name of beasts reported to have inhabited the northern plains of India during the fourth century B.C. They were described as having saw-edged, bonelike protrusions from their foreheads with which they attacked their foes. The Aeternae were also said to have attacked and destroyed several of the soldiers of Alexander the Great's army who were foolish enough to provoke the Æternæ into combat.
References 7

ÆTHON, AETHON
These are variations on the name of a horse in the classical mythology of Greece and Rome. Æthon, which means "to Burn" or "Fiery," is one of the team of Horses of the Sun that pulled the golden chariot that Hephaestus had made for the sun-god Helios. Like the other horses, Æthon is described as the

The Aeternae were described as having saw-edged, bonelike protrusions from their foreheads with which they attacked their foes. (Rose Photo Archive, UK)

purest white with flaring, fire-breathing nostrils. Each morning the nymphs of time, the Horae, harnessed Æthon, along with the other Horses of the Sun, to the chariot for their journey across the sky. When the journey was finished at dusk, they browsed on magical herbs in the Islands of the Blessed, until they were harnessed for the next day.
References 138, 177
See also Horses of the Sun

ÆTOLIAN BOAR
This huge beast is also known as the Calydonian Boar in classical Greek mythology. It was sent by the goddess Artemis to ravage the Greek region of Ætolia in retribution for the lack of sacrifice from Oerieus, whose son, Meleager, was charged with the destruction of this monstrous boar. He called on all of the most famous heroes of Greece, and the brutal hunt, during which the boar savaged many heroes to death, was finally brought to a conclusion when Atalanta succeeded in shooting the beast with an arrow. Meleager finished it off with his spear and promptly gave the creature to the plucky heroine. However, division of the prized carcass was disputed by the other hunters, especially the uncles of Meleager, and a battle ensued. In the escalation of

hostilities that followed, Meleager was prophesied to lose his life.
References 138
See also Battleswine, Beigad, Boar of Beann-Gulbain, Buata, Cafre/Kafre, Calydonian Boar, Erymanthean Boar, Hildesuin, Pugot/Pugut, Sachrimnir, Twrch Trwyth, Ysgithyrwyn

AFANC

This is the name of an evil Hippocamps or water beast in the folklore of Wales. It may be known in other localities by the name Abac, Abhac, Addanc, or Avanc. In Ireland it is called Gorborchinu. Afanc is related to the Horseheads of Native American mythology, the Kelpies of Scotland, and the Nixies of Scandinavia. Variously described as a supernatural crocodile, a giant beaver, a dwarf, or a water demon, Afanc was supposed to have lurked and awaited victims from the depths of river pools near Brynberian Bridge, in Llyn yr Afanc above Bettws-y-Coed, in Llyn Barfog ("Bearded Lake"), or in Llyn Llion. This huge water monster not only seized anyone foolish enough to fall into the water there but also caused terrible flash floods when it thrashed about in the waters that overflowed and swamped the surrounding region. According to legend, such floods were the equivalent of Noah's Great Flood, drowning all the inhabitants of Britain except one man and one woman: Dwyfan and Dwyfach, the ancestors of the present British people.

The monstrous Afanc was such a terror that it had to be destroyed. Two folktales describe this event. (1) The Afanc was caught in chains and dragged from the pool by Hugh Gadarn's great oxen and, once on dry ground, was powerless. (2) The Afanc was enthralled by the caresses of a brave young beauty from the village who let him sleep on her knee. During his enchanted slumbers, men from the village bound Afanc with chains attached to oxen. Roused by this harsh captivity Afanc thrashed about furiously, wrenching the body of the young virgin in his attempt to break free and regain the safety of his pool. Then Afanc was dragged to Llyn Cwm Ffynnon, where he is said to be lurking to this day. (Another version, under the name of Adanc, tells how he was killed by Peredur.) Among other heroes said to have done battle with and killed Afanc are King Arthur and one of his knights of the Round Table, Sir Perceval.
References 7, 21, 54, 64, 89, 128, 159, 182
See also Addanc, Hippocamp, Horse-heads, Kelpy, Nixies, unicorn

AFREET

This is an alternative spelling of the name Afrit, referring to the grotesque cloven-hooved Djinn in Arabic and Islamic legends.
References 20, 38, 64, 74, 124, 159, 160
See also Afrit, Djin

AFRIT/E

The Afrit is not one single being but a classification of the five types of the powerful Jinns of Muslim and Arabic mythology and folklore. They also go by the names of Afreet, Afrite, Efreet, Efrit, Ifreet, and Ifrit in various Arabic regions. The Afrit are described as being enormous both in height and girth and, often, as having horns on the head and hooves instead of feet. The tales associated with these beings tell of their extremely malicious behavior toward any human victim, such that the mere mention of their name inspires unspeakable terror. Ordinarily they inhabit desert wastelands, but the people of Kenya on the east coast of Africa believe that they lurk in the muddy depths of pools and rivers. There, like the English Nursery bogie Jenny Greenteeth, they seize unattended children by the legs and drag them to their deaths. According to Arabic legend, King Solomon compelled an Afreet to become his servant. Lord Byron, ever interested in the romantic legends of the Middle East, wrote an Afrit into his work "The Giaour."
References 20, 38, 63, 64, 74, 124, 145, 159, 160
See also Djin, Jenny Greenteeth, Nursery bogies

AGATHOS DAIMON, AGATHODEMON

These are variations on the name of a supernatural guardian of the individual or abode in the mythology of ancient Greece and Rome. The Agathos Daimon was described as a hovering winged serpent. In the household that it protected, an offering of wine would frequently be reserved for this protective being. It was later regarded in most accounts as a spirit.
References 62, 74, 125, 145
See also Aitvaras

AGLAOPHEME

This is the name of one of the Sirens of classical Greek and Roman mythology.
References 177
See also Siren

AGOG-MAGOG

This is the name of a monster in the legend and folklore of Armenia. The tale is of the legendary Armenian hero Badikan, who vanquishes the monster for the people of the region. There is a remarkable resemblance between the name Agog-Magog and those of the biblical Gog and Magog (Revelations 20:8), as well as those of Brut and Gogmagog in the legends of Britain. One possibility is that the development of these legends occurred with the early medieval travelers and pilgrims to the Holy Land who promulgated the name of the original from the Holy Land on their return journeys.
References 55
See also Gog and Magog, monster

Triton and a Siren. Aglaopheme was one of the Sirens of classical Greek and Roman mythology. (On Monsters and Marvels by Ambroise Paré, trans. by Janus L. Pallister, University of Chicago Press, 1982)

AGRIPPA, TALL AGRIPPA, GREAT AGRIPPA

These are variations on the name of a character from the popular Victorian children's book *The English Struwwelpeter, or Pretty Stories and Funny Pictures* by Dr. Heinrich Hoffmann, published in Britain in 1847. In the story of the *Inky Boys*, which tells of three children, Ned (Edward), William, and Arthur, who were racially harassing an innocent neighbor, Agrippa, "so tall he almost touched the sky," is depicted as a gigantic elderly sage in monk's habit and fez, standing in front of an outrageously huge ink-stand and quill. This giant had observed the boys' behavior and warned them that something might happen to them if they persist. And so it did.

> Then great Agrippa foams with rage—
> Look at him on this very page!
> He seizes Arthur, seizes Ned,

> Takes William by his little head;
> And they may scream and kick and call,
> Into the ink he dips them all.

The perpetrators are indeed punished by Tall Agrippa for their victimization of an innocent neighbor.

Although these stories were written as edifying moral tales for youngsters, the instruments of justice, such as Tall Agrippa and the Red-Legged Scissor-Man, quickly became known in the Victorian children's repertoire as monsters of the Nursery bogie type.

References 97, 181

See also Nursery bogies, Red-Legged Scissor-Man

AGRIUS

This is the name of a giant in the classical mythology of Greece and Rome. Agrius is one of the Gigantes and, like his brothers, was said to have been engendered from the blood that fell on the earth from the castrated Uranus. These giants were born fully mature and clad in full battle armor. They waged war on the Olympian gods after the defeat of the Titans and were themselves defeated. In that battle, Agrius, whose name means "Untamable," was vanquished in the final attack.

References 24, 132, 168, 177
See also Aloadae, Cyclops, giant, Gigantes

AGUNUA

This is the alternative name for Hatuibwari, the cosmic serpent in the traditions and beliefs of the people of San Cristoval Island in Melanesia.

References 38, 125
See also Hatuibwari, serpent

AHI

This is the name of the cosmic serpent or dragon in the Vedic mythology of India. Ahi is an alternative name for Vritra, but it may also be used to indicate a completely separate identity. This monster is described as so vast that it ingested all the waters of the earth and then coiled itself around and on top of the mountains. The god Indra attacked and slew the monster with his thunderbolts, thereby releasing all the waters that had been withheld from the parched earth. The monster is therefore often interpreted as the personification either of drought or of winter, when the snows of the mountains hold the waters that melt with the coming of spring.

References 24
See also Aapep, dragon, monster, serpent

AHUIZOTL

This is a cannibal creature from the folklore and legends of Mexico. Although the name Ahuizotl means "Water Opossum," its appearance does not resemble this creature. It is described as looking somewhat like a dog in size and shape but with the paws of a monkey and a human hand at the extremity of its tail. This prehensile tail and hand were the means by which it seized its victims from the water's edge (where they had been lured by its cries) and dragged them down into the murky waters of its abode. Fishermen were often victims of the Ahuizotl. Its ruse was to make the small fish and frogs of the waters leap about so as to attract the attention of fishermen hoping to catch a large fish. Once they had taken their flimsy boat to the spot, it was a simple matter for the Ahuizotl to reach its handed-tail over the side of the boat and secure its next meal. Relatives always knew what had befallen their loved ones as the corpses would float to the surface exactly three days later with the eyes, teeth, and nails removed.

These were the delicacies sought by the Ahuizotl. Since this creature was believed to be the servant of Tlalocs (the rain-gods), only the priest could remove the body for burial ceremonies, as it was then considered to be a special sacrifice to the gods. Nobody ever actually looked for the creature, however, as the sight of it was an omen of imminent death.

References 7, 24, 89
See also cannibal

ÄI

This is a name used in southern Estonia for the Aiatar, a class of dragons or serpents in the folklore of Finland.

References 119, 159
See also Aiatar, Aitvaras, dragon, serpent

AI TOJON

This is the name of a creature in the folklore of the Yakut peoples of Siberia. Ai Tojon is described as a giant two-headed bird resembling an eagle. His abode is the very pinnacle of the great world tree from which he sheds the light required for the human race.

References 125

AIATAR

This semisupernatural being is known as the "Devil of the Woods" in Finnish folklore. It may also be called Ajatar or Ajattara in different regions of Finland. Manifesting in the shape of a serpent or dragon, Aiatar is described as an evil female that inhabits the forest and lonely places of the Tundra regions. It is said to suckle snakes, and any human who encounters or sees one of these creatures in the forest may become seriously ill. It is comparable with the Äi, Äijo, or Äijätär of southern Estonia.

References 119, 159
See also Aitvaras, dragon, serpent

AICHA KANDIDA

This is the name of a malicious cannibal water djinn in the folklore of Morocco. When luring her human victims she is described as a beautiful young woman, but this enchantment conceals her gigantic size and hideous nature. A predatory being, she lurks on the banks of the River Sebu, around the Aquedal at Marrakech, and sometimes in the Sultan's Palace grounds, awaiting any lone man foolish enough to be taken in by her. Once he has approached her there is no escape, for soon she will reveal her true shape and consume him under the water. She hates humans and if her quarry cannot reach another human or inhabited dwelling in time, he is doomed. Sometimes she may be magnanimous and release back into his world a man who gratifies her willingly, laden with

rich gifts. Her husband is the Afrit known as Hamou Ukaiou.
References 122, 159
See also Afrit, Djin, Hamou Ukaiou

AIDA WEDO
This is the alternative name for Ayida, who is the consort of the Rainbow Snake known as Damballah.
References 24, 132
See also Ayida, Rainbow Serpent, serpent

AIDO HWEDO, DAN AYIDO HWEDO
These are variations on the name of the great Rainbow Serpent or Rainbow Snake in the mythology and folklore of the peoples of Dahomey in West Africa. A vast creature, Aido Hwedo assisted the creation of the universe and the earth by transporting the god Mawu through the cosmos. It ingested great quantities of iron to sustain its strength, but occasionally, when there was insufficient supply, it would greedily devour its own enormous tail. Wherever Aido Hwedo had rested for the night it would deposit vast piles of excrement, which became the mountains of the earth. But soon the god Mawu realized that the earth was becoming too heavy and would fall through the cosmos unless its great weight were supported, so he decreed that Aido Hwedo should support the earth on its vast coiled body. The heat generated by this effort caused Aido Hwedo such agony that the waters of the oceans were created to cool its body. However, this remedy is not always successful, and Aido Hwedo's writhing with discomfort shakes the earth violently, causing humans to experience an earthquake. As Aido Hwedo is no longer above the earth, the amount of iron to be consumed under the sea is diminishing. When the iron is gone the Rainbow Serpent will have only its own tail to consume, and when that is gone, the whole earth, no longer supported on the serpent's coils, will fall completely into the oceans.
References 7, 24
See also Aapep, Rainbow Serpent, serpent

AIGAMUCHAS
This is an alternative name for the Aigamuxa, man-eating monsters in the mythology of the Khoisin people of South Africa.
References 7, 24, 47, 78, 132
See also Aigamuxa

AIGAMUXA (pl.), AIGMUXAB (sing.), AIGAMUCHAS (pl.)
In the mythology of the Khoisin people of South Africa, the Aigamuxa are man-eating monsters that inhabit the dunes of the Kalahari Desert. These curious humanoids are described as having their eyes placed either in the instep or on the heels of their feet, so that they are obliged to stop and lift a foot in order to see where they are going. Although they otherwise look relatively like humans, their huge bodies and heads make them fearsome adversaries, mainly because of their enormous fanglike teeth. Any human overtaken and seized by one of these monsters would be torn to bits and devoured. However, like many of the ogres of North European legends, the Aigamuxa were frequently fooled by their quarry, who then escaped. There is an amusing tale of the Trickster Jackal being hunted by the Aigamuxa. It tells how Jackal, when almost overtaken, scattered tobacco dust on the ground where the Aigamuxa would run, irritating their eyes so much that they could neither run nor see. The clever Jackal then escaped, laughing at their stupidity.
References 7, 24, 47, 78, 132, 159
See also monster, ogre

ÄIJÄTÄR
This is a name used in southern Estonia for the Aiatar, a class of dragons or serpents in the folklore of Finland.
References 119, 159
See also Aiatar, Aitvaras, dragon, serpent

ÄIJO
This is a name used in southern Estonia for the Aiatar, a class of dragons or serpents in the folklore of Finland.
References 119, 159
See also Aiatar, Aitvaras, dragon, serpent

AILLÉN TRECHENN, TRECHEND
This is the name of a monster in the folklore and mythology of Ireland. In Irish Gaelic, Aillén Trechenn means "Triple-Headed," for indeed this creature had three heads extending from its enormous body. Aillén Trechenn variously inhabited (according to the informant) either a cave in the mountainside or an ancient burial mound at Cruachain in County Roscommon. This creature loathed humans, especially the warriors of Emain Macha and the ancient stronghold of Tara. It was during a particularly malicious episode, on the eve of the major Celtic festival of Samain (now celebrated as Halloween), that Aillén Trechenn attacked the community, bent on devastating all the people of Ireland. The creature was finally destroyed by Amaigin.
References 128
See also monster

AIRAVANA
This is an alternative name for Airāvata, the snow-white elephant in the Vedic mythology of India.

References 112, 132
See also Airāvata

AIRĀVATA, AIRAVANA

These are variations on the name of one of the Lokapala Elephants in the Hindu mythology of India. The name is derived from the word *iravat*, meaning "child of the water." Airāvata is described as a vast cosmic creature. Pure white in color, it is one of the sixteen elephants supporting the earth on their backs. Airāvata stands as the guardian of the east quadrant of the world, with the god Indra on his back. There are two traditions that give both Airāvata's origins and description:

1. In the Hindu mythology given in the *Mātangalīlā*, the god Brahma took a cosmic egg and opened it, holding a half in each hand. After he had chanted seven mantras over the two halves, eight pure-white male elephants, each with four huge tusks, emerged from the shell in his right hand. The first and chief of these was Airāvata. From the shell in the left hand of Brahma emerged eight similar female elephants. These sixteen cosmic elephants were placed by Brahma at the eight cardinal compass points to support the weight of the earth in the universe.

2. In the Vedic mythology of the *Mahābhārata*, Airāvata was created out of the "Churning of the Waters" at the beginning of time. This milk-white elephant with wings was so beautiful that the god Indra immediately acquired it as his war elephant. When it flew through the air its trunk siphoned up all the waters from under the earth and sprayed them down to the surface as the gift of rain for human needs. The many progeny of Airāvata also had wings; but as the result of disturbing a sage while he was teaching, by landing heavily above him on a tree, the holy teacher decreed that they should no longer have the ability to fly but should serve humans from that time onward. The rare white elephants are still considered to be descendants of Airāvata, having the beauty, grace, and supernatural properties of their ancestor. Consequently such an elephant would be reserved for the royalty, the maharajahs, and given as royal gifts. As their status precluded these white elephants from any useful normal work duties, the phrase *white elephant* came to mean a useless gift that was beautiful but expensive to maintain.
References 7, 24, 112, 132
See also Lokapala Elephants

AITVARAS

This is the name of a flying dragon of Lithuanian folklore that assumes various shapes according to his environment. In the home he is described as resembling a black cat or black cockerel, but when traveling outside he may take on the appearance of a flying dragon or serpent with a fiery tail. These are the physical manifestations of a supernatural "luck-bringer" that may be "purchased" from the Devil for one's soul. Like the Basilisk of medieval European folklore, the Aitvaras is hatched from the egg of a seven-year-old cockerel or brought home unrecognized until too late. Once in the home, it is dislodged only with great difficulty if the occupant is an honest God-fearing person. The Aitvaras's responsibility is to make his owner rich by any means. This task is usually accomplished by the theft of milk, corn, and gold, frequently at the expense of the neighbors. He demands only the sustenance of omelettes in return for the goods he brings. The first mention of this supernatural creature was in an account of 1547, when the suspicious acquisition of wealth by a villager was investigated. Another account described how a new wife could not understand why the grain she was grinding from the corn bin for her new mother-in-law never ran out. Taking a consecrated candle from the church, she investigated the contents of the bin, where an Aitvaras was seen disgorging constant streams of corn. The sacred candle was the instrument of its demise, for the Aitvaras rose up in the air and was never seen again. The mistress of the house grieved for the loss of her wealth as well as for the damnation she incurred for pledging her soul as payment for the riches the Aitvaras would bring.
References 7, 119, 120, 125, 159
See also Basilisk, dragon, Pukis

AJATAR, AJATTARA

These two names are used in southern Estonia for the class of dragons or serpents known as the Aiatar in the folklore of Finland.
References 119, 159
See also Aiatar, Aitvaras, dragon, serpent

AKHEKHU

Accounts of this semisupernatural being are derived from the folklore and legends of Egypt and absorbed by medieval travelers into European folklore. It is described as a serpent having four legs and inhabiting the desert wastelands. In some respects it resembles the European Griffin.
References 89
See also Griffin

AKHLUT

This is the name of a semisupernatural gigantic killer whale in the folklore and legends of the Inuit people of the Bering Sea coast of Alaska. According to Tennant and Bitar (1981), the folktales describe how this being emerges from the ice-floes to hunt for human beings in the guise of an enormous wolf. The Inuit, upon seeing huge wolf tracks that terminate at the edge of the ice, know that they are in peril and are quick to retreat. They recognize this spot as

dangerous territory, for it is the place where an Akhlut has changed back into its killer whale form and may reemerge to kill them.
References 77

AKŪPĀRA

This is the name of the gigantic cosmic tortoise in the Hindu mythology of India. It is upon Akūpāra that the entire earth was decreed to be supported in the universe.
References 24
See also Lokapala Elephants

AL

This is the name of a semisupernatural creature, or fiend, in the folklore of Libya in North Africa. It manifests as a being that is half human and half beast with glowing red eyes. In its humanlike hands it is said to hold a pair of iron scissors with which to attack humans that wander into the sandy wastes. The Al is fond of hunting women and preys especially upon those about to be delivered of a child.
References 7
See also Pontianak

AL BORAK
See Borak, Al

AL BORAQ, BORĀQ
See Boraq, Borāq, Al

ALAN

This is a group of semisupernatural creatures in the folklore of the Tinguian peoples of the Philippine Islands. The Alan are described as humanoid with birdlike qualities and wings, but with fingers and toes that point backward. They inhabit the jungle and other deeply wooded places, where, like bats, they rest hanging upside-down from the topmost branches of trees. However, according to folklore, they are also supposed to have dwellings on the ground constructed of pure gold. Although they can be both malicious and simply mischievous, the Alan are usually benevolent; indeed, they are considered to be the helpers of many of the mythical heroes of the islands.
References 7, 119, 159

ALBASTOR

This is the name of a semisupernatural being in the folklore and beliefs of the Cheremis/Mari peoples of one of the former USSR republics. Also known as Labasta, it may manifest in the bath-houses of humans as a giant with long flowing hair. It sometimes appears in the guise of a man or woman, but when it travels through the air, it takes on the appearance of a shooting star with a trail of sparks. Though said to

originate as the soul of an unbaptized illegitimate infant, it is capable of shape-shifting to that of any animal while on the ground. The Albastor's activities include sexual intercourse with humans, and it punishes those who overindulge by providing such sexual excess as to cause their death from exhaustion. The attentions of the Albastor may be discerned by a sore left on the victim's lips from its kiss. The human lover of a woman visited by an Albastor will also become ill. The Albastor may be defeated in two ways, either by catching it and breaking the little finger of its left hand, thereby breaking its power, or by placing a cross over each door, thus preventing its entry.
References 159, 164
See also Aitvaras, giant

ALBION

This is the name of a giant in two different traditions:

1. According to the classical literature of Roman mythology, Albion is the son of the sea-god Neptune. Along with his brother Dercynus (also a giant), he posed a threat to the hero Hercules as he passed through their territory in the (now French) region of Liguria near the river Rhone. Hercules was obliged to do battle with the two giants, who together would be insuperable. However, with the aid of the king of the gods, Jupiter, who sent a shower of stones, Hercules was able to destroy them. The place of this battle was thereafter named "Campus Lapideus," the Plain of Stones.

2. Albion is also the name of a giant in the medieval history and annals of Britain written by Geoffrey of Monmouth and later printed in William Caxton's *Chronicle of England* (1480). In this account, Albion is the brother of the legendary giants Gog and Magog of the same tradition. The three giants, together with numerous others, inhabited the lands of Britain. When Brut (or Brutus) came to these islands from the Mediterranean with his armies, the British giants were vanquished in many battles. Although Brut was the ultimate conqueror, it was the name of Albion that came to represent the ancient kingdoms of Britain. The English mystical poet and artist William Blake (1757–1827) portrayed Albion with symbolic effect lying asleep in the British landscape. He also identified this giant with the Titans of classical mythology.
References 54, 78, 132, 173, 177
See also giant, Gog and Magog, Taulurd, Titan

ALCHENDIC

This is the name of a giant in medieval European Arthurian legends at the time of the first Crusades. Merlin prophesied that Alchendic would commit murder to become a king, and indeed the giant ordered the assassination of the ruler of the city of Sarras and then usurped his throne. Curiously, after

such a violent ascendancy, he proved to be a good ruler; when the Crusaders under the leadership of King Richard of Jerusalem laid siege to the city to expel him, his population loyally defended both him and the city. The process of combat by champions was embraced for the long siege, and when several of the Crusaders' champions had been defeated, they all sued for peace. This outcome was negotiated on the understanding that Alchendic would accept the Christian faith, which he did a month after the truce. He was then baptized.
References 54
See also giant

ALCYONEUS

This is the name of two beings from the classical mythology of Greece and Rome.

1. One of these beings is a gigantic ass that destroyed everything in its path. It was probably the manifestation of the wind known as the Sirocco.

2. The other being is one of the Gigantes, who were engendered from the blood of Uranus's castration when it fell upon the earth. Alcyoneus, whose name means "the Brayer," with another giant, Porphyrion, was one of their leaders. They were described as being of enormous humanoid proportions, but with serpents for legs and the serpents' heads for feet. At their first appearance they were already fully formed adult warriors complete with spears and clad in shining armor, ready to do battle. They attacked the Olympian gods immediately. Alcyoneus was a perfect choice for leader of the Gigantes since he retained the special connection with Gaia, his mother earth, whereby he was invulnerable while ever his feet touched the ground. During his battle with the mortal hero Heracles/Hercules, the goddess Athena revealed this secret to the hero. Heracles/Hercules therefore immediately lifted the giant Alcyoneus up off the earth and carried him away to be destroyed.
References 7, 138, 168, 177
See also Clytius, Enceladus, Eurytus, giant, Gigantes, Hecatonchieres, Hundred-Handed Giants, Mimas, Pallas, Pelorus, Polybutes, Porphyrion, Rhaetos, Typhon

ALECTO

This is the name of one of the Furies in the classical mythology of Greece and Rome. Alecto was engendered, like her sisters and the Hundred-Handed Giants, from the drops of blood that fell from the castrated Uranus onto the earth. She is described as a hideous human-shaped hag with the head of a dog and the wings of a bat. Her name means "the Unceasing," and she is believed to be the monstrous supernatural means of war, pestilence, and ultimate revenge.

References 74, 125, 159, 168, 177
See also Erinyes, Eumenides, Furies, giant, Hundred-Handed Giants

ALICANTO

A semisupernatural creature of the night that materializes in the shape of a monstrous bird, the wings of which give out a golden or silvery light. It inhabits the mountains and forests of Chile. The Alicanto has a taste for gold and silver, and when it locates a vein of ore, it feasts until it is unable to fly. There are two types of Alicanto, one that favors silver and takes on a silvery glow when feeding on the ore, and the other similarly attracted to gold. Any human prospectors who think that they can follow the Alicanto's light in the dark to find a source of gold will be deceived by it, as the Alicanto will flicker its wing-light enticingly until it lures them to their doom, usually over the edge of a cliff.
References 18, 78, 159
See also Fearsome Critters

ALICHA

This is a gigantic beast or dragon in the myths and beliefs of the Buriat people of ancient Siberia.
References 7, 55, 132
See also Aapep, Alklha, dragon, monster, Rahu, T'ien Kou

ALICORN

This is an alternative name for the unicorn of European medieval legend.
References 89
See also unicorn

ALIFANFARON

This is the name of a giant featured in the literature created by the Spanish author Miguel de Cervantes Saavedra (1547–1616) in his novel *Don Quixote*. While traveling through the Spanish countryside with his faithful companion Sancho Panza, in search of adversaries, the "hero" Don Quixote came upon a flock of sheep. The don declared that these were the soldiers of the giant Alifanfaron with whom he was determined to do battle.
References 20
See also giant

ALKLHA

This is a gigantic beast or dragon in the myths and beliefs of the Buriat people of ancient Siberia. Alklha, also known by the names Alicha and Arakho, is described as a winged dragon of such a size that its black wings, when spread, covered the entire sky, allowing no light whatsoever to penetrate to the earth. In its abode in the heavens, this monster periodically engulfed either the sun or the moon, but their heat was too much for it to consume and Alklha would be obliged to regurgitate them. If the Buriat people saw that there was a bite taken from either the sun or the moon, they would throw stones at the monster to prevent the sun from being swallowed completely. However, the gods reached a better solution whereby they severed Alklha in half, the rear portion falling to the earth. Thereafter, when it attempted to swallow either of the heavenly lights, they simply came out of the open cut in the middle and were safely restored to the sky. The marks that can be observed on the moon today are the indentations caused by the fangs of Alklha in failed attempts to swallow it.

References 7, 55, 132
See also Aapep, dragon, monster, Rahu, T'ien Kou

ALKONOST

This is the name of a fabulous creature in the folklore and legends of Russia. The Alkonost is described as having an upper half in the shape of a young woman and a lower half in the shape of a huge bird. She has a counterpart known as the Sirin and is said to be one of the hosts that lives in the land of the dead called Rai. Her task is to torment the souls of the damned by wailing her fearful songs and giving eternal punishment.

References 55
See also Angka, Garuda, Harpy, Parthenope, Podarge, Ptitsy-Siriny, Siren, Sirin, Solovei Rakhmatich, Unnati, Zägh

ALLOCAMELUS

This is a term used in English heraldry for a beast depicted in coats of arms and other heraldic devices. The Allocamelus is portrayed as having the head of a donkey or ass and the body and legs of a camel.

References 7

ALMAS

This is the name of a gigantic monster in the folklore of the federal state of Siberia. The Almas is described as being an enormous humanoid covered in shaggy brown-black fur, much like the Bigfoot or Sasquatch of the United States.

References 61
See also Bigfoot

AL-MI'RAJ

See Mi'raj, Al-

ALOADAE, ALOADES, ALOIDS, ALOIDÆ

These are variations on the collective name denoting the sons of Aloes in the classical mythology of Greece and Rome. They were giants born of Iphimedeia, the wife of Aloes/Aloeus; but some accounts maintain that they were the sons of Poseidon by her. The Aloadae were twin brothers named Ephialtes and Otus who, from birth onward, grew at a rate of nine inches each month. They were so vast that by the time they were nine years of age they were already twenty-six feet in girth and nearly sixty feet in height. Though portrayed as gross and uncouth, they were said to have founded cities and inspired the veneration of the Muses. When their mother and sister were threatened, they rescued them.

According to the version of their story in Homer's *Iliad*, the Aloadae laid claim to the throne of Olympus and to the goddesses Artemis/Diana and Hera/Juno. In their bid for these prizes they imprisoned the god of war, Ares, in a bronze pot for over a year. They assailed Olympus by heaping the mountains of Ossa and Pelion on top of Mount Olympus. But the new gods, led by Zeus, were not to be vanquished so easily. There are several versions of their demise. One details how they were slaughtered by Apollo. Another tells how they were tricked by Artemis/Diana, who, disguised as a deer, ran between them. Both twins were so anxious to make the kill that they lunged forward with their weapons just as the deer eluded them, piercing each other to death. In yet another version they were captured and bound together back-to-back in the depths of Tartarus, with chains of enchantment fashioned from serpents.

References 24, 125, 138, 173, 177
See also Ephialtes, giant, Otus

ALOÉS

During the periods when European travelers and armies were sent to the New World, there were many accounts of strange creatures. One such creature, the Aloés, was described in the sixteenth century both by Thevet in his sixteenth-century work *Cosmography* and quoted by Ambroise Paré (1517–90), during the same period in his work *On Monsters and Marvels*. Purported to be a sea creature that resembled both a fish and a terrestrial goose, it had a head body resembling a bird with a very long neck and, instead of legs and feet, four large flippers. This creature was reportedly seen near the "Spanish Isle," which one may conjecture was the recently discovered Island of Hispaniola.

References 146

ALOIDS

This is an alternative spelling of the name Aloadae, who were giants in the classical mythology of Greece and Rome.

References 24, 125, 138, 173, 177
See also Aloadae, Ephialtes, giant, Otus

ALOUS

In the classic literature of medieval Italy, the author Boccaccio (1313–1375) wrote numerous tales. One of

The Aloés, a sea creature that resembled both a fish and a terrestrial goose (On Monsters and Marvels *by Ambroise Paré, trans. by Janus L. Pallister, University of Chicago Press, 1982)*

these mentions that the giant from biblical times called Alous was the father of the Aloids (a group of giants in the classical mythology of Greece and Rome). Boccaccio also states that Alous was one of the sons of Terra and Tytan, and that they engendered, through their descendants, the human race.
References 173
See also Aloids, giant, Tytan

ALPHITO
In the classical mythology of Greece, this being was worshiped as the goddess of barley in the region of Argos. Her name symbolizes the whiteness of the grain kernel as well as the bone bleached in the earth. Little by little Alphito was denigrated by this very whiteness, which came to represent the corruption of disease and death. Ultimately she became known as a grotesque hag that lurked in the gloom to threaten naughty children. Her mythological career descended later into that of a folkloric Nursery bogie.
References 38
See also Nursery bogies

ALSVID
This is the name of one of the giant horses in Norse and Teutonic mythology that pulled the chariot of the sun-maiden Sol (or Sunna) or of the moon. Alsvid, whose name means "All Swift" and thus symbolizes the dawn, was also known as Alswider.
References 20, 24, 89
See also Aavak, Horses of the Sun

ALSWIDER
This is the name of one of the giant horses in Norse and Teutonic mythology. Alswider, whose name means "All Swift," was also known as Alsvid.

References 20, 24, 89
See also Aavak, Alsvid, Horses of the Sun

AMALA

This is the name of a gigantic being in the mythology and folklore of the Tsimshian Native American peoples of the northwest coast of the United States. Amala is obliged to hold the weight of the earth balanced and spinning on a pole above his back. Once each year this painful duty is relieved by the application of duck-oil to his muscles by a servant. It is said that when there is no longer any duck-oil because all the ducks have been wantonly hunted to extinction, the servant will not come to ease Amala's back. When Amala ultimately feels too exhausted to hold the earth, it will tumble from the pole and be destroyed.
References 77
See also Atlas

AMAM

The name of a gigantic semisupernatural monster in the mythology of ancient Egypt. Amam is also known as Amermait.
References 24, 38, 89, 138, 168
See also monster

AMAROK

This is the name of a gigantic wolf in the folklore and mythology of the Inuit of the United States and Canada. Amarok will overtake and devour any person foolish enough to hunt alone at night.
References 7

AMBIZE

This is a monster said to exist in the seas off the West Africa coast, especially around the delta of the River Congo. The Ambize is also known as the Angulo or the Hog Fish. It was first mentioned by European sailors and travelers during the sixteenth century. Its curious description mentions the head of a pig or ox on the body of an enormous fish. It had human hands instead of fins and a tail that was round and flat like that of a beaver; it was also said to be shaped like an archery target. The Ambize was much sought after by the local Congolese fishermen, who stated that its flesh, when cooked, tasted very much like the best pork. However it was extremely difficult to catch, as it weighed over 500 pounds.
References 7, 89
See also monster

AMDUSCIAS

This is an infernal monster portrayed in nineteenth-century France as having a huge humanoid body, but with the head and horn of a unicorn.

References 63
See also Ass (Three-Legged), Chio-Tuan, Karkadan, Ki Lin, Kirin, Koresck, Mi'raj (Al), monster, Onyx Monoceros, unicorn

AMERMAIT

The name of a gigantic semisupernatural monster in the mythology of ancient Egypt is also known as Ammit, Am-Mit, Ammut, or Amam. The name Amermait is variously translated as "the Corpse-Eater," "the Bone-Eater," or "the Devourer." The creature is portrayed in the *Book of the Dead* as a hybrid between a hippopotamus, a lion, and a crocodile, resting either beside the god Osiris or at a temple gateway. Amermait performs the duties of ritual cleansing of the guilty by waiting in the Halls of Justice, where the departed souls are judged. When any of the souls are condemned for their earthly crimes, Amermait would immediately pounce to eat out the heart of the condemned.
References 24, 38, 89, 138, 168
See also monster

AMHULUK

In the beliefs and folklore of the Native American people living in the state of Oregon, the Amhuluk are lake serpents known by the name of the enchanted waters in which they live. These supernatural serpents undergo many metamorphoses, each more formidable than the last. The waters of Amhuluk can also transform into monsters any other creatures that fall into them.
References 133
See also Atunkai, serpent

A-MI-KUK

This is the name of a monster in the folklore of the Inuit peoples of the Bering Straits region of Alaska. The A-mi-kuk is described as being like a huge animal with a pelt that is moist and slimy. Instead of legs it has four extended humanoid arms, even though its habitat is normally the sea. This horrific creature preys upon human beings. It hunts fishermen and people bathing, but if they make for the beach, it will burrow and "swim" through the earth to reach them. The people in the region of St. Michael firmly assert that the A-mi-kuk has been known to travel in this manner from the sea to certain crater-lakes far inland to pursue its prey.
References 133
See also monster

AMMIT, AM-MIT, AMMUT

These are alternative names for the monster Amermait, the hybrid crocodile and hippopotamus monster of the ancient Egyptian underworld.

References 7, 24, 38, 89, 125, 132, 159, 168
See also Amermait

AMPHIPTERE

This is the name of a hybrid creature depicted in the devices of European heraldry, especially that of Britain. Portrayed as having the body of a serpent with wings, it closely resembles the Guivre of French heraldry and folklore. These monsters were greatly feared by the European peoples of the medieval period; therefore anyone displaying such a creature in their coat of arms would be regarded as fearsome, especially in battle.
References 7, 89
See also Guivre

AMPHISBAENA

This is a type of reptile in European legends, folklore, and heraldry especially of the medieval period. This creature is also known by the name Amphivena; the names are derived from the Greek word meaning "to go both ways." The classical writer Lucan described the Amphisbaena in his work *Pharsalia* as inhabiting the deserts of North Africa, where, like most reptiles, it laid and hatched its young from eggs in the sands. This monster is also frequently portrayed in the margins of medieval bestiaries as a winged, two-legged dragon with a head on the end of its long prehensile tail, which is usually clasped behind the head by the jaws of its other head. In this manner it was said to be able to bowl along the ground like a cart wheel. Equipped with eagle legs and claws, it was a formidable adversary, capable of running at great speed in either direction. Its bites were extremely venomous, and even in the dark nobody was safe from it, as its glowing eyes could penetrate the gloom. The two classical writers Pliny the Elder and Lucan wrote of the properties of a captured Amphisbaena for medical purposes. Its dried skin, they said, was supposed to cure rheumatism, but while alive it was reputed to be a talisman for pregnancy! Although this creature was exaggerated to monstrous proportions, no doubt by the "embellished" traveler's tales, it was based on a factual reptile that exists in the Libyan deserts, and is capable of running in either direction, having a tail that raises like a head at the threat of danger.
References 7, 14, 18, 20, 63, 89, 148, 184, 185
See also dragon, Hoop snake, serpent

AMPHISIEN

This alternative name for the Cockatrice is used in reference to European heraldic devices. The creature is similarly portrayed as a reptile with the head and legs of a cockerel. However, unlike the usual Cockatrice, which possessed only one head, the Amphisien had a second head at the end of its tail. Its glance was supposed to kill its adversaries or to turn them to stone. Its depiction as an emblem on the shield of a medieval knight would have been considered quite fearsome.
References 5
See also Amphisbaena, Cockatrice

AMPHITRITES

This is an alternative name for the Abgal of Sumerian mythology.
References 63
See also Abgal

AMPHIVENA

This is an alternative name for the monstrous Amphisbaena in the legends and folklore of medieval Europe.
References 7, 14, 18, 20, 63, 89, 148, 184
See also Amphisbaena, dragon, serpent

ANAKIM

This is the name of a race of giants in biblical literature. Said to have inhabited the valley of Hebron at the time of the Hebrews' attempt to retake the Promised Land, they are described as the enormous, humanoid, terrifying children of Anak. Accounts of these giants are recorded in the Books of Deuteronomy and Numbers in the context of their clashes with the tribes of Israel and their attacks on the neighboring peoples of Moab and Egypt. In these respects they are linked with the other biblical races of giants, the Nephilim and the Rephaim. In his *Opera* (1.9), Hugh of St. Cler states that "after the Flood, these giant sons of Anak had been born in the Hebron valley, had traversed to Egypt, and were known as the Titans." (*Post diluvium etiam nati sunt alii gigantes in Hebron filii Enach, qui transierunt in Ægyptum, et dicti sunt "Titanes."*)
References 63, 173
See also giant, Nephilim, Rephaim, Titans

ANANTA, ANANTA SESHA, ANANTA SHESHA

Ananta is the epithet of the cosmic serpent Shesha, in the Hindu mythology of India. The name may be translated as "Endless" or "Infinity," thus implying the immensity of the serpent's proportions. This vast creature is described as having a thousand heads and during the night of Brahma, the world serpent coils its vastness so that the sun-god Vishnu may repose, shaded by seven huge heads, until he arises at dawn. In this aspect, Vishnu is called Ananta-Shayana, which may be translated as "One Who Sleeps on Ananta."

The origins of Ananta Sesha are various, but one tradition relates how Balarama, the sun-god's brother, fell asleep on the sea shore. As he slept a vast serpent emerged from his mouth and, in the process, took all the body of the sleeper, leaving only the bodiless head as witness to the transformation.

It was with the aid of this cosmic serpent, when tied to Mount Mondara by the gods and then swirled violently, that the Churning of the Oceans produced the magical *amrita,* the elixir of immortality.

Ananta's heads are not only venomous but also spew out fire. Thus, at the end of each period, or *Kalpa,* allotted to the earth, the vast serpent destroy all creation.

References 47, 78, 112
See also Anantaboga, serpent

ANANTABOGA, ANANTA BOGA

These are variations on the name of a dragon in the myths and legends of Java in Indonesia. In the traditions of the *Wayang* (oriental popular "opera"), which draws on the ancient traditional myths as the source of the performances, Anantaboga, King of the Dragons, holds the underworld of the dead as his domain. His wife and consort is called Dewi Nagagini. Both may be compared, in terms of names and status, with the Hindu serpents Ananta Shesha and the Naga and Nagini.

References 113
See also Ananta, dragon, Naga/s

ANASKELADES

This is the name of a semisupernatural beast in the ancient folklore and beliefs of the people of the Island of Crete in the Mediterranean Sea. In the more distant past they were said to resemble a donkey wandering the roads, presenting an apparently free ride. Should anyone be foolish enough to mount the beast, it would immediately expand in size until it was as big as the surrounding mountain range, tossing the victim to the ground far below. In more modern times the story has changed somewhat to become the presentation of a bobbin lying in the road. When the curious traveler goes to inspect it, it turns into a huge donkeylike beast.

References 7, 132
See also Callicantzari

Anantaboga is a dragon in the myths and legends of Java in Indonesia (Rose Photo Archive, UK)

ANAYE

This is the name of a group of beings in the folklore and beliefs of the Navajo peoples of the United States. They are subdivided into four types: the limbless Binaye Ahani, the headless Thelgeth, the feathered Tsanahale, and another unnamed being. This latter monster clung to the rocks in the desert by its fur, which grew like roots into the rock face. From this vantage point it assuaged its cannibal appetite by devouring the occasional unwary traveler.

The Anaye are considered to have been the progeny of wicked women, without a human father, who were destined to generate the causes of fear, wickedness, and misery in the world. All these progeny were giants or monsters of grotesque proportions, but they were ultimately defeated by the sons of the sun and water. However, the siblings of the Anaye—Cold, Famine, Old Age, and Poverty—could not be defeated and continue to plague humans to this day.

References 7
See also Binaye Ahani, Thelgeth

ANCALAGON THE BLACK

This is the name of one of the dragons in the literary works of the English academic and author J. R. R. Tolkien (1892–1973), who wrote *The Hobbit* in 1937 and *The Lord of the Rings* in 1955. Ancalagon the Black is one of the Fire-Drakes bred by the evil Morgoth in the Pits of Angband during the period of the First Sun. When Ancalagon the Black was killed in the Great Battle during the War of Wrath, all the other Fire-Drakes were similarly defeated.

References 51
See also dragon, Fire-Drake, Glaurung, Urulóki

ANCIENT ONE

This is the honorary name given to a monster in the folklore of the people of Estonia on the Baltic Sea. Tradition has it that a lake in the region of Viitna was described as being the Black Lake, where, no matter how many fish were placed there, the only items to be fished out of it were rotten logs. Puzzled by the loss of what should have been a good catch year after year, the local fishermen decided to drag the bottom of the lake. The whole village took part, waiting to see what emerged. The fishermen in one boat netted an extraordinary monster that was part fish and part some sort of hairy creature. As they hauled in the net and headed for the shore, the waves rose around them. Soon the waves were higher than the vessel, becoming so high that they might be sunk. In terror they released the net, which, with the creature inside, was weighing them down. To their amazement, the minute the net was released, the lake became completely calm. Nobody fishes in the lake anymore.

References 133
See also monster

ANCIENT SERPENT

The Ancient Serpent is the translation of the honorary name given to a monster in the folklore and beliefs of the Piute Native American peoples of Nevada in the United States. It is said to be a gigantic water serpent that inhabits Lake Pyramid. When the whirlpools and frothing of this lake took place, the Piute would not go near the lake for fear that the Ancient Serpent was looking for his next victim there.

References 133
See also serpent

ANDROSPHINX

In the mythology of ancient Egypt the Sphinx was a guardian relating to the cosmos and astrology. It is referred to as the Androsphinx when it is depicted with a human head. It is also known, in the astrological sense, as Hor-em-akhen. The latter name may be translated as "Horus of the Horizon," which the Greeks referred to as Har-machis. A vast sculptured representation of the Androsphinx is located next to the Great Pyramid at Giza, where its female human head bearing the pharoic headdress rests on the body of a lion.

References 89
See also Hieracosphinx, Sphinx

ANDURA

This is the alternative name for the Hoga, the monster of Mexican lakes, in the folklore of the peoples of South America.

References 146
See also Hoga

ANGBODA

This is the name of a giantess in the Nordic mythology of Scandinavia whose name may be translated as "Bringer of Sorrow" or "Boder of Anguish." Angboda, also known as Angrboda, Angrbodha, or Angur-Boda, was the wife of the trickster god Loki by whom she bore Hel the goddess, who ruled the underworld of the dead; Fenrir the gigantic wolf, which was responsible for the demise of the gods at Ragnarök; and the gigantic world serpent Jormungandr, which slept beneath the ash tree Yggdrassil. Angboda also bore Gerda by the giant Gymir.

References 24, 61, 78, 125, 132
See also Fenrir, Gymir, Jormungandr, serpent

ANGKA

This is the name of a fabulous bird in the folklore of the Arab peoples of the Middle East, especially Saudi

Arabia. The Angka was described as having the face of a human and as resembling the Persian Simurgh or the Griffin of European medieval tradition. It was said to inhabit the Kaf Mountains, where it devoured anything living that it came across. In this it was so successful that it hunted everything to extinction, resulting in its own demise.

References 7, 89
See also Alkonost, Bahri, Garuda, Griffin, Harpy, Parthenope, Podarge, Ptitsy-Siriny, Simurgh, Siren, Sirin, Solovei Rakhmatich, Unnati, Zägh

ANGONT

The name of a gigantic serpent in the beliefs and traditions of the Huron people of the United States. A vicious and deadly venomous reptile, it was said to inhabit lonely and desolate places in the lakes, rivers, caves, forests, and cold dank depths of the world. From its abode it could reach out deadly long coils and bring disasters and disease to human inhabitants. Medicine men went in search of this gigantic reptile in order to use it for the purposes of working magic medicine. But because even the slightest portion of the Angont's skin was deadly, no good was ever to be expected of one who carried such a talisman.

References 133, 168
See also serpent

ANGRBODA, ANGRBODHA

These are alternative names for Angboda, a giantess in the Nordic mythology of Scandinavia who was the wife of the trickster god Loki.

References 24, 61, 78, 125, 132
See also Angboda, giantess

ANGULO

This is an alternative name for the Ambize, a monster said to exist in the seas off the West Africa coast, especially around the delta of the River Congo.

References 7
See also Ambize

ANGUR-BODA

This is an alternative name for Angboda, a giantess in the Nordic mythology of Scandinavia who was the wife of the trickster god Loki.

References 24, 61, 78, 125, 132
See also Angboda, giantess

ANIWYE

This is a monster in the beliefs and folklore of the Ojibwa peoples of the United States. It is described as resembling an enormous skunk with the same destructive spray as the real-life animal. The Aniwye, however, is a grotesque hunter of human flesh with the ability to understand and communicate with humans; it tracks them wherever they are hiding and kills them with its spray. It is so huge that it can be seen from afar, thus allowing time to escape. One story tells how all the people in a village had been warned that an Aniwye was approaching. They hurried away as fast as possible, leaving one old woman who was too infirm to escape. She was still cowering in her abode when the Aniwye tore off the roof and demanded to know where the villagers were. She said that she was too infirm to run away with them, whereupon the monster told her that he would cure her. Then he sprayed her to death. The villagers, meanwhile, had reached the safety of Fisher Lake in the domain of the Giant Fisher, a supernatural hero.

References 77
See also monster

ANJANA

This is the name of one of the Lokapala Elephants in the Hindu mythology of India. Anjana (known as Saumanasa in other legends) stands as the guardian of the west quadrant of the world with the god Varuna on his back.

References 7, 24, 112
See also Lokapala Elephants

ANJING AJAK

This is the name for a Werewolf in the beliefs and folklore of the people of Java in Indonesia. Like his counterpart in European legends, the Anjing Ajak is the transformed body of an evil man who becomes a cannibal wolf at night.

References 113
See also Werewolf

ANTAEUS

This is the name of one of the early giants in the classical mythology of Greece and Rome. Antaeus, also spelled Anteus or Antaíos, was the progeny of Poseidon/Neptune and Gaia/Terra, who, because he was a son of the earth, could gain superlative strength whenever he touched her. This giant inhabited a region of Libya, where he terrorized the travellers by challenging anyone who came there to a wrestling bout that only he could win. The penalty for losing was death. It was only when Heracles/Hercules traveled to this region and Athena divulged the secret of the giant's strength that the hero was able to wrestle. Heracles/Hercules summoned all his strength and lifted the giant off the earth long enough for him to become weaker, whereupon the hero strangled the giant in midair and threw him down much as he had done with his own victims. Antaeus is said to be buried at Tingis in modern-day Mauritania.

References 20, 78, 125, 138, 168, 173, 177
See also Gaia, giant

ANTAÍOS

This is an alternative spelling of Antaeus, one of the early giants in the classical mythology of Greece and Rome.

References 20, 78, 125, 138, 168, 173, 177
See also Gaia, giant

ANTERO VIPUNEN

The name of a primeval being in the mythology and folklore of the people of Finland. Antero Vipunen, whose name derives from a phrase meaning the "cross of Saint Andrew," is a giant of such immense proportions that he lay with the earth as a blanket. His story is given in Song 17 of the ancient *Kalevala* cycle. While the giant slept, whole communities of forest dwellers and the forests themselves grew and thrived over his body. This giant knew all the secrets of the earth, along with its magic, songs, and lore. His wisdom was renowned throughout Finland. It was for this reason that the hero Väinänöinen sought the help of Antero Vipunen. The hero was in the process of making a special ship using incantations at each crucial stage of the process. However, when the boat was almost complete, Väinänöinen realized that he had omitted to obtain the last three important spells. He was advised to go to Tuonela, the underworld where the giant lay, to ask Antero Vipunen for his help. After an eventful journey, the hero found the giant but, alas, could not wake him. His efforts were so puny that the giant just sniffed and then made an enormous yawn that sucked in the astonished hero; then the giant just carried on sleeping. Inside Antero Vipunen's belly the hero took out the ship-building tools he had brought with him and constructed a forge. The burning on the inside of the giant woke him up with a start, and he spewed the hero and his forge back out, along with a torrent of songs and the very magic that Väinänöinen had come for. Thus the giant had been awakened and Väinänöinen could return and finish his ship.

References 24, 78, 132
See also giant, Ymir

ANTEUS

This is an alternative spelling of Antaeus, one of the early giants in the classical mythology of Greece and Rome.

References 20, 78, 125, 138, 168, 173, 177
See also Gaia, giant

ANTHROPOPHAGUS

This is an ogre or hideous cannibal giant in English drama of the late eighteenth century. Anthropophagus, whose name literally means "Eater of Humans," appears as a somewhat ridiculous figure of terror in much the same manner (though with less sophistication) as had been used by Rabelais in his portrayal of Gargantua. The significance of Anthropophagus is explained by reference to William Ware's play *The Ogre and Little Thumb; or The Seven League Boots,* which features two shady characters, called Will o' the Wisp and Jack o' Lantern, whom any person of the period would have recognized as the lesser spirits or demons that led travelers astray on dark nights near marshes. These characters are of course *ignes fatui.* These two demons are the means by which Anthropophagus has an abundance of travelers at his gloomy castle, where he will dispose of them as his next meal. This horror play of the period was performed in 1807 at the Covent Garden, London.

References 159, 181
See also cannibal, Gargantua, giant, ogre

ANTICHRIST

According to the Christian New Testament in the Book of Revelations (1:8), Thessalonians (2:1–12), and the Epistles of St. John (1, 2:18, 22), the Antichrist is the opponent of God and of Christ. His appearance on the earth is said to herald the imminence of the Second Coming of the Lord, the final destruction of the earth, and the beginning of the Last Judgment. In fact, it is in the Hebraic Book of Daniel (9:17) that the description of the Antichrist is given. He is a gigantic being of 10 cubits in height (equivalent to 18 feet 3 inches in Hebrew cubits or to 15 feet in English cubits). This was possibly a reference to the fearsome Anakim of biblical literature yet the possible derivation of this ultimate opponent of God is said to be from the rebellious Babylonian Tiamat. In addition, many real-life people have been "identified" as the Antichrist (according to the prevailing period of strife), including the Pope during the time of the Reformation, Frederick II during the eighteenth century, Napoleon Bonaparte during the nineteenth century, and Adolf Hitler during the twentieth century.

References 20, 173
See also Anakim, giant, Tiamat

ANTIGONUS

This is the name of the Town Giant of Antwerp in the folklore of Belgium. Antigonus was said to have terrorized the town and its inhabitants. He would demand tribute from anyone passing through his domain, but those who refused were punished by him by chopping off their hands. Eventually a heroic prince named Brabon killed the tyrannical giant, an event from which the "hand-tossing" epithet for the town is believed to have derived. During the course of the ensuing centuries, the fame of this event transformed the giant into a "personality" associated with the town until Antigonus in effigy actually came to represent the town of Antwerp, in much the same

way as Gog and Magog in London. Effigies of
Antigonus are recorded as taking a prominent role in
the town's cultural and political events. In 1534,
according to Fairholt, Antigonus was designed and
built by the court painter to the Emperor Charles V.
The giant was again paraded in 1550, and in 1685 for
the visit of Philip II of Spain.

References 173
See also giant, Gog and Magog, Town Giants

ANTIPHATES

The name of a king of the Laestrygones in the classical
myths of Greece and Rome. The Laestrygones were
cannibals who were antagonists of Ulysses during his
voyages.

References 177
See also Cannibal, Laestrygonians

ANTUKAI

In the beliefs and folklore of the Native American
people living in the state of Oregon, in the United
States, this is a monstrous creature resembling an
otter. It was originally a grizzly bear, but because it
roamed by the wells inhabited by the lake serpent
Amhuluk, it was lured into the water and
transformed into the monster.

References 133
See also Amhuluk, monster, serpent

ANZU

This is the alternative name for the Zû, a huge dragon
or storm-bird in the mythology of Mesopotamia,
Sumer, and Babylon.

References 7, 47, 89, 125, 132, 165
See also Zû

AO CHIN, AO CH'IN

These are two spellings of the name of one of the four
great Dragon Kings in the mythology and beliefs of
ancient China; the other three are Ao Jun, Ao Kuang,
and Ao Shun. Together they control the rains and the
waters of the seas as well as in their own regions of
the earth. They all inhabit great palaces of crystal and
pearl in the depths of the ocean, where the sea
creatures fulfil the role of servants. When there is a
serious water shortage, or flood on the earth, it is the
assistance of the local region's Dragon King that is
sought.

References 138, 165
See also Ao Jun, Ao Kuang, Ao Ping, Ao Shun, Dragon
King, Oriental Dragon

AO JUN

This is the name of one of the four great Dragon Kings
in the mythology and beliefs of ancient China; the
other three are Ao Chin, Ao Kuang, and Ao Shun.

Together they control the rains and the waters of the
seas as well as in their own regions of the earth.

References 138, 165
See also Ao Chin, Ao Kuang, Ao Ping, Ao Shun,
Dragon King, Oriental Dragon

AO KUANG

This is the name of one of the four great Dragon Kings
in the mythology and beliefs of ancient China. Ao
Kuang is the king of these Dragon Kings; the other
three are Ao Chin, Ao Jun, and Ao Shun. Together
they control a region of the seas and earth under the
direction of the August Personage of Jade. They are
responsible for the distribution of the rains and the
waters in their own regions of the earth as well as in
the seas. They are attended by crayfish, lobsters, and
crabs as guards, and by scaly fish as servants, in their
ocean palaces of crystal and pearl. When droughts or
floods occur on the earth, the humans in the region
petition their Dragon King to intercede with the
August Personage of Jade to rectify the water
problem. If there is no response, an effigy of the
regional Dragon King is left exposed in the roadside
to wake him up by humiliation. Ao Kuang was
succeeded in the status of king by his son Ao Ping.

References 138, 165, 180
See also Ao Chin, Ao Jun, Ao Ping, Ao Shun, Dragon
King, Oriental Dragon

AO PING

This is the name of the son of the king of the Dragon
Kings, Ao Kuang, in the beliefs and mythology of
ancient China. Ao Ping, however, was said to have
fought on behalf of the last emperor of the Shang
dynasty, Chou Wang (Chou Hsin) (1154–1121 B.C.),
during the Battle of the Ten Thousand Spirits, which
took place simultaneously with the earthly Battle of
Mu. During the spiritual battle Li No-cha destroyed
the Dragon King Ao Ping.

References 180
See also Ao Chin, Ao Jun, Ao Kuang, Ao Shun, Dragon
King, Oriental Dragon

AO SHUN

This is the name of one of the four great Dragon Kings
in the mythology and beliefs of ancient China; the
other three are Ao Chin, Ao Jun, and Ao Kuang.
Together they control the rains and the waters of the
seas as well as in their own regions of the earth. They
all inhabit great palaces of crystal and pearl in the
depths of the ocean, where the sea creatures fulfil the
role of servants. When there is a serious water
shortage, or flood on the earth, it is the assistance of
the local region's Dragon King that is sought, who
then intercedes on their behalf with the August
Personage of Jade.

References 165
See also Ao Chin, Ao Jun, Ao Kuang, Ao Ping, Dragon King, Oriental Dragon

AONBÁRR
This is the name of a fabulous horse in the mythology and folklore of Ireland. Aonbárr, whose name in Irish Gaelic means "Unique Supremacy," is also known by the name Enbhárr, which may be translated as "Froth" or "Foam." He is the steed of Manannán mac Lir and, as the name implies, was capable of dashing over any surface, whether mountain, marsh, or sea.
References 128
See also Horses of the Sun, Pegasus, unicorn

APALALA
This is the name of a terrifying water serpent or dragon in the Buddhist mythology of the state of Pashawar in India. Legend tells how Apalala inhabited and controlled the source of the River Swat in the Highlands of Peshawar, now in Pakistan. The fearsome monster was tamed and converted by Buddha, an event often portrayed in the Buddhist art of the region.
References 24
See also dragon, serpent

APEP
This is an alternative spelling of Aapep, the cosmic serpent in the mythology of ancient Egypt.
References 7, 24, 49, 89, 138, 159
See also Aapep, serpent

APER CALYDONIUS
This is an alternative name for the Calydonian Boar in the classical mythology of Greece and Rome.
References 105
See also Calydonian Boar

APIS
This is the name of a semisupernatural bull in the mythology of ancient Egypt. Apis, also known as Hap, or by the Greek name Epaphus, was the representative of the god Ptah. This gigantic bull was depicted as wearing the *uraeus* (a royal solar disc) between its horns and as having a black body, a white eagle on its back, a white square or triangle on its forehead, a scarab beneath its tongue, and double-thick tail hair. This mythological creature demanded an earthly representative, so a real-life bull was sought whose mother had been struck by lightning and whose body and head bore the sacred marks. This bull was taken to the temple at Memphis and revered as being the representative of the celestial Apis of the gods and as having the power of an oracle. When the bull died it was embalmed and

taken to the appointed catacombs at Zaqqara. It would later be succeeded by other bulls with the required features.
References 24, 38, 63, 89, 168
See also Buchis

APKALLU
This is an alternative name for the Abgal of Sumerian mythology.
References 63
See also Abgal

APOCALYPTIC BEAST
This is the name given to a monster in the beliefs and folklore of Ireland. Also known as the Dragon of the Apocalypse, it is described as being part serpent and part salmon, and as breathing fire like a dragon. The Apocalyptic Beast is said to inhabit the murky depths of Loch-Bél-Dracon, which is the Irish name meaning "Lake of the Dragon's Mouth." It has been identified with the dragon of the Apocalyptic Beasts, which will arise to signal the destruction of the earth and the Second Coming of the Lord before the Day of Judgment. The Apocalyptic Beast itself is said to be in Ireland to avenge the death of Saint John the Baptist by rising on Saint John's Day at the time of the Apocalypse. The medieval symbolism of the dragon's mouth, as portrayed in numerous bestiaries and missals of the period, was the opening to Hell. In this respect the symbolism of the location of this beast has deep Christian significance.
References 63, 133
See also Apocalyptic Beasts, dragon, Piast, serpent, Sisiutl

APOCALYPTIC BEASTS
These are monsters which are described in the Christian New Testament section of the Bible, specifically in the Revelations of Saint John. There is some controversy over the exact nature of these monsters, which, as their collective name implies, are connected (in terms of their appearance on the earth) with the coming of the Apocalypse, the Second Coming of the Lord, and the Day of Judgment. Although a larger number is implied, only three Apocalyptic Beasts are described, as follows:

1. The first is a beast that rises up out of the waters of the sea. It has the body of a leopard, a bear's paws, seven heads like those of a Hydra, and lions' jaws. Each head has ten horns bearing ten crowns. One of these heads is described as having a fatal wound that has somehow been healed.
2. The second beast rises out of the earth. It is described as having the same appearance as the

The Apocalyptic Beast, also known as the Dragon of the Apocalypse (Rose Photo Archive, UK)

first, but with one head, short horns, and the voice of a dragon.

3. The third beast, named as the Scarlet Beast, has the same appearance as the beast from the sea, except that it is red in color. This monster is the steed of the "Whore of Babylon," who, bedecked with sumptuous scarlet and purple robes trimmed with precious jewels, sits astride the monster.

The mystical symbolism associated with these monsters has long been the subject of theological discussion. As scarlet specifically is a color anciently associated with harlotry, the symbolism of the Scarlet Beast is that of prostitution in the corrupt political and theological sense of the word. This has been taken to infer decadence, which will be the source of the world's destruction. What is believed to be the prophetic nature of this section of the *Book of Revelations* still stimulates fervent interest and discussion.
References 63, 89, 133
See also Apocalyptic Beast, dragon, Hydra

APOP, APOPHIS, APOPIS
These are alternative names for Aapep in the mythology of ancient Egypt.
References 7, 24, 49, 89, 138, 159
See also Aapep, serpent

APOTAMKIN
This is a monster in the folklore of the Maliseet-Passamaquoddy peoples of the northeast coastal region of the United States. According to both Prince (1921) and Fisher (1946), it manifests as a type of bogey described as a humanoid covered in long hair and having enormous teeth. The Apotamkin is essentially a Nursery bogie, for it is by reference to the predations of this monster that cautious parents prevent their adventurous children from wandering onto beaches unaccompanied or venturing onto thin ice in the wintertime. The Apotamkin and the Ponca bogey called Indacinga are probably one and the same.
References 77
See also Hagondes, Indacinga, monster, Nursery bogies, Owner-of-a-Bag

APOTHARNI
This is a name chosen by the author Conrad Lycosthenes, who included references to a race of monsters in his work *Prodigorum ac ostentorum chronicon,* published in Basel, Switzerland, in 1557. The description of these beings as half horse and half human may be compared with the centaurs of classical Greek and Roman mythology. However, unlike the centaurs, who were always male, the Apotharni could be either male or female. The females were described by Lycosthenes as being bald-headed but having hair on the chin resembling a male beard. He also stated that they inhabited marshy areas. Like many of his contemporary European authors writing of the fabulous races of the period, Lycosthenes relied heavily on the ancient classical literature, embellished by tales from contemporary travelers.
References 7
See also centaur, monster

ARACHD
This is the alternative spelling of the Arrach, a monster of the traditions and folklore of Scotland.
References 128
See also Arrach

ARAKHO
This is a gigantic beast or dragon in the myths and beliefs of the Buriat people of ancient Siberia.
References 7, 55, 132
See also Aapep, Alklha, dragon, monster, Rahu, T'ien Kou

ARANDA
This is the name of an enormous serpent in the beliefs and folklore of the Native Australians of the Emianga region of Australia. Aranda was said to inhabit the depths of deep billabongs and river stretches where the currents are so deep that they do not disturb the surface, for it is here that unwary humans go to draw water or to fish, ignorant of the danger lurking below. When in an unguarded moment of preoccupation the human is alone, Aranda seizes the victim and descends again, leaving no trace, as the victim is swallowed whole in one gulp.
References 165
See also serpent, Yurlunggur

ARASSAS
This is the name of a curious monster in the folklore of France. The Arassas was a grotesque hybrid creature having the torso and legs of a lizard but the head of a cat. It was said to inhabit caves and caverns high in the French Alps.
References 133
See also Dard, monster, Stollenwurm, Tatzelwurm

ARAXA
This is one of the giants named in the genealogy created by the Italian monk Annius of Viterbo (Giovanni Nanni, c. 1432–1502), to justify the noble descent of the Gauls from a giant biblical race.
References 138, 173
See also giant, Noah, Priscaraxe

ARAXA JUNIOR

This is the name of a monstrous humanoid serpent said to be derived from the mythology of ancient Greece. The character of Araxa Junior was used by the poet Lemaire (1473–1524) and was derived from Araxa Prisca in the genealogy created by the Italian monk Annius of Viterbo (Giovanni Nanni, c. 1432–1502). Under whichever name, this character was asserted to be an ancestor of the French royal house, in the same manner as Melusine.
References 173
See also Araxa, Melusine, Prisca, Priscaraxe

ARCADIAN HIND

This is an alternative name for the Cerynean Hind of classical Greek and Roman mythology. It was chased by the hero Heracles/Hercules as the third of his twelve "labors."
References 24
See also Cerynean Hind

ARCTOPHONOS

This is the name of one of the great hunting dogs of the giant Orion in the classical mythology of Greece and Rome. It was reputed to have the strength and endurance to kill bears. Orion's other enormous semisupernatural dog was Ptoophagos.
References 20
See also giant, Orion, Ptoophagos

AREPYIAI

This is an alternative name for the Harpies of classical Greek and Roman mythology. Arepyiai may be translated as "Slicer" or "Tearer," which graphically renders the viciousness of the deeds of these Griffin-like monsters. The name Harpy means "to Transport" or "to Snatch," connotations that are somewhat less intimidating than Arepyiai.
References 89
See also Griffin, Harpy, monster

ARGES

Arges is one of the three gigantic Cyclopes in the classical mythology of Greece and Rome. His brothers were Brontes and Steropes. Arges's name may be translated as "Thunderbolt," and, like his brothers, he had only one eye located in the center of his forehead. The Cyclopes were born of Gaia and fathered by Uranus, who threw them into the depths of Tartarus as punishment for their rebellion. In his work *Theogony* (c. 750 B.C.), Hesiod describes them both as giants and as Titans, but the Cyclopes were distinct from both.
References 78, 138
See also Brontes, Cyclops, Gaia, giant, Steropes, Titan, Uranus

ARGOPELTER

This is a monster of the Fearsome Critter variety coined by the lumberjack community of the United States. The Argopelter was rarely seen, and no distinct description thus exists; however, it was said to inhabit hollow tree trunks in the forest. From its vantage point, the creature could await any unwary traveler or lumberman and hurl wooden splinters and branches at its victims. Although the human could sustain serious injury, there is no record of any assault beyond the initial bombardment.
References 7
See also Fearsome Critters

ARGUS, ARGOS, ARGUS PANOPTES

These are variations on the name of a monster in the classical mythology of Greece and Rome. Argus was a giant with, according to different sources, either one hundred or one thousand eyes and, for this reason, also had the name Argus Panoptes, literally "Argus Who Sees Everything." Argus never slept in the conventional manner, for while half his eyes were closed, the others kept watch. When Zeus/Jupiter had an affair with Io, his jealous wife Hera/Juno set the giant to the task of watching the young woman. The king of the gods found out where his wife had hidden Io, whom the goddess had transformed into a cow, now one of many in a herd guarded by Argus. Zeus/Jupiter then sent Hermes to try to rescue Io, but first Hermes lulled Argus to sleep, each eye gently closing while Hermes played lullabies on his lyre. When every eye had closed, Hermes killed Argus and cut off his head to prevent the giant's from reviving and informing Hera/Juno. When the queen of the gods found her guardian giant slain, she carefully gathered up all his eyes and placed them on her beloved peacock's tail.
References 7, 20, 24, 38, 125, 132, 138, 165, 168
See also giant, monster

ARIES

This is the name of a fabulous ram in the classical mythology of Greece and Rome. Of enormous proportions, it had wings and could fly through the air. But its greatest asset was its fleece of pure gold, for which reason it is referred to in the myths as the "Ram with the Golden Fleece." Its epithet is thus Chrysomallus. When Phryxus was accused by his stepmother of being the cause of famine in the land of his father, Athamus, it was on Aries's back that he made his escape. Having safely crossed into Colchis, Phryxsus gave thanks to Zeus, king of the gods, by sacrificing Aries. The beautiful golden fleece was given to the ruler of the region, King Ætes. It was the fame of this wonderful fleece that led the hero Jason and his Argonauts to take it back again.

Aries, the fabulous ram in the classical mythology of Greece and Rome, was also known as the "Ram with the Golden Fleece," which was slain by Jason in the tale of the Argonauts (A Wonder Book for Boys and Girls and Tanglewood Tales by N. Hawthorne, J. M. Dent, London)

Zeus is said to have been so moved by the sacrifice of the wonderful ram that he set it in the heavens as the constellation named Aries. This became the zodiac symbol governing the astrological period March 21 to April 20.
References 20

ARIMASPI, ARIMASPIANS

These are alternative names of a people said by ancient historians to inhabit the regions variously named as Scythia, the Ural Mountains, and, more vaguely, the North of Europe. Both Pliny and Herodotus described these people as having one eye in the middle of the forehead (although they were not gigantic like the Cyclopes) and as living in the land inhabited by the Griffins. As the Griffins were capable

of finding and hoarding great quantities of gold, the Arimaspi constantly attacked the monsters in order to take possession of their gold.
References 7, 18, 63, 168, 177
See also Cyclops, Griffin, monster

ARIMBI

This is the name of a giantess in the legends and folklore of Java in Indonesia. She is a character in the traditional theater/opera known as *Wayang*, which draws upon national myths and legends. Arimbi's son by the warrior Bima is a warrior hero who can fly with the aid of a magic jacket.
References 113
See also giantess

ARION

This is the name of a fabulous horse in the classical mythology of Greece and Rome. Arion, meaning "Martial," was created by the god of the sea, Poseidon/Neptune—some say, by smiting the earth with his trident, and according to others, by having intercourse with Demeter, the goddess of corn, both in the form of horses. Arion was part human in that its right feet were human ones, and on his great back were eaglelike wings. He had the power of both speech and prophecy as well as physical strength. Arion competed and was successful in the Archemoros games. Among his many riders and companions were Adrastus and the hero Hercules.
References 7, 20, 138, 168, 177
See also Horses of the Sun, Pegasus

ARRACH, ARACHD

These are variations on the name of a monster of Scottish beliefs and folklore. In Scottish Gaelic the name may be translated as "Mannikin." It is akin to the Biast, also known as Piast in Irish Gaelic. The Arrach has been described as huge and grotesque, but able to disappear so quickly as to avoid being seen clearly enough for a more detailed description. It is said to lurk in the clefts and rocks on the high moors and mountains of the Highlands.
References 128
See also Biast, monster, Piast

ARRACHD

This is an alternative name for the Fuath, a class of monsters in the Gaelic folklore of Scotland, and may be a variant of the Arachd (see above).
References 7, 128, 159
See also Fuath, monster

ARRAK

This is the name of a fabulous horse in the Norse mythology of Scandinavia. The name may be

translated as "Early Awake." Arrak is a huge semisupernatural horse that, together with Alsvid, pulls the chariot of the sun across the sky from the dawn each day.
References 7
See also Alsvid, Horses of the Sun

ARUSHA AND ARUSHI
These are two great horses of the sun in the Hindu beliefs and mythology of India. The chariot of the sun-god Suraya is pulled by seven great red horses. The lead horse is the fabulous red stallion Arusha, and of the six red mares the primary one is Arushi. When they are seen traveling across the horizon, their color symbolizes either the dawn or the sunset.
References 112
See also Horses of the Sun

ARVAAK, ARVAKR, AAVAK
These are variations on the name of one of the great horses of the sun in the Norse legends of Scandinavia and Iceland. Arvaak, also spelled Aavak, was one of two horses that pulled the chariot of the sun-goddess Sol/Sunna across the sky. Arvaak may be translated from the Old Icelandic as "Early Awake." The other horse of the pair was called Alsvid, which means "All Swift."
References 89, 125
See also Alsvid, Horses of the Sun

ARZSHENK
This is the name of a grotesque monster in the Zoroastrian religion of Iran. Arzshenk is a king of the Devs, who are demons and servants of the supreme evil, Ahriman, who, with his demonic band, are constantly combating the good works of the Amshaspands or Izeds, who represent good. Arzshenk is described as a gigantic humanoid being with the head of a bull. It was prophesied that, in the final battle with the hero Rootsam/Rustam/Rustem, Arzshenk would at last be brought down and have his head cut off by the hero.
References 159
See also Arzshenk, Asterion, Minotaur, monster, Shen-Nung

ASCAPARD
The name of a giant in the folklore and legend of England. According to the legend of the heroic giant Bevis and his love Joisyan, after a number of thrilling adventures, including a fight with a dragon, Bevis eventually met with the giant Ascapard. The two giants fought at Ports Down, a place outside the present town of Southampton in Hampshire. They fought until Ascapard was finally defeated and buried, it is said, under a huge mound there.

References 89, 182
See also Bevis, dragon, giant

ASDEEV
This is the name of a dragon in the mythology of ancient Persia (now Iran). Asdeev—unlike most European, Middle Eastern, or Oriental dragons—is white. This monstrous dragon was the adversary of Rustam/Rustem/Rootsam, the hero of the myths, who, like the classical hero Heracles/Hercules of Greek and Roman mythology, must undertake a number of tasks and defeat adversaries in order to achieve his final victories.
References 20
See also dragon, Oriental Dragon

ASHUAPS
Also known as the monster of Lac Saint-Jean in Canada, this is a water monster of the Loch Ness Monster type. The name Ashuaps is actually derived from Ashuapmouchouan, the name of the river where it was first seen. The monster was described as being about fifty to sixty feet long, able to lift itself about three feet out of the water, and either black or dark blue in color. It was first definitely recorded as being in the lake in 1950, then again in July 1977, when a party in a boat bound for L'Isle au Couleuvres (Grass-Snake Island) saw a huge creature foaming and disturbing an otherwise calm lake surface. In 1978 the members of a terrified Native American family from the local Ouiatchouan Reservation were violently thrown from their canoe. On the same day Ashuaps had been seen by two other parties in the River Ashuapmouchouan, which joins the same lake. By 1980 several sightings had been recorded, and the news media as well as researchers were interested in the legends that had long been known in the Montagnais Native American community.
References 133
See also Loch Ness Monster, monster

ASIN
This is a cannibal girl or woman in the beliefs and folklore of the Alsea Native Americans of the northwest coast of the United States. Asin is a humanoid female monster who inhabits the forests and woodlands near human habitation. She will trap any lone human unwarily wandering on the edge of or into the forest. According to the writings of Frachtenberg (1920), Asin is even more attracted to small children and will encourage them to follow her into the forest where they quickly become her next victims. She can sometimes be heard laughing when she has spotted a likely victim. For a medicine man to have a nightmare about her would spell disaster for the community. Asin is effectively invoked as a

Nursery bogie to prevent adventurous children from wandering unattended into the forests.
References 77
See also cannibal, Dzoo-Noo-qua, nursery bogies, Snee-nee-iq

ASIPATRA

The name of a fabulous bird in the beliefs and folklore of India. The Asipatra, which may be translated as "Sword-Wing," is far from being the normal feathered type for it is monstrous. Although it looks much like an ordinary bird, it has claws resembling knives and its wings are sharp and scythelike that slice through the air and anything else in the way. It is the bird that tortures the condemned sinners in Yamapura, the underworld, where it awaits its gruesome duty, watching from the branches of trees constructed of spears.
References 112
See also Amermait

ASP TURTLE

This is an alternative name for the Aspidochelone of European medieval travelers' lore.
References 14, 89, 184
See also Aspidochelone

ASPIDOCHELONE, ASPIDOCHELON, ASPIDODELONE

These are variations on the name of a monster of the sea recorded since ancient times in European travelers' and sailors' lore. It is mentioned by the ancient Greeks as the Aspidochelon and Aspidodelone, whereas it is known as the Asp Turtle or Fastitocalon in the *Physiologus*, reputedly written in the second century B.C. in Alexandria, Egypt. This work was very widely distributed in Europe by the Middle Ages. During the same period the monster was known in bestiaries by the Greek name Aspidochelon and by the Latin name Aspido-Tortoise in twelfth- and thirteenth-century manuscripts. It was also known in the Middle East, no doubt from the Alexandrian library source, as the Zaratan. This creature was said to be vast, such that its huge stony body resembled an island in the sea. Its back was capable of growing shrubs and trees in the soil that accumulated there. It lived on a diet of fish attracted to the supposedly sweet smell emitted from its open mouth while floating in the sea. As soon as enough fish had entered its enormous jaws, they would snap shut on its victims. Thus it was reputedly the creature that swallowed Jonah of the biblical tale, as well as the model for medieval Christian depictions of the mouth of Hell. It was also the subject of a medieval horror story about sailors who, in need of rest and water, came upon an uninhabited "island" where they would scramble ashore. They would not suspect that the beach upon which they had lit their fire was alive, until it roared with pain and, with an almighty swoop, threw itself into the air and dived deep into the sea, dragging with it the ship, sailors, and all.
References 10, 14, 89, 184
See also Imap Umassoursa, Jasconius, monster, Zaratan

ASPIS (sing.), ASPISES (pl.)

Although the name Aspis means "Serpent," this monster was in fact a dragon in the legend and folklore of medieval Europe. It was described as being smaller than a full-sized dragon, but with only two feet. It may or may not have had wings according to different sources. The Aspis was said to be so poisonous that touching even the skin of a dead one would be fatal. Its bite meant instantaneous death for any living thing. However, there was one way of escaping its attention, and that was by distracting it with music. Aware of this flaw in its strategy for capturing its victims, the Aspis dulled its sensitivity to music by jamming the end of its tail in one ear while pressing the other to the ground. In this pose it was almost certain to allow the victim's escape.
References 10, 77
See also dragon, serpent, Wyvern

ASS (THREE-LEGGED)

This creature is no ordinary ass but, rather, one of spiritual significance in the Zoroastrian religion of Persia (now Iran). The Three-Legged Ass is an enormous creature described in the *Bundahish* (the ninth-century supplement to the works of the prophet Zoroaster) as being pure white with a golden branching horn in its forehead. It has two eyes in the usual place and a further two in both the forehead and the crown of its head. In its face it has three mouths (each the size of a house), a further three in its forehead, and three more on its body. It also has two ears. With this array it is able to know whatever evil is being plotted in an attempt to destroy it. The creature is so vast that the hooves of its three legs, as it stands in the ocean, cover an area large enough for a thousand sheep, and the spurs of each hoof would cover a thousand maneuvering horsemen. The Three-Legged Ass is the symbol of righteousness as well as the beneficent agent of Ahura Mazda in the fight against evil. It purifies the putrid oceans with its urine, and the amber that washes up on the shores is said to be its dung.
References 7, 18, 89
See also Alicorn, Amduscias, Biasd Na Srognig, Chio-Tuan, Karkadan, Ki Lin, Kirin, Koresck, Licorn, Mi'raj (Al), Onyx Monoceros, Scythian Ass, unicorn

ASS-BITTERN

This is the name of a creature depicted in British heraldry. It is a hybrid being with the head of a bittern (a large water bird) and the body of an ass.
References 7

ASTERION

This is the correct name of the Minotaur in the classical mythology of Greece and Rome. It was born of the union between the wife of the king of Crete, Pasiphae, and the Cretan Bull. Asterion was a humanoid monster with the head of a bull; more horrifying still was his cannibal appetite. He was kept confined in a labyrinth that Daedalus built specifically for him under the palace at Knossos. There Asterion was fed a diet of tributary slaves from the Greek mainland until he was killed by the hero Theseus.
References 165
See also Arzshenk, Cretan Bull, Minotaur, Shen-Nung

ASTREUS, ASTRÆUS

These are variations on the name of one of the Titans in the classical mythology of Greece and Rome. From his union with Eos, who symbolized the dawn, came Boreas, the god of the winds. Astreus is also mentioned in the later Italian literature of Boccaccio (1313–1375).

References 20, 173
See also Titan

ASTROPE

This is the name of a horse in the classical mythology of Greece and Rome. Astrope is one of the team of Horses of the Sun that pulled the golden chariot that Hephaestus had made for the sun-god Helios. Like the other horses, Astrope is described as the purest white with flaring, fire-breathing nostrils. Each morning the nymphs of time, the Horae, harnessed Astrope, along with the other Horses of the Sun, to the chariot for their journey across the sky. When the journey was finished at dusk, they browsed on magical herbs in the Islands of the Blessed, until they were harnessed for the next day.
References 138
See also Horses of the Sun

ATCEN

This is the name of an ogre in the beliefs and folklore of the Montagnais Native Canadians. This grotesque being not only preyed on sleeping humans in the forest but also chopped off their heads and then devoured them.
References 133
See also cannibal, ogre

Theseus slays the Minotaur, whose true name was Asterion (A Wonder Book for Boys and Girls and Tanglewood Tales *by N. Hawthorne, J. M. Dent, London*)

ATHACH

This is a monster in the folklore and beliefs of the people of the Highlands of Scotland. The name Athach in Scottish Gaelic may be translated as "Giant" or "Monster." Although descriptions of it are vague, it is said to inhabit lonely places such as the sides of lochs and deep gorges between the mountains. The Irish Fachan is one type of Athach.
References 128
See also Bocanách, Direach, Fachan, giant, monster

ATLAS

This is one of the Titans in the classical mythology of Greece and Rome. The name, according to various sources, means "the Bearer" or "Daring" or "Sufferer." Atlas was the son of the Oceanid Titaness Clymene/Klymene and the Titan Japetus/Iapetus; his step-brothers were Prometheus, Menoetus, and Epimetheus; and he was the father of the nymphs known as the Pleiades, Hyades, Hesperides, Calypso, Maia, Harmonia, Electra, and Dione. Atlas was also the ruler of Atlantis, a vast region of the earth flooded and destroyed by the newly emerging gods headed by Zeus. In vengeance, Atlas, with the other Titans, waged war on the new gods of Olympus. However, when the Titans were defeated, Atlas was condemned to hold the sky forever on his shoulders at the edge of the known world in North Africa. During this labor he was able to have but one period of rest—when the hero Heracles/Hercules, needing his help, took his place. However, when the hero Perseus returned on the winged horse Pegasus via Atlas's place of restriction, bearing the head of the Gorgon known as Medusa, Atlas saw the head and was instantly turned to stone. He became the mountains bearing his name in what is now the country of Morocco. When a very early compendium of maps of the countries of the world was printed, the cover bore an image of the Titan holding the world; from this image we now have the word *Atlas,* which to this day refers to a group of such maps.
References 20, 24, 38, 47, 78, 132, 165, 168, 173
See also Epimetheus, giant, Gorgon, Iapetus, Medusa, Pegasus, Prometheus, Titan

ATUNKAI

This is the name of a monster in the beliefs and folklore of the Native American people of Oregon in the United States. In the mountains of this state are the Wells of Amhuluk, which contain great water serpents. These serpents and wells are said to be capable of transforming into some monstrous form any living thing that falls in the water. The Atunkai monster, which resembled a huge grotesque otter, was originally said to have been a grizzly bear that fell and drowned in the Wells of Amhuluk.
References 133
See also Amhuluk, monster

AUDUMLA, AUDHUMBLA

These are variations on the name of a gigantic cow in the Norse and Teutonic mythology. According to Snorri Sturluson in the *Prose Edda,* written about 1220 A.D., she was the second being created from the melting of the ice in Niflheim. (The first was the giant Ymir, who also emerged from the melting ice.) While Audumla found nourishment from the salt of the frozen waters, she provided sustenance for the giant. But as the ice was removed by the rasping of the giant cow's tongue, she uncovered another being, Buri, whose grandsons, Odin, Ve, and Vili, became the first gods. These gods killed Ymir, creating the earth from his remains.
References 24, 61, 132, 138
See also Bestia, Dun Cow of Warwick, giant, Ymir

AUFHOCKER

This is the name of a giant demonic dog in the folklore of Germany. It has many of the same characteristics as the Belgian Black dog known as Kludde. The name Aufhocker may be translated as "Leap Upon." This monster might appear as a domestic animal that terrorizes night-bound travelers on lonely roads. It would also manifests as a Black dog when it would suddenly appear and pad along on its hind legs, raising itself higher and higher until it reached the throat of its victim. Its most usual manifestation was as a horse that encouraged the tired and the foolish to ride it. Its victims would be unable to get off until after a horrific ride, at which point they were usually ejected into a swamp, marsh, or river. The Aufhocker's other means of attack was to jump on the back of its victim and cling with its talons, becoming increasingly heavy as the terrified person tried to dislodge it. They might even be so exhausted that they could die from the trauma. However, if the Aufhocker was caught in the dawn light or if a nearby church bell was heard, then its victim might be saved.
References 58, 93, 159
See also Black dogs, Kludde, monster, Oschaert

AUGERINO

This is a monster of the Fearsome Critter variety coined by the lumberjack community of the United States. As the Augerino was rarely seen, no distinct description exists; however, it was said to inhabit the dry lands of Colorado. It was a burrowing creature whose movements were subterranean, and it disliked water and required a completely dry environment.

Atlas the Titan (Rose Photo Archive, UK)

These characteristics led it to attack all the water courses that the workers had dug, which would release vast quantities of water from the dams and ditches that they had constructed.
References 7, 24
See also Bunyan (Paul), Fearsome Critters, monster

AUGHISKY

This is the spelling of Eaċh Uisge (the Scottish water horse) that the author W. B. Yeats used in his work.
References 128
See also Eaċh Uisge

AUNYAINÁ

This is a cannibal monster in the beliefs and folklore of the Tupari people of Brazil. Aunyainá was described as an enormous humanoid being with tusks projecting from its face like those of a wild boar. This monster hunted humans for its food and chased unwary people, especially children, who wandered along the edge of the village, far into the forest. There Aunyainá would trap them, gore them to death, and devour their mangled bodies. One day the children whom Aunyainá was hunting climbed into a tree along some lianas to escape, but the creature followed awkwardly. A parrot saw the small intended victims' plight and flew to the tree, where it bit through the lianas, causing them and Aunyainá to crash to the jungle floor far below. The children, realizing their safety in the canopy of the trees, never came down again and became the monkeys of the forest. Meanwhile, the cannibal's smashed body still oozed life; from within it came the reptiles and lizards that now inhabit the rivers and swamps of the earth.
References 132
See also cannibal, monster

AURGELMIR

This is an alternative name for the primordial giant Ymir in the Norse mythology of Scandinavia.
References 61
See also giant, Ymir

AUVEKOEJAK

This is the name of a sea monster in the beliefs and folklore of the Inuit of Greenland and Northern Canada. Auvekoejak is said to manifest in a shape much the same as a merman of the Icelandic and Scandinavian countries (being known as the Havstrambe), but being covered in fur instead of scales. When Otto Fabricius was writing about this sea monster at the end of the eighteenth century, he conjectured that the relationship between the Auvekoejak, the Havstrambe, and the local Stellar' Sea Cow (also known as Buffon's Manatee) might be more than incidental. However, the local Inuit, despite calling the fur seal by the same name, insisted that the Auvekoejak and the seal were two distinct beings.
References 133
See also Havstrambe, merman, monster

AVAGRÁH, AVAGRAHO

In the Sikkata language, these are variations on the name for the Nyan, a monstrous serpentine creature in the traditions and legends of Burma.
References 81
See also Nyan

AXEHANDLE HOUND, AXHANDLE HOUND

These are variations on the name of a creature from the folklore of the lumberjacks and forest workers, especially in Wisconsin and Minnesota in the United States, during the nineteenth and early twentieth centuries. The Axehandle Hound belongs to a group of beings affectionately known as the Fearsome Critters, whose exaggerated proportions and activities not only explained the weird noises of the lonely landscape but also provided amusement in the camps. The Axehandle Hound was described as having a long thin body in the shape of an axe handle, squat little legs, and a head resembling an axe head. Its diet reputedly consisted of axe handles left unattended.
References 18
See also Fearsome Critters

AYIDA

This is the name of a great serpent in the folk beliefs of the people of the Island of Haiti in the Caribbean. Ayida, also known as Aida Wedo. She is the great Rainbow Snake who is the cosmic partner of the voodoo cosmic serpent Damballah.
References 132
See also Damballah, Rainbow Serpent, serpent

AZEMAN

This is the name of a blood-sucking monster in the folk beliefs of the people of Surinam on the north coast of South America. Azeman is almost always a woman who at night puts on the shed-dried skin of an animal and becomes a vampire, preying on the blood of her relatives and neighbors. There are a number of ways in which this outcome can be counteracted and the Azeman caught, as follows:

1. Lay a broom across the doorway at night; the Azeman reputedly cannot cross it.
2. Place several brooms in the middle of the floor; the Azeman is obliged to count each bristle and may be caught if dawn arrives before she has finished.

3. Cast rice or corn grains all over the floor; the Azeman is obliged to pick up and count each one in turn and may be caught by the same method as above.
4. Find the shed-dried animal skin and cover it with pepper, thus preventing its reuse.

References 24
See also Legarou, Loup garou, Sukuyan, vampire, Werewolf

AZI DAHAKA, AZIDAHAKA, AZHI DAHAKA, AŽI DAHAK

These are variations on the name of a supernatural monster in the Persian Zoroastrian creation myth. In the old Avestan language the prefix *aži* may be translated as "snake;" however the modern rendition of *ažidahakā*, in the Farsi language of the area, translates as "dragon." The description of the monster falls somewhere between these two images, inasmuch as Azi Dahaka is portrayed as a winged dragon-snake with three heads representing Pain, Anguish, and Death, each with six eyes and three pairs of fangs. The wings themselves are so vast that, when spread, they obliterate the heavens.

However, Azi Dahaka is described in the Shānāmah as humanoid in shape but with two serpents issuing from the his neck.

The creature was said to have been the son of the female demon Autak and to be the descendant and servant of Angra Mainu, the spirit of ultimate evil. At first Azi Dahaka consumed only cattle; but soon he turned his attentions to humans. He conspired to overthrow and destroy the first human being, Yima, and when he succeeded, he was in turn bound in chains under Mount Demavand and thus made powerless by the hero Thrāētona, or Ātār, depending on the source. This would be a temporary confinement, however, for it is predicted that at the end of time Azi Dahaka will break free, destroying a third of the human population in his vengeance, until ultimately defeated by Keresāspa.

References 24, 47, 64, 78, 125, 132, 138, 159
See also dragon, Fenrir, monster, serpent

AZ-I-WÛ-GÛM-KI-MUKH-'TI

The European traveler E. W. Nelson, when writing about the fauna of Greenland (Nelson 1899, pt. I, pp. 442–443), described this creature as one that inspired great fear in the Inuit people of the region. According to their beliefs and folklore, the Az-i-wû-gûm-ki-mukh-'ti resembled a walrus but had the head of a dog with fangs, four dog's legs, shiny black scales, and the tail of a giant fish. A thrashing blow from its tail was said to kill a man outright. Nelson dubbed it the "walrus-dog" without giving the Inuit translation of the name.

References 133
See also monster

AZRAIL

This is the name of a giant in the legends and folklore of Armenia. Azrail was said to be invincible, and when he took as hostage the brother of three fairies and held him enslaved, it was thought that nobody could save the victim. However, one hero, identified only as "the Apprentice" (signifying his apparent youth and inexperience), said that if he were given eleven goblets made of gold with which to bargain, he might save all the giant's slaves from the castle. As nobody else had succeeded, and the remaining people were all afraid, the king of the region readily gave the goblets as well as suitable armor and weapons to the young man. The Apprentice traveled to the vicinity of the giant's castle on Mount Djandjavag, where he was attacked by two of Azrail's gigantic servants. While they were distracted, the Apprentice managed to get the better of them; then he killed them. The noise attracted the attention of Azrail, who, armed with seven battle maces, swords, bows, and arrows, immediately challenged the upstart youth and launched a barrage of all his weaponry at him. But the Apprentice, having managed to dodge them all, heaved the king's battle mace at the side of the giant's head, knocking him from his horse. Leaping from his own horse, the youth chopped the giant's head from his neck and then chopped it into halves. Azrail instructed the youth to chop again, but the Apprentice wisely knew that this third stroke would restore the giant and left him as he was. Thus the hostages and slaves were freed.

Since Azrail is the name of one of the principal angels of death in the Judeo-Christian and Islamic literature, it is very possible that this folkloric character owes much to this derivation.

References 55
See also giant

AZURE DRAGON

This is an alternative name for the Blue Dragon of the Fêng Shui geomantic system of China.

References 89
See also Blue Dragon

B

BABA IAGA, BABA JAGA

These are alternative spellings of the name Baba Yaga, a monstrous female in the folklore and traditions of Central Europe and Russia.

References 20, 24, 55, 132, 159, 165

See also Baba Yaga

BABA YAGA, BABA JAGA, BABA IAGA

In Russian and East European folklore, Baba Yaga is a monstrous, supernatural, cannibal hag of entirely malicious intent. She is known in Poland both as Jezda and as Ienzababa and in the Czech Republic as Jezi Baba. She entices human victims, especially children, to a horrific death and, in folklore, is said to travel with Death, eating the souls of his victims. She is described as a hideous ogress, with fangs of stone or knife-blades, and her eyes petrify anyone upon whom she looks. When she sees a victim approaching, she may simply let drop her jaw, which is so huge that it could be mistaken for a cave, and swallow the victim whole. She is so enormous that when she lies down, her head is at one end of her little hut and her feet at the other, with her blue hooked nose touching the ceiling. The hut itself constantly whirls around on hen's legs, in a clearing in the forest, behind a fence of victims' bones decorated with their skulls with the remaining eyes glowing in their sockets. She travels by flying through the air either in a mortar propelled by its pestle or in an iron kettle, sweeping the air with a fiery broom. She is sometimes described as having sisters of the same name, all equally vile.

Baba Yaga is associated with other monsters such as Chudo Yudo and Koshchei, dragons that are under her vicious control.

References 20, 24, 25, 55, 61, 125, 132, 159, 165, 181

See also Black Annis, Cailleach Bheur, cannibal, Chudo-Yudo, dragon, Koshchei, Monster, ogress

BABE THE BLUE OX

This is a legendary gigantic ox in the folklore of nineteenth- and early-twentieth-century lumberjacks in the northwestern forests of the United States. This enormous creature was said to have been white originally, but became blue under the snow of the Winter of Blue Snows. This workmate and companion of the legendary gigantic hero Paul Bunyan was described as being ninety-three hands high, with a breadth of over forty-two axe handles. Babe's diet of hay was consumed with baling wire intact, and a crew of workers was employed full-time to pick it from Babe's teeth. His feet and tread were so huge that he was responsible for sinking the holes that filled to become the lakes of Oregon and Michigan, and by dragging a pick inadvertently behind him, he made a split in the earth that was later called the Grand Canyon. He was similarly responsible for creating Puget Sound. Babe's enormous appetite and love of hot cakes was to be his demise, for one day Babe could not wait and consumed not only the almost-cooked cakes but also the stove on which they were baking. The Black Hills of Dakota were said to be the mound that Paul Bunyan placed over his faithful companion's grave.

References 20, 24

See also Bunyan (Paul), Fearsome Critters, giant

BÄCKAHÄST

This is the name of a monstrous semisupernatural creature and an alternative form of the Näcken in Scandinavian folklore. The Bäckahäst was said to inhabit freshwater lakes and rivers, where it manifested at the water's edge in the shape of a water-horse. But there were times when it also resembled an upturned boat or a drifting log. Those who were transfixed and tempted into the water by it were doomed to be dragged to the bottom and consumed.

References 133, 159

See also Cabyll-Ushtey, Eačh Uisge, Kelpy

BAGWYN

This is the name of a hybrid humanoid creature in the heraldic repertoire of Europe.

References 5

Baba Yaga and Peter (Wonder Tales from Many Lands *by K. Pyle, Geo. Harrap and Co.)*

BAHAMUT

In the mythology associated with Islam, this is the name of a vast creature that supports the earth. Bahamut is described as an immense and dazzlingly bright fish with a head resembling that of a hippopotamus or elephant. According to one account, it was created to support a gigantic bull, which in turn supported an enormous ruby, on which stood an angel holding six hells above which was the earth and its seven heavens. According to another source, Bahamut supported a layer of sand on which stood a gigantic bull, on whose forehead rested a mountain of rock holding the waters in which the earth was located. Whatever the description and hierarchy, Bahamut's proportions were such that no human could imagine the size of the creature. Uniquely in the four hundred and ninety-sixth tale in the *Tales of the Thousand and One Nights* are we told that Isa (Jesus) was the only one ever to be granted the privilege of seeing Bahamut in all its magnitude. We are further told that beneath Bahamut, bearing all the fires of hell, is the monstrously vast serpent of hell called Falak.
References 18, 63, 89
See also Behemoth, Falak, Kujata

BAHRI

This is the name of a hybrid creature in the mythology associated with Islam. Bahri is shaped like a bird but has the head of a human being.
References 89
See also Alkonost, Angka, Borak (Al), Garuda, Harpy, Parthenope, Podarge, Ptitsy-Siriny, Siren, Sirin, Solovei Rakhmatich, Unnati, Zägh

BAKBAKWAKANOOKSIWAE, BAKHBAKWALANOOKSIWAY

These are variations on the name of an enormous man-eating bird-monster in the folklore and beliefs of the Kwakiutl people of the northwest region of Canada. It is also known as the Cannibal-at-the-North-End-of-the-World, a vast, vicious bird called Hokhoku, who, with his wife, Galokwudzuwis, hunts down human victims.
Bakbakwakanooksiwae, in the form of Hokhoku, smashes in the skull of his victims and devours the exposed brains. A dance drama is performed by the Kwakiutl people in which a youth is symbolically captured and transformed into Bakbakwakanooksiwae. He then has to be captured and tamed by the villagers with mystical chants, dancing, and songs. During the performance, huge symbolic masks depicting the birds' heads are worn by the participants.
References 77, 89
See also cannibal, Galokwudzuwis, monster

BAKU

In the folklore of the people of Japan, this is a benevolent semisupernatural monster that looks something like an enormous tapir. The Baku is described as having the body of a horse, the head of a lion, and the legs and paws of a tiger. This creature fulfills a role for humans during their early waking moments: if they have suffered a bad dream, all that is necessary is to call upon Baku to eat it up. The obliging monster will then devour the nightmare and restore the humans to a peaceful day.
References 7, 113
See also monster

BALAM

This is a general term for a group of semisupernatural guardians in the beliefs of the Quiché peoples of Mexico. The Balam, whose name means "Tiger" or "Jaguar," were originally gigantic terrifying manifestations of these big cats of the forest, assigned as guardians of the Four Directions. Their names were Iqi-Balam (Moon Jaguar), Balam-Agab (Nocturnal Jaguar), Balam-Quitzé (Smiling Jaguar), and Mahu-Catah (Famous Name)—names that may have been euphemisms intended to ward off the predations of these beasts. In the modern Mayan folklore, all four have been relegated to the role of guardians of nature. The Balam now protect the inhabitants, the villages, and their agricultural land.
References 119, 159

BALAM-AGAB

This is the name of one of a group of terrifying beings, known as the Balam, that were semi-supernatural guardians in the beliefs of the Quiché peoples of Mexico. The name Balam-Agab means "Nocturnal Jaguar." The Balam were originally gigantic terrifying manifestations of these beasts of the forest.
References 119, 159
See also Balam

BALAM-QUITZÉ

This is one of a group of terrifying beings, known as the Balam, in the beliefs of the Quiché peoples of Mexico. The name Balam-Quitzé means "Smiling Jaguar." The Balam were assigned as guardians of the Four Directions. These were originally gigantic terrifying manifestations of these beasts of the forest.
References 119, 159
See also Balam

BALAN

This is the name of a giant in the folklore and literature of medieval France. Balan was renowned for his strength and courage. He was the father of the giant Fierbras, and, according to the legend, both were ultimately defeated by the hero and emperor Charlemagne.

References 20

See also Ænotherus, Charlemagne, Fierabras, giant

BALENA

This is the name of a female sea monster in the folklore of the late medieval travelers and sailors of Europe. Many writers of the time derived their "knowledge" from the Alexandrian *Physiologus*, written about the second century A.D. This monstrous description was further compounded by illustrations and fanciful descriptions from such works as the bestiaries produced during the medieval period. Consequently, no clear description ever emerged. When the head of a walrus was sent to the papal court of Pope Leo X, from Norway in 1520, the Balena was described as its wife. This statement to the Pope did not appear to be accompanied by any further description.

References 133

See also Aspidochelone, monster

BALI, BALIN

These are variations on the name of a group of semisupernatural monsters in the Hindu beliefs of India. There are two types of being with this name, as follows:

1. Bali: Members of the group of Danavas and Daityas in the Hindu beliefs are malicious giants, the main one being Bali (also known as Mahabali). Bali is the grandson of an incarnation of Ravana (called Hiranyakasipu), whom he usurped as the ruler of the heavens and earth. The gods temporarily lost their power and domain to Bali, and Vishnu was requested to take another incarnation, as a dwarf Brahmin, to overthrow this evil giant. Vishnu visited Bali's abode as a guest and was granted his right of request—in this case, the territory covered in three paces. Vishnu immediately assumed his real form and the powerful god took two paces, which covered the entire universe. Bali acknowledged defeat and with the third pace Vishnu banished Bali to the underworld to reign there or, alternatively, to live in a mud hut in the form of a donkey.

A different version of the demise of Bali tells how Indra defeated the giant in a battle led by Jalandhara and his demons. When the giant was slain, instead of blood spurting from the severed body, a cascade of jewels poured from his mouth. Indra, out of curiosity, chopped up Bali's corpse and there came pearls from his teeth, rubies from his blood, sapphires from his eyes, crystals from his flesh, diamonds from his bones, and emeralds from the marrow.

2. Bali (also known as Balin) is the name of a gigantic prince of the apes and monkeys and the step-brother of Sugriva, their king. He is described as having been generated from the hair of his mother and, therefore, while resembling an enormous human in shape, was covered with hair and had an extremely long tail. By usurping his step-brother and taking the kingdom for himself, this enormous semisupernatural creature angered the gods and was ultimately shot and killed by Rama.

References 24, 38, 64, 125, 138

See also giant, Ymir

BALIOS, BALIUS

These are variations on the name of a semisupernatural horse in the classical mythology of Greece and Rome. It was one of a pair of horses, the other being Xanthos, that were the offspring of Podarge (one of the Harpies) from her union with Aeolus, the spirit of the winds. Balios, whose name means "Swift," and Xanthos were given by the sea-god Poseidon/Neptune to Pelops to draw his chariot through the skies. The two horses later pulled the chariot of the Greek hero Achilles during the Trojan Wars.

References 7, 89, 132

See also Harpy, Horses of the Sun, Podarge, Xanthos

BALOR, BALOR OF THE BALEFUL EYE, BALOR OF THE DREADFUL EYE, BALAR

These are variations on the name of the terrifyingly vast giant king of the Fomorians in the mythology and folklore of Ireland. Balor was not only enormous but had just one eye in the middle of his forehead from which a single glance would destroy all it beheld. This resulted from his willful curiosity as a child, when he peered into the druids' brewing cauldron; his one eye had received the full venomous vapor from the magic herbal poisons being prepared. As he grew, this eye grew even larger until four men were required to raise the eyelid. To be successful in battle, the Fomorians needed only to raise the eye of Balor and let him look at their enemies. That was the case until a seer prophesied that Balor's own grandchild would defeat him. So Balor kept his daughter Eithne guarded constantly by twelve loyal women. However, a hero of the Tuatha dé Danann, called Cian mac Cainte, gained their confidence by dressing as a woman; then he seduced all of them. They all gave birth, but the children were drowned by the irate Balor—that is, all but one of Eithne's triplets named Lug the Long-Handed. After a lengthy exile, Lug returned as a warrior of twentyone years, and claimed his membership of the Tuatha dé Danann at the court of Tara. Meanwhile, Balor had waged war on the Tuatha dé Danann at the first Battle of Mag Tured (Moytura), and had killed hundreds with one look of his raised eye. At the second Battle of Mag Tured, Lug employed the strategy of waiting out of range of the Baleful Eye until the eyelid became weary and closed. Although many warriors lay dead around him, Lug waited for the split second when the eyelid would raise, but not enough for the pupil of the killing eye to be active. At that moment, Lug sent a stone missile from his slingshot. It was so fast and accurate that it took Balor's eye clean through his brain and out through the back of his head, killing twenty-seven warriors behind him. Thus the grandson Lug killed Balor as prophesied.

References 24, 54, 78, 165
See also Cyclops, giant, Goliath

BANDERSNATCH

This is a little-explained monster in the poem "Jabberwocky," which appeared in the work *Through the Looking Glass* by Lewis Carroll (Charles Lutwidge Dodgson, 1832–1898), the eminent English author of *Alice's Adventures in Wonderland*, still popular today. It is described only as "frumious" (a combination of furious and fuming, according to Dodgson). Lewis Carroll enigmatically declared that it is best avoided at all costs.

References 7, 40
See also Boojum, Fearsome Critters, monster

BAPETS

This is the name of the female form of a race of monstrous humanoids, called the Siats, in the legends and folklore of the Southern Ute Native American people of the Great Basin region of the United States. Described as cannibals that were particularly prone to kidnapping children, the Bapets were even more malevolent, and with their enormous breasts full of poisonous milk suckled and killed any child instantly. These beings were almost immortal but could be killed with an obsidian arrow. It is possible that these monsters were invoked by anxious parents to prevent their adventurous small children from coming to harm.

References 77
See also cannibal, nursery bogies

BAPHOMET

This is the name of a humanoid monster in the mysteries and cult of the fourteenth-century European Knights Templar. The Baphomet is portrayed as having a female torso with a double head on its single neck, one female and the other male. The explanation of the symbol is that this curious monster was the subject of an idolatrous and decadent worshipping practice of the prophet Mohammed/Mohamet brought as an accusation during the high-profile papal heresy trials in 1307–1310. Following the suppression and disbanding of the Templars, their power now destroyed, the Baphomet was taken as a device in the heraldry of continental Europe.

References 7, 20
See also monster

BAR YACHRE

This is the name of a huge bird in the legends of the Jewish people from ancient times. It was said to resemble the Roc in terms of both its vast eaglelike appearance and its appetite for herds of cattle or even humans. During the Middle Ages, reports of Marco Polo's travels also contained an account of the Bar Yachre.

References 7
See also Griffin, Roc

BARGHEST

Barghest is an alternative spelling of the name Barguest in the folklore of northern England. This creature usually takes the form of an enormous malevolent dog.

References 7, 21, 24, 37, 93, 119, 159, 169
See also Barguest, Black Dogs

BARGUEST

This is the name of a monstrous bogie, a supernatural beast that usually takes the form of an enormous dog. In the northern English counties of Durham, Northumberland, and Yorkshire, it is also known as Barvest and Boguest, which might be derived from the German *Bahrgeist* meaning "Spirit of the Bier." The Barguest is variously described as a black dog the size of a mastiff, with horns, fangs, and fiery eyes; as a large shaggy-haired dog; or as a bear with huge claws and eyes like glowing coals. In some accounts it drags a chain; in others it is wrapped in chains. It has also been described as a headless man, a "Headless Woman," a white rabbit, and a cat or dog that disappears in flames. Whatever its manifestation, the Barguest is always associated with a particular locality. The mere sight of it bodes disaster or death, and if anyone tries to approach it or pass in front of it, it will inflict a terrible wound that never heals. Around the area of Leeds (Yorkshire), a Barguest was said to appear and to set all other dogs of the city howling when anyone of importance was about to die.

References 7, 21, 24, 37, 93, 119, 159, 169
See also Black Dogs, Black Shuck, Freybug, Gytrash, Mauthe Dhoog, Padfoot, Rongeur d'Os, Skriker, Trash

BAROMETZ

This is the name of a conglomerate beast-vegetable in the legends of medieval Europe. Also known as the

Boramez, the Chinese Lycopodium, the Lycopodium, the Jeduah, the Scythian Lamb, and the Vegetable Lamb of Tartary, it is described by medieval European travelers to the Middle East and then embellished in travel books of the period. The following description was given by the pseudoexplorer Sir John Mandeville in his famous *Travels* written about 1360 A.D.: "And there growethe a maner of Fruyt, as though it were Gowrdes; and when thei ben rype men kutten hem ato, and men fynden with inne a lytylle Best, in Flesche, in Bon and Blode, as though it were a lytylle Lomb with outen Wolle." [And there grows a type of fruit, like gourds; and when they are ripe men cut them in two, and find within a little beast with flesh, bone and blood like a little lamb without wool.]

By the seventeenth century, embellishment had made this creature even more extraordinary. As Sir Thomas Brown wrote in *Pseudodoxia Epidemica* (1646), "Much wonder is made of the Boramez that strange plant-animal or Vegetable Lamb of Tartary, which wolves delight to feed on, which hath the shape of a Lamb affordeth a bloody juyce upon breaking and liveth while the plant be consumed about it."

In general, the Barometz was believed to be a creature with roots that held it fast in one place. It resembled a lambsheep with golden colored fleece. The stalk allowed it to browse the surrounding pasture, but as soon as this was consumed, the creature died of starvation. Humans or wolves then came and harvested the body, which was said to taste like crab meat. Its hooves were made of hair, which, like its fleece, was used by humans for weaving clothes.

There are two possible explanations for the development of the legend surrounding this creature, whose presence clearly mystified the early travelers. The first is that it is a strange description of the cotton plant; and the other, that it is a strange description of a woolly fern (*Cibotium barometz*) that grows in the Middle East, the down of which has been used like cotton wool to stem the flow of blood from wounds.
References 7, 18, 20, 89, 179

BARONG

This is the name of a fearsome dragon in the literature, drama, and folklore of the Balinese people of Indonesia. Barong features in a play drama known as *Tjalon Arang* in which the widow or witch, called Ranga, is an adversary of Barong. It is portrayed as having a huge hideous dragon head with leering protruding eyes and enormous fangs over a lolling protruding tongue, attached to a long tortuously winding body.
References 24
See also dragon

BARUSHKA MATUSHKA

This is the name of a magnificent fabulous horse in the legends of Russia. Barushka Matushka, also known as Sivushko or Kosmatushka, was the wondrous magical steed of the *bogatyr'* (hero knight of all the Russias) called Il' ya Muromets.
References 55
See also Sivushko

BARVEST

Barvest is an alternative spelling of the name Barguest in the folklore of northern England. This creature usually takes the form of an enormous malevolent dog.
References 7, 21, 24, 37, 93, 119, 159, 169
See also Barguest

BASA-ANDRE

This is the name of the wife of the ogre Basa-Jaun. She is depicted as a type of siren who sits combing her long hair and luring mortals to their demise in the malignant power of Basa-Jaun. However, if she is entreated by some youthful victims, she may help them to escape.
References 24, 159
See also Basajaun

BASAJAUN, BASA-JAUN

These are variations on the name of a being in the Basque folklore of northwestern Spain. (The French name for this hairy man of the woods is Homme de Bouc.) Basajaun, who takes the shape of an ogre or a faun, is credited with teaching humans about agriculture and iron-working. He is also mischievous and plays tricks on others. Basajaun lives high in the Pyrenean Mountains, in the woods and caves where he protects the flocks of sheep and goats. But he has a malignant nature and will trap and torture humans if they stray into his domain. His wife, called Basa-Andre, is depicted as a type of siren who sits combing her long hair and luring mortals to their demise. However, when entreated by some youthful victims, she may help them to escape.
References 24, 119, 125, 159
See also faun, ogre, Siren

BASILCOC, BASILCOK

These are alternative names for the Basilisk in the medieval legends and folklore of Europe.
References 7, 24, 37, 78, 89, 94, 148
See also Basilisk

BASILIC

This is the name of a dragon in the folklore of France. The Basilic plagued the countryside around the town of Vienne not only with its monstrous predations, taking both cattle and human victims, but also with its hideous stare, petrifying all it gazed upon. The town was diminished and terrified until the hero Fretard, a knight of medieval renown, defeated the Basilic and banished it to the bottom of the Well of Colaine. But that was not the end of this turbulent beast, for it was said to ascend and resurface every ten years. However, if it were seen before it could stare at its observer, it was said to be sent back to the bottom; but if nobody ever saw it arrive at the surface edge of the well, the region would once again be doomed.

References 94
See also Basilisk, dragon

BASILI-COC

This is an alternative name for the Basilisk in the medieval legends and folklore of Europe.
References 7, 20, 24, 78, 89, 94, 148
See also Basilisk

BASILISK

The Basilisk is a fabulous creature of European and Middle Eastern legend and folklore. It has many descriptions according to the various sources, which range from ancient times to about the seventeenth century, when its popularity waned. At first it was described simply as a small reptile resembling a grass snake, but with the distinction of its thorax that remained erect and out of contact with the ground when it moved and a protrusion resembling a crest or crown on its head. It is from this crown that the name derives, as the Greek word *basileus* may be translated as "king." Accordingly, it was designated the king of the reptiles. What accounts for this otherwise unremarkable reptile's reputation, however, was its sheer venom. Every part of the Basilisk meant death to any living thing it touched, breathed on, or saw. Its bite, its smell, its saliva, and its glance were fatal. Nothing could survive an encounter with this monstrous creature. It could even spit its venom at birds flying past and thereby kill them, and its glance, like that of the Gorgon Medusa, was sufficient to kill instantly. Its destructiveness was such that it was said to have been responsible for bringing about the deserts of Libya and the Middle East, where it lived. The Basilisk is mentioned in such ancient texts as the Hebraic *Book of Jeremiah* (8:17) and the *Psalms* (91:13) as being symbolic of the Devil to be defeated by the coming Messiah. It was similarly described by Pliny the Elder in his *Historia Naturalis* (A.D. 77).

During the medieval period, however, the description was varied by the accounts from travelers' and pilgrims' tales. Bestiaries of the eleventh and twelfth centuries maintained Pliny's basic description but included references to a much larger body with either white spots or stripes along it, a mouth that emitted fiery breath, a death-invoking bellow, and the ability to drive people mad through the hydrophobia it induced. It was then conjectured that there were three ways to avoid death from this terrifying creature. The first (probably derived from the classical myth of Medusa) was to carry a crystal globe and reflect the creature's stare back at it, thereby causing it to kill itself; the second was to carry a weasel, said to be the enemy of the Basilisk and to have an equally venomous bite; and the third was to carry a cockerel, as the Basilisk was thrown into a fit by the crowing of this bird, from which it died. (As the weasel is not only wild but also a venomous creature, the carrying of a cockerel on journeys through the deserts became the reason for the Basilisk's changed description and name.)

By the fourteenth century, the English author and diplomat Chaucer (1345–1400) mentioned the Basilisk in his "Parson's Tale" in the *Canterbury Tales* under the name of the Basilicok. This name later developed into Cockatrice, giving testament to the folkloric tale of its having been hatched for nine years by a toad from a seven-year-old cockerel's egg (like the more recent Aitvaras). Previously described as a serpent, it was now said to have the head, neck, and legs of a cockerel, the tail of a serpent, often with a cockerel's head, a human face, and the wings of a dragon. Its killing potential had also increased such that it could now kill a human who attempted to spear it by causing its own poison to travel back up the length of the spear; in addition, it could rot the fruit off trees from a distance and pollute the water where it drank so as to be poisonous for centuries. So great was this monster's reputation for inflicting instantaneous death that its name was given, during Tudor times, to an enormous brass cannon and, later, to a venomous lizard of Armenia.

The Basilisk increasingly became the subject of literature, as in Spenser's *The Faerie Queene* (Act IV, Scene 8, line 37) and Shakespeare's *Richard III*, and of illustrations such as in Androvandi's "Natural History of Serpents and Dragons," where it retained a reptile's scales but was given eight cockerel's legs. It was through literary exposure that the demise of belief in this fabulous monster was evidenced. As the Spanish poet, author, and diplomat Francisco Gomez de Quevedo y Villegas (1580–1645) wrote in his work on the Basilisk:

Si está vivo quien te vio,
Toda su historia es mentira,
Pues si no murió te ignora,
Y si murió no lo afirma.

This poem may be translated as follows: If the person who saw you is still living, then your whole story is lies, since if he didn't die, he has no knowledge of you, and if he died he couldn't confirm it.

However, the Basilisk and its alter ego the Cockatrice were so firmly embedded in the images of European society that they persist in the heraldic devices of families, nobility, and institutions to this day.

References 5, 7, 14, 18, 20, 24, 63, 78, 89, 91, 94, 148, 167, 184

See also Aitvaras, Basilicoc, Cockatrice, dragon, Gorgon, Medusa, serpent, Skoffin, Uraeus, Wyvern

BATTLESWINE

These are the heroic yet fearsome wild-boar adversaries of the heroes and gods in the Norse mythology of Scandinavia. The two protagonists are Hildisuin and Sachrimnir.

References 89

See also Ætolian Boar, Beigad, Boar of Beann-Gulbain, Buata, Cafre, Calydonian Boar, Erymanthean Boar, Hildisuin, Pugot/Pugut, Sachrimnir, Twrch Trwyth, Ysgithyrwyn

BAUGI

This is the name of a giant in the Norse mythology of Scandinavia. He was the brother of the giant named Suttung, who was the owner of the mead of inspiration called *Kvasir*. This mead had been obtained from the dwarfs who had killed their father Gilling, and was taken in revenge for the killing. However, the mead was desired by the gods, especially Odin, so Suttung made his daughter Gunnlöd guard it in the cavern where it was hidden. But Odin knew that Baugi was weak and, by offering his services while in disguise, obtained information about the mead's hiding place. Changing himself into a serpent, the god then slithered into the cavern through a fissure that he had persuaded Baugi to drill for him in the rock wall. Once inside, Odin was able to seduce the giant's daughter and gain the mead.

References 138, 165

See also giant, Gunnlod, serpent, Suttung

BAYARD

Bayard is the name of a fabulous horse in the literature and folklore of medieval France and Italy. In particular, Bayard features in the romances of Charlemagne—namely, Boiardo's *Orlando Innamorato* (1486) and its continuation, Ariosto's *Orlando Furioso* (1516). The horse was not only immortal, and faster than any other, but also able to adjust its size to fit the rider. Originally said to belong to the Emperor Charlemagne, it was given by him to the four sons of Aymon. When only one son rode the horse, it remained the same size as other horses, but as the other sons mounted the beast one behind the other, it elongated to accommodate them all.

In all probability, the Cheval Bayard of French more modern folklore is derived from the Bayard of the Age of Chivalry.

References 7, 20

See also Ænotherus, Balan, Charlemagne, Cheval Bayard, Fierabras

BE CHASTI

This is the name of a giant in the traditions and beliefs of the White Mountain Apache Native American people of the United States. Be Chasti, also known as Metal Old Man, is a giant almost entirely covered in plates of black obsidian. Only the armpits remain uncovered, and it is these vulnerable places that are targets for the arrows of the hero when Be Chasti meets his end.

References 24

See also giant, Golem, Talos

BEANNACH-NIMHE

This is a monster in the folklore of Scotland. Beannach-nimhe, which may be translated as "Horned Poison," is said to be a huge, terrifying creature with horns that roams the Highlands.

References 128

See also monster

BEAST

The legends of the Beauty and the Beast feature in the folklore of many countries worldwide. In general, they revolve around a disfigured, monstrous beast or ogre, befriended or cared for in some way by an innocent, beautiful, and trusting young woman who shows no fear. When the Beast is threatened by some external danger, the loving care of the heroine is demonstrated in some way, usually by tears or a kiss. This is sufficient to break the magic spell that bound and transformed the Beast from being a handsome young man of royal blood. Naturally the pair live happily ever after.

The most famous is perhaps the French version rewritten by Madame Leprince de Beaumont, in which the Beast is leonine. In other versions, from the Basque region between France and Spain, the Beast is a huge serpent, whereas in Hungary he is a huge pig, in Lithuania he is a white wolf, in Armenia he is a dragon, and in South Africa the heroine licks the tears from a monstrous crocodile. More than any other folktale motif, this one signals triumph over adversity in an overtly romantic theme.

In a strange modern twist to the motif, the film *King Kong* (1933) exploits the same theme; but because the "beast," an enormous ape, cannot transform, it is destroyed.

References 138, 181
See also King Kong, Loathly Lady, monster, Odz-Manouk, ogre, Rhinocéros, Riquet à la Houppe, Serpentin Vert

BEAST OF LETTIR DALLAN, THE
This monster in the early legends of Ireland is described as a humanoid creature having a vast bulbous body like a fire bellows and the head of a man. The account of the Beast of Lettir Dallan derives from Old Irish of the tenth century but was written into the Triads of Ireland at the end of the fourteenth century. The story tells of a local priest's daughter who is seduced late one night along the lakeside by a monstrous water horse. The Beast of Lettir Dallan was the progeny of this union.
References 133
See also Kelpy, monster

BÉBINN
This is the name of a beautiful giantess in Irish mythology. In the Fenian cycle it is told how she is murdered by Aeda, whose suit she refused while under the ineffectual protection of Fionn.
References 128
See also giantess

BEGDU SAN
This is the name of a giant in the folklore and legends of the northeast region of China. Apparently Begdu San originally lived in the north of Korea. He was so vast that for sustenance he consumed vegetation for miles and so tall that he eventually blocked the sunlight from the entire region, so he was banished to the mountain ranges of the far north. There he existed happily until he had consumed all the forests and drunk all the rivers dry. So he wandered farther east and started to drink the sea. This made him ill and, as he collapsed, his body formed the Begdu San Mountains, while the released waters became the rivers Tumun and Yalu, and the "dragon pool" Yong Dam.
References 132
See also giant, Ymir

BEHEMOTH
This is a monster in the religious traditions of the Hebrew, Christian, and Muslim faiths. Behemoth is described in both the Hebraic books of *Enoch* (40:7–9) and *Job* (51:15–24) as the male counterpart of the female Leviathan. It is of enormous proportions, so vast that the desert of Dendain extends across its upper body; its bones are as of brass; its huge jaws consume thousands of acres of vegetation at one gulp and the river Jordan at one swallow.

It was prophesied in Jewish tradition that at the coming of the Day of Judgment and the Messiah, the

Behemoth and Leviathan (Rose Photo Archive, UK)

Leviathan and Behemoth would be locked in combat to the death. The resulting bodies would be food for the "chosen," who had lived their lives in righteousness.

In European medieval Christian tradition, Behemoth was regarded as a most powerful tempter that manifested in the shape of a grotesque elephant. His domain is that of the "delights of the belly," and he is charged by the Devil with tempting humans into the vice of overindulgence.

In the Muslim tradition, Behemoth equates with the monstrous Bahamut, the vast monster that supports the earth in the cosmos.
References 7, 18, 20, 24, 47, 61, 63, 78, 89, 94, 125, 133, 159
See also Bahamut, Leviathan, monster

BEIGAD
This is a semisupernatural boar in the traditional literature and folklore of Iceland. The name Beigad may be translated as "Terrifier" or "Fear-Bringer." Its tale is told in both the *Landnámabók* and the *Vatnsdæla Saga* of old Iceland. This magnificent boar was both terrible and admirable to the people, so when it became known that Beigad was loose among the sows belonging to Ingimund, which had wandered into Svinadal, the people were determined to catch him. The hunt was long and hazardous, but at last, when the hunters thought that Beigad was trapped against the sea, the beast jumped in and swam until his trotters dropped off. The boar needed to reach land, and, exhausted, he scrambled up a nearby hill. But the

Grotesque sea creatures. In the Manx language, Yn Beisht Kione means "the Beast with the Black Head." (Rose Photo Archive, UK)

swim had finished him, and the hunters gained their huge prize at last.

References 337

See also Ætolian Boar, Battleswine, Beigad, Boar of Beann-Gulbain, Buata, Cafre/Kafre, Calydonian Boar, Erymanthean Boar, Hildisuin, Pugot/Pugut, Sachrimnir, Twrch Trwyth, Ysgithyrwyn

BEISHT KIONE, YN

This is the name of a sea monster in the folklore and traditions of the Isle of Man in the British Isles. In the Manx language, Yn Beisht Kione means "the Beast with the Black Head." Fishermen of the south coast of the island dreaded ever seeing it raise its black head above the surface of the waters.

References 128

See also monster

BEITHIR

This is a class of monster in the folklore and traditions of the Scottish Highlands. Although the name may be

derived from an old Norse word for "bear," the Gaelic word tends to be used in reference to some gigantic semisupernatural creature that equates with beast, dragon, or even serpent. The description often mentions a long thick tail but no wings. It was said to inhabit the corries and mountains around Glen Coe. In more modern folkloric tales, the Beithir has metamorphosed into a type of Fuath or haunting supernatural.

References 128

See also dragon, Fuath, monster, serpent

BEL

There are two types of being with this name, as follows:

1. Bel is a dragon mentioned in the Old Testament *Book of Daniel*. It was the object of veneration and worship in the Babylonian empire where Daniel was held captive.

2. Bel is also the name of a Frost Giant in the Norse mythology of Scandinavia. Bel, whose name may be translated as "Storm," is the son of Kari.

References 24, 63
See also dragon, Frost Giants, giant, Kari

BELAGOG
In the Arthurian traditions and romances of Britain, Belagog is the name of a giant. He was said to be the guardian of the stronghold of King Arthur and of the vast cave beneath Tintagel in Cornwall, now known as Merlin's Cave. The name may have much in common with, and appears to have been conflated with, those of the giants Bell and Gog and Magog.
References 54
See also Bell, giant, Gog and Magog

BELL
There are two types of being with this name, as follows:

1. Bell is the wife of the giant Wade in the folklore and traditions of Yorkshire in the north of England. Wade and Bell were said to be responsible for the building of many of the ancient and natural features of the region. The castles of Pickering and Mulgrave were created by them whilst throwing their only hammer back and forth to each other in turn. A long causeway between the two castles is accounted for in the following story. Bell owned a gigantic cow that was set to graze on the eastern moors of the county, but as she and her husband lived on the west side, Wade constructed the causeway so that his wife could milk the cow each day. In fact, it is an ancient Roman road still visible today. During the Tudor period of the sixteenth century, tourist trade to the area was boosted by the "discovery" of the jaw bone of Bell's cow, displayed to visitors in the Castle of Mulgrave. This bone was actually the jaw of a whale; which after the destruction of the castle during the civil wars of the seventeenth century, was still to be seen in the local butcher's shop bearing the signatures of gullible tourists.

2. Bell is also the name of a giant in the folklore and traditions of the county of Leicestershire in England. It was said that he had a sorrel horse and that he intended to get to the other side of the county more rapidly than usual. Bell and his horse covered the distance in three enormous leaps. The places at which he alighted were named accordingly, starting with Mountsorrel. The first stage became Wanlip (meaning "One Leap"); the second, Burstall (where his girths broke); and the third, Bellegrave, for that was where he died of exhaustion and was buried. There are numerous accounts from the seventeenth and eighteenth centuries, but certainly no earlier than the eleventh century, as the names were different before then. Although the spellings and pronunciation of the names have changed over the years, it was probably in an effort to make sense of such evocative names that the tradition arose.

References 54, 182
See also giant, Wade, Weland

BELLERUS
This is the name of a giant in the literature of the English Puritan poet John Milton (1608–1674). In his account of Cornwall, the region had been known to the Roman invaders as Bellerium, which Milton adapted for the name of the giant he placed in that county.
References 20
See also Corineus, giant, Gog and Magog

BEN VARREY
This is the name for the mermaid in the Manx language and folklore of the Isle of Man in the British Isles. She closely resembles the usual description of a beautiful maiden with golden hair whose singing malevolently enchants fishermen to their doom. But the Ben Varrey can be benevolent, as in the tale in Dora Broome's *Fairy Tales from the Isle of Man,* in which a grateful mermaid tells her mortal rescuer where to find a hoard of treasure. However, the rescuer, an uneducated fisherman, does not recognize the value of Spanish Armada gold and simply throws it back into the sea. The merman in the Manx folklore is known as the Dinny-Mara.
References 24, 128, 159
See also Dinny Mara, Havfrue, mermaid, merman

BENDIGEIFRAN, BENDIGEID FRAN, BENDIGEIT VRAN
These are variations on the name of the supernatural heroic giant in the early Celtic narratives of Britain especially of Wales, also known as Brân Llyr. His story is interwoven with those of other heroes such as King Arthur, which are more fully explored here under the heading of Bran.
References 128
See also Bran, giant

BENNU, BENU
These are variations on the name of a fabulous bird in the mythology of ancient Egypt. It is depicted as closely resembling a stork, a large white wading bird with long red legs and a crest of two elongated feathers extending from the crown of its head. According to the legend, recorded on papyri, the Bennu bird rises from a burning tree with such melodious song that even the gods are transfixed by it. Thus the bird became the symbol of the sun-god Ra and his rebirth each morning in a fiery glow of dawn. The Bennu bird has thus in later folklore been equated with the Phoenix motif.
References 7, 89, 91, 168
See also Kerkes, Phoenix

Ben Varrey is the name for a mermaid in the Manx language and folklore of the Isle of Man (Rose Photo Archive, UK)

BERGBUI
This is the name of a class of giants in the Norse mythology of Scandinavia. The Bergbui are the mountain-dwelling type of Jotunar.
References 24
See also giant, Jotun

BERGELMIR
This is the name of a Frost Giant in the Norse mythology of Scandinavia. Bergelmir is one of the ancient giants who existed from the beginning, along with Ymir. When Ymir was slain by his grandsons, the gods Odin Vili and Ve, the blood that flowed from the giant created a vast flood that engulfed the land of the Frost Giants. Only Bergelmir and his wife escaped, according to a myth that parallels that of the biblical Noah. The descendants of Bergelmir and his wife became the new race of Frost Giants, who constantly seek revenge from the gods for the murder of their ancestors.
References 78, 127, 132, 138
See also Frost Giants, giant, Noah, Ymir

BERGJARL
This is the name of the chief of the Bergbui who are the mountain dwelling giants or Jotunar/Jotuns in the Norse mythology of Scandanavia. His name means "Lord of the Mountains."
References 24
See also giant, Jotun

BERGRISER
This is the name of a class of giants in the Norse mythology of Scandinavia. The Bergriser are the cliff-dwelling type of Jotunar.

References 24
See also giant, Jotun

BERREY DHONE
This is the name of a female giant in the folklore of the Isle of Man in the British Isles. She is represented as a gigantic hag or crone who is extremely aggressive and will stride across seas and mountains to defeat her adversaries.
References 128
See also giant, giantess

BESTIA, BESTLA
These are variations on the name of a giantess in the Norse mythology of Scandinavia. Bestia was the daughter of the primeval giant Ymir (or in some accounts the daughter of the giant Bolthorn) and the sister of Mimir. She married Bor, the son of Buri—the first being to emerge from under the ice melted by the giant cow Audumla. The three sons of Bestia and Buri were the first three of the Aesir—Odin, Ve, and Vili—who later slew Ymir.
References 78, 132, 138, 168
See also Audumla, Bolthorn, giant, giantess, Mimir, Ymir

BETIKHÂN
This is the name of a composite being in the folklore of India. Described as a type of faun, with an animal body but human head and arms, the Betikhân inhabits the woodlands and forests of the Neilgherry Hills and hunts animals for its prey.
References 151, 159
See also faun

BEVIS

In English folklore and legend this is the name of a giant who was said to inhabit the hills of the county of Sussex. He was so enormous that he could wade through the Solent Channel between the coast of Hampshire and the Isle of Wight, using a tree for a staff, without getting his upper body wet. The legend of Bevis includes his romance with Joisyan and numerous challenges, among them a fight to the death with the giant Ascapard. It is said that, after Bevis's victory over the malicious Ascapard, the Earl of Arundel invited Bevis to become the warden of Arundel Castle, where the Bevis Tower was built as his home. It is also said that when he was dying he threw his mighty sword from the top, and that the burial mound called Bevis's Grave is where it landed. A mighty sword of great antiquity, measuring five feet nine inches in length, is still to be seen in the armory of the castle. (This burial motif is also found in the legends of both Robin Hood and King Arthur.) Bevis's wading staff was bequeathed to Bosham Church, where it remained an object of wonder for many generations.

References 182
See also Ascapard, giant

BHAINSĀSURA

This is the name of a monster in the Hindu folklore of India. Described as a vast elephantine creature of destruction with the head of a water buffalo, Bhainsāsura terrorizes villages, destroying crops and fertile fields unless offered a pig. It appears at the time of the rice harvest for its due respect and portion. But if ignored, it reappears at the time of the corn harvest and smashes the ripening corn down to the ground. This monster is derived from a being in Hindu mythology known as Mahisha, which was vanquished by Skanda (according to the legends of the *Mahābhārata*) or by Durgā when fighting the Asuras.

References 7, 24
See also Mahisha, monster

BHIMA

This is the name of a giant in the Hindu mythology of India. Also known by the epithet Vrikodara, which may be translated as "Wolf's Belly," he had a ravenous appetite that frequently left others without food. Bhima was of enormous proportions and extremely strong; he was also capable of flight—a legacy of his father, the wind-god Vayu. He was a great warrior who was very brave on the battlefield; but when crossed by a wicked person or demon, he could be equally cruel. During his youth, a cousin who was jealous of his position and power poisoned Bhima and disposed of the huge body in the Ganges River. The serpents within the sacred river recognized the giant and resuscitated him.

Bhima became the champion of victims; he rescued the Pandavas from Purochana; he killed both Jayadratha and Kitchaka for attempting to rape Draupadi; and, later, rescued her from death. Bhima married Hindimba, the sister of the demon Hidimba, after slaughtering him in battle. By her he had a son called Ghatotkacha. Later he married the Princess of Kasi, called Balandhara, who bore him a son named Sarvaga. He killed many other demons, including Vaka, and the gods were so impressed that they gave humans a reprieve from their slaughter by the gods.

As a great warrior Bhima was able to take on many demons and supernatural adversaries, and he fought in the great battles detailed in the *Mahābhārata.* In this epic, his victories over Bhishima and the princes of Magadha, Duhsasana, and Duryodhana are recorded. Later, in revenge, King Dhritarashtra tried to lure Bhima to his death by inviting him to the palace for a celebration. But the god Krishna protected Bhima by sending an iron replica in the giant's place. The replica was crushed to bits instead.

References 112
See also giant

BIALOZAR

In the legends and folklore of Poland, this is the name for the fabulous gigantic bird of Russia known as the Kreutzet.

References 7
See also Kreutzet, Roc, Simurgh

BIASD BHEULACH

This is the name of a semisupernatural monster in the traditions and folklore of the Isle of Skye in the Hebridean Islands off the coast of Scotland. The Biasd Bheulach, which haunted the locality of Ordail Pass, usually manifested as a grotesque man with only one leg, although it was sometimes described as a monstrous beast or huge greyhound. At night it could be heard howling and shrieking, causing terror to all who heard it or needed to travel through the pass. One morning, a workman was found dead with horrifying wounds to both his leg and side; but after this, the Biasd Bheulach never reappeared.

References 24, 128, 159
See also Fachan, Nashas, Paija, Shiqq

BIASD NA SROGNIG, BIASD NA SROGAIG

These are variations on the name of a creature in the traditions and folklore of the Hebridean Islands of Scotland. The Biasd na Srognig is described as an ungainly water horse or as a creature resembling a horse with vast legs that make it look very awkward. However it is the horn that protrudes from the top of its head that gives it its name, which may be translated as "the Beast of the Lowering Horn." Indeed, it is a form of the fabled unicorn said to inhabit the lochs of the Isle of Skye.

References 7, 89

See also Alicorn, Amduscias, Ass (Three-Legged), Chio-Tuan, Karkadan, Ki Lin, Kirin, Koresck, Licorn, Mi'raj (Al), Onyx Monoceros, Scythian Ass, unicorn

BIAST

This is an alternative spelling of the Piast, a monster in the legends and folklore of Ireland.

References 133

See also Apocalyptic Beast, monster, Piast

BICHA

This is the name of a monster in the legends and folklore of Spain. It has been depicted since ancient times as having the body of a bull and the head and face of a human.

References 89

See also Lamassu, monster

BICORNE

This is a female monster in the legends and folklore of medieval Europe. Also known as the Bulchin during the sixteenth century, it was fat, resembling a well-fed panther with a human face and broad grin. It was said to live on a diet of "hen-pecked" husbands. In the chauvinist attitudes of the period, such a diet was conjectured to have provided a great quantity of fodder for the beast. Her malnourished counterpart, the Chichevache, fed only on "hen-pecked" wives! Both the Bicorn and the Chichevache were frequently depicted in the church furniture of the period, especially on the misericords.

References 7

See also Chichevache, monster

BIG EARS

This is the name of a demonic cat in the legends and folklore of the Highlands of Scotland. A monstrous being with enormous ears and evil leering yellow eyes, it was summoned as part of a satanic ritual in which real cats were tortured in the ceremony known as Taghairm during the seventeenth century.

References 128

See also Cat Sith, Cath Paluc

BIG FISH OF ILIAMNA, THE

This is a monster in the folklore and legends of the Tanaina people of the subarctic regions of Alaska in the United States. The Big Fish of Iliamna is a terrifying monster that pursues fishing boats across the semifrozen sea and bites chunks out of the bottom until the fishermen within fall to their horrible fate.

References 77

See also monster

BIG HEADS

This is the name of a class of monsters in the traditions and beliefs of the Iroquois Native American people of the United States. The Big Heads, also known as the Flying Heads, are described as huge disembodied heads with flashing fiery eyes and cavernous gaping mouths; they are covered in vast amounts of long, straggly hair from which two grotesque paws with talons emerge. Sustained by this hair during tempests, the Big Heads fly through the stormy skies searching for unwary humans.

References 38, 138

See also Flying Heads, Pontianak

BIG MAN-EATER

This is the name of a gigantic cannibal in the folklore of the people of Alabama in the southeast United States. The Big Man-Eater had a voracious appetite but was both lazy and useless when it came to hunting for game. So he eventually turned to killing unwary humans. But when even this became too much of an effort, he demanded that his wife cut off her limbs to supply him with food. She fled and told her outraged family what had become of her husband. Her brothers immediately killed him, throwing the body on a fire. As he burned, swarms of black birds and winged stinging insects flew out from his corpse.

References 89

See also cannibal, giant

BIG OWL

This is the name of a monster or giant owl in the traditions and beliefs of the Apache Native American people of the United States. The description of Big Owl differs according to each of the traditions. In the legends of the Chiricahua and Mescalero Apache, he is an evil giant; in the legends of the Jacarilla Apache, he is a vicious cannibal monster that petrifies human victims with his evil stare in order to trap and devour them. A similar type of legend in the traditions of the Lipan describes Big Owl as a deceitful giant who encourages his daughter to become the wife of a culture hero, so that Big Owl has him in his power and can be killed by him. However in the legends of the White Mountain Apache, he is the gigantic offspring of the Sun, along with his brother who is a culture hero. Out of sheer malice Big Owl destroys not only the humans in the world but also his own brother.

References 24

See also giant, monster

BIGFOOT

This is the name of a humanoid creature in the traditions and folk beliefs of the people of the United States and Canada. The Bigfoot, alternatively known as Sasquatch, is also known by many other names to the Native American peoples. This being is popularly described as a giant man-ape of seven to eight feet in height, with enormous feet and hands and a body that is covered in long black or brown-black hair and slightly inclined like a Langlauf skier when walking. Reputed to be exceptionally strong and credited with snapping huge pine trees like matchsticks, the beings inhabit deep gloomy ferny forests, particularly in the Goad Mountain range and the Sierra Nevada of California, but also on Mount Saint Helens, Mount Adams, and Mount Rainier in the Cascade Mountains and the coastal range of Oregon. These creatures are said to be ever-present in certain locations; though not observable themselves, they observe humans (especially children) who are camping, lumberjacks and loggers at work, and people whose cars have broken down on the highway.

Although the Bigfoot has long been established in legend and folklore, and over 3,000 sightings have been described, no sighting was actually recorded until October 20, 1967, when Roger Patterson, Harry Lund, and John Waters succeeded in filming, for several minutes, the movements of what appeared to be a large female Bigfoot in the forest at Bluff Creek, in Northern California in the United States. Anthropologists and scientists, among them Dr. Henry Farrenback, are still analyzing samples of hair and other debris that they believe have come from these creatures.

The Bigfoot equates with many other mysterious anthropoid beings such as the Yeti of Nepal, the Yowie of Native Australia, and the Mountain Man of Japan.
References 16, 78
See also Fsti capcaki, Mountain Man, Seatco, Yeti, Yowie

BILDAD

This is a creature from the folklore of lumberjacks and forest workers in the United States, especially Wisconsin and Minnesota, during the nineteenth and early twentieth centuries. The Bildad was described as being about the size of a beaver, but with a hooked beak, webbed feet, and curiously enormous flexible hind legs that could project it through the air for a distance of up to 130 feet. It caught its food in the streams and rivers it inhabited, usually by waiting in the reed beds until a large trout came to the surface. Then it would leap and land just ahead of the fish, scooping it up even before the ripples on the water had formed. The Bildad belongs to a group of beings affectionately known as the Fearsome Critters, whose exaggerated proportions and activities not only explained the weird noises of the lonely landscape but also provided amusement in the camps.
References 7
See also Fearsome Critters

BINAYE AHANI, BINAYE ALBANI

These are variations on the name of a class of monsters in the beliefs and folklore of the Navajo peoples of the United States. The Binaye Ahani manifested as limbless twins with grotesque torsos; they were full of malice toward the other creatures upon whom they preyed. Any living thing that ventured close and saw them was slain by the power of the monsters' eyes. They were related by birth to the headless Thelgeth and the feathered Tsanahale, with whom they constituted the group of monsters known as the Anaye.
References 7, 119, 159
See also Anaye, giant, monster, Thelgeth, Tsanahale

BINGBUFFER

This is the name of a monster in the legends of the Ozark Native American people in the United States. The Bingbuffer was reported by Randolph (1951) to be a lizard-like monster that inhabited the Ozark Mountains.
References 94
See also Fillyloo, Golligog, Gowrow, monster, Stollenwurm

BIRD-MAN

This is the name of a monster in the mythology and folklore of Japan. It is depicted as a humanoid creature with a bird-shaped head, human ears, a cock's comb, beak, and wattles, and human hands on the ends of thin wings. Dressed in traditional Japanese garments, it resembles some of the depictions of the Tengu.
References 149
See also monster, Tengu

BISCLAVERET, BISCLAVARET

Though not commonly used now, these variations on the name for the Werewolf in the Breton dialect of northwestern France may be found in the twelfth-century lays of Marie de France. The modern Breton names are Bleiz-Garv and Den-Bleiz, but Loup-Garou is the more usual term denoting this human-monster.
References 128
See also Loup Garou, monster, Werewolf

BISHOP FISH

This is the name of a monster in the folklore and traditions of medieval Europe. The Bishop Fish was

described as a giant fish but in place of the usual pectoral fins it had two projections resembling claws. Its tail fins resembled legs wearing a fisherman's thigh boots, while its dorsal fin extended about the body. The head, neither truly fish nor truly human, was crowned by a projection resembling a bishop's miter. It is portrayed in a work by Swiss naturalist Konrad von Gesner entitled *Historia Annimalium* (1551–1558), and its description was recorded at a time when "duplicate beings" were believed to exist not only on the earth but also in the sea or the air. Consequently if a sea creature were discovered, it was often categorized under that of an earthly being. Perhaps the Bishop Fish could originally have been a beached squid.
References 7, 89
See also monster

BISTERN DRAGON, THE

This is the name of a dragon in the traditions of the Berkeley family of Bistern in the county of Hampshire, England. The legend, set down in an Old English document some time before the sixteenth century (and still in Berkeley Castle), relates how Sir Moris Barkley (Sir Maurice de Berkeley) encountered a terrifying dragon that had been ravaging the countryside killing any who attempted to get rid of it. Sir Moris, the son of Sir John Barkley of Beverston, is described in suitably heroic terms, as is his manner of killing the dragon, and his own tragic death, along with those of his dogs, in the battle. These testify to the cause for their depiction in the coat of arms of the Berkeley family.
References 182
See also dragon

BLACK AGNES

This is an alternative name for the monstrous female ogre known as Black Annis in the traditions of the English county of Leicestershire.
References 159
See also Black Annis

BLACK ANNIS

This is the name of an evil monstrous hag, also known as Black Agnes, who inhabited the Dane Hills near Leicester in the English county of Leicestershire. The original character may have been derived from the Celtic goddess Danu, but in this form, she was a powerful and terrifying supernatural hag with long claws and yellow fangs. Black Annis lived in a cave called Black Annis's Bower, which she is said to have clawed from the rock. She was considered to be responsible for raiding the vast herds of sheep in the area while they were lambing. More horrifying still, she was a cannibal, enticing and devouring local

*The Bishop Fish is a giant fish with two clawlike projections in place of fins. (*On Monsters and Marvels, *trans. Ambroise Pare., J. L. Pallister, University of Chicago Press, 1982)*

children whom she caught at dusk when they strayed into the Dane Hills. She skinned their flesh before she devoured them, scattering their bones and hanging the skins on a tree to dry. Her terrifying power over horror and death were used to good effect by parents as a Nursery bogie to prevent their children from straying too far.
References 67, 159, 169, 181
See also Baba Yaga, cannibal, Nursery bogies

BLACK DEVIL

This is the name of a type of Centaur figure in the traditions and legends of the people of Yucatan in Central America. A monstrous, black-clad humanoid horse, it is first described by the Spanish chronicler Bernal Diaz del Castillo (1492–1581) in *Historia de la*

Conquista de la Nueva España (1576). In this work, Castillo explains that the Native Americans of the period mistook the horse and rider for a single destructive monster.

The legends of this monster spread so widely that the Shoshone Native American people of the United States also have a tradition of a Black Devil, said to be a huge black cannibal stallion.
References 133
See also cannibal, Mares of Diomedes, monster

BLACK DOGS

This is the name of a class of monstrous beings found in folklore throughout most of the southern and eastern English counties, and sometimes in Scotland. Black dogs appear under many different names in other regions as well. Some take the shape of a huge shaggy-haired black dog (said to be about the size of a calf), with enormous glowing, fiery red eyes; others are malicious; still others are quite benevolent at times. Black dogs, also called Black hounds, are usually encountered on lonely tracks, ancient roads and crossroads, bridges and entrances—the places of transition in human lives. Normally benign if left alone, they are often said to be guardians of an ancient treasure such as the one at Lyme Regis in Dorset or guardians of a sacred place such as the ancient burial mounds in Wambarrows, Somerset.

If anyone attempts to strike out or engage the Black dogs in any way, they can display frightful powers, inflicting savage wounds, paralysis, and death, then vanishing before the eyes of any survivor. Merely seeing one is supposed to portend death within the year; however, in some parts of England, such as Weacombe, Somerset, instances of Black dogs appearing to lost travelers or frightened girls traveling alone and guiding them safely home are well known.

The most famous anecdote is of the Black dog of Bungay, which Abraham Fleming (d. 1607) reported as having terrified and killed those attending the Church of Bungay, near Norwich, on Sunday, August 4, 1577. (A report of the same incident in Stow's *Annales,* published in 1600, makes no mention of a dog!) Numerous local reports in Dartmoor (including one involving a white "Black" dog) were the inspiration for Sir Arthur Conan Doyle's famous *Hound of the Baskervilles.* Other famous Black dog traditions may be found at Oakhampton Castle in Devon, Newgate in London, Cromer in Norfolk, Torrington in north Devon, and Tring in Hertfordshire. Indeed, hundreds of Black dog sightings have been recorded over the last four hundred years in Britain, as well as in Brittany (France), Denmark, and other areas of Scandinavia. More recently, the author has been given anecdotes of otherwise inexplicable police car crashes on a dark empty road in Hampshire, which were ascribed to the appearance of the local supernatural Black dog.

In other countries with a Celtic tradition are counterparts of the English Black dogs such as the Cu Sith of Scotland, the Gwiyllgi of Wales, the Mauthe Dhoog of the Isle of Man, the Coinn Iotair and Saidhthe of Ireland, and the Ki Du and Dogs of Youdic of Brittany in northwestern France.
References 7, 21, 24, 27, 101, 128, 133, 159, 182
See also Barguest, Black Shuck, Coinn Iotair, Cu Sith, Gwyllgi, Gytrash, Ki Du, Mauthe Dhoog, Padfoot, Rongeur d'Os, Saidhthe, Skriker, Suaraighe, Trash, Youdic dogs

BLACK SHUCK

This is the name of a class of monstrous dog, also known as Shuck, Shuck Dog, or Old Shuck, in the folklore of East Anglia, England. The name is possibly derived from the Anglo-Saxon *Scucca,* meaning "demon." Black Shuck is described as about the size of a shaggy black donkey with huge glowing red eyes, or a single eye, which shower sparks of green or red fire. At Clopton Hall near Stowmarket, however, this monster is described as resembling a monk with the hound's head. Its abode is variously the salt marshes or the sea itself, from which Black Shuck emerges only at dusk to patrol the lanes, marshes, river banks, and graveyards. This creature may be encountered on the roads, where its icy breath and shaggy pelt can be felt as it draws alongside a traveler. In Suffolk it offers no harm if left alone, but death soon follows for any who challenge it. In Norfolk merely seeing the Black Shuck was enough to invoke sickness or death. One variant of this monster, said to have the face of a monkey, haunts the area between Balsham and Wratting in Cambridgeshire, where it is known as the Shuck-Monkey. Another variant, the Essex Shuck, however, is a benevolent creature that has been known to guide lost travelers and protect those under attack. The fact that it haunts gallows, gibbets, or cemeteries links it with the evil Shuck.
References 5, 7, 21, 24, 67, 96, 119, 145, 159, 169, 182, 186
See also Barguest, Black dogs, Black Shuck, Gytrash, Mauthe Dhoog, Padfoot, Rongeur d'Os, Skriker, Trash

BLACK TAMANOUS

This is a terrifying monster in the mythology and folklore of the Native Americans of the North Pacific coast. When the "Transformer" cleansed the earth of all the gigantic creatures of evil, the Black Tamanous was somehow overlooked and remained to plague the earth with its predations. This monster was reputedly a cannibal that stalked its human victims in the wilderness.
References 24, 119, 120
See also cannibal, monster

BLATANT BEAST

This is the name of a beast or monster that appears in the work *The Faerie Queene* (Books V and VI) by the English poet Edmund Spenser (1552?–1599). The Blatant Beast, whose name was probably coined by Spenser and may have been derived from the old term *blate,* meaning "to bellow," is also known as the Questing Beast. It was said to have been the progeny of the hideous dog Cerberus and the monster Chimaera, both from the classical mythology of Greece and Rome. The Blatant Beast is described as a hideous creature with a hundred venomous tongues that was muzzled by the hero Sir Calidore and dragged in chains to Fairyland. Unfortunately, it escaped, causing even more terror.
References 7, 20
See also Cerberus, Chimaera, Questing Beast

BLEDLOCHTANA

These are monsters in the legends and folklore of Ireland. In Irish Gaelic, Bledlochtana may be translated as "Monsters." These terrifying beings, which resurface only on the anniversary of the Battle of Mag Tuired, emit horrific howls that cause fear in all who hear them.
References 128
See also monster

BLEDMALL, BLADMALL, BLEDMAIL

These are variations on the name of a group of monsters in the legends and folklore of Ireland. In Irish Gaelic the name may be translated as "Sea Monster." According to early narratives, the local sailors were terrified of them.
References 132
See also monster

BLEIZ-GARV

This is the modern Breton name for the Werewolf of Brittany in northwest France.
References 128
See also Bisclaveret

BLEMMYES (pl.), BLEMYAE (pl.), BLEMYA (sing.)

This is the name of a race of people said to inhabit ancient Ethiopia during the time of the Roman empire. The Blemmyes were described by Pliny the Elder in his *Historia Naturalis* (A.D. 77) as humanoid beings that had no head but had eyes and a mouth located in their chests. They were said to inhabit the upper part of the land beyond Egypt then known as Numibia. The later legends, such as the "Romance of Alexander," transformed the descriptions of the Blemmyes to golden-colored giants with eyes and a mouth in their chests, on which grew such a profusion of hair that their lower limbs were

obscured. By medieval times, such travel writers as John Mandeville had claimed that this race of people still existed and that they inhabited the deserts of Libya. These accounts no doubt influenced explorers of the American continent who stated that they, too, had seen such a people on the River Caora.
References 20, 63, 167, 177
See also Acephalos, People of Caora

BLOODY-MAN

This is the alternative name for the giant called Grim in the classical literature of England. He appears in John Bunyan's *Pilgrim's Progress,* which was published in 1682.
References 20, 31
See also giant, Grim, Maul, Pagan, Pope, Slay-good

BLUE DRAGON, AZURE DRAGON

These are variations on the name of a dragon that has great symbolic significance in the geomantic system of Fêng Shui in China. The Blue Dragon, also known as the Azure Dragon, is symbolic of all the high places of the earth such as the hills, rocks, and mountains that constitute the Yang principle. His counterpart the White Tiger represents the Ying principle and is therefore symbolic of the low regions of the earth such as valleys, estuaries, and lowlands. Practitioners of Fêng Shui assess all the implications of the power of the Blue Dragon and his counterpart before anyone seeks to build on or make use of a piece of land, to ensure that the plans are auspicious.
References 89
See also dragon, Oriental Dragon

BLUE MEN OF THE MINCH

This is the name of a class of evil mermen unique to the Minch Passage of the Outer Hebrides off Scotland. The Blue Men, whose name in Gaelic is *Na Fir Ghorma,* are found only in the folklore of the Outer Hebrides, where they are reputed to have been seen floating in the Minch, known in Gaelic as *Sruth nam Fear Gorma* ("Channel of the Blue Men"), located between the Isle of Lewis and the Shiant Isles off the Scottish mainland. They have the appearance of humans but are entirely blue with grey beards.

The seas around these islands are particularly treacherous and the weather is said to be calm as long as the Blue Men and their chieftain are in their underwater caves. When they appear, they summon up fearsome storms and swim out to any vessel whose captain is foolhardy enough to attempt to make a run through the Minch. Their intention is to wreck the ship and send the sailors to their doom. However, the local skippers know that the Blue Men might be thwarted, since they love rhyming contests and will challenge the captain before condemning the ship. If the captain has an agile tongue and can always get the last word, then the Blue Men will spare the vessel and its crew.

There is strong evidence that these beliefs were derived from the Moorish slaves who were pressed into sailing the Viking longships, and were marooned by the Norsemen in the Minch during the ninth century. These unfortunates wore long blue robes and grey-blue veils, as do their descendants, the present-day Tuaregs of North Africa.

References 21, 24, 67, 128, 159, 169
See also Havhest, Havmand, merman

BLUNDERBORE, BLUNDERBOAR

These are variations on the name of a giant in the traditional English tale of "Jack-the-Giant-Killer." Blunderbore, the brother of another giant named Cormoran, lived in a castle and terrorized the region, demanding food and goods as tribute. Jack, after many others had been killed in the attempt, was persuaded to try to rid the area of the giant's menace. He went as a guest to the castle and was shown his bed where he knew that the giants would kill him if he slept there. So Jack wrapped a block of wood and placed it under the covers, then crawled under the bed to sleep. Sure enough, Blunderbore came into the room during the night and beat the block to a pulp. The giants were most surprised to see Jack come down to breakfast the following morning.

Jack had another trick in store. Having secretly placed a bladder within his shirt, he called for more food every time that his breakfast bowl was empty. What Blunderbore did not realize was that he was spooning the food into the bladder through the top of his shirt, which was getting fatter and fatter. The stupid giant, refusing to be bested by a mere boy, also kept calling for more food until his stomach was so expanded that he could hardly move. When the bladder under Jack's shirt was bulging fit to burst, Jack declared that he would relieve the tension and, taking a knife, slit the bladder so that all the food spilled out. The giant, again unwilling to be outdone, did the same and killed himself.

References 20, 24, 54, 181
See also giant

BMOLA

This is the name of a monster in the mythology and folklore of the Western Abanaki Native Americans of northeastern United States. The Bmola, also known as the Wind Bird, is an enormous flying creature associated with the freezing winds from the north.

References 77
See also monster

BOA

This is a type of fabulous serpent in the ancient descriptions of European natural histories. Details of the creature were given by Pliny the Elder in his Historia Naturalis (A.D. 77), which employed the word bos (meaning "cow"). The name of the Boa is presumed to have been derived from this word, in connection with the belief that the creature attached its mouth to the udders of cows and suckled their milk until they were dry or dead. In the later Physiologus and bestiaries of the Middle Ages, the Boa was depicted as a serpent with large ears, small wings, and, sometimes, two legs.

References 20, 89, 148
See also serpent

BOAR OF BEANN-GULBAIN

This is the name of an enormous boar in the legends of Ireland. The Boar of Beann-Gulbain had once been the mortal son of Angus, who had also fostered the son of Duibhne named Diarmaid. During a jealous quarrel, Diarmaid had slain the son of Angus, who refused the customary death gold as compensation. Angus instead chanted over the corpse of his son, then striking it with his wand, at which point the young man metamorphosed before his eyes into an enormous boar with neither tail nor ears. Angus further declared that Diarmaid would have exactly the same life expectancy as the animal, for they would be the death of each other. Time passed and as he grew into a warrior, Diarmaid fought alongside the hero Finn to rid the region of a huge wild boar that ravaged the region of the Fianna. The howling of the hunting dogs alerted them to its presence one night, and they tracked the beast to the heights of Beann-Gulbain where his geis ("supernatural taboo") is made known to him by seers that hunting a wild boar will bring his death. While Finn watched in the darkness, Diarmaid waited for the beast's charge; but when it came, his dogs, his sword, and his spear were no match for the might of the Boar of Beann-Gulbain. It then charged Diarmaid and gored him without mercy as he took what was left of his scabbard and thrust it to the hilt in the body of the boar. As the two lay expiring on the ground, Finn came to the warrior, who begged for water from his magical healing hands. Twice Finn went to the well and twice he let the water drip from his fingers. By the third attempt the vengeance of Angus was secured in Diarmaid's death.

References 7, 54, 78, 105
See also Ætolian Boar, Battleswine, Beigad, Calydonian Boar, Erymanthean Boar, Hildesuin, Sachrimnir, Twrch Trwyth, Ysgithyrwyn

BOBALICÓN

In the folklore and traditions of Spain, this is an ogre whose name may be translated as "Silly Idiot." He is represented as a very tall humanoid being with an enormous head and a horrible leering grin who hovers terrifyingly over potential victims. But the fear of the Bobalicón is countered by his potential for being duped by a human being. Famously portrayed by Francisco J. de Goya y Lucientes (1746–1828) in a series of etchings created around 1819, this ogre still features frequently in the festivals of Spain, in much the same way as the more northern Town Giants.
References 181
See also giant, ogre, Town Giants

BOBI-BOBI

This is the name of a giant snake in the Dreamtime mythology of the Native Australians. Bobi-Bobi is described as a serpent being that inhabited the heavens, rather like the Rainbow Snake. However, Bobi-Bobi saw that humans were in need of more than just water to survive, and introduced game. But as humans did not know how to catch their food, he threw them one of his own ribs to create the first boomerang. The humans learned well and were pleased with their food and weapon, so one day they decided to go through the cloud barrier through the sky to visit their benefactor. They used the boomerang to make a hole and tore into the cloud barrier. Bobi-Bobi was so displeased with their violence that he refused to help them again and withdrew from the region altogether.
References 132
See also Rainbow Serpent, serpent

BOCANÁCH

This is the name of a monster in the folklore of Ireland. The Bocanách is described as a vast menacing goat that terrifies night-bound travelers on lonely roads.
References 128
See also Black dogs, Gaborchend, Glaistig, Goayr Heddagh

BOCHICA

This is the name of a giant in the mythology of the ancient Chibcha and Muyscaya peoples of Colombia in South America. Bochica was a benevolent giant who supported the sky on his shoulders so that it would not fall on the humans below. According to tradition, when an earthquake occurs it is because Bochica is tired and is changing the position of the sky upon his shoulders.
References 132
See also Atlas, giant

BOCKMAN

In German folklore, this is the name of a humanoid monster of the forest who, like the satyr, is part man and part goat. His existence is used by parents as a Nursery bogie to frighten children into staying away from the forests.
References 151, 159
See also Nursery bogies, satyr

BOGEY

Bogey is an alternative name for the Owner-of-Bag in the traditions and folklore of the Arapaho Native American people of the United States. However, there are monsters designated as bogeys in other traditions as well, such as the Indacinga of the Ponca people, the Apotamkin of the Maliseet people, and the Hagondes of the Seneca Native American people. All of these are Nursery bogies to protect or curb the behavior of adventurous children.
References 77
See also Apotamkin, Bogyman, Hagondes, Indacinga, Nursery bogies, Owner-of-a-Bag

BOGUEST

Boguest is an alternative spelling of the name Barguest in the folklore of northern England. It takes the shape of an enormous malevolent dog.
References 7, 21, 24, 37, 93, 119, 159, 169
See also Barguest

BOGYMAN, BOGEYMAN

This is a type of frightening monster that is also known as a Booger Man in the folklore of the mainland areas of Britain, and as Booman in the Orkney and Shetland Islands off the north coast of Scotland. It appeared in a fearsome and grotesque human shape in lonely places, terrifying people traveling alone on the roads at night. More recently its use has been more in keeping with that of a Nursery bogie.
References 21, 24, 58, 74, 119, 124, 145, 159, 182
See also Bogey, monster, Nursery bogies

BOLLA

This is the name of a monster in the form of a snake in the traditions and folklore of the Altanain people of southern Albania. The Bolla, also known as Bullar, is a predatory being that preys upon humans, but fortunately it is in hibernation most of the time. Should it see a human on Saint George's Day (April 23) when it opens its eyes for the first time after waking up, that person will be killed and consumed. It is said that this creature metamorphoses into the terrifying Kulshedra after a period of twelve years.
References 125
See also Kulshedra, monster, serpent

Many monsters combine human and animal parts, such as the Bockman, which, like the satyr, is part man and part goat. (Rose Photo Archive, UK)

BOLTHORN

This is the name of a giant in the Norse mythology of Scandinavia. Giant Bolthorn is described in some versions, such as the *Prose Edda,* as being the father of Bestla, the giantess who was the mother of the first gods Odin Ve and Vili. In other versions, Bestla's father is the primeval giant Ymir.
References 125, 168
See also Bestia, giant, giantess, Ymir

BOMBOMACHIDES

This is the name of an ogre in the folklore and traditions of early nineteenth-century England. He is described as an enormous figure with three heads who is particularly fond of threatening children. Bombomachides belongs to a class of Victorian Nursery bogies which were used to keep unruly or adventurous children from straying into harmful situations.
References 181
See also Agrippa, giant, Nursery bogies, ogre

BONACHUS, BONASUS

These are two alternative names for the Bonnacon in ancient and medieval European legends.
References 7, 89, 148, 184
See also Bonnacon

BONNACON, BONACONN

These are variations on the name of a fabulous animal said to inhabit the deserts and scrublands of Asia, that appears in the ancient texts of Europe. The Bonnacon, also called the Bonachus and Bonasus, is described by Pliny the Elder in his *Historia Naturalis* (A.D. 77) as a bovine creature with the mane of a horse and enormous incurving horns. (In later texts these are described as green.) This otherwise unremarkable creature possessed a defense mechanism that was more effective than its horns: when pursued, it would defecate so voluminously that the dung was said to cover over two acres and be so acrid as to burn trees, grass, hunters, and dogs alike. The bestiaries of the eleventh and twelfth centuries depict this event most graphically.
References 7, 14, 89, 91, 148, 184

BOO-BAGGER

This is an ogre in the folklore of eighteenth- and nineteenth-century England. The Boo-bagger is described as a giant who carries an enormous bag on his back. He is particularly fond of tracking and ensnaring any young children that have strayed from their guardians. He is of course a type of bogie that belongs to the class of Nursery bogies used by parents and minders to ensure that their charges do not stray.

References 181
See also giant, Nursery bogies, ogre, Owner-of-a-Bag

BOOBRIE

This is the name of an enormous bird in the traditions and folklore of Scotland. It was described as similar to a Great Northern Diver, but with white markings and huge webbed feet and a terrifying roar instead of a normal bird call. The Boobrie was said to be the metamorphosed form of the Each Uisge or monstrous water horse of the Highlands, especially in the region of Argyllshire (now Strathclyde). Like its alter ego, it devoured anything that went to the water's edge of the loch that it inhabited.
References 7, 24, 89, 128, 133
See also Eačh Uisge, monster

BOOJUM

This is the name of a monster that appears in the work *Sylvie and Bruno* (1889) by the English academic and author Lewis Carroll (Charles Lutwidge Dodgson, 1843–1898). Carroll does not actually give a definition, or even a real description, but the image of its victim suddenly vanishing away is quite sufficient for his readers to be very cautious about this monster.
References 7, 40
See also Bandersnatch, Jabberwock, monster, Snark

BORAK, AL

This is the name of the fabulous bird/steed of Islamic mythology. It is also known as Al Boraq, Borāq, and Burak in various regions of the Islamic world, but essentially the name may be translated as "the Lightning," "Shining," or "the Bright One." Al Borak is described as having a human head; variously the face of a woman or man, but with ears resembling those of a donkey; a fine neck with a long mane; a body like that of either a donkey or a horse from which eaglelike wings extend; and a tail resembling that of a peacock. Al Borak is pure white, but its mane, wings, and tail are studded with pearls and precious stones that sparkle with colors, as do its eyes. Its breath was said to be of the most precious perfumes, and it could understand all human speech, although various accounts dispute whether it could reply or not. It was originally the steed of the archangel Gabriel and was so swift that it could travel at one pace farther than the human eye could see.

In the traditions of Islamic mythology it is upon Al Borak that the prophet Mohammed made his Night Journey, known as the *isrā*, from Mecca to Jerusalem and returned the same night. Thus the prophet was able to pick up a pitcher, which had overturned as he left, before it reached the floor as he returned. Through rather extended connections with this event, it became a tradition that Mohammed ascended into heaven upon Al Borak.
References 7, 20, 24, 61, 63, 89, 132
See also Alkonost, Angka, Garuda, Griffin, Harpy, Parthenope, Pegasus, Podarge, Ptitsy-Siriny, Siren, Sirin, Solovei Rakhmatich, Unnati, Zägh

BORAMETZ, BORAMEZ

These are alternative spellings of the name of the Barometz (also known as the Vegetable Lamb of Tartary), a legendary part animal-part vegetable creature of medieval Europe.
References 7, 18, 89
See also Barometz

BORAQ, BORĀQ, AL

These are variant spellings of Al Borak, the fabulous bird of Islamic mythology.
References 7, 24, 61, 63, 89
See also Borak (Al)

BORARO

These are humanoid, semisupernatural monsters of the Amazon forests in the folklore of the Tukano people. The name Boraro may be translated as "the White Ones." They manifest in human shape and are described as tall, pallid, hairy-chested beings with protruding ears and enormous phalluses. They materialize without knee joints and with their feet pointing backward, so that if they happen to fall over they have difficulty righting themselves. The Boraro are cannibal monsters who carry a stone implement when hunting in the forest, where they track and devour unwary humans.
References 47, 159
See also cannibal, monster

BORBYTINGARNA

This is one of the alternative names for the Trolls of Norse legends and Scandinavian folklore. At one time these beings were fearsome ogres that roamed the forests and mountains, inhabiting caverns and fissures in the earth. However, the image of their fierce nature has been eroded by the coming of modern times, and many local names such as Borbytingarna have long been forgotten.
References 181
See also ogre, Troll

BOROGOVE

This is the name of a monstrous bird in *Through the Looking Glass*, the classic work by English academic and author Lewis Carroll (Charles Lutwidge Dodgson, 1832–1898). The beast appears not in the actual narrative but in the poem "Jabberwocky," within a book which Alice sees and decides to read. The

Borogove is described as an "extinct kind of Parrot. They had no wings, beaks turned up and made their nests under sundials. Lived on veal" (246, p. 267).
References 7, 40
See also Jabberwock

BOROKA

This is a terrifying composite creature of the traditions and folklore of the people of the Philippine Islands. Looking rather like a Harpy, the Boroka is described as having a human woman's head and body, the wings of an eagle, and four horse's legs and hooves. She is a malicious cannibal who tracks and ensnares any humans who wander into her territory, and she is especially fond of young children. She has, of course, all the characteristics of a nursery bogie.
References 113
See also Baba Yaga, cannibal, Harpy, Nursery bogies

BORR, BOR

These are variations on the name of one of the first of the primeval giants in the Norse mythology of Scandinavia. Borr is the grandson of Ymir and the husband of Bestia/Bestla. His progeny by her were the first three gods of the Aesir: Odin, Ve, and Vili.
References 78
See also Bestia, giant, Ymir

BRAG

This is the name of a class of malicious beings and monsters in the folklore of the Northern Counties of England. Like the Phooka of Irish folklore, it often appeared as a grotesque horse and as other monstrous shapes. The Brags were seen in fields, on moorlands, and in lonely roads. But instead of being the friendly farm animal expected, the Brags were deceptive beings that frequently misled travelers into dangerous situations.
References 24, 159
See also Grant, Phooka

BRAN, BRAN THE BLESSED, BRÂN LLYR

These are variations on the name of a supernatural heroic giant in the early Celtic narratives of Britain, especially of Wales, where he is also known as Bendigeifran, Bendigeid Fran, or Bendigeit Vran. His story is interwoven with those of other heroes, such as that of King Arthur in other narratives, but it is mainly from the fourteenth-century Welsh epic *Mabinogion* that the legend of Bran is known.

Bran, whose name is derived from the Welsh *brân* meaning a "raven" or "crow," was the son of Llyr, the supernatural king of the sea, and a mortal woman, Penardun. He also had a brother named Manwydan, a half brother named Evissyen, and a sister named Branwen. According to different versions of the legend, his son was called either Gwern or Caradog (the latter being identified with Caractacus, the British opponent of the invading Romans in 43 B.C.).

Bran is described as being of such immense stature that all other humans were as dwarfs beside him. He was the King of the Island of the Mighty, and a marriage that had been arranged between his sister and the King of Ireland was the commencement of his demise. His wicked half brother, Evissyen, was so consumed with jealousy when he was not invited to the feast that he slunk into the stables and mutilated all the horses of the Irish. The Irish king took his revenge on his bride, Branwen, when they returned to his stronghold in Ireland. There he made her work as a servant in his kitchens until Bran heard of the insult and made ready to invade Ireland to rescue her.

So vast was his stature that when Bran invaded Ireland with his Celtic forces he waded the Irish sea ahead of the ships with his army, and then stretched his body as a bridge across the River Shannon for his men to walk over him to the other bank. There he deposed the Irish king, placing his own son Gwern on the throne in the Irish king's stead. But the evil Evissyen fought with Gwern and thrust him into a fire, where he was burnt to death. Bran pursued both his murderous half brother and the forces of the King of Ireland, and a great battle ensued.

Unfortunately, as an act of appeasement after the wedding, Bran had given the Irish king a magic cauldron, the brew from which would restore to life all who had been slain in battle. With this aid, the forces of Bran were soon defeated, until only he and seven of his bravest warriors, among them Taliesin, remained alive. But Bran had received a mortal blow from a poisoned spear. He commanded his men to sever his head from his body and take it for burial on the summit of "the white hill" in London, with the face toward the coast of France, to protect his land against invasion. (This "white hill" has often been identified as the White Tower of the Tower of London, as "white" signifies holiness in the Welsh language.)

The warriors took the head (which did not decay like a human's and became known as *Urdawl Ben*, "Noble Head") back to the mainland as commanded. However the journey was extended by an enchanted sojourn of three years in Harlech listening to the birds of Rhiannon and a further eighty years locked in the stronghold at Gwales (Gassholme Island). Eventually the head of Bran was placed as he commanded, but an account in the Welsh "Triads" accuses King Arthur of having removed the protective head of Bran, returning it to Gwales, in order to assume the role of Britain's protector for himself. The genealogy of King Arthur in the *Bonedd yr Awar,* by both his maternal and paternal lines, traces his ancestry to Bran.

Many of the mysterious places in Britain are associated with these legends, including the Iron Age hill-fort named Dinas Bran ("Bran's Stronghold"); the later stone castle was named as Corbin (Old French for "raven" or "crow") in Malory's (d. 1471) version. This is purported to be the legendary Castle of the Holy Grail of the Fisher King with his crippled foot, who is named Bron in the earliest legend.
References 54, 78, 128, 132, 182
See also giant

BRANDAMOUR

This is the name of an ogre in the folklore and traditions of eighteenth- and early-nineteenth-century England. Described as an enormous figure with either two or three heads, he is particularly fond of threatening children. Brandamour belongs to a class of Victorian Nursery bogies that were used by parents to keep unruly or adventurous children from straying into harmful situations.
References 181
See also Agrippa, Bombomachides, giant, Nursery bogies, ogre

BRASH

This is an alternative name for the Skriker, a class of monstrous dog-like beings in the folklore of the north of England.
References 7
See also Skriker

BRIAREUS

This is the name of a giant in the classical mythology of Greece and Rome. Briareus is one of the Hundred-Handed Giants who were the sons of Gaia and Uranus. He is also referred to as Ægæon. Like his brothers, Cottus and Gyges, he had fifty heads and one hundred arms. All three giants were born fully mature and clad in full battle armor. They waged war on the Olympian gods and were defeated. Briareus is described by Virgillio in the *Purgatorio* (12:28–30) to Dante, who expresses a desire to see this great giant. Dante concludes that his monstrosity was his lack of intellect rather than his gigantic stature, which he declared was quite in proportion.
References 7, 20, 78, 132, 138, 168, 173, 177
See also Cottus, Gaia, giant, Gyges, Hundred-Handed Giants, Uranus

BRINGUENARILLES

This is the name of a giant in the classical literature of France. Bringuenarilles is one of the characters described by the author François Rabelais (1494?–1553?) in *Pantagruel* (1532) and, later, in *Gargantua* (1534). He is not only vast but misshapen and threatening to the human population of the Island of Ruach, which he inhabits. This giant menaces humans in a more extraordinary manner than do giants of the conventional legends, in that he demolishes and devours windmills, the technology upon which people of the period relied for their industry and trade. At the time, such behavior would have been both terrifying and ludicrous. Even more ludicrous was the fact that Bringuenarilles was defeated not by a conventional hero but, rather, by choking himself to death on a simple pat of butter.
References 173
See also Gargantua, giant, Pantagruel

BROBDINGNAGIANS

This is the name of a race of gigantic people in classical English literature. The land of the Brobdingnagians was where Gulliver found himself on his second voyage in *Gulliver's Travels* (1726), by author and politician Jonathan Swift (1667–1745). Unlike the giants of classical mythology and European folklore, Swift describes a gentle race with respect for his hero despite Gulliver's relatively minute size.
References 20, 176, 181
See also giant

BROBINYAK

This is the name of an ogre in the folklore and traditions of eighteenth- and early-nineteenth-century England. Brobinyak is described as a huge menacing figure with the eyes of a dragon and enormous long fangs. He is particularly fond of threatening children and initially appears in the children's moralizing publication *Blabberhead, Bobblebud and Soak*, as a similar character to Agrippa in *The English Struwwelpeter*. Brobinyak belongs to a class of Victorian Nursery bogies that were used to keep unruly or adventurous children from straying into harmful situations.
References 181
See also Agrippa, Bombomachides, Brandamour, giant, Nursery bogies, ogre

BRONTE

This is the name of a horse in the classical mythology of Greece. Bronte, whose name means "the Thunderer," is one of the team of Horses of the Sun that pulled the golden chariot that Hephaestus had made for the sun-god Helios. Like the other horses, Bronte is described as the purest white with flaring, fire-breathing nostrils. Each morning the nymphs of time, the Horae, harnessed Bronte and the other eight Horses of the Sun to the chariot for their journey across the sky. When the journey was finished at dusk, they browsed on magical herbs in the Islands of the Blessed, until they were harnessed for the next day.

References 138
See also Horses of the Sun

BRONTES

This is the name of one of the three gigantic Cyclopes in the classical mythology of Greece and Rome. His brothers were Arges and Steropes. Brontes's name may be translated as "Thunder," and, like his brothers, he had only one eye located in the center of his forehead. They were born of Gaia and fathered by Uranus, who threw them into the depths of Tartarus for rebelling against him. In *Theogony* (c. 750 B.C.), Hesiod describes Brontes and his brothers both as giants and as Titans, but the Cyclopes were distinct from both.

References 20, 78, 138, 168, 177
See also Brontes, Cyclops, Gaia, giant, Steropes, Titan, Uranus

BRUCKEE

This is a type of water monster in the traditions and folklore of Ireland. The Bruckee is an enormous creature that has four feet but is said to inhabit the Lough of Shandangan.

References 133
See also Loch Ness monster

BRUYER

This is the name of a giant in the literature of France. He is cited in the genealogy of Pantagruel as an ancestor of the giant Pantagruel, by the author François Rabelais (1494?–1553?) in his work *Pantagruel* (1532). In the genealogy of Pantagruel, Rabelais describes various attributes of the giant's prowess as well as epithets of distinction. As Bruyer has been derived from a cultural tradition in which he was known as the mighty opponent of a culture hero, he provides a mighty dimension to the ancestry of Pantagruel.

References 173
See also Bruyer, Chalbroth, Daughters of Cain, Etion, Gabbara, Galehaut, Gargantua, giant, Happemousche, Hurtaly, Morguan, Noachids, Noah, Pantagruel

BUATA

This is the name of a semisupernatural monster in the traditions and folklore of the peoples of New Britain. Described as a creature with enormous tusks, it is said to resemble a wild boar, but is vastly bigger and stronger. The Buata has the ability to speak and understand the human beings it hunts as prey, but like most ogre-beings of folklore it has little intelligence and may be tricked into losing its victim.

References 113

See also Ætolian Boar, Battleswine, Beigad, Boar of Beann-Gulbain, Cafre/Kafre, Calydonian Boar, Erymanthean Boar, Hildisuin, monster, ogre, Pugot/Pugut, Sachrimnir, Twrch Trwyth, Ysgithyrwyn

BUCHIS

This is the name of a gigantic bull in the mythology of ancient Egypt. Buchis (the Greek word for the "bull") is also known as Bukhe. It was described by Macrobius as looking much like a normal bull except for its size and the fact that the hair of its hide grew in the opposite direction and that, like the skin of a chameleon, changed color at least twelve times a day. Buchis was the symbol of the god Menthu in the temple complex at Hermonthis in ancient Egypt.

References 138
See also Apis, Epaphus, Hap

BUCKLAND SHAG

This is the name of a monster in the folklore of Buckland in the county of Devon in England. The Buckland Shag is described as a water horse that pursued and trampled its victims to death. Indelible red stains on a large rock were said to be the result of the Buckland Shag having taken its victims there to be slain. Few people dared to venture alone in this vicinity for fear of encountering the Buckland Shag, until the vicar of Buckland exorcised the creature with bell, book, and candle.

References 67, 159
See also Cabyll-Ushtey, Kelpie, monster, Neugle, Shag foal

BUGBEAR/E

This is a class of semisupernatural beings and monsters that are objects of terror in English folklore. The bugbear is a malevolent being thought to take the shape of a bear or large beast. It was later said to be fond of devouring naughty children and used mostly as a Nursery bogie to threaten children into good behavior.

References 21, 124
See also monster, Nursery bogies

BUGGANE

This is the name of a class of particularly malevolent semisupernatural, monstrous beings in the Manx folklore of the Isle of Man in the British Isles. It may take the shape of a giant with or without a head, a grotesque black cow with or without a head and tail, or a large shaggy dog with a white collar. Whichever of these forms it takes, it always has vast glowing eyes and a long black mane of hair. Bugganes have been said to be the servants of evil magicians. Always

terrifying, they pursue humans but rarely do actual harm to them. They can, however, be destructive.

There are several stories about the evil deeds of Bugganes, but the most widely known is that of the tailor and the church of St. Trinian. The locals called this church *Keeill Brisht*—"the Broken Church"—because when it was being built, each time the stone masons went home at night a Buggane emerged from under the ground in the aisle and smashed to pieces all their hard work. Nobody knew what to do until a brave tailor named Timothy sat in the chancel after the masons had left, determined to make a pair of breeches before the Buggane appeared. He had almost finished when the floor was rent and the Buggane started to emerge, ranting at the intrusion of this foolhardy mortal. Whatever the Buggane threatened, the terrified tailor gave the appearance of calm as he replied "I see, I see." Finishing his work, Timothy leapt through the window just in time, for the Buggane pulled down the entire roof as he emerged more completely. The tailor ran as fast as he could for the consecrated ground of the Marown churchyard. The Buggane, unable to pursue him, in its rage tore off its own head and threw it over the wall at the tailor, where it shattered into little pieces. Since that time the Buggane was never seen again either with or without its head, while the brave tailor's scissors and thimble were displayed at an inn on the Douglas to Peel road where all could hear the story.
References 24, 111, 128, 136, 159
See also giant, monster

BUJANGA

This is the name of a monster in the traditions and folklore of the people of West Malaysia and Java. It is described as a dragon or as a huge winged creature that dwells within the jungles and forests. The Bujanga has a reputation for understanding all creatures and forest lore, and is therefore seen more as a protector than as an adversary.
References 113
See also dragon, monster

BUKHE SEE

This is the name of a gigantic bull in the mythology of ancient Egypt. The Bukhe is also known by the Greek name Buchis.
References 138
See also Apis, Buchis, Epaphus, Hap

BULAING

This is the name of a class of mythical serpents in the traditions and beliefs of the Karadjeri Native Australian people. Bulaing are monstrous serpents of the Dreamtime.
References 125
See also Yulunggu

BULCHIN

This is a female monster in the legends and folklore of medieval Europe; it is also known as the Bicorne. The name Bulchin was used from the sixteenth century. This fat monster resembled a well-fed panther with a human face and a broad grin.
References 7
See also Bicorne, monster

BULL OF HEAVEN

This is an alternative name for the monster bull created by the god Anu in the mythology of ancient Sumer.
References 89
See also Gudanna

BULL OF INDE

This is the name of a monstrous type of ox that was said to inhabit India. The Bull of Inde was described as a huge creature with an impenetrable yellow hide and massive horns that pivoted on its head in whichever direction it required. It was almost impossible to catch, and no weapon could kill it through its hide. Furthermore, if it thought it was about to be trapped, it would gore itself to death sooner than be captured.
References 7, 89

BULL OF MEROE

This is an alternative name for Merwer, a sacred bull in the mythology of ancient Egypt.
References 138
See also Merwer

BULLAR

This is the name of a monster in the form of a snake in the traditions and folklore of the Altanain people of southern Albania. The Bullar is also known by the name Bolla.
References 125
See also Bolla, Kulshedra, monster, serpent

BULLEBAK

Bullebak is the name of a giant Nursery bogie mentioned in the autobiography of Isabella de Moeuloose, written in 1695. This book describes seventeenth-century childhood fears as they were experienced in the country now known as Belgium, including references to monsters that were used by parents to threaten their children into good behavior.
References 181
See also giant, monster, Nursery bogies

BULUGU

This is the name of a humanoid reptile in the Dreamtime mythology of the Gunwinggu people of

Arnhem Land in northern Australia. Bulugu is the name of a Water-snake man who stole the intended wife of Jurawadbad.
References 38, 132
See also Jurawadbad

BUNGISNGIS
This is the name of a giant in the traditions and folklore of the people of the Philippine Islands. The name Bungisngis may be translated as "Showing His Teeth," which suggests the malevolent amusement of this huge being who laughs at the sight of humans. He is a cannibal giant described as having such an enormous top lip that it can be put over his head like a hat. Bungisngis hunts and tracks down humans who stray into his territory so that he can kill and devour them. Once he has a grip on someone, there is no escape, for his strength is prodigious. However, the hero Suac managed to steal the powerful club with which Bungisngis kills his victims. He then used this club to kill the enemies of his people.
References 113
See also Gergasi, giant

BUNYAN, PAUL
This is the name of a hero giant of the lumberjacks of the nineteenth century in the United States. Paul Bunyan was generally depicted as a jovial and immensely strong giant of a man. With the aid of his massive Babe the Blue Ox, and his loyal crewmen such as Brimstone Bill, Johnny Inkslinger, and Sourdough Sam, Paul Bunyan was said to be responsible for such features of the American landscape as the Grand Canyon, the great lakes of Oregon and Michigan, and Puget Sound. With his faithful ox, there was no task too big or any deed too difficult for him to accomplish for those in need.

The origins of the name and the character of Paul Bunyan may be derived from the French or Irish settlers and backwoods people of the early nineteenth century. References are made in some versions to the giant fighter of the Papineau Rebellion of 1837. There was also a "Bon Jean," meaning "Good John," and a Paul Bonhomme in the French logging community of Canada. Later Native American and Scandinavian forest features were incorporated into the "tall" tales of this amiable, resourceful, and immensely strong giant hero of the logging communities all over North America. The stories of Paul Bunyan and Babe the Blue Ox were mostly folklore that were first turned into comic types of publications, mostly for advertising the products of the logging and paper industry around 1910. These were swiftly followed by paperbacks and booklets for general distribution. The first of these in 1914 by W. B. Langhead was for the Red River Lumber Company of Minnesota (1914–1916).

Soon wherever there was a lumber community, and often where there was none, festivals and contests for logging strength took place in the name of Paul Bunyan. His image has entered the general folklore of the United States to such an extent that the English composer Benjamin Britten composed the music for an opera by the poet W. H. Auden based on the exploits of this now world-famous logging folk hero.

Like the Fearsome Critters of the lumberjack community, Paul Bunyan and Babe the Blue Ox gave a wry insight into the lives of a community and the major tasks they undertook in difficult times and are rightly established in folklore.
References 24, 26, 94, 134
See also Babe the Blue Ox, Fearsome Critters, giant

BUNYIP
This is the name of a class of horrifying monsters in the traditions and legends of the Native Australian people. The Bunyip is also known by many other names according to the region, such as Good Hoop and Universal Eye in Tasmania, and King Pratie and Tuntabah in other regions of Australia. It is described as a huge dark hairy creature with long arms and enormous claws on the ends of its hands. The Bunyip inhabits inland waters, swamps, and billabongs, where it devours any creature that enters its domain, including humans. Even the young of the Bunyip are harmful to humans; should one be abducted by a human for any reason, its mother will set up the most terrible howl. Then she will make the waters rise and pour into the dwellings of the humans to retrieve the child. No place is safe from this flooding; even if a hill is climbed, the waters will rise up and over that, too. Any humans touched by this flood water will instantly be turned into black swans.

There are several legends and traditional tales concerning the Bunyips and their powers. One such tells of a man of the Frog tribe who went fishing with his wife. As it grew dark, she warned him to come back to the bank quickly because she thought that there might be a Bunyip near. Sure enough, they heard a movement in the reeds. As the Frog-man reached the bank he threw his catch to his wife, but as he got out he saw the long arm and claws of the Bunyip tighten around his wife's arm and drag her into the billabong. Exhausted, he bravely tried to track them, but to no avail as the Bunyip left no trail. So he hit on the idea of tying frogs to his spear: as they called in the night air the Bunyip might come for them. Several nights went by before the Bunyip came with the Frog-man's wife, looking an empty dirty creature with glazed eyes. The Frog-man threw his spear deep into the belly of the Bunyip and followed it with his throwing stick. But his wife was under a spell and followed the crashing Bunyip back to a tree

on an island. This time the husband was able to follow the trail. But as he came close and reached out to his wife who was holding out her arms, he found he could not move. Like her, he was caught and transfixed in the circle of the Bunyip's power. Days, weeks, months, and seasons passed while the husband and wife remained transfixed like a tableau, until one day the rains came and the violent storm broke the circle of power. When they were free, the Frog-man remembered how he had used frogs to find his wife, and the whole tribe never hurt frogs again.
References 7, 20, 61, 78, 89, 152, 153
See also monster

BURACH BHADI

This is the name of a water creature in the folklore of the Western Isles off the coast of Scotland. The Burach Bhadi, also known as the Wizard's Shackle, was described as a creature resembling a huge worm or leech that had nine eyes in the top of its head. This creature inhabited the shallow waters of the lochs and the fords of rivers on the Isles as well as in the county of Perthshire in the Lowlands. Anyone riding a horse through these waters had to be on the lookout for the Burach Bhadi, as it would smell the horse and swiftly attach itself to the animal's legs, pulling it under to be consumed.
References 7, 89

BURAK, BURĀK, BURĀQ

These are variant spellings of the name of Al Borak, the fabulous bird of Islamic mythology and legend.
References 7, 20, 24, 61, 63, 89
See also Borak (Al)

BUSO

This is a class of monsters and demons in the folklore of the Bagobo Malay peoples of the Philippine Islands. They are described as tall, thin humanoid beings with curly hair, flat noses, an ugly mouth with two protruding teeth, and a single huge yellow or red eye like a Cyclops. Like most ogres of this type, they appear to be terrifying but in fact are so stupid that they can be easily duped by their

human prey. They inhabit the deep jungles and forests, as well as the rocks and trees in cemeteries. Here they consume the rotting flesh of the dead and constantly try to ensnare the living humans who stray into their territory. Many folktales describe how the Buso may be outwitted. One very amusing story tells how a cat agreed that the Buso may eat her human owner, but only after the Buso had counted every hair on the cat's tail before morning came. As soon as the Buso got near to completing its task, the cat flicked its tail until the pale light of dawn showed through the window and the Buso was compelled to disappear.
References 119
See also Cyclops, Kappa

BUSSE

This is the name of a hybrid animal in the folklore and legends of medieval Europe. The Busse was described as being about the size and shape of a bull but grey-brown, with the head and horns of a stag. This remarkable creature had the ability to change its color when it was being pursued. It was said to inhabit the area between Greece and Turkey known as Scythia. Its description, along with many of the travelers' and sailors' tales of the period, may have had a basis but was much exaggerated to increase the awe of the audience.
References 7

BUTATSCH-AH-ILGS

This is the name of a terrifying monster in the folklore and traditions of Switzerland. It was described as an enormous swollen amorphous mass, rather like the bag of a stomach, covered with leering eyes from which flames were emitted. The Butatsch-ah-Ilgs was said to inhabit the depths of the Luschersee, a lake in the vicinity of Grisons that was renowned for being the gateway to hell and the eternal fires of damnation. No fishermen ever fished there; neither would the shepherds graze their flocks on the hills that bordered the lake.
References 133
See also Cuero, Hide, monster

C

CABEZUDO (sing.), CABEZUDOS (pl.)

These are the singular and plural names of the enormous Town Giants whose effigies are paraded in the festivals of Spain. The singular form literally means "Big Head," and, indeed, as with most Town Giants and ogres, their big heads often denote the terror evoked by their size and their gullibility against human adversaries. The traditions surrounding the Cabezudos may have developed over many centuries, and often there is a complicated "historical" giant's tale in association with their representation, as in the cases of Cara Vinaigre, Carneros, and Tarasca. They are always depicted as having huge heads and terrifying bulbous piercing eyes, and are usually wearing the costume of the seventeenth or eighteenth century.

References 181
See also Caravinaigre, Carneros (Los), giant, Tarasca, Town Giants

CABYLL-UISGE

This is the Gaelic spelling of the Anglicized name of the Cabyll-Ushtey in the folklore of the Isle of Man in the British Isles.

References 24, 128, 133, 159
See also Cabyll-Ushtey

CABYLL-USHTEY

This is the name of a monster in the folklore and traditions of the Isle of Man in the British Isles. A fierce semisupernatural water being, it is also known in the Manx language as Cabyll-Uisge ("Water-Horse") or Each Uisce ("Water Monster"). The Cabyll-Ushtey may take the form of a water-horse but can transform into the shape of a handsome young man. It is said to attract humans or their livestock into the water where they are torn to pieces. But it is even more likely to incite terror, thereby scattering the herds so that it can take a weak victim.

References 24, 128, 133, 159
See also Ceffyl-dŵr, Eaċh Uisge, Glaistig, Kelpy, Neugle

CACTUS CAT

This is a creature from the folklore of the lumberjacks and forest workers of the United States, especially Wisconsin and Minnesota, during the nineteenth and early twentieth centuries. The Cactus Cat was described as having fur like that of a hedgehog or porcupine, that consisted of spines, and its ears were also covered in spines. But the spines on its legs were particularly long spiky protuberances of sharp bone, and a similarly armored tail that branched out in several directions. The Cactus Cat had a penchant for the fermented juice of cacti and at night would slash their trunks to make the juice flow from several in succession, returning to them as fermentation occurred. Then it drank the juice and quickly became intoxicated, after which humans heard its wild shrieks throughout the night. This creature belongs to a group of beings affectionately known as the Fearsome Critters, whose exaggerated proportions and activities not only explained the weird noises of the lonely landscape but also provided amusement in the camps.

References 7, 24
See also Fearsome Critters

CACUS

This is the name of a monster in the classical mythology of Greece and Rome. Cacus, whose name means "Wicked," is described as having an enormous spherical body like that of a huge grotesque spider, from its single neck were three fire-breathing human heads, and its body was supported by long legs like tree trunks. Cacus was said to be the progeny of the Gorgon Medusa and the god of fire Hephaestus/Vulcan. It inhabited a cave in the cliff of the River Tiber by day, but at night it terrorized the region with its predations and devoured any creature, whether livestock or human, that entered its territory. When Heracles/Hercules returned from one of his twelve labors, driving the herd of Geryon before him, he camped for the night near the River Tiber. Cacus saw the cattle and while Heracles/Hercules slept, the

monster dragged some of the livestock back to his lair. In the morning the lowing herd was answered by the cattle in the cave and the hero went to investigate. But the monster had blocked the entrance with a boulder. At last, after many attempts, the hero tore the cliff apart and Cacus poured venomous fire toward him. Heracles/Hercules seized the monster by the neck and tied it in a knot, leaving it to strangle itself because it was unable to disentangle its three heads. Then the hero threw the monster to the vultures and departed with his herd.
References 7, 20, 24, 89, 132
See also Geryon, monster

CAFRE

In the traditions and folklore of the peoples of the Philippine Islands, this is the name of a monster that closely resembles the monster called the Buata in New Britain. The Cafre, also known as the Kafre, is described as an enormous being with huge fearsome tusks. It looks similar to a wild boar but is black in color and vastly bigger and stronger. This semisupernatural monster has the ability to walk upright on its hind legs like humans; it is also able to talk and understand their language, so it represents a terrifying adversary. It tracks human beings in the jungle as its prey. However, like most ogre-beings of folklore, it has little intelligence and may be tricked into losing its victims.
References 113
See also Ætolian Boar, Battleswine, Beigad, Boar of Beann-Gulbain, Buata, Calydonian Boar, Erymanthean Boar, Hildesuin, monster, ogre, Pugot/Pugut, Sachrimnir, Twrch Trwyth, Ysgithyrwyn

CAILLAGH NY GROAMAGH, CAILLAGH NY GUESHAG

These are variations on the name of a supernatural monstrous old hag. The Caillagh ny Groamagh, whose name means "Old Woman of Gloom" in the Manx language of the Isle of Man in the British Isles, is regarded as a weather spirit in the local traditions and folklore. However, as the Caillagh ny Gueshag or "Old Woman of Spells," she is a giantess who was thrown into the Irish Sea for practising her evil magic. On St. Briget's Day (February 1), she was cast up on the Manx shores, where she gathered sticks for a fire to dry herself. The ensuing spring was wet, and every year thereafter this Caillagh ny Groamagh goes to gather sticks on St. Briget's Day. If the day is fine, she will have plenty of fuel for a wet spring; if the day is wet and she cannot go out, she is obliged to ensure a dry spring for her own comfort.
References 24, 111, 128, 159
See also Baba Yaga, Cailleach Bera, Cailleach Bheur

CAILLEACH BEINNE BRIC

This is the Scottish variant of the name of the giantess known as Cailleach Bera in the legends and folklore of Ireland.
References 24, 120, 128, 159
See also Cailleach Bera

CAILLEACH BERA, CAILLEACH BEARA, CAILLEAC BHÉARRA, CAILLEACH BHÉIRRE, CAILLEACH BÉIRRE, CAILLEACH BÉARRA, CAILLEACH BHEARE, CAILLEACH BHÉARA, CAILLEACH BEARE, CAILLEACH BHÉRRI, CALLIAGH BIRRA

The Cailleach Bera, whose name means "Hag of Beare," is in Irish mythology a supernatural being of strength and cunning who derives from the Celtic corn spirit of Irish folklore. She is a giantess who is associated with the Beare Peninsula near Cork, which she carried as stones in her apron until they formed the rocky promontory when the strings broke. In this way she is also credited with the formation of the Islands of the Hebrides (Scotland), where she goes by the name of Cailleach Beinne Bric. The variant names indicate a tradition in each area of Ireland, especially Cork, Sligo, Munster, and Ulster, where she is deemed responsible for building mountains and the deposit of islands while carrying stones for her abode. By each of her several husbands she is said to have been the ancestor of the people of Ireland.
References 24, 120, 128, 141, 159
See also Cailleach Bheur

CAILLEACH BHEUR

The Cailleach Bheur, whose name means "the Blue Hag," is a giantess in the folklore and traditions of the Highlands of Scotland. Also known by the phonetic spelling Cally Berry, she is described as a huge, hideous, blue-faced hag wearing a plaid and carrying a mallet or a strong staff. The Cailleach Bheur fulfills the role of guardian of wild deer, boar, goats, cattle, and wolves; her plants are the gorse and holly. She also guards the Highland streams and wells. From Halloween (October 31, the Celtic festival "Samhain") until Beltane Eve (the eve of May Day in the old Celtic calendar), she is the personification of winter, turning the ground hard by beating it with her staff to prevent new growth and bring on the snow. In this role she is represented as the hideous hag, the daughter of Grianan, the lesser Celtic winter sun. She lives in a cave beneath Ben Nevis where the "Summer Maiden" is her captive, enduring torments until rescued by one of the Cailleach Bheur's compassionate sons on St. Bride's Day (February 1). This event prompts the Cailleach to unleash the *Faoiltach* ("Wolf Storms") in an effort to prevent Summer from existing. When Beltane (May Day) and spring return, she casts away her staff under a holly or gorse—where no other plants may thrive. The Cailleach Bheur is then transformed, some say, into a beautiful maid, sea-serpent, or land serpent, until next Halloween.

The Cailleach Bheur and her two sons are responsible for changing the landscape; like the Cailleach Bera, she created land features—in this case, the Hebridean Islands—when the rocks she was carrying fell through holes in the container. In her role as guardian of the springs, she accidentally created Loch Awe when she forgot to cover the spring of Ben Cruachan. Her two sons, who are constantly arguing, cast rocks at each other across Invernessshire. In Colonsay in the County of Strathclyde (formerly Argyllshire), she is known as Cailleach Uragaig.
References 7, 21, 24, 25, 45, 96, 128, 159, 169
See also Baba Yaga, Cailleach Bera, Cailleach Uragaig

CAILLEACH URAGAIG
This is an alternative name for the Cailleach Bheur, used exclusively in the Isle of Colonsay in the Clyde estuary in the County of Strathclyde, Scotland. In the traditions of the island, the Cailleach Uragaig is a giantess who, representing winter, entraps the spirit of summer and keeps her captive. She foils any attempt at rescue by becoming a dangerous, constantly shifting rocky promontory, until she is defeated.
References 128
See also Cailleach Bheur, giantess

CALCHONA
This is the name of a giant beast in the traditions and folklore of the people of Chile. The Calchona is described by Julio V. Cifuentes as resembling a huge dog, but with a thick tangled beard and a long white shaggy coat like the fleece of a long-haired sheep. It inhabits mountain passes and traps late-night travelers, scaring them out of their wits and panicking the horses. Although malicious, it seems to do little more harm than stealing food from the frightened humans and then retreating.
References 18, 89
See also Padfoot

CALIBAN
At the time that the English playwright William Shakespeare (1554–1616) wrote his play *The Tempest* in 1609–1613, the European scene was buzzing with the wonders of the Americas and the fabulous creatures that may or may not have existed there. One of the many horrors that preyed upon the European mind was the possibility of being killed by these beings, and a *frisson* was added to the tales if those beings were said to be cannibals. With the inclusion of Caliban, quite clearly an anagram of the word *canibal* (spelling was not formally regularized until the twentieth century), Shakespeare readily added this *frisson* of the unnatural and horrific for his audience, without further explanation being necessary. Caliban is described in the text as "(. . .A freckled whelp, hag-born,) not honoured with/A human shape," and also as "Thou poisonous slave, got by the devil himself/Upon thy wicked dam . . ." (*The Tempest*, Act I, Scene 2).

Caliban was the hybrid humanoid progeny of the witch Sycorax; he was later enslaved by Prospero, the Duke of Milan.

Yet, Shakespeare makes the argument, in the wretched monster's words, that when Caliban was alone on the island in whatever condition the Europeans considered monstrous and uncouth, he was at least his own master and happy in it. But with the coming of the Europeans, the treasures that he had shown them were only returned by the dubious gift of their language, then by accusations of rape and the final injustice of slavery.
References 20, 46, 181
See also cannibal, monster, Wildman

CALIGORANTE
This is the name of a giant in the literary tradition of Italy. Caligorante, like Morgante and other literary giants, is derived from the "Romance" traditions of medieval Europe.
References 173
See also giant, Morgante

CALLICANTZARI
This is an alternative spelling of the name of the satyr-like monster in the modern folklore of Greece.
References 7, 17, 24, 168
See also Kallicantzari, satyr

CALLITRICE
This is the name of a monster in the folklore and traditions of medieval Europe. The Callitrice is described in a twelfth-century bestiary as a humanoid being resembling a satyr but with a copious beard and a long, thick tail. It was said to inhabit the desolate regions of Ethiopia where it existed without hindering humans, from whom it hid.
References 7, 184
See also satyr

CALOPUS
This is the name of a monster in the traditions of medieval Europe. Also known as Chatloup, it was described as having the body of a wolf but with horns on its head and spines on its body. Although a

fearsome and terrifying adversary, if it were lured into scrubland it would easily become entangled. This monstrous beast was said to inhabit the banks of the river Euphrates in what is now Iran. Its image was adopted into the repertoire of European heraldry and may still be seen on ancient armorial shields.
References 7
See also monster

CALYDONIAN BOAR

This is a monstrous boar in the classical mythology of Greece and Rome, also known as the Ætolian Boar. It was sent by the goddess Artemis/Diana to plague the region of Ætolia as punishment for the King of Calydon having omitted to make the sacrifices due to her. The boar destroyed much of the countryside, the crops and dwellings of the people, even the people themselves. Ultimately the king's son, Meleager, called all the heroes of Greece to join the greatest hunt for the creature. Their adventures were many before the beast was finally brought to bay, shot by Atalanta and slain by Meleager. The division of its head and hide as trophies of the monster caused rifts between the heroes that led to further conflict.
References 20, 24, 168
See also Ætolian Boar, Battleswine, Beigad, Boar of Beann-Gulbain, Buata, Cafre/Kafre, Erymanthean Boar, Hildesuin, Pugot/Pugut, Sachrimnir, Twrch Trwyth, Ysgithyrwyn

CALYGREYHOUND

This is the name of a heraldic beast from the Tudor period of England. It is described as having the body of an antelope with the hind legs of a bull and the forelegs of an eagle. This monstrous hybrid, which represents speed, has been specifically used since 1513 in the heraldic devices of the de Vere family on achieving the earldom of Oxford.
References 7

CAMAHUETO

This is the name of a sea monster in the traditions and folklore of the people of the Chiloé Islands off the coast of Chile. The Camahueto is described variously as a giant, a small bull, or a sea horse that starts its life in the upper reaches of the rivers and migrates to the sea as it grows, consuming all the fish and wildlife of the region as it moves. Whatever its description, it is said to be a predatory monster with huge clawed feet and fangs in its mouth with which it gouges out the gullies and coves in the coastal cliffs. In these places it lies in wait to trap its human victims who have been shipwrecked there; then it devours them.
References 133
See also monster

The heraldic antelope, the Calygreyhound, and the Camel-Leopard were placed on English coats of arms (Rose Photo Archive, UK)

CAMEL-LEOPARD, CAMELEOPARDEL

These are variations on the name of a monstrous hybrid beast in the heraldry of Europe. It is described as being part leopard and part camel, but unlike both creatures it has a pair of horns.
References 5

CAMOODI

This is the name of a gigantic serpent in the traditions and beliefs of the people of Guiana in South America. A report of a hunting party made in 1896 describes the party as resting on a vast fallen tree in the gloom of the jungle. At length, one of the men declared that the "tree" had started to move, and as they all leapt to their feet it heaved itself up and slithered into the undergrowth. The men declared that this being was the gigantic protector of the region known as Camoodi.
References 133
See also serpent

CAMPACTI

This is the name of a dragon in the beliefs and traditions of the people of Mexico. It is a vast primeval beast that was defeated and from whose body the earth was made.

References 7
See also dragon, Tiamat, Ymir

CAMPE

This is the name of a monster in the classical mythology of Greece and Rome. When the Titans were making war on the Olympian gods led by Zeus, he was obliged to go for the help of the Hundred-Handed Giants and the Cyclopes who were kept guarded in Tartarus by the monster Campe. Zeus released the giants from their captivity, and they helped the gods to defeat the Titans.

References 138
See also giant, Hundred-Handed Giants, monster, Titan

CAMPHURCII

This is the name of a fabulous creature described by Thevet in his sixteenth-century work *Cosmography*. The Camphurcii was supposed to have inhabited the Island of Molucca. It was described as an amphibious being that had a body resembling that of a deer with the forelegs of the same animal, while its rear legs were purportedly webbed like those of a goose. The Camphurcii was, however, more remarkable for the massive horn that protruded for some three and a half feet from the front of its forehead like that of a Unicorn and was considered by humans to be a remedy for poison. This creature inhabited the coastal regions of the island and lived on fish.

References 146
See also unicorn

CANNIBAL

The name Cannibal was first applied to the Caribes, a Native American people of the West Indies, in an account written by Christopher Columbus (1451–1506), who described their activities as bloodthirsty and specified that they ate their own kind. The name then became synonymous with those activities and, in 1553, was used as a term for the consumption of one's own people. There was a great fear of the unknown dangers associated with the explorations and discoveries of fifteenth century by Europeans, and in accounts that were made for the "home" audience, this aspect of danger was undoubtedly enhanced to give a *frisson* to the popularity of the traveler's publication. The term *cannibal* entered popular literature and the English playwright William Shakespeare (1554–1616) employed this term in his play *Othello:* "The Canibals that each others eate" (Act I, Scene 3, line 43).

Shakespeare also used the term in his play *The Tempest*, in which one of the main grotesque characters is named Caliban, a clear anagram of *canibal*—thereby implying to informed members of the audience the nature of the being that was so named. In more recent years, the term *cannibal* has been used to describe not only a creature that eats its own kind but also, in popular works, a creature that devours humans as its main prey.

Cannibals and cannibalism, as well as the trapping and consuming of humans as prey, feature in the mythology and folklore of many different societies. They are especially prevalent in Native American traditions and folk beliefs, where they are often characterized in terms of the duplicity and stupidity associated with ogres in European legends. The fear of being eaten alive has a very potent symbolism for humans, and this powerful fear has been manifest in the mythology and traditions of most cultures from very ancient times and is still invoked in modern literature.

1. In the classical mythology of ancient *Greece* and *Rome,* at the beginning of time Uranus devoured his own offspring, as did others such as Asterion the Minotaur, the Harpies, the Laestrygonians, and the Mares of Diomides.
2. In the more modern legends of the *British Isles,* there are cannibalistic beings such as Anthropophagus in English drama, giant Maul and giant Slay-good in the works of John Bunyan, the Torogs in the literature of the English academic and author J. R. R. Tolkien, Giant Holdfast in the traditional English folktale, and Cutty Dyer, Hobyah, Child Guzzler, and Black Annis of folklore.
3. In *China* is the legend of the cannibal-turned-saint of Buddhism, known as He-Li-Di or Kishimojin.
4. In *France,* Torto-giant appears in the folklore of the Basque, and Lustucru (Le Grand) appears in French nursery folklore.
5. In the legends of *Germany,* der Kinderschrecker is a Nursery bogie.
6. In *India,* the Pey are cannibalistic vampires of Tamil mythology, and in Hindu mythology there are beings such as Kirata, Hidimba, and Loha-Mukha; and Hariti belongs to the Buddhist tradition.
7. In *Japan,* Karitei-mo belongs to the Buddhist tradition.
8. In the Native American legends of *Canada* are the Atcen of the Montagnais; Tammatuyuq of the Inuit people of the eastern Hudson Bay area; Snee-Nee-Iq or "Narnauk," Gwagwakhwalanooksiwey, Dzoo-noo-qua, and Bakbakwakanooksiwae of the Kwakiutl of British Columbia; and Irraq and Nulayuuiniq of the Inuit.

9. In the Native American legends of the *United States* are the Stonecoats called Jokao; also Hagondes, Ganiagwaihegowa, Deadoendjadases, and Ongwe Ias of the Seneca and Iroquois; the Black Devil and Dzoavits of the Shoshone; Bapets and Siats of the Southern Ute; Raw Gums of the Arapaho; the Kiwahkw giants of the Maliseet Passamaquoddy; Paiyuk of the Ute; Wendigo of the Algonquin; Anaye of the Navajo; Asin of the Alsea; Big Man-eater of the people of Alabama; Gather-on-the-water of the Tsimshian; Haakapainizi of the Kawaiisu; Big Owl of the Jacarilla Apache; and the Black Tamanous of the North Pacific Coast.

10. In the folklore of the lumberjacks and others of the United States, especially Wisconsin, is the curious Hidebehind.

11. In the legends of *Indonesia* is the cannibal giant known as Gergasi.

12. In the legends of the *Philippine Islands* are the Boroka and Bungisngis.

13. In the Dreamtime legends of the Native Australians in *Australia* are Thardid Jimbo and Cheeroonear.

14. In the legends of *Central and South America* are Ahuizotl of Mexico, Aunyainá of the Tupari people of Brazil, and Boraro of the Tukano people of the Amazon.

15. In *Eastern Europe* are the Drake of the Gypsy community of the Balkan states and Baba Yaga of Russian and East European folklore.

16. In the legends of *Pacific Islands* are Abere of Melanesia, Ngani-vatu and Flaming Teeth of the Islands of Fiji in the Pacific, and Kewanambo of western Papua New Guinea.

17. In the legends of *Africa* are Sasabonsam of the Tschwi and Ashanti people of West Africa and Aicha Kandida of Morocco.

References 5, 7, 18, 20, 24, 25, 27, 31, 38, 46, 47, 51, 55, 61, 64, 67, 77, 78, 89, 95, 112, 113, 119, 120, 122, 125, 125, 132, 133, 138, 151, 153, 159, 165, 168, 169, 177, 181
See also Abere, Ahuizotl, Aicha Kandida, Anaye, Anthropophagus, Asin, Asterion, Atcen, Aunyainá, Baba Yaga, Bakbakwanooksiwae, Bapets, Big Man-eater, Big Owl, Black Annis, Black Tamanous, Boraro, Boroka, Bungisngis, Caliban, Child Guzzler, Cutty Dyer, Deadoendjadases, Drake, Dzoavits, Dzoo-noo-qua, Flaming Teeth, Ganiagwaihegowa, Gather-on-the-water, Gergasi, Giant Holdfast, Gwagwakhwalanooksiwey, Haakapainizi, Hagondes, Hariti, Harpy, He-Li-Di, Hidebehind, Hidimba, Hobyah, Irraq, Kewanambo, Kinderschrecker, Kirata, Kishi-mojin, Kiwahkw, Laestrygonians, Loha-Mukha, Lustucru (Le Grand), Mares of Diomides, Maul,

Minotaur, Ngani-vatu, Nulayuuiniq, Ongwe Ias, Paiyuk, Pey, Raw Gums, Sasabonsam, Siats, Slay-good, Snee-Nee-Iq, Tammatuyuq, Thardid Jimbo, Torogs, Torto, Wendigo

CANNIBAL-AT-THE-NORTH-END-OF-THE-WORLD

This is an alternative form of the name of the giant bird Bakbakwakanooksiwae in the traditions and beliefs of the Kwakiutl Native American people of Canada.
References 77, 89
See also Bakbakwakanooksiwae

CAORÁNACH

This is the name of a female monster in the folklore and beliefs of Ireland. Also known as Keeronagh, it was said to have existed in Donegal at the time of Saint Patrick and to have been troublesome to the people there. Not only was the monster itself terrifying, but its progeny were said to be devils. The saint relieved the people's distress by sending the monster to the bottom of Lough Derg, where it is said to be to this day.
References 128
See also monster, Muirdris, Oilliphéist

CAPALUS

This is the alternative name for a monstrous supernatural cat named Chapalu in the legends and folklore of Wales.
References 7
See also Chapalu

CAPANEUS

This is the name of a giant in Italian literature. He features in the "Inferno" section of the *Divina Commedia* by Dante Alighieri (1265–1321).
References 173
See also giant

CAPRICORNUS

This is the name of a hybrid monster in the early mythology of ancient Mesopotamia. The Capricornus was the attendant of the god Ea. It was described as having both a fish head and a human head over the body of a fish. Like the later Sumerian ram-fish known as Suhur-mas, it was associated with the constellation of Capricorn. In the classical mythology of Greece and Rome, the Capricornus was created by Zeus, the king of the gods, when the monster Typhon was chasing the goat-god Pan who jumped into the Nile river. Typhon was changed into a fish with a goat's body and head, then preserved by Zeus as the constellation.
References 7, 20, 89
See also Sagittarius

CAPRI-PEDES

This is an alternative name or epithet for certain monsters in the classical mythology of Greece and Rome. The word *capri-pedes* may be translated as "having goat's feet" and, as such, is applied to monsters having cloven hooves—for example, the satyrs, the fauns, and such gods as Pan.

References 177

See also faun, monster, satyr

CARAVINAIGRE

This is a giant character in the folklore and legends of Spain. The name Caravinaigre may be translated as "Vinegar Face," signifying the sour expression prevalent on the face of this giant. He is portrayed as having a huge head with a lantern jaw, looking rather like Mr. Punch of English and Italian folklore. He wears a tricorne hat and the white trousers and blue jacket associated with sailors in eighteenth-century Spain. Once a frightening figure of Spanish legend, he has now been demoted to the status of Nursery bogie and of the carnival giant known as a Cabezudo. Caravinaigre can be seen in the parade that marks Saint Jermin's feast in Pamplona in the Basque region of Spain.

References 181

See also Cabezudo, giant, Nursery bogies

CARBUNCLE

This is the name of a fabulous creature in the European fables of South American exploration of the sixteenth century. The Carbuncle was never truly described except by the priest Martin del Barco Centenera in his work *Argentina* (1602). In it he states that this creature possesses a precious jewel in its forehead and that he had glimpsed it shining when in Paraquay. He and many others sought this creature for many years, but to no avail.

References 18

CARL OF CARLISLE

This is the name of a giant in the folklore and Arthurian legends of England. Carl had been turned into a giant through the placement of a spell, and it was not until Sir Gawain, Sir Kay, and Sir Baldwin visited his castle that there could be any release. This outcome was made possible by the terrible ordeal of allowing Sir Gawain to cut off the giant's head, at which point he was released from the spell and became Sir Carl of Carlisle once more, knighted by King Arthur. Sir Gawain then married his daughter.

References 54

See also giant

CARN GALVER

This is the name of a giant in the traditions and folklore of the county of Cornwall in England. He was reputed to be not just of enormous proportions but also extremely mild and well disposed toward his human neighbors, such that he would play games with the children. The sad tale describes how instead of using a ball, Carn Galver was so simple-witted that he would throw boulders, which one day accidentally fell on a little boy and crushed him to death. The giant was so devastated by this occurrence that he pined to death after mourning in isolation for seven years. The place of his death is said to be a logan or rocking stone near the town of Penzance.

References 128

See also giant

CARNEROS, LOS

This is the name of a monster in the folklore of the town of Frontera on the Island of El Hiero in the Canary Islands. Los Carneros, which means "the Rams," is a giant effigy of a monstrous ram with huge horns—yet another example of the Cabezudos of Spanish folklore, which are representations of the Bogey figures of local legends demoted to the status of Nursery bogies and carnival giants. In this case, the enormous ram's head and body with thick projecting horns menaces the local children, especially during their festival.

References 181

See also Cabezudo, giant

CARROG

This is the name of a monster in the folklore and traditions of Wales. Carrog, also known as Torrent, was said to inhabit the region of the Conway valley in the county of Gwynedd.

References 128

See also monster

CARTAZONON

This is the name of a class of Unicorn. Aelian (c. A.D. 200) mentioned a beast that he said is called the Cartazonon of India. It was described as being like a horse, yellowish-red in color, with a black horn and long mane. It was also said to be very aggressive and to inhabit the deserts and wastes of the mountains, where it was the enemy of the lion. According to legend, the beast could be killed but never taken alive.

References 81

See also unicorn

CAT SITH

This is the name of a monstrous cat in the Gaelic legends and folklore of Scotland. The Cat Sith is described as a huge black beast, about the size of a large dog, with a white mark on its front, shaggy rough fur like bristles, and a menacingly arched back.

The Highlanders of its domain firmly believed that this evil creature was the metamorphosed form of a witch.
References 128
See also Big Ears, Cath Paluc

CAT-FISH
This is a hybrid monster from the medieval period of Europe whose lower half is a fish and whose upper half is a cat. It is derived from the belief that in the heavens and the seas there were creatures that were the counterparts of those existing on land. The Cat-Fish survives today as a heraldic beast depicted in the coat of arms of certain European families.
Undoubtedly, stories of this creature gave rise to the name of the actual sea creature known today as the catfish.
References 7
See also monster

CATH PALUC, CATH BALUG, CATH BALWG
These are variations on the name of a monstrous supernatural cat in the legends and folklore of Wales and the Arthurian legends of Europe. (In Welsh the word *palug* means "clawing.") It is also known as Palug's Cat or Chapalu in English and as Capalu or Capalus in the Arthurian legends of France. It is described in the Welsh "Triads" as an enormous fabulous creature that hunted both warriors and its own kind to satisfy its enormous appetite. According to legend, it was the progeny of a monstrous pig called Henwen, whose owner tried to drown the feline creature by throwing it into the sea. However, it was rescued from the water at the Isle of Mona (Anglesey), where it was eventually killed by Cai (Sir Kay). Under the name Chapalu or Capalu, it also features in many of the Arthurian legends of Europe, where it was supposed to have defeated King Arthur during a battle in a swamp associated with the Mont du Chat ("Mountain of the Cat") in the Savoie region of France and, then, to have invaded Britain.

Whatever the origins of the legend, the conjectured historical derivation seems to be the story of a leopard that may have been kept as a fearsome pet by one of the Welsh kings on Anglesey.
References 54, 128
See also Cat Sith, Chapalu, Palug's Cat

CATOBLEPAS
This is the name of a creature first mentioned by the Roman naturalist Pliny the Elder in his *Historia Naturalis* (A.D. 77). The Catoblepas, which in Greek means "That Which Looks Downward," was described by him as a beast with an enormously heavy head that drooped downward on its thin neck. Pliny considered this very fortunate, for it was

asserted that any human who actually looked at its eyes would instantly drop dead. This creature was said to inhabit the wastes of Ethiopia and southern Egypt. Descriptions of it were included in many early travelers' accounts, and the bestiaries of medieval Europe portrayed it as having enormous pink eyes (though how could this have been communicated if one were killed by it?) and the head of a pig on its scrawny black body. By the seventeenth century its description had been much modified. Edward Topsell, who called it a Gorgon, described it as covered in scales, with wings like a dragon, gigantic teeth, and hands instead of paws or hooves. The terror it engendered was such that the French author Gustave Flaubert (1821–1880) included it as one of the horrors to be endured by Saint Antony in his work *La Tentation de St. Antoine* (1874).

The historical derivation of this curious beast may very well have been the real-life gnu or wildebeest of the African Rift Valley.
References 7, 18, 89
See also Basilisk, Gorgon

CAWR
This is the word for "giant" in the Welsh language. It is used frequently in the folklore and traditional tales of Wales where no actual name has been recorded.
References 128
See also giant

CCOA
This is a malicious, semisupernatural, cat-shaped monster in the mythology of the Quechua people of Peru. The Ccoa is described as having a grey body with darker horizontal stripes and a very large head from which glow huge fiery eyes that spit out hail. It is associated with foul weather and the ruination of crops, which it brings about on the orders of the Aukis spirits. To prevent his anger and the blight he might inflict, humans placate Ccoa with frequent offerings during the growing season.
References 7, 24, 119, 159
See also monster

CE SITH
This is the Gaelic name for the formidable, monstrous dog of Scottish folklore. The Ce Sith, also known as the Cir Sith or the Cu Sith, was said to be as large as a bullock or a two-year-old cow and to have an entirely dark-green shaggy pelt. It was also distinguishable by paws the size of human hands and a tail so extensive that it was coiled in a huge plait over its back. The Ce Sith was as swift as the wind and could be heard galloping with vast strides and bellowing as it cornered its human prey. Although its name means "Fairy Dog," like its English counterparts this

semisupernatural beast would bring disaster to humans who encountered it in the Highland moors of its domain. Any travelers who heard the beast behind them would have been well advised to seek their home before hearing it bark for the third time, signaling its victims' demise.

References 7, 21, 159
See also Black dogs

CECROPS, KÉKROPS

These are variations on the name of a ruler in ancient Greece who was said to have been engendered from the union of the sperm dropped from King Erechtheus of Attica, upon the earth. Like his father, Cecrops (spelled in Greek as Kékrops) was humanoid from the waist up but a serpent from the waist down. He was said to have founded the city of Athens in honor of the goddess Athena, for whom he gave the verdict in arbitration against the god Poseidon. When he ruled Attica after his father's death, Cecrops instituted many innovations such as marriage and monogamy, bloodless sacrifice, the burial of the dead, and the skill of writing.

References 7, 24, 89, 125
See also Fu-Hsi, Nu Kwa

CEFFYL DŴR, CEFFYLL-DŴR

This is a semisupernatural monster in the traditions and folklore of Wales. The Ceffyll-dŵr, whose name means "Water Horse," is a fearsome and evil inhabitant of mountain pools and waterfalls. In the northern counties of Wales it is said to take the shape of a grey horse with a glow of light that illuminates its surroundings, but in the south it is described as having wings rather like those of Pegasus. It has also been known to appear as a goat, or as a handsome young man. Although seemingly "solid" (and, indeed, humans have been known to mount and ride it, to their cost), the Ceffyll-dŵr will "evaporate" into insubstantial mist. The beauty of this creature belies its true nature, for it will leap out of the water at any lone traveler and, by gripping their back and shoulders, squeeze, kick or trample the victim to death. If anyone is brave enough to attack and kill the Ceffyll-dŵr, no horse's body would be found, but an amorphous mass of something resembling floating lard would remain on the water.

References 70, 119, 128, 133, 159
See also Cabyll-Ushtey, Glaistig, Kelpy, Neugle, Pegasus

CELAENO

This is the name of one of the Harpies in the classical mythology of Greece and Rome. The name Celaeno may be translated as "Black," but that indicates her nature rather than her color. It must have been before

Celaeno was transformed into one of the monstrous Harpies, along with her sisters, that the god Poseidon united with her, producing two sons. Their offspring were both renowned: Eurypylus distinguished himself in the Trojan Wars and later became one of Jason's Argonauts, while Lycus became the ruler of the Fortunate Isles. Neither seemed to have inherited their mother's monstrous nature or form.

References 138, 177
See also Harpy, monster

CELESTIAL STAG

This is a class of creatures recorded in the myths and folklore of China by S. Willoughby-Meade during the nineteenth century. The Celestial Stag manifests as a quadruped having the appearance of a stag but with the human attributes of language and the ability to understand human speech. It inhabited not the heavens but, rather, the subterranean passages of the mines, where it tormented the miners with its promises to show them the richest veins in return for being taken to the surface. If any were foolish enough to allow the beast to come the surface, it would transform into a foul amorphous jelly full of decay and disease.

References 18

CELPHIE

This is a monstrous hybrid creature in the traditions of medieval Europe. It was described as having a body resembling a cow but with five legs, each of which was human from the elbow down to the hands instead of feet. The Celphie was said to inhabit the wastes of Ethiopia. This curious creature was one of the many described and exaggerated by travelers, crusaders, and pilgrims to a gullible audience at home.

References 7
See also Centycore, monster

CELTES

This is the name of a giant in a work by the Babylonian priest Borosus (third century B.C.). Borosus wrote several books on the history of the Babylonians. Among them was an account of the hero Hercules Libyus, who destroyed the giants of Asia Minor and then, in similar fashion, sailed to Italy to remove the tyrannical giants oppressing that land. Borosus also related an episode of romance between the hero and the giantess Galatea, daughter of the giant Celtes, resulting in the birth of Galathes. In the pseudohistory written during the Middle Ages by Jean Le Maire de Belges for the Duke of Bourbon, this genealogy is incorporated into the ancestry of the emperor Charlemagne, in order to justify a dynastic derivation of monumentally heroic proportions.

References 173
See also Charlemagne, Galatea, Galathes, giant, Hercules Libyus

CENTAUR

This is the name of a class of hybrid beings in the classical mythology of Greece and Rome whose description was developed in later travelers' tales and bestiaries of medieval Europe. Centaurs, also spelled Kentaure or Kentauros, are described as having the body and hind quarters of a horse but the head and torso of a man. These beings were variously said to have been engendered from the union of the queen of the gods Hera/Juno with Ixion or from that of Centaurus (son of Apollo) and the Stibia (the Mares of Magnesium). They were also said to inhabit the mountains at Erymanthus in Thessaly or the countryside of Clyon. For the most part the Centaurs were kind, hospitable, sporting, generous, and wise. However, they had some faults that proved their downfall on many an occasion, such as being bawdy and quick to fight, and having no tolerance for alcohol, which made them aggressively drunk.

One notable Centaur was Pholus. Another was Cheiron, who was erudite and wise, and so well educated in the arts and medicine that he was chosen by the gods to educate heroes such as Jason and Theseus. When Cheiron was accidentally killed, Zeus/Jupiter, the king of the gods, set the Centaur in the heavens as the constellation Sagittarius. However, other Centaurs such as Nessus and Eurytus were quarrelsome and rude. The latter caused the battle with the Lapiths at the wedding of Pirithous, resulting in many deaths.

There were many different names for the Centaurs, depending on the culture, the version of the myth, or the type being described. These include the Apotharni, the Hippocentaurus, the Ichthyocentaurus, the Ipopodes, the Monocentaurus, and the Onocentaurus.

During the medieval period, Centaurs were frequently depicted on church furniture and in the bestiaries of religious houses. They were considered to symbolize the suffering of Christ as the Man and the revenge taken upon his betrayal. When they were portrayed as shooting a bow, the arrow in flight was said to be the flight of the soul. However, other sources state that the Centaurs represented the duplicitous nature of man as both pious and literally beastly in his behavior. Where this latter symbolism was employed, the Centaur was usually depicted along with a Siren or mermaid.

To this day the Centaur is also a frequently used image in the repertoire of heraldry in European coats of arms.

References 5, 7, 10, 18, 20, 24, 61, 63, 78, 89, 91, 125, 132, 138, 165, 167, 168, 185
See also Apotharni, Cheiron, Eurytus, Gandharvas, Hippocentaur, Ichthyocentaur, Kimprushas, Kinnara, mermaid, Monocentaur, Nessus, Onocentaur, Pholus, Sagittarius, Satyr, Sileni, Siren

CENTAURO-TRITON

This is the name of a hybrid being in the classical mythology of Greece and Rome. The Centauro-triton is described as resembling a centaur, but with a dorsal fin and the tail of a dolphin. Unlike the Ichthio-centaur, it has no scales.
References 91, 168, 177
See also centaur, Ichthyocentaur, Triton

CENTICORE

This is the French version of the name of the beast in European legend and heraldry known in English as the Yale.
References 184
See also Yale

CENTIMANES

This is the alternative name for the Hundred-Handed Giants, who are also known as the Hecatoncheires in the classical mythology of Greece and Rome. There were three of these gigantic monstrous humanoids, called Briareus, Cottus, and Gyges. They are described as having fifty heads and a hundred hands each; hence the name Centimanes, which literally means "One Hundred Hands." These giants took part in the wars between the giants and the gods of Olympus.
References 78, 138
See also Briareus, Cottus, giant, Gyges, Hundred-Handed Giants

CENTIPEDE

This is a monster in the folklore and traditions of Japan. The gigantic Centipede terrorized the region of the northern mountains, lying in wait for cattle and humans as its prey, and devouring all who strayed into its territory. The terrified people pleaded for someone to rid them of the monster. Eventually the hero Hidesato stalked the creature and slew it with an arrow straight through the head. His reward was a never-emptying bag of rice for his family, given in recognition of his bravery by the Dragon King of Lake Biwa.
References 113
See also Dragon King, monster

CENTYCORE

This is a monstrous hybrid creature in the traditions of medieval Europe. It was described as having a

body resembling a lion, the head of a bear with enormous mouth and ears, the limbs of a horse, and a human-like voice. The Centycore was said by the classical historian Solinus to inhabit the plains of India. This monstrous creature was one of many described and exaggerated by travelers who tried to convey the likeness of strange animals, by reference to ones they already knew, to an audience at home.
References 7
See also Celphie

CERASTES
This is the name of a monstrous serpent in the traditions of medieval Europe. The Cerastes is also known by the name Hornworm. It is described in bestiaries of the period as being a serpent of considerable proportions with, on the front of its head, four protruding horns, like those of a ram. The serpent traps its prey by burying itself in the sands of the desert that it inhabits, leaving only the horns on the surface. When animals or humans go near to investigate, the Cerastes leaps up in the air, sinks its poisonous fangs into their flesh, and drags them down to be consumed.
References 89
See also serpent

CERBERUS
This is the name of a monstrous dog in the classical mythology of Greece and Rome. Cerberus, also spelled Kerberos, is described as a huge dog with three heads, each of which was covered in strands of writhing snakes instead of fur. In some versions the dog has fifty heads, while in others it has a hundred, along with snakes' heads on several tails. Cerberus was the progeny of the monstrous Echidne and Typhon. It was stationed at the entrance to the underworld to prevent unwanted intruders as well as the escape of those who dwelt within. But some people did try to get past Cerberus, such as Æeneas, who was guided by a sybil who drugged the dog with opium and honey, and Orpheus, who lulled the dog to sleep by playing his lyre. But the most dramatic was the encounter with the hero Heracles/Hercules, whose twelfth and last task was to take Cerberus to the surface world at the orders of King Eurystheus. After the hero managed to cross to the gates of the underworld, he grabbed the dog's throats and held on so tightly that it began to suffocate and went limp. The hero chained and bound the monstrous dog while it was still in this condition and took it via Charon's boat back to the world of the living. However, when Cerberus felt the sunlight, he recovered and went into a violent frenzy, thrashing against the chains and all around. After dragging the dog into the hall of the king, the hero unleashed it.

The terrified king hid behind a pillar, while Cerberus bolted back to Hades as fast as possible.
References 7, 18, 20, 61, 63, 78, 89, 132, 138, 148, 165, 168, 177
See also Black dogs, Echidne, Garmr, monster, Sharameyas, Typhon

CERCOPES
This was a race of malicious humanoids in the classical mythology of Greece and Rome. The Cercopes inhabited the wastes of Lydia in Greece and in the region of Ephasus (now in Turkey). They were monstrously ugly and preyed on travelers and lone people who wandered into their territory. Their evil reputation was such that the hero Heracles/Hercules defeated them and surrendered them to the god Zeus/Jupiter. They were then transformed into babbling apes and removed to the islands called the Pithicusae, meaning "Islands of the Apes."
References 12, 138, 177

CERNE ABBAS GIANT
Cerne Abbas Giant is the name of a giant in the traditions and folklore of Dorset in southwestern England. The folkloric tradition states that this giant terrorized the neighborhood of Cerne Abbas, raiding and devouring the sheep. He was so greedy that on one occasion he ate a whole flock and fell asleep on the hillside where the community crept up on him and killed him. It was also said, specifically by John Gibbons (1670), that the Cerne Abbas Giant took part in a battle on Salisbury plain between King Divitiacus and the Cerngik Giants. The image on the hillside at Cerne Abbas is a chalk figure of immense proportions dating from the second century A.D. This figure, which is scoured into the hillside, shows a gigantic man 180 feet in height wielding a club 120 feet in length in his right hand. His body is naked and his genitalia are so well defined that many descriptions have stated his role as that of a fertility god. Indeed, local people have gone to the giant at night for centuries. Curiously, his image is the only "pornographic" material that is permitted to go through the Royal Mail in England! In later periods, the Cerne Abbas Giant was used by local parents to threaten their children into good behavior.
References 13, 78, 128, 181, 182
See also Albion, giant, Gogmagog

CERYNEAN HIND, CERYNEIAN HIND
These are variations on the name of a fabulous creature in the classical mythology of Greece and Rome. Also referred to as the Arcadian Hind, it was described as an immortal deer with hooves of brass and antlers of pure gold. It inhabited the slopes of Mount Cerynea and was so swift that it could not be

caught; thus it was regarded as sacred to the goddess Artemis/Diana. One of the labors that Eurystheus demanded of the hero Heracles/Hercules was to capture the Cerynean Hind. This the hero achieved by pursuing the hind relentlessly across the Peleponnesus (which at that time was most of the known world) until it was worn to a standstill by fatigue a year later on the banks of the River Ladon. The hero took the Cerynean Hind back to Eurystheus and then let it free again.
References 24, 78, 138

CETUS

This is the name of a fierce predatory monster of the sea in the classical mythology of Greece and Rome. It was described as having the head of a dog, similar to a greyhound, on an enormous bloated body resembling that of a whale or dolphin, with a tail divided into two huge fan-like extensions. According to different sources, this monster had been created either by the king of the gods Zeus/Jupiter or by the sea-god Poseidon/Neptune for the purpose of destroying the Andromeda, daughter of Queen Cassiopea. The queen had bragged about the beauty of her daughter, describing her more favorably than the goddesses and sea nymphs. This so angered the gods that Cassiopea was compelled to chain her daughter to a rocky promontory to await her death in the monster's jaws. Luckily, the hero Perseus came by with the newly chopped head of the Gorgon Medusa and turned Cetus to stone. Andromeda was thus rescued and became the wife of her hero.
References 7, 10, 177
See also Gorgon, Medusa, monster

CEUS

This is the name of a giant, specifically one of the Titans, mentioned in the classical mythology of Greece and Rome. Ceus is later mentioned as a primordial giant in the works of the medieval Italian author Boccaccio (1313–1375).
References 173
See also giant, Titan

CHAARMAROUCH

This is the name of one of the kings of the djinns in the traditions and beliefs of the people of Morocco. Chaarmarouch is said to be a vast being who inhabits a cave on the sides of the range of the Goundafi Mountains. Though never seen, he is considered to be of a malicious nature. His presence, which is to be avoided, may be recognized by the shower of stones that will be cast to blind any human intruder.
References 122
See also Djinn

CHAHNAMEED

This is the name of an enormous giant in the legends and folklore of the Pequot people of northeast United States, described by Speck (1903). Chahnameed was constantly hunting and eating, for his hunger was legendary; so was his size, such that he was also known as "The Great Eater Glutton." He lived on an island and constantly hunted in both the sea and the mainland for food. But one day he saw a beautiful young woman on the beach and desired her. So he waded across to her and wooed her until she consented to be his wife. However, this giant wanted to hunt and feed himself, leaving her alone most of the time; but his enchantment prevented her escape. Her plan became clearer as she thought about how to release herself. She fashioned effigies of herself from her feces, and from shells and paint, and placed them around the lodge. When Chahnameed returned this time, he found that he could not move without one of these effigies screaming at him. He finally escaped the lodge in time to see his wife paddling her canoe as fast as possible to the shore of the mainland. Chahnameed waded after her, but she took a hair from her head and with some enchantment it became a spear that she thrust at the giant as he was about to grab the canoe. He fell into the water, never to rise again, and she returned to her people safely.
References 77
See also giant

CHALBROTH

This is the name of a giant in the literature of France. He is cited in the genealogy of Pantagruel as an ancestor, by the author François Rabelais (1494?–1553?) in his work *Pantagruel* (1532). Chalbroth was said to have existed on the medlar fruit splashed by the blood of Abel after Cain had slain him. But it was the contention of Rabelais's storyteller Alcofribas (an anagram of his own name) that the descendants of Chalbroth survived the Noachian flood because his descendant, Hurtaly, rode on the roof of the ark.
References 173
See also Bruyer, Daughters of Cain, Etion, Gabbara, Galehaut, Gargantua, giant, Happemousche, Hurtaly, Morguan, Noachids, Noah, Pantagruel

CHAMP

This is the affectionately diminutive name for the Monster of Lake Champlain, in much the same way as the Loch Ness Monster is referred to as "Nessie." Champ is the inhabitant of the lake on the border between Quebec in Canada and Vermont in the United States. This lake monster has been described as being extremely long (thirty feet) with a serpentine shape; a thick body, sometimes with humps; and a head resembling that of a horse. There are many

Perseus kills Cetus, the sea monster, by showing it Medusa's head. (A Wonder Book for Boys and Girls and Tanglewood Tales *by N. Hawthorne, J. M. Dent, London*)

reports of its having been seen since the time of Sam de Champlain, after whom both the lake and the monster are named, although Champlain himself never said that he had seen it. Key occurrences include an attack on a boat of fishermen in 1939 at Rouses Point as well as several sightings and photographs taken by local people in the 1970s and 1980s. Meanwhile, the township of Port Henry on the American side of Lake Champlain has "instituted Champ" and taken him into their midst as a tourist feature of the community.
References 78, 133
See also Loch Ness Monster, monster

CHAMROSH

This is the name of a fabulous creature or winged monster in the mythology of the ancient kingdoms of Mesopotamia and Persia. Chamrosh is described as having the body of a dog with the head and wings of a bird. It is also said to inhabit the ground beneath the soma tree that was the roost of the Senmurv. When the Senmurv descended or alighted from its roost, all the ripened seeds fell to the earth. These seeds were gathered by the Chamrosh, which then distributed them to other parts of the earth.
References 89, 125
See also Senmurv

CHAN

This is the name of a monstrous sea creature in the legends and folklore of ancient China. In the records of a historical treatise written by Ssu-ma Ch'ien (c. 145–85 B.C.), Chan is described as a clam of immense proportions. This creature's exhalations were said to consist of a substance that created vast underwater palaces.
References 180
See also monster

CH'ANG HAO

This is the name of a king of the snakes in the mythology and legends of China. Ch'ang Hao was able to vary his size, from small to enormous, depending on which proportions were advantageous during his combat with his enemies. However, when Ch'ang Hao took part in the celestial Battle of Mu between the gods and immortal adversaries, the many changes in his size did not prevent his defeat.
References 180
See also serpent

CHANG LUNG

This is the name of a dragon in the mythology and folklore of China. The legend tells how Chang Lung had originally been a very successful magistrate in the reign of Chung Tsung (A.D. 684). He was respected by

all, especially by his wife and sons, for his piety. However, it became noted that he was increasingly spending long hours at night in the local temple. When questioned by one his sons upon returning home one morning, Chang Lung confessed that his cold and wet appearance was because he was metamorphosing into a dragon protector, and that he was being challenged by another dragon. He asked his sons to help him defeat the dragon in the coming contest. They agreed and went with their father to the temple, where they could identify their father only by the red ribbon he told them he would wear. Armed with bows and arrows, the sons aimed and shot the rival dragon, and their father remained in the temple from that time as the protector of the community. The temple was apparently dedicated to Chang Lung in A.D. 707 and enlarged in 894, and again in 1091, by members of the community, who were grateful for their protection from the effects of an extreme drought.
References 180
See also Oriental Dragon

CHAPALU, CAPALU, CAPALUS

These are variations on the name of a monstrous supernatural cat in the legends and folklore of Wales and the Arthurian legends of Europe. It is also known by the name Capalu or Capalus in France. In the Welsh versions it is known as Palug's Cat, an enormous supernatural and fabulous creature that hunted its own kind to satisfy its vast appetite. According to these versions it was eventually killed by Cai (Sir Kay). However, in the Arthurian legends, Chapalu is especially associated with the Mont du Chat ("Mountain of the Cat") in the Savoie region of France, where it was reputedly killed by King Arthur.
References 7, 54
See also Phantom Cat

CHARLEMAGNE

The emperor Charlemagne, Charles the Great (742–814), who was the king of the Franks and the emperor of Rome, has been the subject of many European legends and the hero of many folktales in much the same way as King Arthur. Together with his champion Roland, Charlemagne is often described as a giant, probably in order to confirm his status by reference to stature, and thus he is also a symbol of patriotism.
References 143, 173
See also Ænotherus, Balan, Cheval Bayard, Fierabras, giant

CHARYBDIS

This is the name of a monster in the classical mythology of Greece and Rome. According to various

accounts, Charybdis, the daughter of Gaia and the sea-god Poseidon, was a young woman who offended Zeus/Jupiter, the king of the gods; in one version, by stealing the cattle of Heracles/Hercules, but by a different offence in other accounts. She was struck by one of the god's thunderbolts and then cast into the sea beneath the cliffs where she had been sitting under her fig tree. There she assumed a new form, that of a disembodied mouth gaping at the surface, sucking air and sea, and spewing them back out in an enormous vortex three times a day. Many craft perished in this whirlpool of a mouth, but the heroes Ulysses and Jason and the Argonauts all survived.
References 24, 138, 165, 177
See also monster

CHATLOUP
This is an alternative name for the Calopus of medieval European traditions.
References 7
See also Calopus

CHEEROONEAR
This is the name of a class of monstrous dog-faced humanoids in the traditions and legends of the Native Australian people. The Cheeroonear are described as having extremely long arms with hands that trail on the ground as they walk, a head and ears resembling those of a dog, and a vast dewlap under the throat that extends in wrinkles to the belly. These monstrous beings are predatory creatures that hunt and devour humans in the Nullabor Plain. One particular legend tells how, during a particularly severe drought, the Cheeroonear turned up at a *billabong* and terrified the humans who had gathered there for the last drops of water in the region. The Cheeroonear male sank to the water level and drank so much that his distended stomach ballooned and made him vomit. There on the ground afterward, to the horror of the human onlookers, were the skull and bone remains of their missing relatives. The Cheeroonear leered at them and declared that they could not live to tell of this incident, and he departed before they could do anything. That night the humans pondered what they could do to protect their families from this predator. They decided that only the *wirinuns* (medicine men) known as the Winjarning brothers could help. The *wirinuns* were sent for quickly and asked how they might protect the tribe. Soon all were busy fetching brushwood, as directed, and laying it in two lines converging at the waterhole. Then the families hid in the rocks while the warriors took their position behind the brushwood. As the dawn rose in the east, the Cheeroonear's pack of hounds came through the scrub and toward the water. Then as the front dog got to the end of the brushwood lines, its head was

severed from its body by the boomerang of one of the *wirinuns,* and as each subsequent dog came, it met the same fate. When all were dead, their tails were cut off and whisked at the end of the lines in the hands of a warrior, to simulate the dogs cornering some prey. Soon a Cheeroonear came to investigate and as he reached the end of the brushwood lines the clubs of the humans smashed his skull. He was pulled out of the way, and in the silence the hidden warriors heard the Cheeroonear's wife coming. Her fate was to be chopped up by the waiting men; but before she expired, what appeared to be a boy emerged from her severed body. This being transformed into a monstrous serpent that slithered into the bush to carry on the Cheeroonears' evil.
References 153
See also cannibal, monster

CHEIRON
This is the name of a Centaur in the classical mythology of Greece and Rome. Cheiron, meaning "Hand," and also spelled Chiron, was the offspring of the Titan Cronus (who had assumed the shape of a

Cheiron the Centaur (Rose Photo Archive, UK)

stallion) and Philyra (an Oceanid nymph). Cheiron was described as having the strong body and legs of a horse and the torso and head of a human. This Centaur was extremely well educated in the arts, medicine, law, and prophesy. He was therefore chosen by the gods to educate such heroes as Aesculapius, Achilles, Jason, Meleagor, Nestor, Peleus, and Theseus.

Cheiron inhabited a cave in the slopes of Mount Pelion. In the fiasco following the marriage feast of Pirithous, it was Cheiron who saved the hero Peleus from the drunken Centaurs. Cheiron was host to the hero Heracles/Hercules during the hunt for the Erymanthean Boar, and to entertain the guests, Pholus opened a jar of wine. However, the aroma brought some unruly Centaurs who gate-crashed, and soon a fight broke out. In the melee Cheiron slipped and was accidentally stabbed by one of the hero's arrows. This injury to a mortal would have meant instant death, for the arrows were dipped in the blood of the Hydra. But Cheiron was immortal and was consumed with agony. Prometheus asked Cheiron to let the gods take his immortality so that he would be spared eternal agony, and this they did. The gentle Cheiron was transformed into the heavenly constellation Centaurus, or, according to some, Sagittarius.
References 20, 24, 61, 78, 132, 138, 165, 168, 177
See also centaur, Cronus, Erymanthean Boar, Hydra, Pholus, Prometheus, Rhea, Sagittarius, Titan

CHERNUBLES DE MUNIGRE
This is the name of a giant in the legends and folklore of France. Chernubles de Munigre was one of the adversaries of the hero Roland, the champion of the emperor Charlemagne's court. He is described in the medieval *Chanson de Roland* as being of nobility and exceedingly strong.
References 173
See also Charlemagne, giant

CHERUFE
This is the name of a monster in the legends and folk beliefs of the Araucanian peoples of Argentina and Chile. The Cherufe is said to inhabit the volcanoes high in the Andes Mountains. Its prey is the gullible humans who wander into its territory, especially young girls.
References 125
See also monster

CHESHIRE CAT
This is the name of a creature that appears in the classic work *Alice in Wonderland* (1865), by the English academic and author Lewis Carroll (Charles Lutwidge Dodgson, 1843–1898). It is part of the repertoire of strange beings that beset the heroine

Alice as she goes farther and farther down the rabbit hole into Wonderland. The Cheshire Cat is depicted as a large striped cat with big eyes and large teeth in its wide mouth, usually sitting on the high branch of a tree with the most enormous grin across its face. This cat belonged to the Duchess and was in the habit of appearing or vanishing very slowly so that only the grin was left where the cat had been. Several explanations have been suggested for the Cheshire Cat and its grin, which were in existence in folklore since the seventeenth century, long before Carroll placed the character in his work. One explanation has to do with the shape in which cheeses were sold; yet another is that cats are amused that the county of Cheshire is a palatinate with wider privileges and a higher status than a normal county.
References 7, 18, 20

CHEVAL BAYARD
In the folklore of Normandy, France, this is a type of supernatural water monster that may appear as a human or as a horse. The Cheval Bayard inhabits the banks of rivers, pools, and marshland. When manifesting as a horse, the beast entices foolhardy humans to attempt to ride it; but as soon as they get on its back, it tosses them into the water or the brush. A story is told of the Cheval Bayard who, in the form of a handsome young man, had taken to calling on a peasant woman whose husband found out. The jealous husband placed a bar of iron to heat in the kitchen fire and, concealing himself in his wife's clothes, sat at her spinning wheel to await the being. Soon enough it entered the room and with loving words inquired "her" name. "Myself," replied the husband, hurling the red-hot iron bar at the sprite who yelled for his comrades to come. The others asked who was attacking him and when the Cheval Bayard told them "Myself did it," they chided him for causing his own harm and departed.
References 15, 159
See also Bayard, Cabyll-Ushtey, Eačh Uisge, Kelpy, monster, Näcken, Neugle

CH'I LIN
This is the name of a fabulous beast in the mythology of China. The Ch'i Lin, also spelled K'i Lin, is described as having a body like that of a large deer, the legs and hooves of a horse, the tail of an ox, and a fine head with a single horn. Its back is the primary colors of red, yellow, blue, white, and black, while its belly is either brown or yellow. Its voice is melodious, and it is so sensitive that it will not eat any live being whether animal or vegetation. The name Ch'i Lin actually indicates two animals, for the male is known as the Ch'i and the female as the Lin; but the species is referred to collectively by the joint name. The Ch'i Lin

is one of the four spiritual beings (the others being the Dragon, the Feng Hwang, and the Tortoise). It is also the essence of the five elements of the world: earth, fire, metal, water, and wood. This gentle creature is the bringer, and signifier, of periods of peace and prosperity. It is a sign of great good fortune when the Ch'i Lin appears. Two such occasions were the reign of the Emperor Huang-ti (2697–2597 B.C.) and the birth of the sage Confucius (sixth century B.C.).
References 7, 61, 89, 180
See also Alicorn, Amduscias, Ass (Three-Legged), Biasd Na Srognig, Chio-Tuan, dragon, Feng Hwang, Karkadan, Ki Lin, Kirin, Koresck, Licorn, Mi'raj (Al), Onyx Monoceros, Scythian Ass

CHI LUNG WANG
Chi Lung Wang is a celestial dragon in the legends and popular folklore of China. His name may be translated as "the Fire-Engine Dragon King." This beneficent oriental dragon was deemed to be "in charge of" the provision of domestic water and, as such, was propitiated for assistance in providing sufficient water and efficient working of the pumps in times of house fire. Chi Lung Wang is derived from the religious cult of the Dragon King, Lung Wang, provider of the earth's water.
References 24, 119, 159
See also dragon, Lung, Oriental Dragon

CHIAI TUNG
This is an alternative name for the Oriental Unicorn also known as the Hai Chiai, in the beliefs and mythology of China.
References 81
See also Ch'i-Lin, Hai Chiai, Oriental Unicorn, unicorn

CHIANG-LIANG
This is the name of a hybrid monster in the beliefs and mythology of China. It is described as having a body like a panther but with very long legs terminating in hooves; having the head of a tiger but with a human face. Represented with a snake between its teeth, it appears in the volumes known as the *T'ai P'ing Kuang Chi*, which may be translated as the *Great Records Made in the Period of Peace and Prosperity*, which were completed in c. A.D. 978 and published in A.D. 981.
References 18
See also Ch'ou-T'i, Ch'uan-T'ou (People of), monster

CHICHEVACHE
This is a female monster in the legends and folklore of medieval Europe whose name means "Scrawny Cow." It was recorded in this spelling by the medieval author and diplomat Geoffrey Chaucer (1345–1400) in his "Clerk's Tale" from the *Canterbury Tales*, where the author changed it from the French name Chichifache, meaning "Thin Face" or "Ugly Face." Also known as the Thingut during the sixteenth century, Chichevache was portrayed as an undernourished cow with a human face and a miserable expression. It was said to live on a diet of "hen-pecked" and obedient wives. In the chauvinist attitudes of the period, such a diet was conjectured to have provided very little fodder for the beast, which would sicken to death for want of nourishment. (Her overindulged counterpart, the Bicorne, fed only on "hen-pecked" husbands!) Anchevache and Bicorne were frequently depicted on the church furniture of the period, especially on the misericords.
References 7, 20
See also Bicorne, monster

CHI'I-LIN
This is an alternative spelling for the Oriental Unicorn known as the K'i-Lin in the legends and mythology of China.
References 7, 61, 89
See also K'i-Lin, Oriental Unicorn, unicorn

CHILD GUZZLER
This is the English version of the name of a cannibal giant known as der Kinderschrecker in the folklore of Germany. He lives on a diet of naughty and runaway children, features in many eighteenth- and nineteenth-century stories, and is of course a Nursery bogie by which parents persuaded their children into good behavior.
References 181
See also cannibal, giant, Nursery bogies

CHIMAERA
This is an alternative spelling of Chimera, a monster in the classical mythology of Greece and Rome
References 165
See also Chimera, monster

CHIMERA, CHIMAIRA
These are variations on the name of a monster in the classical mythology of Greece and Rome. The Chimera, also spelled Chimaera, means "Goat"; and indeed, according to the Greek poet Homer, it has the body of a gigantic goat, but with the hind parts of a serpent and the front part and head of a lion. Sometimes it is portrayed, as in Hesiod's *Theogony*, as having the heads of all three of these animals arranged along its back. The Chimera was said to be the progeny of the monstrous Echidne and Typhon, and its siblings were Cerberus the dog of the underworld, the Nemean Lion, the serpentine Hydra, and the enigmatic Sphinx. Once the monstrous pet of the king of Caria, it escaped and went on a rampage

within the court. Then it inhabited the region of Lycia (now Turkey), where it inflicted damage with its fiery breath and devoured every mortal thing that came its way. The terrified people called for it to be dealt with, and the ruler, Iobates, sent for the hero Bellerophon. Mounted on the flying horse Pegasus, the hero managed to thrust the point of his spear into the Chimera's mouth, where its fiery breath melted it and choked the monster to death.

During the late medieval period, the Chimaera was depicted in various art forms and sometimes in bestiaries where it symbolized the complex nature of evil. However, it ultimately became a byword for "the impossible."
References 7, 18, 20, 24, 61, 63, 78, 89, 94, 125, 132, 135, 138, 165, 168, 181
See also Cerberus, dragon, Echidne, Hydra, monster, Nemean Lion, Orthos, Pegasus, Sphinx, Typhon

CHINESE DRAGON
See Oriental Dragon

CHINESE LYCOPODIUM
This is an alternative name for the Barometz, a legendary creature of medieval Europe that is part animal and part vegetable.
References 7, 18, 89
See also Barometz

CHIO-TUAN
This is a type of Ch'i-Lin in the legends and folklore of China. Described as identical to the Chinese Unicorn, the Chio-Tuan appeared as a warning to the great Genghis Khan to desist from his war policies during the thirteenth century.
References 18
See also Ch'i-Lin, unicorn

CHIRON
This is an alternative spelling of the name of the Centaur known as Cheiron in the classical mythology of Greece and Rome.
References 20, 78, 132, 138, 162, 332, 374
See also centaur

CHITRA-RATHA, CHITRATHA
These are variations on the name of the king of the Gandharvas in the Hindu mythology of India.
References 112
See also Gandharvas, Kinnara

CHIVATO
This is the name of a monstrous humanoid in the legends of the Araucanian people of Chile. The Chivato was believed to be the transformed body of a child kidnapped by witches and metamorphosed over several years into a cannibal beast. A number of Chivatos were said to inhabit the caverns called the "Caves of Salamanca" and some caverns called "Quicavi" near the towns of Ancud and Chiloc. A report in the late nineteenth century detailed the discovery in a cave of two such captive cannibals (or "Encerrados"). The caverns were said to be accessible by way of a tunnel that started in the island of a lake and surfaced some distance away in the caverns themselves. The monsters were supposedly fed by an Ivunche or Trequehuecuve servant who captured young girls drawing water from the lake and abducted them by way of this secret tunnel.
References 133
See also cannibal, Encerrados, monster, Trelquehuecuve

CHONCHONYI, CHONCHÓN
These are variations on the name of a group of evil supernatural monsters or vampires in the folk beliefs of the Araucanian people of Chile. When manifested in visible form, they are described as resembling human heads with enormous fangs and ears so enormous that they are used as wings. The Chonchónyi seek and prey upon humans who are old or sick. They wait until these people are left alone on moonless nights; then they flap down, leap upon them, and drain their life away. There are some secret ways in which these monsters may be defeated; these involve reciting certain chants and prayers, making the sign of a Solomon's seal in the earth, or laying clothing out in their path in a certain manner. According to one story, after a Chonchonyi had been dealt with by someone who knew a secret chant, an enormous birdlike creature fell from the night sky. The villagers immediately decapitated it and gave the head to a dog; then the body was thrown on the roof. The following day the dog's body was horrifyingly swollen, and the village gravedigger reported the burial of a headless person.
References 18, 38, 78, 138, 159
See also monster, Pontianak, vampire

CHORTI
This is the name of a Wildman or humanoid beast in the beliefs and folklore of Guatemala. The Chorti is described as a giant hairy being with reversed feet that point back the way it had traveled and claws of metal. There are numerous instances of this belief in Central America, and a similar being is described in the folklore of the Yaqui peoples of Mexico. The Chorti is regarded as a guardian of the wilderness, much like the Wildman of European folklore, but to see it may bring misfortune.
References 94
See also Abominable Snowman, Bigfoot, giant, satyr, Wildman, Yeti

Bellerophon and Pegasus destroying the Chimaera (A Wonder Book for Boys and Girls and
Tanglewood Tales *by N. Hawthorne, J. M. Dent, London)*

CH'OS-SKYON

This is the name given in Tibet to the eight giants of Buddhism, known in India as the Dharmapālas.
References 24, 132
See also Dharmapālas, giant

CH'OU-T'I

This is the name of a composite hybrid creature in the mythology of China. The Ch'ou-Ti is described as having a beast's body but with a head at each end. It appears in the volumes known as the *T'ai P'ing Kuang Chi,* which may be translated as the *Great Records Made in the Period of Peace and Prosperity,* which were completed in c. A.D. 978 and published in A.D. 981.
References 18
See also Chiang-Liang, Ch'uan-T'ou (People of), monster

CHRISTOPHER, SAINT

This is the name of a giant in the scriptures and texts of the Christian religion of medieval Europe. Saint Christopher, according to the *Golden Legend* by the Dominican monk Jacobus de Voragine (1230–1298), came from Canaan and was possibly one of the ancient Anakim in the Holy Land. He is described as being twelve cubits (approximately eighteen feet) in height. However it was the saint's blessing for travelers, following the tradition of his carrying the Christ Child, from which his image as giant derived. When the travelers required safe passage, church authorities obliged by having gigantic images of Saint Christopher put on the walls of churches and other buildings. This was done so that even from a great distance the images could be seen and the protection would be considered a reality. Thus the pilgrim, the scholar, and the diplomat, along with their servants and those toiling in the countryside, could always be under Saint Christopher's protection and never have the fear of dying a "mala mors" unshriven (that is, without confession). It was a small step for the assumption to be made that the images represented were the real size of the saint.

In the orthodox Christian religion of Eastern Europe and the Middle East, however, Saint Christopher was portrayed as a Cynocephalus, or Dog-Head. This depiction occurred through a spelling error that, in turn, led to an error in semantics; since his designation as a "Canaanite" was mistranscribed as "canine." The Cynocephali were already part of the medieval concepts of other cultures, but the description of the saint as a Cynocephalus was highly problematic for the church authorities. This dilemma was resolved around the thirteenth century by emphasizing the miracle of such a person preaching the gospel and witnessing the Lord. In this tradition Saint Christopher was martyred for his preaching, and the king who ordered his martyrdom was later converted to Christianity. There are still several ancient depictions in Eastern Europe of Saint Christopher with the head of a dog.
References 173, 181
See also Anakim, Corineus, Cynocephali, giant, Town Giants

CHRONOS

This is an alternative spelling of the name Cronus, a Titan in the classical mythology of Greece and Rome.
References 20, 24, 47, 78, 94, 125, 138, 165, 177, 181
See also Cronus, Titan

CHRYSAOR

This is the name of the monstrous son of the sea-god Neptune and the Gorgon Medusa in the classical mythology of Greece and Rome. In another version, he was said to be the brother of the flying horse Pegasus, born of the blood that dripped from the severed head of Medusa. His name means "Armed with a Golden Sword." Chrysaor was also the father Geryon, the adversary of Hercules.
References 138, 177
See also Geryon, Gorgon, Medusa, monster, Pegasus

CHRYSOMALLUS

This is an alternative name for the ram Aries in the classical mythology of Greece and Rome. The word *chrysomallus* is an epithet for the fabulous beast in that it refers literally to the fleece of gold that covered this winged creature.
References 20
See also Aries

CH'UAN-T'OU, PEOPLE OF

These are a monstrous hybrid race in the beliefs and mythology of China, described as having a humanoid body, the head of a person but with a bird's beak, and wings resembling those of a bat (that is, with skin rather than feathers). They apparently existed by catching and eating fish directly from the rivers and sea. The People of Ch'uan-T'ou are mentioned in the volumes known as the *T'ai P'ing Kuang Chi* which may be translated as the *Great Records Made in the Period of Peace and Prosperity,* which were completed in c. A.D. 978 and published in A.D. 981.
References 18
See also Ch'ou-T'i, Chiang-Liang, monster

CHUDO-YUDO

This is the name of a dragon in the beliefs and folklore of Russia. Chudo-Yudo is described as a monstrous many-headed dragon whose mouths emit terrifying flames. It was said to be the progeny of the monstrous Baba Yaga, or even a manifestation of the giantess herself in her most demonic form. It was also said to

be the sibling of Koshchei the Deathless, another evil dragon associated with Baba Yaga. Like the Oriental Dragons, Chudo-Yudo was considered the controller of the waters of the region and, as such, was propitiated during shortages.
References 55
See also Baba Yaga, dragon, Koshchei, Oriental Dragon

CICHOL
This is the name of the monstrous leader of the Fomors in the Celtic legends and folklore of Ireland. The Fomorians are described in the Irish texts known as the *Lebor Gabàla* (The book of invasions), and the *Cath Maige Tuired* (The [second] battle of Mag Tured). They became monstrous humanoids with a human body but the head of either a goat or a horse and only one eye, arm, and leg each. This latter fact did nothing to restrict their evil, and they demanded tribute in kind from everyone within their domain.
References 7, 24, 78, 120, 125, 128, 141, 159
See also Fachan, Foawr, Fomor, giant, monster

CIGOUAVE
This is the name of a monster in the beliefs and folklore of Haiti. The Cigouave is a predatory hybrid creature with a body resembling that of a lion or panther and a head like that of a human, much like the Manticore described in medieval European travelers' tales. It appears within the panoply of Voodoo religious beliefs and is conjectured to have derived, via the missionaries of the sixteenth century, from the Manticore as described in the lands of Africa.
References 184
See also Manticore, monster

CIR SITH
This is an alternative spelling of the Gaelic name for Ce Sith, the formidable monstrous dog of Scottish folklore.
References 7, 159
See also Ce Sith

CIRCHOS
This is the name of a fabulous monster in the folklore of Scandinavia. The Circhos is described by the cleric-historian Olaus Magnus (1490–1558) as a humanoid being with three toes on each foot, one of which was larger than the other. Its body had both black and red markings. This sea monster's gait was so insecure, as a result of its disproportionate limbs, that it was obliged to cling to the rocks during sea swells and to go about only during calm weather.
References 7
See also monster

CÌREIN CRÒIN, CIREAN
These are variations on the name of a monster in the beliefs and folklore of the Highlands of Scotland. The

The Sea Serpent, known in the Highlands as Cìrein Cròin (Rose Photo Archive, UK)

Cìrein Cròin, Cirean

name Cìrein Cròin may be translated from the Scottish Gaelic as "Grey Crest," but this creature is also known as Curtag Mhòr a' Chuain ("the Great Whirlpool of the Ocean"); Mial Mhòr a' Chuain ("the Great Beast of the Ocean"), and Uile Bhéisd a' Chuain ("the Monster of the Ocean"). It is described as the most gigantic sea serpent that ever existed, capable of swallowing several whales whole at one go.
References 24, 128
See also Afanc, Loch Ness Monster, monster, Oilliphéist, serpent

CIUDACH

This is the name of a monster in the beliefs and folklore of Scotland, Ireland, and the Isle of Man. Ciudach is a predatory humanoid monster that inhabits caverns and dark subterranean places in the mountains. It is thought to have originally been the giant of the same name from the region of Roscommon in Ireland who traveled to the Scottish region of Inverness along the Great Glen. This giant, who features in the legends of Ireland, was purported to have been the lover of Gráinne.
References 128
See also giant, monster

CLIFF-OGRE

This is a type of ogre or ogress that features in many folktales of the world. It is a motif of a gigantic being that preys upon travelers and local people as they follow a path along the top of a cliff. When the victims are near enough to the edge, the Cliff-Ogre kicks or hurls them to their death, while hungry offspring wait below at the foot of the cliff. This motif appears especially in the folklore of the Native Americans and in some of the ancient Greek myths.
References 24
See also giant, ogre, ogress

CLYMENE

This is one of the female Titans in the classical mythology of Greece and Rome. Her name may also be spelled Klymene. The daughter of Uranus and Gaia, she was ultimately buried in Tartarus with her siblings.
References 20, 47, 78, 125, 138, 165, 177
See also Atlas, Eurymedon, Iapetus, Titan

CLYTIUS

This is the name of one of the Gigantes in the classical mythology of Greece and Rome. They were engendered from the blood of Uranus's castration when it fell upon the earth. Alcyoneus was one of their leaders; Porphyrion was another. The Gigantes were described as being of enormous humanoid proportions but having serpents for legs and serpents'

heads for feet. At their first appearance they were already fully formed adult warriors, complete with spears and shining armor, ready to do battle. And they attacked the Olympian gods immediately. However, by subterfuge, supernatural powers, and the strength of the hero Heracles/Hercules, they were defeated one by one. Clytius, whose name means "the Renowned," in his turn was vanquished by either Hephaestus or Hecate, depending on the source.
References 7, 138, 168, 177
See also Alcyoneus, Enceladus, Eurytus, giant, Gigantes, Hecatonchieres, Hundred-Handed Giants, Mimas, Pallas, Pelorus, Polybutes, Porphyrion, Rhaetos, Typhon

COCA

In the legends and folklore of Spain, this is a gigantic, predatory, monstrous, female fire-breathing dragon, now carried in effigy in Spanish festival parades. The Coca is probably derived from the Tarasque of southwestern France.
References 181
See also dragon, monster, Tarasca, Town Giants

COCKATRICE

This is the name of a fabulous hybrid monster in the legends and folklore of medieval Europe. It was originally described as taking the form of the Basilisk, but by the fourteenth century the English author and diplomat Geoffrey Chaucer (1345–1400) mentioned the Basilisk in his "Parson's Tale" in the *Canterbury Tales* under the name of the Basilicok. This name was later developed into being Cockatrice, giving testament to the folkloric tale of its having been hatched for nine years by a toad from a seven-year-old cockerel's egg (like the more recent Aitvaras). Previously described as a serpent, it was now said to have the head, neck, and legs of a cockerel, the tail of a serpent, a cockerel's head and human face, and the yellow body and wings of a dragon. Sometimes there was even a head on its tail like that of an Amphisbaena.

Its killing potential had also increased such that it could now kill a human who attempted to spear it by causing its own poison to travel back up the length of the spear; in addition, it could rot the fruit off trees from a distance, pollute the water where it drank so as to be poisonous for centuries, and kill simply by looking at a living thing. William Shakespeare (1554–1616) drew on this killing potential when he wrote the following in *Twelfth Night* (Act III, Scene 4): "They will kill one another by the look, like cockatrices."

Terrified travelers of the period believed that the Cockatrice infested the deserts of North Africa and that the only creature that could counteract its poison was a

cockerel, which they made sure was kept safely with them. Such was the reputation for the instantaneous death inflicted by this monster that its name was given during Tudor times, to an enormous brass cannon and later to a venomous lizard of Armenia. Today, like its counterpart the Basilisk, it appears frequently as a heraldic image on coats of arms in Europe.
References 5, 20, 61, 63, 78, 89, 133
See also Aitvaras, Amphisbaena, Amphisien, Basilisk, dragon, monster, serpent, Wyvern

COCK-FISH
This is the name of a hybrid monster in the heraldic repertoire of Europe. It is portrayed as having the body, foreparts, and head of a cockerel and the tail of a large fish.
References 7

COCO
This is the name of a terrifying semisupernatural giant, ogre, or bogeyman in the legends and folklore of Spain. El Coco was portrayed by Francisco de Goya y Lucientes (1746–1828) in *Los Caprichos,* a series of etchings made about 1795, as a type of bogie with which parents threatened their children into good behavior. Consequently, by the nineteenth century the Coca had already been reduced to the status of a Nursery bogie.
References 181
See also giant, Nursery bogies, ogre

COCQCIGRUES, COQUECIGRUES
These are variations on the name of a class of fabulous beasts or monsters in the legends and folklore of France. They were such obscure creatures that the phrase *A la venue des Coquecigrues,* which may be translated as "When the Coquecigrues arrive," indicates an indefinite period, probably never. This famous phrase was current in the nineteenth century when a character created by the English author Charles Kingsley, the fairy Mrs. Bedonebyasyoudid, referred to it in the moralizing tale called *The Water Babies* (1863, ch. 4).
References 20
See also monster

COEUS
This is the name of a giant in the classical mythology of Greece and Rome. Coeus, also spelled Koios, means "Intelligent." He was the son of Gaia and Uranus, and one of the Titans who were the ancestors of the Olympian gods on whom they made war. Coeus's daughter Leto was the mother of the Olympian god Apollo and the goddess Artemis.
References 165, 177
See also Gaia, giant, Titan, Uranus

COINCHENN, COINCHEND
These are variations on the name of a monstrous female humanoid in the legends and folklore of Ireland. Coinchenn, whose name means "Dog-Headed," was also known as Cennfhata. She is described as having the body of a woman but the head of a dog. Her story is told in the *Echtrae Airt meic Cuinn* (Adventures of Art, the son of Conn). She is the mother of the beautiful Delbeháem and the wife of Morgán. Because there was a prophecy that she would die if ever her daughter was wooed, this monstrous dog-headed woman decapitated every young man who came to see her daughter. Soon the bronze railings surrounding the land of their castle were spiked with all the skulls of past suitors, to repel others. But the hero Art overcame Coinchenn, killed her, and placed her head on a bronze spike beside the others.
References 128
See also Cynocephali

COINN IOTAIR
This is the name of a pack of monstrous gigantic hunting hounds in the legends and folklore of Ireland. Coinn Iotair, meaning "Hounds of Rage" in the Irish Gaelic, belonged to Crom Dubh, a great and legendary chieftain of the Celtic pre-Christian era. His dogs were said to wreak havoc with animals and humans alike.
References 128
See also Saidthe Suaraighe

COLBRAND, COLBRANDE
These are variations on the name of a Danish giant in the legends and folklore of England. A reference to Colbrand appears in the legend of Sir Guy of Warwick, during the reign of the Saxon king of England, King Athelstan. Shortly after his marriage to the Earl of Warwick's daughter, Sir Guy traveled on pilgrimage to the Holy Land; but on his return he was horrified to see the land overrun by Danish invaders. The main encampment was held outside the town of Winchester, at that time the capital of England. Many battles and conflicts during that period were frequently settled by the tradition of single combat, whereby the champion of one side did battle alone with the champion of the other. Whichever man killed the other was not only victorious over the combatant but also ensured the victory of his army over the adversaries. The champion of the Danes was an invincible giant named Colbrand. By his faith and his prowess, Sir Guy undertook the fight with Colbrand and killed him. As a result, the whole of England was freed from the Danish tribute system.
References 2, 182
See also Dun Cow of Warwick, giant

COLD-DRAKES

This is a species of dragon in the literary works of the English academic and author J. R. R. Tolkien (1892–1973), *The Hobbit* (1937) and *The Lord of the Rings* (1955). These monstrous creatures were bred by the evil Morgoth in Angband during the First Age of the Sun. The Cold-Drakes are described as having vast bodies covered in iron scales, wings, enormous fangs, and huge claws. (Unlike their legendary counterparts, they could not fly.) Evil beyond belief, they wrought havoc on the people of the Middle Earth until they were almost completely vanquished in the War of Wrath. However, they arose again during the Third Age of the Sun and tracked down the dwarves who had found rich hoards of gold in the Grey Mountains, killing them by stealth and greedily taking the gold. Then the heroic Fram, a prince of the men of Éothéod, did battle with Scatha the Worm and, having slain their leader, the Cold-Drakes fled and did not return until the year 2570. Again the dwarves were slaughtered and robbed of their gold by these monsters. When the last of the dwarves' kings (Dain I) was killed, the remaining little band of dwarves fled from the Grey Mountains and their mines, leaving them to the Cold-Drakes forever.
References 51
See also dragon

COLO-COLO

This is the name of a type of vampire in the legends and folklore of the Araucanian peoples of Chile. Like the Basilisk of European legends, the Colo-Colo was supposedly hatched from the egg of a cockerel. This monstrous creature hovers over the sleeping body of its victim and drinks their saliva until they are drained of all moisture, become full of fevers, and die.
References 138
See also Basilisk, monster, vampire

COLUINN GUN CHEANN, COLUINN GAN CEANN, COLANN GUN CHEANN

These are alternative names of a semisupernatural monster in the legends and folklore of the Highlands of Scotland. The Coluinn Gun Cheann is also known as the Colann Gan Ceann or Colann Gun Cheann, which may be translated as "the Headless Trunk." Manifesting as a torso and limbs, it roamed the paths of the estate of the Macdonalds of Morar in the Isle of Skye (Inner Hebrides, Scotland). To women and children or men traveling in groups by day it offered no harm; but any male traveling alone at night on the "Smooth Mile" to Morar House was sure to be found dead and mutilated in the morning. It was eventually banished by Maccleod of Raasay.
References 24, 67, 128, 159
See also Acephalos

CON TRAM NU' Ó' C

This is the name of a semisupernatural monster in the beliefs and legends of the Annamese people of Thailand. The Con Tram Nu' ó'c manifests in the shape of a huge water buffalo that is capable of covering vast distances over any surface without difficulty in the shortest time. It is believed that a person lucky enough to see where one has been and to come across a hair will be able to cross any surface, including water, without getting wet.
References 24

CONOPENII

This is the name of a class of hybrid monsters in the legends and mythology of Persia (now Iran). They were said to have a body resembling that of a huge horse, but with the head of an ass. More remarkable was the fact that no human could come near for fear of the fire that they breathed from their mouths and nostrils.
References 7

CORC-CHLUASASK

This is the name of a class of hybrid water monsters in the Celtic legends and folklore of the Highlands of Scotland and of Ireland. The name indicates that these offspring of the Tairbh-Uisge, or water bull, have split ears, a feature that demonstrates their supernatural origin. These split-eared "calves" are described as being much larger than real-life calves, with a velvety pelt instead of the usual hide. If they wander into a herd, they are not only troublesome but may even provoke disaster. Consequently in former years any calves born with only half an ear were killed quickly, for fear that they were the monstrous breed.
References 133
See also Huallepén, monster, Tairbh-Uisge

CORINEUS

Corineus was originally a character in the pseudohistorical work *Historia Regnum Britanniae* (c. 1147) written by Geoffrey of Monmouth (1100–1154). In this account Corineus had been recruited by Brutus, the leader of the Trojans, as one of his lieutenants during his invasion of the Island of Albion (Britain), which had been peopled by a race of giants. The Trojans reputedly vanquished all the giants—including Gog and Magog—and settled the country. However, by the eighteenth century this pseudohistory had become distorted in the retelling and Corineus, who now had the alternative name of Gourmaillon, instead of being described as a leader of the invading Trojans, had become identified with the giants that had been vanquished by them. In this later version Corineus defeated Gogmagog in single combat and threw him off the cliffs and into the sea at

Plymouth not far from Saint Michael's Mount. Consequently, in 1741 the two symbolic giants of the Guildhall in the City of London were described as representing Corineus and Gogmagog.
References 173
See also giant, Gog, Gogmagog, Guildhall Giants, Magog, Town Giants

CORMEILIAN, CORMILAN
These are alternative names for the giant Cormoran in the traditions and folklore of the county of Cornwall in England. He is said to have been responsible for starting to build the island of Saint Michael's Mount near Penzance on the southern coast of Cornwall.
References 128
See also Cormoran, giant

CORMELIAN
This is the name of a giantess in the legends and folklore of Britain. Cormelian is the wife of the giant Cormoran, who was reputed to have built the island of Saint Michael's Mount. More specifically, however, the tale relates how the giant fell asleep with the effort, while his wife Cormelian carried on, but bringing green stones from a place closer than the white ones that her husband had carried from afar. According to one version of the tale, as she was passing him on her way to the newly formed island, he rolled and kicked her, causing her to drop the stones from her apron. The stones fell all the way across the bay and now form the green stone causeway leading to the white granite island.
References 54, 128
See also Cailleach Bheur, Cormoran, giant

CORMORAN
In the traditions and folklore of England, there are two types of being with this name, as follows:

1. In the traditional tale of "Jack-the-Giant-Killer," Cormoran is the name of the giant who was defeated by the hero. Cormoran had been the scourge of the region, but young Jack managed to defeat the giant by tricking him into falling into a huge pit. Jack was rewarded for this feat by the gift of a commemorative belt from King Arthur.
2. Cormoran, also known as Cormeilian, Cormilan, or Gourmaillon, is the name of a Cornish giant who started to build the island of Saint Michael's Mount near Penzance on the southern coast of Cornwall. However, the white granite that he had chosen was very heavy and he had to carry it from a distance, so he soon became tired of his project and fell asleep on the beach. His wife Cormelian, neither so

daunted nor so lazy, continued the task, using the local green stones. When she had almost finished Cormoran awoke and rebuked her, causing her to drop the stones she was carrying. These now form the causeway to the island, one half of which is built from white stones and the other half, green ones.

Both of these giants are associated with Cornwall, as is Corineus, who in turn is associated with Saint Michael's Mount. Both Corineus and Cormoran have the alternative name of Gourmaillon, and it has been conjectured that the traditional tale of "Jack-the-Giant-Killer" may be a further rendition of the early pseudohistory in which Corineus defeated Gogmagog.
References 54, 128
See also Corineus, Cormelian, giant, Gogmagog

CORNU
This is a monstrous black bird in the legends and folklore of Ireland. It was said to have been a demonic monster that Saint Patrick banished to the waters of Lough Derg, to live in Saint Patrick's Purgatory.
References 128

COROCOTTA, CROCOTTA, CROCOTTE, CROCUTA
These are variations on the name of a hybrid monster in the legends and folklore of sixteenth- and seventeenth-century Europe. It is derived from descriptions given by travelers and may have been influenced by descriptions of the Cynolycus reported by the ancient historian Pliny the Elder. The Corocotta was said to have the shape of a lion, but with a wolf-like head. Instead of teeth it had a bone arrangement in its huge jaw with which it crushed its prey before swallowing it whole. And as its eyes did not move within its sockets, the beast had to move its entire head to focus its hideous stare. This monster was reputed to imitate the calls of other beings so effectively that their companions were fooled into following, and, whether cattle or men, once inside the thickets of the Ethiopian scrublands they met their demise. The Corocotta is clearly a modification of the much earlier Leucrocotta.
References 7, 18
See also monster, Leucrotta

COTTUS
This is the name of a giant in the classical mythology of Greece and Rome. Cottus is one of the Hundred-Handed Giants who were the sons of Gaia and Uranus. Like his two brothers, Briareus and Gyges, he had fifty heads and one hundred arms. All three giants were born fully mature and clad in full battle

armor. They waged war on the Olympian gods and were defeated.
References 7, 20, 38, 78, 138, 177
See also Briareus, Gaia, giant, Gyges, Hundred-Handed Giants, Titans, Uranus

COWS OF NÄKKI
These are water monsters in the shape of cows in the traditions and folklore of Estonia. Herded by the monstrous Näkki, who drove them upward along with vast ripples from the bottom of his whirlpool, they are said to be the best providers of milk if only a human were brave enough to capture one and run it with his own herd.
References 133
See also Näkki

CRANA
This is one of the giants named in the genealogy created by the Italian monk Annius of Viterbo (Giovanni Nanni, c. 1432–1502) to justify the noble descent of the Gauls from a giant biblical race.
References 138, 173
See also giant, Noah

CRANUS
This is one of the giants named in the genealogy created by the Italian monk Annius of Viterbo (Giovanni Nanni, c. 1432–1502) to justify the noble descent of the Gauls from a giant biblical race.
References 138, 173
See also giant, Noah

CRATOS
This is the name of a giant in the classical mythology of Greece and Rome. Cratos is one of the Titans born of Gaia from the union with Uranus. Along with his siblings, Cratos made war on their descendants, the Olympian gods.
References 168
See also Gaia, giant, Titan, Uranus

CRETAN BULL
This is a monstrous semisupernatural bull in the classical mythology of Greece and Rome. It was created by the sea-god Poseidon and given to Minos, the king of Crete, to be sacrificed in a special festival for the god. This enormous bull was white with red eyes and breathed and bellowed fire. However, Minos, being covetous, substituted an inferior natural bull from his own herd. In revenge the furious god then made Parsiphaë, Minos's queen and wife, love the Cretan Bull, from which union the Minotaur was created. As a further punishment the god turned the bull mad, and it thrashed about the island, wreaking havoc and chaos in fields and dwellings alike—that is, until the coming of the hero Heracles/Hercules, who had been instructed as his seventh labor to capture the Cretan Bull and take it to King Eurystheus. The hero, with his lion's-pelt cloak, confused the bull into charging, then grabbed its horns and leapt onto its back. He rode the beast until it was "broken" and finally, driving it into the sea, succeeded in making it walk across to be delivered to Eurystheus at Mycenae. Another source tells how Heracles/Hercules picked up the monster and carried it through the sea to Argolis. As a spent force it was no longer worthy of sacrifice and, thereafter, was allowed free to wander the plains of Marathon.
References 24, 132, 138, 165
See also Minotaur, monster

CRIEUS
This is an alternative spelling of the name Crius, one of the Titans in the classical mythology of Greece and Rome.
References 20, 24, 47, 61, 78, 94, 125, 135, 138, 165, 168, 173, 177, 181
See also Crius, Titan

CRIOSPHINX
This is the name of a type of Sphinx in the mythology and art of ancient Egypt. It is portrayed as having the head of a ram with huge horns and the body of a lion, and is usually depicted lying down with head erect in a guarding position. The Criosphinx was regarded as the guardian of the soul of Amun and as the symbol of silence.
References 89
See also Sphinx

CRIUS
This is a giant in the classical mythology of Greece and Rome. The name Crius means "Ram." Also known as Creuis or Kreios, he is one of the Titans and the son of Gaia and Uranus. Along with his siblings, Crius made war on their descendants, the Olympian gods.
References 177
See also Gaia, giant, Titan, Uranus

CROCOTTA, CROCOTE, CROCOTTE, CROCUTA
These are alternative names for the Corocotta, a monster in the legends and folklore of medieval Europe.
References 7, 10, 18
See also Corocotta, monster

CROM CRUMH CHOMNAILL
This is the name of a gigantic humanoid monster in the traditions and folk beliefs of Ireland. This enormous being could spew balls of fire from his huge mouth. Crom Crumh Chomnaill brought terror

and destruction to the people as he strode across their lands on his immense legs. Ultimately the Irish Saint Maccrid managed to entice the monster into the river and trap him at the weir. There, the robes of the saint touched the evil Crom Crumh Chomnaill, who died immediately.
References 7
See also monster

CRONUS, CRONOS, CHRONUS, CHRONOS
These are variations on the name of one of the giants known as the Titans in the classical mythology of Greece and Rome. Cronus, also spelled Kronos, was the offspring of Uranus and Gaia. Although the youngest of the Titans, he instituted the rebellion against Uranus, who had disposed of his previous children by enforcing their stay in the womb of Gaia or in Tartarus, according to the version. Cronus, with Gaia's complicity, took a sickle and castrated his father, from whose blood was produced the giants known as the Hecatoncheires, the Furies, and Aphrodite. Cronus released his sibling Titans, but Uranus prophesied that one of Cronus's own children would overthrow him too. From Cronus's consort, the Titaness Rhea, were born the future Olympian gods; but Cronus, remembering Uranus's words, devoured each of his children as they were born. Then, when the last was born, Rhea hid Zeus and gave his father a rock wrapped in swaddling clothes to swallow. When Zeus was mature enough to challenge his father, Rhea persuaded Cronus to vomit up all the progeny and Zeus led them in a ten-year war against his father and the Titans. In this war they finally defeated Cronus and imprisoned him and the Titans in Tartarus.

Through a semantic error the name Cronus, meaning "Crow," became associated with the homonymic *chronos,* which is the Greek word for "time." Consequently, in subsequent years Cronus became synonymous with time and, indeed, was later known as "Old Father Time," the lesser spirit associated with age.
References 20, 24, 47, 54, 61, 78, 94, 125, 135, 138, 165, 168, 173, 177, 181
See also Furies, Gaia, Hecatoncheires, Rhea, Titan, Uranus

CROOKED BEAK OF HEAVEN
This is a form of the name Galokwudzuwis, a cannibal bird in the traditions and beliefs of the Kwakiutl Native Americans of Canada.
References 77, 89
See also Galokwudzuwis

CROQUEMITAINE
This is the name of an ugly monstrous bogie, originally a hobgoblin, in the folklore of France.

During the late eighteenth and nineteenth centuries, the Croquemitaine was, along with a wife called Madame Croquemitaine, the subject of cartoons and cut-out toys for children. But these are horrific beings. Monsieur Croquemitaine is illustrated as having a grotesque face with a thick mouth and huge teeth, empty eyes, a bulbous nose, pointed ears, a Newgate Frill white beard, thick eyebrows, and spiky white hair. He wears a peasant's jacket, a belt, breeches, stockings, and squared patent shoes. His wife looks equally like a rough peasant with staring empty eyes, thick bulbous nose and lips, and huge teeth. She wears a crossover dress and apron in the eighteenth-century style. The Croquemitaine and his wife are essentially Nursery bogies whose malicious activities were used to frighten children into good behavior.
References 20, 159, 181
See also Father Flog, Nursery bogies, Père Fouettard

CTEATUS
This is the name of one of the monstrous twins known as the Molionids in the classical mythology of Greece and Rome. The Molionids, also known as the Actoridæ or Actorione, were said to be the sons of Molione by either Actor or the sea-god Poseidon/Neptune, depending on the account. According to earlier legends, their names were Cteatus and Eurytus, who were hatched from a silver egg.
References 138
See also Eurytus, Molionids

CU SITH
This is an alternative spelling of the Gaelic name for Ce Sith, the formidable monstrous dog of Scottish folklore.
References 7, 159
See also Ce Sith

CUBA
This is a creature from the folklore of the lumberjacks and forest workers in the United States during the nineteenth and early twentieth centuries. The Cuba belongs to a group of beings affectionately known as the Fearsome Critters, whose exaggerated proportions and activities not only explained the weird noises of the lonely landscape but also provided some amusement in the camps. Mention of this creature was first recorded in the *General History of Connecticut,* written by the Reverend Samuel Peters in 1781.
References 7, 24
See also Fearsome Critters

CUELEBRE, EL
This is the name of a serpent in Spanish folklore. It is described as being a vast winged flying serpent that

inhabits the woods, caverns, and waterfalls. El Cuelebre is reputed to be the guardian of a great treasure, but anyone who finds it will never return to tell anyone else.
References 24
See also Aitvaras, Pukis, serpent

CUERO

This is a giant water monster in the folklore of the people of Chile. The Cuero, whose name means "Hide" in Spanish, was said to have been derived from the hide of a donkey that fell into the river, unfolded, came alive, and then engulfed every other living thing that came its way. It is described as a flat extended skin like a cow's hide, either with eyes around the perimeter and on top where a head would have been or with eyes on the ends of tentacles that are variously described as having claws. This creature lures and sucks unwary humans down into the eddies of the water, where it folds around their bodies and consumes them. It has also been said to climb out onto the land where it lies in the sun, and its return to the water, according to legend, is the cause of violent winds. There has been some speculation that it could have been some form of giant squid.
References 7, 133
See also Butatsch-ah-ilgs, Manta, Trelquehuecuve

CURTAG MHÒR A' CHUAIN

This is an alternative name for the Cìrein Cròin, a gigantic sea serpent in the beliefs and folklore of the Highlands of Scotland. Curtag Mhòr a' Chuain may be translated from the Scottish Gaelic as "the Great Whirlpool of the Ocean."
References 128
See also Cìrein Cròin

CUTER-CUSS

This is an alternative name for the Guyascutus in the folklore of the lumberjacks, forest workers, and, later, fraudsters of the United States, especially Wisconsin and Minnesota.
References 7
See also Guyascutus

CUTTY DYER

This is the name of an evil blood-thirsty cannibal in the local folklore of Ashburton in Somerset, England. Cutty Dyer was said to inhabit the bridge or culvert of the River Yeo, which flowed through the middle of the town. Described as being an enormous man with eyes as big as saucers, he waited at night for unwary travelers to cross the river, from which he would emerge behind them. Then he would either pull them down into the river

to drown them or slit their throats to drink their blood. It is reported that an aged blind man who was born in Ashburton but resided in Taunton, before he died in 1972, recited the following rhyme remembered from his youth:

> Dawn't 'ee go down the riverzide
> Cutty Dyer do abide
> Cutty Dyer ain't no gude
> Cutty Dyer'll drink yer blood.

Parents told young children of this spirit's activities to keep them away from a dangerous stretch of the water. In this respect Cutty Dyer was a Nursery bogie.
References 27, 159
See also Nursery bogies

CWN ANNWN, CWN MAMAU, CŴN CYRFF, CŴN WYBR

These are variations on the name of a class of fearsome monstrous dogs in the tradition and folklore of Wales. The Cwn Annwn, which in the Welsh language means "Hounds of Fairyland/Hell," are also known as the Cwn Mamau ("Hounds of the Mothers"), the Cŵn cyrff ("Corpse dogs"), or the Cŵn wybr ("Sky dogs"). They are mostly invisible, but when they appear they take the form of huge white hounds with red eyes and ears. In certain locations they are heard or seen terrorizing the living and howling for the souls of the dead for delivery to hell. The Cwn Annwn are said to search for unbaptized babies, or to attack those living without penitence. Depending on the account, they are led by the Devil, by the monstrous black-faced grey-clad master huntsman known as Gwyn ap Nudd, or by the legendary giant called Bran.
References 7, 96, 119, 159, 172
See also Black dogs, Bran, Cu sith, Devil's Dandy Dogs

CYCLOPEDES

This is the name given to a class of monsters besetting Saint Anthony in the work *La Tentation de St. Antoine*, written in 1874 by the French author Gustave Flaubert (1821–1880). The Cyclopedes were described as long-haired humanoid beings having a single arm extending from their chest, a single leg extending from their torso, and a vast foot upon which they hopped. (At other times, they propelled themselves by using their one hand as a second foot.) During the heat of the day they rested under the shade of their foot and lazed away the afternoons. These monsters derived from the Sciapods, which were described by the Roman naturalist Pliny the Elder in his *Historia Naturalis* (A.D. 77).
References 63
See also Catoblepas, monster, Sciapod

The Cwn Annwn and Gwyn ap Nudd (Fairies and Enchanters *by A. Williams-Ellis, Thomas Nelson, UK, p. 33*)

CYCLOPS (sing.), CYCLOPES (pl.)

These are the singular and plural forms of the name of a class of giants in the classical mythology of Greece and Rome. The Cyclopes, also spelled Kyklopes (meaning "Round Eyes"), were the progeny of Gaia and Uranus and the siblings of the Hundred-Handed Giants. Described as grotesquely ugly humanoids with a single eye in the middle of the forehead, they were crude, ungainly, and given to aggression and cannibalism. According to Hesiod in his work *Theogony* (c. 750 B.C.), they were three in number—Arges, Brontes, and Steropes—and they were thrown by the Titans into Tartarus. But when the Olympian gods made war on Uranus, they rescued the Cyclopes to join the fight. When the gods proved successful, the Cyclopes were given forges under Mount Etna for their services. Here they forged weapons for the gods. In addition, according to Homer in the *Iliad*, they mated with the local women, and a new breed of

Cyclopes was engendered, including Acamas, Pyracmon, and Polyphemus. These later Cyclopes also helped out in the forge, along with the god Hephaestos/Vulcan. The legend of Polyphemus's demise at the hands of the hero Odysseus/Ulysses is told in Homer's *Odyssey* (c. 850 B.C.). The other Cyclopes met their end by the arrows of Apollo, launched in revenge for their having forged the arrows that killed Aesculapius.

References 7, 20, 24, 47, 61, 63, 78, 94, 125, 132, 138, 165, 168, 173, 177, 181

See also Acamas, Arges, Brontes, Gaia, giant, monster, Polyphemus, Pyracmon, Steropes, Titan, Uranus

CYLLARUS

In the classical mythology of Greece and Rome, Cyllarus was one of the centaurs who were present at the marriage of one of the Lapithae called Pirithous. The centaurs were not used to drinking wine, and

Ulysses and the Cyclops (Rose Photo Archive, UK)

when they became drunk, they became lecherous and insulted the bride. In the fight that ensued between the centaurs and the Lapithae, Cyllarus was one of the centaurs who was killed.

References 168, 177
See also centaur

CYMIDEI CYMEINFOLL

This is the name of a giantess in the legends and folklore of Wales. She is also known as Kymideu Kymeinvoll. Her story is told in the second branch of the *Mabiniogi*, the story of *Branwen*. Cymidei

Cymeinfoll is described as being of vast proportions, much larger than her giant husband Llassar Llaes Gyfnewid. Together they are the guardians of the cauldron of immortality. Matholwch plots to kill the couple by setting fire to their abode, but they escape and are given shelter by Bran. In return, they give Bran the magic cauldron.

References 128
See also Bran, giant, giantess

CYNOCEPHALI (pl.), CYNOCEPHALUS (sing.), CYNOCEPTALES (pl.), CYNOSCEPHALI (pl.)

The Cynocephali are a race of hybrid humanoids in the ancient texts of Europe and the medieval Christian beliefs of Eastern Europe. In Greek the name means "Dog-Heads," and, indeed, these beings are described as having a black, hairy, humanlike body and the head of a dog. They were most often described as vegetarian, but a few versions depict them as hunting mammals, although cannibal activities were sometimes though rarely incorporated in some versions. Various accounts such as that of Ctesias the Greek historian, writing in Persia during the fifth century B.C., described them as having huge necks like those of a horse. Herodotus (485–425 B.C.) suggested that they breathed fire, barked, and were inhabitants of Ethiopia. According to Marco Polo (1254–1324), they dwelt on the Andaman Islands in the Indian Ocean. A later account from the *Travels of Sir John Mandeville*, written about A.D. 1360, sets their domain as the Isle of Macumeran. The most famous of the Cynocephali was the Christian Saint Christopher.

References 63, 81, 89, 177, 179
See also Christopher (Saint), Cynoprosopi

CYNOPROSOPI

This is the name of a type of dragon in the legends and folklore of the Mediterranean countries. The Cynoprosopi are described as having the body, legs, claws, and wings of a dragon, but the head of a dog. In addition, they are covered in fur and have beards. They communicate through sharp calls and hissing, and prey upon the local antelope and goats of the northern Saharan Desert where they live.

References 63
See also Cynocephali, dragon

D

DA

This is the name of the cosmic serpent in the beliefs and traditions of the Fon people of Dahomey in West Africa. Da is the Rainbow Snake with its vast male/female body the colors of the spectrum, from the male red-headed end through to the blue female end. But Da was also capable of changing hue according to the period of the day. People may see glimpses of the great serpent whenever there is a rainbow, or when there is iridescence on the waters of the earth. Within the seven thousand coils of this cosmic serpent were held the primordial ocean, the waves of which were the undulations of Da's supporting coils, and the air currents, which supported, similarly, the heaven over it. The earth was formed when the god Mawu was carried in the mouth of Da across the universe. Where the pair rested, the excrement from Da created the mountains, and as it moved the earth was formed behind them. Then Da rested, supporting the universe and the earth, on four pillars set at the cardinal directions.
References 24, 133
See also Airāvata, Akūpāra, Damballah, Lokapala Elephants, Mehen, Rainbow Serpent, serpent, Yurlunggur

DABBAT, DABBATU 'L-ARD

This is the name of a monster in the beliefs and traditions of Islam. The Dabbat takes the form of a vast serpent that is destined to arise from out of the earth on the Day of Judgment.
References 20
See also Apocalyptic Beasts, monster, serpent

DADHIKRA, DADHIKRAVAN

This is the name of a gigantic horse in the Hindu mythology of India. It is represented as beautiful, swift, and having huge wings, like those of an eagle, having a remarkable resemblance to Pegasus of Greek mythology. The Dadhikra symbolized the sun on its path across the sky.
References 7
See also Borak (Al), Horses of the Sun, Pegasus

DAHAK

This is the name of a dragon in the Zoroastrian beliefs and traditions of Persia (now Iran). Dahak was an evil being bent on destruction of all that was worthy on the earth. After many adventures, the hero Thraetona, although he could not kill it, overcame the beast and chained it under a mountain for eternity. It is prophesied that at the approach of the final battle and the end of the earth Dahak will break free of his chains and cause vast destruction.
References 166
See also Apocalyptic Beasts, dragon, Fenrir

DAHDAHWAT

This is the name of a class of fabulous beasts in the beliefs and traditions of the Seneca Native American people of the United States. These monsters pursued and bit the culture hero Ganyadjigowa, and they were responsible for the death of Shodieonskon.
References 77
See also monster

DAITYA, DAITEYA

This is a class of giants and demons, in the Hindu mythology of India. The Daityas were the progeny of the goddess Diti and her consort, Asyapa/Kasyapa. The Daitya, like the Danavas, had considerable strength and took part in the Churning of the Waters at the beginning of the universe. However, they were constantly opposed by the good works of the gods and tried to prevent the proper sacrifices and sacraments from taking place. They were later destroyed or, according to some sources, banished to the underworld to be chained to the caverns and guarded by Varunna, from where their writhings cause the earthquakes felt above.
References 112, 125, 133, 156, 160
See also Danavas, giants

DALHAM

This is the name of a Djinn in the Islamic mythology of the North African coasts and the Arabian

peninsula. Dalham is said to materialize as a man riding on a camel. This ferocious Djinn inhabits desert islands, where he causes ships to be wrecked. There he devours the bodies of the shipwrecked sailors who have been brought there by his powers.
References 64
See also Djin/n, Siren

DAMASTES
This is an alternative name for the giant Procrustes in the classical mythology of Greece and Rome. Damastes, whose name may be translated as "the Tamer," also known as Polypemon, meaning "the Injurious," was a monstrous giant of Eleusis who offered a bed for the night to belated travelers in a mountainous region with murderous intent.
References 78, 133, 178
See also giant, Polypemon

DAMBALLAH, DAMBALLA, DAMBALLA WEDO
This is the name of the great cosmic serpent in the beliefs and traditions of voodoo on the island of Haiti. Damballah forms the arch of the heavens, and when he comes to the earth the deep valleys and clefts of the earth are made as he passes. He basks his vast coils on the surface in the sun, or swims through the oceans, creating great waves as he travels. As the rainbow he is coupled across the universe with his consort, Ayida, also a Rainbow Snake. It is thought that both Damballah and his consort were derived from the cult of Da when the Fon peoples were taken to the Caribbean during the sixteenth and seventeenth centuries.
References 24, 133
See also Ayida, Da, Rainbow Serpent, Yurlunggur

DAN AYIDO HWEDO
This is an alternative name of Aido Hwedo, the Rainbow Serpent in the legends of the people of Dahomey in West Africa.
References 159
See also Aido Hwedo

DANAVAS
This is a class of enormous demonic monsters and giants in the Hindu beliefs and traditions of India. The evil Bali is counted among one of their leaders. The Danavas, like the Daityas, made war on the gods and, when ultimately defeated, the god Indra sent them to the depths of the oceans for eternity.
References 112, 125
See also Bali, Daitya, giant, monster

DARD
This is the name of a monster in the legends and folklore of Austria. This creature is a hybrid monster described as having the body of a lizard or a snake with four legs, but its neck had a mane like that of a horse and the head of a cat.
References 134
See also Arassas, dragon, serpent

DAUGHTERS OF CAIN
These were said to be the descendants of Cain in the Hebrew and Christian beliefs and traditions. It was conjectured that the daughters of Cain, the first murderer according to the Book of Genesis, had become not just beautiful but gross, monstrous, and evil. When the grandsons of Noah, by the son Seth, took wives who were from the descendants of Cain, a further race of monsters and the first giants were produced. This was a philosophy propounded during the late Middle Ages for the deluge and the Flood that was purported to have eliminated all giants from the earth but one, according to the French author Rabelais; this was Hurtaly, who rode on the roof of the ark.
References 174
See also Chalbroth, giant, Hurtaly, monster, Noah

DDRAIG GOCH, Y
This is the correct name in the Welsh language for the Red Dragon of Wales. The legend tells how the Saxon King Vortigern was bent on conquering and settling the whole of the British Isles. When he tried to build a fortress in the Welsh mountains of Snowdonia, every morning the building stones were gone. He was advised that a child sacrifice must be made of a fatherless boy. When eventually such a boy, called Emrys (Ambrose), was brought to the site, they were told by him that their problem lay with the dragons in a cavern beneath the site. Instead of sacrificing the youth, Vortigern's men dug until they saw, sure enough, in a huge cavern beneath the site for the castle, two dragons, one white the other red. With the break into their domain, the dragons became locked in combat. When the white "Gwiber" was defeated and the victorious guardian, y Ddraig Goch remained, it was then that the boy disclosed their symbolism. The Gwiber represented the invading forces of Vortigern and his Saxons, and y Ddraig Goch was the guardian of the Welsh, and the cavern was Britain, from which they would be completely driven. Emrys later became the master of the castle.

This Celtic legend was substantially rewritten by Geoffrey of Monmouth (1100–1154) in his *Historia Regnum Britanniae* (c. 1147), and the informant was changed from a potential child sacrifice to the supernatural Merlin, son of a demon and a nun. It is speculated that adoption of the standard of the guardian y Ddraig Goch of Wales is largely due to the popularity of this latter version.

References 128, 183
See also dragon, Gwiber

DEA

This is a type of creature or reptile that is described in an English bestiary of 1220 as a salamander. The Dea is illustrated as a monstrous lizard that consumes and exists within fires.
References 14
See also Bingbuffer, Fillyloo, Golligog, Salamander, Stellio, Stollenwurm

DEADOENDJADASES

This is the name of a monstrous humanoid cannibal in the traditions and folklore of the Seneca and Iroquois Native American peoples of the northeastern United States. This monster hunts for humans within his territory and takes them back for his three sisters (hags) to prepare. They inhabit his lodge, surrounded by a garden of strawberry plants, in the middle of the forest. This strawberry garden is watched over by the inflated flayed pelt of one of Deadoendjadases's human victims, a man who was called Hadjoqda. Through the spells of his people, Hadjoqda is able to help a hero of the Turkey clan in bringing about the death of the cannibal Deadoendjadases and his sisters, and the strawberry garden is liberated for all the clans to enjoy.
References 77
See also cannibal, monster

DEGEI

This is the name of a cosmic serpent in the beliefs and traditions of the people of Fiji. Degei is described as so vast that he inhabited the whole sky. As Degei watched from his heavens, he saw a hawk called Turukawa lay two eggs in a nest, and the warmth of Degei incubated them. Soon the eggs hatched and a male and female human emerged, but they were hungry, so the serpent gave them bananas and later yams and taro roots as they grew. He gave them the knowledge of fire, cooking, and communication. And it is from these two that the earth was populated.
References 113
See also Rainbow Serpent, serpent

DEHOTGOHSGAYEH

This is the name of a giant in the beliefs and folklore of the Iroquois and Onondaga Native Americans of the northeastern United States. The name "Dehotgohsgayeh" may be translated as "Split-faced Being" or "Wry-face," for this giant is reputedly ugly, and his body is red on one side and black on the other. He wears the huge pelt of a bear tied with a hickory tree bark belt and carries a staff made from the trunk of a hickory tree as well as a huge rattle that

all can hear from wherever they are. Dehotgohsgayeh inhabits the forests at the darkest edges of the earth where it is always night. This enormous being is benevolent toward human beings and protects them from harm.
References 77
See also giant

DEINO

This is the name of one of the Græe in the classical mythology of Greece and Rome. Deino, also spelled Dino, may be translated as "Dread."
References 24, 133, 166, 169
See also Græe

DELGETH

This is the name of a primordial monster in the beliefs and folklore of the Navajo Native Americans in the southern United States. The Delgeth is described as a monstrous type of antelope that pursues and devours human beings. It was hunted down and eliminated along with the other primordial monsters by the twin culture heroes, Nagenatzani and Tjhobadestchin.
References 166
See also monster

DELPHYNE

This is the name of a female monster in the classical mythology of Greece and Rome. She was described as being female to the waist and from there a serpent, like Melusine in the legends of France. Delphyne was the sister of the monstrous Typhon, who set her to guard the king of the gods of Olympus, Zeus, when Typhon had captured him.
References 7, 133
See also Melusine, monster, serpent, Typhon

DEN-BLEIZ

This is one of the modern Breton words for the werewolf of Brittany in northwestern France.
References 128
See also Bisclaveret

DERCYNUS

The son of the sea god Neptune in the classical literature of Roman mythology, he was the brother of Albion (also a giant), and together they posed a threat to the hero Hercules as he passed through their territory in the region of Liguria (in what is now France) close to the Rhône River. Hercules had to do battle with the two giants, who together would be insuperable. However, Hercules prayed for help from the king of the gods, Jupiter, who sent a shower of stones to harass the giants. Hercules was thus able to destroy them. The place of this battle was thereafter named "Campus Lapideus," the Plain of Stones.

References 54
See also Albion, giant

DERKETO

This is the name of a monster in the mythology of ancient Babylon and Mesopotamia. Derketo is described as having the body of a whale and the foreparts of a dragon. It was the creation of the goddess Ishtar and the cause of a vast inundation that covered the earth.
References 78
See also monster

DESPAIR, GIANT

This is the name of a giant in the classical literature of England. He appears in the classic allegorical work *Pilgrim's Progress* written by John Bunyan and published in 1682. Giant Despair, who lives in Doubting Castle, found the pilgrims asleep in his grounds, accused them of trespassing, and marched them back to his castle, where he threw Christian and Hopeful into the depths of his worst dungeon. On the advice of his giantess wife, Diffidence, Giant Despair beat the two with a crab-apple trunk and told them to kill themselves. However, after many days of such treatment, Christian remembered that he had a universal key called Promise. This he took out and found that it unlocked all the doors and gates to the castle, and they escaped. Although the giant eventually heard the last creaking gate, he could not pursue them, for the fits that he suffered prevented his legs from leaping from his bed.
References 20, 31
See also giant, Grim, Maul, Pagan, Pope, Slay-good

DEV

This is the name of a class of demonic, semisupernatural giants in the traditions and folklore of Armenia. The Devs are described as enormous beings with seven heads each, and in the middle of each head is one enormous eye. They can metamorphose into the shape of huge serpents or monsters, inhabiting the caves and forests of the mountains. Their strength is prodigious, and travelers have seen them hurl boulders before escaping the malice of these beings.
References 24
See also Cyclopes, giant, serpent

DEVIL'S DANDY DOGS

This is the name of a pack of semisupernatural monstrous dogs. They are a version of the Wild Hunt in the folklore of Cornwall, England. The demonic huntsman and his enormous demonic dogs are described as black, with fiery eyes and breathing fire. They hunt down the living and rip them to pieces; they also hunt the souls of the damned through tempestuous nights to carry them off, unless saved by the dawn, cock crow, or their prayers.
References 7, 21, 24, 25, 93, 119, 160
See also Black dogs, Cwn Annwn

DEW-MINK

This is a creature from the folklore of the lumberjacks and forest workers in the United States during the nineteenth and early twentieth centuries. The Dew-Mink belongs to a group of beings affectionately known as the Fearsome Critters, whose exaggerated proportions and activities not only explained the wierd noises of the lonely landscape but also provided some amusement at camps. The Dew-Mink was first featured in the *General History of Connecticut* by the reverend Samuel Peters in 1781.
References 7, 24
See also Fearsome Critters

DHAKHAN

This is the name of a hybrid reptile in the traditions and beliefs of the Kabi Native Australian people on the Queensland coast of northwestern Australia. Dhakhan is represented as a giant serpent with the tail of an enormous fish. He inhabits deep pools in the mountains and plains. Occasionally, Dhakhan may be glimpsed as the rainbow, for this is the manner in which he travels from one water hole to the next.
References 47
See also Rainbow Serpent, serpent, Yurlunggur

DHARMAPĀLAS, THE

This is the name of a group of eight giants in the Buddhist beliefs and traditions of India, and in Tibet they are known by the name Ch'os-skyon. The Dharmapālas were so vast that just their heads alone stretched over the whole horizon. Their vast mouths spat a tongue of fire from between huge fangs, and they had three eyes, the third in the middle of their enormous foreheads. Their glare was deadly and searchingly directed at all those who were the enemies of the Buddhist faith. Their leaders are called Devī and Hayagriva.
References 24, 133
See also giant, Hayagriva

DHAUL

This is an alternative spelling of Dhol, a giant cosmic cow, in the traditions and beliefs of India.
References 24
See also Dhol

DHEEYABERY

This is the name of one of many monstrous tribes of people in the legends and folklore of the Kamilaroi

Giant Despair, a giant in the classical literature of England (Rose Photo Archive, UK)

peoples of Australia. The legend tells how one of their young men, named Yooneeara, decided to travel to the setting sun. On his long journey he met many strange people, one tribe of which was the Dheeyabery. They are described as looking like ordinary people from the front, but from behind they were great globes of flesh. When the hero Yooneeara passed through their village, they all wanted to get their hands on him, but he managed to escape.
References 153

DHINNABARRADA
This is the name of one of many monstrous tribes of people in the legends and folklore of the Kamilaroi peoples of Australia. The legend tells how one of their young men, named Yooneeara, decided to travel to the setting sun. He took with him spears for hunting, snares, fire sticks, and a small bandicoot stuffed live into his dilly bag. On his long journey he met many strange people, one tribe of which was the Dhinnabarrada. They are described as looking like ordinary people except that they have the legs and

feet of emus. They are extremely swift and follow the chase, and they make boomerangs expertly; curiously they live only on grubs. When the hero Yooneeara passed through their village, they all wanted to get their hands on him, and he feared that because they ran so swiftly they might. But he opened his dilly bag and out ran the bandicoot, which they chased with glee, and he managed to escape.
References 153
See also Dheeyabery

DHOL
This is the name of a giant cosmic cow, in the traditions and beliefs of India. Dhol, or Dhaul, is a vast white cow upon whose horns the earth rests in the cosmos.
References 24
See also Lokapala Elephants

DHOYA
This is the name of a Fomorian giant who features in a tale written by Irish author W. B. Yeats in 1891. The

giant, who lives in Sligo, falls in love with a fairy and marries her. He is, however, duped into a game of chess with a fairy-man, who turns out to be her fairy-husband. Dhoya has agreed to his fairy-bride as the wager, and when he loses the game he loses her as well.

References 128
See also giant

DHRANA

This is the name of a vast serpent in the Hindu mythology of India. Dhrana is described as being a seven-headed king of the snakes. He is the guardian of the god Pārsva, like the Naga King Muchalinda. The god is periodically under attack from the evil of Meghamalin, and Dhrana provides his vastness for protection.

References 125
See also King of the Snakes, Muchalinda, Naga, serpent

DHUMAVARNA

This is the name of the king of the sea serpents in the mythology and folklore of India. Dhumavarna, which means "Smoke-colored," is a vast serpent from the waist down, but his upper parts are human. He saw the handsome son of King Yayati, called Yadu, as he strolled along the seashore one evening and kidnapped him for his daughters. Dhumavarna took the prince to his underwater palace, where the five mermaid-daughters of the king sea serpent were given as his brides to Prince Yadu, who fathered many children by them.

References 112
See also serpent

DIFF ERREBI

This is a name used as a euphemism for Chaarmarouch in the traditions and beliefs of the people of Morocco. Diff Errebi, which means "Noble One," is the polite form used for referring to a king of the Djinns in order to invoke his goodwill. Any direct reference was considered to be both impolite and likely to cause offense, thus invoking the wrath of this vast being and possible death under a shower of stones.

References 122
See also Chaarmarouch, Djinn

DILLUS FARFOG, DILLUS FARFAWG, DILLUS VARVAWC

This is the name of a giant in the legends and folklore of Wales and Ireland. Dillus Farfog may be translated as "Dillus the Beard," and it is the strength and length of his beard that makes it the subject of a task to be accomplished by the hero

Culhwch. In order to marry Olwen, Ysbaddaden, her giant father, had demanded that some nigh-impossible tasks be completed successfully. One task was to catch the gigantic boar Twrch Trwyth and to make a leash for it from the hair of the beard of Dillus, which was done with the death of the giant.

References 128
See also giant, Twrch Trwyth, Ysbaddaden

DING BALL

This is a creature from the folklore of the lumberjacks and forest workers, especially in Wisconsin and Minnesota in the United States, during the nineteenth and early twentieth centuries. The Ding Ball belongs to a group of beings affectionately known as the Fearsome Critters, whose exaggerated proportions and activities not only explained the wierd noises of the lonely landscape but also provided some amusement at camps. The Ding Ball is also known as the Ding Maul and Plunkus.

References 7, 24
See also Fearsome Critters

DINNY MARA

This is the name of a type of merman in the Manx folklore of the Isle of Man in the British Isles. This being is also known as the Doinney Marrey and Dooinney Marrey, which means "Man of the Sea" in the Manx language. He was regarded as more benevolent than the mermen of the mainland. However, no one was ever allowed to whistle on board the ship for fear of attracting his attention and, with him, more wind than was required.

Some time ago there was a fishing vessel called *Baatey ny Guillyn* (The Boys' Boat) crewed by only seven single young men. Every time they set sail they made an offering of herring to the Dinny Mara, who rewarded them each time with a full net. The other crews were curious, and the "admiral" (fleet controller) requested that they show the others where the herring congregated in such quantity. Willingly they told them that they had fished off the Calf of Man, and accordingly the fleet set sail. During the night the Dinny Mara was heard by the crew of the *Baatey ny Guillyn* to say, "*Te kiuneas aalin nish agh bee sterrym Çheet dy gerrid*" (It is calm and fine now but a storm is coming shortly.) The crew drew in their nets and regained the harbor just as a fierce storm arose, and the rest of the fleet was lost. Since that time it has been decreed by the fleet controller that crews should have both single and married men.

References 24, 128, 160
See also Ben Varrey, Havhest, Havman, Havmand, mermaid, Merrow

DINO

This is an alternative spelling of Deino, one of the Græææ in the classical mythology of Greece and Rome.
References 133, 166
See also Deino

DIONE

This is the name of a giantess in the classical mythology of Greece and Rome. Dione was one of the Titans who were the offspring of Gaia and Uranos. They made war on their descendants, the Olympian gods, except for Dione, who was the lover of Zeus, the king of the gods. According to some sources she was the mother of Aphrodite by him.
References 166
See also Gaia, giantess, Titan, Uranos

DIRAE

This is an alternative name in classical Greek mythology for the three avenging female supernatural humanoid monsters known as the Erinyes. These terrifying beings are described as black, their hair formed of snakes and their hands entwined with snakes. They have wings resembling those of a bat. Their head is that of a dog with suppurating eyes and stinking breath.
References 20, 24, 28, 38, 47, 62, 70, 124, 125, 127, 160, 161, 169, 178
See also Erinyes

DIREACH, DIREACH GHLINN EITIDH

This is the name of a type of giant also known as the Dithreach in the legends and folklore of the Highlands of Scotland. The Direach is a horribly disproportionate humanoid monster that has but one leg, one hand and arm protruding from his chest, and his head has both an eye and a wiry tuft of hair on top. This grotesque monster inhabits the Glen of Eiti, or Eitidh, said to be near Ballachulish.
References 7, 128
See also Nesnas, Palesmurt

DIS SAMOTHES

This is the name of a giant in the traditions and legends of France of the later Middle Ages. It was conjectured that the Gauls that anciently inhabited most of France were the descendants of the giant Dis mentioned by Julius Caesar. The Italian monk Annius of Viterbo (Giovanni Nanni, c. 1432–1502) in his genealogy conjectured that the descent from this line, via the ancestor Japheth of the Bible, was the first king of the Gauls. Dis Samothes was credited with establishing codified laws and administration and education systems to those people. There was much speculation amongst authors concerning this genealogy, and this character is also said by Jean

Tixier de Ravisy (alias Ravisius Textor, c. 1480–1524) to be the grandson of the Biblical giant Noah. From him this French medieval writer constructed a line of descent that included the giant descendants named as Bardus, Bardus Junior, Celtes, Dryiudes, Longo, Magus, Namnes, and Sarron. All of these giants were purported to be Celtic kings of ancient Gaul.
References 174
See also Celtes, giant, Japheth, Noah

DISEMBOWELLER, THE

This is the name of a monstrous female cousin of the moon in the traditions and folklore of the Inuit of Greenland. She was banished to the earth for cruelty, and there she stalked and killed the human inhabitants. If no one was out at night walking by themselves and vulnerable to her attacks, the Disemboweller would whisper ludicrous jokes to guests inside and make them laugh until their sides literally burst and killed them.
References 133
See also monster

DITHREACH

This is an alternative spelling of Direach, a type of giant in the legends and folklore of the Highlands of Scotland.
References 7, 128
See also Direach

DIWE

This is the name of a group of monsters in the folklore of Iran. The Diwe are described as huge creatures with horns, which hunt and devour any human beings that wander into their territory.
References 125
See also monster

DIWRNACH WYDDEL

This is the name of a giant in the legends and folklore of Ireland and Wales who is also known as Dyrnwch Wyddel. He is the steward to King Odgar fab Aedd and the keeper of a great cauldron in Ireland. This great cauldron, which would never cook the food of a coward, had been demanded by Ysbaddaden the giant before his daughter, Olwen, could marry the hero Culhwch. Diwrnach Wyddel's cauldron is so huge that it is required to cook the marriage feast, but the giant does not wish to part with it. It is seized by Arthur, who escapes with it to Wales.
References 128
See also giant, Ysbaddaden

DJIEIEN

This is the name of a gigantic spider over six feet in height in the beliefs and traditions of the Seneca

Native American people of the northeastern United States. In order to survive any attacks from other predators, including humans, this enormous spider keeps its heart buried in the earth beneath its lodge. However, in one attack by Otheigwenhda, the hero took a branch from a nearby tree and thrust it at the spider. It missed Djieien but went straight into the earth and through the heart where it was buried. The vast spider immediately expired.
References 77
See also Dzoo-noo-qua, Tsuchi-Gumo, Ungoliant

DJIN/N
This is the name of a class of semisupernaturals that may take monstrous form. The Djinns feature prominently in the traditions and folk beliefs of the peoples who follow the faith of Islam, especially of the Saharan regions of North Africa and some countries of the North and Eastern Mediterranean. The name is variously spelled as Dgen, Dschin, Genie, Ginn, Jann, Jinn/i, Jinnee, or Jnun. The Islamic traditions declare that Allah created these beings from the Saharan wind (the Simoon). Taranushi was the first Djinn charged with controlling the rest, but the Djinns rebelled, and Azazel and Iblis became their most terrifying leaders, bent on leading the rest on a rampage of violence and evil against all other creations.

The Djinns have many different descriptions according to the culture in which they are a part of the belief system. They mostly take the shape of a gigantic human but may be invisible or take other shapes, such as that of a vast and grotesque beast. They may be beautiful or hideously deformed. When they appear as a beautiful woman, their deception may be detected because they will have vertical eyes and the feet of a goat or a camel. However, by the time a human is close enough to observe this, it is usually too late to be saved. They may be beneficent or thoroughly evil but can never be trusted. Djinns inhabit the desert, isolated ruined places, even the sea coast, water sources, or remote islands, where they may be solitary or congregate to work their terror on the community. Their most famous descriptions are to be found in *Tales of the Thousand and One Nights*.

When benevolent, they may fall in love with and have children by human partners. Their offspring can walk through walls, fly, and age very slowly. Djinns can bring great wealth, beauty, and fabulous possessions to those they like or to magicians who can control them. To those they dislike or have been directed to harm, they will bring disasters, nightmarish tortures, and horrifying death.

Morocco. Djinns have many different shapes, many of which are grotesque beasts and distorted human shapes. They inhabit dark and isolated places as well as water sources. They come in roughly three categories: Earth Djinns dwell in drains, wash places, lavatories, cemeteries, and ruins. They will exact terrible retribution if the correct procedures are not observed when disturbing their domain. Water Djinns inhabit any water source such as rivers, fountains, and wells. They are particularly malevolent and will entice humans into the water for the pleasure of killing them. Tree Djinns inhabit the trees and are mostly benign, except the Djinn of the fig tree, who will incite hatred between any humans that rest together under it.

Egypt. In the traditions of Egypt the Djinns are malevolent toward humans and will pelt or shower them with stones from any height. They are rarely seen, for they usually travel in the whirlwinds across the desert. These Djinns will abduct women and children and threaten all with violence. Calling on the name of Allah will bring protection, and shooting stars are thought to be retribution sent to quell their activities.

Serbia and Albania. Here, Djins are evil monstrous creatures that inhabit the remote areas of the mountains and forests. They will terrify and lead astray any unwary traveler who does not respect them, an event often recorded near the Lake of Skutar.
References 20, 62, 74, 107, 122, 124, 125, 146, 160, 161
See also Afrit, Aicha Kandida, Chaarmarouch, Diff Errebi, Jinn, Lalla Mira, Maezt-Dar l' Oudou, Moulay Abdelkader Djilani, Redjal el Marja, Sidi Hamou

DOBHARCHÚ
This is the name of a fearsome monstrous otter in the traditions and folklore of Ireland. The Dobharchú, also known as the Dorraghow, is also designated the "King of the Lakes," but its name in the Irish Gaelic means "Otter." However, this is no simple creature but a malicious hunter of humans and their animals, which it will devour immediately.
References 128

DOGS, SEA
These are hybrid creatures to be found in the heraldic repertoire of England. These dogs resemble the old English hunting dog known as a Talbot, but instead of having fur their entire bodies (including the tail) have fish scales. They do not have paws but have webbed feet with which they travel in the water. Depictions of these creatures are to be found on coats of arms in England, especially where there is a connection with the sea.
References 7

DOGS OF FO
These are hybrid guardian creatures in the legends and folklore of China. The Dogs of Fo are portrayed

The Djinn Danhaseh and victim (Rose Photo Archive, UK)

101

as having the body of a lion with wings, the broad head of a dog sometimes with a single horn on the forehead, and a bushy, feathery tail. The male is depicted with one paw resting on a globe, while the female has a puppy by her paws. They appear in pairs in paintings and sculptures of the Imperial periods, usually in front of a temple or the gates of a palace.
References 89

DOINNEY MARREY, DOOINNEY MARREY

These are alternative spellings of Dinny Mara, a type of merman in the Manx folklore of the Isle of Man in the British Isles.
References 24, 128, 160
See also Dinny Mara

DONESTRE/S

This is the name of a race of humanoid monsters in the beliefs of medieval Europe. The beings, whose description is given in the legend of Alexander, closely resembled the form of humans with the head of a lion, huge eyes, round furry ears, and a long mane extending over the shoulders. The Donestres were reputed to know all the languages of humans, and with this facility would greet lone travelers, duping them with familiar language into trusting the monsters. As soon as any traveler dropped his guard, the Donestres would kill and devour the traveler, leaving only the bodiless head. Then, astonishingly, the monsters would sit beside the victim's head and weep.
References 45
See also Cynocephali, Minotaur

DONN OF CUÁLGNE

This is the name of an enormous semisupernatural bull in the legends and folklore of Ireland. The Donn of Cuálgne was so vast that a whole army could stand in its shadow from the noonday sun; its back was so huge that games and entertainment could be indulged in by more than fifty people. It was a source of great pride that just the melodic lowing of this great beast was enough to sire calves by every cow that heard him. Naturally such a beast was a great prize, and the tales that involve the Donn of Cuálgne center on the *Cattle Raid of Cooley*.
References 7

DOONONGAES

This is the name of an enormous horned serpent in the beliefs and legends of the Seneca Native American people in the northeastern United States. This is an enormous reptile that has two horns protruding from the top of its head. Although this reptilian form is the most usual, Doonongaes has been known to metamorphose into the shape of a human being for the purpose of pursuing a human mate. Doonongaes may be seen sunning himself sometimes on the banks of the rivers and lakes, where he normally resides in the deep, still pools. No human would dare to enter even a finger in the water where he is known to reside for fear of losing it to the monster serpent. This vast being hunts large animals and humans for its prey, and the monster turtle, Skahnowa, assists him in this. Just talking about Doonongaes can be dangerous, and therefore one must wait until he is in his winter slumbers and unable to hear.
References 77
See also Horned Serpent, serpent, Skahnowa

DORRAGHOW

This is an alternative name for the Dobharchú, a fearsome monstrous otter in the traditions and folklore of Ireland.
References 128
See also Dobharchú

DOSSENUS

This is the name of a monster in the literary and dramatic traditions of ancient Rome. Dossenus, meaning "Ever-chomping," was a hybrid human-animal-monster that was portrayed as one that ate and chomped its way through everything in the comic theater, along with another called Manducus.
References 182
See also Manducus, monster

DRACO

This is the Latin word for a dragon that was derived from the ancient Greek word *draconta* with the same meaning. However, the description of the creature was not as the modern dragon but rather a type of serpent. The Draco was depicted in the classical art of Greece and Rome as a vast serpent with wings resembling those of a bat, possibly breathing fire from its flickering tongue. By the middle of the twelfth century the description had been somewhat modified, and a bestiary of that period written in Latin described the Draco as a vast serpent with a crest on its head and having only a small mouth. It was purported to have the ability to rise in the air and dazzle its victims with the luminescence emitted around the length of its body. It lay in wait, often encircling trees or at the sides of tracks, for its prey, which it would crush in its muscular body in the manner of a python. It was also reputed to thrash its victims with its enormous muscular tail. The Draco was said to inhabit the caves and subterranean places of India and Ethiopia, where it was said to destroy and devour an elephant with ease. The bestiaries equated this creature with foolish pride and considered it a symbol of the Devil, drawing in the foolish to be destroyed.

References 10, 63, 89, 185
See also dragon, serpent

DRACONCOPEDES

This is the name of monstrous serpents in the traditions and folklore of medieval Europe. They are portrayed as vast serpents with the head and face of a woman. It was conjectured that it was a Draconcopede that entered the Garden of Eden and tempted Eve with an apple from the Tree of Knowledge. Consequently, many illustrations of this theme from the medieval period in Europe portray a Draconcopede entwined around the tree.
References 7
See also serpent

DRACONTIDES

This is the name of a dragon in the classical mythology of Greece and Rome. It is the name given to the heroic Cecrops in a work by Aristophanes, after the hero had been changed into a dragon.
References 178
See also dragon

DRACS

This is the name of a group of water monsters reported on by the English Gervaise of Tilbury during the twelfth century. The Dracs were said to inhabit the Rhône River depths. They were predatory beings that would swim to the surface just by a boat with humans on board and float some glittering item to attract the hand or arm of a woman or child. When the victim had reached for the item in the water, the Dracs would surface quickly and grab them, dragging them down to be devoured.
References 134
See also monster

DRACULA

This is the name of the character in the classic horror story *Dracula* (1897) by the Irish author Abraham (Bram) Stoker (1847–1912). The Count Dracula of the novel is described as a clean-shaven old man with a high forehead over his aquiline nose. His eyebrows were so thick that they seemed to meet; his eyes appeared to be as one in a fever; and he wore a gray moustache over his ruddy mouth, from which sharp, pointed teeth protruded and his stinking breath exhaled. His ears were curiously pointed at the hair line, while the hands with which he gripped his visitors were white with hairs in the center of the palm, and the long fingers were extended by pointed, clawlike nails. He was dressed entirely in black, which made his pallid skin appear almost blue. Dracula was a vampire and a Transylvanian count who lived in his castle high in the mountains, from

which he made sorties every night with his wolf pack and other vampires to terrorize the local population. In the novel, Dracula visits the British Isles, and because he must return to his vault each night (sharing with the Trolls of Norse mythology his demise should sunlight fall on him), he had to take some Transylvanian earth with him.

The character of Dracula was well researched by Bram Stoker and was derived from such as the memoirs of W. Wilkinson, the sometime British consul in Bucharest, which Stoker read in Whitby in North Yorkshire, a town featured in the novel. The character's name was founded on Voïvode Dracula (c. 1448), who was a fearless Wallachian general. The Wallachian name Dracula means "Devil" and was said to be an epithet for one recognized as brave or very cruel. These memoirs also gave a reference to the actual person on whom the character of Dracula was based, Vlad the Impaler, an evil and sadistic ruler who was said variously to be either a cannibal or a vampire.
References 69, 94
See also cannibal, Troll, vampire

DRAGON (EPIDAURIAN)

This is the name of a dragon in the folklore of Greece. It is described as being a golden color and more unusually benevolent and tame toward human beings. It inhabited the region of Epidaurus in harmony with its human neighbors.
References 7
See also dragon

DRAGON (ETHIOPIAN)

The Ethiopian dragons were described as extremely huge and some 20 cubits in length (approximately 35 feet), with either one or two pairs of wings. They were, according to the medieval European legends and travelers' tales, efficient predatory beasts whose main prey was local elephants. However, as they lived in the hinterland of the Ethiopian coast, the area was quite arid. Few elephants came in drought years, so, according to some accounts, these vast creatures entwined themselves together to form a living raft and set across the sea to the Arabian shore opposite. There was a strong belief that a precious stone, the Dracontias, was lodged in the brain of these dragons. It was a great prize for the alchemist and much sought. However, the stone, to be effective, had to be taken from a dragon while it was still alive. The method was to drug the beast with specially prepared herbs and then remove the stone—the problem was first to find the dragon.
References 7
See also dragon, Dragon at Uffington

DRAGON (OCCIDENTAL)

The Dragon is probably the most easily recognized of all the fabulous and mythological monsters, as it seems to exist in some form in the majority of cultures throughout the world. Since there are certain characteristic differences, the Occidental (Western) dragons and Oriental Dragons are discussed under separate entries.

The most general description of the Occidental Dragon is very similar to that of the Oriental Dragon, being an enormous, elongated, scale-covered body like that of a crocodile, often with vast wings like those of a bat, and having huge legs like those of a lizard with long claws. It may have a toothed dorsal ridge extending to a long serpentine tail, usually barbed. Its head may be like that of a vast lizard or crocodile but with either a crest or horns on the head, while its gross nostrils and huge fanged mouth breathe fire and noxious fumes. However, this is not the only description of such a monster, for they may have composite features from many other beasts, such as the head of an elephant in India, that of a lion or bird of prey in the Middle East, or numerous heads of reptiles such as serpents. Their body color may range from green, red, and black to unusually yellow, blue, or white dragons. Dragons generally inhabit isolated places such as swamps, mountains, deserts, ruined castles, caverns, and forests. They are highly predatory creatures whose victims are livestock and humans. They are usually propitiated with the sacrifice of young maidens by the terrified population, a ritual that forms the basis of many of the Dragon-slaying myths (although this predatory nature is not always the case for the Occidental Dragon and there are many instances of benevolence recorded). They may be massive independent beings, in predatory communities with a king, or the evil servant of a sorcerer.

Historically, the Dragon was something resembling a vast serpent, often with wings. The early Sumerians, Babylonians, and Assyrians all had the Dragon in their culture as a potent force, such as Tiamat. A cylindrical seal from Sumer of 4,000 B.C. depicts a Dragon behind the goddess Bau. These may well have been originally derived from the serpent cultures of Aapep and Typhon in ancient Egyptian mythology. From the ancient Middle East the development of the Dragon concept migrated with different people and metamorphosed in its description east across the Indian subcontinent to the Orient and west through the European cultures. From the association with the early Earth Goddesses and the Serpents of Chaos, the Dragon was regarded as a powerful being whose associations with elements of earth, water, fire, and flight through the air made them either horrific adversaries or supernatural associates. They had to be either vanquished or propitiated and were frequently held responsible for eclipses by way of their aggression toward the sun and the moon.

The name "Dragon" is derived from the ancient Greek *draconta* or *drakon*, meaning "to watch" or "to look at," which was applied to the monster by way of the attribute of guarding something. This might be golden apples, as in the Greek myths, or hoards of treasure, as in other western European cultures. There are numerous accounts in myths and literature concerning Dragons in the Greek culture, such as the Dragon-soldiers, the Sparti who were raised when Cadmus sowed the teeth of the defeated serpent. The goddess Ceres was said to be drawn in her chariot by two Dragons, as was the enchantress Medea. The golden apples of the Hesperides were guarded by a Dragon, and a benevolent Dragon, by licking his eyes, restored the sight of Plutus in the temple of Aesculapius. Alexander the Great, in his massive expeditions across the known world, was said to have encountered Dragons in India that fought with elephants.

The Latin word for "Dragon" is *draco*, which was derived from the ancient Greek word (above). However, the description of the creature was not as the modern Dragon but like the Greek one, more like a winged type of serpent. The Draco was depicted in the classical art of Rome as a vast serpent with wings resembling those of a bat, possibly breathing fire from its flickering tongue. There are again numerous Dragons in the myths and literature of ancient Rome, deriving from such as the account by the Greek poet Homer of the shield of Hercules upon which was coiled a fire-breathing Dragon. A whole array of Dragons, said to be descended from the Python at Delphi, guarded a grove sacred to the god Apollo, as did a single Dragon for the sacred grove of the goddess Juno and another of the goddess Diana. Pliny the Elder in his *Historia Naturalis* (A.D. 77) also gives an account of Dragons in the land of Ethiopia; he hastens to add that although they are not as big as those of India they are still 20 cubits (about 60 feet) in length.

In the Jewish and Hebraic traditions Dragons were mentioned in the scriptures and incorporated into the Christian texts. In the Old Testament of the Bible, the Serpent of Eden is sometimes referred to as a Dragon. Another instance is that of Bel and the Dragon told in the apocryphal Book of Daniel. In this account the beast is destroyed by Daniel, for which he was cast into the lion's den. The Beasts of the Apocalypse are also compared with Dragons in the scriptures as well as in the religious texts and later folk beliefs. There is a curious legend of a Dragon that pined for the unrequited love of a woman during the reign of King Herod.

In the pre-Christian mythology of western Europe, Dragons had ambivalent relationships with human beings. The Celtic Dragons were both harmful and protective, a primary example of the latter being y Ddraig Goch, the Red Dragon of Wales. Indeed, the proud Welsh title "Pendragon," later incorporated into the genealogy of King Arthur, reflects the protection of the Dragon. But the Celtic Dragons of southern Wales and Ireland were not so well disposed. In the legend of the Táin Bó Fraích (the Cattle raid of Fraích), a Dragon is the mortal adversary and is slain by the Irish hero Fráech. The typical Anglo-Saxon Dragon with which y Ddraig Goch did battle may be identified with Grendel from the great Anglo-Saxon epic poem *Beowulf*. This horrific being terrorized an area of Scandinavia and also reflects the terror of the dragon Fafnir in Norse mythology.

With the coming of Christianity to the region, all Dragon beings were demonized and said to be agents of the Devil. Consequently, the conceptual symbolism of the legends and folklore changed with this influence. A great wealth of Dragon-slaying saints evolved in the Christian texts and traditions, the most famous possibly being that of Saint George (third century A.D.). Others of note were from Biblical times: Saint Phillip the Apostle (first century A.D.), Saint Michael the Archangel, and Saint Margaret (no date); in Britain Saint Keyne (sixth century A.D.?), Saint Guthlac (eighth century A.D.), and Saint Samson (sixth century A.D.); in France Saint Paul Aurelian (sixth century A.D.), Saint Cado, Saint Clement, Saint Florent, Saint Martha, Saint Maudet, and Saint Romain (no dates).

During the Middle Ages Dragons under various names such as the Amphisbaena, the Draco, and the Wyvern became incorporated into the texts of bestiaries throughout Europe, where the symbolism of evil was thoroughly exploited. The alchemists of the same period took the Dragon as the symbol for mercury, and subsequently it became the symbol for alchemists. Also at that time, the great prevalence of the codes of chivalry gave rise to numerous romances detailing the vanquishing of evil in the form of a Dragon; Dragons became associated with the trials and achievement of knighthood. It is from this period, especially at the time of the Crusades, that many of the legends originated such as the Dragon of Wantley, the Loathly Worm, and the Lambton Worm ("Worm" is an ancient name for a Dragon-serpent).

With the passing of the Age of Chivalry, the Dragon concept was still widely found in literature and folklore such as the Dragon of Saint Leonard's Forest, but in the Western world it never retained the power for the general population as it had in the Orient. Revivals of interest in these magical and awesome beings have been achieved in the surge of interest in the Otherworld and in literature such as

that of J.R.R. Tolkien (1892–1973)—*The Hobbit* (1937) and *The Lord of the Rings* (1955)—in which he created a whole dynasty of Dragons under the names of Drakes, Fire-Drakes, Ancalagon, Scatha, and Smaug.

From ancient times the image of the dragon was the symbol of power and a heroic and worthy adversary for warriors. As such it formed the battle banner of the Persians, the Romans, the British, and the Norse Scandinavians, among others. Today the dragon also has enduring symbolism and recognition as one of the most widely used heraldic motifs of Europe.
References 5, 7, 10, 14, 18, 20, 24, 49, 51, 55, 61, 63, 78, 81, 89, 91, 94, 105, 128, 133, 139, 149, 150, 174
See also Ancalagon, Apocalyptic Beast, Apocalyptic Beasts, Ddraig Goch (y), Dragon (Epidaurian), Dragon (Ethiopian), Dragon at Uffington, Dragon Maid, Dragon of Ladon, Dragon of Saint Leonard's Forest, Dragon of the Apocalypse, Dragon-maid, Dragon-Tygre, Dragon-wolf, Drake, Fafnir, Fire-Drake, Gandareva, Gargouille, Girtabili, Grendel, Lambton Worm, Loathly Worm, Mušhuššu, Oriental Dragon, Python, Scatha, Serpent of Eden, Smaug, Tarasque, Tiamat, Vitra, Wyvern

DRAGON AT UFFINGTON

This is the name of a very famous earth mound upon which rests the White Horse, a hill figure in the chalk downs of Berkshire, England. It is a massive 365 feet in length, and there are numerous theories as to its origins. There is no doubt that it is ancient, but many speculate as to whether it is prehistoric or Celtic. The stylized hill figure has not absolutely been identified as a horse, and many believe that it is the dragon itself. However, a dragon was supposed to have terrorized the area in ancient times. A local rhyme attributes the slaying of the dragon to "King George," while the local church is dedicated to Saint George, who slew the dragon of Beirut. If, as is conjectured, the hill figure is indeed a dragon, argues Hugh Massingham (1926), then the mound associated with it would actually indicate the burial of a great Celtic chief, or Pendragon.
References 13
See also dragon

DRAGON KINGS

This is a particular class of Oriental dragon usually associated with command of an entire element or the element of a particular region, especially in the traditions and legends of China and Japan. They are usually powerful and splendid dragons inhabiting splendid crystal palaces but subservient to and the emissaries of the gods. The four great Dragon Kings of China responsible for the waters of the earth are Ao Chin, Ao Jun, Ao Kuang, and Ao Shun, while the Lung Wang is responsible for the element of fire. The

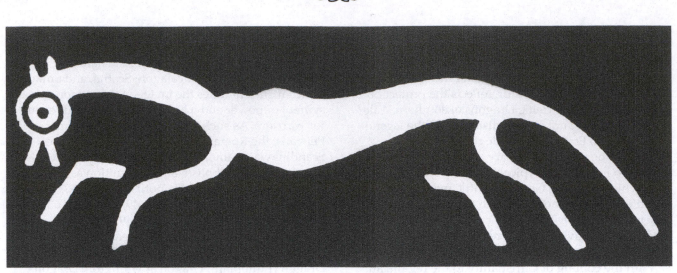
White Horse/Dragon at Uffington (Rose Photo Archive, UK)

Dragon King of Japan associated with the element of water is called Ryujin.
References 139
See also Ao Chin, Ao Jun, Ao Kuang, Ao Shun, Lung Wang, Ryujin

DRAGON MAID, THE
This is the name of a young lady whose story is told in the *Travels of Sir John Mandeville* (1366). The Dragon Maid, also known as the Lady of the Land, was turned into a hideous dragon.
References 180
See also Lady of the Land

DRAGON OF IZUMO
This is the name of a mighty dragon in the traditions and legends of Japan. It is described as being of enormous size and having eight huge heads. It terrorized the people of Izumo in Japan until the hero Takehaya Susanowo, whilst in exile, met with and defeated this monster. While inspecting and dismembering the corpse, he found in its tail a magnificent enchanted sword. Such was its power that he named it "Kusanagi-no-Tsunegi," which may be translated as "Grass-cutting Sword," which implies that it will cut down anything before it. In a gesture of subservience, Takehaya Susanowo gave the sword to Ama Terasu, who passed it to her descendant, who became the first emperor of Japan. And this is the legend as to how the present Imperial Sword came to the emperors.
References 113
See also dragon, Eight-Forked Serpent of Koshi

DRAGON OF LADON
This is a monstrous dragon in the classical mythology of Greece and Rome. It is described as having an enormous, scale-covered body and two hundred fiery eyes on a hundred heads. The Dragon of Ladon is variously described as the offspring of Phorcys and Ceto, of Gaia, or of Typhon and Echidne, or was the creation of the goddess Hera. However, it was Hera who had placed it in the garden of the magic apple tree belonging to the Hesperides, where it coiled itself around the trunk of the tree as its guardian. However, the hero Hercules/Heracles wanted the apples as the eleventh of his Twelve Labors and shot the Dragon of Ladon so accurately that it died instantly without a fight, and he took the apples. When Hera discovered her dead dragon, she set it in the heavens as a constellation, known to the ancient world as the serpent, Draco. Heracles/Hercules, to celebrate his victory, had an image of the Dragon of Ladon placed upon his shield.
References 20, 24, 89, 125, 178
See also dragon

DRAGON OF SAINT LEONARD'S FOREST
This is the name of a dragon or serpent that was reported in the forest of Saint Leonard's in the county of Sussex, England, in August 1614. The report was made by a man called John Trundle, who told of the great destruction and havoc that this monster was wreaking around the town of Horsham. It was said to be responsible for the disappearance and killing of both cattle and men.
References 134
See also dragon, serpent

DRAGON OF THE APOCALYPSE
This is the associated name given to a monster in the beliefs and folklore of Ireland. This creature is also known as the Apocalyptic Beast.

References 134
See also Apocalyptic Beast

DRAGON-CARP
This is a hybrid creature in the legends and folklore of Korea. It has the head of a dragon and the tail of a massive carp, which has the power of human speech. The legend relates how a poor fisherman hauled in the monster and was very pleased with his catch until it spoke to him and begged to be let go. The startled fisherman was moved by its eloquence and gently lowered the monster back over the side of the boat. He had in fact shown mercy to the son of the Dragon King and as a result ever afterward went home with a fine catch in his nets.
References 113
See also dragon

DRAGON-HORSE
This is a hybrid monster in the traditions and beliefs of China. It is described as having the body of a dragon but the front quarters of a horse. This massive creature had the ability to fly between the heavens and the earth and was the heavenly messenger of the gods. It is a Dragon-Horse that is credited with revealing the symbolism of the Yin and Yang to the Chinese emperor that depicted for human beings how the cosmos is in a natural balance.
References 7
See also monster

DRAGON-MAID
This is a supernatural monstrous woman in Celtic mythology and folklore. She is much like Melusine of French legend in that she is part woman and part dragon. She has the ability to confer progeny for previously barren couples who treat her well but curses those who don't.
References 7
See also dragon, Melusine

DRAGON-TYGRE
This is a hybrid monster with the head of a tiger and the body of a dragon, found in the heraldic repertoire of European coats of arms.
References 7
See also dragon-wolf, monster

DRAGON-WOLF
This is a hybrid monster with the head of a wolf and the body of a dragon, found in the heraldic repertoire of European coats of arms.
References 7
See also Dragon-Tygre, monster

DRAKE
There are two traditions that have the name "Drake" as follows:

1. This is a dragon in the traditions and folklore of the Gypsy community of the Balkan states of southeastern Europe. The Drake is described as resembling a dragon or a cannibal ogre with a vast humanoid body. He travels about on horseback and lives in a glittering palace with a human wife. Any human that wanders into his domain is likely to be devoured unless they can convince him that they are his relatives.

2. This is the alternative name for a giant serpent or Lindorm in the traditions and beliefs of Sweden as reported by Sven Magnus Johannsson during the early nineteenth century. He said that he had climbed over what he thought was a huge log on the banks of Lake Södreg, which to his horror moved and turned out to be a Drake, which slithered into the lake.
References 7, 134
See also dragon, Lindorm, ogre, serpent

DRIFTA
This is the name of a giant in the Norse mythology of Scandinavia. Drifta, whose name may be translated as "Snowdrift," is one of the Hrim-Thursar, or Frost Giants. He is the son of Thrym and the sibling of Frosti, Johul, and Snoer.
References 24
See also giant, Frost Giants, Thrym

DRUGGEN HILL BOGGLE
In the folkore of this district of Cumberland in the northwest of England, a story is told of the disappearance of a pedlar in the nineteenth century. This coincided with the appearance of the monstrous Black dog, considered to be a type of bogie beast that terrorized and attacked travelers in the district at night. The local people connected the incidents, and when the pedlar's body was found and interred in the churchyard, the Black dog was no longer reported. The horrific injuries that it had inflicted on its victims at last started to heal.
References 67, 160
See also Black dog

DRUON
This is the name of a giant in the legends and folklore of Belgium. He is described as being the adversary of the hero Gravius by the humanist and poet Lemaire (1473–1524). Druon is later celebrated as the Town Giant of the city of Antwerp from the time of the Emperor Charles V (1500–1558) and is now paraded in effigy as part of the city's festivals.
References 174
See also giant, Town Giant

DUINEACH

This is an alternative name for the Cailleach Bheur of the folklore and traditions of Ireland.

References 128

See also Cailleach Bheur

DUMBELDORS

This is the name given by the English academic and author J.R.R. Tolkien to a race of monstrous insects. They are described in one of the Hobbit's poems as being ferocious and having enormous wings. But they have apparently become extinct, and nothing else was known about them.

References 51

DUN COW OF WARWICK, THE

This is a monstrous beast in the traditions and folklore of England. There are various versions of its origins, either as reputed from the tenth century, the gigantic cow of the giants who had built the vast stone circle of Staple Hill in Shropshire as her pen; or as a fairy cow from an enchanted Iron Age barrow. Whatever the version, she was a gigantic and enchanted cow that provided an inexhaustible supply of milk to those who treated her well. However, one silly, greedy woman not only filled her pail but attempted to fill her sieve with the cow's precious milk. The Dun Cow became enraged and grew into a terrifying monster rampaging all about the village and the countryside. Eventually, Sir Guy of Warwick trapped the beast on Dunsmore Heath and killed it. For some considerable time an exhibit in Warwick Castle was said to be one of the horns of the Dun Cow; in all probability it was the tusk of an elephant.

References 7, 183

See also Colbrand, monster

DUNNIE

This is a semisupernatural monster in the traditions and folklore of the northeast of England. It is much like the Brag in that it materializes as an oversized familiar beast. The Dunnie inhabits the area around Haselrigg in the county of Northumberland (now the administrative region of Northumbria). It will most frequently materialize in the form of a donkey, plough-horse, or pony to be harnessed by an unsuspecting human at the start of some errand. They will usually be left holding the empty harness after being dumped in the mud, with the monster laughing as it gallops off.

References 21, 25, 93, 160

See also Brag, Kelpy, Pooka

DYRNWCH WYDDEL

This is the alternative spelling of the name of the giant Diwrnach Wyddel in the legends and folklore of Ireland and Wales.

References 128

See also Diwrnach Wyddel, giant

DZOAVITS

This is the name of a giant in the traditions and beliefs of the Shoshone Native American people of Nevada and Utah in the United States. Dzoavits was an enormous cannibal ogre who hunted for children. The legend tells how the giant stole either Dove's two eggs or her two tiny children, whom she managed to recover. But she was seen and tracked by Dzoavits, who was intent on devouring them all. Dove enlisted the help of the other creatures, who gave her some tallow, a stomach paunch, and some feathers. When she was being pursued by the giant, Crane made a bridge over the river by extending his leg and letting them run across it; then the animals lost the giant in a maze of tunnels while she escaped. But Dzoavits was only temporarily delayed, so she used the tallow from Eagle to create a chasm to halt her pursuer, but he overcame that. Then she used the stomach paunch that transformed into a cliff face, and after that she used the feathers that became a dense fog. Each time Dzoavits was delayed but overcame the obstacle until Badger dug two holes and put Dove and her children in one and directed the giant to the other, and when he was down the hole she threw in hot rocks on top of him until the hole was sealed. Then Dove and her children were free of Dzoavits for ever.

References 24, 47, 77, 133

See also cannibal, giant, ogre

DZOO-NOO-QUA

This is the name of an enormous giantess in the traditions and legends of the Kwakiutl Native American people in the Canadian province of British Columbia. She is a cannibal monster who seeks the children of humans to enslave or devour. Dzoo-noo-qua inhabits the depths of the forest in a lodge, under the floor of which she kept her spirit so that she would be invulnerable. However, one day the hero Sky Boy tracked her to her abode and in attempting to shoot her missed, and the arrow went through a hole in the floor directly into her hidden spirit. The giantess was killed instantly, and all the remaining captive children were set free.

References 77

See also Asin, Djieien, Snee-nee-iq

DZU-TEH

This is the name for the giant Yeti in the traditions and beliefs of the people of Tibet. There are believed to be three different types of Yeti, named according to their size. The others are the Meh-Teh and the Yeh-Teh.

References 78

See also Abominable Snowman, Bigfoot, Meh-Teh, Yeti

E

EAČH UISGE

This a supernatural monster whose name, Eačh Uisge, means "Water Horse" in Scottish Gaelic in the Highland folklore of Scotland. It is distinguished from the Kelpie in that it haunts only saltwater and the inland lochs; the Kelpie haunts fresh-running-water courses. The Eačh Uisge, also known as the Ech-Uskya and Ech-ushkya, sometimes appears as a handsome young man with seaweed in his hair, or as a bird known as the Boobrie; however, its most usual form is that of a beautiful horse prancing on the shores of the loch. If anyone is foolish enough to mount and ride the Eačh Uisge, it will head for the water immediately, the rider transfixed to its back and unable to dismount. The Eačh Uisge submerges to its underwater lair, where it will devour its victim, leaving only their liver floating on the surface. This monstrous being is reputedly most active during the Celtic feast of Samhain, when it may devour both cattle and humans lured to the waters.
References 24, 25, 89, 119, 128, 134, 160
See also Bäckahäst, Boobrie, Cabyll-Ushtey, Kelpy, Näcken, Neugle

EALE

This is an alternative spelling of the name of the Yale, a beast of the traditions of medieval Europe.
References 10, 14, 89
See also Yale

ECHENEIS

This is the name of a creature in the traditions and legends of European travelers, fishermen, and sailors. The Echeneis, also known as the Remora and the Mora, was described by Pliny the Elder in his *Historia Naturalis* (A.D. 77) as a sea serpent, but no more than six inches in length. Yet this creature apparently had the ability to latch onto the hull of a ship at sea with such a strong grip that it could prevent it from moving away. It was said to inhabit the polar seas and to be able to freeze the air around it; thus any ships sailing in northern seas would know if the Echeneis was present if the ship started to be held in frozen waters. It was considered to be the enemy of the Salamander that existed in fire, and the Echeneis was sought by physicians to remedy ailments, especially of women during pregnancy. Pliny was confirmed of the opinion that Mark Antony lost the Battle of Actium because he was held fast by one of these creatures on the hull of his ship. The creature was commonly portrayed in bestiaries of the thirteenth century in Europe.
References 18, 89, 185
See also Murex

ECHIDNE, ECHIDNA

This is the name of a monster in the classical mythology of Greece and Rome. Echidne was described as having the body and head of a beautiful woman to the waist but the lower half of a hideous serpent. She was the daughter, according to different versions, of Gaia and Tartarus, or Callirrhoe and Chrysaor, or Ceto and Phorcys. She inhabited a cavern near either Arimi or Scythia, from which she half-emerged to attract any male human foolish enough to be lured by her charms. However, once she had him within her abode she would quickly embrace him in a grip of death and consume him. Echidne mated with the monstrous Typhon, and their terrifying offspring were Cerberus (the dog of the underworld), the three-headed goat-beast Chimaera, the Dragon of Colchis, the Dragon of Ladon, the winged Harpies, the multiheaded Hydra, the Nemean Lion, Orthos (one of the dogs of Geryon), the cannibal Scylla, and the Greek Sphinx. She was destroyed by the many-eyed giant Argos Panoptes. In his work *The Faerie Queen*, English Elizabethan poet Edmund Spenser (1552?–1599) suggested that Echidne was the mother of the Blatant Beast.
References 7, 20, 24, 38, 61, 63, 89, 125, 139, 169, 178, 182
See also Argus, Blatant Beast, cannibal, Cerberus, Chimera, Chrysaor, Dragon of Ladon, Gaia, Harpy, Hydra, Medusa, Nemean Lion, Orthos, Phorcys, Scylla, Sphinx, Typhon

ECH-USKYA, ECH-USHKYA
These are alternative spellings of the name of the monstrous Eaċh Uisge in the Highland folklore of Scotland.
References 24, 25, 89, 128, 134, 160
See also Eaċh Uisge

EER-MOONAN
This is the name of a group of monsters in the legends of the Dreamtime of the Native Australian people.
References 154
See also monster

EFREET, EFRIT
These are alternative spellings of the Djinn in Islamic legend known as Afrit.
References 4, 20, 124, 146, 161
See also Afrit, Djinn

EGEON
This is the spelling given in his work by the Italian author Boccaccio (1313–1375) for the giant Ægæon. He is derived from the Titan son of Terra/Gaia and Typhon in the classical mythology of Greece and Rome.
References 174
See also Ægæon, Gaia, Titan, Typhon

EGGTHER
This is the name of a giant in the Norse mythology of Scandinavia. He is described as an enormous being, a great warrior of the giant fraternity, and an accomplished musician. Eggether's main role, however, is as the guardian of the farthest boundaries of all the realms of the Aesir gods, the lands of the Frost and Fire Giants, as well as that of the mortals on earth.
References 139
See also Fire Giants, Frost Giants, giant

EIGHT-FORKED SERPENT OF KOSHI
This is the name of a monstrous, many-headed serpent in the legends and traditions of Japan. This legend prominently features the Japanese favoring of the number eight, which is regarded not only to symbolize multiples but also mystery and enchantment. The Eight-Forked Serpent of Koshi is described as having eight heads and tails on its vast body. The eyes of each head glowed vibrant, deep red, while the rest of its body was so huge that the surface supported pine trees and mosses right to the top of each head. As it moved it created furrows of eight valleys and mountains in between, but the effort scraped scales and blood from its underbelly. Each year for seven years the Eight-Forked Serpent of Koshi demanded one of the king's daughters for its prey or it would devour the entire population. When the eighth year came the last daughter, Princess-Comb-Ricefield, was about to be sent to her fate on Serpent Mountain when the heroic god Brave-Swift-Impetuous-Male made a plan to save her. He built a compound in which he placed eight enormous tower gates with platforms on the upper story. He placed an enormous vat full of rice beer on each and waited for the eight heads of the Eight-Forked Serpent of Koshi to appear. Sure enough, the anticipated damsel and the smell of the rice alcohol attracted the vast reptile, which slithered ahead quickly into each vat on the top of the eight gates. Very soon the intoxicated serpent was slumbering soundly. Then as quickly and accurately as possible the hero sliced each vast head from its neck, flooding the area with torrents of blood from the slain creature. On inspecting the vast corpse the hero discovered in its tail the enchanted sword, now in the shrine at Atsuta. In honor of the great victory, the mountain was renamed Eight Cloud Mountain; the hero Brave-Swift-Impetuous-Male, of course, married the valiantly rescued Princess-Comb-Ricefield, and the image of the defeated Eight-Forked Serpent of Koshi was placed on Japanese currency.
References 18
See also Dragon of Izumo, Fafnir, Hydra, serpent

ELBST
This is the name of a water monster in the folklore of Switzerland. The Elbst has had many different descriptions, from the earliest reporting in 1584 to the latest in 1926. It has been described as a long serpentine creature with a large head and four feet with claws, much like a dragon; or as a bulky creature much the size of two boats side by side in the water but with a huge head resembling the shape of a pig; or as a vast fish with legs. Whatever the description, the Elbst is said to inhabit the depths of the Selisbergsee, a calm lake in the canton of Uri near Lucerne. This monster terrified the people who lived in the vicinity by leaving the lake at night and raiding the herds of sheep in the Alpen pastures, leaving behind their mutilated bodies. In the water it would suddenly surface at the side of a boat and frighten the occupants, then swim or dive swiftly away again. This latter behavior was said to precede an imminent storm. Many people regarded the Elbst as the Beast of the Apocalypse.
References 134
See also Beast of the Apocalypse, dragon, monster

ELEPHANT-TIGER
This is a hybrid beast in the traditions and legends of Thailand. It is described as having the body of an elephant with the head of a giant tiger and was

reputed to be as ferocious as the tiger and as indomitable as the elephant. This fabulous beast was reputed to inhabit the deepest parts of the dense jungle, but King Phan of Nakhon Pathom City wanted the beast for his herds. So three of the best trackers were sent to hunt and trap the beast and bring it to him. After many treks through the jungle, they at last succeeded in finding its habitat, constructing a pit trap and taking the beast alive. With further difficulty, they brought the great beast to the palace of their king and were greatly rewarded for their difficult task. The keepers of the king's herds mated the fantastic beast with the best of the elephants, and a new breed of war elephants was established. When the neighboring King Kong of Chiasi waged war on King Phan, it was this herd that routed the enemy. The victory is celebrated to this day with a festival in which an effigy of the elephant-tiger takes pride of place.
References 113
See also Town Giants

EMOGOALEKC
This is the name of a human who metamorphosed into a monster in the traditions of the Kathlamet Native American people of the northwestern coastal region of the United States. Emogoalekc had fallen in love with a slave girl in the tribal community, but as the son of a chief, this was against the community laws, and he was taken to task by his father, the chief. The distraught son threw himself into the nearby lake to drown himself, but instead he was transformed into a water monster. Sometime later Emogoalekc's friend came to the lake and when confronted by the monster recognized the chief's lost son. Emogoalekc swore him to secrecy, but somehow the villagers found out his whereabouts and were so afraid that they went to the lake to kill Emogoalekc, who mistakenly accused his friend of breaking his promise. However, the friend helped him escape and was told that in the future any human who saw him would one day be a chief.
References 77
See also monster

EMPUSA, EMPUSAE (pl.)
In the classical mythology of ancient Greece, Empusa was a terrible female supernatural hybrid monster. She was described as having one leg of brass, the other that of an ass. The Empusa was sent by the goddess Hecate to torment and terrify travelers on dark country roads, and they were accused of being the monsters that devoured their corpses when terrified to death.

In the folklore of modern Greece she is a shape-shifting evil spirit. She may manifest in the form of an ox, a dog, a mule, or a beautiful woman. She is a frightening spirit to humans but is considered responsible for causing injury to the sheep on the mountains during the noonday heat.
References 7, 17, 125, 160, 169, 178
See also Black dog, Kludde, Padfoot

EMUSHA
This is the name of an enormous black bear in the Hindu creation mythology of India. When the earth was being created from the churning waters of the cosmos, the powers of evil, represented by the demon Hiranyaksha, constantly attempted to prevent the emergence of the earth. The massive bear Emusha was sent to push up the earth and defeat the demon.
References 112

ENAY
This is the name of a giant in the classical literature of France. Enay is one of the giant ancestors of Pantagruel in the famous work *Pantagruel* (1532) by the French author François Rabelais (ca. 1494–ca. 1553). But Enay does not appear in the original edition; he is an addition to later versions by Rabelais, as a means of establishing the genealogy of Pantagruel. Eryx, along with five other giants—Etion, Gabbara, Galehaut, Happemousche, and Morguan— is credited with inventing something concerned with drinking, however Enay and Gayoffe seem not to have any other function than to establish the ancestry.
References 174
See also Bruyer, Chalbroth, Daughters of Cain, Eryx, Gabbara, Galehaut, Gargantua, giant, Happemousche, Hurtaly, Morguan, Noachids, Noah, Pantagruel

ÉNBARR, ENBHÁRR
This is the name of a fabulous horse in the mythology and folklore of Ireland. Enbhárr, which may be translated as "Froth" or "Foam," is also known by the name Aonbárr. He is the steed of Manannán mac Lir and, as the name implies, was capable of dashing over any surface, whether it be mountain, marsh, or sea.
References 128
See also Aonbárr, Horses of the Sun, Pegasus, Unicorn

ENCELADUS
This is the name of a giant in the classical mythology of Greece and Rome. Enceladus, whose name means the "Buzzer," is one of the Gigantes and, like his brothers, was said to have been engendered from the blood that fell on the earth from the castrated Uranus. These giants were born fully mature and clad in full battle armor. They waged war on the Olympian gods after the defeat of the Titans and

were defeated. In that battle Enceladus fought with the goddess Athene, who threw the island of Sicily at him. Some accounts state that he was imprisoned by her under Mount Etna, where his movements create earthquakes; other accounts say that Enceladus was killed by Zeus.

References 20, 24, 139, 169, 174, 178

See also Briareus, Cottus, Gaia, giant, Gyges, Hundred-Handed Giants, Pallas, Uranus

ENCERRADOS

This Spanish word, which may be translated as "captive" or "recluse," is used to describe a class of monstrous being in the folklore and beliefs of the people of Chile. These monsters were said to have been formulated from the abducted children in the region of Chiloé whose orifices had been sewn up by evil witches. These Encerrados were then fed on the flesh of goats and other child victims until they metamorphosed into the hairy grey cannibal creatures served by the Invunche and Chivato and, in some cases, became an Invunche or Chivato. In the dank subterranean passages these creatures were supposedly used for horrific satanic rituals.

References 134

See also cannibal, Chivato, Invunche, monster

ENDROP

This is the name of a water monster in the legends and folklore of Rumania. In a version of the Alexandrian *Physiologus* the Endrop is described as a type of Hippocamp or water horse. Like the Kelpie of Scottish folklore this monster would also entice foolhardy humans onto its back, but the Endrop would race headlong for the water, where it would drown and devour its victims if they had not called upon the Lord Jesus to save them.

References 89

See also Hippocamp, Kelpy, monster

ENFIELD

This is the name of a fabulous hybrid beast in the heraldic repertoire of the British Isles. According to J. Vinycomb (1906), this beast had the torso of a lion with the tail and legs of a wolf but, instead of paws, had the claws of an eagle, all surmounted by the head of a fox. It appeared on the coats of arms of some Irish families.

References 7

ENGULFER

This is the name of the Hînqûmemen, a lake in the traditions and beliefs of the Coeur d'Alene Native American people of British Columbia in Canada.

References 134

See also Hînqûmemen

ENIM

This is the name of a race of giants mentioned in the Hebrew texts that now comprise the Old Testament of the Christian Bible.

References 13

See also giant, Noah, Zamzumin, Zuzim

ENTS

This is the name of a class of giants in the literary works of the English academic and author J.R.R. Tolkien (1892–1973), *The Hobbit* (1937) and *The Lord of the Rings* (1955). The Ents are described as hybrid beings, part tree and part human. Depending on their age, they reached about fourteen feet in height and at first had smooth trunks that later gnarled with age; from these they had arms that branched and legs with feet like roots. Their trunks extended to their heads from which grew their twiggy hair. Although seemingly wooden, they could sway along remarkably quickly. The Ents were wise and gentle but were also strong and determined, and once their anger had been aroused they were terrible adversaries. Their leader was called Fangorn, and they inhabited the Forest of Arda, where they were the shepherds of the trees for the Queen of the Earth Yavanna. Here they lived peacefully, taking their magical liquid refreshment and occasionally holding a communal meeting, or "Entmoot." Their Entwives were especially skilled in the art of horticulture and encouraging their progeny, the Entings, in the forest ways. They disliked any being that wielded an axe anywhere near their trees and were constantly on guard against the Dwarves. Then at the end of the Second Age of the Sun the Entwives and Entings were suddenly no more when the Orcs destroyed their gardens and rampaged through the forest with their steel weapons. The Ents' wrath was terrible to behold, and they marched on Isengard fortress and tore it to pieces and destroyed the Orcish forces completely. But with the loss of the Entwives and Entings their lives changed, and slowly they dwindled, peacefully living in the Entwood.

References 51

See also Entwives, Fangorn, Fimbrethil, Finglas, Flandrif, giant, Orc

ENTWIVES

This is the name of the wives of the hybrid tree giants known as the Ents in the literary works of the English academic and author J.R.R. Tolkien (1892–1973), *The Hobbit* (1937) and *The Lord of the Rings* (1955). The Entwives were skilled in the arts of horticulture and agriculture and inhabited the plains and valleys, while their husbands were guardians of the forest trees. Their progeny were called the Entings, who learned those skills as they developed. During the

War of the Ring the gardens and groves were destroyed by the Orcs, and many of the Entwives and Entings were slain. The others disappeared, and the Ents went to wreak their vengeance upon the Orcs.
References 51
See also Ents, giant, Wandlimb

ENYO
This is a hideous monster of a hag in the classical mythology of Greece and Rome. Enyo is one of the Graiæ, who were the guardian sisters of the murderous monsters, the Gorgons.
References 178
See also Gorgons, Graæ, monster

EOUS
This is one of the Horses of the Sun in the classical mythology of Greece and Rome. The classical poet Ovid (43 B.C.–A.D. 17) mentions Eous as well as Acthon, Phlegon, and Pyrois, who were vast majestic beasts. They all had wings like Pegasus and drew the chariot of the sun daily across the sky.
References 89, 139
See also Horses of the Sun

EPAPHUS
This is the Greek name for the sacred bull Apis in the mythology of ancient Egypt.
References 24, 63, 169
See also Apis

EPHIALTES
This is the name of one of the sons of Aloes in the classical mythology of Greece and Rome. The name "Ephialtes" may be translated as "Leaper." They were giants born of Iphimedeia, the wife of Aloes/Aloeus, but some accounts say that they were the sons of Poseidon by her. Some sources say that they were derived from the blood of the castrated Uranus and that they emerged in full armor at the Peninsula of Pallene near Phlegra. The Aloadae were twins, Ephialtes's brother is Otus, both of whom from birth grew at the rate of nine inches each month. They were so vast that by the time they were nine years of age they were already twenty-six feet in girth and nearly sixty feet in height. Although portrayed as gross and uncouth, they were said to have founded cities and inspired the veneration of the Muses. When their mother and sister were threatened, they rescued them.

In Homer's *Iliad,* they laid claim to the throne of Olympus and the goddesses Artemis/Diana and Hera/Juno. In their bid for these prizes they imprisoned the god of war, Ares, in a bronze pot for over a year. They assailed Olympus by heaping the mountains of Ossa and Pelion on top of Mount

Olympus. But the new gods, led by Zeus, were not to be beaten so easily. There are several versions of their demise, but Ephialtes was in most, slain by the god Apollo.
References 20, 125, 139, 174, 178
See also Aloades, giant, Otus, Uranus

EPIDAURIAN DRAGON
See dragon (Epidaurian)

EPIMACUS
This is an alternative name for the Opinicus, a type of Griffin in the heraldic repertoire of Europe.
References 7, 20
See also Griffin, Opinicus

EPIMETHEUS
This is the name of one of the giants in the classical mythology of Greece and Rome. Epimetheus was one of the progeny of the Titan called Japetus and the Oceanid nymph Clymene according to Hesiod in his work *Theogony* (ca. 750 B.C.), but according to Aeschylus (525 B.C.–456 B.C.) his mother was Themis. His siblings were the giants Atlas, Prometheus, and Menoetius. Epimetheus was responsible for endowing the creatures of the world with certain attributes such as speed and strength and helped Prometheus with the forming of human attributes, encouraging him to take fire from the gods for them. His wife was Pandora, whose curiosity allowed the troubles of the world to be unleashed and her husband to be changed by Zeus, the king of the gods, into a monkey for his meddling with the domain of the gods.
References 139, 166, 169, 178
See also Atlas, giant, Japetus, Menoetius, Prometheus, Titan

EPIROTES
This is the name of an vast semisupernatural serpent in the classical mythology of Greece and Rome. It was the vast guardian of a walled garden in which the sun god, Apollo, kept a number of fabulous dragons. These dragon descendants of the Python of Delphi were the subject of divining the future for the surrounding population. Each year a naked maiden was sent to offer food to the dragons; should they refuse the gift, the year would be full of disasters; should one of the dragons take the food, the year would be full of success.
References 89
See also dragon, Python, serpent

EQUUS BIPES
This is the Latin term that literally means a "two-footed horse." It has been applied, since the classical

times of Greece and Rome, to fabulous horses, mainly those now known as the Sea horse. The general description is that of the body and tail parts of a fish, covered in scales and with a vast, fanlike tail, but with the foreparts and head of a horse. Although the beings are said to be monstrous, there is rarely any indication of threat associated with them and human beings. There are, however, sightings recorded by sailors and travelers wherever the concept of a horse is known. Consequently, tales of such sightings were related from the fifteenth century on the coast of West Africa and from the sixteenth and seventeenth centuries in the Americas. One notable sighting was reported in the Ansedik River off the Island of Brion in New France (now Canada), by Father Louis Nicholas in his *Natural History* of 1675. It is now conjectured that the creature that was then accorded this name was possibly a walrus.

References 134
See also monster, Sea horse

ERESHIGAL

This is the name of a monstrous hybrid in the ancient Sumerian mythology of the Middle East. The image of Ereshigal is taken from an ancient cuneiform text, and the description is of a fish's scaly body but with the hind quarters and hind legs of a dog. She has the upper body of a woman, with human arms and hands, but a head resembling that of a kid (young goat), including the horns. Her abode was the underworld of the dead.

References 7
See also monster

ERICHTHONIUS

This is the name of a hybrid humanoid monster in the classical mythology of Greece and Rome. Erichthonius was described as part male infant and part serpent. He was said to have been engendered from the result of the splashed seed from the god Vulcan/Hephaestus's aborted attempt to rape the young goddess Athena/Minerva. The sperm that fell into the earth developed instantly into a child, and Athena/Minerva took him to her Acropolis to be cared for by Cecrop's daughters with the proviso that they should never look at him directly. When they did, each was so terrified that they fled straight off the edge of the Acropolis and were dashed to death on the rocks beneath.

References 166
See also monster

ERINYES, ERINYS

This is the name in classical Greek mythology for the three avenging female supernatural humanoid monsters. They were also known as Dirae,

Eumenides, Furies, and Semnai, but individually they were known as Alecto, Magæra, and Tisiphone. These terrifying beings are described as black; their hair is formed of snakes and their hands are entwined with snakes. They have wings resembling those of a bat. Their head is that of a dog with suppurating eyes and stinking breath. The robes they wear are soiled and stinking, and they carry flaming torches, snakes, and scourges. These monstrous supernaturals were engendered, according to some sources, from the spilled blood of the castrated Uranus and thus are the siblings of the Hundred-Handed Giants. Other sources say they are the daughters of Cronos and Eurynome. The Erinyes inhabited the underworld until they emerged to pursue those guilty of blood crimes against the family, or the people who had oppressed others, and they exacted a terrible retribution. This monstrous description from the writing of Hesiod (ca. eight century B.C.) and Æschylus (525 B.C.–456 B.C.) was later much ameliorated and developed into more acceptable avenging deities.

References 20, 24, 28, 38, 47, 62, 70, 124, 125, 127, 160, 161, 169, 178
See also Alecto, Dirae, Eumenides, Furies, Hundred-Handed Giants, Magæra, Semnai, Tisiphone, Uranus

ERQIGDLIT

This is the name of a class of monster in the legends and beliefs of the people of Greenland and Baffin Island. The Erqigdlit, which are described as a group of blood-drinking monsters, are also known as the Adlet in the mythology and folklore of the Inuit people of the Labrador and western Hudson Bay coasts in Canada.

References 24, 77
See also Adlet, monster

ERYMANTHEAN BOAR

This was a gigantic boar in the classical mythology of Greece and Rome. It was a colossal monster of a beast that supplemented its diet of ravaged fields and crops with the slaughter of local populations. The Erymanthean Boar inhabited the forests of Mount Lampeia in Arcadia and into Achaia, through the cyprus groves beside the river of Erymanthus, where no mortal dared to hunt it. The hero Heracles/Hercules was given the task, by the tyrant Eurystheus, of capturing this monster alive as the fourth of his Twelve Labors. The hero accomplished this task by pursuing the boar relentlessly up beyond the tree line of the mountain until, beyond the snow line, the beast hurtled forward into a massive drift in which it became stuck. Hercules/Heracles bound the Erymanthean Boar in strong chains and threw it over his shoulders for the journey back to Mycenae. When

The dead boar and warriors (Rose Photo Archive, UK)

Eurystheus saw the hero with the monstrous beast coming to his palace, the cowardly tyrant was so terrified that he fled and took refuge in a bronze jar.
References 7, 24, 78, 133, 139
See also Ætolian Boar, Battleswine, Beigad, Boar of Beann-Gulbain, Buata, Cafre/Kafre, Calydonian Boar, Hildesuin, Pugot/Pugut, Sachrimnir, Twrch Trwyth, Ysgithyrwyn

ERYX

This is the name of a giant in the classical literature of France. Eryx is one of the giant ancestors of Pantagruel in the famous work *Pantagruel* (1532) by the French author François Rabelais (ca. 1494–ca. 1553). But Eryx does not appear in the original edition; he is an addition to later versions by Rabelais as a means of establishing the genealogy of Pantagruel. Eryx, along with five other giants—Etion, Gabbara, Galehaut, Happemousche, and Morguan—is credited with inventing something concerned with drinking.
References 174
See also Bruyer, Chalbroth, Daughters of Cain, Etion, Gabbara, Galehaut, Gargantua, giant, Happemousche, Hurtaly, Morguan, Noachids, Noah, Offotus, Pantagruel

ESTAS

This is the name of a fabulous bird in the folklore and mythology of the Carrier people of British Colombia, Canada. It is from this great bird that the people were saved from the freezing cold by his benevolent gift of fire.
References 169
See also Kaneakeluh, Prometheus, Thunderbird

ETASA

This is the name of one of the semisupernatural horses in the Hindu mythology of India. Etasa was one of the beautiful horses that pulled the chariot of the sun god across the sky.

References 7
See also Alsvid, Arrak, Horses of the Sun

ETION

This is the name of a giant in the classical literature of France. Etion is one of the giant ancestors of Pantagruel in the famous work *Pantagruel* (1532) by the French author François Rabelais (ca. 1494–ca. 1553). But Etion does not appear in the original edition; he is an addition to later versions by Rabelais as a means of establishing the genealogy of Pantagruel. Etion, along with five other giants—Eryx, Gabbara, Galehaut, Happemousche, and Morguan—is credited with inventing something concerned with drinking.
References 174
See also Bruyer, Chalbroth, Daughters of Cain, Eryx, Gabbara, Galehaut, Gargantua, giant, Happemousche, Hurtaly, Morguan, Noachids, Noah, Pantagruel

EUMENIDES

This is a euphemistic term for a group of monstrous supernaturals in classical Greek mythology. The name, which means the "Good-tempered Ones" or the "Kindly Ones," was used in placatory terms for the avenging beings known as the Erinyes. They were also known in Roman mythology as Furies. These beings were horrific hags, said to have been engendered by the spillage of the blood of the castrated Uranus and thus are the siblings of the Hundred-Handed Giants.
References 20, 38, 160, 166, 178
See also Alecto, Furies, Hundred-Handed Giants, Uranus

EURALE, EURYALE

This is the name of one of the Gorgons in the classical mythology of Greece and Rome. Unlike her sister, Medusa, Euryale whose name means "Wanderer," was immortal, but she shared the same horrific

description. They were originally beautiful women but turned to monsters with snakes for hair, bodies of bronze (or scales, according to some sources), with brass hands and wings; they petrified all living things that they beheld. The giant Orion was said to be the son of Euryale and the sea god, Poseidon/Neptune.
References 89, 139, 178
See also Gorgon, Medusa, Orion

EURYMEDON
This is the name of a Titan in the classical mythology of Greece and Rome. He took part in the rebellion against the new gods of Olympus. He is said to have been the father of Prometheus by the Titaness Clymene and by another, the father of Periboea. Eurymedon was the king of the giants in Epirus.
References 78, 178
See also giant, Prometheus, Titan

EURYTION
This is the name of two characters in the classical mythology of Greece and Rome.

1. This is the name of a centaur who was invited as the guest of the bridegroom, King Peirithous the Lapith, to the wedding feast. Unfortunately, centaurs rarely drank wine and easily became drunk, and this is what happened to Eurytion. What was worse was that in his drunken state the centaur insulted the bride by trying to abduct her on her wedding day. The irate King Peirithous appealed to the visiting hero Theseus to intervene, and Theseus expelled the centaur from the feast. Still drunk Eurytion returned with a band of his fellow centaurs ready for a fight. In the ensuing battle one of the centaurs was killed, and the rest were routed to the edge of the domain and the foothills of Mount Pindus.

2. This is the name of the giant who was the guardian of the red oxen of the gigantic monster Geryon. Eurytion patrols the herd of giant oxen day and night with his monstrous dog Orthrus. It was one of the tasks of the hero Hercules/Heracles to slay the giant and his dog in order to carry off the herd and thus win the hand of his love, Deianeira.
References 7, 139, 178
See also centaur, Geryon, giant, Orthrus

EURYTUS
There are two types of being with this name, as follows:

1. This is the name of one of the Gigantes who is also known as Rhaetos in the classical mythology of Greece and Rome. They were engendered from the blood of Uranus's castration when it fell upon the earth. Alcyoneus, with Porphyrion, was one of their leaders. They were described as being of enormous humanoid proportions but having serpents for legs with the serpents' heads for feet. At their first appearance they were already fully formed adult warriors complete with spears and in shining armor ready to do battle. And they attacked the Olympian gods immediately. However, by subterfuge, supernatural powers, and the strength of the hero Hercules/Heracles, one by one they were defeated. Eurytus, whose name means the "Rapids," in his turn was vanquished, according to different sources, by Dyonysus/Bacchus with his thyrsus (staff).

2. This is the name of one of the monstrous twins known as the Molionids in the classical mythology of Greece and Rome. The Molionids, also known as the Actoridæ, or Actorione, were said to be the sons of Molione by Actor or the sea god, Poseidon/Neptune. In earlier legends they were two, Eurytus and Cteatus, who were hatched from a silver egg.
References 7, 139, 169, 178
See also Alcyoneus, Clytius, Enceladus, giant, Gigantes, Hecatonchieres, Hundred Handed Giants, Mimas, Molionids, Pallas, Pelorus, Polybutes, Porphyrion, Rhaetos, Typhon

EWAIPANOMA
This is the name of a monstrous race of people in the legends of Venezuela. These people were described in a report by the English voyager Sir Walter Raleigh on his second expedition to the region in 1617. There he heard from a chief of the region of a race of headless people called the Ewaipanoma. These people, he said, had their mouths in their chests. It is conjectured that the people referred to may have been the Carib tribe of Yekunana, who apparently consider their permanently raised shoulders to be a sign of beauty.
References 76
See also Acephalos, Blemmyes, Hsing-T'ien

EXEDRA
This is an alternative name for the monstrous Hydra in the classical mythology of Greece and Rome.
References 18, 78, 133, 185
See also Hydra

F

FACE OF GLORY, THE

This is an alternative name for Kirtimukha, a monstrous being in the Hindu mythology of India. The Face of Glory was described as a monstrous head.
References 7, 24
See also Kirtimukha, T'ao-Tieh

FACHAN, FACHIN

A hideous being sometimes represented as a giant or as a dwarf in the folklore of Ireland and the Scottish Highlands. He is described as having one hand that protruded from his chest, one leg from his hip, one eye, and one tuft of hair on his head, all of which were usually concealed by a cloak of rough, matted feathers. This evil creature belongs to the group known as the Fuaths. The Fachan inhabited deserted places and would attack any mortal who strayed there. The Fachan is one of the Athach type of monsters.
References 7, 24, 128, 160, 170
See also Acephali, Athach, Cyclops, Fuath

FACHTNA FÁTHACH

This is the name of a giant in the legends and folklore of Ireland. The Irish Gaelic epithet "fáthach," which may be translated as "sagacious," indicates that he was regarded as wise. Fachtna Fáthach was the king of the region of Ulster in northern Ireland and, by his wife Ness, was the father of Conchobar mac Nessa. He was succeeded, however, not by his son but by his brother, who married his widowed Ness.
References 128
See also giant

FAFNIR, FAFNER

This is the name of a terrible dragon in the Norse mythology of Scandinavia and the Teutonic mythology of what is now northern Germany. Fafnir was one of three sons born to the dwarf Hreidmar, the others being Otr and Regin. When the god Loki mistook Otr for a real otter and killed him by mistake, Hreidmar demanded his "blood money." So the wily trickster god said that he would fill the otter's pelt with gold. This he did but, within it, put a ring that not only brought its owner wealth but also eternal misfortune, too. The minute it was taken the curse was laid. Fafnir was so desirous of the gold that he conspired with his brother to steal it from his father, whom he killed. But he did not wish to share the treasure, so he ran to Gritaheid, where he lay down on the hoard and metamorphosed into the most hideous wingless dragon. Meanwhile, Regin had discussed this with a mortal called Sigurd, whom he persuaded to kill the dragon. So Sigurd dug a trench in the path that Fafnir would take and jumped into it himself. When Fafnir came Sigurd was able to thrust his sword into the dragon's underbelly and kill it. He cut out the heart and cooked it over a fire; whilst doing this he burned himself and licked his hand. The taste of the dragon's blood endowed him with the understanding of all languages. Thus he learned that he was meant to be killed in his turn by Regin, so he was able to kill Regin and kept the gold. In the *Ring of the Nibelung* by Richard Wilhelm Wagner (1813–1883), Sigurd is called Siegfried while the two brothers are renamed Alberich and Mime.
References 7, 24, 78, 89, 105, 125, 133, 139, 166
See also dragon

FALAK

This is the name of a gigantic serpent in the mythology associated with Islam. It is within this cosmic serpent, lying below the vast bulk of the supporting Bahamut, that the fires of hell and eternity are located.
References 18, 63
See also Bahamut, serpent

FALCON-FISH

This is the name of a hybrid monster in the heraldic repertoire of Europe. It had the body of a fish and the head and legs of a falcon but with, curiously, the ears of a dog. It is found, occasionally, on the coats of arms of European families and institutions.
References 7

FAMA

This is the name of a monstrous female in the classical literature of Virgil (70–19 B.C.). She was envisaged as a huge female with multiple mouths and multiple tongues within each. She was the Latin personification of the concept of rumor.
References 125

FANGORN

This is the name of the leader of a class of giants called the Ents in the literary works of the English academic and author J.R.R. Tolkien (1892–1973), *The Hobbit* (1937) and *The Lord of the Rings* (1955). Fangorn, also known as "Tree Beard," had a mossy, gnarled trunk over which hung his long, grey beard. He had deep glowing brown eyes that in a certain light seemed to twinkle green; he was renowned for his wise counsel.
References 51
See also Ents, giants

FÁRBAUTI

This is the name of a giant in the Norse mythology of Scandinavia. Fárbauti, whose name means "Dangerous Striker," is credited with the release of fire from stones by striking them together. He is the father of the trickster god Loki.
References 61, 139
See also giant

FARIBROTH

This is the name of a giant in the classical literature of France. Faribroth is one of the giant ancestors of Pantagruel in the famous work *Pantagruel* (1532) by the French author François Rabelais (ca. 1494–ca. 1553). The other three primary ancestors are Charibroth, Hurtaly, and Sarabroth. They all appear in the first edition, which was subsequently edited with many more additional giant ancestors.
References 174
See also Bruyer, Chalbroth, Daughters of Cain, Eryx, Gabbara, Galehaut, Gargantua, giant, Happemousche, Hurtaly, Morguan, Noachids, Noah, Pantagruel

FARRACUTUS

This is an alternative name for the giant of French literature also known as Ferragut.
References 174
See also Ferragut

FASTITOCALON

There are two types of being with this name, as follows:

1. This is an alternative name for the Aspidochelone of European medieval travelers' lore. In the "Physiologus," reputedly written in the second century B.C. in Alexandria, Egypt, the Fastitocalon is described as a stone-skinned sea monster. An Anglo-Saxon bestiary from England, however, suggests that the name means "Floater on Ocean Streams." This text describes the creature as being about the size of a whale and rocklike in appearance, with seaweed and waves lapping at its edges, but extremely aggressive and dangerous to humans. It suggests that the monster encouraged ships' crews to take it for an island, so that when they are most relaxed by their fire on its back it can dive to the bottom of the ocean, taking its victims to be devoured. The bestiary also suggests that if there are no human prey to be had the creature manufactures a sweet perfume from its vast open mouth that is attractive to huge shoals of fish. When they are within its jaws the trap is sprung and they are swallowed in their thousands. This is given as an allusion to the gullibility of humans who are beguiled by repose or sweet perfumes into sinful ways.

2. A monster in the literary works of the English academic and author J.R.R. Tolkien (1892–1973), *The Hobbit* (1937) and *The Lord of the Rings* (1955). These monstrous creatures were taken directly from the traditions of the Anglo-Saxon bestiary beast of the same name and were described by him as a class of turtle-fish so vast that people took it for a deserted island. When they camped there the Fastitocalon sank with all and drowned them.
References 18, 51, 89
See also Aspidochelone, monster

FATHER FLOG AND MADAM FLOG, MOTHER FLOG

These are the names of two ogres in the English and American parents' repertoire derived from a translation of the early nineteenth century French tale produced for an American comic of the 1930s. These two gruesome figures were employed as a threat to naughty children to improve their behavior. Father Flog was portrayed as a tall, evenly proportioned man with a battered top hat covering his hair, which ended in a queue over the top of his high-collared shirt and jacket. He also wore breeches, stockings, and buckled shoes of the period. He is illustrated in the "penny dreadfuls" of the time, birching and abducting naughty children in his pannier to the local jail. He cuts out the tongues of children who tell lies and puts overactive little girls into a cage.

Madam Flog is portrayed as a stout person with a huge frilled bonnet and wearing a voluminous jacket over vast skirts and has buckled shoes on her feet. She hides herself in an outsized saucepan to catch greedy children in the act of theft; she puts a dunce's cap on a lazy little girl; catches and abducts, in her pannier, boys who play truant. But she also gives sweets to those who are good and releases those who repent of their misdemeanors.

These Nursery bogies of England and the United States are derived from the character of Père Fouettard in France.

References 182

See also Nursery bogies, ogre, Père Fouettard

FAUN

These beings are the offspring of the classical Greek demigod Faunus, which resembled him in their semihuman form with the legs, hooves, and horns of a goat but the torso and head of a human male. They are likened to the Satyrs and are guardians of the wild life of the woods and fields they inhabit.

References 7, 20, 133, 146, 160, 178, 189

See also Betikhân

FEARSOME CRITTERS

These are the fabulous creatures that were invented to explain the horrors and difficult experiences that were part of the desolate environment of the lumberjack community in the early history of the United States. Some were, of course, invented as a part of the entertainment in exaggerated "tall tales" for more relaxed moments, the teasing of newcomers, and pranks on fellow workers and, ultimately, gullible cityfolk. These creatures range from the humorous animals, birds, reptiles, and insects through to bizarre hybrids of terrifying description. For the most part the name usually indicates some aspect of the nature of the creature, such as the Come-at-a-Body and Hide-behind, or the fact that it is derived from an Old World origin such as the Fibbertigibbet (a witch's familiar's name) or Harpy-hag (a classical monster).

The stories became part of the folklore of the community and were collected enthusiastically by such as the Reverend Samuel Peters for his *General History of Connecticut* (1781). Later enthusiasts were T. Cox (1910), C. Brown (1935) and H. H. Tryon (1939).

The following is a list that may prove useful for researchers, although only those marked with an asterisk are described in this volume:

Albotritch, Argopelter*, Augerino*, Axhandle Hound*, Ball-tailed Cat, Bed Cat, Billdad, Cactus Cat*, Camp Chipmunk, Central American Whintosser, Clubtailed Glyptodont, Columbia River Sand Squink, Come-at-a-Body, Cougar-Fish, Cuba*, Dew-Mink*, Ding Ball*, Dismal Sauger, Dungaven -Hooter, Flibbertigibbet, Flitterick, Funeral Mountain Terrashot, Gazerium, Giddy Fish*, Glawackus*, Goofang*, Goofus Bird, Gumberoo, Guyascutus*, Hang-down, Happy Auger, Hidebehind*, Hodag*, Hoop Snake*, Hugag, Humility*, Hymampom Hog Bear, Jay Hawk, Kankagee, Kickle Snifter*, Leprocaun*, Log Gar, Lucive*, Luferlang, Milamo Bird, Moskitto*, Mountain Rabbit, Mugwump*, Philamaloo Bird*, Pigwiggen, Pinnacle Grouse, Prock Gwinter*, Rachet Owl, Roperite*, Rumptifusel, Rubberado*, Sandhill Perch, Santer, Screbonil, Shagamaw, Shmoo*, Slide-rock Bolter, Sliver Cat*, Snipe, Snoligoster, Snow Snake*, Snow Wasset Snydae, Splinter Cat*, Squonk*, Swamp Auger, Teakettler*, Tote-Road, Treesqueak, Tripoderoo*, Upland Trout, Wampus Cat, Wapaloosie, Whang Doodle, Whappernocker*, Whiffenpuff, Whifflepoof(le), Whirligig Fish, Whirling Wimpus, Wiggle-Whiffit, Will-Am-Alone, Windigo*, Wunk.

References 7, 24

See also Argopelter, Augerino, Axehandle Hound, Bunyan (Paul), Cactus Cat, Cuba, Dew-Mink, Ding Ball, Giddy Fish, Glawackus, Goofang, Guyascutus, Hidebehind, Hodag, Hoop Snake, Kickle Snifter, Leprocaun, Lucive, monster, Moskitto, Mugwump, Philamaloo Bird, Prock Gwinter, Rubberado, Shmoo, Snow Snake, Splinter Cat, Squonk, Teakettler, Whappernocker, Windigo

FEI LIAN

This is the name of a celestial hybrid monster in the folklore and mythology of China. Fei Lian, who is also known as Feng Bo, which means "Wind Lord," is the controller of the winds, which he kept in a bag and released as required. This monstrous being is described as having the head of a sparrow with bull's horns, the body and legs of a stag, but with the markings of a leopard and the tail of a serpent. Fei Lian and Chi Song-Zi, the rain god, conspired to overthrow Fei Lian's father, the ruler Huang Di. But the coup was a disaster, and Fei Lian was exiled to a cavern high in the mountains. Even there the monster released vicious wind storms until his bag of wind was punctured by the arrows of the archer Yi. The celestial archer then hamstrung the monster and brought him to sweep the ground in parades before the chariot of his father, the king.

References 133

See also monster

FENG HWANG, FÊNG HUANG

This is the name of a class of fabulous bird in the mythology of China. The Feng Hwang is in fact two birds, the Feng being the male and the Hwang being the female, always referred to as paired. The Feng Hwang may also be referred to as the Fum Hwang or the Fung Hwang and is portrayed as beautifully graceful with the body of a swan but the hind parts of a Unicorn with twelve tail feathers, a sinuous neck, and the head of a swallow-throated fowl. Its plumage is striped and colored black, green, red, white, and yellow. The Feng Hwang is a huge bird said to be about nine feet tall. It is considered to be the Chinese

Phoenix, although it does not die in the same way; it was born of fire and is considered to presage good fortune and the reign of a just ruler. It is one of the spiritual creatures of China, the others being the Dragon, the Tortoise, and the Ch'i Lin. When it flies it is surrounded by all the birds of the air, and when others make music, its sweet trill can be heard joining them. It was said to have been seen with the Ch'i Lin at the end of the reign of Yellow Emperor Hwang Ti, acknowledging his benevolence to his people; then again after the death of Hung Wu (A.D. 1399). Its image was reserved for royalty and most especially for the Empress.
References 7, 20, 61, 89, 181
See also Fei Lian, Fum Hwang, Fung, Ho-o, Hwang, Luan, Ping Feng, Shui Ying, Ti-Chiang, Yoh Shoh

FENIX
This is an alternative spelling of the Phoenix in European bestiaries, especially those written in Latin during the early Middle Ages.
References 185
See also Phoenix

FENODYREE, FENODEREE
This is the name of a giant hairy being in the Manx folklore of the Isle of Man in the British Isles. Although he is supposed to belong to a class of Brownie, the Fenodyree manifests in monstrous form. The Fenodyree, also known as Finnoderee, Fynnoderee, Phynnodderee, and Yn Foldyr Gastey (the "Nimble Mower"), is described as a huge hairy being that is amazingly strong and very ugly. He was said to have been one of the Ferrishyn (Manx fairy), transformed into an ugly monster as a punishment for falling in love with a human girl in the Glen of Rushen. Because of this he committed the offense of missing the appointed revels of his own kind. The Fenodyree works extremely hard at farm tasks such as the herding, mowing, reaping, and threshing, all accomplished between dusk and dawn. His only reward was the comfort of his food and drink from the farm. A grateful farmer innocently lost his services by offering, as a reward, the insult that all types of Brownies fear—a suit of new clothes.
References 24, 25, 64, 111, 152
See also giant, monster

FENRIR, FENRISWULF, FENRISÚLFR
This is the name of a gigantic evil wolf in the Norse mythology of Scandinavia. Fenrir, also known as Hrodvitnir, was the first of the monstrous progeny of the giantess Angboda from the trickster god Loki. His siblings were the terrible hell-hound Garmr and the goddess of the underworld, Hel. Fenrir is described as so huge that his upper jaw reaches the heavens and his lower jaw the earth. As the cub grew he became so destructive that when he reached full growth the gods were terrified of his strength and evil force. They conspired to bind Fenrir, but each time the beast broke loose and was even more destructive than before. However, the Dark Elves made a magic rope called Gleipnir that was fashioned from the nerves of a bear, the foot-fall of a cat, a hair from the beard of a woman, the breath of a fish, the roots of a mountain, and the spittle of a bird. Fenrir was curious about the gods' intentions and suggested that he would trust them if one of them put his hand in the wolf's jaws. Tyr volunteered, and, when the enraged wolf realized that he was bound, bit it off, but this time the magical rope held. However, with the coming of Ragnarök, Fenrir will be unleashed, Skoll will devour the sun, and the gigantic wolf will swallow the god Odin on Sleipnir and in turn be killed by Vidar.
References 7, 20, 24, 61, 78, 89, 125, 136, 139, 166, 169
See also Angrboda, Garm, giant, Midgardsormr, Skoll, Sleipnir

FER CAILLE
This is the name of a monstrous humanoid in the legends and traditions of Ireland. The Fer Caille, whose name may be translated as the "Man of the Woods," is described as being huge-looking like a man but having only one eye in his head, one hand, and one foot. He is evidently not restricted by this, since he is occupied with controlling the great herds of beasts and frequently seen carrying a huge black pig over his shoulders and followed by an extraordinarily ugly hag. It is in the *Togul Bruidne Da Derga*, the epic of the *Destruction of the Hostel of Da Derga*, that we are told of how Fer Caille waylays the hero Conaire on his way to Da Derga.
References 128
See also Direach, Fachan

FERRAGUT, FERRAGUS, FERRACUTE
This is the name of a giant in the classical literature of France. Ferragut, also known as Farracutus, is derived in part from the biblical traditions of David and Goliath. He first appears in a chronicle of the twelfth century, the *Pseudo-Turpin Chronicle*, and later in the *Chanson de Roland* as the leader of the Saracen army against whom the hero Roland does single combat for the retreating armies of Emperor Charlemagne. It is related that after this battle Ferragut was converted to Christianity. He appears also in the romance of *Valentine and Orson* as the giant of Portugal, a massive brazen head that could speak and was able to deliver the answers to anything from its omniscient intellect.
References 20, 144, 174
See also Charlemagne, giant

Fenris wolf (Fenrir) bound (Rose Photo Archive, UK)

FIERABRAS, FIEREBRAS

This is the name of a giant in the legends and the literary traditions of Europe, especially France. Fierabras, whose name in French may be translated as "Proud Arms," is the son of King Balan of Spain and is described as being of enormous stature, strength, and battle prowess. In the twelfth-century legends of Roland, Fierabras is a member of the Saracen army who does combat with Oliver, the friend of Roland, and is defeated. After the battle, Fierabras is reported to have been converted to Christianity.

In later literary works Fierabras the giant is cited in the genealogy of Pantagruel as an ancestor, by the author François Rabelais (ca. 1494–ca. 1553) in his work *Pantagruel* (1532). He is given the occupation of having been the personal servant of Emperor Nero and has a son named Morgante.

References 20, 144, 174
See also Charlemagne, giant, Morgante, Pantagruel

FILLYLOO

This is the name of a giant lizardlike monster in the legends and folklore of the Ozark Native American people of the United States. This monster was reported by V. Randolf in 1951 as having inhabited the Ozark Mountains during the nineteenth century.
References 94
See also Bingbuffer, Golligog, Gowrow, monster

FIMBRETHIL

This is the name of one of the Ents, a class of tree giants in the literary works of the English academic and author J.R.R. Tolkien (1892–1973), *The Hobbit* (1937) and *The Lord of the Rings* (1955). The Entwife of Fimbrethil, who was called Wandlimb the Lightfoot, was killed by the Orcs during the War of the Ring.
References 51
See also Ents, Entwives, giant, Wandlimb

FINGLAS

This is the name of one of the Ents, a class of tree giants in the literary works of the English academic and author J.R.R. Tolkien (1892–1973), *The Hobbit* (1937) and *The Lord of the Rings* (1955). Finglas, also known as "Leaflock," was so shocked by the devastation caused by the Orcs and the War of the Ring that he retreated into his tree-being and, unmoving, was left alone to exist as one of the trees he guarded.
References 51
See also Ents, giant

FINNODEREE

This is an alternative spelling of the Manx semisupernatural giant known as the Fenodyree in the legends and folklore of the Isle of Man in the British Isles.
References 24, 25, 64, 111, 152
See also Fenodyree

FIORGYN

This is the name of a giantess in the Norse mythology of Scandinavia. Fiorgyn, also known as Jörd, is the wife of the king of the Aesir, the god Odin. By him she is the mother of the god Thor.
References 24
See also giantess

FIR CHREIG

This is the name of the giants in the ancient folklore of the Isle of Lewis, one of the islands in the Outer Hebrides off the coast of Scotland. The Fir Chreig, which may be translated as the "False Men," were a gigantic race of people said to have inhabited the island long before the advent of Christianity. When Saint Kieran came to the island to preach the gospel, the Fir Chreig refused to build a church for him and refused baptism. The saint cursed them, and the giants turned into stones together when they next met. The resulting huge and impressive circle of standing stones has since been known as the Giants of Callanish and is thought to date from approximately 2000 B.C. This stone circle was long venerated in the Celtic calendar long after Christianity was introduced to the island and certainly into the early part of the twentieth century.
References 183
See also giant

FIRE DRAGON

This is the name of a celestial being in the creation mythology of the Huron and Iroquois Native American people of the northeastern United States. The legend relates how a young woman was desired by the "Chief of All the Earth"; her name was Ataentsic. She had to take a number of tests to prove her worthiness before she could make the journey to the heavens to be his bride. After having made the journey and stayed there some time, she grew big with child. But the Chief of All the Earth disputed that it was his and grew unreasonably suspicious of the Fire Dragon. As a result, Ataentsic and her child were cast down to earth through the clouds and, guided by the other sympathetic creatures, became the ancestors of the human race.
References 139
See also dragon

FIRE GIANTS

This is a race of giants in the Norse mythology of Scandinavia. The chief of these giants is called Surt, or Surtur. The Fire Giants come from a place of great heat called Muspelheim where dwells the great giant Muspel and his sons, the flames. It is they who will precipitate the final destruction of Ragnarök.
References 127, 139
See also giant, muspel, Sutr

FIREBIRD

This is a fabulous bird in the legends of old Russia. It was a celestial creature with feathers of pure gold and eyes of the brightest crystals. It grazed in the magnificent garden of Tzar Dalmet, but it had a fondness for the beautiful apples in the garden of Tzar Vyslav Andronovich and would steal them from time to time. This czar was envious of his neighbor's bird and resolved to take it from him and called upon his three sons, Dimitri, Ivan, and Vasili, to find a way. Eventually, Ivan, aided by a magical wolf, located and trapped the fabulous bird but was ambushed and killed by his jealous brothers. Dimitri and Vasili then brought back the Firebird to their father. Unbeknown to them, the Firebird had actually been won fairly by Ivan's completing a task for Czar Dalmut, and when the magical wolf restored the prince to life he exposed the would-be murderers. Ivan kept the Firebird, and his brothers were thrown in jail for their conspiracy to murder him.

In another traditional tale, the Tzar of all the Russias was presented with a feather from the tail of the Firebird, by one of the Bogatyrs. Instead of being content, the Tzar demanded that the warrior bring the bird itself. In terror, the warrior despaired of this task, for the Firebird was vast and notoriously aggressive. He managed to trap the bird by strewing maize in a huge field and hiding in a tree until the bird swooped down. Then his magic horse pranced nearer and nearer to the fabulous Firebird until it pranced onto the huge glowing outstretched wings and fastened the bird to the earth. The Firebird was then bound with strong ropes and taken to the Tzar.

His magic horse pranced nearer to the fabulous Firebird until it pranced onto the outstretched wings and fastened the bird to the earth (A Staircase of Stories edited by L. Chisholm and A. Steedman, Thomas Nelson, UK)

References 42, 55
See also Feng Hwang, Phoenix

FIRE-DRAKE
There are two types of being with this name, as follows:

1. This is a species of dragon in the Celtic and Teutonic legends of Europe. They are described as great fire-breathing, flying dragons that may inhabit the wetlands and fens of the British Isles, or the deep caverns of the mountains of northern Europe. Whatever their abode, their main task is that of treasure-guardian, and they are fearsome adversaries. It is against the Fire-Drake that the hero Beowulf, in the eighth-century English epic of that name, does his final battle.

2. This is a species of dragon called the Urulóki in the literary works of the English academic and author J.R.R. Tolkien (1892–1973), *The Hobbit* (1937) and *The Lord of the Rings* (1955). The monstrous creatures are bred by the evil Morgoth and, like their legendary counterparts, flew across the sky on batlike wings, breathing destructive fire on all beneath. The most dreadful of these were Ancalagon the Black, the Dragon of Erebor named Smaug, and Glaurung.
References 7, 20, 24, 51, 89, 160
See also Ancalagon the Black, dragon, Glaurung, Smaug, Urulóki

FISH KINGS
See king of the fishes

FLAMING TEETH
This is the name of a monstrous giant in the legends and folklore of the people of Fiji. Flaming Teeth was a fierce cannibal giant who was described as being of immense size. But the most horrific aspect of this monster was his teeth, which were vast, burning pinnacles in his mouth. He hunted down all the human beings in the region; no matter where they might hide they were not safe, and the people lived in terror. Eventually, all the men gathered together and by a ruse managed to get Flaming Teeth to run beneath a great rock, which they heaved upon his head. Before the giant was cold, everyone from the village brought sticks and set them alight from the giant's teeth, so now the Fijians have fires for their needs.
References 113
See also giant

FLANDRIF
This is the name of one of the Ents, a class of tree giants in the literary works of the English academic and author J.R.R. Tolkien (1892–1973), *The Hobbit* (1937) and *The Lord of the Rings* (1955). Flandrif, also

known as "Skin Bark," was enraged by the devastation caused by the Orcs and battled with them to try to save his Entings and prevent the capture of his birch groves. However, he was so badly hurt during the War of the Ring that he retreated into his tree-being and fled alone to exist as one of the trees near the tree line on the mountains.

References 51
See also Ents, giant

FLYING FISH

This was the descriptive name given to a sea monster caught off the coast of northeastern Italy during the sixteenth century. This creature was reported to have been landed about three miles above a place called Quioze between the cities of Ravenna and Venice in the lagoons. It was described as a huge creature about five feet in length and breadth with a huge head having eyes one on top of the other, with ears and two mouths under a protruding snout. It had holes for breathing on its throat and had vast wings on its body

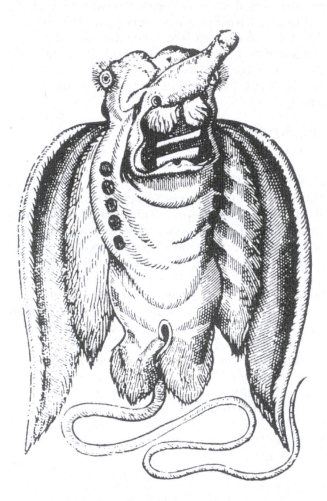

Flying fish, a sea monster caught off the coast of northeastern Italy during the sixteenth century (On Monsters and Marvels by Ambroise Paré, trans. by Janis L. Pallister, University of Chicago Press, 1982)

above an enormously long tail that also had wings. The creature was green and, when reported by the writer Ambroise Paré (1517–1590), was said to have inspired much terror in the court where it was taken. It is suggested that this "monster" may have been a species of cow-nosed ray that had been caught.

References 89
See also monster

FLYING HEADS

This is the name of a class of monsters in the legends and folklore of the Iroquois Native American people in the northeastern United States. They were described as vast ugly heads with huge fiery eyes, rows of enormous sharply pointed fangs that closed like a prison door, straggly hair, and huge wings instead of ears. The Flying Heads fly through the stormy skies, sustained aloft by their hair in the tempests, while they search for unwary humans. This voracious monster preyed on the villagers and their herds alike, swooping down at night and devouring whatever it landed on. Nothing could escape once the jaws had snapped shut, that is, until an elderly woman conceived a plan to defeat it. She carefully built a glowing fire with wood and red-hot coals upon which to roast some chestnuts for her evening meal. As she brought them from the fire, the shell fell off and she ate each delicious chestnut with loud approval. Soon the Flying Head descended and scooped up all the chestnuts in the fire along with the red-hot stones. Like all such monsters, it was not blessed with intellect, and once its jaws had closed the fire stones with the chestnuts could not be released and the Flying Head was burned to death from inside its own mouth.

References 38, 133, 139
See also Pontianak

FOAWR

This is the name of a class of giants in the Manx legends and folklore of the Isle of Man in the British Isles. They are described as huge lumbering humanoids who steal cattle but apparently do not molest humans. The Foawr may possibly have been derived from the Fomorians described in the Irish *Lebor Gabàla*, which is *The Book of Invasions*.

References 128
See also Fomor, giant

FOMOR/S, FOMORIANS, FOMOIRE, FOMÓIRI, FOMHÓRAIGH, FOMHOIRE, FOMHÓIRE, FOMORII, FOMORÉ, FO-MUIR

In the Celtic folklore and legend of Ireland, this race was deemed to be the original people of the land. They were defeated and transformed into grotesque supernatural monsters by the invading Firbolgs, who were themselves defeated by the Tuatha Dé Danann. The Fomorians are described in the Irish texts known as the *Lebor Gabàla* (*The Book of Invasions*), and the *Cath Maige Tuired* (*The* [Second] *Battle of Mag Tured*). Their leader was the hideous Cichol. They became monstrous humanoids described as having human bodies but the head of either a goat or a horse and only one eye, arm, and leg each. This did nothing to restrict their evil, and they demanded tribute in kind from everyone within their domain. If cattle were not forthcoming, then they would descend and take humans instead until the two-thirds demand had been met. If there was any opposition, then they would destroy the face of the resister by slicing the nose off. After the coming of Christianity to Ireland, these monsters were equated with the biblical giants and then demonized. The Fomorians were often later identified in folklore as weather spirits associated with storms, fog, and blighted crops.

References 7, 24, 78, 120, 125, 128, 142, 160
See also Cichol, Fachan, Foawr, giant, monster

FORNEUS

This is the name of a monstrous being described in the medieval European texts associated with necromancy and demonology. It is alternatively described as a monster from the depths of the sea or a demon from hell. The name and description may have been a corruption of the Fornjotr.

References 125
See also Fornjotr, monster

FORNJOTR

This is the name of a primordial giant in the Teutonic and Norse myths of northern Europe. He is described as the immense being from whom the Frost Giants and, according to some sources, the giantess Hler, and the giants Logi and Kari, were descended.

References 125
See also Frost Giants, giant

FRACASSUS

This is the name of a giant in the late medieval literature of Italy. Fracassus is a grotesque giant who appears in the comic work of the Benedictine Teofilo Folengo (1491–1554) writing under the pseudonym of Merlinus Coccaius. In the comic romance *Baldus*, Fracassus is described as the descendant of the giant Morgante, which implies the lack of most uncouth properties of the folkloric giants.

References 174
See also giant, Morgante

FRANKENSTEIN'S MONSTER

This is the name of a monster in the classic literature of England. Frankenstein's Monster was a character in the novel *Frankenstein* (1818) by Mary Wollstonecraft Shelley (1797–1851). The idea for the novel was apparently the result of a nightmare, which Mary Shelley wrote down as her contribution to a competition proposed during a moment of ennui while she was vacationing in Switzerland with the poets Shelley and Byron and their friend Dr. Polidori. The story tells of the creation of a humanoid by a medical student from human corpses. This being, who never receives a name, is animated electrically and from that time after, querying his own existence, sets about destroying others to avenge himself on his maker. Frankenstein ultimately dies during his quest to destroy the creature he created.

Within the novel are the "modern" innovations of electricity and medical developments that raised issues with contemporaries, certainly concerning the ethics of dissection and anatomical studies engendering the trade of "body-snatching." There was already the well-known Jewish legend of the Golem when this tale was written, which also incorporates many of the moral issues that are still current.

References 20, 78, 94, 182
See also Golem, monster

FREKI

This is the name of a monstrous supernatural wolf in the Norse mythology of Scandinavia.

References 7
See also Geri and Freki

FREYBUG

This is the name of a monster in the medieval traditions and folklore of England. It took the form of a monstrous black dog that patrolled the country lanes at night terrifying late travelers and making them flee in horror. It is mentioned in an English manuscript of 1555.

References 160
See also Black dog, monster

FROST GIANTS

This is a class of primordial giant also known as the Hrimthurses, or Thurses, in the Norse mythology of Scandinavia. These immense beings were derived from and inhabited the land of frost, ice, and snow, where it was permanently winter. The most well known of these were Vasty, Hymir, Hrungnir, Bergelmir, and their leader and giant-king, Thrymir. They were the constant adversaries of the god Thor and were always trying to abduct the goddess Freya. They take a prominent part in the final battle of Ragnarök.

References 47, 78, 127
See also Bergelmir, giant, Hrimthurses, Hrungnir, Hymir, Thrym, Vasty

FROSTI

This is the name of a giant in the Norse mythology of Scandinavia. Frosti, whose name may be translated as "Cold," is one of the Hrimthurses, or Frost Giants. He is the son of Thrym, and the sibling of Drifta, Johul and Snoer.

References 24
See also Frost Giants, giant, Hrimthurses

FSTI CAPCAKI

This is the name of a giant in the traditions and beliefs of the Seminole Native American people of Oklahoma in the United States. Fsti capcaki, also known as Tall Man, is described as a monstrous hairy grey humanoid that carries tree trunks as his weapons. In order to get his clubs, Fsti capcaki is so strong that he can rip the limbs from the trees, which die as a result. It is therefore easy to see where Fsti capcaki is—by the dead trees—and avoid the area.

References 77
See also Bigfoot, giant, Yeti

FUATH, FUATHAN (pl.) FUATHS (pl.), FUATH-ARRACHD

This is a general term for a group of monstrous manifestations of an evil being associated with water in the Gaelic folklore of Scotland. The Fuaths are sometimes known by the names Arrachd, or Fuath-Arrachd. They are described as being a hideously deformed human shape often covered in shaggy yellow hair, having a head with no nose, and webbed feet on the end of legs protruding from a green robe, from which emerged a long spiky tail. They are full of malice and evil intent toward human beings but are rarely seen because of the remote terrain that they normally inhabit on the edges of lochs, seashores, and remote rivers. The following also belong to the same class of Fuaths: Beithir, Brollachan, Caoineag, Cuachag, Fachan, Fideal, Glaistig, Peallaidh, Shellycoat, Urisk, and Vough.

References 7, 21, 24, 78, 128, 134
See also Beithir, Fachan, Glaistig, Peallaidh, Urisk

FU-HSI

This is the name of an emperor of China during the period of the mythical third age. Fu-Hsi (2852–2738 B.C.) was described as having the lower body of a serpent but the head and torso of a human. However, he is sometimes portrayed as having the head of a bull with horns emerging directly from his forehead. His empress, Nu-Kwa, was also similarly portrayed as having a human upper body and serpent below the waist. They are usually depicted together entwined while holding symbols of architecture and the arts, emphasizing their gift of these to humanity.

References 89
See also Cecrops, Nu-Kwa, serpent, Shen-Nung

FUM HWANG

This is an alternative name for the Phoenix in the legends and folklore of China. It is more ususally known as the Feng Hwang.

References 81
See also Feng Hwang, Phoenix

FUNG, FUNG HWANG

This is the name of a fabulous bird in the traditions and legends of China. It is a form of the Lwan and is described as looking something like a much larger and more beautiful and graceful type of pheasant. These are alternative types of the Oriental Phoenix in the legends and folklore of China. It is more usually known as the Feng Hwang. However, this bird is capable of changing its body color and is known by different names accordingly. As the Fung, or Fung Hwang, it is red on its head and wings and is regarded as a form of the Lwan.

References 81
See also Feng Hwang, Lwan, Phoenix

FURIES

This is the collective name given to the avenging monstrous supernaturals in the classical mythology of Rome. The Furies, whose name means the "Angry Ones," were also known as the Dirae. But in Greek mythology they were known as the Erinyes, Eumenides, or Semnai. These spirits have been given various origins: as the daughters of the gods of the Earth, or the Night, the daughters of Night and Tartarus, or generated from the blood dropped from the castration of Uranus. In this respect they are the terrible siblings of the Hundred-Handed Giants, the goddess Aphrodite, and the future Olympic gods. They are sisters whose names are Alecto, Tisiphone, and Magæra, described variously as being snake-haired, stinking, human-shaped hags that may have bats' wings or the head of a dog. They avenge the unpunished wrongs committed by humans with horrible zeal to exact revenge even after death. In this respect they were so dreaded that they were only referred to by the euphemisms of Eumenides and Semnai.

References 20, 74, 78, 133, 146, 160, 178, 182
See also Alecto, Dirae, Erinyes, giant, Hundred-Handed Giants, Magæra, Tisiphone

FU-TS'ANG

This is the name of a dragon in the legends and folklore of China. Fu-ts'ang, also known as the Dragon of the Hidden Treasures, as his name

suggests, is the guardian of all the mineral wealth that exists under the earth.
References 89
See also dragon, Oriental Dragon.

FYNNODEREE
This is an alternative spelling of the Manx semisupernatural giant known as the Fenodyree in the legends and folklore of the Isle of Man in the British Isles.
References 24, 25, 64, 111, 152
See also Fenodyree

G

GÆA

This is an alternative name for the primordial giantess Gaia in the classical mythology of Greece and Rome.
References 38, 47, 125, 139
See also Gaia

GAASYENDIETHA

This is the name of an enormous dragon in the beliefs and legends of the Seneca Native American people in the northeastern United States. Gaasyendietha is described as a dragon that is capable of shooting fire as well as crossing the heaven on a trail of fire. In this respect it is also known as a meteor-fire dragon. But although associated with fire, Gaasyendietha inhabits deep pools in the local rivers and lakes.
References 77
See also dragon

GABBARA

This is the name of a giant in the classical literature of France. Gabbara is one of the giant ancestors of Pantagruel in the famous work *Pantagruel* (1532) by the French author François Rabelais (ca. 1494–ca. 1553). But Gabbara does not appear in the original edition; he is an addition to later versions by Rabelais, as a means of establishing the genealogy of Pantagruel. Gabbara, along with five other giants—Etion, Eryx, Galehaut, Happemousche, and Morguan—is credited with inventing something concerned with drinking.
References 174
See also Bruyer, Chalbroth, Daughters of Cain, Galehaut, Gargantua, giant, Happemousche, Hurtaly, Morguan, Noachids, Noah, Offotus, Pantagruel

GABORCHEND, GABORCHIND (pl.)

This is the name of a race of humanoid monsters in the legends of Ireland. The Gaborchind, said to be the most primitive inhabitants of the land of Ireland, were described as having human-shaped bodies with heads resembling those of a dog or a goat.
References 128
See also Coinchenn, Cynocephali

GA-GORIB

This is the name of a gigantic malicious being in the legends and beliefs of the Khoisin people of South Africa. This monster would not let any human pass by unless they performed the challenge of throwing a stone at him on the edge of the pit to make him fall in. What the reluctant travelers did not know was that the stone would boomerang and instead cast the thrower into the pit. Thus Ga-gorib disposed of everyone who attempted to cross his territory. However, the hero Heitsi-Ebib, who had a special magical birth, passed through the territory and was similarly challenged. He refused to rise to the challenge and engaged the monstrous Ga-gorib in distracting chatter and then quickly threw his stone. The challenger was caught off guard and tumbled into his own pit.
References 78
See also monster

GAIA

This is the name of a vast primordial giantess in the classical mythology of Greece and Rome. Gaia, also known as Ge and Gæa, was depicted as a gigantic female being. She was the mother figure who produced Pontus and Uranus and by him the giant races of the Titans, the Cyclopes, the Hecatoncheires (Hundred-Handed Giants), and the Furies. From the depths of Tartarus she produced the monstrous Typhon, and by Pontus she produced Nereus, Phorcys, and Thaumus.
References 38, 47, 125, 139
See also Cyclopes, Furies, giant, Hecatoncheires, Titans, Typhon, Uranus

GAKI

This is a type of Oni or demonic monster in the legends and beliefs of Japan. The Gaki take a somewhat human shape, but their huge-bellied bodies are red or green, having the head of either a horse or an ox with three eyes and grotesque horns and talons. They are tortured incessantly by raging hunger and thirst. These monsters pounce upon the souls of the wicked who are about to die and convey them to the torments of Hell. Gaki may be driven out at the Shinto Oni-yarahi ceremony, and some may lose their malicious character by being converted to Buddhism.

References 47, 78, 139, 160, 166
See also Amermait, Ma Mien

GALATEA, GALATHEA

This is the name of a giantess in the pseudohistorical genealogy of Charlemagne, king of the Franks, in the traditions and literature of France. The Babylonian priest Borosus (third century B.C.) wrote several books on the history of the Babylonians, including an account of the hero, Hercules Libyus's destruction of the giants of Asia Minor. He then detailed Hercules Libyus's voyage to Italy to remove, in similar fashion, the tyrannical giants oppressing that land. However, an episode of romance was related between the hero and the giantess daughter of the giant Celtes, resulting in the birth of Galathes. In the pseudohistory written by Jean Le Maire de Belges (ca. 1473–1524) for the duke of Bourbon, this genealogy is incorporated into the ancestry of Emperor Charlemagne in order to justify a dynastic derivation of monumentally heroic proportions.

References 174
See also Celtes, Charlemagne, Galathes, giant, Hercules Libyus

GALATHES

This is the name of the giant son of Galatea in the pseudohistory of Hercules Libyus written by Borosus (third century B.C.), a Babylonian priest who wrote several books on the history of the Babylonians. However, an episode of romance was related between the hero and the giantess daughter of the giant Celtes, resulting in the birth of Galathes. In the pseudohistory written by Jean Le Maire de Belges (ca. 1473–1524) for the duke of Bourbon, this genealogy is incorporated into the ancestry of Emperor Charlemagne, and the giant Galathes was thus incorporated into the pseudodynasty of the French monarchy.

References 174
See also Celtes, Charlemagne, Galatea, giant, Hercules Libyus

GALEHAUT

This is the name of a giant in the classical literature of France. Galehaut is one of the giant ancestors of Pantagruel in the famous work *Pantagruel* (1532) by the French author François Rabelais (ca. 1494–ca. 1553). But Galehaut does not appear in the original edition; he is an addition to later versions by Rabelais,

as a means of establishing the genealogy of Pantagruel. Galehaut, along with five other giants—Etion, Gabbara, Eryx, Happemousche, and Morguan—is credited with inventing something concerned with drinking.

References 174
See also Bruyer, Chalbroth, Daughters of Cain, Enay, Eryx, Etion, Gabbara, Gargantua, Gayoffe, giant, Happemousche, Hurtaly, Morguan, Noachids, Noah, Pantagruel

GALEMELLE

This is the name of a giantess in the classical literature of France. She is given as the mother of the giant Gargantua by the author François Rabelais (ca. 1494–ca. 1553) in his work *Gargantua* (1534). Her consort and the father of Gargantua is given as Grant-Gosier, and both were supposed to have come from the Oriental Mountains. Galemelle was said to have been engendered by the wizard Merlin from the nail parings of the Queen Guinevere and the bones of a cow whale. In the best rock-building traditions of giants, the two are said to be responsible for the building of Tombelaine and Mont Saint Michel. Galemelle died of joy in Brittany when she saw the return of her son Gargantua victorious from the Battle of the Gué de Vède; she was buried there by Merlin on his way to the court of King Arthur.

References 54, 174
See also Gargantua, giant, giantess, Grant-Gosier

GALERU

This is an alternative name for the great Rainbow Snake, also known as Kaleru, in the legends of the Kimberley region of Australia.

References 166
See also Rainbow Serpent, serpent, Ungud

GALLEY-TROT

This is the name of a type of bogie or demonic road monster in the folklore of Suffolk, England. The Galley-trot, also known as the Gilitrutt, takes the form of a large, white, shaggy dog, about the size of a bullock. Like the Shuck and the Black dog–type of demonic road monster, it would silently appear beside humans on lonely roads, engulfing or harassing them. It particularly haunted the area of Woodbridge and Dunwich, as well as a bog called Bathslough, from which it would emerge to chase passing travelers.

References 24, 96, 160, 170
See also Black dogs, Galley-beggar

GALOKWUDZUWIS

This is the name of the monstrous cannibal-bird wife of Bakbakwakanooksiwae in the folklore and beliefs of the Kwakiutl people of northern Canada. She manifests as the Crooked Beak of Heaven and is depicted with a crooked protuberance on her massive beak. She accompanies her husband while they hunt their human victims.

References 77
See also Bakbakwakanooksiwae

GALON

This is an alternative name for the fabulous bird known as the Garuda in the mythology and folk beliefs of Thailand.

References 7
See also Garuda

GAMBIER

This is the name of a giantess in the legends of the Native Australians in the State of Victoria, Australia. She was a vast being that lived in the southernmost mountains, where she gave life to a son named Woo. But Woo was not the vast immobile immortal like his mother; he was so swift that he flew to other parts, where he became corrupted and wicked. The giantess Gambier heard of the wickedness of her only son, and little by little she sank into despair, with a constant stream of tears flowing down her sides. Many years passed and Woo, tiring of his lifestyle, returned to the foot of the mountain home of his mother. He implored her to forgive him and help him, but her sorrow had worn her into a petrified ridged entity surmounting the peaks. She could do nothing but gaze down on her distraught son, who sank to his knees and sobbed till he too died of a broken heart.

References 153
See also giantess

GAMBRIVIUS

This is the name of a giant who appeared in the medieval work *Officina* by the erudite Jean Tixier de Ravisy (alias Ravisius Textor, ca. 1480–1524), who proposed that Tuyscon Gigas was actually a son of the giant Noah whose progeny were the ancestors of European nobility. He constructed a line of giant descendants, Gambrivius being one of many legendary figures.

References 174
See also giant, Noah, Tuyscon Gigas

GANDAREVA

This is the name of a gigantic monster in the Sumerian mythology of ancient Mesopotamia. Gandareva, also known by the name Kundrav, was a being that resembled a dragon but was so immense that while its upper parts were in the skies its lower body was resting in the ocean. It was the destroyer of the land and preyed upon humans as its source of

Gandareva, an immense being that resembled a dragon (Rose Photo Archive, UK)

food, but he was the guardian of another, more dangerous dragon. Gandareva, however, was defied by the hero Keresapa, who was determined to destroy the monster, and a series of horrific battles ensued. In these battles the monster seemed at first to have the upper hand. It killed fifteen horses from under the hero, made him blind, threw him into the scrubland, and abducted his wife and children. But the hero recovered and reversed the battle fortunes; ultimately Gandareva was destroyed and the family rescued.

A survival of this legend is in the name of the Hindu horse of the sun, Gandarva.

References 7

See also dragon, Gandarva, Horses of the Sun, monster

GANDARVA

This is the name of a fabulous horse in the Vedic mythology of India. It is one of the horses of the sun that pull the chariot of the sun god across the sky each day. The name is derived from the Sumerian mythological being known as Gandareva, the sky dragon defeated by the hero Keresapa.

References 7

See also dragon, Gandareva, Horses of the Sun

GANDHABBAS

This is an alternative Pali name for the Gandharvas in the Hindu mythology of India.

References 7, 24, 160

See also Gandharvas

GANDHARVAS

In the classical mythology of India, these semisupernatural beings, also known by the Pali name of Gandhabbas, inhabit the air, forests, and mountains. They are described variously as being shaggy, half-animal hybrids, very similar in form to the centaurs of classical Greek mythology, with the head of a human and a horse's body. But they could also appear as fragrant, richly clothed warriors. The Gandharvas are the companions of the Apsaras and renowned for their beautiful music in the heavens, as entertainers to the gods. They are also the keepers of the celestial wine known as soma and are devolvers of medical knowledge to humans. Their leaders are Chitra-ratha, Visvavasu, and Tumburu, and they lived in fabulous palaces that appeared sometimes on the cloudless horizon like a mirage. They could also be vindictive and made war on the Nagas until the god Vishnu intervened.

References 7, 24, 38, 112, 125, 133, 139, 156, 160, 161

See also centaur, Chitra-ratha, Kinnara

GANIAGWAIHEGOWA

This is the name of a cannibal monster in the legends and folk belief of the Seneca Native American people of the northeastern United States. The Ganiagwaihegowa is described as looking something like a bear but without fur; he is a predatory monster who terrorized the community, stealing and devouring any vulnerable member alone in the forest. Two prominent members of the Seneca tribe named Hadentheni (the Speaker) and Hanigongendatha (the Interpreter) were determined to destroy the monster. So they consulted with a spirit being, Gadjiqsa, who told them first that Ganiagwaihegowa was immortal

except for the soles of his feet and second that he could be duped by representations of humans that would equally excite his greed. So the two heroes traveled to the underworld domain of Ganiagwaihegowa and placed brasswood effigies of men before their lodge. Sure enough, the excited monster came to pounce on what he thought was more vulnerable prey. In the ensuing fight, the heroes managed to shoot the monster through the soles of his feet and cut them off. The rest of the body they destroyed with fire to ensure that Ganiagwaihegowa would never again terrorize their community.

References 77

See also monster

GANJ

This is the name of a dragon in the legends and folklore of Persia (now Iran). The Ganj is a monstrous guardian of a hoard of treasure and preious stones, one of which is lodged in its forehead.

References 63

See also dragon

GA-OH

This is the name of a giant in the traditions and beliefs of the Iroquois Native American people of the United States. Ga-oh is depicted as a vast giant who controls the winds of the four directions. In some versions of the legends he is described as a cannibal giant of a violent nature who destroys the landscape and the vegetation. In other versions he is benevolent and has been described as a gentle spirit.

References 38, 139, 166

See also cannibal, giant

GARA

This is the name in the Bengali language of India, for the Nyan a monstrous serpentine creature in the traditions and legends of Burma and India.

References 81

See also Nyan

GARGAM

This is the name of a giant in the Celtic legends of Brittany in northwestern France. The name "Gargam" in the Breton language may be translated as "Curved High," which would indicate Gargam's immense proportions. He has also been given the nickname "Boiteux," meaning "Lame"; he was said to go about mainly at night, possibly to hide his limp. Gargam is one of the many giants possibly used as a source for the giant Gargantua by the author François Rabelais (ca. 1494–ca. 1553) in his work *Pantagruel* (1532) and later in *Gargantua* (1534).

References 128

See also Gargantua, giant, Gwrgwnt, Pantagruel

GARGAMELLE

This is the alternative name of the giantess Galemelle in the classical literature of France. She is given as the mother of the giant Gargantua by the author François Rabelais (ca. 1494–ca. 1553) in his work *Gargantua* (1534). Her consort and the father of Gargantua is given as the giant Grant-Gosier.
References 174
See also Galemelle, giantess

GARGANTUA

This is the name of a giant in the classical literature of France. Gargantua is one of the characters described by the author François Rabelais (ca. 1494–ca. 1553) in his work *Pantagruel* (1532) and later in *Gargantua* (1534). He is the offspring of the giants Grant-Gosier and Galemelle, engendered on the whim of Merlin from bull and cow whale bones and nail parings of Guinevere. Gargantua, when fully grown, went to the court of King Arthur as a slayer of giants. He disposed of Gos et Magos but found himself challenged by many other giants, whom he defeated in almost a parody of Geoffrey of Monmouth's account of the English Corineus. He is described as a vast being whose insatiable appetite has brought the word "gargantuan" into the English language. His mouth was so enormous that even armies could fall into it when he snored in his sleep. When he took prisoners, he secured them in a hollow of one of his teeth, in which there was also a tennis court. Rabelais makes him the father of Pantagruel. He is derived most probably from many giants in the Celtic folk beliefs, but Rabelais also referred to chapbook legends that had been well known for centuries before and retold in the *Grandes Chroniques*. Gargantua has now become a Town Giant representative of Bailleul in the Nord Pas de Calais region of France.
References 20, 54, 174
See also Corineus, Galemelle, giant, Gos et Magos, Grant-Gosier, Pantagruel, Town Giants

GARGITTIOS

This is the name of one of Geryon's Dogs in the classical mythology of Greece and Rome.
References 20
See also Geryon, Geryon's Dogs

GARGOUILLE, GARGOYLE

This is the name of a dragon in the legends and folklore of northeastern France. It was a monstrous beast that inhabited the marshes of the River Seine in the surrounding countryside about the town of Rouen. This dragon would harry the fishermen by creating great disturbances and waterspouts in the water, upsetting the boats and devouring the men. At other times the beast would take the cattle and the people from the marshes to consume them in the water. Many people had thus perished when, during the seventh century, Saint Romain, the bishop of Rouen, decided enough was enough. He took two condemned criminals to the edge of the marshes, where they were tied to a stake to attract the monster. When the Gargouille appeared, the saint transfixed the beast with the cross, wrapped his clerical stole about its neck, and led it back to Rouen, completely cowed like a dog on a leash, where it was killed by the citizens. From that day the waterspouts that direct the rainwater from the roof of a church building through the mouth of a monster are called gargoyles.
References 7, 20, 57, 89
See also dragon, monster

GARM, GARMR

This is the name of a monstrous dog in the Norse mythology of Scandinavia. Garm is the hound of hell described as a vast, four-eyed, blood-spattered beast that inhabits the cavern of Gripa at the gates to Niflheim. There he stands guard, allowing none out and snarling at those whose miserliness in life prevented them from being kind to the poor. Garm will howl to all at the beginning of Ragnarök and at the end of the battle, when only he and the one-handed god Tyr are left; each will be slaughtered by the other.
References 18, 24, 61, 89, 125, 139
See also Cerberus, Fenrir

GARUDA, GARUDA BIRD

This is the name of a fabulous bird in the Hindu and Buddhist mythologies of India and other Eastern countries with these traditions, especially Indonesia. Garuda, also known as Taraswin, meaning the "Swift One," is variously described as having the body of an eagle that may be gold, green, or red; four human arms; and wings that are golden or scarlet. He has the head of a bird with a human face that may be gold or white. Garuda was hatched from an egg over a period of 500 years, although it is also said that Garuda is the son of Kasyapa and Vinata. When his mother was enslaved by his father's second wife, a Nagini, Garuda undertook to steal the Amrita from the gods as her ransom. After this his hatred for the Nagas knew no bounds, and he became the sworn enemy of these snake beings. Garuda met with the god Vishnu and became the celestial steed of the god. Garuda is not only the symbol of many nobles and royalty in southeastern Asia but also the heraldic symbol of the Indonesian Garuda Airlines.
References 7, 18, 24, 47, 61, 78, 89, 113, 125, 133, 166
See also Alkonost, Angka, Garuda, Harpy, Khrut, Naga, Parthenope, Podarge, Ptitsy-Siriny, Simurgh, Siren, Sirin, Solovei Rakhmatich, Unnati, Zägh

GATHER-ON-THE-WATER

This is the name of a cannibal in the traditions and folktales of the Tsimshian Native American people of the United States. Gather-on-the-Water was taken by his father during the ceremony of the Cannibal Dancers and left in their keeping. He was placed in the high branches of a tree overlooking the dancing. But instead of learning the dance, he was taken over by one of the cannibal beings and forced to eat a child of the village, whom they had killed, under threat of his own death. From that time the tree became his abode and the people of the village his meat. This monstrous metamorphosis was accompanied by the powers of the cannibal beings, for he had become one of them. The terrified villagers banded together to catch him; although they caught him eventually, nothing would kill him or diminish his power. Soon he escaped and killed periodically, but he no longer ate his victims.
References 77
See also cannibal

GAYANT

This is the name of a giant in the legends and folklore of Belgium. It is apparently a giant that inhabited the region around Douai and is now that town's representative in effigy. Gayant has been presented as the Town Giant according to some evidence since 1530, but the name was not regularized and documented reliably until 1781.
References 174
See also giant, Town Giant

GAYOFFE

This is the name of a giant in the classical literature of France. Gayoffe was one of the giant ancestors of Pantagruel in the famous work *Pantagruel* (1532) by the French author François Rabelais (ca. 1494–ca. 1553). But Gayoffe does not appear in the original edition; he is an addition to later versions by Rabelais, as a means of establishing the genealogy of Pantagruel. Eryx, along with five other giants—Etion, Gabbara, Galehaut, Happemousche, and Morguan—is credited with inventing something concerned with drinking, while Gayoffe and Enay are simply additions.
References 174
See also Bruyer, Chalbroth, Daughters of Cain, Enay, Eryx, Etion, Gabbara, Gargantua, giant, Happemousche, Hurtaly, Morguan, Noachids, Noah, Pantagruel

GE

This is an alternative for the name of the primordial giantess Gaia in the classical mythology of Greece and Rome.

References 38, 47, 125, 139
See also Gaia

GEGENEIS

This is the alternative name for the giants otherwise known as the Gigantes in the classical mythology of Greece and Rome. The name Gegeneis may be translated as "Earth-born," from the fact that they were generated from the blood spilled on the earth when Cronus castrated Uranus.
References 24, 133, 169, 178
See also Cronus, Gaia, Gigantes, Uranus

GEIRRÖD, GEIROD

This is the name of a giant in the Norse mythology of Scandinavia. He had two daughters, Gjalp and Greip. During one of the escapades of the trickster god Loki, who was flying in the shape of a bird, Geirröd caught him and kept him without food in a cage until he confessed who he was. The giant extracted the promise that Loki would deliver the god Thor to him without his hammer, gloves, and girdle. Without this power, the giant thought he would kill Thor to avenge the death of Hrungnir. However, while Loki was bringing Thor to the giant, they met the giantess Grid, who lent him her iron gloves, unbreakable staff, and belt of strength. While they were attempting to cross a river, the floodwaters suddenly rose, threatening to engulf them, until Thor realized that the menstruating giant's daughter Gjalp had been told to stand in the river. Thor threw a huge rock to stop up her vagina and allow them to reach safety. When they reached the abode of Geirröd, they were given an iron hut to sleep in. Suddenly the chair he was sitting in was being heaved up to the iron roof, and he might have been crushed to death if he hadn't used Grid's unbreakable staff to prop between the floor and the ceiling. However, he soon found out the source of the problem, for a loud crack and sudden descent to the floor revealed the two dead daughters of the giant. They had been heaving the floor up to kill him but had broken their own backs. The next day Thor was attacked by Geirröd, who threw a huge piece of white-hot iron at him from the fire. But Thor caught it in Grid's iron gloves and flung it back, striking straight through the pillar supporting the building and through the stomach of the giant. The whole edifice came crashing down on the dead giant, and Thor killed off any of Geirröd's men that might have survived.
References 133, 139, 166
See also giant, giantess, Grid, Hrungnir

GELDEGWSETS

This is the name of a race of giants in the traditions and folklore of the Coos Native American people in

western Oregon in the United States. These giants lived by the rivers, where they existed on a diet of fish. They coexisted peacefully as neighbors with humans.
References 77
See also giant

GEMMAGOG

This is the name of a giant in the literature of France. He is cited in the genealogy of Pantagruel as an ancestor by the author François Rabelais (ca. 1494–ca. 1553) in his work *Pantagruel* (1532). Gemmagog is credited with the "invention" of the pointed style in the toes of shoes current at the period. It is not too difficult to conjecture that Rabelais's giant's name derived in great part from that of Gog and Magog of biblical fame, or the Gogmagog of the British and Breton Celtic legends.
References 174
See also Bruyer, Chalbroth, Daughters of Cain, Etion, Gabbara, Galehaut, Gargantua, giant, Gog and Magog, Gogmagog, Happemousche, Hurtaly, Morguan, Noachids, Noah, Pantagruel

GERD, GERDA, GERDAR, GERDR

This is the name of a giantess in the Norse mythology of Scandinavia. Gerd was the daughter of the giantess Angboda and Gimir, the Frost Giant. She was a fair and comely woman whose beauty attracted many suitors, among them the god Freyr. He was so despairing of being able to win her that he sent Skirnir, his servant, to persuade her to meet him and would give Skirnir his magic sword if he succeeded. At first Skirnir tried gentle wooing words that she rejected, but she agreed when he tricked her with some runes.
References 20, 24, 61, 139
See also Angur-boda, Frost Giants, giant, giantess, Gymir, Jotun

GERGASI (sing.), GERGASIS (pl.)

This is the name of a giant in the traditions and folklore of the people of the islands of Indonesia. Gergasi is a cannibal giant; he hunts and tracks down any human that strays into his territory so that he can kill and devour them. Once he has his grip on anyone there is no escape, for his strength is prodigious. However, a hero managed to steal the powerful spear with which Gergasi killed his victims and used it to kill the enemies of his people.
References 113
See also Bungisngis, giant

GERI AND FREKI

These are the names of two enormous wolves or wolfhounds in the Norse mythology of Scandinavia.

Geri, whose name means the "Ravener," and Freki, whose name means the "Glutton," are the monstrous hounds of the king of the Aesir gods, Odin.
References 7

GERJIS

This is the name of a ferocious monster in the legends and folktales of the people of West Malaysia. The Gerjis is described as being an enormous beast that looked something like a tiger, but it preyed upon every living thing. Nothing was safe from this vast predator, and neither man nor beast could cross its territory and survive. The animals of the jungle were very soon depleted, and the remaining ones gathered together to discuss their fate. They knew that only some plot could save them, so while they dug a pit, Kanchil the Mousedeer was elected to persuade the monster to get in it. Kanchil achieved this by convincing Gerjis that the sky was about to fall in on them all and offered to help save him in a special dug-out area. When they duly arrived at the pit and Gerjis jumped in, Kanchil threw the earth back over him, then the elephant threw a tree on top and crushed Gerjis's skull.
References 113
See also monster

GERYON

This is the name of a gigantic monster in the classical mythology of Greece and Rome. This giant humanoid being had three bodies, three heads, and six arms but a single body from the waist down. He was the son of Chrysaor and Callirrhoë. Geryon ruled in the land known as Epirus, now the Iberian Peninsula in the region according to some sources, of Partessus, or Erythea, or Gades according to others. The chief delight of this monster was the breeding of his great herd of gigantic red oxen that were guarded night and day by the giant Eurytion and his monstrous dog Orthrus. It was given to the hero Hercules/Heracles to slay the giant guard and capture the herd of oxen as the tenth of the Twelve Labors he had to perform to gain the hand of Deianeira.
References 7, 20, 24, 133, 139, 166, 169, 183
See also Eurytion, giant, Orthrus

GERYON'S DOGS

These were the monstrous dogs of the giant Geryon in the classical mythology of Greece and Rome. Their names were Gargittios and Orthrus, the latter being more ferocious by way of having two heads. They, with the giant Eurytion, guarded the massive herd of red oxen that the hero Hercules/Heracles was determined to capture. In the fight to gain the cattle, their guardians were all killed by the hero.
References 20, 24, 133, 183
See also Geryon, giant

GĒUSH URVAN

This is the name of a gigantic primordial cosmic bull (or cow) in the mythology of Persia, now Iran. Gēush Urvan, also known as Gōshūurūn, was a celestial being that was so vast that it held within it the seed of every animal and plant species. Gēush Urvan grazed the earth for more than three thousand years before being killed, according to some sources, by Mithra, in others, by Angra Mainyu. From the vast body there emerged a pair of cattle and 282 pairs of other animals, while from its legs came sixty-five species of herbal plants and grain plants.

References 24
See also Audhumla, Ymir

GHADDAR

In the traditions of the Yemen and Upper Egypt, the Ghaddar are the Djinn offspring of the supremely evil Iblis. These beings manifest as ugly, giant humanoids. They are responsible for ensnaring gullible humans, whom they terrify and torture, eventually abandoning their victims in some remote place.

References 64, 160
See also Djin/n

GHAWWAS

This is the name of a Jinn that inhabits the water in the Islamic beliefs of Saudi Arabia.

References 115
See also Jin

GHOUL/E, GHUL/I

This is the name of a species of Djinn in Islamic traditions and beliefs. In pre-Islamic times they were identified as the male Qutrub and the female Gulah. Other spellings of the name are Ghol, Ghool, Ghowl, and Goul, while Ghulah is the female form. The Ghouls are fiends known and feared from the north of Africa, across the Middle East, to the Indian continent and beyond. They are said to inhabit the wilderness, or lonely forests, islands, and caves as well as their more usual place of abode—where humans have died or are buried. The Ghouls have been described as dark, hairy, quick-witted, and lustfully attracted to humans. Another manifestation is as a grotesquely ugly being resembling an ostrich with only one eye. However, these evil semisupernaturals are shape-shifters that can transform themselves to any guise in order to seduce humans. Ghouls prey on the unwary traveler and may kidnap them or terrorize them. They may haunt the sites of human tragedy, such as battlefields, murder sites, and cemetaries, devouring the bodies of the recent dead in deserted graves.

References 64, 74, 78, 94, 120, 146
See also Baba Yaga, Djinn, Pey

GIANT

This is a general term for a being of immense stature that may be applied as a superlative to any being that is of abnormal size. However, within the realms of mythology, legend, folk belief, allegory, and literature this term usually indicates a fabulous being that may or may not have had a basis in reality. The one uniting feature is the immense size, but Giants have their different characteristics according to the culture, the region, and the purpose of their existence; however, they exist in the narrative repertoire of virtually every culture in the world.

The word "giant" is derived from the classical mythology of Greece in which a race of Giants, known as the Gigantes, the progeny of Gaia and Uranus, were described as being monstrous creatures, part human and part serpents born of the blood from their castrated father. These primordial monsters fought with the Olympian gods in revenge for the defeat of their siblings, the Titans, who were of equally monstrous size but in human proportions. All were finally defeated by the Olympian gods aided by the culture hero Heracles and condemned to eternal imprisonment in either Tartarus or under mountains and volcanoes. A further group, the Cyclopes, were vast humanoid monsters with a single eye in their foreheads. This mythology was later adapted within the Roman myths, retaining the characters but adapting the names to a Latinized version.

The Middle East also had its Giants, such as the primordial Upelleru in the ancient Hurrian beliefs of the place now known as Anatolia; later there was a giant called Azrail in the legends of Armenia. Those mentioned within the Hebraic scriptures were various races of gigantic people called the Anakim, the Enim, the Rephaim, and the Zamzummim who inhabited the lands the length of the River Jordan. There were also the Nephilim, who were a race that intermarried with humans. Probably the most well known were Gog and Magog, Og of Bashan, and Goliath of Gath, whose exploits and defeat are also chronicled within Pentateuch books of the Old Testament of the Christian Bible. These Giants posed a serious problem for the religious discourse of the early Christian periods, since the disappearance of such peoples had not been accounted for simply by the Flood and the subsequent survival of Noah and his family. They were there in the Promised Land as inhabitants long after that period and encountered by the spies sent by Moses. In Rabbinical literature a tradition developed that Og of Bashan had survived the flood when he was allowed to sit astride the roof of Noah's Ark and was the last of the Giant race.

In the later medieval periods of Europe some theories and indeed fabrication, by such persons as the Italian monk Annius of Viterbo (Giovanni Nanni,

A giant (Rose Photo Archive, UK)

ca. 1432–1502), asserted that the biblical Noah was a giant. From this viewpoint he developed a genealogy of Giants, descended from Noah through Dis Samothes, to account for the distribution of certain peoples and noble lines in Europe. These Giants, far from being the wicked opposition to humans, were positively assessed in cultural terms and integrated into the cultural traditions for that period. The occasional discovery of Giant's bones (dinosaurs) added credance to the theories.

There were, of course, legends that existed within the cultures of Europe concerning Giants, many of which centered on Celtic mythology. Giants had supposedly inhabited all the islands of Britain until colonized by the "Trojans" under Brutus, according to Geoffrey of Monmouth (1100–1154) in his *Historia*

Giant

Regnum Britanniae (ca. 1147). In this pseudohistory the biblical names of Gog and Magog became conflated into that of a single Giant called Gogmagog. He was defeated by the "Trojan" Corineus, who in later versions was also deemed to be a Giant. The folklore and traditions of Britain, like much of the rest of Europe, has a rich variety of its own Giants ; indeed the ancient name of Britain—Albion—was said to be derived from a Giant. In Wales there is Wrnach and the gentle Bendigeidfran, who crossed to Ireland where, like the Cornish Giants, the Giants were as fierce and hostile as the Scottish ones.

The Norse and Teutonic mythology of Scandinavia and what is now Germany had a hierarchy of Jotuns, vast Giants who inhabited the various regions of their world. The earth, according to their myths, had been derived from the primordial Giant Ymir, and from his dead body all things had been generated. There were also the Frost Giants, the Fire Giants, and the Earth Giants, all of whom were immense beings with powers that challenged the gods. In Finland there were also primordial Ice Giants, namely Antero Vipunen and Joukahainen.

The number of mythological Giants in the Asian countries is comparatively few, since Djinns and demons prevail, but Giants feature as primordial beings in many cultures. In the Vedic mythology of India are Purusha, Madhu, Kaitabha, and Bali, one of the Danavas and Daityas in the Hindu beliefs.

Two Giants feature as emissaries of the god of wealth, Phra, in the mythology of Thailand. They were sent with a miraculous pillar to the city of Nobapuri, where the citizens were being plagued by dishonest traders. The pillar emitted virtue, and soon all were trading honestly and were happy. As time went on, the people forgot their prayers of gratitude to Phra In, so he sent the Giants to remove the pillar, and the people returned to dishonesty and poverty.

The primordial Giants whose bodies became the world and its creatures in the mythology of China were Pangu and Begdu San, while in the legends of Mongolia Manzaširi is the name of a primordial giant in the legends and folk beliefs of the Kalmyk people. The vast primordial being in the legends of Micronesia was called Puntan, and in the Pacific Island of Siau there is a tradition of Giants who resemble trees and whose very touch is death.

There is a very rich tradition of Giants in the mythology of the Native Americans of both Canada and the United States. These Giants may be benevolent toward humans, such as the Dehotgohsgayeh of the Iroquois, Gedegwsets of the Coos, and Inugpasugssuk of the Netslik peoples. But more often they are responsible for terrorizing humans and creating disasters in the environment. Particularly evil ones are cannibals, like the Kiwahkw

of the Maliseet and child abductors like the Dzoo-Noo-qua of the Kwakiutl people and Nahgane of the Slavey people. Others are just malevolent, like Chahnameed of the Pequot peoples, Nulayuuiniq of the Povungnituk people, and Tsavoojok of the Paviotso people.

Giants also belong to other traditions than mythology; they also have a place in the folklore of the people rather than in the organized mythological structures of religion. It is within folklore that a further rich source of Giants may be found around the world. The Giants may be credited with the construction of some massive natural feature, such as Paul Bunyan's gouging of the Grand Canyon in the United States; Cailleach Bheur creating the Hebridean Islands of Scotland; and Cormeilian, credited with creating Saint Michael's Mount in Cornwall, England; or unnatural features such as the standing stones of ancient Europe, Stonehenge, known as the Giants' Dance in England, and a similarly named circle of stones in Russia; the Giant's Causeway in Ireland; and glacial features called the Giant's Cauldron in Germany, Norway, and the United States. In these legends the Giants themselves are often said to be turned to stone either by the force of sunlight or the Christain condemnation of dancing on the sabbath. Many of the legendary figures of history whose heroic deeds became of national importance were often turned into folkloric Giants, such as Emperor Charlemagne and his bodyguard Ænotherus.

Giants also passed into the literature of cultures, which spread rapidly after the invention of printing (c. 1439) in Germany by Johannes Gensfleisch Guttenberg (1400–1468). The early literature of Europe was handwritten by poets and chroniclers, and many such manuscripts survive. The account of the raids of a Celtic giant called Ingcél Caech, in the literature of early Ireland, was told in *Togail Bruidne Da Derga* (The Destruction of Derga's Hostel). The Giant Farracutus first appears in a chronicle of the twelfth century, the *Pseudo-Turpin Chronicle*, and later in the *Chanson de Roland*. Many Giants appear in early Italian literature, such as the *Divina Commedia* by Dante Alighieri (1265–1321), and in the work of Boccaccio (1313–1375). The later Italian works, such as *Orlando Innamorato* by Matteo Maria Boiardo (1434–1494), *Il Morgante Maggiore* by Luigi Pulci (1432–84), the work of the monk Annius of Viterbo (Giovanni Nanni c.1432 –1502), and *Baldus* by the Benedictine Teofilo Folengo (1491–1554) under the pseudonym Merlinus Coccaius, would all have benefitted from the invention of printing in reaching the literate of Italy. In France the fascination with Giants in literature was just as strong and featured in the works *Pantagruel* (1532) and later in *Gargantua* (1534), written by François Rabelais (c. 1494–c. 1553), as well as in Spain by the author Miguel de Cervantes Saavedra (1547–1616).

In England the Giant Albion, brother of the legendary giants Gog and Magog, featured in the *Historia Regnum Britanniae* (ca. 1147) written by Geoffrey of Monmouth (ca. 1100–1154) and later printed in William Caxton's *Chronicle of England* (1480). A tradition of literary Giants featured in the later works of John Milton (1608–1674), the English Puritan poet, as well as the author and politician Jonathan Swift (1667–1745), and continues in such works as *The Hobbit* (1937) and *The Lord of the Rings* (1955) by the academic and author J.R.R. Tolkien (1892–1973).

The Giants in the above works were for the most part taking a serious, if sometimes satirical, role in the narrative; however, Giants also appear in folklore and folkloric literature in the guise of cautionary beings, as in fairy tales and nursery rhymes. Such giants in England were Woglog in *The Tale of Tommy Trip* (1767), probably by John Newbery; the Sandman, a Nursery bogie in the fairy tale written by E.T.A. Hoffmann in 1817; Agrippa, a character from the popular Victorian children's book *The English Struwwelpeter, or Pretty Stories and Funny Pictures,* by Dr. Heinrich Hoffmann published in Britain in 1847; while Bombomachides, Brandamour, Brobinyak, the Boo-bagger, and Thundel all belong to a class of Victorian Nursery bogies. There were equally horrific giants in the folk traditions of Germany, such as the Kinder-fresser and Kinder Schreker, which became popular from the invention of printing in Germany during the Middle Ages. In Belgium, Bullebak was a giant Nursery bogie mentioned in the autobiography of Isabella de Moeuloose (1695). Giant Grumbo features in the traditional tale of *Tom Thumb,* in print in 1724 as the French *Le Petit Poucet;* Croquemitaine, along with a wife called Madame Croquemitaine, was the subject of cartoons and cut-out toys for children during the late eighteenth and nineteenth centuries; and also we have Le Grand Lustucru in the nursery traditions of France. There were also the Alphito of Greece, the Tengu in the folklore of Japan, and Yara-ma-yha-who in the folklore of the Native Australian people. In the Native American traditions of Canada and the United States, there were the Pot-Tilter of the Choctaw Native American people, the Windigo in the traditions of the Ojibwa people, Apotamkin of the Maliseet-Passamaquoddy peoples of the Northeast coastal region, the Indacinga of the Ponca Native American people in the Plains, Skatene, and Hagondes—all Giants used traditionally in some way to control the behavior of adventurous children.

From these traditions have also evolved the Town Giants, originally legendary Giants who became representatives or guardians of some settlement such as Gog and Magog of London and Giant Onion in the town of Silchester in England. There are Druon and Antigonus of the city of Antwerp, Jean le Boucheron of Steenvoorde, and the Giant Gayant of Douai, all in Belgium. In Spain the town giant is el Zangarrón, while in Holland, Belgium, and France in the towns of Anvers (Belgium), Ath (Belgium), Hasselt (Holland), Lierre (Belgium), Malines (Belgium), Nieupoort (Belgium), Nivelles (Belgium), and Troyes (France) their Town Giants were all given the name of Goliath.

Although originally these giants may have had a protective role, their significance has dwindled, and many are still paraded today but with the frisson of the terror somewhat diminished. They have become gigantic effigies in town parades, especially in France and Spain, where they are called Bobalicón, Cara Vinaigre, and Cabezudos. However, these town giants may also still play a representative role in the heraldic devices of their towns, such as Gog and Magog, who feature in the coat of arms for the Guildhall of London in England.

References 7, 13, 20, 24, 51, 61, 77, 78, 94, 113, 125, 128, 137, 174, 180, 182, 183

See also Agrippa, Albion, Alphito, Anakim, Antero Vipunen, Antigonus, Apotamkin, Ænotherus, Bali, Bendigeidfran, Bobalicón, Bombomachides, Boo-bagger, Brandamour, Brobinyak, Bullebak, Cabezudos, Cailleach Bheur, cannibal, Cara Vinaigre, Chahnameed, Charlemagne, Corineus, Cormeilian, Croquemitaine, Cyclopes, Daityas, Danavas, Dehotgohsgayeh, Dis Djinn, Druon, Dzoo-Noo-qua, Enim, Farracutus, Fire Giants, Frost Giants, Gaia, Gargantua, Gayant, Gedegwsets, Giant Grumbo, Giant Onion, Gigantes, Gog and Magog, Gogmagog, Goliath, Hagondes, Indacinga, Ingcél Caech, Inugpasugssuk, Jotun, Joukahainen, Kinder-fresser, Kinderschreker, Kiwahkw, Le Grand Lustucru, Madame Croquemitaine, Nahgane, Nimrod, Noah, Nulayuuiniq, Og, Pantagruel, Paul Bunyan, Pot-Tilter, Purusha, Rephaim, Samothes, Sandman, Skatene, Tengu, Thundel, Titan, Town Giants, Tsavoojok, Uranus, Windigo, Woglog, Yara-ma-yha-who, Ymir, Zamzummim, Zangarrón

GIANT DESPAIR
See Despair, giant

GIANT DINGO
This is the gigantic cannibal beast that terrorized the Native Australian people of Western Australia during the period of the Dreamtime. Together with a monstrous snake, the Giant Dingo took so many victims that the survivors were too terrified to light a fire for warmth or for cooking, and the tribe sickened. So Jitta-Jitta the Willy Wag-Tail Man and his companion, Kubiri the Robin Man, decided to try to

kill the beasts. They waited until the wind was in the right direction and lit a huge fire at the entrance to the cave of the Giant Dingo. In rushed Jitta-Jitta, who attacked and killed the Giant Dingo. When he came out he saw Kubiri hiding in the tree, shaking with fear. Kubiri was so ashamed of his cowardice that he killed the snake in the same manner, and the people rejoiced in their freedom. Since then neither the wagtail nor the robin is ever threatened, for they freed humans from their danger.
References 159

GIANT HOLDFAST

This is the name of the giant or cannibal ogre in the traditional English folktale of Jack and the Beanstalk. Giant Holdfast lives in a castle that can be reached only through the clouds at the top of the beanstalk. He is the guardian of a great treasure hoard and the abducted king's daughter, both eventually liberated by Jack.
References 78
See also cannibal, giant, ogre

GIANT OF CARDIFF (N.Y.)

This was a "petrified" giant, twelve feet high and four feet in breadth, that was "found" in the diggings for a well by a farmer in 1869. For some considerable time the arguments raged over whether it was a primeval giant of human origin. Eminent people from universities and Ralph Waldo Emerson examined the "corpse" and made comments, but none reached any conclusions. Even the entertainer P. T. Barnum tried to purchase the American Goliath, it had created such an interest. However, eventually the commissioner of the Jenny Hanniver admitted the hoax had been made from gypsum, and the game was up.
References 174
See also giant, Goliath, Jenny Hanniver

GIANT OF MONT SAINT MICHEL, THE

This is the name of a giant in the Arthurian legends of Brittany in northwestern France. The Giant of Mont Saint Michel had abducted and killed the niece of the king of Brittany, Helena. King Hoel had then enlisted the help of King Arthur and his knights, Sir Bedevere and Sir Kay, who together brought the giant to bay and killed him.
References 54
See also giant

GIANT OF SMEETH

This is the name of a giant in the folklore of England. The Giant of Smeeth was said to be a vast and aggressive being who inhabited a cavern in the common of Smeeth near to the East Anglian town of Wisbech during the eleventh century. This giant was

so malicious that the local people would go twice the length that their journey should take in order to avoid crossing the common. A certain young man of great stature and little wit, called Tom, who spent his time eating and doing little to support his widowed mother, was set to work delivering ale for a brewer in Kings Lynn. On his journey he saw no good reason for taking the long route and set out across the common. Out came the outraged Giant of Smeeth, wielding the most enormous club and ready to smash him to pulp like so many others before. But Tom simply lifted the cart and took off the enormous cart wheel and then took out the axle to use as a shield and club. The stupefied giant had never met resistance before, and Tom took the advantage and swiped at the giant's head, knocking it from his shoulders. With the giant defeated, Tom explored the cavern and, to his amazement, found a treasure hoard that would keep himself and his mother for the rest of their lives.
References 183
See also giant

GIANT OF TRAPANI

This was a giant that was reported from an account by the Italian author Boccaccio (1313–1375) as having been discovered in Sicily. Apparently during the digging for the foundations of a village house, a cave with a sealed entrance was uncovered. When the peasant builders broke through and entered the cave they saw the body of an enormous man seated and propped up by a staff the size of a ship's mast. Soon half the village had come to see this immense individual, which crumbled to a pile of dust when touched. Only part of the scull, three teeth, and a thigh bone were left with the metal core of his staff. These were used by mathematicians of the time to calculate his height, which they estimated at 300 feet.
References 174
See also giant

GIANT OF WALES, THE

This is the name of a giant in the folklore of the county of Shropshire on the English borders of Wales. The folktale relates how the Giant of Wales, who was a vast being, was particularly enraged by the inhabitants of the town of Shrewsbury, so he took it into his mind to dam the River Severn and cause a flood that would drown all who lived there. So he took a great shovelfull of earth and set out with it, but having little by way of intellect, he did not know which way to go. After a long time on the road and growing weary of carrying so much earth, he met a cobbler who had just walked the few miles from Shrewsbury with a load of worn shoes and boots to mend. The giant asked the man for directions to Shrewsbury, but the cobbler, wary of the giant and his

The Giant of Wales (English Legends by H. Bett, Batsford Books, UK, 1950)

load of earth, asked the reason for the giant's journey. So the giant unsuspectingly told the man what he was going to do. The cobbler then told the giant that he would never make the journey within less than two days and said that he had worn out all those pairs of shoes on his long journey from that town. The stupefied Giant of Wales dropped the shovel of earth right there and scraped another pile from his boots. And this is the reason for the Wreakin Hills and the smaller hill of the Ercall.
References 183
See also giant

GIANT ONION
This is the name of a giant in the folklore of the county of Hampshire, England. It was conjectured in ancient times that the many massive Roman towns, which lay in ruins, had been the work of an ancient giant race that had inhabited Britain in pre-Christian times. One such belief manifested in the name of Giant Onion, whose name was associated with the

ancient Roman town of Calleva Atrebatum, now the town of Silchester. The English traveler and writer Camden noted in 1610 that the postern gate in the ancient city walls had been called Onion's Hole, and the many hoards of Roman coins found there were designated Onion's Pennies. Camden also noted that locals believed that, as the walls had obviously been of an enormous height, the giant builder must similarly have been huge, but no further information concerning the giant was made known.
References 183
See also giant, Town Giant

GIANTESS
This is the female form of the name "giant" in the mythology and folklore of many cultures. The giantess is usually massive and cumbersome but, unlike the giants, they are often beautiful, like Gerd in Norse mythology. They are usually of reasonable intellect, unlike the giants, and often benevolent toward humans. They are sometimes, especially in Celtic mythology, portrayed as hags with an ambivalent attitude toward humans. They are frequently held responsible for the creation of geographical features such as islands and mountain ranges.
References 78, 133, 139, 169
See also Angrboda, Bébinn, Cailleach bera, Cormelian, Cymidei Cymeinfoll, Dzoo-noo-qua, Galemelle, Gerd, giant, Giantess of Loch Ness, Giantesses of Putney and Fulham, Gougou, Iarnsaxa, Muilearteach, sGrolma, Thökk, Tytea Magna

GIANTESS OF LOCH NESS, THE
There is a legend in the Highlands of Scotland that suggests that the name "Loch Ness" is derived from the name of the daughter of a giantess who drowned there centuries ago.
References 183
See also giantess

GIANTESSES OF PUTNEY AND FULHAM, THE
According to a local legend dating from 1787, two giantesses built the churches of Putney and Fulham on either side of the River Thames in London, England. Tradition tells that they had only one hammer between them and they created a code to let the other know when it was going to be flung across the river to the other. On the south point of the river, in Surrey, the giantess would shout "Put it nigh," while on the north side of the river she would shout "Heave it full home." The settlements around the church later became known as "Putnigh" and "Fullhome" and contracted to the present Putney and Fulham. This is a very fanciful legend for place names that may have borrowed heavily from the legend of Bel, the wife of the giant Wade.

References 183
See also Bel, giantess, Wade

GIANTS OF CALLANISH, THE
This is the alternative name for the Fir Chreig in the folklore of the Isle of Lewis in the Outer Hebridean Islands of Scotland. This particular name is used mostly to refer to the standing stones into which the giants were turned.

References 183
See also Fir Chreig, giant

GIBBORIM
This is the name of a race of giants in Judeo-Christian tradition and in the Book of Genesis (6:4), in the Old Testament. The Gibborim were a gigantic antediluvian people that were said to be wiped out by the Flood that Noah and his family survived. These giants were regarded by the Hebrew people to be, along with the Nephilim, the first historical peoples of the earth, but by the first century A.D. a discourse by Philo of Alexandria had already considered them to be allegorical rather than historical fact.

References 99, 174
See also giant, Nephilim

GIDDY FISH
This is a creature from the folklore of lumberjacks and forest workers, especially in Wisconsin and Minnesota, during the nineteenth and early twentieth centuries. The Giddy fish belongs to a group of beings affectionately known as the Fearsome Critters, whose exaggerated proportions and activities not only explained the wierd noises of the lonely landscape but also provided some amusement at camps. The Giddy fish is also known as the Gillygalloo or the Whiffenpoof.

References 7, 24
See also Fearsome Critters

GIGANTES
The Gigantes were a class of giants in the classical mythology of Greece and Rome, and it is from their name that the word "giant" is derived. According to differing accounts, they were the progeny of Coelus and Gaia or engendered from the blood of the castrated Uranus when it fell on the earth. The Gigantes were also called Gegeneis or Ge Geneis, which may be translated as "earth-born" from this origin. These earth giants were therefore invincible whilever they were in contact with their earth mother, and immortal whilever they ate a certain herb, "ephialtion," that grew there. Their names are given variously as: Agrius, meaning "Untamable," Alcyoneus, meaning "Brayer," Aloeus, meaning "Of the Threshing Floor," Clytius, meaning "Renowned," Enceladus, meaning "Buzzer," Eurytus, meaning "Rapids," Gratium, meaning "Grater," Hippolytus, meaning "Stampede," Mimas, meaning "Mocker," Pallas, meaning "Handsome," Polybutes, meaning "Cattle-lord," Porphyrion, meaning "Purple One," Thoas, meaning "Fast," and Tityus, meaning "Risker." In some versions Phoetus is included, while in others Ephialtes and Otus are included, but they are otherwise said to be the sons of Aloeus and known as the Aloades. Still other versions include Briareus, Cottus, and Gyges, the three Hundred-Handed Giants. These monstrous giants were variously described as breathing fire or having multiple heads and limbs.

After the defeat of their siblings, the Titans, the Gigantes made an attack on Mount Olympus, having constructed a mound high enough to reach them. In some versions the gods were so terrified that they escaped to Egypt, taking the form of beasts until they had summoned sufficient powers to fight the Gigantes. But when the Gigantes reached a par with Mount Olympus they started to throw rocks, and when the sun shone at dawn the Olympian gods saw their leader Alcyoneus and knew what was happening. The goddess Athene had enlisted the help of the hero Heracles/Hercules, who shot Alcyoneus with an arrow as the sun dazzled him, then beat him to death as he was falling and unable to regenerate by touching his mother earth. Clytius in his turn was vanquished, according to different sources, by Hephaestus or Hecate. Enceladus was crushed under the weight of Sicily, which had been broken off Italy for Athene to use as a missile. Ephialtes had almost defeated Ares when he was shot with arrows from both the god Apollo and the hero Heracles/Hercules. Eurytus in his turn was vanquished, according to different sources, by Dyonysus/Bacchus with his "thyrsus," while Mimas and Pelorus were killed according to some sources by the god Ares, who transfixed the giant with his sword, or by Jupiter/Zeus with a bolt of lightning. Pallas was defeated in single combat by Athene, who added his name to hers as a celebration of her victory. Polybutes in his turn was vanquished after being pursued by the sea god Poseidon/Neptune and finally buried under the Island of Nysirus, torn by the god from the Island of Cos. Porphyrion was vanquished when he attempted to avenge his brothers but was diverted by Zeus/Jupiter, who compelled the giant with lust for the goddess Hera. While he was thus distracted, Porphyrion was felled by one of Zeus/Jupiter's thunderbolts and shot by the hero Hercules/Heracles with a poisoned arrow.

With the demise of these Gigantes, those that survived made a final attack at Trapezus but were all brought down. They were heaved into great chasms within the earth, their bodies covered by mountains and volcanoes to keep them from regenerating and

fighting again. However, when they stir they cause earth tremors and earthquakes felt on the surface. It is possible that these myths were the creation of an explanation for quantities of dinosaur bones that have been found continuously in the region of Trapezus.
References 24, 133, 169, 178
See also Agrius, Alcyoneus, Aloadae, Aloés, Clytius, Cyclopes, Enceladus, Ephialtes, Eurytus, Gaia, giant, Gratium, Hippolytus, Mimas, monster, Otus, Pallas, Phoetus, Polybutes, Porphyrion, Rakshasas, Thoas, Titans, Tityus, Typhon, Uranus

GILITRUTT

This is an alternative name for the demonic road monster, also known as the Galley-trot, in the folklore of Suffolk in England.
References 24, 96, 160, 170
See also Galley-trot

GILLING

This is the name of a giant in the Norse mythology of Scandinavia. Two evil dwarfs, Fjalar and Galar, murdered a wise and gentle man called Kvasir and collected his blood to make a magic mead of knowledge and eloquence. Soon the fame of the mead brought many to seek the dwarfs, few realizing how they had come by it. Two such visitors were the giant Gilling and his wife, who came as guests to the table of the dwarfs but were murdered by them. When they did not return from their visit, the giant Suttung, the nephew of Gilling and his wife, went in search of them. When he reached the abode of the dwarfs and he too drank some of the magic mead, he knew immediately what had befallen Gilling and his wife. He slew the dwarfs and took the mead back to the giants.
References 64, 127, 133, 160
See also Baugi, giant, Suttung

GILLYGALOO

This is a creature from the folklore of lumberjacks and forest workers, especially in Wisconsin and Minnesota in the United States, during the nineteenth and early twentieth centuries. The Gillygaloo belongs to a group of beings affectionately known as the Fearsome Critters, whose exaggerated proportions and activities not only explained the weird noises of the lonely landscape but also provided some amusement at camps. The Gillygaloo is described as a curious type of bird that laid its nest on the slopes of the Pyramid Forty constructed by the hero giant Paul Bunyan. This fabulous bird had adapted its eggs to the precarious nature of its perch by laying eggs that were cubes and did not roll down the sides. This were highly prized by the lumberjacks, who hard-boiled the eggs to use as gaming dice.

References 18
See also Bunyan (Paul), Fearsome Critters

GIRTABLILI, GIRTABLULU

This is the name of a monstrous humanoid in the legends and mythology of Babylon in Mesopotamia. The Girtablili is described as having a human upper body and head but having the lower body and tail of a scorpion. These scorpion men were a type of dragon race that assisted the monster Tiamat at the time of the creation of the earth. She decreed that Girtablili would guard the entrance to the Mashu Mountains, but Girtablili allowed the hero Gilgamesh to pass, warning that none ever returned. Girtablili was a symbol of boundary guardianship, and his image was used on many of the Babylonian seals.
References 7, 89
See also dragon, monster, Tiamat

GLAISTIG, GLAESTIG, GLASTIG

The Glaistig is a complex being and a member of the group known as Fuaths in the folklore of the Highlands of Scotland. The Glaistig is also known as the Maighdean uaine, which in Scottish Gaelic means the "Green Maiden." She is able to shape-shift from the form of a monstrous woman, to half woman and goat, or completely the form of a goat, but is always dressed in green. As a semisupernatural associated with water, the Glaistig might beg to be carried across a stream by an unsuspecting mortal. Her treatment of her victims varies from simply leading them astray to slitting their throats and draining them entirely of their blood. As a benign household familiar, she might willingly do domestic tasks while the family sleeps or herd the cattle for the farm. In this capacity the Glaistig appears to protect the infants, the infirm, and the elderly. As the Green Glaistig she will wail for the imminent departure of one of her charge, much like a Banshee. The Glaistig, although of questionable motives, does not seem to have been totally at fault. One anecdote of a smith who entrapped a Glaistig tells how, when she produced the magic cattle and inviolable house he demanded, seared off her extended hand of farewell. The vegetation in the place where she met this horrible reward, Lochaber, Inverness, is said to be stained red to this day.
References 7, 21, 24, 67, 128, 160
See also Baba Yaga, Fuath

GLAS GAIBLEANIR, GLAS GAIBLEANN, GLAS GAIBHLEANN, GLAS GHAIBHLEANN, GLAS GHAIBHNANN, GLAS GHAIBHNENN, GLAS GHOIBHNEANN, GLAS GAIVLEN, GLAS GAVELEN, GLASGAVELEN

This is the name of a semisupernatural cow in the ancient mythology of Ireland and later folklore of

Scotland. This enormous creature is described variously as gray-white or milk-white with green spots. Whatever the description, its fame rested in its inexhaustible supply of milk to whomever was kind but in need. According to different sources, she belonged either to the smith Goibniu, or to Gaiblin, or to Cian, who let her graze the slopes of Donegal. However, as the fame of this wonderful beast spread, the giant Balor came and, while Cian was distracted, stole the cow, taking her back to Tor Mor (now Tory Island). After many adventures Cian, in disguise, tracked the pair to the island. There Cian wooed and made love to Ethne, the daughter of the giant, who later showed him how to take the cow from its tethering and escape.

References 7, 24, 128
See also Dun Cow, giant

GLASHTIN, GLASHAN, GLAISTYN, GLASTYN

This is a supernatural water monster in the Manx folklore of the Isle of Man in the British Isles. The Glashtin is a form of the Scottish water horse called the Kelpie, the Irish Each Uisge, and the Welsh Ceffyl Dwfr. In his human shape, the Glashtin appears as a handsome, dark-haired young man with huge horses' ears within his curly hair. The Glashtin usually inhabits the banks of rivers and lochs where, in his equine form, he encourages humans to mount his flanks. With his victim firmly in place, he would take the unfortunate to be devoured beneath the waters. A common theme of tales concerning the Glashtin describes how a young woman left at home alone unbolts the door to the cottage to admit someone she thinks is her father caught in the rainstorm. It is only when the stranger uncovers his head to dry by the fire that she notices the horses' ears. The monster makes a grab for her, but the cockerel in the yard is wakened by her piercing screams, and she is saved by the cock's crow.

References 24, 111, 119, 128, 160
See also Cabyll-Ushtey, Ceffyl Dŵr, Eačh Uisge, Kelpy, Neugle

GLAURUNG

This the name of a dragon in the literary works of the English academic and author J. R. R. Tolkien (1892–1973), who wrote *The Hobbit* (1937) and *The Lord of the Rings* (1955). Glaurung is the name of the most destructive and powerful of the Urulóki, the monstrous Dragons bred by the evil Morgoth in the Pits of Angband during the period of the First Sun. Ee was unleashed on the Elves in the Battle of the Sudden Flame during the Wars of Beleriand. Glaurung sired a race of Fire-Drakes and Cold-Drakes. Glaurung was eventually slain by the hero

Túrin Turambar, who was simultaneously killed by the venomous blood of the monster.

References 51
See also Cold-Drakes, Dragon, Fire-Drakes, monster, Urulóki

GLAWACKUS

This is the name of a huge beast in the local folklore of Connecticut and Massachusetts in the United States. It was described as a hybrid beast looking something like a boar, a panther, and a lion. It was reported as having been sighted in 1939 in Glastonbury, Connecticut, and again in Frizzelburg, Massachusetts, where it was said to have attacked a bull in November 1944.

This is a creature from the folklore of lumberjacks and forest workers during the nineteenth and early twentieth centuries. The Glawackus belongs to a group of beings affectionately known as the Fearsome Critters, whose exaggerated proportions and activities not only explained the weird noises of the lonely landscape but also provided some amusement at camps.

References 7, 24
See also Fearsome Critters

GLUMDALCLITCH

This is the name of a gigantic child in classic English literature. The land of the Brobdingnagians was where Gulliver found himself on his second voyage in the work *Gulliver's Travels* (1726) by the author and politician Jonathan Swift (1667–1745). Glumdalclitch was the name of the forty-foot-tall "little" girl who looked after him among her race of gentle giants.

References 20, 177, 182
See also giant

GLYCON

This is the name of a hybrid supernatural demonic serpent in the cult of Mithras in Persia, now Iran. Glycon was a human-headed serpent and the messenger or, according to some sources, the avatar of the god of healing, Asklepios.

References 125
See also serpent

GLYRYVILU

This is the name of a freshwater monster in the traditions and beliefs of the people of Chile. The Glyryvilu, in some districts, might be called the Vulpangue, or fox-serpent, but was considered to be a dragon or monstrous fish. It was described variously as a serpent with a head resembling that of a fox, or as a vast, flat, circular being with eyes around the edges that inhabited the lakes high in the Andes. An account of this creature was given in the *Essay on the Natural*

History of Chile (1782), written by the prelate Juan-Ignacio Molina (1740–1829), who stated that the people were so terrified of the Glyryvilu that they would not enter the water. He conjectured that it might have been some type of manta ray or giant squid.
References 77, 134
See also dragon, Hide, Manta, serpent, Vulpangue

GOAT, SEA
There are two traditions that have a Sea-goat:
   1. In the mythology of ancient Sumer the god Ea or Marduk had as his steed a vast goat that strode through the waters of land and the seas with the god standing on its back.
   2. A type of Sea-goat is described in the mythology of India as a class of Makara.
References 7
See also Makara

GOAYR HEDDAGH
This is a monster in the Manx folklore of the Isle of Man in the British Isles. The Goayr Heddagh is described as a vast, menacing goat that will terrify night-bound travelers on lonely roads.
References 128
See also Black dog, Bocanách, Gaborchend, Glaistig

GOBORCHEND, GORBORCHIND
These are the alternative spellings of Gaborchend, a goat-headed, monstrous race in the legends of Ireland.
References 128
See also Gaborchend, monster

GOBORCHINU
This is the name of a monstrous humanoid people in the legends of Ireland. They, like the Gaborchend, are described as having the head of a beast, in this case that of a horse.
References 89
See also Gaborchend, monster

GODAPHRO
This is an alternative name for the Guyascutus in the folklore of lumberjacks and forest workers (and later fraudsters), especially in Wisconsin and Minnesota in the United States.
References 7
See also Fearsome Critters, Guyascutus

GOEMAGOT, GOEMOT
This is the name of a giant in the early pseudohistory of Britain. The Celtic legend and early history of Britain were substantially rewritten by Geoffrey of Monmouth (1100–1154) in his *Historia Regnum*

Britanniae (ca. 1147), in which he described the islands as being inhabited by a race of giants. He then told how Brutus came from the Roman Empire to invade the islands with an army from Troy. Goemagot, later known as Gogmagog, was given as the adversary of Corineus, the Trojan lieutenant of Brutus. This story was later incorporated by the Elizabethan poet Edmund Spenser (1552?–1599) in his work *The Faerie Queene* (1590).
References 20
See also Corineus, giant, Gog and Magog

GOG
This is the name of a giant in Hebraic and Christian scripture and apocalyptic texts. Gog is described in the Books of Genesis and Ezekiel, where it is said that he originates from a place called Magog. This latter name is used to denote a further giant, however, in the apocalyptic literature, where they are the agents of Satan and the Antichrist.
   Gog features in further legends and folklore as a giant with somewhat different activities but is no doubt derived from the biblical source.
References 24, 61, 166, 174
See also Gemmagog, Gog and Magog, Gogmagog

GOG AND MAGOG
These are the names of two giants in the legends and folklore of Britain. The legend relates that these two, along with others, were the offspring of the wicked daughters of Emperor Diocletian (A.D. 245–313), who ruled Roman Britain. When Brutus and his men came from the Trojan wars, Gog and Magog were taken prisoner and chained to the gates, or were made to become menial porters, at the palace in London. An alternative version states that they were the last of a race of giants that was imprisoned by the Greek commander Alexander the Great (356–323 B.C.) behind massive bronze and iron gates. But during the time of the Celtic King Arthur, they escaped to attack the court. In France the giants, known as Gos et Magos, were vanquished by the French giant Gargantua and thence chained to the palace gates in London. Since that time effigies of Gog and Magog have guarded the entrance gates, first to the palace and then to the London Guildhall, which was built on the site of the old palace. Records of this go back to the time of King Henry V (1387–1422) but those effigies were destroyed in the Great Fire of London (1666) and were replaced by wooden effigies by the carver Richard Saunders in 1708, which were subsequently lost in the bombing raids of World War II in 1940. The present figures of Gog and Magog were created in 1953 for the coronation of Queen Elizabeth II.
References 13, 20, 24, 47, 54, 61, 77, 78, 133, 166, 174, 182
See also Gargantua, giant, Goemagot, Gog

GOGMAGOG

This is the name of a giant in the legends and folklore of Britain. Gogmagag, also known as Goëmagot, was said to be the leader of the giants who inhabited Britain when Brutus and his Trojans came from the Trojan wars to this land. Corineus, one of the generals of the army, defeated the giant in the county of Cornwall and then threw his body over a cliff. In other legends Gogmagog was buried outside Cambridge, and effigies were cut in the chalk hills at Cambridge and on the top of the cliffs at Plymouth in the county of Devon. The name is clearly a conflation of the biblical names of Gog and Magog, incorporated by Geoffrey of Monmouth (1100–1154) in his *Historia Regnum Britanniae* (ca. 1147) as Goëmagot. The gigantic hill and cliff figures have been conjectured to represent either ancient harbor markers or guardians. These chalk hill figures are centuries old and are renewed periodically as ancient monuments, although sadly some were lost in earlier centuries.
References 13, 20, 47, 54, 61, 78, 133, 166, 174
See also Gemmagog, Goemagot, Gog, Gog and Magog, Wandlebury giant

GOLDBRISTLES

This is the name of the gigantic boar Gullinbursti in the Norse mythology of Scandinavia.
References 89
See also Gulinbursti

GOLDEN DRAGON NAGA MAS

This is an alternative name for the Naga Mas, the sea monster of the Malay people of West Malaysia.
References 113
See also Naga Mas

GOLEM

This is the name of a gigantic artificial humanoid being in the Jewish legends of Europe, of which a number were said to have existed. The most famous was created in Prague in the Czech state. The medieval legend is retold in the novel *Der Golem* (1915) by the German author Gustav Meyrink (1868–1932). In the tale, Rabbi Judah Loew ben Bezabel, who was well versed in the use of the holy letters for magical purposes, created from clay an image of human form that was activated by placing the formulaic Ameth or Emet or AMTh (meaning "truth," "reality") on a Shem tablet under the being's tongue. Then the Golem, which means "a clod of earth," would, on command, do menial tasks such as ringing the bells for the synagogue. However, it was essential to remove the tablet from its tongue, for the Golem, being inhuman, never slept and would carry on. One night this was forgotten, and the Golem rampaged through the streets, creating mayhem, knocking down both people and things in its way. At last the rabbi caught it and removed the tablet. The Golem shrank back to its little clay image, which then had the words "Meth" or "Met" or "MTh," meaning "Death," inscribed on its forehead to prevent a recurrence. In another version, when the Rabbi caught up with the Golem and removed the tablet, it simply disintegrated into a pile of dust.

Other Golems for similar tasks were created by Elijah Chelm and Rabbi Jaffe in the region of Prussia, now the eastern sector of Poland. There was some ethical debate as to whether such a creature could be used, not only for menial positions but also to make up the required number for the *minyan* prayer meeting. However, there were inherent problems that came to light, literally, when the Golem of Rabbi Jaffe, unable to differentiate even on the simplest level what was required, set fire to everything in the place.
References 18, 24, 78, 94
See also Be Chasti, Frankenstein's monster, Talos

GOLIATH, GOLIATH OF GATH

This is the name of a giant in the Hebraic and Christian scriptures. Goliath was the champion of the Philistine army that invaded the land of Judah in the time of King Saul. The details are given in the Book of the Old Testament of the Bible, (I Samuel xvii, 4–7): "And there went out a champion out of the camp of the Philistines named Goliath of Gath, whose height was six cubits and a span (eleven feet nine inches). And he had an helmet of brass upon his head; and he was armed with a coat of mail; and the weight of the coat was five thousand shekels of brass. And he had greaves (shin armor) of brass upon his legs, and a target (plate armor) of brass between his shoulders. And the staff of his spear was like a weaver's beam; and his spear's head weighed six hundred shekels of iron; and one bearing a shield went before him."

This Goliath challenged any member of the Israelite army to fight in single combat with him, but they were all terrified. However, David, the son of Jesse, had left his sheep and come with food for his brothers in the army. He heard the challenge and went to the king to volunteer and had to convince everyone of his intentions. So David was given armor, but it was too restrictive, so he set out to face the giant with just his sling and shot. "And the Philistine said to David, Come unto me and I will give thy flesh unto the fowls of the air, and to the beasts of the field.... And David put his hand in his bag and took thence a stone, and slang it, and smote the Philistine in the forehead . . . and he fell upon his face to the ground" (44–49). Goliath was then decapitated, and the Philistine army departed.

In a curious twist to the story of this biblical giant, the ancient Town Giants (from ca. A.D. 1460) of the towns of Anvers (Belgium), Ath (Belgium), Hasselt (Holland), Lierre (Belgium), Malines (Belgium), Nieupoort (Belgium), Nivelles (Belgium), and Troyes (France) were all given the name of Goliath. During the visit of the future King Charles VIII in 1486 to the town of Troyes, their Goliath reenacted the challenge and his defeat by a local "David."
References 20, 61, 99, 166, 174
See also giant, Town Giant

GOLL MAC CARBADA
This is the name of a monster in the legends of Ireland. Goll Mac Carbada is described as a vast, one-eyed monster that was the permanent adversary of the hero Cúchulainn. The hero, after many adventures, eventually tracked down the beast and slew it.
References 128
See also monster

GOLLIGOG, GOLLYGOG
This is the name of a giant lizard-like monster in the legends and folklore of the Ozark Native American people of the United States. This monster was reported by V. Randolf in 1951 as having inhabited the Ozark Mountains during the nineteenth century.
References 94
See also Bingbuffer, Fillyloo, Gowrow, monster

GOLLINKAMBI, GOLLIN KAMBI
Gollinkambi, also known as Vithafnir, is the golden cockerel watch-bird that stays alert on the top of Yggdrasil, the Ash Tree of the World, in the Norse mythology of Scandinavia.
References 7
See also Vithafnir

GONG-GONG
This is the name of an evil demonic dragon in the legends and traditions of China. This gigantic black dragon, which has a huge horn protruding from the front of its head, is accompanied by the monstrous Xiang-Yao. Gong-gong is described as being so vast that in its hatred of the Emperor Yao it impaled the mountain of Buzhou on its horn and ripped it from the earth, causing all the waters from the mountain to flood the earth. Then Gong-gong swung its head into the sky and ripped a hole there, causing great disturbances of the light from the sun and great periods of gloom. All this destruction of the earth was set right again by the goddess Nu-Kwa, re-creating the cardinal directions and earth-sky alignments.
References 125, 160, 166, 174
See also dragon, Xiang-Yao

GOOD HOOP
This is an alternative name for the monstrous Bunyip of Native Australian mythology. The Bunyip is called the Good Hoop in Tasmania, where it is envisaged in a serpentine form.
References 7, 78, 89
See also Bunyip

GOOFANG
This is a creature from the folklore of lumberjacks and forest workers, especially in Wisconsin and Minnesota in the United States, during the nineteenth and early twentieth centuries. This curious fish was so sensitive that it had developed the ability to swim backwards in order to keep the water from hurting its eyes. The Goofang belongs to a group of beings affectionately known as the Fearsome Critters, whose exaggerated proportions and activities not only explained the wierd noises of the lonely landscape but also provided some amusement at camps.
References 7, 24
See also Acipenser, Fearsome Critters

GOOFUS
This is a creature from the folklore of lumberjacks and forest workers, especially in Wisconsin and Minnesota in the United States, during the nineteenth and early twentieth centuries. This is a curious bird, for it built its nest in the shape of an igloo with the exit underneath. No one ever worked out how the eggs remained in it. This bird had also developed the ability to fly backwards in order to watch the scenery that it had just passed. The Goofus belongs to a group of beings affectionately known as the Fearsome Critters, whose exaggerated proportions and activities not only explained the weird noises of the lonely landscape but also provided some amusement at camps.
References 7, 18
See also Fearsome Critters

GORGON, GORGOS (pl.), GORGONES (pl.)
There are three definitions of Gorgon.
1. This is the name of three monstrous sisters in the classical mythology of Greece and Rome. They had been the beautiful progeny of Ceto and the old Man of the Sea, Phorcys; their names were Euryale, Medusa, and Stheno. However, the sea god Poseidon desired Medusa so much that he disguised himself as a white stallion and seduced her in a temple sacred to the goddess Athene. The outraged Athene desired revenge for her desecrated temple and changed Medusa into a hideous parody of her former self. They were described as having the form of women but with wings on their backs, great tusks or fangs in huge gaping mouths from which their tongues lolled, heads

Perseus shows the Gorgon's head (A Wonder Book for Boys and Girls and Tanglewood Tales *by N. Hawthorne, J. M. Dent, London*)

full of writing snakes in place of hair, and brazen clawed hands on their arms. Their most fearsome feature, however, was their eyes, for any mortal who was foolish enough to look at them was instantly turned to stone. They were variously said to inhabit the wastes of Libya, or the east of Scythia, or the edge of the Western Ocean, or Cisthene. Of the three, only Medusa was mortal, and they hid themselves in obscurity, guarded only by their siblings, the Graeae. That was until the advent of the hero Perseus, who stole the eye and tooth of the Graeae and killed Medusa, taking her head back to the avenged goddess Athene. When the name Gorgon is used in the singular it invariably refers only to Medusa.

2. This is an alternative name for the Catoblepas as described in the seventeenth century by Edward Topsell. Its description had been much modified from the original image of the Catoblepas, and he described the beast, which he called a Gorgon, as covered in scales, having wings like a dragon, enormous blood-shot eyes covered by a long mane, gigantic teeth, and hands instead of paws or hooves. It was said to browse only poisonous plants, by which its breath was also made poisonous, as well as having eyes that could petrify any mortal thing if it ever looked upon them.

3. Gorgon is also the name of a monster in the early mythology of Greece. It was said to be generated by Gaia as a creature that could assist the Gigantes in their struggle against the Olympian gods. It was dispatched by the goddess Athene, who decapitated the beast and placed it beneath the meeting place, or *agora*. The confusion of this early legend with the later classical myth involving the hero Perseus has led to the two being totally conflated and the earlier version almost lost.
References 7, 20, 24, 38, 47, 61, 78, 89, 91, 125, 133, 139, 166, 169, 178
See also Catoblepas, Chrysaor, Eurale, Geryon, giant, Gigantes, Graeae, Medusa, monster, Pegasus, Phorcys, Stheno

GORM

This is the name of a giant in the local folklore of the West Country region of Britain. Gorm is a topographical giant, one whose legendary activities were supposed to be the cause of features of the landscape. He is credited with having created the Maes Knoll when he tripped over the Cotswold Hills and dumped a shovelfull of earth, his fallen spade cleaving the earth to form the Wansdyke. When he ran for fear of rebuke he fell and drowned in the Bristol Channel, and his body became the islands of Flatholm and Steepholm.
References 13
See also giant

GORYNICH

This is the name of a fearsome dragon in the legends and folklore of Russia. The dragon Gorynich was the nephew of the evil sorcerer Nemal Chelovek, who had abducted the czar's daughter and imprisoned her in a dark, mountainous castle. The sorcerer intended the princess to be the bride of his monstrous nephew. The czar had offered untold riches for the brave prince who could find and rescue his daughter. Many valiant princes came but failed to find her. At last one of the palace guards, Ivan, said that he would undertake the mission. While he had been on duty he had overheard two crows whispering together where the princess was to be found. Reluctantly the czar equipped Ivan with a magic sword and the necessary things for his journey and let him go on his quest. Ivan, after many adventures, arrived at the fortress of Nemel Chelovek, which was left unguarded because the sorcerer thought that no one could find the place. Ivan searched and eventually found the princess and told her of her betrothal to the dragon Gorynich. Before they could escape from the great hall, the sorcerer entered and, expanding to gigantic size, attacked Ivan. But Ivan was ready with the magic sword, Samosek, which flew from his hands, sliced through the gigantic form of Nemel Chelovek, and then flew into every part of the fortress, slicing through every being that belonged to the sorcerer, including the dragon. With all the adversaries dead, the joyful pair returned to the czar, and Ivan married his princess.
References 55
See also dragon, Goryshche

GORYSHCHE

This is the name of a dragon in the traditions and folklore of Russia. Goryshche is a vast, twelve-headed monster that hunted humans for her brood of dragons that inhabited her cavern in the Sorochinsk Mountains. With each of her raids Goryshche took many young Russians and herded them like cattle into the depths of the caves until the time they were to be devoured. One of the *bogatyrs* (a knight of Holy Russia) Dobrynya Nikitich, vowed to rid the people of this terror and set out to kill them all, but having killed many of Goryshche's progeny he had to flee for his life. Despite his mother's warning, the warrior-hero returned to the mountains and was by the River Puchai bathing when he realized that the dragon was after him. He swam to the opposite bank, where he found the hat of a priest that had power against dragons. Wielding the hat, he sliced through eleven of her heads, and the dragon dropped to the ground, whereupon Dobrynya Nikitich jumped onto her back and was about to dispatch her when the dragon begged to be left to live and vowed never to do harm

again. The *bogatyr* relented, but when he finally returned to Kiev, Goryshche had already abducted the Princess Zabava, the niece of Prince Vladimir Bright Sun. Prince Vladimir hears of Dobrynya Nikitich's encounter with the dragon and orders him to rescue his niece or lose his life. He returned to the house of his mother, who told him to take his father's old mare and, when it grew weary, to put a silken whip across its flank. Reaching the dragon's lair he slaughtered many of her progeny, the poor old horse being wounded severely, but when he put the silken whip to her flank she was instantly revitalized. Then he tackled Goryshche, but the battle lasted for three days, until at last the dragon lay in a vast lake of its own blood. He released all the captives, and when at last he found the princess he took her back to a hero's welcome in Kiev.
References 55
See also dragon, Gorynich

GOS ET MAGOS

This is the name of a giant in the classical literature of France. Gos et Magos is, despite the double name, one of the characters described by the author François Rabelais (ca. 1494–ca. 1553) in his work *Pantagruel* (1532) and later in *Gargantua* (1534). This is the French version of the giants Gog and Magog, later given as Gogmagog (clearly a conflation of the biblical names), which was then incorporated by Geoffrey of Monmouth (1100–1154) in his *Historia Regnum Britanniae* (ca. 1147) as Goëmagot. In the version by Rabelais, who must have been aware also of Geoffrey of Monmouth's work, they were defeated at the court of King Arthur in France by the French giant Gargantua in an almost identical hurling over the clifftop.
References 77
See also Gargantua, giant, Goemagot, Gog and Magog

GOSH, GŌSHŪURŪN, GŌSHŪURVAN

This is the name of a primordial bull or cow in the Zoroastrian mythology of Persia (now Iran). Gosh is more usually known as Gēush Urvan. This vast bull was created at the same time as the first human, Gayomart, as the provider of all things for humans to survive upon the earth. Both Gayomart and Gosh were destroyed through the works of the supremely evil Ahriman.
References 24, 139
See also Audumla.

GOU MANG

In Chinese mythology this is a dragon that always associated with the dragon form of Rou Shou. They are always associated as the messengers of the sky-god and share the form of the double dragon. Gou Mang pressages good fortune and the return of springtime. He is associated with the benefit of longevity, and he always comes from the eastern directions.
References 125, 160
See also dragon, Lung, Oriental Dragon, Rou Shou

GOUGER

This is an alternative name for the Guyascutus in the folklore of lumberjacks and forest workers (and later fraudsters), especially in Wisconsin and Minnesota in the United States.
References 7
See also Fearsome Critters, Guyascutus

GOUGOU

This is the name of a giantess in the traditions and beliefs of the Micmac Native American people of the northeastern United States. The Gougou, also known as the Gugu or Gugwe, is described as a vast female humanoid-shaped cannibal with a hairy face like that of a bear and enormous hands. She was of such proportions that she could wade into the river and pick up an entire boat and crew, put all in a pouch slung about her body, and carry them off. The Gougou was said to inhabit the island off the Baye des Chaleurs in the Saint Lawrence River, from which weird noises were heard, but none dared investigate.
References 134
See also Atcen, cannibal, giantess

GOURMAILLON

This is the alternative name for two giants in the traditions and folklore of the county of Cornwall in England.

1. The alternative for Cormoran, a Cornish giant who started to build the island of Saint Michael's Mount near Penzance on the southern coast of Cornwall.

2. The alternative for Corineus, who in later accounts became a giant who defeated Gogmagog in Cornwall.

The fact that this name has been used to identify both these characters has been conjectured to indicate that one developed from the other and, furthermore, that the later folktale of "Jack-the-Giant-Killer" may be a folk myth derived from the legend of Corineus.
References 47, 54
See also Corineus, Cormoran, giant, Gogmagog

GOWROW

This is the name of a giant dragon in the legends and folklore of the Ozark Native American people of the United States. The Gowrow was said to be a huge, dragon-like monster with tusks from the front of its head and at least twenty feet in length. This monster

was was reported by V. Randolf in 1951 as having inhabited the Ozark Mountains during the nineteenth century.
References 94
See also Bingbuffer, dragon, Fillyloo, Golligog, monster

GRÆÆ

This is the name of the monstrous hags who were the sisters of the Gorgons in the classical mythology of Greece and Rome. The Græææ, also spelled Graiai, Graiae, or Graii, are also known as the Phorcides, from their descent from Phorcys the Titan. They are described variously as having the bodies of swans or of women, but their lank, gray hair covered their hideous, eyeless faces. They had one removable eye and one tooth between them, which they transferred from one to the other so that each in turn could eat or watch over their monstrous sisters, the Gorgons. Originally, according to Hesiod (ca. eighth century B.C.), there were only two, but later versions give the names of three: Deino/Dino, Enyo, and Pemphredo/Pephredo. When Perseus came to slay Medusa before gaining access to the Gorgon's lair, he had to go past the Græææ at the entrance to Cisthene. He cunningly waited for the transfer of the tooth and eye when none could see and snatched both eye and tooth. They gave him a pair of winged sandals, a cap of invisibility, and the directions to Medusa. On his return with the head of Medusa in the pouch, some versions related that he returned the tooth and eye as he departed.
References 24, 38, 125, 133, 166, 169
See also Deino, Enyo, Gorgon, Medusa, Pemphredo, Phorcys

GRÁHA, GRAHO

This is an alternative name to the Avagráh, the name in the Sikkata language for the Nyan, a monstrous serpentine creature in the traditions and legends of Burma.
References 81
See also Nyan

GRAIAI, GRAIAE, GRAII

These are alternative spellings of the name Græææ, the monstrous sisters of the Gorgons in the classical mythology of Greece and Rome.
References 24, 38, 125, 133, 166, 169
See also Græææ

GRANAUS

This is one of the giants named in the genealogy created by the Italian monk Annius of Viterbo (Giovanni Nanni, ca. 1432–1502) to justify the noble descent of the Gauls from a giant biblical race.

References 139, 174
See also giant, Noah

GRAND LUSTUCRU, LE

See Lustucru (Le Grand)

GRANDFATHER

This is an alternative name for the giant known as Haduigona in the traditions and beliefs of the Iroquois Native American people of the United States.
References 136
See also giant, Haduigona

GRANDGOUSIER, GRANDGOUSIR, GRANT-GOSIER

This is the name of a giant in the classical literature of France. Grandgousier is one of the characters described by the author François Rabelais (ca. 1494–ca. 1553) in his work *Pantagruel* (1532) and later in *Gargantua* (1534). He was engendered by the wizard Merlin in the court of King Arthur, from whale bones mixed with the blood of the knight Lancelot. His consort Galemelle was similarly engendered from the nail parings of Queen Guinevere and the bones of a female whale. Grandgousier was the parent of Gargantua, and he was a warrior giant, wise, generous, forgiving, and magnanimous to his defeated enemies.
References 174
See also Galemelle, Gargantua, giant, Pantagruel

GRANT

A semisupernatural creature described by Gervaise of Tilbury, the thirteenth-century English chronicler, as taking the form of a yearling colt with glowing, fiery eyes, much like the Brag. It traveled only on its hind legs and presented a terrifying aspect for those who saw it. Although frightening, the Grant seems to have been delivering a warning to the town when it appeared during the heat of the day or at sunset. This monstrous being would set the dogs barking and chasing it in vain, which alerted residents to an imminent fire somewhere in one of the buildings of the town.
References 7, 21, 24, 160, 170
See also Brag

GRANT-GOSIER

This is an alternative spelling of Grandgousier in the classical literature of medieval France.
References 174
See also Grandgousier

GRATIUM

This is the name of a giant in the classical mythology of Greece and Rome. Gratium is one of the Gigantes

and, like his brothers, was said to have been engendered from the blood that fell on the earth from the castrated Uranus. These giants were born fully mature and clad in full battle armor. They waged war on the Olympian gods after the defeat of the Titans and were defeated. Gratium was one of those who survived until the final attack and was defeated and buried under mountains in the earth.
References 24, 133, 169, 178
See also Aloadae, Cyclopes, giant, Gigantes

GREAT AGRIPPA
This is the alternative name for Agrippa, or Tall Agrippa, a character from the popular Victorian children's book *The English Struwwelpeter, or Pretty Stories and Funny Pictures,* by Dr. Heinrich Hoffmann and published in Britain in 1847.
References 97, 182
See also Agrippa

GREAT GALACTIC GHOUL
This is the name of a cosmic monster that floats in the voids of the universe. It is portrayed as a huge, amorphous, blue-and-pink body with a vast mouth. The Great Galactic Ghoul has been blamed for many of the failed missions and destroyed modules that have been sent to the planet Mars both by the Russians and the Americans. It was reported that between 1970 and 1990 as many as fourteen Russian Mars missions had disappeared without trace, as had several from the United States. This monster has entered the folkloric domain of the mission scientists in the Pasadena Launch Control. It was they who named the cosmic monster as being responsible for the destruction of craft bound for that planet in order to safeguard its secrets. The mission of July 4, 1997, successfully escaped the clutches and oblivion in the mouth of the Great Galactic Ghoul.
References 56, 131
See also monster

GREAT HORNED SERPENT
This is the title of the messenger of the lake monster of Iroquois Native American legends and beliefs in the United States. The Great Horned Serpent is portrayed as a vast, swollen rattlesnake in pictograms and paintings around the Great Lakes. This being was apparently invoked as a protector for difficult crossings of the waters in turbulent weather.
References 134
See also Horned Serpent

GREAT, LONG-LEGGED SCISSOR-MAN, THE
This is an alternative name for the Red-Legged Scissor-man, a nineteenth-century Nursery bogie of England and Germany.

References 97, 182
See also Agrippa, Nursery bogie, Red-Legged Scissor-man

GREAT LYNX
This is an alternative name for the water serpent–monster Mishipizhiw of the Ojibwa Native American people of the United States. The Great Lynx was described as a catlike monster of the Great Lakes that had a saw-toothed protuberance the length of its back and a vast prehensile tail with which it ensnared and dragged its victims under the water.
References 134
See also Mishipizhiw

GREAT SERPENT OF HELL
This is the name of a monstrous being in the legends of the Peigan Native American people of Canada. The story relates how a Sioux wife named Onwi-Menocha, meaning "Moon-woman," was made to perform the "dance of the secret loves" when he suspected her odd disappearances. From her green body paint and the writhings of her performance it was assumed that her lover was a forest serpent. Her death was demanded immediately, but she disappeared before this could be accomplished. The husband was later assured by her in visions that she was indeed with the Great Serpent of Hell but would still protect his hunting.
References 134
See also serpent

GREAT SERPENT OF LORETTE
This is an alternative name for the monstrous serpent known as Oyaleroweck that lived in the great waterfall of the Saint Charles River.
References 134
See also Oyaleroweck, serpent

GREAT TALL TAILOR
This is an alternative name for the Red-Legged Scissor-man, a nineteenth-century Nursery bogie of England and Germany.
References 97, 182
See also Agrippa, Nursery bogie, Red-Legged Scissor-man

GREAT TIGER
This is an alternative name for the water serpent–monster Mishipizhiw of the Ojibwa Native American people of the United States. The Great Tiger was described as a cat-like monster of the Great Lakes that had a saw-toothed protuberance the length of its back and a vast prehensile tail with which it ensnared and dragged its victims under the water.
References 134
See also Mishipizhiw

GRENDEL

1. This is the name of a monstrous creature in the great Anglo Saxon epic *Beowulf* dating from the eighth century and written in England, probably in Northumbria, about a hero of Scandinavia. The epic derives from earlier oral traditions of about the sixth century but the only surviving manuscript, in the British Museum, dates from about A.D. 1000. There is little by way of actual description of Grendel except that this vast, monstrous being, possibly some sort of dragon, inhabited the fetid swamps of Denmark close to the mead-hall called Heorot (the Hall of the Stag) built by King Hrothgar. However, this evil creature of the swamps could not stand to hear people enjoying themselves in the mead-hall. Grendel descended upon the place at night while all were sleeping and killed thirty of the warriors, then dragged their bodies back to be devoured in the swamp. The following night the same happened and yet again until the court of King Hrothgar fled to a safer abode. Years later, Beowulf of the Geats sailed to Denmark and offered to rid the land of Grendel. He and his men stayed in the mead-hall, and when Grendel appeared and devoured one of his men Beowulf heroically fought the monster and succeeded in mortally wounding it and severing one of its arms as proof. When King Hrothgar returned in the morning they could see the limb hanging from the rafters of the hall. Then they followed the bloody track back to the swamp, where the water was red with the dying monster's blood. But while they rejoiced with great feasting for the death of Grendel, Grendel's mother came to be avenged for the death of her son.

2. This is also the name of one of the Water Giants or Jotuns in the Norse mythology of Scandinavia. Grendel was the progeny of Aegir or Hler and Ran, and his siblings were Gymir and Mimir.
References 7, 13, 20, 47, 78, 105, 134, 166, 182
See also dragon, Grendel's Mother, Gymir, Jotun, Mimir, monster

GRENDEL'S MOTHER

This is the name of a monstrous creature in the great Anglo Saxon epic *Beowulf* dating from the eighth century and written in England, probably in Northumbria, about a hero of Scandinavia. When Beowulf dispatched the monstrous Grendel, neither he nor his men, nor those of King Hrothgar, suspected that there were two monsters lurking in the fetid swamp near their mead-hall. While they were asleep from their feasting, this vast and gruesome monster came in the night, took the bloody arm of her son from the rafters of the hall, then seized and devoured one of the champions of the king. In the morning the hero Beowulf armed himself and went to the bloody swamps after Grendel's mother. There he swam to the bottom of the mere, and a mighty battle ensued under the water. All the anxious onlookers thought the hero had been killed when the water boiled with blood. But a weary Beowulf finally emerged from the swamp to a hero's welcome and feasting. Many years later he was to lose his life whilst killing a dragon.
References 7, 13, 20, 47, 78, 105, 134, 166, 182
See also dragon, Grendel, monster

GRIDR, GRID

This is the name of a giantess in the Norse mythology of Scandinavia. Gridr was the mother of the god Vidar; this son will be one of the only beings to survive the final battle of Ragnarök after killing the wolf Fenrir. Gridr gave birth to her son by the god Thor, whom she rescued from the scheming of Loki and the giant Geirröd by giving Thor her own magic gloves, belt, and staff. In some versions he is her son by Odin, the king of the gods.
References 125, 133, 139
See also Fenrir, Geirröd, giantess

GRIFFIN, GRIFFON, GRIFFEN, GRIPHON, GRIFFETH

This is the name of a fabulous monster in the legends and folk beliefs of Europe. The Griffin, whose name means "to Seize," also spelled as Gryffon or Gryphon, is derived from the Greek word *gryps* and the Latin word *gryphus*. They are described as hybrid monsters having the body of a lion and the head, torso, and legs of an eagle with large ears. They had large red eyes, their body was brown, but the wings were either blue or white. It was said to be the progeny of a lion and an eagle. The Griffins were said to be malicious, greedy, and terrifying creatures that would attack any living thing that entered their domain, taking them in their vast talons through the air to their nests in the mountains.

This monstrous beast was known in the ancient cultures of Mesopotamia and Egypt, where its image has been dated back to 3300 B.C. In classical times they were said to draw the chariots of the gods Apollo, Jupiter, and Nemesis. The Griffins were said to guard hoards of treasure in the mountains or to guard mines of gold in the regions of northern India and the eastern Mediterranean lands. Early legends tell of attempts to take these treasures and of their fight with a one-eyed race called the Arimaspians. One legend tells of how Alexander the Great (356–323 B.C.) was supposed to have harnessed eight Griffins to a basket, into which he had enticed them with food on a spear, to fly him into the heavens. The legends concerning these creatures were promulgated by such authors as Aelianus, Aristeas, Herodotus, and Pliny during the classical period of ancient Greece and Rome. Griffins were later incorporated into many of

Heraldic Griffin on a helmet crest (Rose Photo Archive, UK)

the medieval Books of Hours, psalters, and bestiaries of Europe, in which they were described as hating horses and considered in an Italian bestiary to symbolize the devil. However, this was not the general view, for in both the *Etymologies* of Isidore of Seville (ca. 560–636) and the work of Dante Alighieri (1265–1321) the Griffin symbolized both the mortal and the divine in Christ. During the late Middle Ages, travelers' tales incorporated accounts of the Griffins. The fourteenth-century *Travels of Sir John Mandeville* tells of Griffins in the land of Bactry whose bodies were eight times the size of a lion, with vast horns on their heads that were made into drinking horns. The Griffin was a popular beast despite its fearsome reputation and was incorporated into the *Mock Turtle's Story* in the classic work *Alice in Wonderland* (1865) by the English academic and author Lewis Carroll (Charles Lutwidge Dodgson, 1843–1898). It is part of the repertoire of strange beings that beset the heroine

Alice as she goes further down the rabbit hole into Wonderland.

The Griffin was widely depicted in art forms throughout these periods as well as being used as an emblem in battle for regal courage. It has become well established in the heraldic repertoire of European coats of arms, especially for nobility and the crest of the family named Griffin.

References 5, 7, 14, 18, 20, 40, 61, 63, 78, 89, 149, 167, 180, 185

See also Akhekhu, Angka, Arimaspi, Bar Yachre, Griffin Vulture, Kargas, Kirni, monster, Senmurv, Simurgh

GRIFFIN VULTURE

This is a monstrous bird in the classical mythology of Greece and Rome. It was the offspring of the monstrous Echidne and the monster Typhon and was to be the instrument of the torture of Prometheus. Every day the terrible bird feasted on the liver of the immortal giant Prometheus, and every evening, because he was immortal, the liver regrew, and the process of his agony was thus repeated. That is, until the advent of the hero Heracles/Hercules, who killed it by shooting it in flight with an arrow. In modern times a vulture, *Gryps fulvus*, has been named after this mythological monster.

References 7

See also giant, Griffin, monster, Prometheus

GRILLUS (sing.), GRILLI (pl.)

This is an alternative spelling of the ancient classical and medieval European monster called the Gryllus.

References 182

See also Gryllus, monster

GRIM

This is the name of a giant in the classical literature of England. He appears in the classic allegorical work *Pilgrim's Progress*, written by John Bunyan and published in 1682. Giant Grim is also known as Bloody-Man because of his reputation for slaughtering pilgrims and devouring them. When he comes upon the pilgrims and Great-heart surrounded by lions, he challenged them and was attacked by Great-heart the guide, who felled him to the ground. Then the pilgrims passed even the lions that they found to be chained up and unable to attack.

References 20, 31

See also Despair (Giant), giant, Maul, Pagan, Pope, Slay-good

GRINDYLOW

This is the name of a monster in the folklore of Yorkshire, England. It is described as a humanoid monster, with excessively long arms and fingers,

The death of Giant Grim (Rose Photo Archive, UK)

inhabiting the marshes and deep, stagnant pools. There it awaits any unwary children unattended by parents to venture to the edge. The Grindylow will swoop on the unsuspecting child and drag it to be devoured in the depths of the murky waters. Grindylow is, of course, a nursery bogie whose activities were used by anxious parents to keep their children safe from stagnant waters.

References 24, 160
See also Jenny Greenteeth, Kappa, Nellie Long Arms, Nursery bogies, Peg Powler

GROOT SLANG

This is the name of a monster in the legends and folk beliefs of West Africa. It was reported by the European travelers to the Congo as being huge, like an elephant, with the tail of a serpent. It inhabited the caverns and swamps of the West African coast. The Groot Slang resembles the Mokêle-Mbêmbe and the Iriz Ima.

References 7, 47, 63, 89
See also Iriz Ima, Mokêle-Mbêmbe

GRUAGACH

The Gruagach of Scottish folklore are also known as the Groagach, Grogach, or Grogan. They are variously described as hairy beings with long, golden hair. In Ulster, Northern Ireland, they are described as a large-headed, soft-shaped, almost formless hairy ogre, resembling a Woodwose or Wildman. (In other accounts it is a brownie-type of spirit about the height of a man's knee and without clothes.) Whatever the description, the Gruagach can be both malicious and benevolent around the homestead or the farms in which it abides. Its protective qualities and cattle-herding abilities make up for the other mischief that it may wreak on the household.

References 128, 183
See also ogre, Red Etin

GRUGYN SILVER BRISTLES

This is the name of a monstrous boar in the Celtic legends and folklore of Ireland and Wales. Grugyn Silver Bristles was the son of the gigantic Twrch Trwyth, and together with this monster and other siblings they ravaged the whole of Ireland. Then the heroic King Arthur was called upon to rid the land of these monstrous beasts, and three ferocious battles took place before the brood was driven from Ireland. Undaunted, the tribe of gigantic boars swam the Irish Sea to the coast of Wales, where they were once more bent on destruction. Arthur and his heroic knights pursued the beasts from the Wye River across the land. One by one the boars were killed, with many warriors gored and slain, until only Twrch Trwyth and his sons, Grugyn Silver Bristles and Llwydawg the Hewer, were left. A vicious battle ensued, but

Grugyn Silver Bristles, by then exhausted, was hacked down among the slaughtered warriors at a place now called Garth Grugyn, which commemorates his demise.

References 105
See also Gullinbursti, Llwydawg the Hewer, Twrch Trwyth

GRUMBO

This is the name of a giant in the traditional tales of seventeenth- and eighteenth-century Europe derived from older folkloric traditions. Giant Grumbo features in the traditional tale of Tom Thumb, the mighty miniature fairy-child. The stories appeared in print in 1724 as the French *Le Petit Poucet* (Tiniest Thumb) and were translated into English during that year. The tale related how Tom Thumb had many adventures as a result of his size, one of which was that he accidentally fell into a bowl of porridge that had been prepared for Giant Grumbo. Whilst trying to extricate himself from the mess, Tom found himself first on a gigantic spoon and then down the gigantic throat. But Tom's wriggling in the giant's throat tickles so much that the giant vomits the tiny chap out of his castle window and into the sea. There Tom's adventures continue, with his being swallowed by a fish. The fish was shortly caught and served up for the meal of the legendary King Arthur—with Tom still aboard!

References 182
See also Agrippa, Bombomachides, Brandamour, giant, Nursery bogie, ogre

GRYFFON, GRYPHON

These are two alternative spellings of the name of the Griffin, a fabulous beast in the legends and folk beliefs of Europe.

References 5
See also Griffin

GRYLIO

This is the name of a fabulous creature in the bestiaries of medieval Europe. It was described as looking similar to a large salamander and was equally poisonous both to man and animal. According to the authors of the bestiaries, this reptile would climb up into fruit trees when the fruit was ripening and deliberately poison the fruit. This ensured the certain death of anything that either ate the fruit or, if the fruit fell into water, the death of those who drank there.

References 7
See also Dea, salamander, Stellio

GRYLLUS, GRYLLI (pl.), GRILLUS (sing.), GRILI (pl.)

This is the name of a monstrous hybrid humanoid creature in the ancient legends and art forms of the

Circe and Gryllus (A Wonder Book for Boys and Girls and Tanglewood Tales by N. Hawthorne, J. M. Dent, London)

eastern Mediterranean countries. The Gryllus was depicted as part beast and part human with another human face in the center of the belly. These Stomach-Faces, as they were also known, were depicted on jewelry and other art forms in ancient Egypt, Greece, Rome, and other Mediterranean countries of the Greco-Roman period. Pliny the Elder in his work (ca. A.D. 77) tells of a number of artists specializing in the portrayal of Grilli but does not give details of the images. However, the Greek historian and philosopher Plutarch (A.D. 46–ca. 120) related a version of the Homeric myth, concerning Odysseus's encounter with the sorceress Circe, in which she had turned men into grotesque swine. When Odysseus tried to have the men disenchanted from their metamorphosis, one of their number gave an elegant argument for the retention of his grotesque and brutish state. When asked, Circe gave the name of this man as Gryllus. In Homer's earlier version of the myth, he had used the word *sus* for "swine," but Plutarch cleverly used the root for the Greek "to grunt," *gryl.* (Plutarch's dialogue was later used in erudite discourse of the seventeenth century for philosophical discussion concerning the difference between human and animal states.)

During the medieval period the Gryllus became a familiar drollery in the visual imagery of psalters and Books of Hours as well as on stonework and wood carvings in ecclesiastical buildings, where its symbolism was that of human folly and vice. The character of Grylle, the beastly man, was introduced in *The Faerie Queene* by the English Elizabethan poet Edmund Spenser (1552?–1599). The original ancient meaning of the Gryllus has long been lost but was regarded in ancient times as a powerful and potent amulet.

References 89, 182
See also Acephalos

GRYPS, GRYPES

This is an alternative name for a class of Griffin in the classical mythology of Greece and Rome. Gryps are variously described as having the body of a lion but the head of an eagle, or the body of a horse and the head of an eagle. They were designated the duty of guarding the mineral wealth to be found in the region of Scythian Arimaspi (an area corresponding to the modern Middle East and northwestern Asia), especially the deposits of gold to be found there. The Gryps were much used as a symbol of guardianship by the Romans and can still be seen on intaglio rings from the period.

References 89, 178
See also Griffin, monster

GUARDIAN OF THE FISHES

This is the name of a water monster in the legends and folklore of the Estonian people. The Guardian of the Fishes is described as a monstrous, fish-shaped creature of gigantic proportions that "walks" on feet on land but mostly inhabits the waters. It is to be recognized not only by its vast shape but also from the massive, saw-toothed ridge that projects from the length of its back.

References 134
See also King of the Fishes, monster

GUDANNA

This is the name of a monstrous bull in the mythology of ancient Sumer. Gudanna was described as a vast creature with such poisonous breath that it was capable of killing over two hundred warriors at a time. It was created by the god Anu at the behest of the goddess Ishtar to wreak vengeance on the hero Gilgamesh for refusing her advances. Gilgamesh, with the help of his friend Enkidu, managed to slaughter and dismember Gudanna. This so enraged the god that Enkidu was slain in revenge.

The Guardian of the Fishes is a water monster with a saw-toothed ridge that projects from its back. (Rose Photo Archive, UK)

Guardian of the Fishes

References 7, 89
See also Cretan Bull, Minotaur

GUGU

This is an alternative spelling of Gougou, the name of a giantess in the traditions and beliefs of the Micmac Native American people of the northeastern United States.
References 134
See also Gougou

GUGWE

This is an alternative spelling of Gougou, the name of a giantess in the traditions and beliefs of the Micmac Native American people of the northeastern United States.
References 134
See also Gougou

GUHYAKA

This is the name of a race of giants in the Hindu mythology of India. The Guhyaka are a race of troglodyte gigantic men who act as the guardians of the treasures that Kubera has hoarded in the caves.
References 112
See also giant

GUILDHALL GIANTS

This is the alternative title for the Town Giants of London, England. Their individual names are Gog and Magog; their derivation is not only biblical but also from the legendary past of the British Isles.
References 174
See also giant, Gog and Magog, Town Giants

GUIRIVULU

This is the name of a monster in the legends and folklore of South America, especially Chile. The Guirivulu is described as a beast that has the shape of a puma with a head resembling that of a fox. It has the curiously adapted tail that ends in a massive claw. Because of its features it is sometimes called the fox-snake. This monster inhabits the deepest pools and waters of the rivers, where it will attack not only animals but any human that is foolish enough to go near it. Should it come upon a victim, they are quickly enveloped in the enormous mouth and swallowed into the body, which expands and extends like that of a snake, to take the victim whole.
References 7, 134
See also monster

GUITA, GUITAS (pl.)

This is the name of a dragon in the legends and folklore of Spain. The name "Guita" may be translated as "Kicking Mule," which hardly sounds like the name for a dragon. The legends have been long eroded from fire-breathing monsters and lost from the original. Now this dragon is paraded as an effigy, like a Town Giant, to protect its inhabitants from evil in the festivals of Corpus Christi at the Patum of Berga in Catalonia. The Guita is an enormous, serpentine, green dragon with an extended neck like the Loch Ness Monster. Its face is black with huge fangs and leering eyes above a vast open red mouth. To simulate the original fiery breath, it now contains rockets and fireworks to give a frisson to the festival crowd.
References 182
See also dragon, giant, Town giant

GUIVRE

This is the name of a hybrid monster in the legends and folklore of medieval France. It is described in the bestiaries as having the body of a serpent but with the head of a dragon with horns protruding from its forehead. The Guivre was said to inhabit pools, woods, forests, and damp lonely places. It was said to be a particularly vicious beast and would attack humans at every opportunity. It is now most frequently seen in the armorial heraldry of France.
References 89
See also Amphiptere, Wivre, Wyvern

GULAH

This is the name of a female Ghoul in pre-Islamic traditions and beliefs. In later times they were identified as a species of Djinn.
References 64, 74, 78, 94, 120, 146
See also Baba Yaga, Djin/n, Ghoul, Pey

GULINBURSTI, GULLINBURSTI

This is the name of a gigantic wild boar in the Norse mythology of Scandinavia. Gulinbursti, whose name may be translated as "Goldbristles," was associated with the god Freyr as the creature that drew his chariot over any type of terrain, whether air, sea, or land. As his name implies, Goldbristles was made entirely of golden bristles that glowed so much that they illuminated the entire region in which he traveled. Like Hildesuin and Slidringtanni, they were frequently the wild, vicious, rapid steeds of the gods through the underbrush of the forests and into a battle or the chase.
References 7, 78, 89, 105
See also Ætolian Boar, Beigad, Boar of Beann-Gulbain, Buata, Cafre/Kafre, Calydonian Boar, Erymanthean Boar, Hildesuin, Pugot/Pugut, Sachrimnir, Slidringtanni, Twrch Trwyth, Ysgithyrwyn

GULON

This is the name of a monster in Swedish folklore that is also known as Jerff in the northern parts of Sweden. It was described by the traveler Olaus Magnus in 1555 as having a long, fur-covered body somewhere between that of a lion and that of a hyena with the tail of a fox and enormous claws. It inhabited the northern snowfields, where it existed on carrion. It would eat anything ravenously and would swell with the gasses of the putrefying flesh it had consumed. Then it would find two trees growing close together and squeeze its body between them and dislodge the swelling so that it could gorge some more. It was during this process that the Gulon was most vulnerable, and it could be killed for its fur. Although its flesh was never eaten, its blood was said to have been mixed with honey and drunk at weddings.

References 7, 77, 89
See also monster

GUMBEROO

This is a creature from the folklore of lumberjacks and forest workers, especially in Wisconsin and Minnesota in the United States, during the nineteenth and early twentieth centuries. The Gumberoo belongs to a group of beings affectionately known as the Fearsome Critters, whose exaggerated proportions and activities not only explained the weird noises of the lonely landscape but also provided some amusement at camps. The Gumberoo was described as a beast resembling a bear, but instead of fur it had a rotund body of hairless leather that seemed invulnerable to whatever was shot at it. Bullets and arrows and any other missile simply bounced off it. Should anyone wish to kill this beast they had to use fire, for that was all that could defeat the Gumberoo.

References 7, 24
See also Fearsome Critters

GUNAPIPI

This is an alternative name for the gigantic female monster known as Kunapipi in the legends of the Dreamtime of the Native Australians.

References 38, 125, 133
See also Kunapipi, monster

GUNNLOD

This is the name of a giantess in the Norse mythology of Scandinavia. When her father, the giant Suttung, went to avenge the killing of his father, he brought from the dwarfs who had done this a magic mead called Kvasir. When Suttung returned he hid the Kvasir and asked his daughter Gunnlod to guard it. But Odin, the king of the gods, was determined to retrieve the magic mead. He duped Baugi, Suttung's brother, into showing him the hiding place and seduced Gunnlod into allowing him to the brew, which he immediately swallowed. Then Odin assumed the form of an eagle and flew away with Suttung in the same shape, but the giant's powers failed; he fell from the skies and was killed.

References 133, 139
See also Baugi, giant, giantess, Suttung

GURANGATCH

This is the name of a water monster in the Dreamtime mythology of the Native Australian people of New South Wales. Gurangatch is described as a hybrid lizard-fish of immense size. He was never hunted until Mirragen the Cat-man went fishing and required the honor of being the best fisherman of the village. So he went to the deep pool he knew was inhabited by Gurangatch and used spells and charms, learned from the *wirinuns* (shaman), to bring the monster to the surface. But try as the pursuer might, the monster evaded capture. So he went for some poison bark to drug the water of the pool. While Cat-man was absent, Gurangatch departed by burrowing through the solid rock as easily a swimming in the deep pool. Cat-man could not believe his eyes, for a third river had started where the pool of the two rivers raced in a torrent through the channels made by Gurangatch's escape. For days the monster evaded Mirragen, until Gurangatch went directly to his village, taking the torrents through it and scattering the villagers. Then Mirragen went for help, and only the Bird-people would dive to look for the monster. Finally, Diver-bird brought back a single scale from the monster, and the torn, bleeding, fatigued Mirragen took that as the token flesh from its body for them to eat. But to this day the many rivers and Jenolan and Whambeyan caverns of New South Wales testify to his ferocious pursuit of Gurangatch.

References 154
See also monster

GUYANOOSA

This is an alternative name for the Guyascutus in the folklore of lumberjacks and forest workers (and later fraudsters), especially in Wisconsin and Minnesota in the United States.

References 7, 24
See also Fearsome Critters, Guyascutus

GUYASCUTUS

This is a creature from the folklore of lumberjacks and forest workers (and later fraudsters), especially in Wisconsin and Minnesota in the United States during the nineteenth and early twentieth centuries. The Guyascutus was described as being a gigantic monster reportedly like a dragon. In later tales it is like a ten-foot-long alligator with a covering of shell-plates like those of an armadillo but with a dorsal ridge of fierce horns. In other, even later accounts it resembled a white-tailed deer with the ears of a rabbit but with ferocious fangs in its jaws. Whatever the description, the most notable feature were its legs, which were

shorter at one side than the other, as they were able to telescope to the desired angle of the slope. This was presumably so that it could get around the mountainsides easily, but in case this did not happen its prehensile tail would curl around a suitable rock until it could get its balance. It seemed that the mountains were a natural habitat, but in 1844 a Guyascutus was reported to be lodged in a massive poplar tree, and they were also recorded in the farming territory of Vermont. Although some were supposed to be predatory, this must be an exaggeration, since in 1855 they were reportedly eating hyacinth roots.

This creature belongs to a group of beings affectionately known as the Fearsome Critters, whose exaggerated proportions and activities not only explained the weird noises of the lonely landscape but also provided some amusement at camps. The Guyascutus is also known as Cuter-Cuss, Godaphro, Gouger, Gwinter, Guyanoosa, Hunkus, Lunkus, Mountain Stem-Winder, Prock, Prock Gwinter, Sidehill Dodger, Sidehill Ganger, Rickaboo Racker, Rockabore, Sauger, Sidewinder, and Sideswipe.

There are several tales concerning the Guyascutus, notably one that tells of a traveling wild animal show. The proprietors arrived with their charge in a small town in the Midwest and promptly advertised the showing of their gigantic Guyascutus. The show was a sellout, and one night the tent was packed with the curious townspeople. Then one of the men stormed into the tent in a state of horror and screamed that the terrifying Guyascutus had escaped. The audience fled in terror, leaving the showmen to escape with their takings.

Showmen were not the only ones apparently to use the talents of the Guyascutus. It seems that the farmers of Vermont bred their sheep with the Guyascutus for the development of legs that would adapt to the mountain pastures. One of these farmers later recalled how one of these domesticated Guyascutus had followed him like a pet, and he remembered he was most unhappy when the poor thing tried to follow him on the flat road with its uneven legs.
References 7, 24
See also Fearsome Critters

GWAGWAKHWALANOOKSIWEY

This is the name of a cannibal bird in the traditions and beliefs of the Kwakiutl Native American people of Canada. Gwagwakhwalanooksiwey is a metamorphosed form of the Raven, also known as Hokhoku, and is ultimately also metamorphosed from Bakbakwakanooksiwae, the Cannibal-at-the-North-End-of-the-World. As Gwagwakhwalanooksiwey, he preys upon unwary humans, breaking their heads with his long hard beak to pick out and devour their eyes. He has an equally terrifying wife known as

Galokwudzuwis, and together their images feature in Kwakiutl ceremonies.
References 77, 89
See also Bakbakwakanooksiwae, Galokwudzuwis

GWENHIDWY, GWENHUDWY

This is the name of a mermaid in the folklore of Wales. Her flocks of sheep were the waves, and every ninth one was a ram. The Bard Rhys Llwyd ap Rhys ap Rhuert wrote in the sixteenth century:

> Haid ddefaid Gwenhudwy
> A naw hwrdd yn un a hwy
> (A troop of the sheep of Gwenhuwy
> And nine rams along with them.)

There does not seem to be the same malevolent character attached to Gwenhidwy from the Atlantic side of the British shores as there does with the North Sea or Mediterranean mermaids.
References 84, 160
See also Ben Varrey, Havhest, Havman, mermaid, Merrow

GWIBER

This is the name of a white dragon in the legends of Wales. The Gwiber is a winged snake, a type of dragon like a Wyvern; the word now means "adder" or "viper." The Celtic legend tells how the Saxon King Vortigern was bent on conquering and settling the whole of the British Isles. When he tried to build a fortress in the Welsh mountains of Snowdonia, every morning the building stones were gone. He was advised that a child sacrifice must be made of a fatherless boy. When eventually such a boy, Emrys (Ambrose), was brought to the site, they were told by him that their problem lay with the dragons in a cavern beneath the site. Instead of sacrificing the youth, Vortigern's men delved until they saw, sure enough, there in a huge cavern beneath the site for the castle, two dragons—one white, the other red. With the break into their domain, the dragons became locked in combat. When the white "Gwiber" was defeated and the victorious guardian, y Ddraig Goch remained, it was then that the boy disclosed their symbolism. The Gwiber, the white dragon, represented the invading forces of Vortigern and his Saxons; y Ddraig Goch, the red dragon, was the guardian of the Welsh, and the cavern was Britain from which they would be completely driven.
References 128, 183
See also Ddraig Goch (y), dragon

GWINTER

This is an alternative name for the Guyascutus in the folklore of lumberjacks and forest workers (and later

Y Ddraig Goch and Gwiber Dragon (English Legends by H. Bett, Batsford Books, UK, 1950)

fraudsters), especially in Wisconsin and Minnesota in the United States.
References 7
See also Fearsome Critters, Guyascutus

GWRGWNT

This is the name of a giant in the Celtic mythology of Wales. Like the Gargam of breton Celtic folklore, Gwrgwnt is said to be a collossal being but is maimed and only roams at night about the mountains and hillsides. He poses no threat to the local population.
References 128
See also Gargam

GWYLLGI

This is the name of a gigantic dog in the traditions and folklore of Wales. It is described as an enormous mastiff that pads along beside late night travelers and terrifies them.
References 128
See also Black dog

GYES

This is the name of a giant in the classical mythology of Greece and Rome. He is also referred to as Gyges.
References 7
See also Centimanes, Gyges

GYGES

This is the name of a giant in the classical mythology of Greece and Rome. Gyges is one of the Hundred-Handed Giants who were the sons of Gaia and Uranus. He is also referred to as Gyes. Like his two brothers, Cottus and Briareus, he had fifty heads and a hundred arms. They were born fully mature and clad in full battle armor. They waged war on the Olympian gods and were defeated.
References 24, 78, 139, 169, 178
See also Briareus, Centimanes, Cottus

GYGR

This is the female designation for the giantesses in the Norse mythology of Scandinavia. They are the female counterparts of the Jotuns, or giants. The Gygr, such as one called Juternsaxa, were renowned for their beauty, and were frequently the wives of the gods .

The Gytrash follows travelers on lonely moorland roads and brings misfortune and terror to those who are too slow to get away.
(Lancashire Ghosts by K. Eyre, Dalesman Books, UK)

References 24
See also Jotun, Juternsaxa

GYMIR

This is the name of a giant in the Norse mythology of Scandinavia. Gymir had a daughter called Gerda, who was so beautiful that the god Frey fell instantly in love with her and ultimately, after some adventures and with Gymir's consent, married her.

References 139
See also Angboda, Gerd, giant

GYTRASH

This is the name of an evil, monstrous, supernatural dog in the folklore of the North of England, especially in Yorkshire and Lancashire. Gytrash is also known as Guytrash and is a portent of death and disaster. It is usually described as having the body of an animal such as a horse, cow, mule, or dog but with a fierce, thick-set head like a mastiff with huge, glowing eyes. It is most frequently seen as a large, shaggy-haired dog with glowing eyes. The Gytrash, like the Padfoot, follows night-bound travelers on lonely moorland roads and brings misfortune and terror to those who are too slow to get away. Charlotte Brontë describes the Gytrash in *Jane Eyre* (1847).

References 20, 24, 37, 146, 160
See also Barguest, Black dogs, Black Shuck, Mauthe Dhoog, Padfoot, Rongeur d'Os, Skriker, Trash

H

HAAKAPAINIZI

This is the name of a monstrous grasshopper in the legends and traditions of the Kawaiisu Native American people from the Great Basin of the United States. This gigantic creature was a predatory cannibal that hunted for humans, using a great basket to carry them off. Haakapainizi especially trapped little children to abduct and devour. Then the hero Mouse managed to dispose of the monster by tricking it into swallowing a hot coal; it turned into stone from the inside out.

References 77
See also monster

HADHAYŌSH, HADHAYĀOSH

This is the name of a primordial ox or bull in the Zoroastrian mythology of Persia, now Iran. Hadhayōsh, also known as Sarsaok in the Pahlavi language, carried the first humans across the primordial ocean known as Vourukasha. This great beast will provide from a mixture of its fat and the white haoma herbs of sacrifice, the draft of immortality, for the coming resurrection of all righteous people.

References 24
See also Gēush Urvan

HADUIGONA

This is the name of a giant in the traditions and beliefs of the Iroquois Native American people of the United States. Haduigona, who is also referred to as Twisted Face and Grandfather, is described as an enormous humanoid being with a very long, distorted face, with huge eyebrows over deep-set eyes. His long nose and huge mouth have a pronounced twist to the right, showing his fang-like teeth. The legend relates how Haduigona believed that he was the creator of the world in which he lived, but when the Creator met Haduigona on the far side of the Rocky Mountains, this was disputed. Haduigona agreed to a test in which both would sit with their backs to the mountains and by their powers bring a mountain to

them. Haduigona managed to move the mountain a little, but the Creator brought the mountain directly and, as the disbelieving giant turned to look, smashed his face against the mountain at his back. The Creator generously acknowledged the giant's *orenda* power and asked him to cooperate in his great task of healing in the world. Haduigona responded and suggested that offerings of tobacco and respectfully referring to him as "Grandfather" in ceremonies, where his image was worn as a mask, would assure his help. This is said to be the origin of the image of Haduigona as Twisted Face in the False Face Society.

References 136
See also giant

HAFGYGR

This is the name of a giantess or monster in the Norse mythology of Scandinavia. Hafgygr, also known as Margygr, is a type of sea monster or water monster that is part giantess, in much the same manner as the Grendel's mother of the epic *Beowulf*. She is said to inhabit the stagnant pools and inland tarns of murky waters where few humans dare to venture.

See also giantess, Grendel, Grendel's Mother, monster

HAGONDES

This is the name of a cannibal in the traditions and beliefs of the Seneca Native American people of the northeastern United States. This being is now portrayed in effigy with a mask with a long nose. This gives rise to the alternative name "Long Nose" for Hagondes. He is portrayed as a clown with very threatening overtones, especially for little children, whom he will abduct and devour. Hagondes is almost certainly a form of Nursery bogie used by anxious parents to keep their children safe from danger.

References 77
See also cannibal, Nursery bogie

HAI CHIAI

This is an alternative name for the Oriental unicorn in the traditions and legends of China.

HAI HO SHANG

This is the name of a fabulous fish in the traditions and folklore of China. The name was translated by the medieval European writer Guillaume Rondelet as "Sea Buddhist Priest." This was described, in *The Book of Sea Fishes* by Rondelet, as a type of merman or "Monk fish." It was described as a fish except that it had a tonsure like a monk and a scaly type of hood and cloak beneath which extended its fish's tail. This great sea monster was so belligerent that it would attack the fully manned junks in the sea and completely overturn them, drowning all on board. The stench of burning feathers or a ritual dance by a member of the crew might avert disaster.
References 89
See also merman, monster

HAI RIYO

This is the name of a composite fabulous creature in the traditions and legends of Japan. The Hai Riyo, also known as the Tobi Tatsu and the Schachi Hoko, is described as having the body of a bird and bird's claws and wings but with the head of a dragon. This legendary creature's image is to be found on screens in the monastery of Chi-on-in in Kyoto. It is possible that it is derived from the only winged Chinese dragon, the Ying Lung.
References 81, 89
See also Ying Lung

HAIETLIK, HEITLIK

This is the name of a serpent in the traditions and beliefs of the Clayoqut and Nootka Native American people of the Pacific Coast of Canada. Haietlik, also known as the Lightning Serpent, is described as a vast serpent with a body like that of an elongated alligator with a huge head resembling that of a horse. It was said to inhabit the inland coastal waters and lakes and was associated with the activities of hunting and fishing. Many pictograms of the monster are to be found on the rocks in the vicinity of its habitat. The skin of this monster was said to be especially efficacious for catching a whale if carried in the boat. The earliest recorded sighting, however, was in 1791, when a party of men in a canoe were suddenly frightened by the monster close to the shore. There are no recordings of any malice in the creature.
References 89, 134
See also serpent

HAIIT

This is the name of a creature detailed by Thevet in his sixteenth-century work *Cosmography* and again quoted

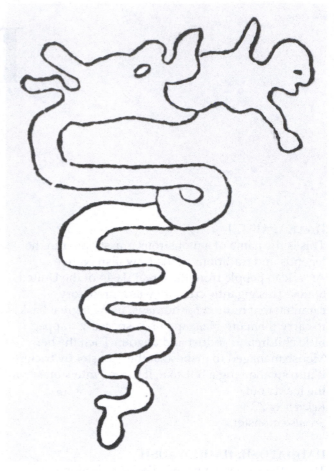

Serpent devouring a child. The Haietlik is one of many legendary serpents. (Rose Photo Archive, UK)

by Ambroise Paré (1517–1590) during the same period in his work *On Monsters and Marvels*. It was purported to be a large beast with a shaggy, furry body and a very small tail, a face similar to that of a human; the three-toed feet had extensive claws with which it climbed the trees. The Haiit was said to inhabit the forests of central Africa where the people sometimes trapped the Haiit, but because it had never been observed to eat, the authors reported that it lived on air. As with many of these European travelers' tales, much exaggeration distorted the concept of what was in all probability a quite familiar anthropoid creature.
References 147

HAIKUR

This is one of three names of the Scandinavian Nicker, or water monster, in the traditions and folklore of the people of Iceland.
References 20, 37, 107, 111, 120, 160
See also Nicker

HAIRY-MAN

This is the name of a giant humanoid beast in the traditions and folklore of the Tanaina peoples of the

subarctic regions of Alaska. The Hairy-Man is described as an upright, two-legged beast covered in gray hair. He has curious eyes that have no pupils. This humanoid inhabits the mountainous regions, where he is benevolent to any humans that he comes across—unless threatened by them.
References 77
See also Bigfoot, Yeti

HAI-URI
This is the name of a monster in the traditions and legends of the Khoisin people of South Africa. This is a terrifying monster described as having only one half of the normal humanoid body, with one arm and leg. Although apparently thus restricted, the Hai-uri is capable of traveling at great speed through the rough terrain that he inhabits, in order to hunt and devour the humans that are his prey.
References 47, 78
See also monster, Nashas

HAIZUM
This is the name of a horse in the sacred book of Islam, the Quran. Haizum is the horse upon which the archangel Gabriel delivers messages to the Prophet Mohammed.
References 20
See also Arion, Balius, Borak (Al), Pegasus, Sivushko, Sleipnir

HAKENMANN
This is the name of a water monster in the Teutonic legends and folklore of the northern German coastal regions. The Hakenmann is described as having the body of a gigantic fish and the torso and head of a man. It is a particularly vicious and predatory being that will hunt down and destroy any humans within its domain.
References 24
See also merman, Skrimsl

HAKULAQ
This is the name of water monster in the traditions and beliefs of the Tsimshian Native American coastal peoples of the Northwest United States. The Hakulaq is described as a huge female sea monster that allows its child to imitate a lost human baby floating in the waters between two islands. When humans take the "child" out of the water and try to "rescue" it, taking it back to land, Hakulaq will follow, accuse them of stealing her child, and swamp them with such stormy waves that all will drown.
References 77
See also monster

HALFWAY PEOPLE
According to the legends and traditions of the Micmac people of eastern Canada, these are sea humanoids resembling the mermaids of European legend. The Halfway People are so called because they have the upper body resembling humans and the lower body of an enormous fish. Unlike their European counterparts, when the Halfway People sang it was to warn the local fisherfolk that a storm was coming. Whilever they were treated with respect, these beings would be benign, but should any human be disrespectful, then they would invoke storms and such turbulence that the fishermen would be drowned.
References 7
See also Ben Varrey, Gwenhidwy, Havfrue, mermaid, mermen

HAM
The Italian monk Annius of Viterbo (Giovanni Nanni, ca. 1432–1502) asserted that the biblical Noah was a giant. He re-created a whole genealogy of giants from Noah and Iapetus to justify the constructed line of descent through the giant Dis Samothes to the ancestry of the French nobility of the period. Within this genealogy Annius asserted that the sons of Noah, Shem, Ham, and Japheth, were also giants.
References 174
See also Noah

HAMOU UKAIOU
This is the name of an evil and malicious Afrit in the folklore of Morocco. He is said to be the husband of the djinn Aicha Kandida, and he pursues women traveling alone at night, as his wife does with men, in order to attack and devour them. It is said that sharpening a knife on the ground may put them to flight.
References 122
See also Afrit, Aicha Kandida, Djinn

HAP
This is an alternative name for the gigantic sacred bull in the mythology of ancient Egypt.
References 24, 169
See also Apis, Buchis

HAPALIT
This is an alternative name for the giant Og of Bashan in the Hebraic scriptures and Rabbinical texts. Hapalit, meaning the "Escapee," refers to his delivery from the Flood sent by Yahweh to destroy the evil of mankind.
References 174
See also Og

HAPPEMOUSCHE

This is the name of a giant in the classical literature of France. Happemousche is one of the giant ancestors of Pantagruel in the famous work *Pantagruel* (1532) by the French author François Rabelais (ca. 1494–ca. 1553). But Happemousche does not appear in the original edition; he is an addition to later versions by Rabelais, as a means of establishing the genealogy of Pantagruel. Happemousche, along with five other giants—Etion, Eryx, Galehaut, Gabbara, and Morguan—is credited with inventing something concerned with drinking.

References 174

See also Bruyer, Chalbroth, Daughters of Cain, Gabbara, Galehaut, Gargantua, giant, Happemousche, Hurtaly, Morguan, Noachids, Noah, Offotus, Pantagruel

HARE, SEA

This is the name given to a sea monster in the traditions and beliefs of medieval Europe. It was described as having the body of a fish but with the legs, head, and ears of a hare, behind which were fins. It was said to be a predatory creature that would attack almost any living thing within its reach, pursuing those that were not. The description comes from a time when travelers and sailors described, and exaggerated, the creatures that they encountered, and also when people generally believed that what existed on land also had its counterpart in the oceans and skies.

References 7

See also monster

HARITI, HĀRITI

This is the name of a demonic female ogress in the mythology of India, of China, where she is known as He-Li-Di, or Kishimojin, and of Japan, where she is known as Karitei-mo. In the mythology of India and China this monstrous female cannibal entrapped and devoured children until converted by the Buddha, who hid one of her own children and she learned what anguish she had caused. Hāriti is now a guardian of children and elevated to the status of a goddess able to bless couples with children and cure sick children. As Karitei-mo, her original Chinese name, she is especially venerated by the Shingon and as Nichiren sects in Japan, where she is represented holding a child or the flower of happiness.

References 61, 125, 139, 160

See also cannibal, ogress

HAR-MACHIS, HARMACHIS

This is an alternative name for the Androsphinx of ancient Egyptian mythology. It was also known in the astrological sense as Hor-em-akhen, which may be translated as "Horus of the Horizon," which the Greeks referred to as Har-machis. The most famous image of Har-machis is the familiar feature in the vicinity of the pyramids, usually known simply as the Sphinx. This colossal hybrid creature, more than 180 feet in length and sixty feet in height, has the body of a lion but the head of a human with the portrait representation face of King Khephren.

References 89, 139

See also Androsphinx, Sphinx

HARPY

In classical Greek and Roman mythology the Harpies were originally wind spirits personifying the storm winds, hurricanes, and whirlwinds and later transformed to the role of vengeful, hideous, monstrous fiends. There are various accounts of their origins: They are the daughters of Thaumas and Electra, or the daughters of Neptune and Terra, or the daughters of Typhon and Echidna. Their number also varies from one to five; Homer mentions Podarge (meaning the "Racer"), Hesiod mentions Aëllo (meaning "Swift as the Storm" or "Hurricane") and Ocypete (meaning "Swift"); others mention Celeno, or Keliano (meaning "Dark" or "Black"), and Aellopus. There are also various descriptions from different sources; some say that they resembled birds with the heads and torso of ugly women, with bears' ears, and having arms with talons for fingers. Other accounts say that they had the body of a vulture with the torso and head of a woman, but their wings and talons were bronze or brass. They lived, according to some sources, on the islands of Strophades or Salmydessus in eastern Thrace.

The Harpies, also known by the name Arepyiai, were not only ugly but foul-smelling, and they contaminated whatever they touched. These cannibal monsters abducted the daughters of Pandareus and delivered them to the Erinyes as servants and preyed on any sailors in the vicinity, such as Aeneas and his men when returning from the siege of Troy. They were sent by the gods, as instruments of torture, to Phineus, the king of Thrace, who was blinded by the Harpies and then prevented from getting any of the food at his table before these monstrous creatures despoiled it. The Harpies feature in the tales of Jason and the Argonauts, who eventually helped to bring about the demise of these terrifying sisters and release Phineus from his plight.

Their image became a familiar feature of European heraldry, and they may be depicted on coats of arms as a vulture with the neck and head of a woman.

References 5, 7, 18, 24, 38, 47, 78, 89, 133, 134, 139, 160, 169, 178

See also Aëllo, Aellopus, Arepyiai, Boroka, cannibal, monster, Ocypete, Podarge, Tsanahale

HATUIBWARI

This is the name of the cosmic serpent in the traditions and beliefs of the people of San Cristoval Island in Melanesia. This vast serpent has an upper body resembling that of a human but with two enormous wings. The head has four eyes and the torso has four pendulous breasts with which to nourish all living creatures. Hatuibwari, also known as Agunua, is the primodial ancestor of the human race.
References 38, 125
See also serpent, Ymir

HAVFINË

This is the name of the mermaid in the traditions and folklore of Norway. These half-woman, half-fish beings were highly unpredictable and given to stormy temperament. It was considered exceptionally dangerous to see one, even more so when they drove their white cattle up on to the shore, for this was a signal for a violent storm.
References 7
See also Havfrue, mermaid

HAVFRUE

This is the name of the mermaid in the tradtions and folklore of Denmark. The Havfrue is very beautiful, with long, golden hair, which she may be seen combing whilst floating on the surface of the sea. She can be both helpful and malevolent. They are regarded as being able to foretell events of importance, and the birth of the Danish King Christian IV of Denmark was foretold by a Havfrue. She may be seen driving her milk-white cattle over the dunes to feed on the shore, or glimpsed through the early summer sea mists hovering on the surface of the water. But these sightings are usually portents of wild and stormy weather. She has been reported as visiting the fishermens' night fires on the shore, in the guise of a beautiful maiden who is wet and suffering from the cold. Any who are unwary and enticed to her side may be taken by her to her watery underworld with all the other bodies of the drowned who never resurfaced.
References 25, 107, 120, 160
See also Havmand, Mermaid

HAVHEST

This is a hybrid monster in the traditions and folklore of Scandinavia. The Havhest is described variously as having the body of a fish and the head of a large horse, or as having a serpentine body with a vast torso and head like a horse, with yellow eyes and a double row of enormous fangs in its huge, fire-breathing mouth. This terrifying monster was reported in 1750 in Norway, again in the late nineteenth century on the Sejord, and in the accounts of local folklore by K. Bugge in 1934.
References 134
See also Horse-heads, monster

HAVMAN, HAVMAND

This is a beneficent merman in Scandinavian folklore. The Havmand is known as the Havstrambe in the folklore of Greenland. He is described as being very handsome in human shape, sometimes with a blue skin, and having either a green or black beard and hair. When not in his water home under the sea, he may be in the cliffs and rock caves along the shore. During the voyage of the *Oldenborg* from Denmark to the East Indies in 1672, the crew saw a Havman off the Cape of Good Hope and reported it to the ship's doctor, who drew it in his book. This representation by J. P. Cortemünd is preserved in the Royal Danish Library. Another sighting in 1719 was reported to the bishop of Bergen (Norway), Bishop Pontoppidan, as a twenty-eight-foot monster with the face of a man and front paws like those of a seal calf, beached at a place called Nordland. For the most part the Havmand is regarded as benign if left undisturbed.
References 24, 25, 107, 120, 134, 160
See also Havfrue, mermaid, merman

HAVSTRAMBE

This is the name of a sea monster in the traditions and folklore of the people of Greenland. The Havstrambe is described as having the body of an enormous fish but the torso and head of a man with green hair and beard. He is also known as the Havman in Danish legends.
References 134
See also Havman, merman

HAYAGRIVA

This is the name of a demonic giant in the classical mythology of India. Hayagriva, whose name means "Horse's Neck," is described as a little, pot-bellied human torso with a horse's head. In the mythology of the Vedas, this evil member of the Daityas stole the scriptures but was ultimately defeated by Vishnu in the avatar of a fish.

In Tibetan Buddhism Hayagriva, known as a Dharmapāla, is converted from his wickedness and transformed into a protective deity who guards humans from the demons' attacks. For the Buddhists of Mongolia, after his conversion to Buddhism, the gigantic Hayagriva became the protector of horses. In Tibetan Buddhism, this monstrous giant, known there by the name of rTa-mgrin, became, after his conversion, the Lord of Wrath.
References 24, 47, 64, 125, 133, 160
See also Daitya, giant

HAYICANAKO

This is the name of a giantess in the traditions of the Tlingit Native American people of the northwestern United States. Hayicanako, whose name may be translated as "Old Woman Underneath Us," is described as so vast that she is capable of supporting the world. In some versions she keeps watch over the stability of the earth as it is supported on the leg of a beaver. Sometimes she loses her concentration because of hunger, and the result is a series of earthquakes. Her hunger is assuaged when humans throw fats into their hearths.
References 77
See also giantess

HECATE

This is a monstrous deity in the classical mythology of Greece and Rome. Hecate was originally one of the Titans and the offspring of Gaia and Uranus. She was described as a hideous female with snakes on her head instead of hair, like that of the Gorgons and Medusa. She helped the Olympian gods in their wars against the giants and was later elevated to being the goddess of the underworld, revered for her domain of boundaries, crossroads, cemetaries, and the black arts associated with the evil of the night.
References 38, 125, 166
See also giant, Gorgon, Medusa, Titan

HECATONCHEIRES, HEKATONCHEIRES

This is the name of three giants in the classical mythology of Greece. In Roman mythology they are called the Centimanes and are otherwise referred to as the Hundred-Handed Giants. They were enormous beings with fifty heads and a hundred arms and hands, which is the meaning of their name.
References 78
See also giant, Hundred-handed Giants

HEDAMMU

This is the name of a vast demonic serpent in the mythology of the Hurrian people, the biblical Horites, of Mesopotamia. Hedammu was a vast, all-consuming sea serpent that engulfed anything in its domain.
References 125
See also serpent

HE-LI-DI

This is the name for the ogress Hārītī in the legends and traditions of Buddhist beliefs in China.
References 61, 125, 139, 160
See also cannibal, Hārītī, ogress

HELIODROMOS

This is the name of a fabulous creature in the traditions and folklore of medieval Europe. It was said to be a hybrid between a vulture-like bird and a winged beast, resembling a Griffin.
References 7
See also Griffin

HEMICYNES

This is the name given to a fabulous tribe of people in the traditions of medieval Europe. The Hemicynes were part human and part dog, as the name implies. They were said to live in the extreme north of the known world and were the subject of exaggerated travelers' and sailors' tales.
References 178
See also Cynocephali

HENKIES

In the folklore of the Orkney and Shetland Islands off the northern coast of Scotland, the Henkies are a form of the native Trows, or Trolls. Because they had a pronounced limp, or *henk*, when they danced, they were called by this name.
References 24, 160
See also Troll

HERCULES

There are several characters in mythology and European traditions who bear the name "Hercules." The first and foremost is the hero of classical Greek mythology, who is not a giant but whose character was "borrowed" by the giantologist and genealogist of medieval France, Jean Tixier de Ravisy (ca. 1480–1524) for one of the descendants of the biblical Noah. In this work, Hercules is not only a giant descendant of Noah—through his reputed giant son Tuyscon Gigas—but also a sibling of the giants Gambrivius, Herminon, Hunnus, Ingaevon, Istaevon, Marsus, Suevus, Teutanes, and Vandaluus. These were conjectured as the giant race from whom the Gauls and ultimately the French monarchy were supposed to be descended. (Many of these names are taken from the names of the races of people who invaded Europe from the east, after the collapse of the Roman Empire circa 400 A.D.) The list was utilized extensively in the genealogy of Pantagruel as ancestors by the French author François Rabelais in his work *Pantagruel* (1532).

The third Hercules is also a giant and is usually known as Hercules Libyus.
References 174
See also Dis Samothes, Gargantua, giant, Hercules, Noah, Pantagruel, Tuyscon Gigas

HERCULES LIBYUS

This is the name of a giant in the biblical traditions of medieval Europe. This Libyan Hercules was not the hero Hercules but was included in the work by the

Hercules and Atlas (A Wonder Book for Boys and Girls and Tanglewood Tales by N. Hawthorne, J. M. Dent, London)

genealogist Le Maire de Belges (ca. 1473–1524) from an earlier Babylonian script. The Babylonian priest Borosus (third century B.C.) wrote several books on the history of the Babylonians, including an account of Hercules Libyus's destruction of the giants of Asia Minor. He then detailed Hercules Libyus's voyage to Italy to remove, in similar fashion, the tyrannical giants oppressing that land. However, an episode of romance was related between the hero and the giantess daughter of the giant Celtes, resulting in the birth of Galathes. In the pseudohistory written by Jean Le Maire de Belges for the duke of Bourbon, this genealogy is incorporated into the ancestry of the Emperor Charlemagne in order to justify a dynastic derivation of monumentally heroic proportions.

The Italian monk Annius of Viterbo (Giovanni Nanni, ca.1432 –1502) in his genealogy conjectured that the descent from this line, via the ancestor Japheth of the Noachian giants, was part of the qualifying heritage of the Spanish rulers of the time, Ferdinand and Isabella. This must have been the result of Hercules Libyus's defeat of the Iberian monstrous Geryon. The "honorable" line of descent was in fact an expedient for the publication of his book in their realm.
References 174
See also Celtes, Galatea, Galathes, Geryon, giant, Hercules, Japheth, Noachids

HERENSUGUE

This is the monstrous manifestation of a demon in the folk beliefs of the Basque people of northern Spain and southwestern France. The Herensugue is said to appear either as a deformed being with seven heads, or as a snake that may fly through the air like the Aitvaras, or as a dragon to do its evil deeds.
References 24, 125, 160
See also Aitvaras, dragon

HERMINON

This is the name of a giant who appeared in the medieval work *Officina* by the erudite Jean Tixier de Ravisy (alias Ravisius Textor, ca. 1480–1524), who proposed that Tuyscon Gigas was actually a son of the giant Noah whose progeny were the ancestors of European nobility. He constructed a line of giant descendants, of whom Herminon was one of many legendary figures.
References 174
See also giant, Noah, Tuyscon Gigas

HIDE

This is a class of waterborne monster in the beliefs and folklore of the people of Chile. According to the author Julio Vicuña Cifuentes, this monster is described as looking like an enormous cowhide

stretched out and floating in the water, with enormous glaring eyes all around the circumference. There is a form of a head that also has four glaring eyes. This monster is highly predatory, and as soon as any living being, whether cattle or human, enters the water, it is immediately engulfed and consumed by the Hide.
References 134
See also Butatsch-ah-Ilgs, Cuero, monster

HIDEBEHIND

This is a creature from the folklore of lumberjacks and forest workers, especially in Wisconsin and Minnesota in the United States, during the nineteenth and early twentieth centuries. The Hidebehind belongs to a group of beings affectionately known as the Fearsome Critters, whose exaggerated proportions and activities not only explained the weird noises of the lonely landscape but also provided some amusement at camps. This monster was able to hide around the trunks of the trees or behind the huge piles of logs. It was so fast that no matter how swiftly the person turned after hearing it, it was still able to get behind them. The Hidebehind was a predatory cannibal beast that lurked around the loggers' camps until one was alone long enough to be grabbed and carried away to be consumed. The Hidebehind was described as a huge, strong beast, but because it was never seen by those still alive no real description of it exists.
References 7, 18
See also Fearsome Critters, Guyascutus

HIDIMBA

This is the name of a cannibal in the Hindu mythology of India. Hidimba belongs to a class of monsters and demons known as the Asuras. He lived in a cave strewn with the bones of his victims in the depths of the forests. Hidimba used his beautiful sister Hidimbaa as a decoy to lure unsuspecting travelers to his cave for their meals, little knowing that they would be the meal. However, one day Hidimbaa enticed Bhima and was so attracted to him that she warned him of the danger and offered to help him escape. Bravely, Bhima engaged the terrible Hidimba in a ferocious struggle to the death and succeeded in killing the cannibal. When the terrified Hidimbaa returned, she was to become his bride.
References 112
See also cannibal

HIERACOSPHINX

This is the name of a particular type of Sphinx in the mythology of Egypt. The Hieracosphinx is described as having the body of a lion and the head of a falcon. It is the representative of the god Horus and his solar power.

References 89
See also Androsphinx, Criosphinx, Har-machis, Lamassu, Sphinx

HIINTCABIIT

This is the name of a water monster in the traditions and beliefs of the Arapaho Native American people of the western United States. Hiintcabiit is described as a huge serpent with horns on the top of its head that inhabits the rivers and lakes of the mountains. One legend tells of a Hiintcabiit who takes two wives; when the second wife, River-woman, gives birth to a child, the first wife, Crow-woman, drowns her. Beaver Foot, the grieving brother, takes his sister's child in his arms and searches for her body along the river. Then Hiintcabiit rises to the surface of the water with River-woman to feed the crying child but, in doing so, causes such a flood that the village is almost swamped. Fortunately, Beaver Foot manages to hold back the flood, and when his sister resurfaces in the water a hunter shoots Hiintcabiit, and River-woman is restored to her people.

Another legend tells of Lime Crazy, the dissolute brother of a powerful chief who takes Lime Crazy across the river and abandons him in the mountains. When Lime Crazy finds an eagle's feather at the edge of the river, a hawk tells him to address the keeper of the river to be able to cross. A Hiintcabiit emerges, and Lime Crazy ties the eagle's feather to its horns and climbs on the monster's back. Despite being attacked by the monster, Lime Crazy gets to the shore and returns to his village.

There is a story of a woman called Hairy Face who refused to eat fish because she had a special relationship with the river beings and Hiintcabiit in particular. One day her grandson disobeyed her wishes and gave her food with fish in it, from which she died in 1876.
References 77
See also serpent

HILDESUIN, HILDESVIN

These are the names of a gigantic wild boar in the Norse mythology of Scandinavia. Hildesuin, whose name may be translated as "Battle Swine," was associated with the goddess Freya. Like Gulinbursti and Slidringtanni, the Hildesuin were frequently the wild, vicious, rapid steeds of the gods through the underbrush of the forests and into a battle or the chase.
References 7, 78, 89, 105
See also Ætolian Boar, Beigad, Boar of Beann-Gulbain, Buata, Cafre/Kafre, Calydonian Boar, Erymanthean Boar, Pugot/Pugut, Sachrimnir, Slidringtanni, Twrch Trwyth, Ysgithyrwyn

HIMAPANDARA

This is the name of one of the Lokapala Elephants in the Hindu mythology of India. In the *Ramayana*, Himapandara, whose name may be translated as "Snow Palace," stands as the guardian of the north quadrant of the world with the god Kubera on his back.
References 7, 24, 112
See also Lokapala Elephants

HIND OF MOUNT CERYNEIA

This is an alternative name for the Cerynean Hind, also known as the Arcadian Hind, of classical Greek and Roman mythology. It was chased by the hero Hercules as the third of his Twelve Labors.
References 78
See also Cerynean Hind

HÎNQÛMEMEN

This is the name of the strangest monster, for it is a body of water. The Hînqûmemen, also known as the "Engulfer," is the name for a lake in the traditions and beliefs of the Coeur d'Alene Native American people of British Columbia, Canada. Should anyone inadvertently take water and carry it back to their dwelling, the Hînqûmemen will pursue them until it has enveloped them, carried them back, and then drowned them. Consequently, the lake is regarded with terror and avoided at all costs.
References 134
See also monster

HIPPOCAMP, HIPPOCAMPUS

This is the name of the water horse in the classical mythology of Greece and Rome. The Hippocamp, also known in more modern times as the sea horse, is generally described as having the upper half of a horse and the lower half of a fish. The classical Hippocamp was the steed that pulled the water chariot of the sea god Poseidon/Neptune and, in some depictions, has the lower half of a dragon or serpent. There is some version of the sea horse wherever there has been a horse culture, such as in ancient Mesopotamia, Greece, and India, and is depicted on bronzes, silverware, and in paintings from the classical period through to the Baroque period of Europe for over four thousand years. The Hippocamps were not just steeds but also, in later depictions, much more sinister in their activities.

The Hippocamp has become a symbol associated with the heraldic repertoire of Europe, but the image is quite different from that of the classical Hippocamp. In this category it is depicted as having the head and torso of a horse but a mane that is like the dorsal fin of a fish, webbed feet on its front legs, the tail of a fish, and sometimes wings like those of a flying fish.

References 7, 20, 89
See also Afanc, dragon, Eačh Uisge, Endrop, Goborchinu, Hydrippus, Sea Horse

HIPPOCENTAUR

This is the correct name for the most usual image of the centaur of classical Greek and Roman mythology. As the name implies, this hybrid being had the full body and legs of a horse and the torso and head of an man. Centaurs in general could be a compilation of other creatures. The centaur in general had the full form of a human with only the hind quarters of a horse. Other hybrid Centaurs were the Onocentaur, the Ichthyocentaur, and Apotharni. Pliny the Elder, in his *Historia Naturalis* (A.D. 77), describes a Hippocentaur that he asserts was brought from Egypt to Rome preserved in honey. Its description was later included in the works of Isidore of Seville (ca. 560–636) and in bestiaries of the medieval period.
References 7, 20, 78, 89, 91, 125, 133, 167, 178
See also Apotharni, centaur, Cheiron, Eurytus, Ichthyocentaur, Nessus, Onocentaur, Saggitarius

HIPPOCERF, HIPPOCERVUS

This is the name of the hybrid creature in the medieval lore and later heraldic repertoire of Europe. It is described as having the head and foreparts of a stag or deer, but with the hind parts of a horse. It was symbolic of indecision.
References 7

HIPPOGRYPH, HIPPOGRIFF

This is the name of a fabulous monster in the traditions and folklore of Europe. The Hippogriff is, as the name implies, part horse and part Griffin. It is described as having the front parts of a Griffin with the head of an eagle, lion's legs, and eagle's talons, with the rear part formed of a winged horse. It was said to inhabit the Rhiphaean Mountains in the far frozen north of Europe. The Hippogryph features in the work *Orlando Furioso* (1516) by Italian author Ludovicio Ariosto (1474–1573), in which the wizard Atlantes tames it and has it as his steed. Ariosto was said to have used a phrase from Virgil—*Iungeant iam grypes equis,* translated as "to cross griffins with horses" and meaning to try to do the impossible—for the derivation of this fabulous creature.
References 7, 18, 20, 89
See also Griffin, Pegasus

HIPPOLYTUS

This is the name of a giant in the classical mythology of Greece and Rome. Hippolytus is one of the Gigantes and, like his brothers, was said to have been engendered from the blood that fell on the earth from the castrated Uranus. These giants were born fully mature and clad in full battle armor. They waged war on the Olympian gods after the defeat of the Titans and were defeated. In that battle Hyppolytus, whose name means "Stampede of Horses," was not defeated until the final attack. He was buried, like the others, in deep chasms within the earth, upon which mountains and volcanoes were piled.
References 24, 133, 169, 178
See also Aloadae, Cyclopes, giant, Gigantes

HIRGUAN

This is the name of an evil monster in the beliefs of the people of the Island of Gomera in the Canary Islands. He is described as a gigantic humanoid beast covered in shaggy hair. This evil being is the adversary of the god Orahan, worshipped anciently on these islands.
References 125
See also monster

HOBYAH

This name has two character meanings:
1. In English folktale and nursery lore of the nineteenth century, these Nursery bogies were said to be terrifying cannibals that trapped unwary children in cupboards or the cellars of the home. The only thing of which the Hobyahs were afraid were Black dogs, one of which eventually destroyed them all.

2. During the nineteenth century these Nursery bogies must have emigrated with the settlers bound for Australia and interbred with the native Bunyips, for the Hobyahs appear in the European Australian folklore as fearsome monsters. They are described as lurking in the bush close to swamps, waiting to trap unwary travelers and drag them under to be devoured.
References 24, 160, 182
See also Bunyip, monster, Nursery bogie

HODAG

This is a creature from the folklore of lumberjacks and forest workers, especially in Wisconsin and Minnesota in the United States, during the nineteenth and early twentieth centuries. The Hodag was described as a huge beast with extensive horns and tail; from its back protruded a line of fearsome spikes. This monster searched the swamps it inhabited for the humans that were its prey; once it spotted prey with its huge, protruding eyes, this formidable beast could easily overcome its victim. There was one way in which this creature could be outwitted: Because of its heavily spiked body, it could not lay down to sleep, as it could get stuck in the swamp; instead it leaned against a tree. If that tree could be found and partially sawn through, it would fall and be at the mercy of its intended victim. The Hodag belongs to a group of beings affectionately known as the Fearsome Critters, whose exaggerated proportions and activities not only explained the weird noises of the lonely landscape but also provided some amusement at camps. The Hodag may be compared with the European Achlis, from which it may have been derived.

References 7, 24, 134
See also Achlis, Fearsome Critters

HOFAFA

This is the name of a Jinn that has wings and can fly in the Islamic beliefs of Saudi Arabia.

References 79
See also Jin

HOG, SEA

This is the name of a monster of the sea reportedly found in the North Sea in 1537. It was described as having the tail of a fish, the legs of a dragon, but having the body and head of a pig or boar with tusks. There is the suggestion by later authors that a very large bull walrus was sighted.

References 7, 89

HOGA

This is the name of a monster in the traditions and folklore of Mexico. In South America it is known as Andura. The Hoga is described as being like a gigantic fish creature, with a head and ears like those of a pig, and extremely long barbs or thick whiskers round its mouth in which were great fangs. This creature amazingly had the ability to change color and could be red, green, or yellow. The Hoga was said to inhabit the lake of the city of Themistitan, where it grazed on the leaves of the hoga tree at the shoreline. Humans were afraid of it since it was reported to take vast fish and even land animals if they strayed too close to the water's edge.

References 147
See also monster

HOGFISH, HOG FISH

This is an alternative name for the Ambize, a monster said to exist in the seas off the West African coast, especially around the delta of the River Congo.

References 7, 89
See also Ambize, monster

HOK BRAZ

This is the name of a giant in the Celtic mythology of Brittany in northwestern France. Hok Braz was not only enormous, but his prodigious appetite was not even assuaged by his consuming the three-masted ships that passed by the coastline near his abode.

References 134
See also giant

HOKHOKU

This is the grotesque cannibal bird monster, also known as Bakbakwakanooksiwae in the folklore and beliefs of the Kwakiutl people of northwestern Canada. Hokhoku is depicted as having a long, thin, but strong beak with which to smash the skulls of his human victims and devour the exposed brains.

References 77
See also Bakbakwakanooksiwae, Galokwudzuwis

HO-O

This is the alternative name for Feng Hwang, the Oriental Phoenix, in the legends and folklore of Japan.

References 7, 89
See also Feng Hwang, Oriental Phoenix, Phoenix

HOOP SNAKE

This is a creature from the folklore of lumberjacks and forest workers, especially in Wisconsin and Minnesota in the United States, during the nineteenth and early twentieth centuries. The Hoop Snake belongs to a group of beings affectionately known as the Fearsome Critters, whose exaggerated proportions and activities not only explained the weird noises of the lonely landscape but also provided some amusement at camps. The Hoop Snake was described as a highly colored snake that had the ability to move by taking its tail in its mouth and bowling along like a hoop. It was a highly poisonous, predatory reptile and would launch itself at its prey at great speed. Humans were able to outwit it and escape by jumping through the center of its hoop, thus confusing it long enough as it bowled past, for it could not turn around to give chase.

References 7, 24
See also Fearsome Critters

HORDESHYRDE

This is the name of a dragon in the Norse mythology of Scandinavia and Britain. Hordeshyrde is a vast dragon guardian of a treasure horde and is slain by the hero Beowulf in the eighth-century English epic of that name.

References 89

HOR-EM-AKHEN

This is an alternative name for the Androsphinx of ancient Egyptian mythology. It is also known in the astrological sense as Hor-em-akhen, which may be translated as "Horus of the Horizon," which the Greeks referred to as Har-machis.

References 89
See also Androsphinx

HORNED ALLIGATOR

This is the name of a water monster in the traditions and beliefs of the Kiowa Native American people of the United States. The "horns" are especially regarded

The Hoga, a monster in the traditions and folklore of Mexico (On Monsters and Marvels by Ambroise Paré, trans. by Janis L. Pallister, University of Chicago Press, 1982)

as prized possessions for their properties in the assistance with healing, poisoning, hunting, and war.
References 134
See also monster

HORNED SERPENT, GREAT SERPENTS
The Horned Serpents are a particular genre of creature to be found mostly in the legends and traditions of the Native American people of Canada and the United States. The characteristics of these creatures are their immense length and vast head with huge, gaping jaws and two horns on the top of the head. Sometimes there are eyes or horns on the neck as well. These Horned Serpents are ambivalent in their relationships to humans and can be both benign and malevolent, in much the same way as the water horses of Northern Europe.

Some legends tell of the magical pacts humans made with the Horned Serpent for the magic of their powdered blood, only to find that it causes the downfall of the recipient. Such a legend is that of Tijaiha of the Hurons, who, after sacrificing his mother-in-law to the Horned Serpent to kill his enemies, is forced to flee and live with them to escape the wrath of his own people, who later kill him. A legend of the Mandan people tells of the cooking and eating of such a serpent, which then turns the person into a water serpent and guardian of the Missouri River. In the legends of the Mississagnas, people always avoided a cavern close by Lake Ontario, where a Horned Serpent swallowed the Iroquois hero Gun-No-Da-Ya, who was rescued by Thunder. The Iroquois believed that storms were caused on the lake when the Horned Serpent was angry. In the legends of the Shawnee people, young women at puberty or during their periods were particularly vulnerable to the attentions of the Horned Serpents, while in the folk beliefs of the Sauk people, a young woman once

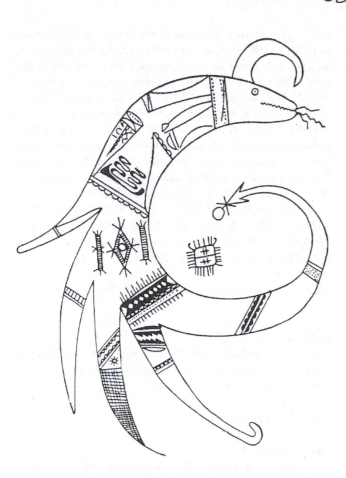

Horned Serpents are to be found mostly in the legends and traditions of Native American people. (Designs on Prehistoric Hopi Pottery by J. W. Fewkes, Dover Publications, New York, 1973)

produced eggs from a Horned Serpent on the shores of the lake that it inhabited.
References 77, 134
See also Doonongaes, Eač Uisge, Kelpy, Kolowisi, Mishipizhiw, Misikinipik, Thunderbird

HORNED WATER SERPENT
This is a class of serpent in the traditions and beliefs of the Pueblo, Hopi, and Zuñi Native American people of the United States. The Horned Water Serpent is described as monstrous, with huge horns emerging from the top of its head. This fearsome creature is, however, revered and incorporated into many important ceremonies.
References 24
See also Kolowisi, To Kas

HORNWORM
This is the alternative name for the Cerastes, a monstrous serpent in the traditions of medieval Europe. It is described in bestiaries of the period as being a serpent of considerable proportions having,

on the front of its head, four protruding horns like those of a ram.
References 89
See also Cerastes

HOROMATANGI
This is the name of a monster in the legends of the Maori people of New Zealand. Horomatangi, also known as Ihu-maataotao, was one of the class of monsters known as the Tanihwa that preyed upon the Maori when they went to hunt or fish. It was a huge, hideous creature that resembled a reptile or giant lizard, but unlike most of its class, Horomatangi did not hunt humans. One legend tells how Horomatangi helped the sisters of Ngaatoro when they went to seek his help. Horomatangi was also said to be the cause of the Karapiti blowhole and to have been transformed into a guardian black rock. Horotomangi was believed to be responsible for the many deaths and accidents caused to crews of the canoes and today still attacks the powerboats and upsets them whenever possible.
References 155
See also Hotu-puku, Huru-kareao, Ihu-maataotao, Tanihwa

HORSE, ORIENTAL
The fabulous Oriental Horse in Hindu mythology was described as having the shape of a normal horse but with bejewelled hooves of agate, pearls in its coat, and eyes of ruby in its head. It was further distinguished by a green mane.
References 7
See also Horse

HORSE OF NEPTUNE
This semisupernatural creature was the horse that pulled the chariot of the sea god Poseidon/Neptune in the classical mythology of Greece and Rome. It is described as resembling an ordinary horse in shape but having a bronze mane and hooves. It is derived from the Hippocampus.
References 7
See also Hippocamp

HORSE-HEADS, HORSES-HEAD SERPENTS
This is the name of a class of water monster of which there are numerous examples worldwide. The Horse-Heads are almost entirely aquatic serpents, although some examples of gigantic fish have been recorded. They are usually described as being vast, undulating serpentine creatures with the front part like that of a horse, or in some cases only the head of a large horse. However, unlike a domestic horse, they usually possess enormous fangs and glowing red or yellow eyes, and may breathe fire. Early European examples are the Havhest and Lindorm of Scandinavia. The American examples are the Misiganebic of the Algonquian Native

American people and the Tcipitckaam of the Micmac Native American people of the United States, and the Ogopogo in the folklore of the Okanagan lake area of British Columbia in Canada. The Piranu is a monstrous Horse-Head fish in the folklore of Argentina.
References 89, 134
See also Havhest, Lindorm, Misiganebic, Ogopogo, Piranu, Tcipitckaam

HORSES OF DIOMEDES
See mares of Diomedes

HORSES OF THE SUN
In many cultures around the world where there were horses in domestication, the daily course of the sun god or goddess across the sky may be considered to be powered by a celestial chariot pulled by fiery steeds. In some cultures the sun or dawn might be the steed itself.

In the classical mythology of Greece and Rome these horses were Actaeon, Aethon/Acthon, Aethiops, Amethea, Astrope, Bronte, Erythreos/Eous, Lampon, Lampos, Phlegon, Purocis, Pyroeis/Pyrois, Phaethon, and Sterope.

In the Norse mythology of Scandinavia these horses were Aavak/Avak, Alsvid, Arrak, Hrimfaxi (moon), and Skinfaxi.

In the mythology of Armenia the Horses of the Sun were Enik, Benik, Menik, and Senik.

In India the horses were Gandarva in Vedic mythology, Arusha, Arushi, Dadhikra/Dadhikravan, and Etasa in Hindu mythology.
References 7, 139

HOTU-PUKU
This is the name of a monster in the legends of the Maori people of New Zealand. Hotu-puku was one of the class of monsters known as the Tanihwa that preyed upon the Maori when they went to hunt or fish.

It was a huge, hideous creature that resembled a reptile or giant lizard but was covered in warts and spines. It was so strong and fast that no man could outrun it, and they were soon overtaken and devoured in its vast mouth. However, a hunting party vowed to kill this creature and plotted a strategy. The hunting party found the cave where the creature slept and laid a trap of woven nooses. Then the bravest taunted Hotu-puku from the mouth of the cave until it ran at the warrior in fury straight into the trap of the ensnaring nooses. When it was firmly entangled, the other warriors hauled the ropes until the Tanihwa was firmly held while the others speared it until every breath was gone. When the vast belly of Hotu-puku was slit many of the missing villagers' bodies were found.
References 155
See also Horomatangi, Huru-kareao, Ihu-maataotao, Tanihwa

HOUNDS OF RAGE
This is the English translation of the Irish Gaelic name Coinn Iotair, monstrous dogs in the legends and folklore of Ireland.
References 128
See also Coinn Iotair

HOUYHNHNMS
The Houyhnhnms and Yahoos appear in the novel *Gulliver's Travels* by the satirist Jonathan Swift (1667–1745). Houyhnhnms were essentially the shape of horses but with high intellect and the power of human speech.
References 63, 177
See also Yahoos

HRAESVELG
This is the name of a monstrous bird in the Norse mythology of Scandinavia. The Hraesvelg resembled

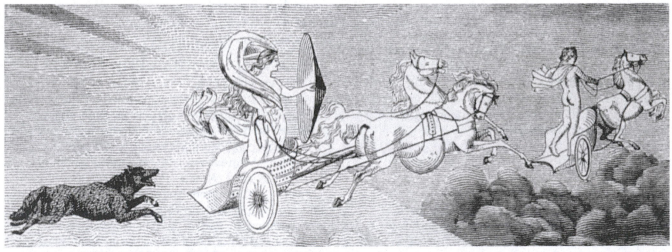

Fenrir chasing the Horses of the Sun (Rose Photo Archive, UK)

a gigantic eagle that inhabited the icy wastes at the peak of the mountains of the extreme north of the world. Its eaglets were the icy, blasting winds that were dispatched to wreak havoc when Hraesvelg flapped her great wings.

References 133
See also Roc

HRIMFAXI

This is the name of the celestial horses in the Norse mythology of Scandinavia. Hrimfaxi, whose name means "Frost-mane," is the supernatural horse that pulls the chariot of the night; the chomping of the bit produces the dewdrops that fall nightly to the earth.

References 20, 89
See also Horses of the Sun, Skinfaxi

HRIMTHURSES

This is the name of the massive giants of the frozen north in the Norse mythology of Scandinavia. The Hrimthurses were the Frost Giants, whose domain was the towering mountain ranges and the frozen wastes of the northern limits beyond the Bifrost bridge and over the River Ifing. They were as powerful as their evil was terrible, and it is they who will cause destruction at the time of the final battle of Ragnarök.

References 47, 78, 127
See also Bergelmir, Frost Giants, giant, Hrungnir, Hymir, Thrym, Vasty

HRODVITNIR

This is an alternative name for the gigantic evil wolf known as Fenrir in the Norse mythology of Scandinavia.

References 7, 20, 89, 169
See also Fenrir

HRUNGNIR

This is the name of a giant in the Norse mythology of Scandinavia. Hrungnir was a Stone or Earth Giant who bragged about his strengths and his horses. One day while the king of the gods, Odin, was traveling through his territory, Hrungnir admired the god's eight-legged steed Sleipnir but said he had one better. Odin took up the challenge of a race, but no matter how far Hrungnir thought he was ahead, whenever he crossed the brow of a hill Odin on Sleipnir was ahead. At last the weary giant, who had been tricked into the gates of the god's abode in Asgard, had to admit defeat. The gods were amused and the giant was invited to feast with them, but when he was drunk Hrungnir was so furious that he vowed to destroy Asgard. Odin then called on the mighty god Thor to do battle with Hrungnir, and the two faced each other, Hrungnir with his vast stone club and Thor with his hammer. As they lay into the fight Hrungnir parried the swipe of Thor's hammer with his club, which splintered into a thousand pieces. One

piece caught Thor in the head, and he let fly with the hammer, which felled the giant and killed him.

References 24, 47, 133, 139, 166
See also giant, Jotun, Sleipnir

HRYM

This is the name of a giant in the Norse mythology of Scandinavia. Hrym is one of the Frost Giants who spends his time boat-building and navigating his great ships. He will play an important part in the final destruction of the world in the last great battle of Ragnarök. The great ship *Nagalfar,* which Hrym constructs from the nails from the toes and fingers of the human corpses, will be the transport of the Frost Giants from their abode to make their great attack on the Aesir.

References 133
See also Frost Giants, giant

HSIAO

This is the name of a hybrid monster in the traditions and mythology of China. It is described as having the body of an anthropoid with a dog's tail, the head of a bird, and the face of a human. The Hsiao appears in the volumes known as the *T'ai P'ing Kuang Chi,* (Great Records Made in the Period of Peace and Prosperity), which was completed ca. A.D. 978 and published in A.D. 981.

References 7, 18
See also Alkonost, Angka, Garuda, Harpy, monster, Parthenope, Podarge, Ptitsy-Siriny, Siren, Sirin, Solovei Rakhmatich, Unnati, Zägh

HSING-T'IEN

This is the name of a humanoid monster in the traditions and legends of China. It was a semisupernatural creature that had fought against the gods in the great Battle of Mu, where it was decapitated. It is described as having human shape and gait but with a mouth at its navel and eyes in its chest, like the Acephali of Greek mythology. The Hsing-T'ien is doomed to wander the scrublands of China in search of its head, but when it encounters human beings it is said to be extremely aggressive, brandishing its axe and shield.

The Hsing-T'ien appears in the volumes known as the *T'ai P'ing Kuang Chi* (Great Records Made in the Period of Peace and Prosperity), which was completed c. A.D. 978 and published in A.D. 981.

References 7, 18
See also Acephali, Blemmyes, Ewaipanoma

HUA-HU-TIAO

This is the name of a monstrous elephant in the traditions and Buddhist legends of China. The Hua-Hu-Tiao is described as a supernatural white elephant with gigantic wings, but it was contained and restricted by its Diamond King of Heaven in a bag

made of a panther's skin. It was a ferocious beast that the Diamond King would release from time to time, when it would wreak havoc and destruction on the human race, killing and devouring all before it. This monster was eventually killed by having its stomach ripped apart after swallowing the warrior Yang Ching, who continued to fight it from within its body.
References 7
See also monster

HUALLEPÉN

This is the name of a hybrid beast in the traditions and folklore of Chile. It is described as having the body of a sheep and the head of a calf with twisted legs. It inhabits the pools and water courses of desolate places but will seek out and mate with either cows or ewes in pastures near its abode. The resulting offspring are always recognizable from their twisted muzzles or hooves. Although the animal itself is not particularly dangerous, sighting one or its progeny would be disastrous for any pregnant woman, as her child would undoubtedly be born with twisted legs.
References 18, 78
See also Corc-chluasask

HUGI

This is the name of a giant in the Norse mythology of Scandinavia. When the god Thor, with his companions Thjalfi and Loki, arrived in the kingdom of Utgardloki, they were expected to prove themselves worthy of the abode of the giants before they would receive hospitality. Loki was pitted in an eating contest against the giant Logi, while Thjalfi was pitted in a running contest against the giant Hugi. No matter how fast the god ran, he could not outmatch the giant and had to admit defeat. Thor was also defeated ignominiously by the cat and the mother of the giant Utgardloki. The contest, in fact, was an illusion, and the adversaries had been unbeatable things such as "fire" and "old age"; in the case of Hugi the giant was "thought" itself, which even the gods could never outrun.
References 139
See also giant, Utgard-loki

HUGIN, HUGINN

This is the name of a monstrous raven in the Norse mythology of Scandinavia. Together Hugin, whose name may be translated as "Thought," with the raven Muninn, whose name may be translated as "Memory," are the supernatural birds of Odin, the Norse king of the gods. At dawn each day these monstrous birds flew above the earth and saw and heard everything in the worlds of humans, giants, and gods. They returned before sunrise to deliver all the information to their master.
References 7, 139
See also Yata Garasu

HUI

This is the name of a hybrid monster in the traditions and folklore of China. It is described as looking like a gigantic dog with the head of a man. It is extremely fleet of foot and able to take great bounds to clear any obstacles; it has no fear of humans. Its appearance was regarded with foreboding, as it was said to appear when a typhoon was imminent. It was said to have been named for the Mountain of Hui. The Hui appears in the volumes known as the *T'ai P'ing Kuang Chi* (Great Records Made in the Period of Peace and Prosperity), which was completed ca. A.D. 978 and published in A.D. 981.
References 18
See also monster

HULD

This is the name of a Troll in the traditions and folklore of Scandinavia. Huld is a she-Troll who featured in a story told for the Norwegian royal family by the historian Sturla Thordarson.
References 105
See also Troll

HUMAN SNAKES

This is a class of humanoid monster in the traditions and folk beliefs of the Seminole Native American people of Oklahoma and the southeastern United States. These are powerful beings that spread evil among normal humans. One tale relates how a young man was seduced at a dance by a beautiful girl and followed her to her home. To his horror, under the tree in a cavern, all her family were vast serpents. Although he escaped physically, he was still in their power and sickened every day. The villagers managed to get him to tell them what had happened and went to look for themselves. To eradicate the menace of the Human Snakes the medicine men made a medicine bundle of a deer skin containing the ashes of menstrual blood. This they took with a menstruating woman to the lair of the Human Snakes, where she was the one to lower the medicine bundle into their cavern. The effect was that the monstrous forms metamorphosed from serpents to that of distorted humans and half-snake humans who writhed in agony until they died.
References 77
See also monster, serpent

HUMBABA

This is the name of a monstrous giant guardian in the mythology of ancient Mesopotamia. Humbaba, also known as Huwawa and Kumbaba, is the guardian of the cedar forests and may originally have been a deity of nature. It was later demoted to the status of a giant demonic monster and the adversary of Gilgamesh. It was described as having a vast humanoid body with scale plates all over it, with the legs of a lion ending in vulture's talons; on its head were horns like those of a bull; the tail was long and had a snake's head at the end. Humbaba features in the Sumerian mythological epic of Gilgamesh, who ventures into the forests with his companion Enkidu. After a battle with the giant, the heroes defeat Humbaba.

References 7, 18, 47, 125, 160, 166
See also giant

HUMILITY

This is a creature from the folklore of lumberjacks and forest workers, especially in Wisconsin and Minnesota in the United States, during the nineteenth and early twentieth centuries. The Humility belongs to a group of beings affectionately known as the Fearsome Critters, whose exaggerated proportions and activities not only explained the weird noises of the lonely landscape but also provided some amusement at camps. This creature was first featured in the *General History of Connecticut* by the Reverend Samuel Peters in 1781. It was described as a bird like an eagle with eagle's eyes, but more piercing, and exceedingly swift, outflying the sharpest shot.

References 24, 178
See also Fearsome Critters

HUNDRED-HANDED GIANTS

This is the name of a class of giant in the classical mythology of Greece and Rome. They were the three original sons of Gaia and Uranus and primordial monsters born of vast proportions with fifty heads and a hundred arms and hands, as the name implies. They were also known as Hecatoncheires (Greek) and Centimanes (Roman), both meaning "having a hundred hands." They were originally three in number—Briareus, Cottus, and Gyges—but others, such as Enceladus, were named later. Uranus was so disgusted by their appearance that he cast them into the darkness of Tartarus. They were the siblings of the Titans and related to the Olympian gods, who made war on the Titans. Gaia informed the king of the Olympian gods that the Hundred-Handed Giants were in Tartarus and could help defeat the Titans. When they were released, they helped the gods, and when the Titans in turn were cast into Tartarus by the victorious gods the Hundred-Handed Giants were given the task of being their guards.

References 133
See also Briareus, Cottus, Gaia, giant, Gyges, Titan, Uranus

HUNKUS

This is an alternative name for the Guyascutus in the folklore of the lumberjacks and forest workers (and later fraudsters), especially in Wisconsin and Minnesota in the United States. This version of the creature was so highly adaptable that if it were being pursued it was able to roll around itself to turn inside-out and escape the opposite way.

References 7
See also Guyascutus

HUNNUS

This is the name of a giant who appeared in the medieval work *Officina* by the erudite Jean Tixier de Ravisy (alias Ravisius Textor, ca. 1480–1524), who proposed that Tuyscon Gigas was actually a son of the giant Noah whose progeny were the ancestors of European nobility. He constructed a line of giant descendants, of whom Hunnus was one of many legendary figures.

References 174
See also giant, Noah, Tuyscon Gigas

HURTALY

This is the name of a giant in the classical literature of France. Hurtaly is one of the giant ancestors of Pantagruel in the famous work *Pantagruel* (1532) by the French author François Rabelais (ca. 1494–ca. 1553). The other three primary ancestors are Charibroth, Sarabroth, and Faribroth. They all appear in the first edition, which was subsequently edited with many more additional giant ancestors. In his description, Rabelais equates Hurtaly's reign with that of Og of Bashan, being at the time of the biblical Flood, and that he survived by sitting astride the roof of the Ark and being fed by Noah. Thus Rabelais accounts for the survival of the ancestral line of his giants and attests to the good and generous nature of Hurtaly.

References 174
See also Bruyer, Chalbroth, Daughters of Cain, Eryx, Gabbara, Galehaut, Gargantua, giant, Happemousche, Hurtaly, Morguan, Noachian giants, Noah, Pantagruel

HURU-KAREAO

This is the name of a monster in the legends of the Maori people of New Zealand. Huru-kareao, said to be the relative of Horomatangi, was one of the class of monsters known as the Tanihwa that preyed upon the Maori when they went to hunt or fish. It was a huge, hideous creature that resembled a reptile or giant lizard and inhabited a lake near Tongariro, upon which floated a sacred log. These Taniwha looked after the people of the local village. When two of their women were treated badly by a neighboring village, the monsters stirred the waters so violently that they flooded the valleys and drowned the rivers. When the Europeans came to the land they insisted that the log and the lake be used to construct a church on the site, but the lake soon returned and the church decayed and fell to bits and the men who cut the wood died mysteriously.

The Huspalim, a monster of Ethiopia described during the late medieval period (On Monsters and Marvels by Ambroise Paré, trans. by Janis L. Pallister, University of Chicago Press, 1982)

References 155
See also Hotu-puku, Horomatangi, Ihu-maataotao, Tanihwa

HUSPALIM
This is the name of a monster of Ethiopia described during the late medieval period in Europe by the traveler and physician Ambroise Paré (1517–1590). It was said to look like a giant marmot with a huge, round head, tiny round ears and monkey-like face, round paws, and bald, red-spotted skin. It was reported to be kept in cages by the people of the Island of Zacotera as a source of rather indigestible meat unless beaten thoroughly.
References 147
See also monster

HUWAWA
This is the name of a monstrous giant guardian in the mythology of ancient Mesopotamia. Huwawa, also known as Humbaba and Kumbaba, is the guardian of the cedar forests.

References 7, 47, 160, 166
See also Humbaba

HVCKO CAPKO
This is the name of a monster in the traditions and beliefs of the Seminole Native Americans of Oklahoma in the southeastern United States. The Hvcko Capko, also known as Long Ears, is described as a monstrous being with a gray body, a tail like that of a horse, and the head like that of a wolf but with enormous ears. The Hvcko Capko is easy to detect from afar by the stench of its body. It is said to inhabit desolate, rocky places; although it does not seem to be a predatory threat, it is best to stay away from it, as it can infect humans with disease.
References 77
See also monster

HWA YIH
This is the name of a fabulous bird in the traditions and legends of China. It is a form of the Lwan and is described as looking something like a much

larger and more beautiful and graceful type of pheasant. However, this bird is capable of changing its body color and is known by different names accordingly. As the Hwa Yih it is the white form of the Lwan.
References 81
See also Fung, Lwan, Phoenix, To Fu, Yu Siang

HWANG
This is an alternative name for the Feng Hwang or Oriental Phoenix in the legends and mythology of China. It is symbolic of beauty, sensitivity, and serenity and as such will never make an appearance unless the kingdom is at peace. Consequently, the evidence of a great and peaceful reign of an emperor is signified by the appearance of the Hwang.
References 81
See also Ch'i Lin, Feng Hwang, Phoenix

HWCH DDU GOTA
This is the name of a monstrous pig in the traditions and folklore of Wales. The Hwch Ddu Gota, which may be translated as "Bob-tailed Black Sow," is described as a huge black pig that was believed to seek as its victim the last of the revellers at the Celtic festival of Samain. When Christianity was introduced and the festival became that of Halloween, the Hwch Ddu Gota was equated with the devil.
References 128

HYBRIS
This is the name of an individual satyr in the classical mythology of Greece of Rome. They are described as having human faces, pointed ears, horns, and hairy male bodies; below the waist they have the body and legs of a goat. They were the attendants of their drunken leader Silenus and the god of wine, Dionysus/Bacchus. They inhabited the woods, mountains, and countryside, where they pursued the nymphs and were renowned for aggregating, drunken sexuality, lechery, rudeness, and love of playing pranks. This is reflected in some of their names; here, Hybris means "Insolence."
References 7, 14, 24, 89, 125, 160
See also satyr

HYDRA
This is the name of a monster in the classical mythology of Greece and Rome. The Hydra was also known as the Exedra and, more usually, as the Lernean Hydra because it inhabited the marshes at Lerna in Argolis. The Hydra was said to be the progeny of the monstrous Echidne and Typhon. It was described as a vast, dog-like body from which sprouted, according to different sources, nine, fifty, a hundred, or even a thousand serpents' heads whose

breath stank with poison. One of these heads was immortal, but should the others be severed, then more would grow in their place. Slaying the Hydra was the second of the Twelve Labors given to the hero Heracles/Hercules by King Eurytus. At first the hero slashed at the heads and was faced with more than ever. Then he called his charioteer, Iolaus, to help, and he set fire to the trees and took a burning branch. With this he seared each neck stump before more heads could grow. Little by little, the Hydra's heads and strength were spent until only the immortal head remained. The hero chopped up the body and dipped his arrows in the poisonous fluids, then buried the hissing head under the heaviest rocks, from which it would never emerge.

The Hydra was later used to equate with the monstrous apocalyptic beasts in the Book of Revelations of Saint John in the Christian New Testament scriptures. In this interpretation the Hydra was said to be the adversary of Saint Michael the archangel at the final battle before the Day of Judgment. In this guise the Hydra was usually portrayed as a two-legged dragon with as many as nine heads, but otherwise looking like a Wyvern. It was also a frequent subject to be found in the bestiaries of the medieval period, where it was the symbol of luxury and hypocrisy. The Hydra is still to be found in the heraldic repertoire of European coats of arms, where it is depicted as a many-headed dragon.
References 5, 7, 18, 20, 61, 78, 89, 91, 133, 134, 139, 178, 182, 185
See also Apocalyptic beasts, dragon, Echidne, monster, Typhon, Wyvern

HYDRIPPUS
This is the name of a hybrid creature in the traditions of medieval Europe. It is described as having the foreparts of a horse and the hind parts of the tail of a fish covered with golden scales. This creature was described in the medieval bestiaries as the leader or king of the fishes; those that did not follow were doomed to be caught in the fishermens' nets.
References 7
See also Hippocampus, Sea Horse

HYDRUS
This is the name of a serpent in the medieval bestiaries of Europe. The Hydrus, also known as the Idrus, was a curious serpent that inhabited the banks of the River Nile in Egypt. It was portrayed as a triple-headed snake or dragon and was sometimes confused with the Hydra of Greek mythology. The Hydrus was the enemy of the crocodile, and when it met one on the river bank it would roll itself in the mud. Then, when it was completely slippery, it would

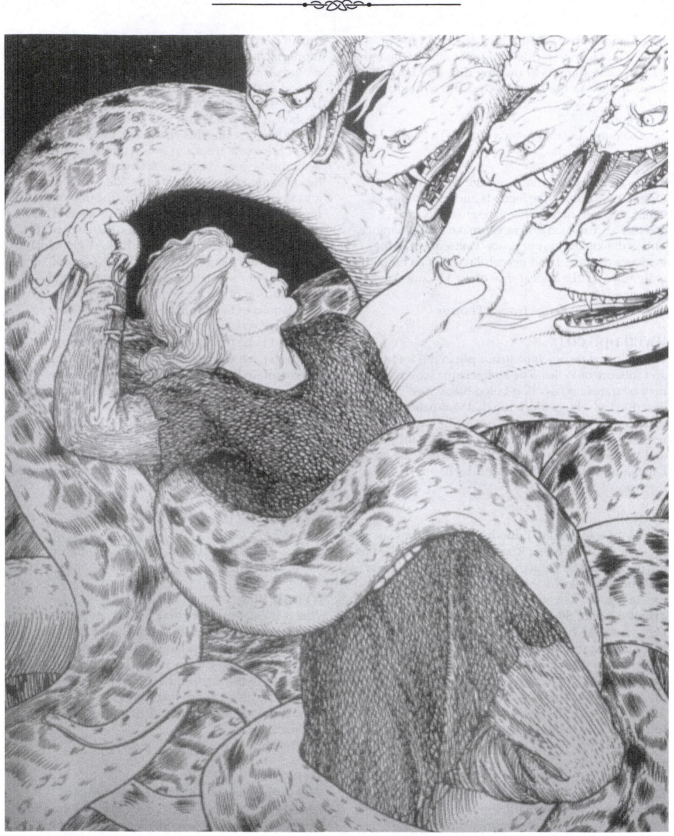

Should the heads of the Hydra be severed, more would grow in their place. (Rose Photo Archive, UK)

enter the gaping jaws of the reptile and go down the gullet. Once inside the beast, the Hydrus would burst through the stomach wall and come out through the beast's side, killing it. This curious behavior was explained by the ecclesiastical community of medieval times as the symbol of Christ's descent into hell and His resurrection and release of those who were unjustly condemned.

References 14, 91, 149, 185
See also dragon, Hydra, serpent

HYLÆUS

This is the name of a centaur in the classical mythology of Greece and Rome. Hylæus, also known as the "Woodman," was enamored of the lovely Atalanta and pursued her endlessly until she retaliated and killed him. Another source relates that Hylæus met his end in the battle between the Centaurs and the hero Heracles/Hercules.

References 169, 178
See also centaur

HYMIR

This is the name of a giant in the Norse mythology of Scandinavia. Hymir was the father of the two gods Tiw and Tyr, but this did not lessen his hatred of the gods known as the Aesir. He lived at the eastern edge of the universe and possessed a brewing pot as vast as the heavens. When the gods planned a great feast, all their pots were not big enough to hold the quantity of mead required, so Thor was sent to borrow Hymir's pot. Hymir said that he would consider it, but in the meantime they would have a

fishing contest. Taking two of his prized bulls, the giant and the god set out in his boat and used the cows as bait. Whoever hooked the greatest fish would win. Hymir fished out two vast whales, but Thor's bait was taken by the world-serpent, the Midgardsormr. In some versions of the myth Hymir threw himself into the sea in terror and drowned. In other versions the giant cut the line and the pair took the whales to land, where they consumed them. Hymir was still not satisfied and challenged Thor to a drinking contest and to afterwards smash the drinking vessel. Try as he would he could not break it, and the only surface hard enough to smash the vessel was the giant's own forehead. In some versions of the myth, at this juncture Hymir agreed to let Thor take the pot; in other versions Thor grabbed it and ran off. But Hymir was not finished and pursued the god with an army of giants. Thor then took his mighty hammer and laid death and destruction about him, then took the mead vat back to Asgard.

References 47, 125, 133, 139, 166
See also giant, Midgardsormr

HYPERION

This is the name of one of the Titans in the classical mythology of Greece and Rome. Hyperion is the son of Uranus and Gaia; by the Titan Theia he was the father of the primal gods Eos of the dawn, Helios of the sun, and Silene of the moon. He also fathered the nymphs Lampetie and Phaëthusa.

References 20, 38, 125, 133, 166, 178
See also Gaia, Theia, Titan, Uranus

I

IACULUS
This is the alternative spelling of the Jaculus in European Latin bestiaries of the medieval period.
References 14
See also Jaculus

IAK IM
This is an alternative name for the Yagim, which is described as a creature that resembles a vast shark, but in the ceremonies of the Tsetseka, it is represented by a huge, red-fringed mask.
References 77
See also Yagim

IAPETIONIDÆ
This is the collective name of the giants Atlas, Epimetheus, Menætius, and Prometheus in the classical mythology of Greece and Rome. They were the sons of Iapetos and were thus called the Iapetionidæ or Japetidæ.
References 178
See also Iapetus

IAPETUS
This is the name of a Titan in the classical mythology of Greece and Rome. Iapetus, also spelled Japetus, was the son of Gaia and Uranus, against whom, with his siblings, he rebelled. He was the father, by the Titaness Clymene, of the giants Atlas, Epimetheus, Menætius, and Prometheus, who were thus called the Iapetionidæ or Japetidæ.

In the later medieval writing of the Italian Boccaccio (1313–1375), Iapetus is identified with the son of the biblical Noah, Japetus (Japheth). This was a source used by the Italian monk Annius of Viterbo (Giovanni Nanni, ca. 1432–1502) in his genealogy when he conjectured that the descent of Dis Samothes from this line, via the ancestor Japheth, was the first king of the Gauls. Annius re-created a whole genealogy of giants descended from Noah and Iapetus to justify the noble ancestry of the French nobility of the period.

References 20, 47, 125, 139, 169, 174, 178
See also Atlas, Dis Samothes, Epimetheus, Gaia, giant, Menœtius, Noah, Prometheus, Titan, Uranus

IARNSAXA
This is the name of a giantess in the Norse mythology of Scandinavia. Iarnsaxa, also spelled Jarnsaxa, was the wife of the god Thor. By him she had two sons: Magni, meaning "Strength," and Modi/Mothi meaning "Courage."
References 78, 169
See also giantess

ICE GIANTS
This is the name of giants in the legends of the Maliseet Passamaquoddy Native American people of the United States. The Ice Giants are known as the Kiwahkw and are predatory cannibals who track down and devour any humans in their territory.
References 77
See also giant, Kiwahkw

ICHTHYOCENTAUR, ICHTHYOCENTAURUS
This is the name given to a class of centaur in the *Physiologus,* an ancient work of natural history said to have been written in Alexandria during the third century A.D., and was later included in bestiaries of the medieval period. The Ichthyocentaur is described as having the torso and head of a man but the forelegs of a horse (or sometimes a lion), with the hind part formed of the tail of a dolphin. There are numerous images of these beings of the sea, often identified with the Tritons, but no classical written evidence seems extant. They were mentioned from the earliest times by the Byzantine writers Claudian, Lycophron, and John Tzetzes and also in later bestiaries. Their images continued to decorate pottery and metalware well into the eighteenth century in Europe.
References 7, 18, 20, 78, 89, 91, 125, 133, 167
See also Apotharni, centaur, Onocentaurus, Triton

ICHTHYOPHAGI

This is the name given to a type of wild people in the legends of medieval Europe. The name "Ichthyophagi" literally means "Fish-eaters." Their image is to be seen in the medieval manuscript in the Bibliotheque Nationale in Paris known as the *Légende d' Alexandre* (1450–1480), where they are depicted as hairy humanoid water beings.
References 134

IDRIS

This is the name of a giant in the folklore and legends of Wales. His "seat" is the Cader Idris (the chair of Idris), a *cwm* at the top of the mountains, where no bird will fly. It is said that anyone who stays there overnight will emerge either supremely eloquent or insane.
References 20
See also giant

IDRUS

This is the alternative spelling of Hydrus, the monster of Egypt detailed in medieval bestiaries of Europe. It is named in this fashion in a bestiary of 1220 in the Bodleian Library at Oxford.
References 14
See also Hydrus

IÉMISCH

This is the name of a monster in the traditions and folklore of the people of Patagonia, South America. This creature is described as having the foreparts of a fox but the tail of a serpent. When any potential victim appears, this prehensile tail is used to entwine the body like a boa constrictor, dragging the victim down to be consumed.
References 134
See also Glyryvilu, Vulpangue

IENZABABA

This is a name for Baba Yaga used in the folklore of Poland.
References 25, 125, 160
See also Baba Yaga, Jezda

IFREET, IFRIT

These are alternative spellings of Afrit, which is one classification of the five types of the powerful Jinns of Muslim and Arabic mythology and folklore.
References 20, 38, 63, 64, 74, 124, 146, 160, 161
See also Afrit

IGPUPIARA

This is the name of a class of mermaid or merman in the folklore of the people of Brazil. The Igpupiara, a name that derives from the local name "Hipupiara," meaning "Dweller in the Water," was described as a humanoid torso on a mass of flesh resembling a fish's tail. The head was somewhat like that of a seal, but its gigantic arms had five webbed fingers. This creature was said to attract humans into the waters, where it consumed only the eyes, nose, breasts, genitalia, fingers, and toes of the victim. When bodies with this mutilation appeared on the beaches, the terrified villagers refused to fish. Numerous sightings were reported between 1575 and 1585 in the region of the coast of San Vicente and others in the early seventeenth century when terrified locals and Portuguese travelers shot and hacked at the beasts. It has been conjectured that these were sightings of the Brazilian dolphin.
References 134
See also mermaid, merman

IHUAIVULU

This is the name of a monster in the traditions and folklore of the peoples of South America. It is described as a vast creature with seven heads breathing fire and inhabiting the craters of volcanoes. It is dangerous to any living thing.
References 7
See also monster

IHU-MAATAOTAO

This is an alternative name for Horomatangi, a class of monstrous Tanihwa in the legends of the Maori people of New Zealand.
References 155
See also Hotu-puku, Horomatangi, Huru-kareao, Tanihwa

IKALU NAPPA

This is the name of a type of sea creature in the traditions of the Inuit of the Arctic regions. The Ikalu Nappa is described as being a female torso and head, with the lower half being that of a fish living under the ocean.
References 77
See also mermaid

IKUUTAYUUQ

This is the name of a monster in the traditions and beliefs of the Inuit of eastern Hudson Bay in Canada. The Ikuutayuuq, whose name means "One Who Drills," had a brother equally monstrous, and together they hunted down any humans in their territory. When they trapped someone, the evil pair tortured them to death by holding them down, splayed on their backs, and drilling holes through their body. Then the monsters covered the body with a pile of stones. The Inuit know that a victim had been murdered by Ikuutayuuq and his brother when a new *inuksuut* pile of rocks appeared. The pair of murderers were eventually hunted down and fought by one of

the original people or *tuniit,* who succeeded in defeating Ikuutayuuq, whose brother fled and was never seen again.
References 77
See also monster

ILLUYANKAS, ILLUJANKA

This is the name of a dragon in the Hittite mythology of ancient Mesopotamia, now Syria. This dragon of chaos was portrayed as a vast, monstrous, serpentine creature with numerous heads. There are two versions of the demise of Illuyankas. The first version tells how the goddess Inaras prepared a great feast for the greedy dragon, who had just defeated the weather god Taru. At the feast, with constantly replenished fare, Illuyankas became so bloated and drunk with the wines that Inaras and her lover, Hupasiyas, were able to bind the monster. Then the weather god was able to slaughter the monster and scatter it over the earth. The second version tells how Illuyankas had encircled each of the gods in its vast coils and swallowed their eyes and hearts so that they were powerless. So the son of Taru took the daughter of the dragon as his lover and persuaded her to give him the eyes and hearts as a gift. When he had them all they were given to the gods, who then slaughtered Illuyankas.
References 47, 89, 125, 133
See also dragon

IMAP UMASSOURSA

This is the name of a gigantic sea monster in the traditions and folklore of the Inuit of Greenland. This gigantic creature was so vast that it was mistaken for a flat island. The Imap Umassoursa was greatly feared by the local fisherfolk, for if the water appeared to be more shallow than usual it was possible that the boat was directly over the monster. When the monster rose to the surface it could tip a boat and any crew into the water, where they would be unable to save themselves in the freezing temperatures.
References 134
See also Aspidochelone, Cuero, Hide, Kraken

IMDUGUD

This is the name of a demonic yet benevolent monster in the mythology of ancient Mesopotamia. Imdugud was portrayed as having an eagle's head or, later, a double eagle's head on the body of a winged lion. Imdugud was benevolent, with the thunder of its wings bringing the benefit of rains, but it would also hover over and threaten to destroy domestic animals.
References 89, 125, 133, 160, 166

I-MU KUO YAN

This is the name of a race of monstrous people in the legends and folklore of China. They are described as having only one eye in the middle of their foreheads, like the Cyclopes in the classical mythology of Greece and Rome. The I-Mu Kuo Yan appear in the volumes of the *Great Imperial Encyclopaedia* and were no doubt derived from exaggerated travelers' tales in much the same way as those that influenced the medieval bestiaries of Europe.
References 181
See also Cyclopes, Nieh-Erh Kuo Yan, San-Shen Kuo Yan, Ting Ling Kuo Yan, Yü-Min Kuo Yan

INDACINGA

This is the name of a class of gigantic monster in the legends and folklore of the Ponca Native American people in the Great Plains of the United States. The Indacinga are described as enormous, strong beings that often uproot the trees of the deep forests they inhabit. They are even capable of ripping up the peoples' lodges from their foundations and scattering them about like matchsticks. These powerful beings of the dark woods are used as a deterrent by anxious parents to control their children and as such may be classed as Nursery bogies.
References 77
See also Apotamkin, Hagondes, monster, Nursery bogie, Owner-of-a-Bag

INGAEVON

This is the name of a giant who appeared in the medieval work *Officina* by the erudite Jean Tixier de Ravisy (alias Ravisius Textor, ca. 1480–1524), who proposed that Tuyscon Gigas was actually a son of the giant Noah whose progeny were the ancestors of European nobility. He constructed a line of giant descendants, of whom Ingaevon was one of many legendary figures.
References 174
See also giant, Noah, Tuyscon Gigas

INGCÉL CAECH

This is the name of a Celtic giant in the literature of early Ireland. Ingcél Caech, whose name in the Irish Gaelic means "One-eyed," was described as a giant, vicious pirate who had but one huge eye, with three pupils, in the middle of his head. This giant came from the mainland of Britain or, in some accounts, from the area of Cornwall. The account of his raids was told in *Togail Bruidne Da Derga* (The Destruction of Derga's Hostel), in which the giant with, among others, the sons of Donn Désa destroyed and pillaged Derga's settlement.
References 128
See also Cyclopes, giant

INHABITANTS OF ISLANDS NEAR DONDUN

These are descriptions of giants and monsters from a work purported to have been written by the English

pseudoexplorer Sir John Mandeville in his famous *Travels*, written about 1360 A.D. In the work there are several unnamed islands that were purported to have inhabitants of a most curious nature. Some were one-eyed giants like the mythical Cyclopes; some were headless like the Acephalos of Greek legends; others had featureless faces or abnormal lips or ear lengths; while other peoples were reported to have horse hooves or to go on all fours and climb trees. It was ultimately these fabulous descriptions that lost the work its credibility, although *Travels* continued for reference material centuries after its publication.
References 180
See also giant, monster

INUGPASUGSSUK

This is the name of a giant in the traditions and folklore of the Inuit people of Canada. Inugpasugssuk was described as an enormous being who was so huge that even the lice on his body were the size of the arctic lemming. He lived on the fish, whales, and seals of the inlet that he inhabited and was so well disposed to humans that he would help them with their catch whenever possible. If his gigantic strides into the sea threatened to swamp a village with the waves he created, then he would move the village and save the people. The tale relates how Inugpasugssuk fell in love with a human woman and persuaded her husband to exchange her for his own wife. But Inugpasugssuk's attempt at intercourse split her in two; the human husband entered the giant's wife, never to be seen alive again (only his bones fell out of her). Inugpasugssuk was so unhappy at the consequences of all this that he and his wife adopted the human son of the family and brought him up as their own. The boy started to develop into a gigantic form and soon was helping Inugpasugssuk, but he still yearned after his home village. The boy persuaded Inugpasugssuk to let him journey back with the aid of a magic token to find his way. He was disappointed when he arrived, for he was now so huge that he could no longer be recognized or enter a human home. So the boy went back to his foster father Inugpasugssuk and lived as a giant.
References 77
See also giant

INVUNCHE

This is the name of a monster in the legends and folklore of the people of Chile. The Invunche, also known as "Master of the Hide," is described as a "beast-man" that is a vast, inflated pelt, like a balloon, that inhabits a cave that can be accessed only through a tunnel going under a lake. The Invunche never leaves its lair but has a minion known as the Trelquehuecuve that lures young girls swimming or getting water from the edge of the lake. These victims are then abducted and taken under the lake to the Invunche, who drains them of their blood like a vampire. In the many legends concerning an Invunche, the hero must find the subterranean entrance to the cave, kill the Trelquehuecuve, and then kill the Invunche by piercing it like a bladder.
References 134
See also Camahueto, Chivato, Hide, Trelquehuecuve, Vampire

IÖRMUNGANDR

This is an alternative spelling of Jormungandr, the World-Serpent in the Norse mythology of Scandinavia.
References 133
See also Jormungandr

IPOPODES

This is the name of a type of Centaur in the classical mythology of Greece and Rome. The Ipopodes are described as being almost totally humanoid but with the legs and hooves of horses. They were said to inhabit the region known as Scythia.
References 7
See also centaur

IQI-BALAM

This is one of a group of terrifying beings, known as the Balam, in the beliefs of the Quiché peoples of Mexico. Iqi Balam means "Moon Jaguar." The Balam were assigned as guardians of the Four Directions.
References 119, 160
See also Balam

IRIZ IMA

This is the name of a monster in the legends and folk beliefs of West Africa. It was reported by European travelers to the Congo as being huge like an elephant with the tail of a serpent. It inhabited the caverns and swamps of the West African coast. The Iriz Ima resembles the Groot Slang and the Mokêle-Mbêmbe.
References 7, 47, 63, 89
See also Groot Slang, Mokêle-Mbêmbe

IRRAQ

This is the name of a monstrous child in the traditions and folklore of the Inuit people of Alaska in the United States. Irraq is described as a baby that, as the result of neglect of tradition, became a cannibal. The tradition is that any child of any age would be offered *akutaq*, a type of ice cream, which was eaten with enjoyment during festivities. Even the tiniest babies would be given some on their mouths to lick. On this occasion the child was neglected and the tradition was not observed. Later in the day the family saw the child on its own with its mouth covered in blood. To their horror there was no sign of the mother or father but a quantity of blood in the home. An amulet was made and put on Irraq, who was then sent far away into the mountains.

References 77
See also cannibal

ÍRUSÁN

This is the name of a gigantic cat in the traditions and legends of Ireland. Írusán, or "King of the Cats," was described as being the size of an ox and inhabited a vast cave in the mountains at Knowth. Írusán had incredibly acute hearing; when he heard the poet Senchán Torpéist reciting a satire about cats, the monster raced to take revenge. The monstrous cat came and, before anyone could do anything, had tossed the poet on his back and made off with the terrified human across the country. The commotion was heard by Saint Ciarán, who grabbed a red-hot poker from the fire as the cat and its passenger passed by Clonmacnoise. The saint threw the poker at Írusán and killed it, rescuing the grateful poet and releasing the region from the monster's predations.

References 128
See also Chapalu, Phantom Cat

ISTAEVON

This is the name of a giant who appeared in the medieval work *Officina* by the erudite Jean Tixier de Ravisy (alias Ravisius Textor, ca. 1480–1524), who proposed that Tuyscon Gigas was actually a son of the giant Noah whose progeny were the ancestors of European nobility. He constructed a line of giant descendants, of whom Istaevon was one of many legendary figures.

References 174
See also giant, Noah, Tuyscon Gigas

ITHERTHER

This is the name of an enormous primordial ox in the mythology of the Kabyl people of Algeria. This myth tells of the creation of the beings of the earth and how Itherther was, along with a female, Thamuatz, and male calf, Achimi, the first beings to emerge from Tlam, the darkness. The bull-calf mated with his mother and drove Itherther into the mountains, and while his progeny were becoming the domesticated servants of newly emerged humans, Itherther remained in the mountains. There, each time the vast ox remembered Thamuatz, his mate, his seed fell into the bowl of rocks and from this came all the wild animals that populated the earth.

References 47

IWANČÏ

In the beliefs of the Jívaro people of the Amazon region of Equador, the Iwančï are demonic serpent monsters. The Iwančï may manifest in the shape of the terrifying Macančï, a monstrous water snake, or appear as an enormous engulfing Paņi, the deadly anaconda, in order to kill its victim.

References 90, 160
See also serpent

IYA

This is the name of a giant or monster in the traditions and beliefs of the Lakota Native American people of the United States. Iya is described as a vast, monstrous being, or *wakanpi*, that has stinking breath and is thoroughly malevolent toward humans.

References 77, 125
See also giant, monster

J

JABBERWOCK, JABBERWOCKY

This is the name of a monstrous creature in the classic work of the English academic and author Lewis Carroll (Charles Lutwidge Dodgson, 1832–1898), entitled *Through the Looking Glass*. The beast appears not in reality but in a poem within a book that Alice sees and decides to read. As she is through the looking glass, the writing is reversed, but when viewed properly the words are still rather incomprehensible. Thus when Tenniel, the artist commissioned for the publication, created his image of the Jabberwock, that too was based on conjecture. The first verse of the poem itself was created by Dodgson as an exercise in pseudo-Anglo-Saxon verse and written into the family magazine that he had produced. The later verses give something of the description as follows:

"Beware the Jabberwock, my son!
The jaws that bite, the claws that catch!"

and

The Jabberwock, with eyes aflame,
Came whiffling through the tulgey wood,
And burbled as it came!

But this is as far as the image is relayed before the thing is despatched by the "vorpal blade." Tenniel's image, however, shows us a monstrous pseudodragon with bat's wings, gigantic, spider-like eagle's talons, and a vast dragon's tail stretching into the wood from which it emerged. The head was something of an evil humanoid with globular eyes, huge incisors, whiskers, and sinuous horn protrusions. There is a sense of the ridiculous, however, as the vast, scaly body sports a waistcoat! This image was considered too terrifying for its original place in the volume as its frontispiece and was placed instead in the text of the book.
References 7, 40, 182
See also Bandersnatch, dragon, Fearsome Critters, monster

JACULUS (sing.), JACULI (pl.)

This is the name of a monster in the traditions of Europe. The Jaculus, also spelled Iaculus, is mentioned by the Latin poet Marcus Annaeus Lucanus, known as Lucan (A.D. 39–65), in his work the *Pharsalia* (ix, 720) and in later medieval manuscripts such as the bestiary. The monster is described as a vast serpent with wings, sometimes depicted with two forelegs. It was regarded as particularly terrifying in its method of attack, for it would get up into tall trees and wait in the branches. When a likely victim approached the tree the Jaculus would launch itself onto the victim's back and kill it by sinking its fangs into the neck. Jaculus, meaning "Javelin," is taken from this action.
References 14, 149, 185
See also monster, serpent, Wyvern

JAGUAR-MAN

This is a type of Werewolf in the legends and folk beliefs of the people of Paraguay as well as many peoples of the Amazon Basin. The Jaguar-men are in normal life quite indistinguishable from any other, but at night they use sorcerers' powers to enable them to stalk their human prey as jaguars.
References 24
See also Werewolf

JALA-TURGA

This is the name of a supernatural monster in the Hindu mythology of India. The Jala-Turga is described as a water horse that is a predatory being in lonely stretches of water.
References 112
See also Kelpy

JALL

This is the alternative name for the fabulous beast of medieval Europe known as the Eale or the Yale.
References 89
See also Yale

JAPETIDÆ

This is an alternative name for the Iapetionidæ, the giant sons of Iapetos, in the classical mythology of Greece and Rome.
References 178
See also Iapetionidæ

JAPETUS

This is the alternative spelling of the name Iapetus in the classical mythology of Greece and Rome. Japetus is the name of a Titan.
References 174
See also Iapetus

JAPETUS JUNIOR

This is one of the giants named in the genealogy created by the Italian monk Annius of Viterbo (Giovanni Nanni, ca. 1432–1502) to justify the noble descent of the Gauls from a giant biblical race.
References 139, 174
See also giant, Noah

JAPHETH

The Italian monk Annius of Viterbo (Giovanni Nanni, ca. 1432–1502) asserted that the biblical Noah was a giant. He re-created a whole genealogy of giants from Noah and Iapetus to justify the constructed line of descent through the giant Dis Samothes to the ancestry of the French nobility of the period. Within this genealogy Annius asserted that the sons of Noah, Shem, Ham, and Japheth were also giants.
References 128, 174
See also Noah

JARAPIRI

This is the name of a monster in the legends and beliefs of the Native Australians of the Wimbaraka region. Jarapiri is described as being in the form of a human in the upper body, with the form of a serpent in the lower parts of his body. He inhabited the area northwest of Alice Springs known as Wimbaraka and became integrated with the land.
References 166
See also monster

JARNSAXA

This is the name of a giantess in the Norse mythology of Scandinavia. Jarnsaxa, also spelled Iarnsaxa, was the wife of the god Thor. By him she had two sons: Magni, meaning "Strength," and Modi/Mothi, meaning "Courage."
References 78, 169
See also giantess

JASCONIUS

This is the name for a gigantic fish in the traditions and legends of Ireland. Jasconius was the vast creature upon which the boat of Saint Brendan was beached, the crew thinking that it was an island.
References 128
See also Aspidochelone, Imap Umassoursa, Zaratan

JATAYA

This is the name of a huge, fabulous, human-headed bird in the Hindu mythology of India. Jataya is the progeny of Garuda, the steed of the god Vishnu, and the sibling of a similar bird called Sampati. Jataya had been destroyed by the demon king of Sri Lanka, Ravana; his brother Sampati avenged his death.
References 112
See also Garuda, Sampati

JAZI BABA

This is a name for Baba Yaga in the folklore of the Czech Republic.
References 25, 125, 160
See also Baba Yaga

JEDUAH

This is an alternative name for the Barometz, which is a legendary part animal, part vegetable creature of medieval Europe. It is also known as the Vegetable Lamb of Tartary.
References 7, 18, 89
See also Barometz

JENNY GREENTEETH

This is a monstrous being in the folklore of the county of Lancashire in northwestern England. Jenny Greenteeth is evil and malignant, inhabiting stagnant lakes and pools of water. She is a predator of humans and in particular awaits the unwary child who may go too close to the water. When this happens, she grabs the child in her long, green fangs and drags them down under the water to drown. Jenny Greenteeth may be found in any pool or pond that is covered with green slime or scum. She is a monstrous, demonic being that belongs to a class of Nursery bogies described with vigor by watchful nursemaids and anxious parents in order to prevent the untimely death of children in such fearful places.
References 21, 24, 160, 170, 183
See also Kappa, Nellie Longarms, Peg Powler

JENNY HANIVER

This is the name given to any fake monster made for the purpose of deception, to pass off as the real thing to gullible people, during the later Middle Ages through the twentieth century in Europe and the United States. During the earlier periods, Jenny Hanivers were made to prove the existence of fabulous creatures such as the Basilisk, the Cockatrice, dragons, and mermaids when travelers or sailors returned to their sponsoring lords of the late medieval world. The term "Jenny Haniver" is supposed to reflect the name of the town of Anvers (Antwerp in modern Belgium), where many of these "beings" were made, but many were manufactured in China, Japan, and the Middle East. Later fakes were made for the veneration of "saints'" relics or to display the Dragon of the Apocalypse (Prague 1648), curiosities for the exhibition and circus world (United States, Barnum's Circus 1848 and as recent as 1933), and in today's modern world by persons wishing to be credited with the discovery of some long-dead species; even the "missing link" of ancient humans has been subject to such fraud as the notorious Piltdown Man in England.

Jenny Hanivers were generally made from the body of a real species that was artificially sewn with parts from another species, then dried and treated with chemicals so effectively that even "experts" have been seriously duped for years. Today they have become collectors' items in their own right.
References 7, 89

JERFF
This is an alternative name for the Gulon of Swedish folklore. It was described by the traveler Olaus Magnus in 1555 as being the name given to this creature in the northern parts of Sweden.
References 7, 89
See also Gulon

JEZDA
This is a name used for Baba Yaga in the folklore of Poland.
References 25, 125, 160
See also Baba Yaga, Ienzababa

JEZI BABA
This is the name of Baba Yaga used in the folklore of the Czech Republic.
References 25, 125, 160
See also Baba Yaga

JIDRA
This is the name of a curious humanoid monster in the traditions and folk beliefs of the Middle East according to medieval European travelers. The Jidra is described as emerging from the ground like a plant, from which it never becomes detached. Although permanently attached to the earth by its "root," it consumed everything about it, whether plant, animal, or human. It was a vicious and voracious beast. However, its bones were highly prized and a valuable commodity, which encouraged people to brave its ferocity. If one was not to be consumed by this creature, it had to be detached from the earth; the only method of killing it was by shooting arrows to sever

the "root." Like the Mandrake, from which it is probably derived, it was said to scream as this happened.
References 63
See also Borametz

JIN, JINN/I
This is the name given to monstrous, semisupernatural beings in the traditions and beliefs of Saudi Arabia. In an account said to emanate from the Prophet Mohammad, there are different types of Jinn:

1. Those that inhabit the depths of the earth and manifest as monstrous creatures such as a serpent.
2. Those that manifest as monstrous Black dogs.
3. The *hofafa* that has wings and can fly.
4. The *so'la* that devours human beings.

Apparently any Jinn that goes about only at night is known as a Ghoul, while one that inhabits water is known as a Ghawwas.

They are said to inhabit all the areas where excrement, rubbish, cleansing, and burial take place.

Jin is the spelling used in Bhasa Melayu language in West Malaysia for the Djinn of Islamic folk belief elsewhere in the Islamic world.
References 79, 80
See also Black dog, Djinn

JIN GENDANG
This is the name of a Jinn in the beliefs of the Malay people of West Malaysia. Jin Gendang is the guardian of the state "royal musical instruments" whose duties associate him with the Jinn of the state known as Jin Karaja'an. He is subject to the king of the Jinns, Sang Gala Raja.
References 166
See also Sang Gala Raja

JIN KARAJA'AN
This is the name of a Jinn in the beliefs of the Malay people of West Malaysia. Jin Karaja'an is the Jinn of the state and is subject to the king of the Jinns, Sang Gala Raja.
References 166
See also Sang Gala Raja

JIN NAUBAT
This is the name of a Jinn in the beliefs of the Malay people of West Malaysia. Jin Naubat is the guardian of the state "royal musical instruments" whose duties associate him with the Jinn of the state known as Jin Karaja'an. He is subject to the king of the Jinns, Sang Gala Raja.

References 166
See also Sang Gala Raja

JIN NEMFIRI, JIN LEMPIRI

This is the name of a Jinn in the beliefs of the Malay people of West Malaysia. Jin Nemfiri, also known as Jin Lempiri, is the guardian of the state "royal musical instruments" whose duties associate him with the Jinn of the state known as Jin Karaja'an. He is subject to the king of the Jinns, Sang Gala Raja.
References 166
See also Sang Gala Raja

JIN SEMBUANA

This is the name of a Jinn in the beliefs of the Malay people of West Malaysia. Jin Sembuana is the guardian of the state "royal weapons" whose duties associate him with the Jinn of the state known as Jin Karaja'an. He is subject to the king of the Jinns, Sang Gala Raja.
References 166
See also Sang Gala Raja

JINSHIN UWO

This is the name of an eel-fish of enormous size in the legends and traditions of Japan. It is so vast that where it lies in the middle of the ocean it supports the entire islands of the country of Japan upon its great back. Its massive head is located beneath the city of Kyoto while its tail is located seven hundred miles north, under Awomori. In order to prevent Japan from falling off its great back, there is a rivet that goes through a stone in the temple gardens of Kashima that secures the country to Jinshin Uwo. However, when this great beast of the ocean rolls or lashes its tail, then an earth tremor, earthquake, or tsunami will affect Japan.
References 7, 18, 89
See also Jishin-Mushi, Kami, Midgard Serpent

JISHIN-MUSHI

This is the name of a subterranean monster in the legends and traditions of Japan. Jishin-Mushi, also known as the "Earthquake Beetle," is described as having a thick body covered in scales, ten enormous legs with hairs, claws like that of a spider, and the head of a dragon. This monster is the subterranean counterpart of the monstrous eel-fish known as Jishin Uwo, and it is said that the burrowing of Jishin-Mushi causes the earthquakes in Japan.
References 18
See also dragon, monster

JOHUL

This is the name of a giant in the Norse mythology of Scandinavia. Johul, whose name may be translated as "Glacier," is one of the Hrim-Thursar, or Frost Giants. He is the son of Thrym and the sibling of Frosti, Drifta, and Snoer.
References 24
See also Frost Giants, giant

JOKAO

This is the name of a class of cannibal giant in the traditions and beliefs of the Iroquois and Seneca Native American peoples of the United States. The Jokao are also known as the Stonecoats, as these enormous humanoids are entirely covered in stone plates for their skin, which holds the secret of their power. They were said to have been engendered by winter itself or during a particularly severe winter when famine wracked the earth; the people of a northern village started to eat their neighbors and finally their own families. Some escaped and went to the warm south across the rivers, but those who remained soon turned into the monsters that developed the stone coats. One who realized what he had become got as far as the river but was too frightened of the water. He called for help to a man in a canoe, who gave him hot deer fat to warm him, and as soon as he drank it the stone coat fell away and he was free. There are many ceremonies and legends where the Jokao are associated with the False Faces.
References 77
See also cannibal, giant, monster

JÖRD, JÖRDH

This is the name of a giantess in the Norse mythology of Scandinavia. Jörd, also known as Fiorgyn, is the wife of the king of the Aesir, the god Odin. By him she is the mother of the god Thor.
References 24
See also giantess

JORMUNGANDR, JÖRMUNGAND

This is the name of the world serpent in the Norse mythology of Scandinavia. Jormungandr, also spelled Iörmungandr and also known as the Midgardsormr, or Midgard Serpent, was the progeny of the trickster god Loki and the giantess Angboda. Its siblings were Hel, the goddess of the underworld, and Fenrir, the horrific wolf bound by the gods until the last battle of Ragnarök. When this monster was born the gods were so horrified that they threw it into the ocean, where Jormungandr grew so huge that he encircled Midgard and became known as the Midgardsormr. The arches of this serpent's coils, when they rose in the air, were deemed to be the rainbow. Many of the gods who feared the serpent had encounters with it, in particular the god Thor when he went fishing with the giant Hymir. At the coming of Ragnarök, Jormungandr will rise up out of the oceans, bringing

Jormungandr grew so huge that he encircled Midgard and became known as the Midgardsormr. (Rose Photo Archive, UK)

devastation and poisoning the earth. His adversary will be the god Thor, and they will kill each other in the final battle.

References 7, 24, 47, 61, 133, 169
See also Angboda, Fenrir, giant, giantess, Hymir, Midgardsormr, Rainbow Serpent, serpent

JOTUN, JOTAN, JÖTUN, JÖTEN, JÖTUNN, JOTUNAR (pl.), JÖTNAR (pl.) (GYGR feminine)

This is the general term for the giants in the Norse mythology of Scandinavia and the Teutonic mythology of what is now northern Germany. These giants lived in Jotunheim in the northeastern sector of Asgard, the place also inhabited by the Aesir gods. These were the primordial beings, the gigantic forces and elements, which they represented in their subdivisions as:

- Air Giants, the Hrimthursr, whose chief was Kari, meaning "Tempest"; his sons were Bel, meaning "Storm," and Thiassi, meaning "Ice"; his daughter was Skadi, meaning "Winter."
- Ice Giants, the Thursar, whose chief was Thrym, meaning "Frost," whose progeny were Drifta, meaning "Snow-drift," Frosti, meaning "Cold," Johul, meaning "Glacier," and Snoer, meaning "Snow."
- Mountain Giants were subdivided into Bergbui, the "Mountain Dwellers," whose chief was the Bergjarl, or "Lord of the Mountains," and the Bergriser, or Cliff Giants. Some of these took their names from the mountains and cliffs that they inhabited, such as Senjemand.
- Water Giants were Grendel, Gymir, and Mimir, who were descended from Aegir, or Hler.

All these giants were said to be descended from Ymir through his line by Bergelmir, and they had an ambivalent relationship with both humans and the gods. Sometimes they were fearsome and aggressive; at other times they were benevolent and hospitable. Their general description was vast, humanoid, and rough with few graces, their main occupation being building, feasting, and drinking when they were not quarreling.

The giantesses, also known as Gygr, were renowned for their beauty, such as Juternsaxa, and were frequently the wives of the gods, such as Gerda.

References 24, 78, 125, 169, 182
See also Bel, Bergbui, Bergelmir, Bergjarl, Bergriser, Drifta, Fire Giants, Frost Giants, Frosti, giant, giantess, Grendel, Gymir, Johul, Juternajesta, Juternsaxa, Kari, Mimir, Senjemand, Skadi, Snoer, Starkadr, Thiassi, Ymir

JOUKAHAINEN

This is the name of a Frost Giant in the mythology of Finland. Joukahainen was a vast being that was a primordial giant who had developed from the meltings of a great icicle in the furthermost part of the world. He inhabited the icy wastes of the northern lands until the culture-hero Väinämöinen swam ashore and started to clear the land to plant food crops. This enraged the giant, who came to kill the hero. But Väinämöinen was well versed in the magic arts, and he held the rainbow as his bow and shot hawks as arrows, which turned Joukahainen into a vast pillar of ice that was condemned to melt into the tundra beneath him. When the giant promised that he would give Aino, his sister, as Väinämöinen's wife, the hero let the giant go free. However, Aino was horrified and killed herself, so Väinämöinen went in search of a wife in the land of the Ice Giants in Pohjola. But Joukahainen came after him again, blaming him for the death of his sister. He swamped the boat and left the hero to drown out in the frozen seas, but he was rescued, and Joukahainen returned to his icy castle in the far north.

References 78, 133
See also Frost giants, giant, Ymir

JOVIS BELLUS

This is the name given to the giant son of Nymbrotus in the study of world history from the time of Noah undertaken by the Italian monk Annius of Viterbo (Giovanni Nanni, ca. 1432–1502).

References 174
See also giant, Nymbrotus

JOVIS SAGA

This is an epithet by which Noah is called in the study of world history undertaken by the Italian monk Annius of Viterbo (Giovanni Nanni, ca. 1432–1502)

References 174
See also giant, Noah, Nymbrotus

JULUNGGUL, JULUNGSUL

This is the alternative name for the Rainbow Snake, also known as Yurlunggur, in the Dreamtime mythology of the Native Australian people of Arnhem Land in northern Australia.

References 38, 133, 166
See also Rainbow Serpent, serpent, Yurlunggur

JUMAR

This is a monstrous hybrid described as the offspring of an ass and a bull. It was described in *Natural Magick,* a work by the sixteenth-century English writer John Baptist Porta. This was a monstrosity that

never existed but intrigued the readership of the period.
References 7
See also monster

JURAWADBAD
This is the name of a man-snake in the Dreamtime legends of the Gunwinggu people of Arnhem Land in northern Australia. Jurawadbad wanted a particular woman of the tribe of humans for his wife, but she refused him, and she and her mother both made fun of him. Sometime later the young woman took as her lover Bulugu, a water-snake-man, and the distraught Jurawadbad plotted his revenge. He slithered into an enormous hollow log when he knew that they were foraging for food. Soon the daughter peered into the log searching for grubs. Jurawadbad closed his eyes so that the log appeared to have food possibilities, but when the mother looked in, he opened his eyes so wide that she thought she saw daylight at the other end. So both women put their hands into the log to get the food they thought was within, and Jurawadbad bit and killed them both. This is a story that has been enacted by the Urpar cult as a rain-bringing ceremony.
References 38, 133

JURIK
This is the name of a monstrous flying supernatural serpent in the legends and beliefs of the people of Sunda in Indonesia. It takes the form of a fiery dragon or serpent flying through the night sky.
References 113
See also Aitvaras, dragon, serpent

JUTERNAJESTA
This is the name of a giantess in the Norse mythology of Scandinavia. Juternajesta was loved by Torge, and when the Mountain Giant Senjemand, a Jotunar identified with the island of Senjen, was rejected by her, he tried to shoot her with a massive arrow of stone. Torge, her lover, deflected it in time with his hat and ran after Senjemand who leaped on his horse and fled.
References 24
See also giant, Jotun, Senjemand

JUTERNSAXA
This is the name of a giantess in the Norse mythology of Scandinavia. Juternsaxa was a female Jotun known as the Gygr, and she was renowned for her beauty.
References 24
See also Gygr, Jotun

K

KABANDA, KABANDHA

This is the name of a monstrous humanoid in the legends and Hindu mythology of India. Kabanda, whose name means "Barrel," is one of the Rakshasas. He is described as an ugly, hairy giant without a head or legs. His single eye and enormous mouth, which is full of sharp fangs, are in the middle of his body, and his eight vast arms serve as his legs, like a gigantic spider. In the epic Indian legend *Ramayana*, Kabanda had originally been a Gandharva; however, he had quarrelled with the god Indra, who dealt him such a blow that his head and legs were swallowed up into his body. In this metamorphosed state he became the monster Kabanda, swelling like a barrel, his eye and mouth emerging though his huge, hairy torso. As Kabanda he quarrelled with Rama, who destroyed the monster with *vajra* (lightning fire), from which he reemerged in his original form as a Gandharva. In gratitude the Gandharva helped in Rama's wars against the king of the demons, Ravana.
References 24, 112, 125, 160, 166
See also Gandharvas, monster, Rakshasa

KA-EN-ANKH NERERU

This is the name of a gigantic cosmic serpent in the mythology of ancient Egypt. Ka-en-ankh Nereru is described in the *Book of the Coming Forth into Day* as a vast serpent whose entire body stretches through the total darkness of the night skies. When the old sun in the shape of the god Ra in his celestial boat reaches the horizon, the god and his boat enter the tail of Ka-en-ankh Nereru. They emerge on the eastern horizon, and the rejuvenated Ra begins his daily journey across the skies once more.
References 89

KAFRE

This is an alternative spelling of the name of a monster called Cafre in the traditions and folklore of the peoples of the Philippine Islands. Kafre closely resembles the monster called the Buata in New Britain.

References 113
See also Ætolian Boar, Battleswine, Beigad, Boar of Beann-Gulbain, Buata, Cafre, Calydonian Boar, Erymanthean Boar, Hildesuin, monster, ogre, Pugot, Sachrimnir, Twrch Trwyth, Ysgithyrwyn

KAI TSI, KAI TSU

These are alternative names for the Oriental unicorn in the legends and folk beliefs of China.
References 81
See also unicorn

KAIA

This the name of a group of demonic monsters in the traditions and beliefs of the people of the Gazelle Peninsula in New Britain, Melanesia. The Kaia were originally creator spirits but have since been demoted to the status of monsters. They appear as terrifying snakes, eels, or pigs, and sometimes as humanoid hybrids of these creatures. The Kaia inhabit the depths of the earth or volcanoes from which they emerge to bring destruction to humans.
References 125, 160
See also monster, serpent

KAITABHA

This is the name of one of two terrifying giants in the Hindu creation mythology of India. Together with Madhu, the other giant, Kaitabha plotted to kill the young god Brahma as he was emerging from the god Vishnu. So while Vishnu reposed on the lotus of the world, the two giants hid in his ears to await the moment when Brahma came up from the navel of the great god. But the moment of Vishnu's awakening, and with it the new era, was at hand, and he knew instantly where Kaitabha and Madhu were and what they intended. He seized the two giants and destroyed them and, from their marrow, created the new world and all in it.
References 112
See also Ymir

201

KALERU

This is an alternative name for the great Rainbow Snake, also known as Galeru, in the legends of the Kimberley region of Australia.
References 166
See also Rainbow Serpent, serpent, Ungud

KALEVANPOJAT

This is the name of a group of demonic giants in the legends and folklore of Finland. The Kalevanpojat, whose name means "Sons of Kalevala," are malevolent toward all beings, especially humans. They will wreak havoc in the arable fields, turning them into wastelands full of stones, and smash and flood the beautiful forests.
References 125
See also giant

KALIYA

This is the name of a monstrous serpent in the Hindu mythology of India. Kaliya is described as a five-headed, bejewelled snake that inhabited the deepest parts of the River Yamuna, or Jumna. Kaliya was the king of the serpents who emerged from their depths at night to lay waste to the surrounding countryside and then sleep in a particular tree. One day the young god Krishna climbed this very tree and dived into the water beneath. The vast, heated wave that he created burned the tree. The outraged Kaliya summoned his serpent hordes and encircled Krishna, ready to destroy him. But the god easily escaped and danced on the head of Kaliya. All his powers were drained, which so terrified the serpents that Kaliya and they departed to the oceans forever. For this gesture of good will, Krishna promised that Garuda, who killed serpents, would never touch them.
References 24, 112, 133
See also Garuda, Hydra, serpent

KALKES

This is the alternative name for the dog- or goat-like monsters in modern Greek folklore called Kallicantzari. They are called Kales in the district of Ponorio.
References 7, 160, 169
See also Kallicantzari

KALLICANTZARI

This is the name of a monstrous creature in the modern legends and folklore of Greece. There are two types of Kallicantzari, also spelled Callicantzari, the first being a type of dwarf-like hairy being with a long tail; the others are a race of giant creatures much like the Satyrs in classical mythology of ancient Greece, from whom no doubt they were derived. These evil and malignant monsters are also known as Kalkes in the district of Panorio.

The giant Kallicantzari are described as being humanoid beings but with a head resembling that of a dog or goat with a beard and rough, shaggy hair over their bodies and cloven hooves. They walk on their hind legs and range in height from taller than a man to a terrifying twenty-five feet or more. This gigantic race is subterranean and credited with trying to destroy the World Tree (a similar concept to the Ash Tree Ygddrasil of Norse legends) by gnawing its roots. But as the Kallicantzari are nocturnal, their chances to kill the tree through its roots diminish as the winter nights approach. At the time of Christmas through to Epiphany (the Twelve Days of Christmas to January 6), the Kallicantzari roam above ground, creating havoc, abducting women, destroying crops, groves, and dwellings, killing livestock, and even making travelers dance with them until exhausted, when they may be set upon and devoured. As troglodytes, the Kallicantzari were terrified of sunlight, and anyone who could keep them above ground by making them dance until cock crow would be saved. Any child born during this period was viewed with suspicion, and there was a practice in Chios of branding the child on the heel to make sure that it would not turn into a Kallicantzari. When these beings returned to their lair after the festive period and the lighter nights started to come again, the World Tree had recovered sufficiently, but they would start to gnaw it again.
References 7, 17, 24, 160, 169
See also giant, monster, satyr

KALSERU

This is an alternative name for the great Rainbow Snake in the Dreamtime legends of northwestern Australia.
References 24
See also Rainbow Serpent

KAMA-DHENU, KAMADHENU, KAMDHAIN, KAMDHENU

This is the name of the great cosmic cow in the Hindu mythology of India. There are two versions of how Kama-Dhenu came to exist; she was said to be the first being that was created from the Churning of the Ocean, or produced as the offspring of the goddess of the sun, Rohini. Kama-Dhenu, also known by the names Savala and Surabhi, gave an everlasting supply of milk with which to nourish all. But she was capable of much more, and when her sometime owner, Vasishtla, made a wish, whatever he desired was there. Kama-Dhenu was so powerful that she was also responsible for delivering an army of warriors to defeat Arjuna.

References 24, 112, 133
See also Audumla, Dun Cow, Glas Gaibleanir

KAMAPUA'A

This is the name of the primordial giant boar in the mythology of the people of the Hawaiian Islands. Kamapua'a, whose name may be translated as "Pig-child," raised, with his snout, from the bottom of the ocean's mud all the earth and mountains of the islands. And where depressions were left by him from pounding with his trotters, these became the sounds between the islands and lakes within them. Kamapua'a was sexually very aggressive and pursued both goddesses and human women and produced many monstrous beings. The goddess of fire, Pele, rejected him outright, so with an army of his subjects he tried to trample out all her flames. Fortunately, the gods came to her rescue and banished Kamapua'a to the lowlands and Pele to the hills, which she filled with her fires. It is said the earthquakes experienced there are the two joining in turbulent relations from time to time.
References 47, 133

KAMI

This is the name of a gigantic fish in the mythology of Japan. The Kami is described in the sacred literature of Japan as being a vast fish that resembles a catfish whose body is in the great ocean beneath the islands of Japan. It was the movement of this enormous fish that made many of the earthquakes above it in the islands. However, after one such episode the Great Deity of Deer Island took an enormous sword and speared it deep through the earth down into the great ocean and straight through the head of the Kami, transfixing it forever. Henceforth, whenever the Kami wriggled beneath the islands, the Great Deity would take hold of the hilt of the sword and apply pressure to the head of the Kami until it was still. This great sword is carved from a granite rock in the temple, and during the seventeenth century one of the lords of the island had his men dig to find the point. After six days the point of the sword had still not been reached, and they gave up.
References 18
See also Jinshin Uwo, Jishin-Mushi, Midgardsorm

KANEAKELUH

This is the name of a giant fabulous bird in the legends and folklore of the Kwakiutl Native American people of British Columbia, Canada. Kaneakeluh is said to be responsible for delivering the gift of fire to humans.
References 169
See also Estas

KAPPA

These are aquatic monsters in the mythology and folklore of Japan. They are variously described as being small and in the shape of monkeys, with scaly skin and webbed fingers, or as having the body of a tortoise with the head of a monkey. Whatever the description, they are reputedly green, and their heads have a depression in the top of the skull in which there is a fluid that gives them their life force. The Kappa, also known as Kawako, which means "Child of the River," as the name implies, inhabit ponds and rivers. They are particularly malicious and entice humans and animals into the water, where they devour their victims and drink their blood. If a human is clever enough to negotiate with the Kappa, he may keep his life, and if befriended by offering the preferred cucumbers as food, they may teach the person about medicine. If, however, the Kappa is intent on consuming the victim, its potency may be drawn from it by making a low bow, which must be returned; in doing so, the liquid, which is the source of the Kappas's power, will drain from its head.
References 7, 24, 38, 60, 89, 113, 125, 133, 137, 160, 166
See also Buso, Jenny Greenteeth, Llamhigyn y Dwr, Peg Powler

KARASA TENGU

This is the name of a monster in the traditions and folklore of Japan. The Karasa Tengu is described as a huge, bird-like creature with gigantic talons on its legs, animals' ears, and a vast, red beak big enough to carry a man through the air.
References 7, 89, 113, 160
See also Tengu

KAR-FISH

This is the name of a class of gigantic fish in the Zoroastrian mythology of Persia (now Iran). These fish are described as having the keenest eyesight of living beings and are so huge that they surround the Gaokerena, the Tree of Immortality created by Ahura Mazda. However, the force of evil, Angra Mainyu, constantly seeks to undermine and destroy the sacred tree, so Ahura Mazda created the Kar-Fish to guard it against the great lizard of evil. Their vigilance, with their heads constantly pointing outward against the foe, will continue to the end of days.
References 7, 89

KARGAS

This is the name of a fabulous monster in the legends of Turkey, possibly dating from the tales of medieval European travelers. The Kargas is a hybrid bird that closely resembles a Griffin.
References 7
See also Griffin

KARI

This is the name of a giant in the Norse mythology of Scandinavia. Kari, whose name may be translated as "Tempest," is the leader of a subgroup of storm giants and is one of the Hrim-Thursar, or Frost Giants. Kari has three sons named Bel, Thiassi, and Thrym. His daughter is Skadi.
References 24
See also Bel, Frost Giants, giant, Skadi, Thiassi, Thrym

KARIA

This is one of the local names for the Rainbow Serpent in the Dreamtime mythology of the Native Australian people.
References 159
See also Rainbow Serpent

KARITEI-MO

This is the name for the ogress Hārītī in the legends and traditions of Buddhist beliefs in Japan.
References 61, 125, 139, 160
See also cannibal, Hārītī, ogress

KARKADAN

This is the name of a monstrous creature in the legends and beliefs of Persia and India. It was described by European travelers in 1503 as having a very large body but the legs and cloven hooves of a deer, with thick, hairy legs on the bulky hindquarters. Its head resembled that of a horse with a scanty mane, for it had little by way of a neck. The Karkadan was said to be a russet color, like that of a weasel, and also said to be aggressive. In some descriptions, however, this beast was credited with a single horn from its forehead that was much prized as a means of detecting poison but was used by the beast to kill and carry off its prey.
References 63, 89
See also Alicorn, Amduscias, Ass (Three-Legged), Biasd Na Srognig, Chiai Tung, Chio-Tuan, Ki Lin, Kirin, Koresck, Licorn, Mi'raj (Al), monster, Onyx Monoceros, Scythian Ass, Unicorn

KASHCHEI

This is the name of a monster in the traditions and folklore of Russia. In some versions of the tales Kashchei, also known as Koshchei, is a dragon, but in others Kashchei is a male version of Baba Yaga.
References 55
See also Baba Yaga, dragon

KASHEHOTAPOLO

This is the name of a wild humanoid beast in the legends and folklore of the Choctaw Native American people of the southeastern United States. The name "Kashehotapolo" derives from the words *kasheho*,

which may be translated as "woman," and *tapolo*, which may be translated as "call." Kashehotapolo is described as a humanoid beast with an undersized head and inhabits the marshes and swampy woodlands of the area. If Kashehotapolo sees any of the hunters, he will emit a piercing screech and flee immediately.
References 77
See also Nalusa Falaya

KATYN TAYUUQ

This is the name of a monster in the legends and folklore of the Inuit people of the eastern region of Hudson Bay in Canada. Katyn Tayuuq is described as a vast female head in which is her vulva and from which extend her pendulous breasts and feet. This horrific monster can enter the dwellings of humans at will.
References 77
See also Pontianak, Tunnituaqruk

KATYUTAYUUQ

This is the name of a female monster in the traditions and beliefs of the Inuit of eastern Hudson Bay in Canada. Katyutayuuq is described as having a humanoid shape, but on her small head her breasts are above her mouth and her genitalia below her mouth. She and her male counterpart, known as Tunnituaqruk, follow the humans or seek out their recently abandoned snow-houses to search for discarded scraps. They have a nasty habit of hiding in abandoned bedding and terrifying anyone who might happen upon them.
References 77
See also monster, Tunnituaqruk

KAUKAS

This is a semisupernatural in the legends and folklore of Lithuania. The Kaukas is mostly described as being like the Aitvaras, a kind of flying dragon with a fiery tail, but it may also manifest as a sort of deformed goblin. The Kaukas brings good fortune and stolen goods for the family to which it is attached. It may also be the guardian of treasure hoards.
References 119, 120, 125, 160
See also Aitvaras, Pukis

KEELUT, KE'LETS

This is a malevolent semisupernatural monster in the legends and folk beliefs of the Inuit people of Canada and Alaska. The Keelut appears in the shape of a massive dog but completely without fur.
References 38, 139, 160
See also Black dogs

KEEN KEENGS

This is the name of a race of gigantic people in the Dreamtime mythology of the Native Australian

people. The Keen Keengs were flying men who were descended from the primordial giants that first inhabited the land. They were described as very tall humanoid beings with two fingers and a thumb on each hand, from which extended, the length of their arms, ribbed wings like those of a bat. They inhabited enormous caverns in the cliffs of mountains but were so huge that they bent double to enter. They guarded the flame of their flame god in the center of the cavern complex, and this terrible god demanded human sacrifices. One day two *wirinuns* (shamans), called the Winjarning brothers, happened to be hunting near the caverns of the Keen Keengs. The Keen Keengs had spotted them but knew that they were powerful and had thwarted many of their attempted abductions for sacrifice. Since they knew that the *wirinuns* had never seen them before, the Keen Keengs decided to invite them as guests and then throw them to the flame god. But the *wirinuns* could hear the plot from afar and, when they were invited, accepted the lift on the back of one of the Keen Keengs behind his wings. They stayed and were entertained in the caverns for three days, and with each day the flames of the god's pit grew stronger. Eventually, on the third night, they went to the farthest place in the cave and made their plans to escape. During the frenzy of the women's emu dance the first brother shot out of the cavern, swiftly followed by all the Keen Keengs, but they lost him in the blackness of the night. When they returned they saw to their horror all their women dancing dizzily around with the remaining *wirinun*, and one by one they all tumbled into the pit of the flame god. The male Keen Keengs raced into the throng, but they too were caught up in the *wirinun*'s dancing and eventually dizzily hurled themselves to their flame god. Then as both the *wirinuns* left the accursed place at dawn, the flames of the mountain reached to such a height that the mountain where the cavern had been imploded in a roar of fire. Later in the day only a flat plain full of ants could be seen where they had been.
References 154
See also giant

KEERONAGH

This is the alternative name of a monster in the folklore and beliefs of Ireland usually known as Caoránach.
References 128
See also Caoránach

KEINNARA

This is an alternative spelling of the name Kinnara, a group of semisupernatural beings, or Gandharvas, in the mythology of India, Indonesia, and Thailand. They are variously described as being like birds with a human head.

References 89, 120, 125, 160
See also Chitra-ratha, Gandharvas, Kimpurushas

KÉKROPS

This is an alternative spelling of the name of the king of Attica in Greek legend known as Cecrops.
References 24, 89, 125
See also Cecrops

KELERU

This is the name used for the great Rainbow Snake in the Dreamtime mythology of the Native Australian people of the Kimberley region of Australia.
References 125, 166
See also Rainbow Serpent, Yullunggur

KELPY, KELPIE

This is the fearsome, malevolent, semisupernatural water monster of Scottish folklore. Although it could assume the form of a rough, shaggy old man or a handsome young man, the Kelpy mostly took the form of a black or gray horse with flashing eyes and silken coat. It could be identified by the green rushes that always clung to its hair. The Kelpy was to be found on the shores of the lochs, at fords, and at ferry points. To see a Kelpy is considered a portent of drowning or other waterborne catastrophe. In human form it could leap on to the horse behind the rider and crush the terrified traveler to the point of death. It would appear to unsuspecting young women as a lover, eventually abducting and then devouring them under the water. The Kelpy would also entice wandering children or unwary young men to mount him in the guise of a sleek horse on the side of the loch. The monster would then gallop off into the water, dragging down his victims and devouring all but the entrails, which would float to the surface. If anyone could get a bridle over the Kelpy's head, it was said that it would do the work of several horses. The Kelpy was also known to keep the waterwheels of the mills turning at night; he was just as capable of destroying them, too. A legend tells how the Laird of Morphie once bridled a Kelpy and made it work hard, dragging the stones for the building of his castle. On completion the released monster cursed the laird never to enjoy the building, and the curse remained with the Grahams of Morphie ever since.
References 10, 12, 16, 20, 21, 24, 25, 37, 78, 89, 120, 124, 128, 134, 160, 170
See also Bäckahäst, Cabyll-Ushtey, Cheval Bayard, Eaċh Uisge, Näcken, Neugle

KENTAURE, KENTAUROS

These are alternative for the names for the centaur in the classical mythology of Greece and Rome.

The Kelpy mostly took the form of a black or gray horse with flashing eyes and silken coat. (Rose Photo Archive, UK)

References 125
See also centaur

KÉRBEROS
This is the alternative spelling of the name of the monstrous dog of the underworld, Cerberus, in the classical mythology of Greece and Rome.
References 125
See also Cerberus

KERE
This is the name of a class of unicorn mentioned as being in the legends and traditions of Tibet. It was said to be very aggressive.
References 81
See also unicorn

KERKES
This is the name of the fabulous bird of Turkish mythology that equates with the Phoenix or the Bennu birds of Egyptian mythology.
References 89
See also Bennu, Phoenix

KESHI, KESHIN
This is the name of a monstrous giant horse in the Hindu mythology of India. The Keshi, whose name may be translated as the "Long-haired," was described as a vast, long-maned, entirely malicious beast. It was eventually choked to death when the god Vishnu pushed his hand and arm down into its mouth and down its throat.
References 112

KETO
This is the name of a monster in the classical mythology of Greece and Rome. She was a hideous sea monster and the wife of the sea god Phorkys, by whom she was the mother of the even more hideous Gorgons and their guardian sisters, the Graeae.
References 125
See also Gorgon, Graeae, monster

KEWANAMBO
This is the name of an ogre in the legends and folk beliefs of the people of western Papua New Guinea. Kewanambo is an evil cannibal ogre that will deceive small children with a disguise into thinking that he is a benevolent female, then he will abduct and devour them.
References 113
See also cannibal, ogre

KEYEME
This is a humanoid monster in the traditions and folk beliefs of the Taulipang people of the Amazon Basin in South America. Keyeme, also known as the "Lord of the Animals," by donning a rainbow colored skin, can assume the shape of a gigantic water serpent.
References 125
See also serpent

KHADEM QUEMQUOMA
This is a female Djinn in the folk beliefs of Morocco. The name means "Black Woman of the Copper Pot." This semisupernatural manifests as a gigantic female at night. She is particularly wicked to small children and will wake up a sleeping infant and frighten it, making it cry in the dark.
References 122, 160
See also Djinn

KHARA
This is the name of the cosmic ass in the Zoroastrian mythology of Persia, now Iran. Khara is described as having the gigantic body of an ass with three legs. Its head has six eyes, of which two are on its back, two are as normal, and a further two are on the top of its head. It has a single horn protruding from its forehead and nine mouths. It is an all-seeing beast that helps to deter evil.
References 24

KHOLOMODUMO
This is the name of a gigantic monster in the legends and folk beliefs of the Sotho people of southeastern Africa. Kholomodumo existed from the time of creation and was so voracious that it ate every living human except one. This woman survived by hiding and eventually gave birth to twin boys. They and a dog decided to track and destroy Kholomodumo. When they succeeded, the whole of the devoured humanity was restored and came out from inside it.
References 125
See also giant

KHRUT
This is the alternative name in the language of the people of Thailand for the fabulous Garuda bird of Indian and Indonesian mythology.
References 113
See also Garuda

KHUMBABA
This is the name of a monstrous giant guardian in the mythology of ancient Mesopotamia. Kumbaba, also known by the names Huwawa and Humbaba, is the guardian of the cedar forests.
References 78
See also Humbaba

KHYUNG
This is the Tibetan name for a mythical bird in the legends and folk beliefs of the people of Tibet. Its description is almost identical with the Garuda bird of Indian and Indonesian legends.
References 125
See also Garuda

KI DU
This is the name of a monstrous dog in the legends and folklore of the Breton people of northwestern France. The Ki Du is a Celtic Black dog beast that is said to accompany deceased humans to their "Otherworld" abode until reborn as another individual.
References 128

KIAU
This is the name of a vast water monster in the legends of China. The Kiau was an enormous water serpent that wreaked havoc with the fishing and fishermen in the Chien-Tang River. It was eventually killed in 1129 A.D. by a local hero.
References 181
See also serpent

KICHIKNEBIK
This is the name of a gigantic serpent in the traditions and beliefs of the Native American people of the United States. Kichiknebik the Great Serpent, also known as Manitou Kinebik, was described by Father Louis Nicholas, ca. 1675, as being so vast and strong that it could swallow a buffalo entirely at one go. It was a serpent in shape but had the addition of horns or spines along its back. Despite its size, Kichiknebik could move as swiftly on land as it could in the water.
References 134
See also Manitou Kinebic, serpent

KICKLE SNIFTER
This is a creature from the folklore of lumberjacks and forest workers, especially in Wisconsin and Minnesota in the United States, during the nineteenth and early twentieth centuries. The Kickle Snifter belongs to a group of beings affectionately known as the Fearsome Critters, whose exaggerated proportions and activities not only explained the weird noises of the lonely landscape but also provided some amusement at camps. The Kickle Snifter is also known as the Hickle Snifter.
References 7, 24
See also Fearsome Critters

KIH TIAU
This is the name of a a type of sea monster or sea dragon in the legends and folk beliefs of China. The Kih Tiau was purportedly the creature from which a

preservative similar to that of ambergris was derived, as it was said that the spherical lumps of the substance were the eggs of the beast, brought at great expense to the markets of Canton and Foochow.
References 81
See also dragon, sea-serpent of Memphré magog, serpent

KIJO
This is the name of an ogre in the traditions and folklore of the people of Japan. Kijo inhabited the deep forests and woods of the islands.
References 113
See also ogre

KI-LIN, K'I-LIN
This is the name of a beast in the legends and mythology of China. The Ki-lin, also spelled Ch'i-Lin, is one of the celestial animals, the others being the dragon, the Feng Hwang, and the tortoise. The Ki-lin is described as having the body of a stag, the legs and hooves of a horse, and the tail of an ox; the head, which is like that of a deer, has a single fleshy horn protruding from the forehead. The coat of the Ki-lin was the five sacred colors of red, black, yellow, blue, and white. It was said to live for a thousand years and brought good fortune, but to see one dead or to kill one brought disaster. The Ki-lin was by nature extremely gentle, existing only on those things that were not alive. It walked gently and, like the Feng Hwang, only appeared in the times of a good and just reign. Another variety of the Ki-lin is the Chio-tuan, which seeks peace in times of the country's invasion.
References 7, 18, 89
See also Alicorn, Amduscias, Ass (Three-Legged), Biasd Na Srognig, Chiai Tung, Chio-Tuan, Feng Hwang, Karkadan, Ki Lin, Kirin, Koresck, Licorn, Mi'raj (Al), Onyx Monoceros, Oriental Dragon, Scythian Ass, unicorn

KIMPURUSHAS
This is the name of a class of humanoid monsters in the Hindu mythology of India. The Kimpurushas are described as having the body of a horse with the head of a human, rather like the centaurs in the classical mythology of Greece and Rome. They, like the Kinnaras, are the servant-followers of the evil Kubera.
References 24
See also centaur, Kinnara, monster

KINDER-FRESSER
This is the name of a monstrous ogre in the traditions and folklore of Germany. Kinder-fresser, which may be translated as "Child-guzzler," and the Kinderschrecker, belong to a group of beings used by anxious parents as Nursery bogies to control their

children's behavior. They became popular from the invention of printing in Germany during the Middle Ages and were widely disseminated by the seventeenth century. They have since been associated with effigies in town carnivals.

References 174

See also Coco, Father Flog, Kinderschrecker, Nursery bogie

KINDERSCHRECKER, KINDER SCHRECKER, DER

This is the name for a cannibal giant in the folklore of Germany. He is known in English as the Child-guzzler and is a Nursery bogie.

References 182

See also cannibal, Child Guzzler, giant, Nursery bogie

KINEPIKWA

This is an alternative name for the Msi-Kinepikwa, or Great Reptile, in the traditions of the Shawnee Native American people of the United States.

References 134, 139

See also Msi-Kinepikwa

KING

This is an alternative name for the Oriental Unicorn in the legends and traditions of China.

References 81

See also Ch'i-Lin, unicorn

KING AURIARIA

This is the name of a giant in the legends and folk traditions of the people of Kiribati, one of the Gilbert and Ellice Islands in Micronesia. King Auriaria is described as a giant who had a completely red skin. He fell in love with Neititua Abine, the goddess of vegetation. She died shortly after their marriage, and from her head grew the first coconut palm.

References 113

See also giant

KING KONG

This is the name of a monstrous anthropoid that featured in the classic American horror film of the same name by Cooper and Schoedsack in 1933. King Kong in the story is a monstrous cannibal ape that inhabits a Pacific island. An expedition is mounted by a group of American explorers to bring this monster back to the United States as a spectacle for the public. As with many folkloric motifs, such as the unicorn and the Afanc, King Kong is seduced by the beauty of a woman, in this case portrayed by the actress Fay Wray. From his majestic jungle terrain to the public spectacle is the theme of the mighty being denigrated. The audience is not surprised by the creature's break for freedom and his rampaging through the streets of New York City. The film cleverly focuses attention on the bond and the pity that comes from the relationship between the "Beauty" and the "Beast." But in this story the beast does not have the capacity to transform and is shot down in a spectacular fashion by airplanes buzzing around him atop the Empire State Building.

References 20, 182

See also Afanc, Beast, giant, monster, Unicorn

KING OF THE FISHES

This is the title, almost all over the world, of the monstrous fish that in legend and folklore herds and guards the fish in large inland stretches of water. In the Fino-Ugric speaking nations of Finland and the Balkan states, this being is known as the King, or Queen, of the Fishes. In Teutonic and Gallic areas it may be the Mother, or Guardian, of the Fishes. In the New World the fish has become a water serpent but still with the same qualities. These are all ancient semisupernatural beings whose bodies are often covered in mosses and may have fully mature trees growing on their backs.

References 134

See also serpent

KING OF THE SNAKES, KING OF THE SERPENTS

This is the name given to the monstrous guardian of the serpents in the folklore of Sweden. The King of the Snakes is described as an enormous serpentine dragon with a crest on its head. The folkloric reports, one of them in the *Hamar Chronicle,* tell of someone first seeing and killing a snake, which is followed by successive emergence of others that are subsequently killed. Then the enormous head of the King of the Snakes emerges and either attacks the informant, or the informant flees.

References 134

See also Basilisk, Ch'ang Hao, Dhrana, Dhumavarna, King of the Snakes, Muchalinda, Raja Naga

KING PRATIE

This is an alternative name for the monster known as the Bunyip in the legends of the Native Australians.

See also Bunyip

KINGU

This is the name of a monster in the mythology of ancient Babylon in Mesopotamia. Kingu is variously described as the son or the consort of the monster Tiamat. When Kingu was defeated and slain by Marduk, it was from the blood of this slain monster that human beings were made.

References 61, 125

See also monster

KINNARA

This is a group of semisupernatural beings, or Gandharvas, in the mythology of India, Indonesia, and Thailand. They are variously described as being like birds with human heads, or having the torso of a man and the head of a horse. The Kinnara, also spelled Keinnara, were said to have emerged from the toes of the god Brahma and are the attendants of Kubera. As Keinnara they feature in the mythology of Burma.

References 89, 120, 125, 160
See also Chitra-ratha, Gandharvas, Kimpurushas

KIOH TWAN

This is an alternative name for the Oriental unicorn in the legends and traditions of China.

References 81
See also unicorn

KIRATA

This is the name of a race of monstrous humanoids in the legends and folklore of India. The male Kirata are described as part human and part tiger, being a tiger from the waist upward. The Kirata inhabit the deep forests in the hills of northeastern India. They can live on raw fish but are cannibal monsters preying on any human communities that live in the vicinity. The female Kirata are described as being beautifully golden in color and capable of seducing any nearby humans in the woods.

References 112

KIRIN

This is the name in Japanese mythology for the Ch'-Lin or Oriental unicorn, of China. It is described as being a multicolored animal with a single horn protruding from its forehead. The Kirin is the reward of the good and just and the punisher of those that do evil deeds.

References 7, 89, 113
See also Ass (Three-Legged), Ch'i-Lin, Chio-Tuan, Karkadan, Ki Lin, Mi'raj (Al), Onyx Monoceros, unicorn

KIRNI

This is the name of a fabulous bird in the legends of Japan. The Kirni is described as being very similar to the Griffin of classical medieval legends of Europe.

References 7
See also Griffin

KIRTIMUKHA

This is the name of a massive monstrous head in the Hindu mythology of southeastern Asia. Kirtimukha, also known as the Face of Glory, is described as a vast, disembodied head that has huge, protruding eyes, over which the enormous eyebrows become pointed horns, and a vast, gaping mouth. This is surrounded in a tangle of hair, all of which terminates in heads of Makaras. The tradition relates that when Siva was told that he was unworthy of marrying Parviti, in his rage a monster sprang from his head. This monster, in the form of a hybrid man and lion, immediately attacked the god and demanded a sacrifice. Siva commanded it to take itself, and so it ingested its body, leaving only the entrails, which turned into pearls. Siva then appointed Kirtimukha to be the guardian of entrances. In the images of the Javanese Kirtimukha, flowers also pour from its mouth.

References 7, 24
See also Makara, T'ao-Tieh

KISHI-MOJIN, KISHIMOJIN

This is the name for the ogress Hārītī in the legends and traditions of Buddhist beliefs in China.

References 61, 125, 139, 160
See also cannibal, Hārītī, ogress

KISIHOHKEW

This is the name of a monstrous beast in the traditions and beliefs of the Cree Native American people of Canada. Kisihohkew is described as someimes resembling a great moose or wolf but is at all times the servant of Wesucechak.

References 77

KITCHI-AT'HUSIS

This is the name of a great water serpent in the traditions and beliefs of the Micmac Native American people of the United States. In one particular tradition two shamans decided to work out their differences by transforming themselves into the shapes of their serpent guides. One metamorphosed into Weewilmekq whilst the other took on the form of the great serpent Kitchi-at'Husis. Together they did battle in Boyden Lake in Washington County, Maine. Their writhings caused such turbulence in the water during their battle that the lake has been turbulent ever since.

References 134
See also Horned Water Serpent, Kitchi-at'Husis, serpent, Weewilmekq

KITZINACKAS

This is the name of a gigantic serpent in the traditions and beliefs of the Lenapes and Algonquian Native American people of the United States. In an account by Wassenaer from 1631 in a *Description of New Holland,* the shamans of the people imitated and encouraged the presence of the great serpent Kitzinackas for a sacred celebration.

References 134
See also serpent

KIWAHKW

This is the name of giants in the legends of the Maliseet Passamaquoddy Native American people of the northeastern United States. The Kiwahkw are a class of Ice Giants who are predatory cannibals who track down and devour any humans in their territory. They are apparently derived from corpses that are transformed by witches; they then must devour at least two other humans to transform into Ice Giants. In one traditional tale the hero Glooscap disguises himself as an Ice Giant and is accepted by them, whereupon he performs a magic stamping on the ground and makes the water rise. As he chants a song of metamorphosis, his magic changes the Ice Giants into fish that are taken away in the waters and will cause no more harm.
References 77
See also cannibal, Frost Giant, giant, Ice Giant

KIYO

This is the name of a dragon in the legends of Japan. The legend tells how a novice monk went to a teahouse on the bank of the Hidaka River, where he met and fell in love with a waitress there called Kiyo. They had many meetings, but he was eventually filled with guilt and resolved never to see her again. In despair her love turned to anger and her anger into the desire for revenge. Soon she acquired the knowledge of magical formulas in the temple of Kompera and was able to transform herself into a dragon. In this form Kiyo went to the monastery, where her former lover hid under the great bell. With one blast of fire from her dragon's mouth, Kiyo melted the bell and killed the cowardly man beneath it, who should have been loyal to his vows.
References 113
See also dragon

KLUDDE

This is the name of a malignant shape-shifting demonic monster in the folklore of Belgium. The Kludde would appear as a gigantic dog, cat, frog, bat, or horse to terrorize night-bound travelers on lonely roads. The Kludde could, however, be identified by telltale blue flames flickering ahead of it. This being might jump on the back of the victim and cling with its talons, becoming heavier the more the terrified human tried to dislodge it, until the victim might die of exhaustion. Only dawn breaking or the sound of the church bell could save the traveler. As a Black dog, it suddenly appeared and pranced along the road, stretching on its hind legs until it reached the throat of its victim. Its most usual manifestation is as an old horse that, like the Kelpie, encouraged the unwary to mount on its back, from which they were unable to dismount until, after a horrific ride, they were ejected into a river.
References 93, 160
See also Aufhocker, Kelpy, Oschaert

KLYMENE

This is the alternative spelling of the name of the female Titan Clymene in the classical mythology of Greece and Rome.
References 47, 78, 178
See also Clymene, Titan

KOERAKOONLASED

This is the name of a race of humanoid monsters in the legends and folklore of Estonia, Latvia, and some parts of Lithuania. The Koerakoonlased are described as vertically part human and part dog with one side of the body from each of these beings but with a single eye in the center of their foreheads. In other versions they have the body of a human but the head of a dog like the Cynocephali of classical literature. They inhabited the far icy wastes of the north from which they raided the human settlements. The Koerakoonlased were extremely vicious cannibals who hunted human beings to take for their cattle, to be fattened and eaten.
References 24
See also cannibal, Cynocephali

KOGUKHPUK

This is the name of a type of monster in the legends and folklore of the Inuit of the Bering Sea coast in Alaska, United States. It is described as an enormous subterranean creature that is obliged to remain within the earth, burrowing for its food—but more because the daylight would kill it. Consequently, the Kogukhpuk emerges into the darkness of the night sky in the depths of winter for one night only. Those that have stayed too long on the surface and been killed by the rays of the sun are now massive, bleached bones. This is an explanation of the mammoth bones that have been found in the vicinity.
References 77
See also monster

KOIOS

This is an alternative spelling of Coeus, one of the Titans in the classical mythology of Greece and Rome.
References 20, 24, 47, 61, 78, 94, 125, 136, 139, 166, 169, 174, 178, 182
See also Coeus, Titan

KOIS

This is the name of a Titan in the classical mythology of Greece and Rome. Kois was the father of Leto by Phoibe.
References 125
See also giant, Titan

KOJIN

This is the name of a demonic monstrous humanoid in the legends and traditions of Japan. Kojin is described as being a huge female ogre with thousands of arms. She hated human beings and more especially the children, whom she abducted and crushed to death. She was converted from her wickedness and became a protectress of children.
References 133
See also Hariti, Kishi-mojin, ogre

KOLOWISI

This is the name of a horned water serpent in the traditions and beliefs of the Zuni Native American people of the southwestern United States. Kolowisi is represented as a vast serpent with horns on its head, a massive mouth, and fins along the length of its body; this monstrous being inhabits deep pools and springs. One legend tells how a young girl went to such a spring to bathe and found a tiny baby there, which she took home with her. But she did not tell her parents, and when she slept with the "child" Kolowisi transformed into his true shape, encircled the girl in his coils, and abducted the girl to become his wife in the deep spring. This is told as a warning for young girls not to go to such springs on their own.
References 77, 134
See also Horned Water Serpent, serpent

KOMOS

This is the name of a satyr in the classical mythology of Greece of Rome. They are described as having human faces, pointed ears, horns, and hairy male upper bodies, below the waist having the body and legs of a goat. They were the attendants of their drunken leader, Silenus, and the god of wine, Dionysus/Bacchus. They inhabited the woods, mountains, and countryside, where they pursued the nymphs and were renowned for aggregating, drunken sexuality, lechery, rudeness, and love of playing pranks. This is reflected in some of their names; here Komos means "Revelry."
References 7, 14, 24, 89, 125, 160
See also satyr

KONOHA TENGU

This is the name of a type of Tengu in the traditions and folklore of Japan. Konoha Tengu are described as having giant humanoid bodies with grotesque red birds' heads, long hair, wings, and eagle-like talons on their legs. They are particularly aggressive and inhabit the forests on the mountainsides.
References 7, 64, 89, 113, 166
See also Tengu

KORESCK

This is the name of a type of unicorn in the legends of Persia, now Iran. The Koresck is described as being part goat and part horse. It was regarded as a royal beast.
References 7
See also Ass (Three-Legged), Chio-Tuan, Karkadan, Ki Lin, Kirin, Mi'raj (Al), Onyx Monoceros, unicorn

KOSHCHEI

This is the name of a monster in the traditions and folklore of Russia. In some versions of the tales Koshchei, also known as Kashchei, is a dragon, but in others it is a male version of Baba Yaga. This monstrous being is described as immortal for the simple reason that Koshchei's soul is kept hidden outside its body. In most tales the monster's undoing occurs when it abducts a beautiful young girl, in one version called Vasilissa Kirbit'evna, who finds out where the creature's soul is hidden. A hero, often Bulat the Brave, is then given the task of retrieving the egg with the soul and confronting the creature. The final demise of the dragon is when the egg and soul are smashed against Koshchei's own head.
References 55
See also Baba Yaga, dragon

KOSMATUSHKA

This is the name of a magnificent fabulous horse in the legends of Russia. Kosmatushka, also known as Sivushko or Barushka Matushka, was the wondrous magical steed of the *bogatyr'*, Il' ya Muromets.
References 55
See also Sivushko

KRABBEN, KRAKE, KRAXE

These are alternative names for the monster in European folklore known as the Kraken
References 89
See also Kraken, monster

KRAKEN

Two characters bear this name:

1. This is the name of a sea monster in the traditions and legends of Norway and northern Scandinavia. The Kraken, also known as the Krabben or Sykraken, is described as being a vast length with a breadth of approximately one and a half miles with many fins or horns that extended from the sides of its body with which it encircled any ship and dragged it under the waters. When it descended into the water it made a vast whirlpool, which sucked down with it anything that might have escaped. It was said to hunt humans for its food and to be able to devour an entire fishing fleet. Its excrement was said to be the amber that settled around the shores of the North Sea. When

it was not active, the Kraken floated and basked on the surface of the sea. Like the Aspidochelone of ancient tales, it was said that men mistook it for an island and camped on its body. While most sailors were terrified of encountering the creature, the fishermen said that great schools of fish were driven before it, and if they could keep out of its way they had a wonderful catch. Early reports of the Kraken were made in the sixteenth century; one was said to be stranded at Alstradhang in the year 1680 and another at Rothsay in the Kyles of Bute in Scotland in 1775. The bishop of Bergen, Erik Pontoppidan, included the Kraken in his *Natural History of Norway* (1752), while the English poet Alfred Lord Tennyson (1809–1892) immortalized the Kraken in a poem of that name. It is possible that this creature was based on the giant cuttlefish swept up by the Gulf Stream.

2. The Kraken is also a monster in the literary works of the English academic and author J.R.R. Tolkien (1892–1973), in *The Hobbit* (1937) and *The Lord of the Rings* (1955). These monstrous creatures were bred by the evil Melkor in the Middle Earth kingdom of Utumno. They were huge, tentacled beings that swept through both the land and water. One of them came to the River Sirannon and created a barrier in the waters for its abode. It became known as the "Watcher in the Water," for it would not allow anyone past it.
References 7, 18, 20, 24, 51, 78, 89, 134, 182
See also Aspidochelone, Krabben, monster, Sykraken, Zaratan

KREIOS
This is an alternative spelling of Crius, a Titan in the classical mythology of Greece and Rome.
References 20, 24, 47, 61, 78, 94, 125, 136, 139, 166, 169, 174, 178, 182
See also Crius, Titan

KREUTZET
This is the name of a fabulous gigantic bird in the legends and folklore of northwestern Russia. It was described as resembling a gigantic eagle, much like the Roc of Arabian legend. This bird was also known in Poland as Bialozar.
References 7
See also Bialozar, Roc, Simurgh

KRONOS
This is the alternative spelling of Cronos, a Titan in the classical mythology of Greece and Rome. Kronos, which means "Crow," was the offspring of Uranus and Gaia. Although the youngest of the Titans, he instituted the rebellion against Uranus.
References 20, 47, 125, 133, 182
See also Cronos, Cyclopes, Gaia, giant, Hundred-Handed Giants, Polyphemus, Titan, Uranus

KUA FU
This is the name of a primordial giant in the traditions and mythology of China. Kua Fu wanted to prolong the day and thought that he could do so by stopping the sun from setting. So one day he set off in the morning to prevent the sun from reaching the western horizon, but just as he thought that he could catch the orb he was seized with an immense thirst. As he quenched his thirst, first by drinking the Yangtse River, then the Huang Ho and all the tributaries, the sun had gone. Kua Fu lay down exhausted and fell asleep. In the morning his huge body had become Mount Chiyu in Shan Xi province, and the staff he had carried had become the first peach tree with the immortal fruit of the gods.
References 133
See also giant

KUÇEDRË
This is an alternative name for the demonic female water monster, also known as Kulshedra, in the folklore of Albania. It may manifest in two different forms, the first being that of a hideous hag with ugly pendulous breasts, the second a flying dragon like the Aitvaras, spitting fiery sparks as it travels through the air.
References 125
See also Aitvaras, dragon, Kulshedra, monster

KUDAN
This is the name of a humanoid monster in the legends and folklore of Japan. The Kudan is described as having the body and legs of a gigantic bull with three eyes along each side and a row of horns protruding from its spine. It has the head of a human. It was regarded as a beast that could never deceive and always spoke the truth.
References 7
See also monster

K'UEI
This is the name of a class of dragon in the legends of China. The K'uei are described as two-legged dragons and are depicted on ancient ceremonial vessels.
References 61
See also dragon, Oriental Dragon

KUJATA
This is the name of a vast cosmic creature in the creation mythology of Islamic countries. The Kujata is described as resembling a bull, but its head has four thousand eyes, ears, mouths, and nostrils, and its body has four thousand legs and feet. This immense creature stands upon the cosmic fish Bahamut that is, in turn, supported by the cosmic ocean, which is above an abyss, which is above a vast sea of fire,

which is above the cosmic serpent. The back of Kujata supports an enormous glowing ruby upon which is an angel whose shoulders support the weight of the world.
References 18, 63, 89, 78
See also Atlas, Bahamut, serpent

KUKUWEAQ
This is the name of a monstrous polar bear in the tradtions and folklore of the Inuit people of Alaska in the United States. Kukuweaq is described as a terrifying, gigantic polar bear that had ten legs. The tale relates how a very selfish man killed and kept for himself a walrus in time of hardship. His neighbor, Kucirak, had many children and had to go hunting for whatever was there. He hunted all day and at last found the ice hole of the monster Kukuweaq. Hunger made him quell his fears, and when the monster raised its head Kucirak stabbed it in the eyes with his harpoon. Blinded and in a rage, the monster chased after the man, smelling his trail. Knowing this, Kucirak led the staggering monster into a crevasse and trapped and killed it. Then he took as much as he could carry home to his family and his village. The shamed neighbor was so impressed that he was never selfish again.
References 77
See also monster

KUL
This is the name of a monster in the legends and folklore of the people of Syria. The Kul was described as a humanoid fish, something like the merman and mermaid of European legends. However, the Kul and their many offspring inhabited the muddy bottom of freshwater lakes, pools, and wells. They could be malevolent to humans and would deliberately stir up the mud from the bottom and pollute or, even worse, poison the freshwater. However, as they were susceptible to flattery and music, singing a hymn in their honor was sure to keep them and the water sweet.
References 133
See also mermaid, merman, monster

KULILI
This is the name of a type of dragon and later a merman in the mythology of ancient Sumer. Kulili is sometimes portrayed as a dragon symbolizing chaos, sometimes as a type of fish-man, the forerunner of the Abgal.
References 7
See also Abgal, dragon, merman

KULSHEDRA
This is a demonic female water monster, also known as Kuçedrë, in the folklore of Albania. It may manifest in two different forms, the first being that of a hideous hag with ugly pendulous breasts, the other a flying dragon like the Aitvaras, spitting fiery sparks as it travels through the air. The Kulshedra is entirely evil; it may despoil natural water with its urine, or it may cause a drought. It is thought that a human sacrifice is the only method of placating or averting the evil intentions of the Kulshedra.
References 125
See also Aitvaras, monster

KUMBABA
This is the name of a monstrous giant guardian in the mythology of ancient Mesopotamia. Kumbaba, also known by the name Humbaba, is the guardian of the cedar forests and may originally have been a deity of nature. Kumbaba was later demoted to the status of a giant demonic monster and the adversary of Gilgamesh.
References 78, 139
See also giant, Humbaba

KUMBHAKARNA, KUMBHA-KARNA
This is the name of a giant in the Hindu mythology of India. This giant was eternally hungry from the moment of birth and could consume many herds of buffaloes, cows, goats, sheep, and humans at a single sitting and would wash the lot down with gallons of wine. But Kumbhakarna was also devout and, having made sacrifices to the gods, was entitled to a wish. Instead of the giant wishing for immortality, Brahma managed to trick the giant into wishing for eternal sleep. So the giant hibernated for most of the year and ate solidly for the few days he was awake. When his brother, the evil Ravanna, was attacked by the god Rama, Ravanna sent for Kumbhakarna to fight. But they had to waken the giant by throwing things at him and tempting him with the smell of food. When, after a massive feast, he entered the fray, Rama and his army soon sliced the sluggish giant's body until it was a normal size, then chopped his head off.
References 112, 133
See also giant

KUMUDA
This is the name of one of the Lokapala Elephants in the Hindu mythology of India. Kumuda (or Vamana, according to different legends) stands as the guardian of the southwestern quadrant of the world with the god Sūrya, or Nirriti, on his back.
References 7, 24, 112
See also Lokapala Elephants

KUN MANGGUR
This is a regional name for the Rainbow Serpent in the Dreamtime mythology of the Native Australian people.

References 133
See also Rainbow Serpent

KUNAPIPI, KUNAPIPI-KALWADI-KADJARA

This is the name of a monster in the legends and Dreamtime mythology of the Alawa Native Australian people of Arnhem Land in northern Australia. Kunapipi, also known as Gunapipi, is a water monster that lurked by the streams where young boys went to fish. Then Kunapipi would emerge and swallow them whole down her great gullet. In some versions Eagle-hawk goes and manages to get the monster to regurgitate the boys, who emerge as young men. This is incorporated into many ceremonies and puberty rituals. In other versions of the legends, Kunapipi was given some children to look after, and she instantly swallowed them when the parent was gone. When this was discovered, the warriors went after Kunapipi and trapped her in a swampy pool. There they speared her legs and neck and chopped open her stomach for the children to escape.

References 38, 125, 133
See also monster

KUNDRAV

This is an alternative name for the monster in Sumerian mythology known as Gandareva.

References 7
See also Gandareva

KURANGAI TUKU, KURANGAI TUPU

This is the name of an ogress in the traditions and beliefs of the Maori people of New Zealand. Kurangai Tuku is described as a massive, strong female, having huge legs with which she steps over trees and mountains, with wing membranes extending from her arms, and enormous lips that shoot out from her mouth. With these lips she caught the birds upon which she fed whilst they were flying through the air. One day a man called Hautupatu, who had fallen out with his brothers, was wandering in the forest when he was spotted by Kurangai Tuku hunting birds. She quickly caught him as he tried to escape, took him to her cave, and offered him some of the birds to eat. In the morning she blocked up the cave to go hunting and Hautupatu cooked a bird for his meal, then chanted a *karakia* charm to unblock the cave. But one of the birds escaped too and alerted the ogress to his departure. She immediately strode back over the forest and went after him. Eventually, he came to a huge, seething hot spring and skirted it carefully, but Kurangai Tuku was in such a hurry that she did not notice it. She sank straight into the boiling water and was scalded to death.

References 113
See also ogress

KURDAN

This is an alternative spelling of Kudan, the monstrous bull of Japanese legends.

References 89
See also Kudan

KURMA

This is the name of a gigantic cosmic tortoise in the Hindu mythology of India. Kurma is described as a gigantic being whose upper shell formed the outer limits of the heavens; the lower shell was the basis of the earth, and the interior was the earth's atmosphere. Kurma had been created from a cosmic egg that had been squeezed by Prajapati to form the earth in this way. Consequently, early cartographers in India depicted the subcontinent as on the surface of the tortoise shell, with all other lands around the perimeter.

References 133
See also Lokapala Elephants

KURREA, KURRIA

This is the name of a monster in the Dreamtime legends of the Native Australian people. Kurrea is described as a vast creature with a form resembling that of a gigantic lizard or crocodile that inhabited a fetid swamp. Kurrea was not content with taking the wildlife hunted by the people and was soon eating the people from the region. Toolalla, a brave warrior, was asked to kill this monster before it devoured them all. Bravely, he went to the swamp and threw every spear he had, but they all bounced off. Then Kurrea came after him. Kurrea came out of the swamp and traveled through the earth and rocks, ploughing through them as easily as the water. The monster was too fast, and very soon it was gaining on him. In the distance Toolalla could see his mother-in-law, the bumble tree. She was the only being apart from Kurrea of which he was terrified, so he raced as fast as he could right up to her. As Kurrea drew level and came directly to his mother-in-law, the monster took one look and screeched to a halt, then turned, creating a vast hole in the earth, and fled. Now Kurrea leaves humans alone, and the channels that he dug while pursuing Toolalla fill with refreshing water in the wet season.

References 153
See also monster

KW' ÊN

This is the name of a gigantic fish in the legends of China. The Kw' ên, according to the works of Chuang Tsze, was a vast fish of several miles in length that inhabited the great Northern Sea of China. What was even more remarkable was that this fish was able to metamorphose for part of its life into the gigantic form of the bird called the P' êng.

References 81
See also P' êng

KYKLOPES

This is an alternative spelling for the Cyclopes in the classical mythology of Greece and Rome.
See also Cyclopes

KYLIN

This is an alternative spelling of the Ch'i-Lin, or Oriental unicorn, in the legends and traditions of China.
References 7, 89, 113
See also Ch'i-Lin

KYMIDEU KYMEINVOLL

This is the alternative spelling of the name of the giantess Cymidei Cymeinfoll in the legends and folklore of Wales.
References 128
See also Cymidei Cymeinfoll

L

LA VELUE

This is the name of a monster in the legends and folklore of medieval France. La Velue, which may be translated as the "Shaggy Beast," was also known as the Peluda. It was described as a vast creature with a huge body covered in what seemed to be green, straggly fur, but it was masses of something resembling tentacles with vicious stingers on the ends. It had enormous feet, a long tail, and the head of a snake. It was conjectured that this was a monster that had escaped the biblical Flood and that ravaged the countryside, searing crops with its burning breath and devouring livestock and humans. La Velue inhabited the region bordering the Huisine River, and whenever a search party of men went to hunt it down it would wade into the river, causing vast floods to cover the land. Eventually, after one of its raids, when it took and devoured a young woman about to be wed, it was tracked down and its tail sliced off by her sweetheart. This was La Velue's only vulnerable part; with its tail hacked in two it died instantly, and the region rejoiced.
References 89
See also monster, Peluda

LABASTA

This is the name of a semisupernatural in the folklore and beliefs of the Cheremis/Mari peoples of one of the former Soviet republics. This being, also known as Albasta, may manifest in the bathhouses of humans as a giant with long, flowing hair.
References 160, 165
See also Aitvaras, Albastor, giant

LABBU

This is the name of a monster in the Akkadian mythology of ancient Mesopotamia. It is described as a vast serpentine creature that had associations with the celestial Milky Way. The Labbu was eventually killed by the god Tišpak.
References 125
See also monster, serpent.

LADON DRAGON

See Dragon of Ladon

LADY OF LAKE TRAUN

This is the name of a type of mermaid in the traditions and folklore of Austria. Lady of Lake Traun, also known as the Mistress of the Lake and the Mistress of Aquatic beasts, was described as a mermaid who rode across the surface of the lake on a type of sea-horse. She was the guardian of the inhabitants of the waters, and she was particularly malevolent toward fishermen, whom she would cause to drown.
References 134
See also mermaid, Sa-yin, Sea-horse

LADY OF THE LAND

This is the name of a woman who had been turned into a dragon and whose tale is related in the *Travels of Sir John Mandeville*, published in 1366. The Lady of the Land, also known as the Dragon Maid, was described as a vast, hideous creature that lived in a cavern under a castle on the island of Lango. She was said to have been the once beautiful daughter of Yppocras, who had fallen foul of the goddess Diana. The goddess condemned her to exist in the hideous dragon form until a man would kiss her and love her for herself. Many instances are given, by Mandeville, of men's attempts to release her from the curse, efforts that were prompted by her being surrounded by a great hoard of gold and jewels. Each time they got close to her, their revulsion repelled them so much that they fled; the penalty was their imminent death.
References 180
See also dragon

LAESTRYGONIANS, LAESTRYGONES, LÆSTRYNGONES, LESTRINGONS

This is the name of a cannibal race in the classical mythology of Greece and Rome. The Laestrygonians, also spelled Laestrygones and Lestrigons, are described as a race of giants who inhabited the east region or the northwestern coast of Sicily, according to

The Lady of Lake Traun, a type of mermaid, was the guardian of the inhabitants of the waters. (Fairies and Enchanters *by A. Williams-Ellis, Thomas Nelson, UK)*

the source. These predatory people harassed the ships that passed by their cliffs and pelted them with rocks until the boats were sunk. Then, on a pretense of saving the crew, they took the sailors from the sea and killed and devoured them; sometimes the victims were simply speared in the water and taken. The Læstrygonians were described in the myths concerning the hero Odysseus/Ulysses, who wished to land at a safe haven for freshwater on the island of Sicily, where they lived. But these cannibal giants ate one of the sailors that Odysseus/Ulysses had sent as messengers to their king. The other members of the crew fled in terror, many being slaughtered before they reached the safety of the ship and put to sea. Odysseus and his men escaped the predations of these monstrous people when they met the daughter of their king, Antiphates.

References 20, 166, 169, 178, 182
See also Antiphates, cannibal, giant, ogre

LAIDERONETTE
This is an alternative name for the Serpentin Vert in the tales by the French authoress Marie-Catherine d' Aulnoy (1650–1705).
References 182
See also Loathly Lady, Serpentin Vert

LAIDLEY WORM
This is the name of a monstrous type of serpent in the legends and folklore of the North of England. This is the tale of a beautiful young woman turned into a gigantic serpent by a curse. The Laidley Worm became the terror of the region. But she was set free from her hideous and terrifying form by the kiss of a young man.
References 89
See also Beast, worm

LAILOKEN
This is the name of a class of Wild Man of the Woods in the legends and folklore of Scotland. Lailoken is described as a very hairy humanoid, with the power of human speech, that inhabited the Strathclyde Welsh-speaking region during the sixth century. He was credited with prophecy and called to the court of Rhydderch Hael. In the fifteenth-century legend *Lailoken and Ketigern*, it was suggested that Lailoken considered himself responsible for the deaths at the battle of Arfderydd (c. 573) and confessed this to Saint Ketigern.
References 128
See also Wild Man

LAKHAMU
This is the name of a primordial monster in the mythology of ancient Mesopotamia.

References 78
See also Lakhmu

LAKHMU
This is the name of a primordial monster in the mythology of ancient Mesopotamia. Lakhmu, together with a similar monster, was created by Apsu's union with the monstrous Tiamat. Lakhmu and Lakhamu's progeny are the first gods known as Igigi, Anu, and Anunnaki, who immediately threaten the power of Taimat and Apsu. In the battles that follow all the monstrous beings, including Lakhmu and Lakhamu, are destroyed by Marduk, the great sun god.
References 78
See also monster, Tiamat

Lailoken is a class of Wild Man of the Woods in the legends and folklore of Scotland. (Rose Photo Archive, UK)

LALLA MIRA, LALLA MIRRA

This is the name of one of the kings of the Djinns in the traditions and beliefs of the people of Morocco.
References 122
See also Djinn

LAMA

This is the name of a female guardian in Sumerian mythology. Lama was later associated with the Lamassu of Assyria. Like the Łedu, they were depicted as the winged bull beings that were guardians, especially of gateways to palaces. Their images, in relief and sculpture, are to be seen today as enormous bull/cow representations with human faces and vast wings from their backs.
References 125, 139, 160

LAMASSU

These are benevolent beings in the mythology of ancient Assyria and Babylon. They were portrayed as winged bulls or lions with human heads, or with the head of a bull with the traditional human male beard. The Lamassu may be compared with the Egyptian Sphinx. The Lamassu were regarded as female—their male counterparts were called Šedu or Shedu—and in their most important role they formed the protection of the palaces and temples, where their effigies often remain to this day.
References 7, 64, 89, 139, 160, 161
See also Sphinx

LAMBTON WORM

This is the name of a vast serpentine creature in the legends and traditions of Northumberland (now Northumbria) in England. The legend tells of a young squire named Lambton who went fishing one day and caught a tiny, curious creature that was unfit for food. Thinking nothing of it, he tossed the creature away, and it fell into a nearby well. While the young man was away fighting in the Crusades (1070–1193, no relative time is given in the legend), the "Worm" grew in the well and its appetite swelled with its size until it emerged as a vast serpentine monster. The Lambton Worm then ravaged the countryside, devouring livestock and any creature that came within its range, creating terror and mayhem in the region. When the young Lambton returned from the wars, he was horrified to see the devastation and vowed to slay the creature. He went to the armorer and had a suit of arms made up that was covered front and back with long, protruding blades, resembling a hedgehog. When this strange armor was ready, he put it on and went to the river. There he blew his horn and the "Worm," which had been lying coiled around a nearby hill, slithered toward him at a terrifying speed. He held his position even when the great beast coiled itself around him, but the tighter it coiled to kill him, the more it was sliced on the blades, until it had sliced itself to death.
References 78, 89
See also monster, serpent, worm

LAMIA

Two characters bear this name:

1. This is the name of a female supernatural monster in the classical mythology of Greece and Rome. The Lamia was said to exist in the northern African deserts. She was described as being like a woman to the waist, but thereafter the body was like that of a serpent, though she was able to assume the shape of a completely beautiful woman. There are a number of traditions concerning her origin. The most usual is that she was a Lybian queen loved by the king of the gods, Zeus/Jupiter. He hid her from his consort, Hera, in a fabulous cavern in Africa and, to protect her, empowered Lamia to remove her eyes and leave them to keep watch while she slept. However, Zeus/Jupiter's queen, Hera/Juno, found and transformed Lamia to her hideous appearance, then took her children and destroyed them. Henceforth, Lamia seeks and destroys men and children wherever she can entice them. Later on, her legend was associated with the Empusae, the Vampires of the ancient world, spawning a horrible tribe of offspring known as the Lamya, Lamie, or Lamye. From this earlier legend, used over a thousand years ago as a Nursery bogie for Roman children, the tradition developed to the Lamia described by Burton in *The Anatomie of Melancholy* (1621) and Keats's *Lamia* (1780) of the amorous sorceress, or succubus.

In more modern times she has survived in the dual form of the demonologists' vampire or nightmare or the malignant melancholy fairy road demon of modern Greek folklore.

2. The Lamia is a mermaid of an entirely benevolent nature in the folklore of the Basque people of southern France and northwestern Spain
References 7, 17, 18, 20, 74, 78, 89, 119, 124, 125, 133, 146, 158, 160, 169, 178, 182
See also Baba Yaga, Empusae, Lamya, mermaid, vampire

LAMIE

This is an alternative spelling of the Lamya, the terrifying offspring of the Lamia in the medieval legends of Europe.
References 7, 89
See also Lamya

LAMMIKIN

This is the name of a demonic monster, also known as Long Lankin, in the folklore of Scotland. The ballad relates how the monster creeps into the house and pokes and stabs at any infant until the mother appears to calm the child. Then Lammikin will attack and slice the mother and drain her blood from her. This would seem to be a horror conjured by anxious parents to prevent their child from crying in the night and as such would be classed as a Nursery bogie of a more vicious variety.

References 182
See also Nursery bogie, vampire

LAMPALUGUA

This is the name of a gigantic class of lizard in the legends of the Araucanian people of Chile. The Lampalugua is described as a vast reptile resembling a lizard having the most enormous claws. It is a predatory monster that takes and devours both cattle and humans.

References 134
See also monster

LAMPON, LAMPOS

This is the name of a horse in the classical mythology of Greece and Rome. Lampon, whose name means "Shining Lamp," is one of the team of Horses of the Sun that pulled the golden chariot that Hephaestus had made for the sun god, Helios. Lampon, like the other horses, is described as the purest white with flaring, fire-breathing nostrils. Each morning the nymphs of time, the Horae, harnessed Lampon along with the other Horses of the Sun to the chariot for their journey across the sky; when their journey across the heavens was finished at dusk they browsed on magical herbs in the Islands of the Blessed until they were harnessed for the next day.

Lampos is also given as one of the horses of the chariot of Aurora, the goddess of the dawn.

References 139
See also Horses of the Sun

LAMUS

This is the name of a king in the classical mythology of Greece and Rome. Lamus was a giant, the son of the sea god Poseidon/Neptune and in *Metamorphoses* (xiv, 23) by the Roman poet Ovid (43 B.C.–A.D. 17), the king of the bloodthirsty cannibal race of Laestrygones. He was said to have been responsible for founding both the town of Formiae in Italy and the Latin family of Lamiae.

References 178
See also giant, Laestrygonians

LAMYA, LAMYE, LAMIE

These are the horrible offspring of the Lamia in the legends and beliefs of Rome and, later, medieval Europe. The Lamya are described as hybrid monsters variously with the body of a serpent or a goat having paws on their forefeet and cloven hooves on their rear ones. Their torso was the head, breasts, and arms of a woman. The Lamya were essentially hissing, snake-like vampires that especially preyed on unguarded sleeping children. In later folktales of the medieval period, the Lamya became forest-dwellers who emerged at night from their retreat to attack any human within their range. It was said that the only cure for the unhealing wound was to hear the Lamia herself.

References 7, 18, 89, 133, 158, 169, 178, 182
See also Baba Yaga, Lamia, vampire

LANGAL

This is a regional name for the Rainbow Serpent in the Dreamtime mythology of the Native Australian people.

References 133
See also Rainbow Serpent

LASKOWICE

This is the name of a class of Wild Men of the Woods in the mythology and folklore of the Slavic people. The Laskowice, also known as Leschia, are described as resembling satyrs, with their hairy bodies, goats' feet, and the upper parts like a man. They are the guardians of the forests and the creatures that reside there, with a particular affinity with the wolf.

References 125, 160
See also satyr, Wild Man of the Woods

LEGAROU

This is the name for both the vampire and the Werewolf in the folk beliefs of the people of the island of Haiti in the Caribbean. The name clearly derives from the French words *loup garou*, meaning "werewolf," and was probably brought to the island with the folklore of the French colonists of the seventeenth century onward.

References 24
See also Azeman, Loup garou, Sukuyan, vampire, Werewolf

LEI

This is the name of the Thunder Dragon who is the father of Lei Chen-Tzu in the mythology of China.

References 133, 160, 181
See also Lei Chen-Tzu, Oriental dragon

LEI CHEN-TZU, LEI JEN ZU

This is the dragon form of a supernatural hero in the legends of ancient China. He is said to have been

hatched from an egg that was the result of a thunderclap from his father, Lei the Thunder Dragon. Lei Chen-Tzu was adopted by Wen Wang, the god of literature. After many adventures, Lei Chen-Tzu discovered that his adoptive father, Wen Wang, had been taken prisoner and thus sought a way to rescue him. This he did by eating two apricots sent by the Thunder Dragon; when he swallowed them he was transformed into a dragon. He became a huge, winged, green dragon, having a boar's face with tusks and a long, pointed snout and shining eyes. Then he effected the supernatural rescue.
References 133, 160, 181
See also Oriental dragon

LENAPIZKA

This is the name of a monster in the traditions and beliefs of the Peoria Native American people of Illinois in the United States. The Lenapizka is described as a lake monster that was amphibious and also known as the "True Tiger."
References 134
See also monster

LEPROCAUN

This is a creature from the folklore of lumberjacks and forest workers, especially in Wisconsin and Minnesota in the United States, during the nineteenth and early twentieth centuries. The Leprocaun belongs to a group of beings affectionately known as the Fearsome Critters, whose exaggerated proportions and activities not only explained the weird noises of the lonely landscape but also provided some amusement at camps. The name is derived from that of the Irish Gaelic little spirit, the Leprechaun, who wreaks havoc on human lives in its native Ireland. No doubt he emigrated with his Irish humans to the American continent during the nineteenth century and entered the lumberjacks' folklore.
References 7, 24
See also Fearsome Critters

LERNEAN HYDRA

This is the name of a monster in the classical mythology of Greece and Rome. This monster is more usually known simply as the Hydra.
References 24, 78, 139
See also Hydra, monster

LESCHIA

This is an alternative name for the Laskowice, a type of Satyr in the legends and folklore of the Slavic people of eastern Europe.
References 125, 160
See also Laskowice, satyr

LESHAK

This is an alternative name for the Leshii of Russian folklore.
References 38, 64, 103, 133, 139, 152, 160, 166
See also Laskowice, Leshii

LESHII, LESHIYE, LESHY

This is the name of a semisupernatural humanoid very similar to the English Green Man in the folklore of Russia. The Leshii, also known as the Lesovik, Leshak, Lesnoi, Lisun, Lieschi, Ljeschi, and Lychie, is regarded as the guardian of the animals and forests. His name is derived from the word *les,* which means "forest." He is described as having the shape of a human but with strangely pallid flesh, green eyes, green beard, and long, straggly hair, wearing his bast boots on the wrong feet and throwing no shadow. The Leshy was a shape-shifter that could stand as tall and in the likeness of the forest trees, or assume the size of a blade of grass. He knew and could make every noise of the forest, deceiving humans who strayed there. There was usually one Leshii in each forest unless it were very large. Each was thought to have a wife called Lesovikha and children called Leshonki. In the spring, when he had just emerged from his winter death, he would rage with other Leshii, bringing storms and floods at the thought of their autumn demise, but soon they calmed down. He would call to humans traveling through the forests and lead them off the track until they were in a bog or thoroughly lost, then disappear into the trees laughing. Knowing these and other pranks of the Leshii, herdsmen and hunters thought it best to propitiate them regularly with the traditional offerings of salt and bread. Another way of outwitting the Leshii was to imitate him by turning all one's clothing and boots back to front until the safety of the edge of the forest had been reached.
References 38, 64, 103, 133, 139, 152, 160, 166
See also Laskowice

LESNOI

This is an alternative name for the Leshii of Russian folklore.
References 38, 64, 103, 133, 139, 152, 160, 166
See also Laskowice, Leshii

LESOVIK

This is an alternative name for the Leshii of Russian folklore.
References 38, 64, 103, 133, 139, 152, 160, 166
See also Laskowice, Leshii

LESTRIGONS

The Lestrigons, also spelled Laestrygones and Laestrygonians, are described as a race of cannibal

giants that inhabited the east region or the northwestern coast of Sicily in the classical mythology of Greece and Rome.
References 20
See also Laestrygonians

LEUCOSIA
This is the name of one of the Sirens in the classical mythology of Greece and Rome. An island near Pæstrum off the coast of Italy, on which she sat to lure sailors to their demise, is now known by her name.
References 178
See also Siren

LEUCROTTA, LEUCROCUTA, LEUCROTA
This is the name of a hybrid monster in the ancient texts and the medieval bestiaries of Europe. The Leucrotta was described by the Latin naturalist Pliny the Elder in his *Historia Naturalis* (A.D. 77) as a creature that resembled an ass with the head of a badger, the neck, tail, and foreparts of a lion, and the legs of a deer with cloven hooves. Its extraordinary head had a mouth that was so huge that it extended right up to the ears, and instead of teeth it had an enormous blade of bone horizontally placed in the upper and lower jaws. The cackle of this monster was said to resemble human speech. Later medieval bestiaries neither embellished nor detracted from this curious description except to suggest that it inhabited the land of India.
References 7, 10, 14, 18, 63, 148, 185

LEVIATHAN
This is the name of a primordial monster in the mythology and scriptures of Hebrew and Christian traditions. The Leviathan, also known as the Livjatan, is described in the Book of Job (41:19–33) in the Old Testament of the Bible:

> Out of his mouth go burning lamps, and sparks of fire leap out.
> Out of his nostrils goeth smoke, as out of a seething pot or cauldron.
> His breath kindleth coals, and a flame goeth out of his mouth. . . .
> The sword of him that layeth at him cannot hold; the spear, the dart, nor the habergeon.
> He esteemeth iron as straw, and brass as rotten wood.
> The arrow cannot make him flee: sling stones are turned with him into stubble.
> Darts are counted as stubble; he laugheth at the shaking of a spear. . . .
> He maketh the deep to boil like a pot; he maketh the sea like a pot of ointment.
> He maketh a path to shine after him: one would think the deep to be hoary.
> Upon this earth there is not his like, who is made without fear.

This vast creature, over 900 miles in length, with seven heads and over three hundred eyes, was invulnerable and encircled the world in the great abyss, or the depths of the cosmic ocean. It was the personification of chaos created at the same time as Behemoth and said to devour the dragons of the earth. The Leviathan is destined to be defeated either by Yaweh or by the Archangel Gabriel and to provide the meat for the feast of the Righteous after the Day of Judgment. The skin of the monster was to provide covering for their roofs and for the walls of Jerusalem. However, the image was probably derived from the Phoenician monster known as Lotan, and there is a similar monster with much the same destiny in Islamic legend, known as the Nun.
References 7, 20, 47, 78, 89, 99, 125, 133, 134, 145, 166
See also Behemoth, dragon, Lotan, Midgard serpent, Nun, Tarasque

LI NO ZHA
This is the name of a giant in the traditions and legends of China. Li No Zha was originally born of the wife of Li Jing by the Unicorn of Heaven as a ball of flesh. When Li Jing sliced open the ball of flesh Li No Zha emerged and proceeded to grow at an immense rate. He was very aggressive, and when fighting with the gods and the son of the Dragon king he shamed his parents. They remonstrated with him, and he was filled with such shame that he committed suicide. But he was immediately regenerated as a vast giant. Li No Zha now had three heads, each with three eyes and eight arms, brandishing weapons over his enormous, sixty-foot body. Li Jing was so horrified that he attacked his own stepson, but the kindness of the gods made peace and appointed the massive Li No Zha as the shield-bearer to the Jade Emperor Yu Huang.
References 133
See also giant, unicorn

LIBAN
This is the name of a mermaid derived from a human in the legends of Ireland. Liban was originally the daughter of Eochaid and Etain who was caught up in the floods of a sacred spring that had been neglected. She was carried to an underwater cavern with her pet dog, whilst the rest of her community, except Conang and Curman, was destroyed. Liban was trapped for a year until she prayed that she might be as the fishes. She was transformed into the body and tail of a salmon below the waist but remained like a human above. Her dog was changed to become an otter. As a mermaid Liban had become free but remained below the water until, after three hundred years, a cleric named Beoc heard her singing. She asked him to bring her out of the water and take her to Saint

Liban was a mermaid derived from a human in the legends of Ireland. (Rose Photo Archive, UK)

Comgall. She was baptized and given the choice of another three hundred years of life or immediate entry to heaven. She chose the latter, but her image may be seen carved on many of the columns and pews in the churches built on the road she took to Saint Comgall.
References 24
See also Ceasg, mermaid

LICORN
This is an alternative name for the unicorn of European medieval legends.
References 89
See also unicorn

LIESCHI
This is an alternative name for the Leshii of Russian folklore.
References 38, 64, 103, 133, 139, 152, 160, 166
See also Laskowice, Leshii

LIGHTNING MONSTERS
This is the name of a class of monster in the traditions and beliefs of the people of Zambia. The Lightning Monsters are described as having the hind quarters of a crocodile but the foreparts and head of a goat. These beings inhabit the heavens, but when there is a storm they may descend to the earth on a glutinous thread like that of a spider's web and rebound to the heavens, thus creating the lightning. Sometimes the thread may break, and unless warriors protected by supernatural charms can find and destroy them, then they will wreak havoc on earth.
References 89
See also Lightning Serpent, monster

LIGHTNING SERPENT, LIGHTNING SNAKE
This is the name of a class of monster in the traditions and beliefs of the Native Australian people. The Lightning Snakes are described as enormous serpents that inhabit the heavens, but when there is a storm they may descend to the earth and rebound to the heavens, thus creating the lightning. And when they make contact from the earth to the heavens the vital rain can be released from the heavens to the earth.
References 89, 134
See also Lightning Monsters, Rainbow Serpent, serpent

LIGIA
This is the name of one of the Sirens of classical Greek and Roman mythology.
References 178
See also Siren

LIK
This is the name of a water serpent in the traditions and folk beliefs of the people of Gran Chaco in South America. The Lik is also known as "Master of the Water" and as such is described as a vast, monstrous guardian of the inland fish of the lakes and rivers. It may be recognized for its age and terrifying power by the mosses that grow on its body and the palm trees growing along its back.
References 134
See also King of the Fishes, serpent

LINDORM, LINDWORM
This is the name of a gigantic serpent, or worm, in the legends and folklore of Sweden and northern Scandinavia. The Lindorm, also known as the Lindworm, was mentioned in the *Hamar Chronicles* and is described as a vast serpent with the head of a horse and a mane down the neck section of its vast body, having red eyes glowing like burning coals. It was said to guard ancient burial mounds and mutate in its later stages to a sea serpent. There are numerous "sightings" registered, especially in the Swedish region of Småland during the period 1878–1885, reported by Ingemar of Arnanäs, Hylten-Cavallius, and Sven Nilsson.

References 7, 134
See also serpent, worm

LION-GRIFFON
This is a hybrid monstrous being in the folklore of the ancient Near East and medieval Europe. The Lion-Griffon, as the name implies, is a class of the Griffin that is described as having the head and foreparts of a lion but the rear and legs of the Griffin bird. Its description was part of the repertoire of medieval travelers' tales. The Lion-Griffon may be seen in the ancient relief sculptures of Assyrian and Persian temples and palaces and has been used in the heraldic devices of Europe.
References 89
See also Griffin

LIOUMERE
In the folklore of the Caroline Islands this was the name of a terrible female ogress. Lioumere was described as appearing in a hideous female human form with metal fangs in her enormous jaws. She caused havoc with her iron fangs, entrapping and devouring any being that was unwary in her domain. She was defeated when a man, who wanted the magic fangs, hired a clown to make the demon laugh. When this happened he leapt forward, smashing out the teeth with a stone and removing her control over the terrified people.
References 47, 160
See also ogre, ogress

LISUN
This is an alternative name for the Leshii of Russian folklore.
References 38, 64, 103, 133, 139, 152, 160, 166
See also Laskowice, Leshii

LITTLE MANITOU
This is the name of a huge water serpent in the traditions and folklore of the Otsitsot Native American people in the United States. The tale relates how a ne'er-do-well named Carcajou, which means "Glutton," sneered at the beliefs of the others of his people and mockingly went to the sacred tree. He heard a noise and then experienced a glaring light, and he realized that he was staring up at the most enormous horned serpent. Sparks of flame danced off this creature, which addressed him and said that it was known as the Little Manitou. Carcajou made a pact with the Little Manitou, and in return neither his bottle nor his pipe was ever empty.
References 134
See also horned serpent, serpent

LIVJATAN
This is an alternative name for the Leviathan of Hebrew and biblical texts.

References 125
See also Leviathan

LJESCHI
This is the name in the traditions and folklore of the Slavic people for the Leshii of Russian folklore. However, the description varies slightly in that he has a blue face and green eyes, hair, and beard. He was a terrifying adversary of anyone who wished to invade his domain by trying to create forest clearings for homesteads.
References 38, 64, 103, 133, 139, 152, 160, 166
See also Laskowice, Leshii

LLAMHIGYN Y DWR
This is the name of a fearful water monster in the folklore of Wales. Llamhigyn y Dwr, whose name means "Water Leaper," is described as having the shape of an enormous toad with a tail and huge wings instead of legs. It was a malignant and vicious monster that inhabited the banks and mud shoals of rivers with plentiful fish and grazing sheep on the banks. The Llamhigyn y Dwr's favorite preoccupation was to give a shriek, then snap the lines of any fisherman, causing him to fall into the water and be dragged down to his death to be consumed in the mud at the bottom of the water. If no humans were fishing, then the Llamhigyn y Dwr would incite the curiosity of the sheep on the bank and lure them into the water to be devoured.
References 24, 84, 160
See also monster

LLASSAR LLAES GYFNEWID
This is the name of a giant in the legends and folklore of Wales. He is the husband of the vast giantess Cymidei Cymeinfoll, and together they are the guardians of the cauldron of immortality. They escape the fire intended to destroy them and eventually give the magic cauldron to Bran.
References 128
See also Bran, giant, giantess

LLWYDAWG THE HEWER
This is the name of a monstrous boar in the Celtic legends and folklore of Ireland and Wales. Llwydawg the Hewer is the son of the gigantic Twrch Trwyth, and together with this monster and other siblings they ravaged the whole of Ireland. Then the heroic King Arthur was called upon to rid the land of these monstrous beasts, and three ferocious battles took place before the brood was driven from Ireland. Undaunted, the tribe of gigantic boars swam the Irish Sea to the coast of Wales, where they were once more bent on destruction. Arthur and his heroic knights pursued the beasts from the Wye River across the

land. One by one the boars were killed, with many warriors gored and slain, until only Twrch Trwyth and his sons, Grugyn Silver Bristles and Llwydawg the Hewer, were left. A vicious battle ensued, but Grugyn Silver Bristles, by then exhausted, was hacked down among the slaughtered warriors. Llwydawg the Hewer carried on as far as Ystrad Yw, goring and savaging as many pursuers as possible until his demise.

References 105
See also Grugyn Silver Bristles, Gullinbursti, Twrch Trwyth

LOATHLY LADY

This is the name of a monstrous female humanoid in the traditional tales of medieval Europe known as Romances. The Loathly Lady features especially in the traditional tales of King Arthur across Europe. She is so cursed with monstrous features that no one will take her as a bride. Through the kindness and understanding of a knight who sees the loveliness of her character rather than her monstrosity, she at last receives a proposal of marriage and the curse that bound her as a monster is broken. This is a counterpart to the romance tale motif of the same period known as the Beauty and the Beast.

References 20, 182
See also Beast, Laideronnette, monster, Odz-Manouk, Rhinocéros, Riquet à la Houppe

LOATHLY WORM

This is the name given in the legends and folklore of England for a hideous type of dragon. The Loathly Worm is usually a massive dragon that has no wings and mostly resembles a serpent with two feet and the forepart of its body. These creatures were frequently depicted in the psalters, books of hours, and bestiaries of medieval Europe. There are numerous examples in the Luttrell Psalter of these monsters, which were credited with devastating large areas of Europe.

References 78
See also Lambton Worm, Lindorm

LOB OMBRE

This is the name for the Werewolf in the folklore of Spain.

References 94
See also Werewolf

LOB OMEM

This is the name for the Werewolf in the folklore of Portugal.

References 94
See also Werewolf

LOBÍSON

This is the name for a type of Werewolf in the traditions and folklore of southern Brazil and Uruguay. The Lobíson usually manifests in the shape of a monstrous dog or huge wild pig to terrorize and devour any of the local inhabitants. In the region of Entre Rios, it is well understood by the local population that the stockyards are the most likely habitat for these monsters, which take human form during daylight hours. Consequently, no young woman will go out with any man that lives in that vicinity.

References 18
See also Werewolf

LOCH NESS MONSTER, NESSIE, NESSY

This is the name of a lake monster in the legends and folklore of Scotland. It is possibly one of the most famous and enigmatic mysteries in the world concerning this type of monster. Although there has never been a clear image, the description has usually been of a huge body, often serpentine, with humps or undulations out of the water, which stretch for some considerable length, up to thirty feet. The head has been described as like that of a dragon, or a serpent's head over a long, sinuous neck. As the monster moves in the water, the head is held erect and the neck creates a bow wave that extends in a great *V* shape, even in perfectly still conditions. The monster inhabits Loch Ness, from which it takes its name, but is almost affectionately called "Nessy" or "Nessie." Loch Ness is an inland channel of about 755 feet in depth and some twenty-three miles long, connected to the North Sea and the Atlantic at either end by freshwater rivers.

Reports of the sightings of the monster are ancient. The first recorded sighting was in the time of the Celtic saints, from ca. A.D. 690 in a hagiography by Adamnans of Saint Columcille (Saint Columba, ca. 521–597). Sightings of the Loch Ness Monster did not reach the public very frequently until the advent of the road running the length of the loch. Then, in 1933 a number of people motoring down the road saw the monster and described it independently, which was reported widely in the press. In 1940 the legend was somewhat jokingly exploited in the *Detective Weekly* with a "Sexton Blake" mystery that "uncovered" a Nazi submarine conspiracy. This theme was taken up in the United Artists film, *The Private Life of Sherlock Holmes,* supposedly set in 1887 and investigating German submarines. Curiously, during the filming the model Nessie sank unexpectedly to the bottom of the loch without trace.

Periodic sightings, photographs, and underwater investigations have taken place over the last thirty years, with little evidence to support or refute the theories concerning the survival of ancient species.

References 20, 61, 78, 94, 128, 134

See also Champ, Lockski Nesski Monsterovich, Seljordsorm

LOCHLONNACH
This is an epithet of the giant in Irish legends known also as Searbhán. The name means the "Norseman." He is described as being extremely skilled in the magic arts and a protector of the magical rowan trees in Dubros, County Sligo.
References 128
See also giant, Searbhán

LOCKSKI NESSKI MONSTEROVICH
This is the name given to a Russian monster reported in the American press in the years of 1962 and 1964. It was described as a vast, serpentine, undulating monster with a huge fin the length of its back and at least thirty feet in length. This water monster was said to have been seen by prospectors on the edge of a lake in eastern Siberia.
References 94
See also Loch Ness Monster, monster

LOGI
There are two giants with this name in the Norse mythology of Scandinavia.

1. This is the name of a primordial giant in the Teutonic and Norse myths of northern Europe. Logi is described as an immense being and is one of the Frost Giants. According to some sources, he, like the giantess Hler and the giant Kari, were descended from Fornjotr.

2. When the god Thor, with his companions Thjalfi and Loki, arrived in the kingdom of Utgardloki they were expected to prove themselves worthy of the abode of the giants before they would receive hospitality. Thjalfi was pitted in a running contest against the giant Hugi, while Loki was pitted in an eating contest against the giant Logi. Although Loki ate great quantities, he could not outeat the vast Logi, who consumed the entire beast, its bones, and the platter upon which it had been served. Thor was also defeated ignominiously by the cat and the mother of the giant Utgardloki. The contest in fact was an illusion, and the adversaries had been unbeatable elements; in the case of Hugi, this giant was "thought" itself, which even the gods could never outrun, while the giant Logi was the element of "fire," which consumes all. Elli, the mother of the giant, was "old age," and the "cat" had been the vast Midgardsormr.
References 139
See also Fornjotr, giant, Hugi, Kari, Midgardsorm, Utgard-loki

LOHA-MUKHA
This is the name of a class of monstrous giants in the Hindu mythology of India. The Loha-Mukha, whose name may be translated as "Iron-faced," have, as the name implies, faces of iron, but they have only one leg and foot. Despite their seeming inability to move, they are cunning cannibal hunters, living entirely on humans foolish enough to wander into their domain.
References 112
See also cannibal, giant

LOKAPALA ELEPHANTS, LOCAPĀLA ELEPHANTS
These are the guardian elephants of the universe in the Hindu mythology of India. There are eight in number that support a guardian Lokapala god upon their backs within a quadrant of the universe known as a Lokapala. Each of the elephants stands within its quadrant, supporting the weight of the world upon its back, with a consort female of the same immense proportions. There are various spellings and different names according to the source, but they are as follows:

- In the northern quadrant the god is Kubera on the elephant Himapandara/Sarvabhauma/Suryabhauma
- In the northeastern quadrant the god is Prthivi/Siva/Soma on the elephant Supratika
- In the eastern quadrant the god is Indra on the elephant Airāvata/Virupaksha
- In the southeastern quadrant the god is Agni on the elephant Pundarika
- In the southern quadrant the god is Yama on the elephant Vamana/Mahapadma
- In the southwestern quadrant the god is Sūrya/Nirriti on the elephant Kumuda
- In the western quadrant the god is Varuna on the elephant Anja/Saumanasa
- In the northwestern quadrant the god is Vāyu on the elephant Pushpadanta

References 7, 24, 112

LONG EARS
This is the alternative name for the Hvcko Capko in the traditions and beliefs of the Seminole Native Americans of Oklahoma in the southeastern United States.
References 77
See also Hvcko Capko

LONG LANKIN
This is the alternative name for the Lammikin, a type of vampire in the folklore of Scotland.
References 182
See also Lammikin, vampire

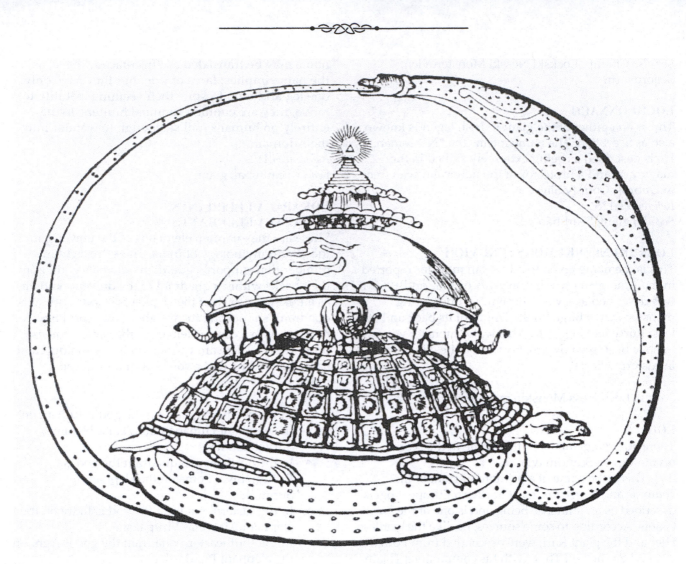

The Lokapala Elephants, Akupara the tortoise, and the World Serpent (Rose Photo Archive, UK)

LONG MAN OF WILMINGTON

This is the name of an ancient chalk hill figure cut in the turf slope of Windover Hill in the county of Sussex in England. The figure measures some 235 feet in length and is allegedly the largest depiction of a human figure. The giant is now a simple outline of a man holding a stave in each hand. Over a hundred years ago an investigation found evidence of a face and a foundation of Roman bricks. Within the vicinity there is the remains of a Benedictine priory and many Iron Age burial mounds.

The folkloric explanation of the giant's presence is that two giants inhabited the two hills of Windover and Firle, facing each other across the Cuckmere Valley. They were mortal enemies and would throw rocks and boulders at each other. The giant on the Windover Hill was struck down, and the place where he fell is etched in the turf. The hollows in the hills are said to be the place where the rocks fell in their battle, but these are actually ancient flint workings. The Long Man takes his name from the local settlement of Wilmington, where he is also known as the Lone Man of Wilmington, the Lankey Man of Wilmington, and the Green Man of Wilmington.
References 13, 78, 183
See also giant

LONG NOSE

This is an alternative name for Hagondes, a cannibal in the traditions and beliefs of the Seneca Native American people of the northeastern United States.
References 77
See also Hagondes

LOTAN

This is the name of a dragon in the mythology of ancient Mesopotamia. In the *Ras Shamra* is the description of this vast, seven-headed dragon, Lotan, and of the god Baal's conquest of the monster. Lotan, like the Leviathan of Hebraic mythology and Tiamat of Babylonian mythology, is a vast serpent dragon of primordial chaos.

References 47, 89
See also Leviathan, Tiamat

LOU CARCOLH

This is the name of a gigantic mollusk-type monster in the folklore of France. It is described as a vast, slimy, snail-like serpent with vast, hairy tentacles and an an enormous shell. It was said to inhabit a huge cavern under the town of Hastingue in the region of Les Landes in southwestern France. The viscous slime could be seen sometimes long before it arrived, but no human dared go near, for any unwary person would be sucked up immediately by one of the tentacles, dragged into the cavern, and engulfed in its vast mouth.
References 134
See also monster

LOUHI

This is the name of an ice giantess in the traditions and folklore of Finland. She was a particularly conniving giantess who used the beauty of her daughter, the princess Pohjola, to trap her suitors into performing difficult tasks for her. When they failed, she set the army of Frost Giants to kill them. Then, the heroes Ilmarinen, Lemminkäinen, and Väinämöinen came courting, and although she got them to create the magic *sampo* of prosperity, before she could make herself the queen of the universe they stole it back and escaped.
References 133
See also Frost Giants, giantess

LOUP GAROU

1. This is the name for the Werewolf in the legends and folk beliefs of France. The Loup Garou has been recorded in French documents since the thirteenth century. The Loup Garou was deemed to be a normal mortal by day but by night transformed to feast in the shape of a wolf on his neighbors and strangers out at night. The Loup Garou is said to be transformed as the result of a curse from a witch, but the metamorphosis could be into other animals, such as a horse or a monstrous black dog. The Loup Garou du Cimitière digs up the corpses freshly buried and devours them. The remedy may be by exorcism, spilling of blood, or actual death.

In other French-speaking countries, such as French Canada and Haiti, the Loup Garou has entered the folk beliefs. In Haiti the monster is described as a red-haired woman who sucks the blood from between the sleeping person's toes and is more like a vampire.

2. This is the name of a giant in the classical literature of France. Loup Garou is one of the characters described by the author François Rabelais (ca. 1494–ca. 1553) in his work *Pantagruel* (1532). The misshapen and monstrous giant is one of the adversaries of the giant Pantagruel.
References 24, 78, 89, 94, 174
See also Azeman, Bisclaveret, Bleiz-Garv, Den-Bleiz, Legarou, Sukuyan, vampire, Vilkacis, Werewolf

LU

This is an alternative name for the Unicorn in the legends of China.
References 7, 89, 113
See also Oriental Unicorn

LUAN

This is the alternative spelling of Lwan, the name of a fabulous bird in the legends of China. It is said at first to be very similar to the Feng Huang, or oriental Phoenix, but as it develops it changes. In its maturity the Luan is famous for its being of five different colors and in each color combination it has a different name. In maturity it also has a call from which the oriental musical scale is derived.
References 181
See also Feng Hwang, Fung, Lwan, Phoenix

LUCIVE

This is a creature from the folklore of lumberjacks and forest workers, especially in Wisconsin and Minnesota in the United States, during the nineteenth and early twentieth centuries. The Lucive belongs to a group of beings affectionately known as the Fearsome Critters, whose exaggerated proportions and activities not only explained the wierd noises of the lonely landscape but also provided some amusement at camps. The Lucive is also known as the Lucivee and the Loup-Cervier, which gives its derivation from the French hybrid wolf-deer.
References 7, 24
See also Fearsome Critters

LUMAKAKA

This is the name of a giant of the seas in the legends of the Maori people of New Zealand. The legend tells how one day two brothers had been fishing and their boat was laden with fish; Lumakaka the sea giant emerged from the waves and demanded to share their catch. So the elder brother threw some of the catch to the giant. Dissatisfied, Lumakaka pursued the brothers until all the catch was gone, and yet he still demanded to be fed. In desperation, the younger brother suggested that he should throw his severed arm. Reluctantly, the elder brother did this, for they were still a long way from the safety of land, but the giant ate this and still demanded more. Lumakaka was not satisfied until he had consumed all the limbs of the youngest brother. The sorrowing elder brother carried the torso back to their grandfather. With

sorrow they buried the youngest brother, from whose body grew the first coconut tree that would supply everything they would ever need.
References 113
See also giant

LUNG
This is the general term for the class of dragon in the legends of China. The Lung is essentially the guardian of the earth's waters and is shown with a scaly serpentine body with four legs (each having four huge claws), a long, sinuous tail, and a head resembling that of a gigantic lizard. Some dragons may be represented with the body of a gigantic carp with the legs of a tiger, the talons of an eagle, and the horns of a stag on their heads. Each is said to have the pearl of wisdom in its gaping mouth. The nostrils breath smoke or fire, and they inhabit the rain clouds. Each class of dragon will have the name of its designated responsibility in front of the name "Lung," as with the Chang Lung, Chi Lung Wang, Lung Wang, Pai Lung, Shen Lung, Tien Lung, Ti Lung, Yu Lung, and Ying Lung.
References 47, 61, 89, 133, 181
See also Chang Lung, Chi Lung Wang, dragon, Lung Wang, Oriental Dragon, Pai Lung, Shen Lung, Ti Lung, Tien Lung, Ying Lung, Yu Lung

LUNG WANG, LONG WANG
This is the name of a dragon in the legends of China. The Lung Wang is the Dragon King, who is also known as the Fire Dragon. Lung Wang may be represented as an Oriental dragon, but at other times it may be represented as a human body with the head of a dragon and horns resembling those of a stag. Other depictions show him with a fish's body with the legs of a tiger and dragon's head. He is the controller of the waters of the seas, the lakes, and other inland stretches of water, where he is responsible for storms and waterspouts. Lung Wang directs other dragons such as Ao Kuang, Ao Ping, and Pai Lung.
References 7, 24, 47, 61, 89, 181
See also Ao Kuang, Ao Ping, Chang Lung, Naga, Oriental Dragon, Pai Lung

LUNKUS
This is an alternative name for the Guyascutus in the folklore of lumberjacks and forest workers (and later fraudsters), especially in Wisconsin and Minnesota in the United States.
References 7
See also Fearsome Critters, Guyascutus

LUPO MANARO
This is the name for the Werewolf in the folklore of Italy.

References 94
See also Werewolf

LUSTUCRU, LE GRAND
This is the name of a gigantic ogre in the nursery traditions of France. Le Grand Lustucru, whose name may be translated as the "Great Would You Believe It," is depicted as an enormous, hideous cannibal ogre with the head of a pig. This being is a terrifying Nursery bogie of the nineteenth century, with whom little children were threatened if they proved reluctant to go to sleep. The nursery rhyme, still current in some French anthologies of children's lullabies, was:

> Entendez-vous dans la plaine
> Ce bruit venant jusqu'à nous?
> On dirait un bruit de chaines,
> Se trainant sur les cailloux.
> C'est le Grand Lustucru qui passe.
> Qui repasse et s'en ira,
> Emportant dans sa besace
> Tous les petit gars qui ne dorment pas.

> Do you hear in the plain
> A noise coming toward us?
> One might say the sound of chains,
> Trailing over pebbles.
> It's the great Lustucru who comes.
> He'll come again then go away,
> Carrying in his knapsack
> All the little children who aren't asleep.
> (M. Warner, No Go the Bogeyman, [1998], p. 219)

References 182
See also cannibal, giant, Nursery bogie, ogre

LWAN, LWAN SHUI
This is the name of a fabulous bird in the traditions and legends of China. It is described as looking something like a much larger and more beautiful and graceful type of pheasant. However, this bird is capable of changing its body color and is known by different names accordingly. These are the Fung, the Hwa Yih, the To Fu, the Yu Chu, and the Yu Siang. These birds were revered as the most eminent such that they commanded the following of other flocks, and when they died they were buried with due ceremony by one hundred of their fellows.
References 81
See also Fung, Hwa Yih, Phoenix, To Fu, Yu Siang

LYCANTHROPE
This is the name for the Werewolf derived from the Greek words lykos, or "wolf," and anthropos, or "man." The term was used widely in Europe, and the belief in Werewolves may be traced to the ancient times in

Lung, the Chinese Imperial five-toed dragon (Rose Photo Archive, UK)

Greece and Rome. The Werewolf was known as the *versipellis,* or "turnskin," in Latin during Roman times. In ancient Greece it was believed that a person could be transformed by eating the meat of a wolf that had been mixed with that of a human and that the condition was irreversible. During the medieval period it was thought that witchcraft was the source of lycanthropy, and numerous people were accused and put to death.
References 0, 61
See also Loup Garou, Werewolf

LYCAON
This is the name of the first monstrous Werewolf in the classical literature of Greece and Rome. Lycaon was the king of Arcadia. In some accounts, such as Theodotius, he was a Titan and the son of Tytan and Terra. The legend related by the classical poet Ovid (43 B.C.–A.D. 17) in his *Metamorphoses* describes how this monstrous cannibal kills his guests in their sleep and preys upon their bodies for his meat. When he is visited by the king of the gods, Zeus, who investigates the rumors, Lycaon tries to test the god by serving human meat. The outraged Zeus destroys the house of the man and condemns him to live forever as part man and part wolf, seeking its food from the passers-by that it might devour. The legend was retold by the Italian poet Boccaccio (1313–1375), which was reproduced in the medieval French literature *La Bible des Poètes,* which contained in its publication of 1493 an illustration of Lycaon baking his gruesome pies in a medieval kitchen.
References 174, 182
See also cannibal, Titan, Werewolf

LYCHIE
This is an alternative name for the Leshii of Russian folklore.
References 38, 64, 103, 133, 139, 152, 160, 166
See also Laskowice, Leshii

LYCIDAS
This is the name of a centaur in the classical mythology of Greece and Rome. Lycidas is one of the centaurs who was present at the marriage feast of Pirithöus and Hippodamia. He was unused to the wine that had been given to guests in great quantities and became so drunk that he, with another centaur, Eurytion, insulted the bride by trying to carry her off. As a result, a fight broke out among the guests, and the centaurs were ejected from the feast. The irate King Pirithoäs appealed to the visiting hero Theseus to intervene, and Theseus expelled the centaur from the feast. Still drunk, Eurytion returned with a band of his fellow centaurs, ready for a fight. In the ensuing battle, one of the centaurs was killed, and the rest were routed to the edge of the domain and the foothills of Mount Pindus.
References 178
See also centaur, Eurytion

LYCOPODIUM
This is an alternative name for the Barometz, which is a legendary part-animal and part-vegetable creature of medieval Europe.
References 7, 18, 89
See also Barometz

LYNX
This is the name of a fabulous beast in the medieval tales and traditions of Europe. It was described in medieval bestiaries as having the body of a panther with the head of a dog. It had immensely bright, far-seeing eyes that could pierce the gloom of night for its sleeping prey.
References 20

LYON-POISSON
This is the name of a fabulous beast in the repertoire of European heraldry. It is described as having the body and tail of a fish and the foreparts and head of a lion. Its modern counterpart is the Merlion in the heraldry and symbolism of Singapore.
References 7

M

MA MIEN

This is the name of the monstrous demonic messenger from hell in the mythology of China. Ma Mien is described as a humanoid monster with the head of a horse, hence the name, which means "Horse-face." He and Nui T'ou are the attendants and messengers of Yen-Lo, the ruler of the dead and those in hell. They were armed with official warrants for the souls of the departed, whom they conducted to the Halls of Judgment.

References 38, 133, 160, 181

See also Amermait, monster

MACAN GADUNGAN

This is the name of a Were-tiger in the legends and folk beliefs of the island of Java in Indonesia. It is described as a predatory tiger with the soul of a sleeping man that has escaped. Other explanations are that men can change themselves by *ngelmu gadungan,* or ritual magic, and roam the villages in search of human prey. It is said that a sure sign of a man who is a Macan Gadungan is that he will not have a dimple in the upper lip of his mouth.

References 113

See also Were-tiger, Werewolf

MACRUS

This is one of the giants named in the genealogy created by the Italian monk Annius of Viterbo (Giovanni Nanni, ca. 1432–1502) to justify the noble descent of the Gauls from a giant biblical race.

References 139, 174

See also giant, Noah

MADA

This is the name of a terriying monster in the mythology and folklore of India. The Mada is described as a huge creature with enormous fangs that protrude from its huge mouth. It has a voracious appetite for any creature and will devour humans just as easily.

References 112

MADHU

This is the name of one of two giants in the Hindu creation mytholgy of India.

References 112

See also Kaitabha

MAEZT-DAR L' OUDOU

This is the name of a vast and terrifying Djinn in the folklore and traditions of the people of Morocco. Maezt-Dar l'Oudou, which may be translated as the "Goat of the Lavatories," is described as a monstrous and very aggressive goat. It has a predisposition to take possession of the baths and lavatories at night and other places where water might be flushed. This Djinn will materialize, attack, and terrify anyone imprudent enough to venture to those places after dark.

References 122, 160

See also Djinn

MAFEDET

This is the name of a hybrid monster in ancient Egyptian and Mesopotamian mythology. The Mafedet is portrayed as having the body of a lion but the head and neck of a serpent. The images of the Mafedet have been found in relief on votive palettes from Heirakonopolis.

References 89

See also monster

MAGÆRA

This is the name of a monstrous, snake-haired supernatural whose name means "Envious Fury" in the mythology of ancient Greece and Rome. She is the dispenser of ultimate revenge. Magæra is one of the Furies who exact retribution from those whose hideous crimes, especially matricide or patricide, remain unpunished by human law.

References 20, 38, 160

See also Erinyes, Furies

MAGNI

This is the name of a giant in the Norse mythology of Scandinavia. Together with his brother, Modi, Magni,

whose name means "Strength," is a son of the giantess Iarnsaxa.
References 78
See also giant, giantess, Iarnsaxa

MAGOG
See Gemmagog, Gog and Magog, Gogmagog, Gos Et Magos

MAHAPADMA
This is the name of one of the Lokapala Elephants in the Hindu mythology of India. In the *Ramayana,* Mahapadma (sometimes Vamana, according to different legends) stands as the guardian of the southern quadrant of the world with the god Yama on his back.
References 7, 24, 112
See also Lokapala Elephants

MAHISHA, MAHISHĀSURA
This is the name of a monster in the Hindu mythology of India. Mahisha is described as a vast creature of destruction with the head of a water buffalo. This monster is vanquished variously by Skanda, according to the legends of the *Mahābhārata,* or by Durgā when fighting the Asuras. In the modern folklore of India this monster terrorizes the villages as Bhainsāsura, destroying the crops and fertile fields unless offered a pig.
References 24
See also monster

MAHU-CATAH
This is one of a group of terrifying beings, known as the Balam, in the beliefs of the Quiché peoples of Mexico. The name "Mahu-Catah" means "Famous Name." The Balam were assigned as guardians of the Four Directions.
References 119, 160
See also Balam

MAIGHDEAN UAINE
This is the name of a type of Fuath in the legends and folklore of the Highlands of Scotland. The name "Maighdean uaine" may be translated as the "Green Maiden."
References 128
See also Glaistig

MAKA
This is the name of a vast cosmic serpent in the mythology of ancient Egypt. Maka is described as a monstrous serpent of the void that constantly attacks the sun god Ra on his journey from horizon to horizon.
References 166
See also Aapep

MAKARA
This is the name of a monster of the sea in the traditions and folklore of India, Thailand, and Indonesia. Indeed, the name may be translated as "Sea Monster," but this being is depicted variously as a gigantic and grotesque crab, or as part crocodile and part bird, or as part deer with the hindquarters of a fish. The name "Makara" is often applied to any composite monster with elements of both fish and mammal and may often have parts of an elephant, especially the trunk, when depicted as a guardian on Hindu temple gateways. It is the steed of the gods Ganga and Varuna and, occasionally, of Vishnu. It is the equivalent of the Western zodiac sign of Capricorn in the Hindu calendar.
References 7, 24, 61, 89, 112, 113
See also Capricorn, dragon, Leviathan, monster

MAKE
This is the name of a gigantic serpent in the traditions and beliefs of the people of Papua New Guinea. Its presence is considered to be an indication of the presence of the sun god Wunekau.
References 125
See also Rainbow Serpent, serpent

MALDAPE
This is the name of a monster in the traditions and beliefs of Native Australians.
References 154
See also monster

MANCOMORION
This is the alternative name for the hybrid beast known as the Manticore in medieval European bestiaries. The Mancomorion was a type of Manticore, or hybrid man-tiger, that was supposed to inhabit India.
References 7, 89
See also Manticore

MANDUCUS
This is the name of a monster in the literary and dramatic traditions of ancient Rome. Manducus—the name means "Jaws"—was a hybrid human-animal-monster that was portrayed in the comic theater as one that had ever-chattering teeth, along with another called Dossenus.
References 182
See also Dossenus, monster

MANETUWI-RUSI-PISSI
This is the name of a lake monster in the legends and beliefs of the Shawnee Native American people of the United States. The Manetuwi-Rusi-Pissi is described as a water tiger and is a guardian monster of the lakes and fishes within it.

References 134
See also Lenapizka

MANIPOGO

This is the name of a lake monster in the folklore of the people around Lake Manitoba, Canada. The Manipogo was said to have surfaced on 12 August 1962 in front of two fishermen who were able to take a rather hasty photograph of the monster as it skimmed the surface of the water. It looks rather like a water serpent with a single undulation in the middle of its serpentine body.
References 134
See also monster, serpent

MANITOU KINEBIK

This is the alternative name of a Kichiknebik, a monstrous water serpent in the legends and traditions of the Native Americans of the United States.
References 134
See also Kichiknebik

MANITOUKINEBIC

This is the name of a monstrous serpent in the beliefs of Native Americans reported during the nineteenth century. Manitoukinebic, also known as Kichiknebik, the Great Serpent, was described as a vast serpent with a huge mouth and spines along its back. It was extremely strong and fast both overland and on water. This serpent was a highly predatory creature that was capable of encircling an entire buffalo and swallowing it whole.
References 134
See also serpent

MANTA

This is the name of a giant seagoing monster in the folklore of the people of Chiloc, Chile. The Manta is said to be the sea-water equivalent of the Cuero. It is described as a flat, extended skin, like a cow's hide, with eyes around the perimeter, four more on the top, where a head would have been, and tentacles and tail with claws. This creature comes to the surface, where it lures and sucks unwary humans swimming there down under the water, where it enfolds their bodies and consumes them. The creature has been known to climb out onto the land, where it lies in the sun, but its return was said to be the cause of violent gales. The fishermen of Chaloc were naturally terrified of the creature and would leave the fishing grounds if a Manta were seen. There has been some speculation that it could have been some form of giant squid.
References 134
See also Cuero, Hide, Trequelhuecuve

MANTICORE, MANTICORA, MANTICHORA, MANTICORY, MANTICORAS

This is the name of a hybrid humanoid monster in the legends of ancient Asia, Mesopotamia, and medieval Europe. The name "Mantichora" was said to be a distortion of the Persian *mardkhora*, which may be translated as "Man-slayer." The Manticore, also known as the Martikhora, Mantiserra, Memecoleous, Mancomorion, and the Satyral, is described as having the body of a lion with a tail fanned at the end with stinging spines; its head is that of a human with a red face, blue eyes, and a triple row of teeth in its vast mouth. It was said to have a call that resembled a trumpet and flute together and to inhabit the region of India or Ethiopia. This monstrous creature is exceptionally fast and will hunt and kill its human prey by shooting them with the stinging quills from its tail. The original description was said to have come from the Greek physician to King Artaxerxes Mnemon (404–359 B.C.) and later transcribed by Pliny the Elder in his *Historia Naturalis* (A.D. 77).

During the medieval period the Manticore was frequently depicted in bestiaries, and a Latin bestiary of the twelfth century and an Anglo-Saxon bestiary of 1220 both retain the basic description first given by Pliny over a thousand years earlier. Surprisingly, it was depicted as the representative of the prophet Jeremiah. In church architecture of the period, it was also portrayed as a scale-covered woman.

In the later folklore of Spain, the Manticore developed into a child-abducting type of Werewolf.
References 7, 10, 14, 18, 63, 89, 148, 185
See also monster, Werewolf

MAN-TIGER

This is the name of a fabulous hybrid monster in the heraldic repertoire of Europe. The Man-Tiger is portrayed as having the body of a tiger and the head of a man but with horn projections from the forehead.
References 5

MANTISERRA

This is an alternative name for the Manticore of medieval European legends.
References 89
See also Manticore

MANZAŠIRI

This is the name of a primordial giant in the legends and folk beliefs of the Kalmyks, a people in western Mongolia. The dismembering of this vast giant of the universe provided the earth from his body; the sun and moon that had been his eyes; his blood became the earth's water; and the fires of the earth were generated from the heat of his own internal organs.

References 125
See also giant, Ymir

MARES OF DIOMEDES

Also known as the Horses of Diomedes, these are a herd of cannibal horses owned by a Thracian king in the classical mythology of Greece and Rome. The eighth of the Twelve Labors of Hercules/Heracles was to tame these wild, flesh-eating, gigantic horses. The hero accomplished this by feeding the king to his own horses, then taking the herd of mares to be dedicated to the goddess Hera in Argos.

References 24, 139
See also cannibal

MARGYGR

This name has two meanings in literature.

1. This is an alternative name for Hafgygr, a giantess or monster in the Norse mythology of Scandinavia.

2. This is the name of a type of mermaid in the traditions and folklore of the people of Greenland.

The Margygr is described as hideously ugly with piercing eyes and a flat face. It is possible that she is derived from the monster of that name in the Norse mythology of Scandinavia brought to Greenland by the Viking settlers.

References 7
See also giantess, Hafgygr, mermaid, monster

MARINE BOAR

This is the name of a sea monster in the medieval sailors' tales and, later, travelers' tales of Europe. It was described as having the scaly body of a huge fish but the head and tusks resembling those of a wild boar. These descriptions come from a time when it was believed that whatever existed on the earth had a counterpart in the seas and the skies.

References 147

MARINE LION

This is the name of a curious creature that was reported to have been captured in the Tyrrhenian Sea. The Marine Lion was described by Ambroise Paré

The Marine Lion, a curious creature that was reported to have been captured in the Tyrrhenian Sea (On Monsters and Marvels by Ambroise Paré, trans. by Janis L. Pallister, University of Chicago Press, 1982)

(1517–1590), in his work *On Monsters and Marvels*, as being like a lion but with its body entirely covered with scales instead of fur and having a voice similar to that of humans. It was taken from the sea around 1540 and presented to Marcel, the bishop of Castre, but it expired soon thereafter.
References 147

MARINE SOW
This was the name given to a sea monster reported by the traveler Olaus Magnus in 1555. The Marine Sow was described as a vast creature of seventy-two feet in length, fourteen feet in depth, and seven feet across from eye to eye on a head that resembled that of a pig. It also had a further six eyes, three located on each side of its scaly body, and a crescent-shaped dorsal fin. When the creature was caught and slaughtered off the Isle of Thylen in Scandinavia, five casks were needed to hold the liver alone.
References 147
See also monster

MARSAYAS
This is the name of a being closely related to the Satyrs in the classical mythology of Greece and Rome. Marsayas was originally a Phrygian demon adopted and transformed to a status similar to that of Silenus after the occupation of their land by the Greeks. The story of Marsayas tells how he found the discarded *aulos*, a type of flute, invented by the goddess Athena, and learned how to play it so well that he challenged the god Apollo to a musical contest. The winner would do whatever he wanted with the loser. Marsayas lost and for his presumption was flayed alive, his flowing blood forming the river that now takes his name.
References 24, 120, 125, 139, 160, 166, 178
See also satyr, Silenus

MARTIKHORA
This is an alternative name for the Manticore of medieval European legends.
References 89
See also Manticore

MÁSAW
This is the name of a giant in the traditions and beliefs of the Hopi Native American people of the United States. Másaw was described as being benign toward humans but an arrogant being in charge of the third world. However, when his control was removed he was given the lesser position of looking after the underworld of the dead until reinstated in a fourth world.
References 78, 91, 134
See also giant

MASHERNOMAK
This is the name of a monster in the traditions and beliefs of the Menominee Native American people of

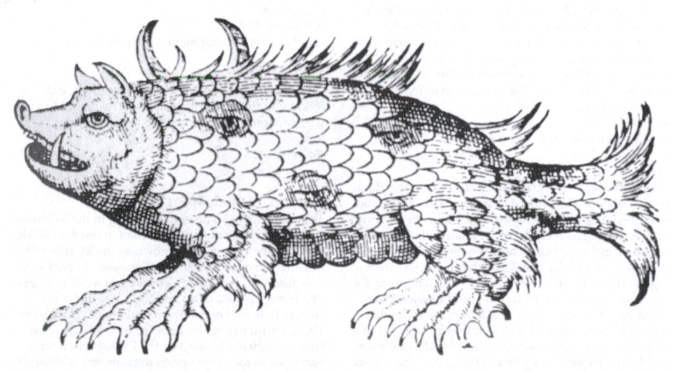

The Marine Sow, a sea monster reported by the traveler Olaus Magnus in 1555 (On Monsters and Marvels by Ambroise Paré, trans. by Janis L. Pallister, University of Chicago Press, 1982)

the United States and Canada. The legend tells how Mashernomak was a predatory lake monster that trapped and devoured any unwary fisherman. One day the hero Manabush also became a victim of Mashernomak and was swallowed whole. Inside the belly of the monster, Manabush discovered his brothers and many other victims, so he took his knife and slashed a huge hole in the side of Mashernomak, allowing its victims to escape and killing it from inside.

References 134
See also monster

MASTER OF THE FISHES

This is an alternative name for Mishipizhiw in the traditions and beliefs of the Native American people of the United States.

References 134
See also Mishipizhiw, Sa-Yin

MASTER OF THE WATER

This is the name of a water serpent known as Lik in the traditions and folk beliefs of the people of Gran Chaco in South America. The Lik is described as a vast monstrous guardian of the inland fish of the lakes and rivers.

References 134
See also Lik

MASUS

This is the name of a giant who appeared in the medieval work *Officina* by the erudite Jean Tixier de Ravisy (alias Ravisius Textor, c. 1480–1524), who proposed that Tuyscon Gigas was actually a son of the giant Noah whose progeny were the ancestors of European nobility. He constructed a line of giant descendants, of whom Masus was one of many legendary figures.

References 174
See also giant, Noah, Tuyscon Gigas

MATAU

This is the name of a giant in the legends of the Maori people of New Zealand. Matau was a vast humanoid that preyed upon the people of the plains in the South Island. The legend tells how the giant stole Manata, a beautiful girl from the village, whom he enslaved with magical bonds. Matakauri, her lover, searched high and low for her and at last discovered where the giant had hidden her. In vain he tried to release her, but it was only when her tears fell on the ropes that the magic was broken. However, they recognized that wherever they hid the terrible giant would find them. So Matakauri went to try to kill the giant. The warrior found Matau sleeping soundly in a hollow of the mountains covered in bracken, and he quickly set fire

to the dry ferns all around him. At first the warmth made the slumbering giant pull up his legs to turn, but soon the raging heat and smoke choked the giant to death before he could escape. The fire raged so fiercely that the huge corpse melted and was consumed deep into the earth, where a vast fissure opened as it sank deeper. But the supernatural heart of the giant kept beating, and long after his death the heart of Matua still pumps the lake waters that have filled the hollow where he was destroyed.

References 155
See also giant

MATCHI-MANITOU

This is an alternative name for the Michi-Pichoux in the traditions and beliefs of the Cree Native American people of Canada.

References 134
See also Michi-Pichoux

MAUL, MAUL THE SOPHIST

This is the name of a giant in the classical literature of England. He appears in the classic *Pilgrim's Progress*, written by John Bunyan and published in 1682. The giant Maul is a cannibal that hunts and devours humans, especially the pilgrims who cross his territory. He stops the pilgrims on their road and challenges them with fallacious arguments concerning their route. The pilgrim's guide, Great-heart, met the giant's attack, and they fought bitterly for a long time until the giant was defeated and decapitated.

References 20, 31
See also giant, Grim, Pagan, Pope, Slay-good

MAULEON

This is the name of a giant in the traditions and folklore of the Philippine Islands. The giant Mauleon was apparently rescued by the hero Don Juan Tinyoso.

References 113
See also giant

MAUTHE DHOOG, MAUTHE DOOG

This is the name of an evil Black dog in the folklore of the Manx people of the Isle of Man in the British Isles. The Mauthe Dhoog, also known as the Moddey Dhoo, inhabits the corridors and battlements of Peel Castle. It is described variously as the size of a calf with eyes like pewter plates, or an enormous spaniel with shaggy hair, that may appear and attack all who see it. There are numerous accounts of people who have some experience of the Mauthe Dhoog, often with varations in the events or on the outcome. One such tale refers to the time that Peel Castle was occupied by military forces in the seventeenth century. A bored

Sleeping giant. Matakauri found Matau sleeping soundly in a hollow of the mountains. (Fairies and Enchanters by A. Williams-Ellis, Thomas Nelson, UK)

soldier on guard duty, after a few drinks, bragged that he would search for the Mauthe Dhoog. His terrified shrieks brought his fellow officers to the corridor where he lay, and they dragged him back to the guard room, jabbering about the "Dhoog," before he died. A similar fate befell a Methodist minister brought in to exorcise the creature.
References 96, 128, 160
See also Barguest, Black Shuck, Gytrash, Padfoot, Rongeur d'Os, Skriker, Trash

MEDUSA

This is the name of one of the Gorgons in the classical mythology of Greece and Rome. Medusa, whose name means "Ruler" or "Queen," had been with her sisters Euryale and Stheno, the beautiful progeny of Ceto, and the old Man of the Sea, Phorcys. The sea god Poseidon desired Medusa so much that he disguised himself as a white stallion and seduced her in a temple sacred to the goddess Athene. The outraged Athene desired revenge for her desecrated temple and changed Medusa into a hideous parody of her former self. She still had the form of a woman but with wings on her back, as well as great tusks or fangs in her huge gaping mouth from which her tongue lolled; from her head grew writhing snakes in place of hair, and she had brazen clawed hands on her arms. Her most fearsome feature, however, was her eyes, for any mortal who was foolish enough to look at them was instantly turned to stone. Of the three, only Medusa was mortal, and the Gorgons hid themselves in obscurity guarded only by their siblings, the Graeae, in the region east of Scythia or the wastes of Libya, or the edge of the Western Ocean, or Cisthene. Then the hero Perseus came in search of Medusa, having vowed to take her head to King Polydectes. By tricking the Graeae during the exchange of their one eye and tooth, he managed to get from them the whereabouts of Medusa. While the ugly sisters were without sight and toothless, Perseus,

Mauthe Dhoog, also known as the Moddey Dhoo, inhabits the corridors and battlements of Peel Castle. (Welsh Legends by D. Parry-Jones, Batsford Books, London, 1953)

aided with the winged sandals and sickle of Hermes and the helmet of invisibility from Athene, came upon Medusa and killed her, guiding the sickle by watching only her image reflected in his shield. As the blood spurted out of her, so too did the winged horse Pegasus and the monstrous Chrysaor. Then Perseus wrapped the head in the pouch that Athene had given him and escaped, invisible under the helmet, past the Graeae. Wherever the blood dropped as he crossed the desert it turned into the venomous snakes that now inhabit the region, and where it fell into the sea it turned into red coral. When the hero gave the head to Athene, she took the blood from the left side, which was destructive, and placed the hideous face on her *aegis* (shield) to petrify her foes. Aesculapius took the curative blood from the right side of Medusa's head for his healing activities. For centuries, images of the Gorgon's head were used on shields for warriors and then on doors and buildings as a means of warding off evil.

In ancient art, Medusa had been depicted as a winged horse like her progeny, Pegasus, and then as a woman's torso and horse's hindquarters, rather like a Centaur with wings on her head, which later were portrayed as snakes. When the name "Gorgon" is used in the singular it invariably refers only to Medusa. The more familiar image came quite late in development but persisted into the medieval period and changed again during the sixteenth century. At this time travelers and others believed that the Gorgon still inhabited North Africa but in the guise of a beast that might be more readily identifiable with the Catoblepas of the medieval bestiaries.
References 7, 20, 61, 78, 89, 133, 136, 166, 178, 182
See also Catoblepas, centaur, Chrysaor, Euryale, Gorgon, monster, Pegasus, Stheno

MEHEN
This is the name of a cosmic serpent in the mythology of ancient Egypt. Mehen is described as a vast serpent that accompanied the sun god Ra on his nightly return journey from the western horizon to the eastern horizon. Ra was constantly under threat from the cosmic serpent Aapep as he journeyed in his sun boat and was vulnerable in the darkness below the horizon. Therefore, Mehen coiled himself protectively over the boat.
References 38, 139, 160
See also Aapep, Naga

MEH-TEH
This is one of the names for the Yeti in the traditions and beliefs of the people of Nepal in the Himalayas. There are three different types of Yeti, categorized according to size and height. The smallest is the Yeh-Teh, from which we derive the general name. The large one is the Meh-Teh, but the largest of all is called the Dzu-Teh.
References 78
See also Yeti

MÉLISANDE
This is the name in France for the monstrous female serpent also known as Melusine.
References 24, 161
See also Melusine

MELUSINE, MELUSINA
This is the name of a hideous female monster in the traditions and folk beliefs of medieval France. Melusine, also known in France as Mélisande, is described as having the head and torso of a beautiful young woman garbed in medieval finery but with the wings of a dragon and the lower half of a monstrous serpent. She is depicted frequently in the Books of Hours of the period.

The story of Melusine was already well known in French folk history before it was written down by Jean d'Aras in 1387. She was the daughter of a fountain Fairy named Pressina by a mortal king, Elinus of Albany (Scotland). When these two married it was on the Fairy pledge that he should never see her in childbed, but he did. The broken vow deprived him of his wife and three daughters, Melusine, Melior, and Platina, who were compelled to return to their Fairy court. When these daughters assumed their full supernatural powers, they took revenge on their father, sealing him forever in a cave in Northumbria (England). Pressina, their Fairy mother, realizing what they had done, cursed each of her daughters, and Melusine was to become a water serpent from the waist to feet once a week. She would never experience love until she found someone who agreed not to see her on that day. If this were broken, she would be condemned to exist only as a hideous winged snake. Melusine met and married Count Raymond of Poitiers, who built the Chateau of Lusignan for her. Most of their children were monsters deformed from the start in some awful manner, but the last two were normal. Eventually the count also broke his vow, and Melusine leaped from the castle ramparts to eternity as the winged serpent mermaid, leaving the noble line of descendants claimed to be the ancestors of the French monarchy.

She is frequently depicted as a mermaid with a double tail in the heraldic repertoire of France and the British Isles.
References 7, 24, 25, 160, 161, 183
See also mermaid, monster, serpent, Tegid Foel

Perseus kills Medusa. (A Wonder Book for Boys and Girls and Tanglewood Tales by N. Hawthorne, J. M. Dent, London)

MEMECOLEOUS

This is the alternative name for the hybrid beast known as the Manticore in medieval European bestiaries. The Memecoleous was the type of Manticore, or hybrid man-tiger, that was supposed to inhabit India.

References 7, 89
See also Manticore

MENOETIUS

This is the name of one of the giants in the classical mythology of Greece and Rome. Menoetius was one of the progeny of the Titan called Japetus and the Oceanid nymph Clymene, according to Hesiod in his work *Theogony* (c. 750 B.C.), but according to Aeschylus (525 B.C.–456 B.C.), his mother was Themis. His siblings were the giants Atlas, Prometheus, and Epimetheus. Both Menoetius and Atlas took part in

the revolt against the gods, and for his part Menoetius was condemned by the king of the gods, Zeus, to the eternal darkness of Erebus.

References 139
See also Atlas, Epimetheus, giant, Japetus, Prometheus, Titan

MENUIS

This is the Greek form of the name "Merwer," a sacred bull in the mythology of ancient Egypt.

References 139
See also Merwer

MERMAID/E, MEREMAIDEN

This is the name of a female water being in the form of a beautiful young woman from the head to the waist, the rest of her body being like the tail of a huge fish. Mermaids have been part of folklore and

Mermaids are often seen holding a mirror and combing their long hair whilst singing and enticing sailors to come closer to the dangerous rocks. (Rose Photo Archive, UK)

mythology of maritime and freshwater cultures since ancient times. The derivation of the English name means both "sea" and "lake" maiden, however there are many different regional names in the British Isles, such as the Ben Varrey, Ceasg, Clytie, Gwenhidwy, Liban, Mari Morgan, Merrow, Roane, and Selkie.

The Mermaids are often seen sitting on rocks holding a mirror and combing their long hair whilst singing and enticing curious sailors to come closer to the dangerous rocks. It is this singing that allies them to the Sirens, luring sailors to their doom. Even the ancient accounts, as well as the more modern ones, mention the appearance of these supernaturals in conjunction with misfortune and disaster, although occasionally they can be benevolent. In regional tales from Scotland, Wales, and Cornwall in England, when rescued they have given humans the knowledge of herbal cures for fatal sickness, other rich gifts, and warnings of storms. They may marry with humans, their offspring having webbed feet and fingers, but they usually return to their watery world, where their consorts are called mermen.

During the medieval period in Europe the Mermaid was considered to be an agent of the devil and a symbol of deceit. She was often depicted on church furniture holding a fish, which symbolized the entrapment of the soul of the Christian drawn to sin by charms and flattery. In later periods through to today, the image of the Mermaid is frequently to be seen in the coats of arms of Europe and is part of the repertoire of heraldry.

There is a rich tradition of folktales and songs about Mermaids from other cultures all around the world, such as the Bonito Maidens of the Solomon Islands; the Saivo-Neita and Havfrue of Scandinavia; the Näkinneito of Finland and the Näkineiu of Estonia; the Imanja and Jamaína from Brazil; La Sirena from Spain; the Halfway People of the Micmac of Canada; the Margygr of Greenland; and the Ningyo from Japan
References 7, 20, 21, 24, 25, 29, 60, 61, 67, 68, 78, 84, 119, 124, 137, 160, 161, 170, 186
See also Ben Varrey, Gwenhidwy, Halfway People, Havfrue, Lamia, Liban, Margygr, Melusina, Merrow, Näkineiu, Näkinneito, Ningyo, Saivo-Neita, Sirena, Siren/s

MERMAN
This is the male counterpart of the sea-dwelling being known as the mermaid. Like her, he appears in the form of a human above the waist with green hair and beard, but below the waist is the tail of a large fish. The Mermen have a reputation for more terrifying behavior than even the mermaids and can be held responsible for violent storms and sinking ships. They are also thought in British legends to be aggressive toward the mermaids and even devour their own offspring, whereas in the Scandinavian legends the Havmand is more benign. The traditions of Mermen may have been derived from the Abgal of ancient Sumer, but more recent folkloric derivations could be from ancient sightings of such creatures as the bull walrus to the strange tales of the Blue Men of the Minch, whose origins are from the press gangs of early European history. Whatever the derivation, the image of the Merman has become familiar in the heraldic repertoire of Europe.
References 25, 67, 120, 124, 160, 170
See also Näkki, Nix, Triton

MERROW
This is the name of the mer-people in the traditions and folk beliefs of Ireland. The Merrows may also be called the Murdhuacha, Moruadh, Moruach, Muir-Gheilt, Samhghubha, or Suire. The mermaids appear as beautiful young women above the waist with pale skin, dark eyes, and long hair, but they look like a fish below the waist. Their mermen are ugly with green skin, teeth, and hair but a sharp red nose and tiny, narrow eyes. They all have webbed fingers and are able to shape-shift from the appearance of land animals or humans to that of marine dwellers by way of a magic red feather cap. If this cap is stolen, they are unable to return to their underwater world, and this is often how a mortal man may gain a Merrow bride. The Merrows are usually of a peaceful and benevolent nature toward humans, often intermarrying; their children may have webbed feet and fingers and even a scaly skin.
References 21, 24, 25, 170
See also mermaid, merman

MERWER
This is the name of a sacred bull in the mythology of ancient Egypt. Merwer, also known by the Greek name "Menuis" and the location name of "Bull of Meroe," was depicted as a massive creature with, according to different sources, a light or black color. This vast being was the sacred beast of the sun god Ra at Helipolis, and like the other sacred bulls it was represented on earth by a real bull that was mummified at death.
References 139
See also Apis, Buchis

MESHEKENABEC
This is the name of a massive lake serpent in the traditions and beliefs of the Native American people of the United States. Meshekenabec is described as having a vast serpentine body with plate-like iridescent scales, a red head, and eyes that radiated a

Celtic mermen (Rose Photo Archive, UK)

red light. This terrifying creature inhabited a lake with many other attending serpents but was eventually vanquished by the culture hero Manabozho.

References 7
See also serpent

METAL OLD MAN

This is an alternative name for the giant known as Be Chasti in the traditions and folk beliefs of the White Mountain Apache Native American people of the United States.

References 24
See also Be Chasti, giant, Golem, Talos

MHORAG

In the folklore of Scotland this is the name of the mermaid or lake monster that inhabited the thousand-foot-deep Loch Morar. She behaves in a similar way to the banshee of Ireland, as she only reveals herself when a member of the clan is about to die. She is said to arise out of the water in three representations that symbolize the death, coffin, and grave of the victim. There have been numerous sightings of Mhorag during the nineteenth and twentieth centuries. Often they describe a monster of at least twenty-five feet in length, serpentine, and green with a humped back. On one occasion in 1969 the monster collided with a boat, from which the terrified occupants fended for themselves with rifles and oars.

References 134
See also Bunyip, Loch Ness Monster, mermaid, monster, Peiste

MIAL MHÒR A' HUAIN, THE GREAT BEAST OF THE OCEAN

This is an alternative name for the Cìrein Cròin, a gigantic sea serpent in the beliefs and folklore of the Highlands of Scotland. The name may be translated from the Scottish Gaelic as the "Great Beast of the Ocean."

References 128
See also Cìrein Cròin

MICHIPICHI, MICHIPICHIK

These are alternative names for the Michi-Pichoux in the traditions and folk beliefs of the Cree Native American people of Canada.

References 134
See also Michi-Pichoux

MICHI-PICHOUX, MICHI-PICHI, MICHIPICHIK, MITCHIPICHI

This is the name of a monster in the traditions and beliefs of the Cree Native American people of

Canada. The Michi-Pichoux is also known as Michi-Pichi, or Michipichik, or Mitchipichi, or Matchi-Manitou according to different sources. This being was described by the French priest Father Louis Nicholas in the *Histoire Naturelle* (1675) as having a vast, hairy body like that of a tiger, but it was over eighteen feet in length with huge clawed feet and a tail somewhat resembling that of a beaver. Its head was huge, and its jaws had fangs of over two feet in length. Michi-Pichoux was the terrifying inhabitant of islands in the estuary of the Saint Lawrence River and was feared for its predatory attitude toward humans. The monster was said to take and devour children who wandered to the shores of the river. It is conjectured that Father Louis Nicholas had seen and emulated the work of Ambroise Paré (1517–1590), *On Monsters and Marvels,* in transcribing the description he was given, along with his appreciation of a "tooth" of the Michi-Pichoux, which he subsequently gave to the administrator of New France.

References 77, 134
See also monster

MICROMÉGAS

This is the name of a giant in a literary French classic. Micromégas appears in the work of the same name by François Marie Arouet de Voltaire (1694–1778).

References 174
See also Gargantua, Pantagruel

MIDCHAÍN

This is an alternative name for Miodhchaoin, a giant in the Celtic legends of Ireland.

References 128
See also Miodhchaoin

MIDGARD'S WORM

See Midgardsorm/r

MIDGARDSORM/R, MIDGARD SERPENT, MIDGARD WORM

This is the name of the world serpent in the Norse mythology of Scandinavia and the Teutonic mythology of what is now northern Germany. The Midgardsorm, which means the "Serpent of Midgard," takes this name from its location, but it is also known as Jormungandr. This vast serpent was the progeny of the trickster god Loki and the giantess Angboda. Its siblings were Hel, the goddess of the underworld, and Fenrir, the horrific wolf bound by the gods until the last battle of Ragnarök. When this monster was born, the gods were so horrified that they threw it into the ocean, where it grew so huge that it encircled Midgard and became known as the Midgardsormr. The arches of this serpent's coils,

Fenrir and the Midgardsormr at Ragnarok (Rose Photo Archive, UK)

when they rose in the air, were deemed to be the rainbow. Many of the gods who feared the serpent had encounters with it, in particular the god Thor when he went fishing with the giant Hymir. Hymir challenged Thor to a fishing contest. Taking two of his prized bulls, the giant and the god set out in his boat and used the bulls' heads as bait. Whoever hooked the greatest fish would win. Hymir fished out two vast whales, but Thor's bait was taken by the world-serpent, the Midgardsormr. In some versions of the myth, Hymir threw himself into the sea in terror and drowned. In other versions, the giant cut the line, and the pair took the whales to land, where they consumed them.

In another legend, Thor was challenged by one of the Frost Giants to prove his strength, but he could not even lift the cat off the floor that he had been given as his task. It was only later that Utgard-Loki explained that he had been deluded into trying to lift the Midgardsorm.

At the coming of Ragnarök, the Midgardsorm will rise up out of the oceans, bringing devastation and poisoning the earth. His adversary will be the god Thor, and they will kill each other in the final battle.

References 7, 24, 47, 49, 61, 125, 133, 134, 169
See also Angboda, Fenrir, giant, giantess, Hymir, Jormungandr, Rainbow Snake, serpent, Utgard-Loki

MIGAS
This is the name of a monster in the traditions and beliefs of the people of the High Congo region of central West Africa. The Migas is described as a huge, flat, aquatic creature with long, tentacle-like protrusions from its fleshy body and inhabited the upper waterways of the Congo River. It was said that anything that got too near was grabbed by these "tentacles" and pulled down into its lair beneath the water.
References 134
See also Cuero, Hide

MIKULA
This is the name of a giant in the ancient mythology of Russia. Mikula was the primordial being who cultivated the mother earth, represented as Mati-Syra-Zemlya. This being was of such gigantic proportions that no human could cover the amount of ground or steer his vast plough. After being elevated as a celestial being, Mikula's image became reduced to

that of a culture hero, or *bogatyr'*, with the coming of Christianity.
References 133
See also giant

MILŽINAS
This is the name of a giant in the folklore and traditions of Lithuania.
References 24
See also giant

MIMAS
This is the name of a giant in the classical mythology of Greece and Rome. Mimas was one of the many Gigantes who had been engendered from the blood of the castrated Uranus. They had sprung directly from the earth in full armor, having beneath their gigantic bodies legs that were serpents whose heads were the giants' feet. His siblings were Alcyoneus, Clytius, Enceladus, Ephialtes, Eurytus, Pallas, Pelorus, Polybutes, and Porphyrion. These beings made war on Zeus and the Olympian gods and they were all defeated. Mimas, whose name means the "Mocker," was killed, according to some sources, by the god Ares, who transfixed the giant with his sword, or by Jupiter/Zeus with a bolt of lightning.
References 139, 169, 178
See also Alcyoneus, Clytius, Enceladus, Ephialtes, Eurytus, giant, Gigantes, Pallas, Pelorus, Polybutes, Porphyrion, Uranus

MIMICK DOG, MIMIKE DOG
This is the name of a fabulous creature in the beliefs of the medieval European travelers concerning the ancient Egyptians. The Mimick Dog was so called because it was said to be able to mimic anything. They were described as looking similar to an ape but having a snout something like that of a hedgehog. They were said to be capable of imitating anything, including human behavior, and were therefore trained as servants for the poorer citizens.
References 7, 89

MIMIR
This is the name of a giant in the Norse mythology of Scandinavia. Mimir was one of the Jotuns and the guardian of the well of inspiration and wisdom, which lay at the roots of Yggdrasil, the World Tree. When Odin, the king of the gods, wanted to drink from this well, Mimir made him leave an eye in payment for his knowledge. Mimir was taken in battle as a hostage by the Vanir, who beheaded him. Odin retrieved Mimir's head, which he kept alive with magic herbs, and continued to advise the lord of the gods.
References 78, 125, 127, 133, 160, 161, 166, 169
See also giant, Jotun

MINATA-KARAIA
This is the name of a monstrous race of people in the traditions and beliefs of the people of the Xingu River basin in central Brazil. The Minata-Karaia are huge like the trees up to the canopy of the forest and have fruits growing from under their arms, which resemble coconuts. This is their food, for they take it out, crack it, then eat. The local people know when they are coming and can get out of the way, for there is a hole in the tops of the heads of the males that emit a high-pitched whistle when they move.
References 47

MINDI
This is a regional name for the Rainbow Serpent in the Dreamtime mythology of the Native Australian people.
References 133
See also Rainbow Serpent

MI-NI-WA-TU
This is the name of a river monster in the traditions and beliefs of the Teton Native American people of Missouri in the United States. Mi-Ni-Wa-Tu is described as a vast body with red fur, having an enormous head with a single eye and horn projecting from its forehead, and a long tail flattened vertically with tooth-like projections on its upper ridge. The Mi-Ni-Wa-Tu was said to move swiftly through the water, creating a wave before it and an iridescence on the water behind. In the spring it was his activities that were said to cause the enormous cracks across the frozen Missouri River. To see this being was terrifying as a sight, and the experience was said to bring about convulsions and even death.
References 134
See also monster

MINOTAUR, MINOTAUROS
This is the name of a humanoid monster in the classical mythology of Greece and Rome. The Minotaur, which means the "Bull of Minos," was described as having the body of a man but with the monstrous head of a huge bull. It was said to be kept in the deep labyrinth beneath the palace of Knossos in the island of Crete during the reign of King Minos. The legend relates how King Minos had been sent the Cretan Bull to make a sacrifice to the gods but substituted one of his inferior, mortal bulls. In punishment, the gods made his wife love the Cretan Bull, and the Minotaur was their hideous offspring, whose name is variously given as Asterion or Asterius. Not able to dispose of this semisupernatural being, the king ordered Daedalus to construct a labyrinth in which it was to be housed and fed. This monster was a cannibal, and King Minos took his tribute from other lands in the youth of their people to feed to the Minotaur. Then the hero Theseus was

Theseus and the Minotaur (Rose Photo Archive, UK)

sent to the island, having taken the place of one of the tribute prisoners. With the aid of a ball of string given to him by the king's daughter, Ariadne, he was able to kill the Minotaur and retrace his way to escape from the labyrinth.

References 7, 18, 20, 24, 47, 61, 78, 89, 125, 133, 166
See also Arzshenk, Asterion, cannibal, Cretan Bull, monster, Shen-Nung

MIODHCHAOIN, MIDCHÁIN, MOCHAEN

This is the name of an enormous and vicious giant in the Celtic legends of Ireland. Miodhchaoin, also known as Midcháin and Mochaen, was an ogre who inhabited and protected a hill in the northern region of Lochlainn. He had three sons, named Áed, Conn, and Corc. He rarely did battle, for he was so vast that his voice penetrated everything and could destroy humans. In the epic *Oidheadh Chlainne Tuireann*, Lug Lámfhota, knowing this, sent the three hated sons of Tuirenn to "take three shouts" from the ogre, with the inevitable result he desired.

References 128
See also giant, ogre

MIQQIAYUUQ

This is the name of a monster in the traditions and folk beliefs of the Inuit of eastern Hudson Bay in Canada. The Miqqiayuuq is described as being a large, faceless being covered in hair that inhabits the depths of the frozen freshwaters. It is a malicious being that will come to the edge of the frozen waters in winter for the express purpose of upending the lowered buckets in the icy water so that they do not fill when the Inuit pull them up again.

References 77
See also monster

MI'RAJ, AL-

This is a creature in the mythology of Islamic countries of North Africa and the Middle East. It is described as a supernatural yellow hare with a single horn protruding from its forehead. Its properties may be compared with the European tales of the unicorn.

References 89
See also Alicorn, Amduscias, Ass (Three-Legged), Biased na Srognig, Chio-Tuan, Karkadan, Ki Lin, Kirin, Koresck, Licorn, Onyx Monoceros, Scythian Ass, unicorn

MISHIPIZHIW

This is the name of a water monster in the traditions and beliefs of the Ojibwa and Algonquian Native American peoples of the United States. Mishipizhiw, also known as Mitchipissy, is described as having the body of a great, cat-like creature with a raised, saw-toothed ridge down its spine, extending to the long, sinuous tail with which it encircles its victims. With this tail, it is also said to raise fierce storms and waves on the surface of the water and whirlpools within the water that suck down unwary people in their boats. Accounts of Mishipizhiw were given as early as the seventeenth century by travelers, and an image of Lake Superior from 1850 shows a huge bow wave ahead of numerous boats for which there was no explanation.

References 134
See also Chief of Fishes, Great Horned Serpent, Great Lynx, Master of Fishes, Miskena, Tcipitckaam, Weewilmekq

MISIGANEBIC

This is the name of a monstrous serpent in the traditions and beliefs of the Algonquian Native American people of the United States. Misiganebic is described as a vast, thirty-foot-long, dark-green serpent that shines in a multitude of colors on the surface. He has a head resembling that of a horse and is sometimes categorized as a Horse-Head Serpent. Misiganebic is said to inhabit the waters of the Blue Sea Lakes, the Cedar Lakes, Lake Bitobi, Lake Deschênes, Lake Désert, Lake Pocknock, and Lake Trente-et-un Milles, where he performs the task of cleaning the waters of the lakes; he is given offerings in thanks at the cardinal points of the Blue Sea Lake. However, it is considered an omen of death to see Misiganebic, but, as his abode is thought to be a cavern in the bottom of Lake Pocknock and he hibernates in winter, this is very rare.

References 134
See also Horse Heads, serpent

MISIKINIPIK

This is the name of a vast earth serpent in the traditions and beliefs of the Cree Native American people of Canada. Misikinipik is described as an enormous primordial serpent with huge horns on its head that lives eternally beneath the land and the waters of the world. He is evil and aggressively allied to Michi-Pichoux and the Water Lynxes in making war on Wesuccechak and on the Thunder Beings.

References 77, 134
See also Michi-Pichoux, serpent

MISIKINUBICK

This is the name of a malicious and evil serpent in the traditions and beliefs of the Algonquian Native American people of the United States. Misikinubick is described as a huge, horn-headed, black serpent covered in fur. There is a legend of a Menominee man who acquired it as a guardian spirit but paid the price for its magic by having to kill his own two daughters.

References 134
See also Horned serpent, serpent

MISKENA
This is the name of a fish-serpent in the traditions and beliefs of the Native American people of Winnipeg, Canada. Miskena was described as a vast serpent with the head and foreparts resembling a gigantic sturgeon fish. Miskena was regarded as the Chief of the Fishes and the guardian of the sturgeon of Lake Winnipeg.
References 134
See also Missipissy

MISSIPISSY
This is the name of a fish-serpent in the traditions and beliefs of the Native American people of the Great Lakes region of Canada and the United States. Missipissy, also known as the Master of the Fishes, was described as similar to or even being the same as the Great Lynx. This monster was considered to be the guardian of the sturgeon fish that inhabited the lakes and hibernated in their depths during the long winters.
References 134
See also Mishipizhiw

MISTRESS OF THE LAKE
This is an alternative name for Lady of Lake Traun, a type of mermaid in the folklore of Austria.
References 134
See also Lady of Lake Traun, Sa-Yin

MITCHIPISSY
This is an alternative name for the Mishipizhiw in the traditions and beliefs of the Ojibwa Native American people of the United States.
References 134
See also Mishipizhiw

MNEMOSYNE
This is the name of one of the female Titans in the classical mythology of Greece and Rome. Her name means "Memory," and she was the daughter of Uranus and Gaia. By Zeus, the king of the Olympian gods, Mnemosyne bore the nine Muses.
References 20, 24, 38, 47, 78, 94, 125, 139, 166, 178, 182
See also Titan

MNEVIS
This is the name of a gigantic bull in the mythology of ancient Egypt. Mnevis, also known as Mnewer, was, like Apis, represented by a real bull of extraordinary stature. Mnevis was sacred to the sun god Ra and, as his "herald" was designated the bull of Heliopolis.
References 125
See also Apis

MOCHAEN
This is the name of an enormous and vicious giant in the Celtic legends of Ireland; Mochaen is also known as Midcháin and Miodhchaoin.

References 128
See also giant, Miodhchaoin

MOCK TURTLE
This is the name of a creature that appears in the classic work *Alice in Wonderland* by the English academic and author Lewis Carroll (Charles Lutwidge Dodgson, 1843–1898). It is part of the repertoire of strange beings that besets the heroine Alice as she goes farther down the rabbit hole into Wonderland. The Mock Turtle is described as looking like a turtle but with the head, rear feet, and tail of a calf. Alice and the Gryphon meet the Mock Turtle on a beach, where he sobs through his life history and demonstrates the Lobster Quadrille.

Mock Turtle Soup was a very well established, middle-income dish of the Victorian era; made of veal, it was a substitute for the real thing eaten by the nobility, hence the Mock Turtle's constant anxiety and sadness and his hybrid form.
References 7, 40
See also Griffin

MODI
This is the name of a giant in the Norse mythology of Scandinavia. Together with his brother, Magni, Modi, whose name means "Courage," is a son of the giantess Iarnsaxa.
References 78
See also giant, giantess, Iarnsaxa

MOKÊLE-MBÊMBE
This is the name of a marine monster in the early travelers' lore of the West African coast. The Mokêle-Mbêmbe was said to be a monster resembling an elephant but having a single horn from its head and a tail resembling that of a crocodile or a scaly serpent. It was said to inhabit the cliff cavern of the Congo coastline and to resent humans so much that it would attack and upturn their boats. The Groot Slang and Iriz Ima are said to be similar monsters of the same region.
References 47, 63, 89
See also Iriz Ima, monster, serpent

MOKO
This is the name of a monster in the traditions and beliefs of the Mangaian people of the Cook Islands in the Pacific. Moko, also known as Tu-Te-Wehiwehi, is described as having the body of a lizard but the head of a man. This Great Lizard was also a master of magic and able to protect his human descendants.
References 113
See also monster

MOLIONIDS
This is the name of monstrous twins in the classical mythology of Greece and Rome. The Molionids, also

known as the Actoridæ or Actorione, were said to be the sons of Molione by Actor or the sea god Poseidon/Neptune. They were hatched from a silver egg. In earlier legends they were two separate beings named Cteatus and Eurytus. However in later myths they were described as having a single body from which two heads, four arms, and four legs emerged. The Molionids joined their uncle, Augeas, in his war with the hero Hercules/Heracles and were killed by him at Cleonæ.
References 139, 178

MOLL WALBEE

This is the name of a giantess in the legends of the Marches country of Wales and the West of England. Moll Walbee was reputed to have built Hay Castle in a single night by taking great stones from the Brecon Mountains; she dropped some stones from her apron in the process, one of which became the enormous standing stone in Llowes churchyard. This giantess was derived from a real historical person called Matilda de Saint Valery, the wife of Baron William de Braose, during the period of the reign of King John (1167–1216). The diminutive of Matilda being Maud or Moll, her name was translated into the Welsh as Malld Walbri. She had a fierce reputation and so successfully resisted the onslaught of the Welsh, in the absence of her husband, at Castell Paen (Painscastle in English), that the place became known in Latin as Castrum Matildis, or Matilda's Castle. Her reputation became legendary in the folklore of her adversaries as the mountain- and castle-building giantess.
References 183
See also giantess

MONK FISH

This is the name of a marine creature widely reported in the travelers' and seafaring tales of the medieval period in Europe. The description given by Ambroise Paré (1517–1590) in his work *On Monsters and Marvels*, was of a type of humanoid-looking fish closely resembling a merman. The Monk fish was credited with the head of a human with a tonsured hairstyle like that of a monk and a monk's cowl on a cape about its shoulders. Its fish-like body, covered in scales, was supported vertically on two extremely large flippers, with similar flippers for arms. Sightings of this creature were reported in Copenhagen, Denmark, off the coast of Norway, and in the northern seas off the coast of Poland between 1200 and 1600. A similar description was given to the Hai Ho Shang in China during the same period.
References 7, 89, 147
See also Hai Ho Shang, merman

MONOCENTAUR, MONOCENTAURUS

The Monocentaur, also known as the Onocentaur, was later included in the works of Isidore of Seville (c.

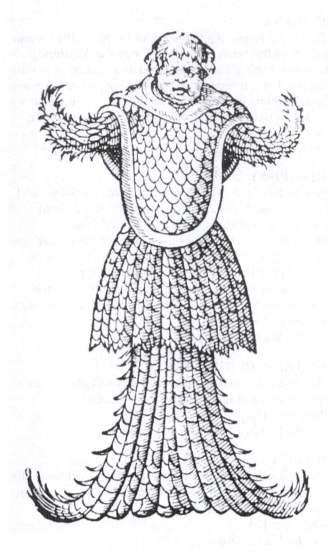

The Monk fish was credited with a tonsured hairstyle like that of a monk and a monk's cowl on a cape about its shoulders. (On Monsters and Marvels by Ambroise Paré, trans. by Janis L. Pallister, University of Chicago Press, 1982)

560–636) and in bestiaries of the medieval period. It is described as having the torso and head of a man but the body and legs of an ass.
References 7, 20, 78, 89, 91, 125, 133, 168
See also centaur, Onocentaur

MONOCEROS

The Monoceros appears in two different contexts in literature.

1. This is the name of a monstrous hybrid first included in the work *Historia Naturalis* (A.D. 77) by the Roman naturalist Pliny the Elder. It was described as having the body of a horse but with the feet of an elephant and a tail like that of a boar, but its head, which was like that of a deer, had the most enormous, straight, black horn protruding from the front of its

forehead to about four feet in length. The Monoceros was considered to be highly dangerous to humans, and although the horn was valued in much the same way as that of the Unicorn, no one was able to get anywhere near without considerable risk to their lives. By the Middle Ages, the Monoceros appeared in many bestiaries, and although it was sometimes confused with the Unicorn, many illustrations showed the characteristic thick feet that distinguished it from the more gentle beast. In an Anglo-Saxon bestiary in the Bodleian Library, Oxford, this monster is credited with a most "horrible bray" and its possibility of being killed but never taken alive. Such was its fame that the "mighty Monoceros with immeasured tayles" (II, xii, 23) was included by the Elizabethan poet Edmund Spenser (c. 1552–1599) in his work *The Faerie Queene* (1590).

2. This is the name of a marine monster in the later travelers' and seafaring tales of the seventeenth century onward in Europe. It was described as a vast, seagoing, serpentine fish that had the most enormous horn on the top of its head with which it attacked and sank ships. This earlier monster (probably a distorted description of the Narwhal) was extended in a famous development of the Monoceros theme in a story by E. Hoffmann Price, *The House of the Monoceros* (1941). In this tale, a terrifying Unicorn sea serpent, with its lair below an old castle in the county of Cornwall in England, was steadily devouring all the young people of the region. The Monoceros was the totemic guardian of the Treganeths of Treganeth Castle, whose guardianship was bought by human sacrifice. It was, of course, finally defeated.
References 7, 14, 63, 134, 148, 185
See also monster, serpent, unicorn

MONOCEROS MARINUS
This is the name given to a marine monster in the region of Westphalia in Lower Saxony (now Germany) and in the Tramin region of Austria during the medieval period. The Monoceros Marinus was depicted in the medieval frescoes at Zillis as a vast, fish-like creature with an enormous extended horn protruding from the center of its head. It was said to inhabit the murky depths of the lake known as the Darmsee. It is possibly one and the same as the Monoceros, shown in medieval bestiaries as inhabiting the *Marae saeculi*, the world's oceans, as an agent of the devil.
References 10, 134
See also Monoceros, monster

MONOCOLI
This is the name of a monstrous humanoid race in the travelers' lore of medieval Europe. The Monocoli

were said to have only one leg and foot and to inhabit the wastes of Ethiopia. Although they had but one foot, this did not prevent them from speedy movement. Furthermore, the foot was so enormous that they could lie on their backs in the midday heat and extend their leg and foot over them to provide shade in the treeless landscape.
References 63
See also Cyclopedes, Monoscelans, Sciapods

MONOSCELANS
This is an alternative name for the Monocoli and Sciapods, races of one-legged people in the lore of medieval European travelers.
References 7
See also Cyclopedes, Monocoli, Sciapods

MONSTER
There has always been a fascination for the monstrous, and depictions of monstrous beings have been known from the earliest times. What actually constitutes a monster depends on the cultural values in which the image is depicted. That which is deemed to be monstrous is against the natural order of what is acceptable, and this is usually the image of nature and human natural forms. Consequently, even some being that is of an abnormal size may be regarded as monstrous yet still be acceptable. It is, however, those beings that constitute a supernatural hybrid mix of other forms that bring the most revulsion and are most likely to be considered monstrous. Composite forms of beings abound in the ancient mythologies, especially of Mesopotamia and Babylon, from where the winged bulls and the eagle-lion Griffin emanated. Ancient Greek mythology gave us the serpent-woman Echidne, the goat-lion Chimera, the many-headed Lernean Hydra, the man-bull Minotaur, the horse-men Centaurs, and many more. In India, the monsters are such as the Makara, a hybrid crocodile and bird, Jataya, a humanoid bird, and the Kimpurushas, who were horse-men. In Europe, especially during the medieval period and the early exploration of other lands, monsters were described in ecclesiastical texts and secular books such as bestiaries. Some were derived from the ancient mythologies, like the Griffin, while others were biblical, such as the Leviathan and the Apocalyptic Beasts; others such as the Aspidochelone were travelers' depictions of possibly exaggerated natural phenomena. In the Americas, the Native American people had a tradition rich in lake monsters such as Mashernomak, Piasa, and Hiintcabiit, cannibal monsters such as Raw Gums, and humanoid monsters such as Nalusa Falaya.

Folklore also plays a part in cultures throughout the world where a similar phenomenon is

Monsters at Roland's descent (Rose Photo Archive, UK)

experienced but is given different names, such as the Werewolf that is known in the shape of animals in most cultures. The vampire has its counterpart in countries as diverse as those in Central Europe, Central America, and South East Asia. These folkloric motifs have also proved a fertile ground for literature and popular culture where horror stories constitute a form of entertainment. Such tales as that of Dracula, Frankenstein's Monster, and King Kong were preceded by over a thousand years with the Anglo-Saxon epic *Beowulf* and the monster Grendel. Ancient monsters are still the subject of investigation, such as the Loch Ness Monster and the Seljordsorm, and new ones are being "discovered," such as Fire-Drakes of J. R. R. Tolkien and the Great Galactic Ghoul of space exploration.

References 24, 77, 94, 113, 147, 174, 186

See also Apis, Apocalyptic Beasts, Aspidochelone, cannibal, centaur, Cerberus, Chimera, Dracula, Fire-Drakes, Frankenstein's Monster, Galactic Ghoul, Grendel, Grendel's mother, Griffin, Hecate, Hiintcabiit, Hydra, Jataya, Kimpurushas, King Kong, Lamia, Leviathan, Loch Ness Monster, Makara, Mashernomak, Melusine, Minotaur, Nalusa Falaya, ogre, Piasa, Raw Gums, Seljordsorm, vampire, Werewolf

MONSTER OF BROMPTON

This is the name given to a monster by way of its habitation as it was sighted at Lake Brompton, also known as Antoné Outunwitti, in the eastern region of the United States. It was described variously as looking like a big, green fish, its back extended eight feet in length above the waters of the lake, or as a grayish silhouette having three humps and a head like a horse but with bristles from its mouth. Whatever its description, it frequently gave a fright to fishermen who came close enough to have to avoid colliding with it, as it swam so fast through the waters that its wake was over 250 feet long. It was sighted several times during the 1970s, but the waters were too murky for any creature to be seen by a search team.

References 134

See also Loch Ness Monster, monster

MONSTER OF LAKE FAGUA

This is the name of a monster in the folklore of the region of Lake Fagua, Chile. It was mentioned in a broadsheet of 1784, now held in the Bibliotheque Nationale of Paris. The description related that this monster had a long, serpentine body with wings and one pointed tail, which it used as a spear, and another with "rings," or suckers, with which it grabbed its victims. Its head was described as having huge ears like that of a donkey, a face like a human, huge horns

from the top of its head, and a long mane like that of a horse. This monstrous creature terrified the whole population with its predations at night, when it emerged from the lake to devour the local livestock.

References 134

See also Guirivilu, monster

MONSTER OF LOCH AWE

This is a monster that was not defined clearly but was described as being of considerable size and inhabiting the depths of Loch Awe in the Highlands of Scotland. This enormous being had considerable strength and could be heard in winter breaking the ice on the surface of the loch as it rose from the bottom.

References 134

See also Loch Ness Monster

MONYCHUS

This is the name of one of the centaurs in the classical mythology of Greece and Rome. Monychus, whose name may mean "Single-hoofed" or "Solid–hoofed," had such great strength that in battle he would uproot trees and hurl them at their adversaries like javelins.

References 178

See also centaur

MOOGIE

This is the name of a monster reported in the legends of the Ozark Native American people in the United States. The Moogie was said to be a lizard-like monster that inhabited the Ozark Mountains.

References 94

See also monster

MORA

This is an alternative name for the Echeneis, or Remora, a monstrous fish described by Roman historians.

References 18, 89

See also Echeneis

MORAG

This is the name of a monster in the folklore of the Scottish Highlands around the thousand-foot-deep Loch Morar. Morag is more generally known as Mhorag.

References 78

See also Bunyip, Loch Ness Monster, Mhorag, Peiste

MORGAN

This is the name of a type of merman in the folklore and traditions of Wales. The Morgan inhabited freshwater lakes and would abduct any unwary or naughty children playing there unattended, devouring them in its murky depths. This being is clearly used as a Nursery bogie, but its origins may

The Morgan is a type of merman in the folklore and traditions of Wales. (Rose Photo Archive, UK)

have been in the Arthurian Morgan le Fay or the Celtic Breton Morgens. The fact that this name is used in Wales for a merman Rhys attributes to the Welsh use of Morgan only as a man's name.
References 24, 120
See also mermaid, merman, Triton

MORGANTE

This is the name of a giant in the early literature of Italy. Morgante was the benevolent giant who featured in the work *Il Morgante Maggiore* (Morgante the Giant, 1481) by Luigi Pulci (1432–1484). Morgante was originally a very fierce and belligerent giant who was later converted by Orlando to Christianity and became a caring and benevolent being who saved Perceforest from condemnation as a heretic. Later in the narrative Morgante took up the trade of brewer. The tale is a mixture of the burlesque and serious debate characteristic of the Middle Ages. Morgante was widely used within later literary works, especially those of Teofilo Folengro (1491–1554), the Spanish author Miguel de Cervantes Saavedra (1547–1616), and the French author François Rabelais (ca. 1494–ca. 1553) in his work *Pantagruel* (1532) and later *Gargantua* (1534), where Morgante was considered to be one of the ancestors of Pantagruel.
References 61, 174
See also Fierabras, Fracassus, giant, Pantagruel

MORGUAN

This is the name of a giant in the classical literature of France. Morguan is one of the giant ancestors of

Pantagruel in the famous work *Pantagruel* (1532) by the French author François Rabelais (ca. 1494–ca. 1553). But Morguan does not appear in the original edition; he is an addition to later versions by Rabelais, as a means of establishing the genealogy of Pantagruel. Morguan, along with five other giants— Etion, Gabbara, Galehaut, Happemousche, and Eryx—is credited with inventing something concerned with drinking.
References 174
See also Bruyer, Chalbroth, Daughters of Cain, Eryx, Gabbara, Galehaut, Gargantua, giant, Happemousche, Hurtaly, Noachids, Noah, Pantagruel

MORHOLT

This is the name of a giant in the Celtic traditions and legends of Britain. Morholt was the half-brother of Moraunt, the king of Ireland who led a raid into Cornwall on the southernmost peninsula of England. They demanded tribute from King Mark. During the ensuing battle, Morholt was killed by Tristan/Tristram, King Mark's nephew born of Queen Elizabeth of Lyonesse. But Tristram received poisoned wounds and was saved by the lovely Iseult, leading to their legendary, ill-fated love affair.
References 54, 133, 174
See also giant

MORMO, MORMOLYCE

This is the name of a monster in the beliefs of the population of ancient Rome. The Mormo, or Mormolyce, possibly meaning "Banewolf" or "Werewolf," was described as a monstrous female who had originally been a queen of the Laestrigonians and had been deprived of her children. The grief had turned her into a monster that abducted and took the children of others in revenge. She later became a sort of Nursery bogie used by Roman mothers to threaten their children into good behavior.
References 24, 64, 125, 160
See also Lamia, monster, Werewolf

MORUADH, MORUACH

These are alternative names for the Merrow in the folklore of Ireland.
References 21, 24, 25
See also mermaid, Merrow

MOSHIRIIKKWECHEP

This is the name of a monstrous fish in the mythology and folk beliefs of Japan. The Moshiriikkwechep, whose name may be translated as "World Backbone Trout," was one of the first beings created, and as a result the fish supports the world upon its back. However, it is so vast that when it writhes it sends shockwaves along the earth over it. So it had to be secured in the mud under the oceans, and two sea gods usually keep it there, but every now and again it wriggles free, causing earthquakes and tsunamis until it is brought under control again.

References 133

See also Jinshin Uwo, Jishin-Mushi, Kami, Midgard serpent

MOSKITTO

This is a creature from the folklore of lumberjacks and forest workers, especially in Wisconsin and Minnesota in the United States, during the nineteenth and early twentieth centuries. The Moskitto belongs to a group of beings affectionately known as the Fearsome Critters, whose exaggerated proportions and activities not only explained the wierd noises of the lonely landscape but also provided some amusement at camps. It almost certainly derived from the swamplands and hot steamy summers, when the true mosquito was a great pest, and developed into a monstrous insect.

References 7, 24

See also Fearsome Critters

MOTHER OF THE FISHES

This is the name of a terrifyingly vast fish said to inhabit the River Elster in the region of Voigtland. Whilst this creature was said to be the guardian of the aquatic creatures there, this monster was also said to bring about catastrophe for the region if it were seen on the surface by any humans.

References 134

See also King of the Fishes, monster, Queen of the Fishes

MOULAY ABDELKADER DJILANI

This is the name of one of the leaders of the Djinns in the traditions and folklore of the people of Morocco.

References 122, 160

See also Djinn

MOUNTAIN MAN

This is the name of a monstrous humanoid in the traditions and folklore of Japan. The Mountain Man is described as an enormous, strong being covered in hair like an ape, living in the woods and forests on the mountainsides. The local population hardly ever sees him, but they are terrified and leave offerings of food to placate him.

References 113

See also Bigfoot, Wild Man of the Woods, Yeti

MOUNTAIN STEM-WINDER

This is an alternative name for the Guyascutus in the folklore of lumberjacks and forest workers (and later fraudsters), especially in Wisconsin and Minnesota in the United States.

References 7

See also Fearsome Critters, Guyascutus

MOUNTAIN WOMAN

This is the name of a demonic giantess in the legends and folklore of Japan. The Mountain Woman is described as being extremely strong and enormous yet able to fly through the air. She lives in the forests and woodlands on the mountainsides, where she will attack and consume any foolish travelers who enter her territory without caution.

References 113

See also giantess

MSI-KINEPIKWA

This is the name of the Great Reptile, also known as Kinepikwa, in the traditions and beliefs of the Shawnee Native American people of the United States. This massive, supernatural serpent apparently is not created in that image from the beginning but, like the earth reptiles, gradually gets to its final form by shedding its previous ones. However, with the Msi-Kinepikwa, as one legend relates, the first stage was that of a fawn with one red and one blue horn that was immersed in its lake. As it grew, it moved to the water's edge, shedding that form until the serpent form of Msi-Kinepikwa finally emerged.

References 134

See also serpent

MUCHALINDA, MUCALINDA

This is the name of the gigantic cobra snake, the king of the Nagas, in the Buddhist beliefs of India. Muchalinda, also known as Mucalinda or Musilinda, perceived that Buddha was unaware of an approaching violent storm as he meditated under the great Bo tree. The king of the Nagas transformed his vast Naga serpent shape and coiled himself around both the Bo tree and the Buddha seven times, then spread his hood to give shelter. When the storm had passed, Muchalinda transformed to the shape of a young man and paid his respects to Buddha.

References 24, 47, 113, 133, 139, 160

See also serpent, Shesha, Naga

MUCHUKUNDA

This is the name of a monstrous giant in the Hindu mythology of India. One legend tells how the borders of India were being threatened by a foreign invader called Kala-Yavana. As the armies moved into the region, the god Krishna went to meet Kala-Yavana and asked him to visit the great cavern of

Muchukunda. As the giant was slumbering, the arrogant King Kala-Yavana poked the giant so hard that he awoke. What Kala-Yavana did not know was the power of the giant's eyes, for the minute they opened they pierced straight to the center of the body of Kala-Yavana, and he was totally consumed with fire, leaving only a pile of ashes where he had stood.
References 112
See also giant

MUGWUMP
This is a creature from the folklore of lumberjacks and forest workers, especially in Wisconsin and Minnesota in the United States, during the nineteenth and early twentieth centuries. The Mugwump belongs to a group of beings affectionately known as the Fearsome Critters, whose exaggerated proportions and activities not only explained the wierd noises of the lonely landscape but also provided some amusement at camps. Even in the twentieth century, this name had come to mean some creature, or even a human, that was completely stupid.
References 7, 24
See also Fearsome Critters

MUILEARTEACH, MUILEARTACH, MUILIDHEARTACH, MUIREATACH, MUIR LEARTACH
This is the name of an evil sea giantess in the folklore of the Scottish Highlands. Like the Caileach Bheur, Muileatach is described as a hideous bald hag with a blue-gray face and one staring eye. She lives in a watery Celtic underworld, and when she rises from it she causes great storms. Sometimes she emerges from the shore as a dripping, pathetic old woman hammering at the door of fisherfolks' cottages begging for shelter. But no one should ever let her in, for once inside she swells up to enormous, terrifying size, wreaking havoc within. She can, however, be benevolent; with the pot of balsam she carries she can heal the sick or wounded, and she can restore the dead to life by poking her wizened finger into their mouths.
References 24, 128, 160, 170
See also Caileach Bheur, giantess, Muircartach

MUIRCARTACH
This is the name of the old hag giantess of the sea in the traditions and Gaelic mythology of Ireland. She is the Irish counterpart of the Scottish Muilearteach, but unlike her, the Muircartach is bald with a black face and a single eye protruding from the middle of her forehead.
References 7
See also giantess, Muilearteach

MUIRDRIS
This is an alternative name for a monster in Irish legend, known as the Sínach, in the later manuscripts of the legends. The Muirdris was described as a fearsome sea creature in the early texts, where the name "Muirdris" is mostly used, and whose adversary, Fergus mac Léti, vanquished the beast in Lough Rudraige in County Down.
References 128
See also Caoránach, Oilliphéist, Sínach

MUIR-GHEILT
This is an alternative name for the Merrow in the folklore of Ireland.
References 21, 24, 25
See also mermaid, Merrow

MUIT
This is a regional name for the Rainbow Serpent in the Dreamtime mythology of the Native Australian people.
References 133
See also Rainbow Serpent

MÛMARKIL
This is the name of monstrous beasts in the literary works of the English academic and author J. R. R. Tolkien (1892–1973) in The Hobbit (1937) and The Lord of the Rings (1955). The Mûmarkil, known to the Hobbits as Oliphaunts, were described as vast elephantine beasts with enormous, pointed tusks, said to be the ancestors of the smaller elephant. The Mûmarkil were brought by Harad as beasts of battle into the War of the Ring during the Third Age of the Sun. They carried great "castles" on their backs full of archers, and those that were not killed in the land of Gondor from these archers were crushed under the mighty beasts or speared on their vast tusks. They were only vulnerable when archers managed to shoot their unprotected eyes, and when this happened the blinded beasts thrashed about in the battlefield, killing anything and everyone, including their own army.
References 51
See also monster

MUNGA MUNGA
This is the name of the monstrous daughter of the female monster Kunapipi in the traditions and beliefs of the Native Australian people.
References 38
See also Kunapipi, monster

MUNINN
This is the name of a monstrous raven in the Norse mythology of Scandinavia. Muninn, whose name may be translated as "Memory," and the raven Hugin,

Sea serpents much like the fearsome Muirdris (Rose Photo Archive, UK)

whose name may be translated as "Thought," are the supernatural birds of the Norse king of the gods, Odin. At dawn each day these monstrous birds flew above the earth and saw and heard everything in the worlds of humans, giants, and gods. Then they returned before sunrise to deliver all the information to their master.
References 7, 139
See also Yata Garasu

MURDHUACHA

This is one of the alternative names for the Merrow in the folklore of Ireland.
References 21, 24, 25, 160, 170
See also mermaid, Merrow

MUREX

This is the name of a creature in the traditions and legends of European travelers, fishermen, and sailors. The Murex was described by Pliny the Elder in his *Historia Naturalis* (A.D. 77) as a monstrous purple fish with such strong jaws that it had the ability to latch on to the hull of a ship in the sea with such a strong

grip that it could prevent it from sailing away. Pliny compared the Murex with the Remora or Echeneis, of which he held the opinion that Mark Antony lost the Battle of Actium because he was held fast by one of these creatures on the hull of his ship.
References 18, 89
See also Echeneis

MURGHI-I-ĀDAMI

This is the joint name of two fabulous birds in the mythology of Islamic countries. These two birds are described as resembling peacocks with human faces and the ability to speak like humans. It was said that, should anyone see them sitting together talking, if they listened carefully they would hear much of interest to them. Tales of these Murghi-i-Ādami were brought to Europe by travelers during the medieval period.
References 89

MURRISK

This is the name of a monstrous deadly marine fish in the legends and folklore of Ireland said to inhabit the

coastal region of Croagh Patrick. The Murrisk was said to be so poisonous that if it disgorged the contents of its stomach into the water all the aquatic life was killed. The fumes from its mouth polluted the air so badly that even the birds fell dead from the sky and all that breathed in the region was infected with sickness.
References 7

MUŠHUŠŠU, MUSHHHUSH, MUSHUSSU

This is the name of a vast cosmic dragon in the mythology of ancient Babylon and Mesopotamia. Mušhuššu, also known as Sirrush, was depicted as having an enormous body of a dragon, ending in the tail of a serpent with a poisonous sting; its hind legs were those of an eagle while its foreparts, including the legs, were those of a lion; its head was that of a snake but with horns and projections from the top of its head down its neck. The whole creature was covered in plate-like scales and was the guardian at the Ishtar gate of the city of Babylon, associated with the god Marduk.
References 7, 89, 136
See also dragon, serpent

MUSILINDA

This is an alternative name for Muchalinda, the King of the Nagas, in the Buddhist mythology of India.

References 139
See also Muchalinda, Nagas, serpent

MUSPEL

This is the name of a giant in the Norse mythology of Scandinavia. He was a Fire Giant that lived in Muspelheim with all his progeny.
References 20
See also Fire Giant, giant, Jotun

MYSTERY OF THE WATERS

This is a collective name for lake monsters in the traditions and beliefs of the Coeur d'Alene Native American people of British Columbia, Canada. The name serves as a euphemism for the monsters, whose appearance could destroy the uninitiated. One tale relates how some young women who were bathing in the Saint Joe River saw a curiously huge fish; four of them swam out to get a better look. They never returned, and only much later were their companions able to identify the four scalps found by the beach of a lake in the mountains as those of their four friends. It was presumed that a "Mystery of the Waters" had consumed them and left their remains by another lake from an underground connection.
References 134
See also monster, Naitaka, serpent

N

NABON
This is the name of a giant in the Arthurian legends of Britain. Nabon was the lord of the island of Servage. He was killed by the Cornish hero Tristan/Tristram, who served King Mark of Cornwall.
References 54
See also giant, Morholt

NÄCKEN
This is the name of the Scandinavian Nicker, or water monster, in the traditions and folklore of the people of Sweden.
References 20, 37, 107, 120, 111, 160
See also Nicker

NAGA MAS
This is the name of a gigantic sea monster in the legends and folklore of the Malay people of West Malaysia. Naga Mas, also known as the Golden Dragon, was the unfortunate son of Raja Budiman and the brother of Prince Lela Muda.
References 113
See also dragon, serpent

NAGA PAHODA
This is the name of a king of the serpents in the traditions and beliefs of Indonesia. Naga Pahoda is described as a vast primordial serpent that is the king of the oceans in which he dwells. He was credited with being instrumental in the shaping of the islands of Indonesia. The tradition relates that when the daughter of the supreme god Batara Guru fell from the heavens toward the primodial ocean, Naga Pahoda waited in the depths to consume her. However, Batara Guru scattered dust down to form a dry place to save her, and when Naga Pahoda writhed up out of the depths to flood the island that had formed, the lord of the heavens again threw iron dust to stabilize the earth that had taken shape. But the evil Naga Pahoda still tried to reach the child and with each writhing broke through the earth or heaved it up such that, although he was unsuccessful, the new land became a group of islands with vast mountains and valleys.
References 133
See also Naga, serpent

NAGA/S, NAGINI/S
These names are applied to different classes of beings in different cultures:

1. These are the names of the male and female serpent beings in the myths and legends of India. The Nagas and Naginis, said to be descendants of Kadru and Kasyapa, are described as being human to the waist and a serpent from the waist down. Sometimes they are described as having many heads and being of different hues. The Nagas live in beautiful underwater palaces in Bhagavati or, according to other myths, under the earth in Nagaloka. Their wives, who are called Naginis, are said to be extremely beautiful. They are ruled by their king, Ananta-Shesha, who protects and supports the god Vishnu and who is equated in the *Ramayana* with Ravana. The Buddha was protected by a Naga king named Muchalinda. In general, their relationship with the deities and humans is ambivalent, sometimes malicious and evil and, at other times, benevolent. Their avowed enemy is the Garuda bird, which will pursue the Nagas to release the earth's waters. The epic *Mahabharata* tells of their being vanquished through the sacrifice of Janamejaya. In modern Hindu belief, Kārkotaka is the king of Nagas that controls the weather, especially the coming of the rains.

2. The Nagas have a quite different description in other cultures. In Indonesia and Thailand the Naga is a five-headed dragon that is usually the guardian of temples. However, in West Malaysia the Nagas are a species of multiheaded marine dragon of horrifying proportions of whom the fisherfolk are terrified.
References 18, 47, 78, 87, 89, 112, 113, 120, 125, 133, 160, 166
See also Ananta, Garuda, Muchalinda, serpent, Shesha, Takshaka, Vasuki

NAGINI BESANDI

This is the name of a Naga female, known as a Nagini, who was born to the Nagas but who took a mortal king, Duttabaung of Burma, as her consort. In both India and in Burma, many royal families trace their descent from Nagas, in much the same way as the French royal family traced theirs from Melusine.
References 41, 160
See also Melusine, Naga, Nagini Besandi

NAHGANE

This is the name of a race of giants in the traditions and folk beliefs of the Slavey/Etchareottine people of British Columbia, Canada. The Nahgane are terrifying Bush Giants that will abduct any unwary or unattended child. In this respect these giants may have been used as a form of Nursery bogie to ensure that children did not wander away from adults.
References 77
See also giant, Nursery bogie

NAITAKA

This is the name of a monster, also known as the Monster of Lake Okonagen, in the traditions and folklore of the Shushwap Native American people of British Columbia, Canada. Naitaka is described as a vast lake monster that inhabited a cave accessible only through tunnels under an island in the middle of the lake. This being was so terrifying in its pursuit of those who tried to cross the lake that humans would take offerings of effigies and paint the image of Naitaka on rocks to prevent its wrath. One legend relates how a family that did not make these observations was swamped by the waters of the lake and disappeared. Their canoe was discovered strangely perched high in the mountains some years later.
References 134
See also monster

NÄKINEITSI

This is an alternative name for the Näkineiu, or mermaid, in the traditions and folk beliefs of the people of Estonia.
References 120, 160
See also mermaid, Näkineiu

NÄKINEIU

This is the name of the female Näkki in the traditions and folk beliefs of Estonia. Näkineiu, also known as the Näkineitsi, is described, much like the British mermaid, as a beautiful, blonde-haired maiden to the waist with the tail of a fish below. She is frequently to be seen on the water combing her long, golden hair or looking after her water cattle in the waves.
References 120, 160
See also Mermaid, Merrow, Näkinneito

NÄKINNEITO

This is the name of the female Näkki in the traditions and folk beliefs of Finland. The Näkinneito is described, much like the British mermaid, as a beautiful, blonde-haired maiden with a gleaming white body to the waist and the tail of a fish below. This female water being is well endowed with such voluptuous breasts that she is able to throw them over her shoulder. Näkinneito is frequently to be seen on the water combing her long, curly hair. However, no matter how alluring she may seem, she is just as dangerous to human fishermen and sailors, whom she lures to their doom in the depths of the waters.
References 120, 160
See also Mermaid, Näkineiu

NÄKKI

This is the name of a fearsome water being in the traditions and folk beliefs of Finland and Estonia. The Näkki is said to be an attendant of the water god Ahto in his underwater kingdom, where they have magnificent, jewelled palaces. In Estonia, however, this monstrous being inhabits the most dangerous whirlpools, which suck down any fishing vessel too close; the crew would all be prey to the monster. At other times the Näkki will surface in the eddies of the whirlpool and drive his herd of cows to the shore, where he may entice human prey.

In western Finland in particular, the Näkki is described as a giant water-horse, much like the Kelpie of Scotland. At other times the Näkki is described as a type of centaur that may emerge onto land by the lakes in the mornings and evenings. This being is a predatory monster that will entice humans closer to him and then will drag them to their doom under the water.
References 119, 134, 139, 160
See also centaur, Cows of Näkki, Kelpy, monster, Nökk

NALMUQTSE

This is the name of a giant figure in the traditions and folk beliefs of the Kutenai Native American people of the United States. Because of his size, Nalmuqtse spent most of his time traveling on all fours. Even when he traveled over vast distances, giving names to the things of the earth, he moved on all fours, leaving great rifts and scars that became topographical features. However, at last he stood up, but as he did so his head smashed against the heavens, tossing his powerful headdress from his head. With his power dislodged, Nalmuqtse could no longer sustain his vitality and died.
References 77
See also giant

NALUSA FALAYA

This is the name of a class of humanoid monsters in the traditions and beliefs of the Choctaw Native American people of the United States. The Nalusa Falaya are described as having hairy human shapes with wizened faces, small eyes, and pointed ears. Their offspring are credited with detaching their skins and traveling as glowing creatures in the swampland edges while their parents call to unwary travelers in the dark. The effect of seeing one of these Nalusa Falaya is so terrifying that a human will collapse. While in this state the monsters will stab the human with sharp spines and instill them with malevolence toward their fellow humans. When the human returns to camp, the human will attack friends without knowing why.
References 77
See also Kashehotapolo, monster

NAMORODO, THE

This is the name of humanoid monsters in the traditions and beliefs of the Native Australian people of northern Arnhem Land in northern Australia. The Namorodo were described as having the shape of humans, but they were only the skeletal structure held by ligaments, through which the winds of the desert howled. In the traditions of the vampires of western Europe, the Namorodo rested during the day but at night flew to the homes of sleeping humans. There, if they could gain entry, they would turn them into Namorodo by draining their blood from their bodies as they slept.
References 133
See also vampire

NAMTAR

This is the name of a gigantic serpent in the mythology of ancient Egypt. Namtar is the guardian of the entrance to the underworld and also the guardian of the sun god Ra when he leaves the western horizon for his night journey through the darkness.
References 125, 160
See also Aapep, Mehen, serpent

NANDI

This is the name of a gigantic bull in the Hindu mythology of India. Nandi is described as an enormous, milk-white creature that is the steed of the god Shiva and leader of the Ganas. This bull was said to be the offspring of Kasyapa and Surahbi, and he has a consort named Nandini. Nandi not only provides the transport for Shiva but is also the guardian of his temples, and his image is to be seen there prominently. This being is also the provider of celestial music for Shiva's dance and is the guardian of all other animals.
References 24, 112, 139, 169
See also Nandini

NANDINI

This is the name of the cow that is the consort of Nandi in the Hindu mythology of India. Nandini is said to be the granter of entreaties and wishes.
References 112
See also Audumla, Nandi

NARA, NARAS

This is a race of horses in the Hindu mythology of India. They are described as huge beautiful horses with wings, like Pegasus in the classical mythology of Greece and Rome. Naras are the transport of the god Kubera in his journeys across the heavens.
References 112
See also Pegasus

NASHAS, NASNAS

The Nashas were a type of Djinn in the pre-Islamic folk beliefs of the Yemen and the Hadramut. They were said to be the offspring of humans and the Shiqq. The Nashas, also known as the Nasnas or Nesnás, are a hideous combination of half-human and half-Djinn, which means that they have only one arm, one leg, and half a head. Another group that inhabited the island of Ráïj in the China Sea appeared with bats' wings. Another type of Nasha had no head or neck, but its eyes and mouth were in its chest, like the Blemyes of medieval European lore; these were hunted by the inhabitants of Yemen as a source of meat.
References 64, 160
See also Biasd Bheulach, Blemmyes, Direach, Djinn, Empusa, Fachan, Hai-uri, Paija, Shiqq

NAUL

This is the name of a gigantic bird in the legends and folklore of Russia. The Naul is described as a hybrid that resembled a dragon with the head and talons of an eagle. It features in a legend concerning Vol'ga Buslavlevich, whose men were hunting birds. In order to trap the birds, they strung nets between the trees, and Vol'ga Buslavlevich transformed himself into a Naul to scare them into the trap.
References 55
See also Roc

NDZOODZOO

This is the name of a type of unicorn to be found in the legends of the peoples of South Africa.
See also unicorn

NEBROD

This is an alternative spelling of the name of the biblical giant Nimrod.
References 99, 174
See also Nimrod

NEE-GUED

This is the name for the legendary Yeti in the traditions and beliefs of the people of Sikkim, India. This gigantic humanoid monster is said to inhabit the slopes in the mountain range of Kanchenjunga.
References 61
See also Bigfoot, Yeti

NEHEBKAU

This is the name of a hybrid monster in the mythology of ancient Egypt. Nehebkau was said to have been created in the form of a human, but after devouring several coils of the world–serpent, Aapep, he sprouted a snake's head and the stinging tail of a scorpion. In this terrible shape he was sent as a guardian to the underworld but used the poisons he possessed to cure humans of the bites inflicted by snakes and scorpions.
References 38, 125, 133
See also monster, Naga

NELLIE LONG ARMS, NELLIE LONG-ARMS

This is the name of a vicious female monster in the folklore of Derbyshire, Cheshire, Lancashire, Shropshire, and Yorkshire in England. Nelly Long-arms is described as a humanoid monster with long, green hair and teeth and enormously extended arms and spidery fingers. She would lurk beneath the surface of stagnant water, waiting for any unwary or naughty child to venture too close. Then she would catch hold of the child and drag it under the water, never to be seen again. She is, of course, a Nursery bogie used by anxious parents to curb the overadventurous child and prevent it from coming to harm.
References 21, 24, 160, 170, 183
See also Grindylow, Jenny Greenteeth, Kappa, Peg Powler

NEMBROTUS

This is the alternative spelling of the giant Nymbrotus in the study of world history from the time of Noah undertaken by the Italian monk Annius of Viterbo (Giovanni Nanni, c. 1432–1502) to justify the noble descent of the Gauls from a giant biblical race.
References 174
See also Nymbrotus

NEMEAN LION, THE

This is the name of a monstrous lion in the classical mythology of Greece and Rome. The Nemean Lion was a scourge of the region of Nemea, devouring humans and livestock alike. It was said, in some accounts, to be the offspring of the two monsters Echidna and Typhon, or Orthrus, or to have been created by the goddess Silene. The lion was virtually indestructible, and this was given as the first labor by Eurystheus to the hero Heracles/Hercules. As the creature could not be killed by bronze, iron, or stone, the hero captured the monster and, taking its neck in his powerful grip, choked it to death. Thereafter, he wore its pelt not only as a trophy but as his armor.
References 20, 24, 70, 78, 89, 133, 139
See also Echidne, monster, Orthos, Typhon

NEPENDIS

This is the name of a hybrid creature in the repertoire of European heraldry. The Nependis is portrayed as being part boar and part ape.
References 132, 161

NEPHILIM

This is the name of a race of giants mentioned in the Hebrew scriptures and the Christian Old Testament as inhabiting the Hebron Valley in the land of Canaan before the Flood in which all but Noah and his family perished. These biblical giants were described in the Book of Genesis as so vast that when humans saw them they were terrified and felt themselves in comparison to be the size of mere grasshoppers. The Nephilim were said to be the sons of Anak and may also be referred to as the Anakim.
References 13, 174, 182
See also Anakim, giant, Gibborim, Noah

NESNAS, NESNÁS

This is an alternative name for the Nasha in the pre-Islamic beliefs of the people of Yemen.
References 7, 18
See also Direach, Empusa, Nashas

NESSIE, NESSY

These are the colloquial and local terms for the being otherwise described as the Loch Ness Monster in the folklore of Scotland.
References 78, 134
See also Loch Ness Monster, monster

NESSITERAS RHOMBOPTERYX

This is the cryptozoological term for the Loch Ness–type of beings that are currently being investigated as possible surviving members of species extinct after the Ice Age.
References 134
See also Loch Ness Monster

NESSUS

This is the name of a centaur in the classical mythology of Greece and Rome. Nessus was the progeny of Ixion and Nephele and a companion of the hero Heracles/Hercules. Nessus was jealous of the hero's wife, Deianira, and when the hero asked if Nessus would carry her on his back across a river the centaur attempted to abduct her. However, Heracles/Hercules shot the centaur with one of the arrows that he had dipped in the poisoned blood of the Hydra. While Nessus was dying, he told Deianira to put some of his blood in a phial because it would ensure the return of her husband if he was ever unfaithful. When she later suspected Heracles/Hercules of infidelity, she remembered this and smeared his shirt with the blood. But Nessus had been clever to the last, knowing that his blood was poisonous; the result was that when it touched her husband's skin, the hero also died in agony.
References 20, 139, 166, 169, 178
See also centaur, Hydra

NEUGLE

This is the name of a fearsome water-horse in the folklore of Scalloway on the mainland of the Shetland Islands north of Scotland. This spirit was also known as Nogle, Noggle, Nuggle, Nuggie, and Nygel. It inhabited Njugals Water and is described as looking like a horse with a green mane and an odd tail like a wheel curling over its back. Like the Each Uisge, it would appear saddled and bridled, prancing on the shore. Should any human be tempted to mount and ride him, the Neugle would immediately enter the water; with the human being unable to dismount, the victim might never be seen again. However, the Neugle was not always as malicious as the Cabyll-Ushtey or the Ceffyll-dŵr, and the rider would often suffer no more than an undignified drenching, whereupon the Neugle would disappear in a dancing blue flame into the water. This water-horse was fond of waterwheels on the mills and would take great delight in causing them to stop and thereby causing great irritation to the millers. It is said to have been seen in British Columbia by Scandinavian and Shetlander immigrants and passed into the folklore of Canada as the Nogle.
References 24, 67, 134, 160
See also Cabyll-Ushtey, Ceffyll-dŵr, Each Uisge, Kelpy, monster, Nogle

NEVINBIMBAAU

This is the name of a terrifying ogress in the traditions and beliefs of the people of Melanesia. Nevinbimbaau is described as a gigantic female with a booming voice. She is associated with the hero-god Ambat. She is invoked during certain ceremonies of initiation, where a bull-roarer symbolizes her call and the ritualized slaughter of her daughters and their husbands is played out in effigy.
References 38
See also ogress

NGALBJOD

This is a regional name for the Rainbow Serpent in the Dreamtime mythology of the Native Australian people.
References 133
See also Rainbow Serpent

NGANI-VATU

This is the name of a monstrous bird in the traditions and beliefs of the people of the island of Fiji. The Ngani-vatu, also known as Ngutu-Lei, is described as so huge that its body blots out the sun from the horizon and the flapping of its wings cause storms over the land. This predatory bird feeds on the animals and especially humans in the Pacific islands. The legend relates how the hero Okova was fishing with his wife in their sailing boat. Suddenly, the sky was blackened as Ngani-vatu circled over the boat and then grabbed Okova's wife and flew away. The anxious hero sailed as fast as possible after the bird but to no avail; it was gone too fast. After searching for a long time for the place where the bird might have landed, he came to the island of Sawailau, where the bird was reputed to land each night. There, in a vast cavern, he found the finger of his wife among a heap of skeletons. He vowed that he would avenge her death and kill Ngani-vatu, so he left to get the help of his wife's brother, Kokoua, and returned to the island. After some time hiding in the cavern, the bird returned with another victim, which it proceeded to devour. While it was thus occupied, the two crept toward Ngani-vatu until they were underneath its legs and then, swiftly, the pair thrust their spears up to the end of the shaft into its underbelly. As it fell, the giant bird caused an avalanche of rock, but the men managed to take a wing feather to replace one of their sails. Then they heaved the Ngani-vatu off the edge of the cliff and into the sea, causing a tidal wave far out to other islands as it submerged.
References 113
See also Roc

NGUTU-LEI

This is the alternative name of the Ngani-vatu, a monstrous cannibal bird, in the traditions and legends of the people of the Islands of Fiji on the Pacific.
References 113
See also Ngani-vatu, Roc

Nessus the centaur (Rose Photo Archive, UK)

NICKAR

This is the name of the Scandinavian Nicker, or water monster, in the traditions and folklore of the people of the Danish Faroe Islands.
References 20, 37, 107, 120, 111, 160
See also Nicker

NICKEL

This is the name of the Scandinavian Nicker, or water monster, in the traditions and folklore of the people in the Danish island of Rügen.
References 20, 37, 107, 111, 120, 160
See also Nicker

NICKER, NICKUR

This is the name of a water monster in the folklore of Scandinavia. The Nicker is called the Näcken in Sweden; the Nickar in the Danish Faroe Islands; the Nickur or Ninnir or Haikur in Iceland; the Nickel in the Danish island of Rügen; the Nikyr in the Manx language of the Isle of Man in Britain; and the Nøkke in Denmark. It is variously described as a beautiful, huge, white horse with its hooves in reverse, or as a handsome youth to the waist with horse's body and legs like the centaurs of classical mythology, or as a golden-haired boy wearing a red cap, or an old man with a green, dripping-wet beard. These water beings inhabit the seas, lakes, rivers, and streams. They are generally benign toward humans if left alone to make their music. However, if anyone tries to ride one in the form of a horse, that person will be taken forever under the water. The Nicker will sometimes desire a human wife and will be a most attentive lover, but if scorned he can be as malicious and terrifying as the Scottish Kelpie. A knife or metal object is placed in the bottom of a fishing boat as a precaution against the Nicker, as iron is supposed to "bind" his power.
References 7, 20, 37, 107, 111, 120, 160
See also centaur, Kelpy

NICKNEVEN

This is the name of a monstrous hag in the traditions and folklore of the Highlands of Scotland. The Nickneven is a malicious giantess or ogre.
References 20
See also giantess, ogre

NICKUR

This is one of the three names of the Scandinavian Nicker, or water monster, in the traditions and folklore of the people of Iceland.
References 20, 37, 107, 111, 120, 160
See also Nicker

NICOR

This is an alternative name for the Nicker, or water monster, in the traditions and folklore of the people of Scandinavia.
References 20, 37, 107, 111, 120, 160
See also Nicker

NIDHOGG, NIDHOGGR, NIDHÖGGR

This is the name of a gigantic serpentine dragon in the Norse mythology of Scandinavia. The Nidhogg, whose name has been variously translated as "Envy Dragon" or "Corpse Tearer" or "Dread Biter," from its tearing at the bodies of the dead in the underworld, threatens the existence of the world by gnawing constantly at the underneath of the roots of the ash tree Yggdrasil, which supports the entire universe. The tree is constantly being renewed by the efforts and magic herbs of the Norns, who guard and water it.
References 7, 47, 78, 89, 107, 125, 133, 139, 160
See also dragon, serpent

NIEH-ERH KUO YAN

This is the name of a race of monstrous people in the legends and folklore of China. The Nieh-Erh Kuo Yan, the "People of the Whispering Ears," are described as having stripes on their bodies like those of a tiger; their ears are so long that if they were not held while they walk the ears would reach waist level. The Nieh-Erh Kuo Yan appear in the volumes of the *Great Imperial Encyclopedia* and were no doubt derived from exaggerated travelers' tales in much the same way as those that influenced the medieval bestiaries of Europe. The description of the Nieh-Erh Kuo Yan appears along with many other fabulous races such as the I-Mu Kuo Yan, the San-Shen Kuo Yan, the San-Shou Kuo Yan, the Ting Ling Kuo Yan, and the Yü-Min Kuo Yan.
References 181
See also Fearsome Critters, I-Mu Kuo Yan, San-Shen Kuo Yan, San-Shou Kuo Yan, Ting Ling Kuo Yan, Yü-Min Kuo Yan

NIGELUNG

This is the name of one of the giants in the legends of Germany. Nigelung is one of the two giant kings ruling, with Schilbung, over twelve giants living in the wilderness of the mountains, forests, and gorges. Their story in the *Nibelungenlied* tells how the rockfalls, cavernous sounds, and water torrents were caused by their grumbling and groans.
References 139
See also giant

NIHNIKNOOVI

This is the name of a monstrous bird-like being in the legends and folklore of the Kawaiisu Tubatulabal

Native American people in the southwestern United States. The Nihniknoovi is described as a predatory being with enormous talons on the end of its legs. It hunts human beings and carries the slaughtered corpses off to a waterhole, where it drains the blood into the red water before devouring the victim.
References 77
See also Bar Yachre, Griffin, Nunyenunc, Roc

NIKKE
This is an alternative name for the Nicker, or water monster, in the traditions and folklore of the people of Scandinavia.
References 20, 37, 107, 111, 120, 160
See also Nicker

NIKYR
This is the name of the Scandinavian Nicker, or water monster, in the Manx language of the traditions and folklore of the people of the Isle of Man in Britain.
References 20, 37, 107, 111, 120, 160
See also Nicker

NIMROD, NEBROD
This is the name of a person in the Hebraic and Christian scriptures in which Nimrod, in the Book of Genesis, is deemed responsible for the construction of the Tower of Babel. He is not actually described as a giant in the scriptures. However, in the later texts of ecclesiastical discourses, especially that of Augustine of Hippo (A.D. 354–430) and the *Etymologies* of Isidore of Seville (c. 560–636), Nimrod, or Nebrod, was conjectured to have been a giant. Following these early commentators, he features as a giant in Italian literature in the "Inferno" section of the *Divina Commedia* by Dante Alighieri (1265–1321). For the temerity of constructing a mighty tower and challenging the authority of the Almighty, Nimrod was condemned, with his companion giants, after the confusion of tongues, to be buried to the waist in the desert. The description of these giants in the desert gives their dimensions as resembling vast towers in the distance.
References 174
See also giant

NINGYO
This is the term for a mermaid in the folklore of Japan. Unike the European one described as being a beautiful maiden to the waist with a fish's tail instead of legs, the Ningyo is depicted as being an enormous fish but with the head of a beautiful woman. Furthermore, she is benevolent and protective toward humans, warning them against misfortune on land and at sea, and does not entice them into danger like her occidental counterpart.

References 7, 24, 120, 125, 160
See also Ben Varrey, Bonito Maidens, Ceasg, Clytie, Gwenhidwy, Halfway People, Havfrue, Imanja, Jamaína, Lamia, Liban, Margygr, Mari Morgan, Melusina, mermaid, Merrow, Saivo-Neita

NINNIR
This is one of the three names of the Scandinavian Nicker, or water monster, in the traditions and folklore of the people of Iceland.
References 20, 37, 107, 111, 120, 160
See also Nicker

NIU T'OU, NIU TU
This is the name of the monstrous demonic messenger from hell in the mythology of China. Niu T'ou is described as a humanoid monster with the head of an ox, hence the name, which means "Ox Head." He and Ma Mien are the attendants and messengers of Yen-Lo, the ruler of the dead and those in hell. They were armed with official warrants for the souls of the departed, whom they conducted to the Halls of Judgment.
References 38, 133, 160, 181
See also Amermait, monster

NIX, NIXE, NIXIE
These are supernatural water beings in the folklore of Scandinavia, Germany, and Switzerland. The name "Nix" is derived from the Old High German word *nihhus*, meaning a crocodile, and was a vast water monster. These beings still retain the monstrous element in their descriptions but are becoming more and more aligned to the spirit form as their folklore develops.

The females are described as being beautiful women above the waist and having the tail of a fish in the manner of a mermaid, but the Nix usually inhabits freshwater. However, it is a malicious, predatory being that uses the beautiful image to entice mortals to their doom in the waters. Their more usual image was wizened with green skin, teeth, and hair, or even as a massive, gray water-horse. There are different descriptions according to the region, and while the above is a general one, in Iceland and Sweden the description of the Nix is more like that of the centaur in the classical mythology of Greece and Rome. However, in the Slavic mythology of eastern Europe, the female beings are described as resembling the Siren of classical mythology, with the torso and head of a woman but the legs and wings of a bird. In the same region, the male Nixes have the torso and head of a wizened old man but the body and brush of a fox and the hooves of a horse.
References 7, 89, 120, 125, 160

The Nix is a malicious, predatory being that uses its mermaid shape to entice mortals to their doom in the waters. (Rose Photo Archive, UK)

See also Centaur, Kelpy, mermaid, Näkinneito, Ningyo, Siren

NOACHIDS, NOACHIAN GIANTS

The Italian monk Annius of Viterbo (Giovanni Nanni, c. 1432–1502) asserted that the biblical Noah was a giant. He re-created a whole genealogy of giants from Noah and Iapetus to justify the constructed line of descent through the giant Dis Samothes to the ancestry of the French nobility of the period. Apart from the biblical Shem, Ham, and Japheth, the names of the other Noachian Giants in Annius's genealogy were: Araxa, Crana, Cranus, Granaus, Japetus Junior, Macrus, Oceanus, Pandora Junior, Prisca, Priscus, Prometheus, Regina, Tuyscon Gigas, Thetis, and Typhoeus. He also included the Titans in this line of descent.
References 174
See also giant, Noah

NOAH

Although in the Hebrew scriptures Noah is a human who survived the Flood with his family and animals, the Italian monk Annius of Viterbo (Giovanni Nanni, c. 1432–1502) asserted that he lived over six hundred years as a giant. Furthermore, because he and his family had survived, they were "good" giants, unlike the monsters and ogres of legends. Annius then proposed that Noah and his family had colonized the mainland of Europe and identified them with the Etruscans. His descendants were the Noachids, or Noachian Giants, that spread throughout Europe into Armenia, Egypt, France, Germany, and Spain. He re-created a whole genealogy of giants descended from Noah and Iapetus to justify the ancestry of the French nobility of the period. In this genealogy he conjectured that the descent of Dis Samothes from this line, via the ancestor Japheth, was the first king of the Gauls. Apart from the biblical Chem/Shem, Ham/Samus, and Japheth/Japetus and their wives, Noela, Noegla, Pandora, and Tytea, the names in Annius's genealogy were: Araxa, Crana, Cranus, Granaus, Japetus Junior, Macrus, Oceanus, Pandora Junior, Prisca, Priscus, Prometheus, Regina, Tuyscon Gigas, Thetis, and Typhoeus. He also included the Titans in this line of descent.
References 174
See also Dis Samothes, Gargantua, giant, Japetus, Noachids, Pantagruel

NOGGLE

This is an alternative name for the Neugle, or water-horse, in the traditions and folklore of the Shetland Islands.
References 24, 67, 134
See also Neugle

NOGLE

This is the name of a water monster in the European traditions of British Columbia, Canada. It is described as a monstrous water creature like a serpentine horse. The Nogle is derived from the Neugle of the Shetland Islands north of Scotland and was "imported" with the immigrants from that part of the world during the eighteenth and nineteenth centuries.
References 24, 67, 134, 160
See also Neugle

NÖKK

This is the name of a water monster in the folklore of Estonia. It is described as a water-horse rather like the Kelpie of Scotland that particularly abducts and devours children. In this respect it was most probably used by parents as a Nursery bogie to keep adventurous children from dangerous stretches of water.
References 134, 160
See also Kelpy, Nicker, Nøkke

NØKKE, NØKKEN (pl.)

This is the name of the Scandinavian Nicker, or water monster, in the the traditions and folklore of the people of Denmark and Finland, where it takes the shape of a water-horse not unlike the Kelpie of Scotland.
References 20, 37, 107, 111, 120, 134, 160
See also Kelpy, Nicker

NO-KOS-MA

This is the name of a monster in the traditions and legends of the Cree Native American people of Canada. It is described as a gigantic, bear-like creature with black hair and a huge, extended snout.
References 134
See also monster

NU KWA, NU-KWA

This is the name of a hybrid human in the traditions and legends of China. Nu Kwa is the consort of the serpent-bodied Emperor Fu-Hsi, and like him she is portrayed as having a human torso and head but the lower half of a gigantic serpent. The two are always depicted as being entwined.
References 89
See also Fu-Hsi

NUCKALEVEE

This is the name of a sea monster in the legends and folklore of Ireland that inhabited the coastal areas. It is depicted as being something like the Centaur in the classical mythology of Greece and Rome, but the Nuckalevee had no skin around its flesh. It was a predatory monster that inflicted the plague with its stinking poisonous breath. It would hunt down any humans foolish enough to enter its domain and devour them, unless they could cross a stream, for it was terrified of fresh running water.

References 7

See also centaur, monster

NUGGLE, NUGGIE

This is an alternative name for the Neugle, or water–horse, in the traditions and folklore of the Shetland Islands.

References 24, 67, 134

See also Neugle

NULAYUUINIQ

This is the name of a monstrous cannibal infant in the traditions and legends of the Inuit people of eastern Hudson Bay region of Canada. The legend relates how a female child grew just after her birth to the proportions of a giantess during a savage period of famine for the village. When people from another village came to relieve them with food, they found only Nulayuuiniq, wrapped in the parka that belonged to her mother, with all the others nowhere to be seen. In fear, the people tried to escape Nulayuuiniq, who ran after them crying like a baby. So seal skins were tossed at her from the sleds, and each skin was sucked down her vast gullet because she still had no teeth. At last unable to keep up with the sleds, Nulayuuiniq sank exhausted to the ground, where she turned into a rock.

References 77

See also cannibal, giant, monster, Raw Gums

NUN

This is an alternative name in Islamic legend for the biblical monster called the Leviathan.

References 7

See also Leviathan

NUNYENUNC

This is the name of a monstrous bird in the traditions and legends of the Native American people of the United States. The Nunyenunc is described as a predatory being that hunts especially for humans. It swoops on unwary travelers and hunters, grasping them in its talons, and takes them to be devoured in the mountains.

References 7

See also Bar Yachre, Griffin, Nihniknoovi, Roc

NURSERY BOGIES

In many cultures there are supernatural beings, ogres, and monsters that never seem to have been taken too seriously by mature adults, although they are spoken of with serious expression, and even reverence, when the audience is children. This class of being is deemed to threaten or caution the activities of children into being those approved of by the social group in which they live. These Nursery bogies have, for the most part, an extremely terrifying appearance and an even worse reputation in dealing with humans who enter their domain.

The following British ones are used as a warning for bad behavior: Agrippa, Auld Scratty, Black Annis, Black Sow, Bodach, Booger Man, Bogyman, Bogie, Bombomachides, Boo-bagger, Brandamour, Brobinyak, Bucca Dhu, Bug, Bug-a-boo, Bugbear, Cankobobus, Child Guzzler, Cutty Dyer, Father Flog and Madam Flog, Hobyah, Jack up the Orchut, Jennie of Biggersdale, Lammikin, Morgan, Mumpoker, Old Bloody Bones, Raw Head and Bloody Bones, Red-Legged Scissor-man, Sandman, the Spoorn, Tanterabogus,Tod Lowery, Tom Dockin, Tom Poker, and Woglog.

The following are used to protect crops from being gathered unripe by greedy children: Awd Goggie, Churnmilk Peg, Clim, the Gooseberry Wife, Lazy Lawrence, and Melsh Dick.

And to keep British children from dangerous waters, the following were named: Grindylow, Jenny Greenteeth, Nellie Longarms, and Peg Powler.

In other countries the following may be used by adults to warn children: Afrit, Alphito, Apotamkin, Asin, Baba Yaga, Bockman, Bogey, Boroka, Bullebak, Caravinaigre, Carneros, Caypór, Coco, Croquemitaine, Hagondes, Indacinga, Katzenveit, Kinder-fresser, Kinderschrecker, Krampus, Lamia, Lammikin, Lustucru, Mormo, Nahgane, Nökk, Omo Nero, Owner-of-a-Bag, Père Fouettard, Pontarf, Pot-Tilter, Seatco, Skatene, Snee-Nee-Iq, Strigae, Stringes, Sri, Tengu, Thundel, Windigo, and Yara-ma-yha-who.

References 24, 160

See also Afrit/e, Agrippa, Alphito, Black Annis, Bogyman, Bombomachides, Boo-bagger, Boroka, Brandamour, Brobinyak, Bugbear/e, Bullebak, Caravinaigre, Child Guzzler, Coco, Cutty Dyer, Father Flog and Madam Flog, Grindylow, Hobyah, Jenny Greenteeth, Kappa, Kinder-fresser, Kinderschrecker, Lamia, Lammikin, Lustucru, Morgan, Mormo, Nahgane, Nellie Longarms, Nökk, Owner-of-a-Bag, Peg Powler

NYAN

This is the name of a monstrous serpentine creature in the traditions and legends of Burma and India. The Nyan, also known as the Avagráh, the Gara, the Gráha, or the Tanti-gáha in different regions, is described as a vast sinuous, worm-like being that inhabited the estuaries and rivers of Burma and Bengal in India. It preyed upon all large creatures that entered its domain and would encircle their body

with its sinuous coils in the water, squeezing and dragging them down to be consumed. It was such a menace to the elephant population that the "Dhammathats," when judging the causes of lost hired work elephants, decreed that there was no liability if they had been taken by a Nyan. Accounts of it were written in the *Amarakosha Abhidhan* and later in the *Kavilakhana dépané,* written by Mingyi Thiri Mahazeyathu. Even the army of King Alaung-mindara-gyé lost several elephants to the Nyan while crossing the Martaban River.
References 81
See also Odontotyrannus, serpent

NYGEL

This is an alternative name for the Neugle, or water-horse, in the traditions and folklore of the people of the Shetland Islands.
References 24, 67, 134
See also Neugle

NYKKJEN

This is the alternative name, in the folklore of Norway, for the Nøkke of Denmark and Finland. As recently as 1983, a woman searching for lost sheep on the mountainside of the Myrkevaten, or Dark Lake, in Norway reported that the monster moved alongside the lake parallel with her but just under the surface. When it reared up out of the water, revealing its vast green body, head, and beard, she fled.
References 134
See also Nøkke

NYKUR

This is the name of a water monster in the traditions and folklore of the people of Iceland. The Nykur is described as being like the Kelpie of Scottish folklore or the Nøkke of Scandinavia. This monster will neigh under the water and, especially when the creaks of the thickly frozen ice move over the waters in winter, it is believed that the monster is calling to his victims.
References 134
See also Kelpy, Nøkke

NYMBROTUS

This is the name of a giant in the study of world history from the time of Noah undertaken by the Italian monk Annius of Viterbo (Giovanni Nanni, c. 1432–1502) to justify the noble descent of the Gauls from a giant biblical race. Annius gives the alternative spelling of Nymbrotus as Nembrotus in his version of how the giant (Nimrod in the biblical account) constructed the Tower of Babel. Annius asserts that Nymbrotus stole the ritual books from Jovis Saga and took his son, Jovis Bellus, and their family to settle a place called Senahar. There he then laid out the city of Babylon and set about constructing the tower. After fifty-six years the Tower of Babel had reached the height of the nearby mountains, but at this point, Annius states, Nymbrotus was taken by the gods and disappeared. Annius's fanciful account of biblical events was taken as a basis for many of the later genealogical ancestries and incorporated into much of European literature, including that of Rabelais.
References 174
See also giant, Jovis Saga, Noah

O

O GONCHO

This is the name of a dragon in the traditions and legends of Japan. O Goncho is described as an enormous, winged dragon that unusually was white and inhabited a stretch of water at Yamahiro. Every fifty years the O Goncho transformed into a type of bird with golden plumage and a call resembling the howl of a wolf. This metamorphosis and the call were indicative of some diasaster, such as a famine.

References 7
See also Oriental dragon

OCEANUS

There are two characters that go by this name.

1. This is the name of a giant in the classical mythology of Greece and Rome. Oceanus, also spelled Okeanus, means "Swift," and was one of the Titans and the progeny of Uranus and Gaia. By his Titaness consort and sister, Tethys, were engendered the nymphs known as the Oceanids and all the rivers of the world. Oceanus represents the cosmic waters but was vanquished in the great battle of the Titans and the Olympian gods.

2. This is one of the giants named in the genealogy created by the Italian monk Annius of Viterbo (Giovanni Nanni, c. 1432–1502) to justify the noble descent of the Gauls from a giant biblical race.

References 7, 14, 38, 63, 78, 139, 148, 174, 178, 185
See also Gaia, giant, monster, Noah, Tethys, Titan, Uranus

OCYPETE

This is the name of one of the Harpies in the classical mythology of Greece and Rome. Ocypete, whose name may be translated as "Swift-flying," was a monstrous female human-bird hybrid. Together with her sisters, she tortured the blinded King Phineus at Salmydessus in eastern Thrace until driven away by Jason and the Argonauts.

References 89, 139, 178

See also Alkonost, Angka, Arepyiai, Garuda, Harpy, Parthenope, Podarge, Ptitsy-Siriny, Siren, Sirin, Solovei Rakhmatich, Unnati, Zägh

ODONTOTYRANNUS

This is a monstrous creature reported in the ancient writings of the Greeks c. 400–300 B.C. and in the later Roman and medieval travelers' tales. The Odontotyrannus was described as a vast black amphibious beast with three horns protruding from its forehead and a mouth so huge that it could consume a whole elephant. It was a predatory monster that inhabited the Ganges River in the north of India, where it was said to have attacked and devoured many of the elephants and men of Alexander the Great's (356–323 B.C.) armies.

References 7, 89
See also Nyan

ODZ-MANOUK

This is the name of a monstrous child in the legends and folklore of the people of Armenia. Odz-Manouk was apparently born to the king and queen of Armenia in the shape of a snake. In horror the child was locked into a secret room, where he metamorphosed into a dragon. There he was well kept but never allowed out, despite the fact that he refused even the most dainty foods. His roars of hunger attracted the attention of the daughter of the chamberlain who entered and was immediately devoured. From that time the palace servants scoured the countryside for suitable maidens to feed the growing royal monster, now so huge that the victim was lowered through a hole in the ceiling—until the day that the beautiful Arevhat was lowered to be consumed. But there were no noises to be heard; the silence was so strange that the king peered into the hole and saw the beautiful girl sitting gently by a handsome young man. The birth curse had been broken by her kindness, and they were later married.

This legend clearly conforms to the Beauty and the Beast motif of other fables and folktales.

References 55

See also Beast, Loathly Lady, Rhinocéros, Riquet à la Houppe

OFFOTUS

This is the name of a giant in the classical literature of France. Offotus is one of the giant ancestors of Pantagruel in the famous work *Pantagruel* (1532) by the French author François Rabelais (ca. 1494–ca. 1553). The name and character appeared originally in the work *Officina* by the erudite Jean Tixier de Ravisy (alias Ravisius Textor, c. 1480–1524). But Offotus does not appear in the original edition; he is an addition to later versions by Rabelais as a means of establishing the genealogy of Pantagruel. Offotus, along with six other giants—Eryx, Etion, Gabbara, Galehaut, Happemousche, and Morguan—is credited with inventing something concerned with drinking. Offotus was in fact the first amended entry credited with such an ability in the description: *Lequel eut terriblement beau nez à boyre au baril*, which may be translated as his having a terribly fine nose because of drinking from the cask. This, of course, is a pun that implies two alternative things about his character: that Offotus was a *bon viveur* who took his drink seriously and savoured it as a connoiseur from the original source, or that Offotus had a red nose from drinking anything straight from the barrel without its having the refinement of bottling.

References 174

See also Bruyer, Chalbroth, Daughters of Cain, Enay, Eryx, Etion, Gabbara, Gargantua, giant, Happemousche, Hurtaly, Morguan, Noachids, Noah, Pantagruel

OG, OG OF BASHAN

This is the name of a giant in the rabbinical and Hebrew texts and scriptures and also the texts of the Old Testament. Og of Bashan, also known as Hapalit, meaning the "Escapee" (i.e., from his delivery from the Flood), is described as having multiple fingers and toes and being such an immense being that the waters only lapped his ankles. In other accounts of the Flood, he persuaded Noah to allow him to sit astride the roof of the Ark. Although seemingly allowed to survive this destruction, Og's character was less than perfect, and when the Ark finally rested he tried to seduce Sarah, the wife of Noah. Exiled and ostracized by the Jewish people, he put every obstacle in their way, including a massive rock to block their exodus from Egypt. When Yahweh struck the rock from his grasp via an army of stinging ants, the rock smashed into the giant's teeth. At this point he was chopped at the ankles and felled by Moses. The fallen giant became the mountain range from which they viewed the Promised Land.

References 133, 174

See also giant, Noah

OGOPOGO

This is the name of a lake monster in the folklore of the Okanagan Lake area of British Columbia, Canada. This monster is variously described as looking like a vast log with a horse's head, an undulating serpentine creature with several humps or saw-toothed ridges on its back, or as a seventy-foot serpentine being with a smooth back with several fins. Whatever its description, there have been several sightings recorded from the 1950s to 1975, when the terrified informants related that the monster caused a violent frothing of the waters of the lake and in one instance smashed through the frozen surface during winter. The creature is seen to disappear suddenly either by Rattle Snake Island or close to the shore, giving rise to the theory of underground connecting caverns so familiar with other such lake monsters.

References 78, 94, 134

See also Champ, Haietlik, Loch Ness Monster, monster, Naitaka, Ponik

OGRE, OGREE

This is a name given in folklore to a particular class of giant. In general an ogre is a gigantic humanoid male of very little intellect, enormously strong bulk, cannibal tendencies, and easily outwitted by a clever human. The name "Ogre" was thought to be the invention of either of two French authors, Charles Perrault (1628–1703), in his *Histoires ou Contes du temps Passé* (1697), or Marie-Catherine Jumelle de Berneville, Comtesse d' Aulnoy (1650–1705), in her story *L' Orangier et l' Abeille* (The Orange Tree and the Bee, 1698). However, it is thought that it was derived originally from the work of the Italian author Giambattista Basile (1575–1632), whose *Sole, Luna et Talia* became the classic *Beauty and the Beast*. Whoever is responsible, the translation of their fairy folktales passed into the English language, including the word "Ogre" for this type of giant. In the case of the Comtesse d' Aulnoy, a further word, "Ogree," was given for the progeny of an Ogre.

Whilst the dialogue between the cannibal ogres may seem gross and bloodthirsty, in the best traditions of fairy tales, there is a certain black humor in the stories, which is usually resolved in the favor of the hero or heroine (whereas in the case of the traditional giant there is little by way of relief from the terror inflicted). The Ogre seems to be more firmly rooted in folklore and folktale than in mythology, and examples of this class of monster can be found worldwide, such as: the character known as

Ogre with cudgel (Rose Photo Archive, UK)

Beast in many countries worldwide; Atcen of the Montagnais Native Canadians; Dzoavits of the Shoshone Native American people; Skatene of the Choctaw Native American people; Drake of the Gypsy community of the Balkan states; Kinder-fresser in the folklore of Germany; the Trolls of Scandinavia; the Gruagach of Scotland; Miodhchaoin in the Celtic legends of Ireland; Tom Dockin in the folklore of England; Bobalicón in the folklore of Spain; Ravagio and Tourmentine in the literature of France; Sasabonsam in the legends of the Tschwi and Ashanti people of West Africa; and Kojin in the legends of Japan.

References 20, 24, 61, 77, 182

See also Atcen, Beast, blunderbore, Bobalicón, Bombachides, Brandamour, Drake, Dzoavits, Ga-gorib, giant, Gruagach, Grumbo, Kinder-fresser, Kojin, Miodhchaoin, ogress, Pot-Tilter, Ravagio, Sasabonsam, Skatene, Thundel, Tom Dockin, Tourmentine, Troll, Yellow Cedar bark ogre

OGRESS

This is the female form of the ogre in the traditions and folklore of Europe, although there are counterparts of the type in other cultures around the world. She is generally considered to be a vast female humanoid with massive body structure but with little intellect. They are usually associated with water, but

An ogress, a vast female humanoid with massive body structure but with little intellect (Rose Photo Archive, UK)

where they accompany ogres as their consorts they are far less cruel or malicious toward humans. Like most ogres, they can easily be duped by a clever human child. The first recorded use of the word "Ogress" appears in the French seventeenth-century author Charles Perrault's rendition of the *Sleeping Beauty in the Wood*, where it is recorded as "Ogresse." References 182
See also ogre

OGYGES
This is the name given to the biblical Noah by the Italian monk Annius of Viterbo (Giovanni Nanni, c.

1432–1502), who asserted that the biblical Noah was a giant. He re-created a whole genealogy of giants from Noah and Iapetus to justify the constructed line of descent through the giant Dis Samothes to the ancestry of the French nobility of the period. Within this genealogy Annius asserted that the sons of Noah—Shem, Ham, and Japheth—were also giants and that they constituted a class known as the Ogyges. When this pseudohistory was developed by Pierre Charron (1541–1603) in his *Histoire Universelle*, he asserted that the Ogyges were responsible for the foundation of the French city of Bourges.

References 174
See also Dis Samothes, giant, Iapetus, Japheth, Noah

OHYNS

This is the name for a monstrous child in the folklore of the Kasubian people of eastern Europe. The Ohyns are children who are born with teeth already through the gums and are regarded as vampires in this culture. Pulling the teeth is regarded as the cure for the condition.

References 24
See also vampire

OILLIPHÉIST, OILLEPHEIST

This is the name of a lake monster in the traditions and legends of Ireland. The name "Oilliphéist" derives from the Irish Gaelic *oll,* meaning "great," and *péist,* meaning "fabulous beast." This vast monster, described as looking something like a dragon, was so huge and of such length that as it traveled it gouged the length of the Shannon River. However, the legend relates that when it heard that Saint Patrick was coming to exorcise it, the hitherto benign Oilliphéist became enraged. It swallowed a drunken piper who happened to be in the wrong place at the wrong time, but, undaunted, the man continued to play in the monster's belly. This made Oilliphéist so irritated that it disgorged the drunkard oblivious to his adventure, who continued his journey playing as before.

References 128
See also Caoránach, Muirdris, Sínach

OKEANUS

This is an alternative spelling of Oceanus, one of the Titans in the classical mythology of Greece and Rome.

References 20, 24, 47, 78, 94, 125, 139, 166, 178, 182
See also Oceanus, Titan

OLD MAN OF THE SEA

In the Arabian *Tales of the Thousand and One Nights,* the story of Sindbad's fifth voyage gives details of this terrifying Djinn. The Old Man of the Sea is described as a monstrous humanoid with a hairy body, wizened face, pointed nose and ears, and a long, trailing beard that inhabits the desert. He is strong and deformed and mounts the backs of men and rides them ceaselessly until they die of exhaustion. Sindbad managed to dislodge and destroy it.

References 53
See also Djinn

OLIPHAUNT

This is the name of monstrous beasts in the literary works of the English academic and author J. R. R. Tolkien (1892–1973) in *The Hobbit* (1937) and *The Lord of the Rings* (1955). The Oliphaunt is the name by which the Mûmarkil was known to the Hobbits. They were described as vast, elephantine beasts with enormous, pointed tusks, said to be the ancestors of the smaller elephant.

References 51
See also Mûmarkil

OLOG-HAI

This is the name of giant Trolls in the works of the English academic and author J. R. R. Tolkien (1892–1973) in *The Hobbit* (1937) and *The Lord of the Rings* (1955). The Olog-hai were a breed of Trolls, described as black-blooded giant cannibals with vast fangs and claws, green, scaly skin, enormous strength, and little intellect. They were armed with massive black shields and huge hammers, with which they slaughtered anything in their path. Like their folkloric Norse predecessors, they were derived from darkness, but the Olog-hai could not be destroyed and turned to stone in the light. They were created during the First Age by the Enemy known as Melkor in the depths of Angband and were sent with the Orcs to rampage through the universe. After being defeated, they were hidden, but during the Second Age the servant of Melkor, named Sauron, imbued them with a dangerous, deceitful mind, and a more evil race was created. By the time the Third Age came there were many different classes of Troll, including a new breed known as the Olog-Hai that could withstand the rays of the sun. But when the One Ring was finally destroyed, and with it their master, Sauron, the Olog-hai were without power or direction and easily overcome and slaughtered in their stupefied state.

References 51
See also cannibal, giant, Troll

OMO NERO, L'

This is the name of a frightening humanoid monster in the folklore of Italy from the medieval period to the nineteenth century. L'Omo Nero, which may be translated as the "Man in Black," was regarded as an evil bogie with which to frighten children into good behavior. In this respect the character, often used in carnivals in the same way as El Coco in Spain, was a Nursery bogie.

References 182
See also Coco, Nursery bogie

ON NIONT, ONNIONT

This is the name of a horned serpent in the traditions and beliefs of the Huron Native American people of the northeastern United States. This vast serpent was held to be responsible for the deep clefts in mountains and rocks as it severed its path with its huge horn on

the front of its forehead. This horn was greatly prized as a talisman if ever anyone were able to get one.
References 7, 169
See also horned serpent, serpent

ONDITACHIAE

This is the name of a hybrid being in the traditions of the Huron Native American people of the northeastern United States. The Onditachiae are described as having the body of a human but the head of a cock turkey and are seen only at a time of storms.
References 77
See also Raicho, Xexeu

ONE WHO DRILLS

This is the alternative name for the Ikuutayuuq in the traditions and folk beliefs of the Inuit people of eastern Hudson Bay in Canada. These are terrifying monsters that reportedly kill their victims by drilling into their bodies.
References 77
See also Ikuutayuuq

ONE-STANDING-AND-MOVING

This is the name of a giant in the traditions and beliefs of the Haida Native American people of the Queen Charlotte Islands and British Columbia, Canada. One-Standing-and-Moving exists beneath the earth and the islands; his movements create the earthquakes felt above.
References 77
See also Jinshin Uwo

ONGWE IAS

This is the name of a giant in the traditions and folk beliefs of the Seneca Native American people of the United States. Ongwe Ias was a cannibal that hunted human prey, but it was trapped and destroyed by the culture hero Hodadenon.
References 77
See also cannibal, giant

ONIARES

This is the name of a water serpent in the traditions and beliefs of the Caughnawaga Mohawk Native American people near Montreal, Canada. The legend tells how Da-Ra-Sa-Kwa, meaning "Moss Collector of the River," went to Lake Caughnawaga to search for a suitable log. Seeing one that looked right, he waded out to it, but as soon as he stood on it he found himself stuck by his feet, with the "log" taking him toward the rapids. The man was dragged over the edge into the watery depths, where he discovered a race of humanoids that gave him a serpent's skin to wear. As he put it on, he and the others transformed into Oniares, the vast, antlered water serpents. But with his transformation he had become one of the predators of his own people.
References 134
See also monster, serpent

ONOCENTAUR, ONOCENTAURUS

This is the name given to a class of centaur in the *Physiologus*, an ancient work of natural history said to have been written in Alexandria during the third century A.D. The Onocentaur, also known as the Monocentaur, was later included in the works of Isidore of Seville (c. 560–636) and in bestiaries of the medieval period. It is described as having the torso and head of a man but the body and legs of an ass. In medieval Christian symbolism it represented hypocrisy and sensuality.
References 7, 10, 20, 78, 89, 91, 125, 133, 148, 168
See also Apotharni, centaur, Cheiron, Eurytus, Ichthyocentaur, Nessus, Saggitarius

ONODRIM

This is the name of a race of giants in the literature of the English academic and author J. R. R. Tolkien (1892–1973) in *The Hobbit* (1937) and *The Lord of the Rings* (1955). The Onodrim are more usually referred to in the work as the Ents.
References 51
See also Ents, giant

ONYX MONOCEROS

This is the name given to the unicorn in the work by the Greek historian and author Ctesias, writing in Persia (now Iran) during the fifth century B.C. He described this inhabitant of the wilds of Persia as having a white body resembling that of a mule, a head colored purple with piercing blue eyes, and a massive horn colored red at the base, then black with a red point.
References 89
See also Alicorn, Al-mi'raj, Amduscias, Ass (Three-Legged), Biasd Na Srognig, Ch'i Lin, Chiai Tung, Chio-Tuan, Karkadan, Ki Lin, Kirin, Koresck, Licorn, Scythian Ass, unicorn

OOSER

This is an alternative name for the Wildman of European traditions and legends.
References 7, 128, 174
See also Wildman

OPHION

There are three beings that go by this name.
1. This is the name of a vast cosmic serpent in the ancient Pelagian mythology of Greece. Ophion was the creation of the goddess Eurynome from a cosmic

egg, from which also emerged all the things of the universe. When Ophion became the mate of Eurynome, the monster took the pride of creator for itself. The enraged goddess vanquished and disfigured the serpent and condemned Ophion to the caverns beneath the earth forever.

2. This is the name of one of the Titans in the classical mythology of Greece and Rome. Ophion was the progeny of Uranus and Gaia; his consort was Eurynome. He was vanquished during the wars with the Olympian gods by both Saturn and Rhea.

3. This is the name of a Centaur in the classical mythology of Greece and Rome. Ophion was the father of Amycus.

References 7, 14, 63, 89, 148, 169, 178, 185

See also centaur, Gaia, giant, monster, serpent, Titan, Uranus

OPINICUS

This is the name given in the heraldic repertoire of Europe to the Griffin when depicted in coats of arms and on other heraldic devices. The name "Opinicus," also known as the Epimacus in heraldic terminology, may be derived from the Greek name "Ophinicus" for the astronomical constellation of the serpent. The Opinicus is depicted with the body of a lion with either two or four legs, an eagle's or dragon's head, the wings of an eagle, and the tail of a camel. This curious composite creature is a feature of the heraldic coat of arms of the London guild of Barber-Surgeons.

References 7, 20

See also Griffin

OPKƏN

This is a fearsome water monster in the folk beliefs of the Cheremis/Mari people of the former Soviet Union. The Opkən is described as a vast, globular being with an enormous mouth. It inhabits large areas of open water, such as wide rivers, lakes, and inland seas, where it appears suddenly to swallow up any boats caught unaware of the danger.

References 165

See also Cuero, Hide

ORC, ORCO

This is the name of a monster described by the Roman naturalist Pliny the Elder in his *Historia Naturalis* (A.D. 77). It was considered to be a vast creature of the ocean with immense jaws full of huge teeth. It was not a whale but said to be much larger and to prey upon the whale. An instance of an Orc consuming a load of cowhides that had fallen overboard from a ship in Ostia harbor during the reign of the emperor Claudius brought terror to the seafarers. This monster, now named Orco, was later used, in the Italian work *Orlando Furioso* (1516) by Ludovicio Ariosto

Three Griffins in the arms of the Earl of Arundel. When depicted in coats of arms, the Griffin is titled the Opinicus. (Rose Photo Archive, UK)

(1474–1573), as the sea monster that threatened Andromeda.

References 7, 20, 174, 178

See also monster

ORIENTAL DRAGON

The Oriental Dragon, usually classified under the general term "Lung" or "Long," does not have a definite description, since this is a generalization and the subclasses of dragon have their individual characteristics. However, the Oriental Dragon may be described as having a long, scaly, serpentine neck and body with legs like those of a lizard and talons like those of an eagle. The head is delicate, like that of a camel, having whiskers and a tufted beard; the forehead has stag-like horns and huge ears. The eyes gleam a fiery red, but the rest of the body may be different colors. It has a pearl under its mouth, from which its breath may be mist or even flames. The Oriental Dragon rarely has wings; the Ying Lung is one example, although they move on the clouds through the heavens and may ascend or descend by way of a waterspout in the sea. The Oriental Dragon can be fierce but is almost always benevolent toward human beings. Although there are instances of malevolence, this is rare, unlike the Occidental Dragon, whose relationship with humans is much more ambivalent. The dragon enjoys the flesh of the swallow and loves jewels, especially jade; it hates centipedes and anything made of iron.

The Oriental Dragon holds a superior place in the legends and mythology of China, where it is responsible for the elements of water and fire and is a celestial being. Consequently, it is associated with the terrestrial position of the emperor, and the five-toed dragon was reserved exclusively in decorating the imperial garments and property. Indeed, some of the emperors were so closely associated with the dragon that one of them, Emperor Yaou (2356 B.C.), was said to have been sired by a dragon. The reigns of other emperors were regarded as most auspicious when the dragons were in evidence in the land. The appearance of the dragons as well as the Feng Hwang and the Ch'i Lin would be regarded as a time of great prosperity and peace. These three, with the Tortoise, form the Four Celestial Beings revered in Chinese mythology. It was said to be a dragon that gave the Pa Kwa spiritual trigrams to the emperor during the fourth millennium B.C. The dragon is also one of the beings representing one of the years in the twelve-year cycle of the zodiac, and the preparation of dragons' bones was a remedy for many medical conditions.

There are many subdivisions of the Chinese Oriental Dragon according to their responsibilities. During the Sung period in the year A.D. 1101, an emperor categorized the dragons as Black Dragons, in charge of mysterious lakes; Blue Dragons, which give compassion and are associated with courage; Red Dragons, which reside in the south, are associated with the pleasures of summer and are in charge of fresh water lakes; Yellow Dragons brought the system of writing to humans and listen and convey prayers to the gods; and the White Dragons extol virtue but may precede a period of famine.

There are Dragon Kings who hold a superior position and answer directly to the August Personage of Jade; they are Ao Chin, Ao Kuang, Ao Shun, and Ao Jun. They in turn command other dragons according to their lesser duties, some of whom are Chang Lung, Chi Lung Wang, Lung Wang, Pai Lung, Shen Lung, T'ien Lung, Shen Lung, Ti Lung, Yu Lung, Ying Lung, Gou Mang, and Rou Shou. These duties range from control of springs, wells, marshes, lakes, rivers, seas, rainfall, storms, fires, and floods.

The Japanese concept of the Oriental Dragon is very much the same as that in Chinese mythology but is termed the "Tatso" or "Hai Ryo." They are described as much more serpentine in shape than the Chinese Dragon and usually as having only three claws but

may have more. Unlike the Chinese Dragons, their relationship with humans can be ambivalent, like the Occidental Dragons. Typical legends include that of the storm god, Takehaya Susanowo. He heard a beautiful young woman weeping and inquired of her parents why Kushiada wept. The god was told that she was the last of eight beautiful daughters who had all been devoured by an eight-clawed dragon. This dragon was evil and had eight tails, eight legs with eight claws on each; its red eyes shot fire, and it was so vast that it dwarfed the hills. Soon she was expecting to be its next victim, and there was nothing that they could do to prevent it. So the god requested that, if he rescued her, she become his wife. Kushiada's parents consented, so Takehaya Susanowo transformed her into a comb, which he secured in his hair. Then he waited for the dragon with a vat of sake, which he offered to the monster when it arrived. The dragon was not used to the sake and was soon very drunk, whereupon the storm god killed it.

Another legend is very similar to the French legend of Melusine and tells of Hi-ko-hoho-da-mi no mikoto, a god who went fishing with his brother's best hook and lost it in the sea. When he went to the depths of the ocean in search of the hook, he met with Toyotama, the beautiful daughter of the sea god, who helped him retrieve the hook. He married Toyotama, but Hi-ko-hoho-da-mi no mikoto wished to return to the upper world and persuaded his pregnant wife to go, too. However, she made him promise never to see her when she slept. When the child was born, Hi-ko-hoho-da-mi no mikoto could not wait till morning and drew back the screens. There was their child, resting in the coils of a vast, black dragon, which fled to the sea forever.

References 18, 81, 89, 94, 113, 181

See also Blue Dragon, Ch'i Lin, Chang Lung, Chi Lung Wang, dragon, Dragon kings, Feng Hwang, Fu Ts'ang, Gou Mang, Hai Riyo, Ki Lin, Kih Tiau, Lung, Lung Wang, Melusine, Pai Lung, Rou Shou, Shen Lung, Tatsu, Tien Lung, Ti Lung, Yellow Dragon, Ying Lung, Yu Lung

ORION

This is the name of a giant in the classical mythology of Greece and Rome. Orion was variously born of the god Poseidon, or of a buried cowhide upon which three gods had urinated, or from Gaia, the great earth mother. He was famed as a hunter, with his dogs Arctophonos and Ptoophagus, and while involved in the chase on the island of Chios he fell in love with Merope. Unfortunately, her father, Œnopion, did not approve of the match. In a moment of madness, Orion tried to take Merope, for which crime her father, aided by the god Bacchus, blinded him. But the god Vulcan sent Cedalion to guide him until he could bathe his eyeballs in the rays of the rising sun; thus his sight was restored. He eventually took as his wife Side but still yearned after others. It was this that proved fatal, for while boasting about his hunting prowess to the goddess Artemis/Diana he was slain by one of her arrows, or in some versions by the sting of a scorpion. The gods then placed him in the heavens as the giant constellation known by his name.

References 20, 61, 166, 169, 178
See also Arctophonos, Gaia, giant, Ptoophagus

ORM

This is a general term in British and Scandinavian traditions and folklore for a vast serpentine or dragon-like monster. The word is derived from the Norse word *ormr,* which means "dragon." The other related names are "Worm" and "Vurm."

References 89
See also Lambton Worm, Lindorm, Vurm, Worm

OROBON

This is the name of a monstrous fish that was reported by medieval travelers and described in bestiaries as a belief of the Arabs of Moun Mazovan in the Red Sea region. The Orobon was described as being about ten feet long and the same in breadth with a hide similar to that of a crocodile. It was considered to be a vicious predator.

References 147
See also Cuero, Hide

ORRIBES

This is the name of a giant in the romances and legends of Spain. Orribes appears in the European

*The Orobon was considered to be a vicious predator. (*On Monsters and Marvels *by Ambroise Paré, trans. by Janis L. Pallister, University of Chicago Press, 1982)*

Arthurian legends as terrorizing Britain until killed by the hero Tritram/Tristan the Younger.
References 54
See also giant

ORTHOS, ORTHROS, ORTHRUS, ORTHUS
This is the name of a monstrous dog in the classical mythology of Greece and Rome. Orthos was the massive, two-headed dog of the giant Geryon. It was the sibling of Cerberus, the monstrous dog of the underworld, both being the offspring of the monsters Typhon and Echidna. Orthos was the guardian of the gigantic Oxen of Geryon, which were to be captured by Hercules/Heracles as one of his Twelve Labors. In the battle for the oxen, Orthos was killed by the hero.
References 7, 20, 178
See also Cerberus, Echidna, Geryon, monster, Typhon

ORTHRUS
This is the alternative spelling of the name of one of Geryon's dogs in the classcal mythology of Greece and Rome.
References 20
See also Geryon, Geryon's Dogs, Orthos

OSCHAERT
This is the name in Belgian folklore for the monstrous Black dog with the same characteristics as the Kludde. The Oschaert was described as looking like a huge horse, or a padding Black dog with fiery eyes. It would seize upon unwary travelers on dark nights, leaping upon their backs, growing heavier the more its victims tried to be free. It particularly oppressed those who were troubled by a guilty conscience, for it would dig its claws deep into their flesh and breathe fiery breath on their necks. The Oschaert was said to inhabit an area surrounding the town of Hamme, near Duendemonde. It is said that a priest of the area finally exorcised the Oschaert and banished it over the seas for ninety-nine years.
References 93, 160
See also Black dogs, Brag, Grant, Kludde, Padfoot

OSHÄDAGEA
This is the name of a giant in the traditions and beliefs of the Iroquois Native American people of the northeastern United States. Oshädagea, also known as Big Eagle of the Dew, is described as a gigantic eagle that is the attendant of Hino. This vast eagle protects humans from the destructive fires caused by evil demons. When the forests are blazing, Oshädagea takes the waters from the ocean in the hollow of his back between his wings and douses the scorching forests and puts the demons to flight.
References 133, 139

OSHUMARE
This is the name of a vast serpent in the traditions and beliefs of the Yoruba people of Nigeria. Oshumare is the Rainbow Snake, equating with the great rainbow snake Aido Hwedo in the mythology of the peoples of Dahomey in West Africa.
References 24
See also Aido Hwedo

OTOHIME
This is the name of a monstrous sea princess in the mythology and traditions of Japan. Otohime is also known as Toyotama.
References 113, 133
See also Toyotama

OTUS
This is the name of one of the sons of Aloes in the classical mythology of Greece and Rome. The name "Otus" may be translated as "Resister." They were giants born of Iphimedeia, the wife of Aloes/Aloeus, but some accounts say that they were the sons of Poseidon by her. Some sources say that they were derived from the blood of the castrated Uranus and that they emerged in full armor at the Pallene Peninsula near Phlegra. The Aloadae were twins; Otus's brother is Ephialtes. From birth the pair grew at the rate of nine inches each month. They were so vast that by the time they were nine years of age they were already twenty-six feet in girth and nearly sixty feet in height. Although portrayed as gross and uncouth, they were said to have founded cities and inspired the veneration of the Muses. When their mother and sister were threatened, they rescued them. Otus is also described as a member of the race of giants known as the Gigantes. This character was also used, along with others, in the classic works of the medieval Italian author Boccaccio (1313–1375), who describes him as a son of Tytan and Terra.
References 139, 174
See also Alodae, Ephialtes, giant, Gigantes, Uranus

OURANOS
This is an alternative spelling of Uranus in the classical mythology of Greece and Rome.
References 47, 166, 182
See also Uranus

OUROBOROS
This is the name of a serpent-dragon in the mythology of ancient Egypt. Ouroboros is the serpent-dragon of eternity and continuity, depicted as a vast cosmic monster continually devouring its own tail. Paradoxically, despite its continuous destruction, it is also continuously reemerging; should the process be disrupted, it is the signal for the end of time.

References 61, 78, 89, 134
See also dragon, serpent

OWNER-OF-A-BAG, OWNER-OF-BAG

This is the name of a monstrous bird in the traditions and folklore of the Arapaho Native American people of the United States. Owner-of-a-Bag, also known as Bogey, is described as a gigantic owl that has a vast bag in which it abducts small children who constantly misbehave. Owner-of-a-Bag is therefore a Nursery bogie used by parents to threaten their children into good behavior.

References 77
See also Boo-bagger, Nursery bogie

OX OF DIL

This is the name of a monstrous cow or bull in the legends and traditions of Ireland. The Ox of Dil was said to be the offspring of the beast of Lettir Dallan when it mated with one of the cattle on the shore of the lake.

References 134
See also Beast of Lettir Dallan, Oxen of Geryon

OXEN OF GERYON

These were monstrous cattle in the classical mythology of Greece and Rome. These oxen were described as having three bodies each and were a vast herd at Erytheia on the Iberian Peninsula. They were guarded day and night by the giant Eurytion and the massive dog Orthos until the hero Hercules/Heracles slew them and took the herd as one of his Twelve Labors to win Deianeira as his bride.

References 7
See also Eurytion, giant, Orthos

OYALEROWECK

This is the name of a lake monster in the traditions and folklore of the region of the Saint Charles River and the Lake of Lorette in Canada. Oyaleroweck, also known as the Great Serpent of Lorette, was described as a vast creature over thirty feet long that inhabited the cavern behind the waterfall above the lake. At night the creature would surface and roam the area of the village and terrify the inhabitants. The legend relates how a Jesuit priest was determined to exorcise the monster and one evening went to the waterfall, where he chanted the rites of exorcism and commanded the monster to emerge. This it did; it slowly dragged its huge form through the village and departed to Lake Saint Joseph.

References 134
See also monster, serpent

P

P' ÊNG

This is the name of a gigantic bird in the legends of China. The P' Êng was the metamorphosed form of the gigantic fish called the Kw' Ên. In its state as a bird this creature was so vast that when it spread its wings the heavens were obliterated from sight. It inhabited the north of the country, but with the onset of the typhoon season the P' Êng rose thousands of feet into the heavens and flew south.

References 81

See also Kw' Ên

PADFOOT

This is the name of a terrifying monstrous being in the folklore of Yorkshire in the north of England. Padfoot, also known as Padfooits, is said to inhabit the moors, particularly around Leeds. It is described variously as taking the form of a monstrous sheep with shaggy fleece and fiery eyes, or of a huge white dog, or even of a massive black donkey with huge, glaring eyes. Whatever shape, it is the soft, eerie padding behind its victim as it draws alongside in the dark that warns of its presence. This is often accompanied by roaring or the sound of chains. Terrified victims have died of fright. Some have attempted to hit it, but this is a bogey beast, not unlike the Barguest, Gytrash, Skryker, and Trash—all supernatural road monsters of northern England that must never be approached or touched.

References 21, 24, 25, 37, 160

See also Black dogs, Black Shuck, Mauthe Doog, Rongeur d'Os, Skriker

PAGAN, GIANT PAGAN

This is the name of a giant in the classical literature of England. He appears in the classic allegorical work *Pilgrim's Progress*, written by John Bunyan and published in 1682. Giant Pagan, with Giant Pope, is considered to be responsible for the slaughter of many people whose bones fill a cave that the pilgrims must pass.

References 20, 31

See also Despair (Giant), giant, Maul, Pope, Slay-good

PAI LUNG

This is the name of a dragon in the traditions and legends of China. The Pai Lung, also known as the White Dragon, was a Dragon King notable for being the only white dragon. Legend tells how a young girl answered the door of their home to an old man requesting shelter from a violent storm. When he had gone in the morning, she was found to be pregnant, and her outraged family ejected her. When the "child" was delivered, it appeared to be no more than a ball of white flesh, which was thrown in the water, where it turned into a magnificent white dragon. The young girl fainted from terror and never recovered consciousness, but the local people revered her as the mother of Pai Lung. When she died she was buried with honor, and her grave became a shrine. Pai Lung had a temple dedicated on Mount Yang Suchow in Kiangsu, where a tablet records the legend.

References 181

See also Oriental Dragon

PAIJA

This is the name of a monster in the folk beliefs of the Innuit and Ihalmiut peoples of Canada. She is described as a huge, grotesque, humanoid female with long, black hair flowing over her body and just one leg that emerges from the region of her genitalia. The Paija is a predatory being that hunts and tracks humans in the winter snows during the long winter nights. She will especially seek men caught in the blizzards to devour them. A single look from her, or merely the sight of her, is instantaneous death, and therefore anyone seeing her twisted, single-foot track in the snow will not venture out until it is safe.

References 138

See also Biasd Bheulach, Fachan, monster, Nasha, Shiqq

PAIYUK

This is the name of a class of monsters in the traditions and beliefs of the Ute Native American people of the United States. The Paiyuk are described

as evil water-elk types of animals that hunt humans as their prey. These cannibalistic creatures are regarded by shamans as having supernatural powers.
References 77
See also cannibal, monster

PALESMURT

This is the name of a curious humanoid monster in the folklore of the Volga region of Russia. The Palesmurt is described as looking like a human but having only one half of the body, one arm and hand, one leg and foot, and a head with only one eye. This horrific being trapped unwary travelers in his territory and choked them to death.
References 7
See also Direach, Nesnas

PALET

This is the name of a giant in the Hebrew scriptures and texts of the Jewish religion. Palet was mentioned by the prophet and leader Moses as being a giant that had survived the Flood with Noah and was now living in Syria. This giant is referred to in other texts as Og of Bashan.
References 174
See also giant, Og

PALLAS, PALLOS

There are two giants with this name in the classical mythology of Greece and Rome.

1. Pallas, or Pallos, whose name means the "Brandisher," was the name of one of the primordial giants born of Gaia. He took part in the wars with the Olympian gods and was vanquished, his skin being flayed by the goddess Athene. Thereafter, she used his skin as a cloak or as the covering for her shield and took the name "Pallas Athene" to commemorate his defeat.

2. Pallas was the name of a Titan who was the progeny of Eurybia and Caius and the sibling of Astraeus and Perses. He was the father of Bia, Cratos, Nike, and Zelos by his consort, Styx.
References 133, 139, 169, 178
See also Gaia, giant, Titan

PALLENES

This is the name of a giant derived from the classical mythology of Greece and Rome and also mentioned in the later Italian literature of Boccaccio (1313–1375).
References 174
See also Aloids, Ephialtes, giant, Otus, Terra, Tytan

PAL-RAI-YUK

This is the name of a type of water monster in the traditions and beliefs of the Inuit people of Alaska. The Pal-rai-yuk were described as very long creatures with two heads, six legs, three stomachs, a saw-toothed ridge on the spine, and two tails. These terrifying monsters were said to inhabit the creeks and estuary swamps of the rivers. To ensure that the Pal-rai-yuk would not molest them, it was the habit to paint their image on the *umiaks* before venturing out into the waters of their territory.
References 77, 134
See also Haietlik, monster

PALUG'S CAT

This is the name of a monstrous supernatural cat in the legends and folklore of Wales and the Arthurian legends of Europe. It is also known as Cath Paluc and Chapalu in Wales and Capalu or Capalus in France. It is an enormous supernatural and fabulous creature that hunted its own kind to satisfy its enormous appetite.
References 7
See also Cath Paluc, Chapalu, Írusán

PALULUKON

This is the name of a class of water serpent in the traditions and beliefs of the Hopi Native American people of the United States. It is said that the earth rests on the backs of two Palulukon floating in the cosmic ocean. When these Palulukon have been badly treated by humans, or when they become tired and turn, earthquakes occur above them, or the water springs may cease to flow.
References 77
See also Aido Hwedo, Kolowisi, serpent

PAMBA

This is the name of a monstrous water being in the traditions and folklore of the people of Tanzania in the region of Lake Tanganyika. The Pamba is described as a vast creature with a mouth so huge that it can engulf a canoe and all the fishermen aboard. When it moves in the water it turns the water red, and when this is observed no boats will leave the shore.
References 134
See also monster

PANDORA JUNIOR

This is one of the giants named in the genealogy created by the Italian monk Annius of Viterbo (Giovanni Nanni, c. 1432–1502) to justify the noble descent of the Gauls from a giant biblical race.
References 139, 174
See also giant, Noah

PANGU, PANGU, P'AN-KU

This is the name of a cosmic giant in the legends of China. This vast primodial being was generated,

according to some legends, from a cosmic egg; the earth and heavens were later formed from the two sections of the shell. In other versions he was a minute speck in Hun Dun (chaos), growing at the rate of six feet each day and becoming a vast giant within 18,000 years. As he grew, he chiseled away at the earth and heavens, pushing them farther apart and forming the undulations of the earth. When all this was done, Pangu expired, but his various parts became the universe: His eyes became the sun and moon, his sweat the waters of the earth, his breath the winds, his voice the thunder, the hair of his head became the stars, his body became the soil of the earth in which his body hair grew as the vegetation of the world, while the human race evolved from the fleas on his body. In some legends his various body parts became the mountains in the different regions of China.
References 7, 125, 133, 166
See also giant, Purusha, Ymir

PANTAGRUEL

This is the name of a giant in the classic early literature of France. Pantagruel appears as the main character in the works by the author François Rabelais (ca. 1494–ca. 1553), in the satires *Pantagruel* (1532) and later in *Gargantua* (1534). The name, according to the author, was derived from the Great Panta, meaning "All," and the Arabic word *gruel,* meaning "thirst," because he was born during a great drought. He was so vast that his cradle was made from ship's beams, and although he was chained into it he broke out by smashing the base of the cradle and released himself. In maturity he became omniscient and outshone everyone in every manner. Pantagruel was the King of the Dipsodes, and his goal was the search for the "Oracle of the Holy Bottle," during which he journeyed to Utopia.
References 20, 174
See also Gargantua, giant

PAPILLON

This is the name of a horse in the classic literature of Italy. Papillon is the supernatural fire-breathing flying horse that features in the work *Orlando Innamorato* (1486) by Matteo Maria Boiardo, Count of Scandiano (1434–1494).
References 7
See also Horses of the Sun, Pegasus

PAPSTESEL

This is the name of a hybrid monster in the medieval accounts of Italy. The Papstesel, also known as the Pope Ass, was described as having the body of a woman with one human arm, the other

being like the trunk of an elephant; the legs were deformed, one being like that of an eagle and the other like that of a cow. The head was said to resemble that of a donkey but with the image of a bearded man's face on the back. It also had a serpent's head on the end of its tail, like an Amphisbaena. This creature was said to have been landed from the Tiber River in the flood of 1496 and was used by Martin Luther (1483–1546), the German religious reformer, in 1523 to call derision on the corruption of the papacy.
References 89
See also Amphisbaena, Monk fish, Pope ass

PARANDUS, PARANDRUS, PARANDER

This is the name of a creature frequently depicted in the bestiaries of medieval Europe. It was described as something between a bear and an ibex with a thick, shaggy pelt, huge horns on its head, and cloven hooves on its deer-like legs and feet. The most remarkable feature was its ability, when pursued, to blend with the environment like a chamaeleon by changing its body color. In an Anglo-Saxon bestiary of 1220 in the Bodleian Library, Oxford, the creature was said to have the footprints of an ibis (a bird), probably a medieval misreading of the word "ibex," and to inhabit the land of Ethiopia. Today it still features frequently in the heraldic repertoire of European coats of arms.
References 10, 14, 89, 148, 185

PARATA

This is the name of a water monster in the legends of the Maori people of New Zealand. The Parata belongs to the class of monsters known as Taniwha that preys upon humans and other creatures. However, the Parata is a vast ocean monster whose mouth is so wide and cavernous that it sucks in all the waters of the seas and then spews them back out. This Taniwha therefore accounts for the tidal motions of the seas.
References 155
See also Tanihwa

PARTHENOPE

This is the name of one of the Sirens in the classical mythology of Greece and Rome. Parthenope, like her sisters, is part woman and part bird or part fish.
References 178
See also Aglaopheme, Alkonost, Angka, Garuda, Harpy, Podarge, Ptitsy-Siriny, Siren, Sirin, Solovei Rakhmatich, Unnati, Zägh

PAUL BUNYAN

See Bunyan, Paul

PEALLAIDH

This is the name of a Urisk, or monster, in the folklore of Perthshire, Scotland. It belongs to a class of semisupernaturals called Fuaths that are evil in nature. The Peallaidh is also known as the "Shaggy One" from its appearance, which, like most of the Fuaths, is covered in shaggy hair. This one inhabits the river-divided forested areas of Perthshire, but a Lowland version of the Peallaidh is known, and this is called the Shellycoat.
References 24, 128, 160
See also Fuath, monster, Urisk

PEG POWLER

This is the name of an evil humanoid monster in the folklore of the border between Yorkshire and Durham, England. She is described as an evil hag, having a hideous female form with green hair and a gaping mouth with green teeth. She inhabits the River Tees and lurks there, awaiting the opportunity to drag unwary humans under the water to her lair, where she may devour them. Peg Powler's favorite prey are the little children who defy their parents to play at the water's edge, and in this respect she is a Nursery bogie. There are two indications of her presence: the froth on the upper reaches of the river, which are known as Peg Powler's Suds, and the green surface scum on the slower sections of the river, called Peg Powler's Cream.
References 21, 24, 25, 60, 170
See also Grindylow, Jenny Greenteeth, Kappa, monster, Nellie Longarms, Nursery bogie

PEGASI

These are monstrous birds in the legends of Greece and Rome. They were described by Pliny the Elder in his *Historia Naturalis* (A.D. 77) as being huge birds with the head of a horse that inhabited the eastern Mediterranean region of Scythia.
References 7
See also Siren

PEGASUS

This is the name of a flying horse in the classical mythology of Greece and Rome. Pegasus was said to be generated from the union between the sea god Poseidon, appearing as a white stallion, and the Gorgon called Medusa prior to her monstrous state. An alternative version states that Pegasus was engendered from the spilled blood of Medusa after she had been decapitated by the hero Perseus. He is depicted frequently in ancient art as a vast but elegant white stallion with golden wings. Pegasus became the mount of Perseus, but when he died Pegasus, who was immortal, flew to Mount Helicon.

The mountain springs and streams had run dry in a severe drought, and the nymphs known as the Muses were grateful when Pegasus, stamping the ground with mournful rage, engendered freshwater springs wherever he went. Today one such spring is known as Hippocrene, or "Horse Spring." When the monstrous Chimera was laying waste to Corinth, the hero Bellerophon was sent by King Iobates to kill the monster. He prayed to the goddess Athene to help him, whereupon she gave him a golden bridle with which to tame and ride Pegasus to do battle with the Chimera. When he was successful, Bellerophon erroneously tried to keep Pegasus for himself and, in his inflated pride, soar to the height of Mount Olympus itself. The king of the gods, Zeus, sent a gadfly to sting Pegasus under the tail and unseat the presumptuous human, who fell to the earth and was killed. Pegasus remained on Mount Olympus with the gods and became one of the steeds of Zeus.
References 5, 7, 20, 24, 61, 78, 89, 94, 106, 133, 166, 169, 178, 182
See also Chimera, Gorgon, Griffin, Hippogryph, Medusa, Poqhiraj

PEISTE

This is the name of a huge water monster in the traditions and legends of Ireland. The Peiste is described as a type of amphibious "worm," or dragon, recorded in early times and said to have been defeated by Saint Patrick. A recent sighting, by a group of friends on an outing, took place in Lough Fadda in the west of Ireland in 1954, and the folk belief still clearly lives on.
References 78, 89, 134
See also dragon, Loch Ness Monster, monster, Worm

PELAGON

This is the name of one of the Hundred-Handed Giants in the classical mythology of Greece and Rome. He is included in later versions of the myths.
References 178
See also giant, Hundred-Handed Giants

PELORUS

The name of one of the Gigantes in the classical mythology of Greece and Rome. They were engendered from the blood of Uranus's castration when it fell upon the earth. Alcyoneus, with Porphyrion, was one of their leaders. They were described as being of enormous humanoid proportions but having serpents for legs with the serpents' heads for feet. At their first appearance they were already fully formed adult warriors, complete with spears and in shining armor, ready to do battle.

Bellerophon on Pegasus (A Wonder Book for Boys and Girls and Tanglewood Tales *by N. Hawthorne, J. M. Dent, London*)

And they attacked the Olympian gods immediately. However, by subterfuge, supernatural powers, and the strength of the hero Hercules/Heracles, one by one they were defeated. Both Pelorus and Mimas were killed by the Olympian god Ares by being run through with a sword.
References 7, 139, 169, 178
See also Alcyoneus, Clytius, Enceladus, giant, Gigantes, Hecatonchieres, Hundred-Handed Giants, Mimas, Pallas, Polybutes, Porphyrion, Rhaetos, Typhon

PELUDA
This is the name of a monster in the legends and folklore of medieval France. The Peluda was also known as La Velue, which may be translated as the "Shaggy Beast."
References 89
See also monster

PEMPHREDO
This is the name of one of the Grææ in the classical mythology of Greece and Rome. Pemphredo, also spelled Pephredo, may be translated as "Wasp."
References 24, 38, 125, 133, 166, 169
See also Græææ

PEOPLE OF CAORA
During the sixteenth-century exploration of the Americas by the Europeans, a number of curious and monstrous forms were often equated with those of the classical mythology of Greece and Rome, or with the fabulous monsters of medieval Europe. The People of Caora undoubtedly come within this category, for they were described by the English geographer Richard Hakluyt (c. 1522–1616) as similar to the Blemmyes in his *Divers Voyages Touching the Discovery of America* (1582). They were said to have their heads below their shoulders, where their eyes were located, and to have their mouths in their belly. They inhabited the banks of the River Caora. Sir Walter Raleigh (1552–1618) also described a similar people as living at the time in the region of Guiana.

There is, in fact, some evidence to support there having existed a race of people in the Americas, whose consideration of fashion and beauty led to the habit of a posture that raised their shoulders permanently. This thus obscured their necks and lowered the position of the eyes and mouth to an observer, which could have been the basis of the legend.
References 20
See also Blemmyes

PEPHREDO

This is the name of one of the Grææ in the classical mythology of Greece and Rome. Pephredo, also spelled Pemphredo, may be translated as "Wasp."
References 24, 38, 125, 133, 166, 169
See also Grææ

PÈRE FOUETTARD

This is the name of a type of ogre in the traditions and folklore of France. Père Fouettard, whose name means "Father Spanker," was introduced into the folklore of France about the beginning of the eighteenth century. He is depicted as a huge, middle-aged countryman in early-nineteenth-century dress with a tattered top hat, high collars and cravat, waistcoat, tailcoat, beeches, stockings, and buckled shoes. Père Fouettard is a threatening ogre who seeks out and deals with all the naughty children by putting them in the pannier on his back and carrying them off to be imprisoned and flogged. In this respect, he is therefore used by parents as a Nursery bogie to encourage their children's good behavior, especially before the festive season, when he is regarded as the counterpart to the generous Père Noël.
References 182
See also Croquemitaine, Father Flog, Nursery bogie, ogre

PERSES, PERSAIOS

This is the name of a giant in the classical mythology of Greece and Rome. Perses is a Titan and the father of the Olympian goddess Hecate.
References 20, 125
See also giant, Titan

PERYTON

This is the name of a hybrid monster reported by a Rabbi from Fez, most probably Jacob ben Chaim, during the sixteenth century, as being detailed in a now lost book from the library at Alexandria. The Perytons were said to inhabit the land of Atlantis and described as having the body and wings of a green-feathered bird but with the legs and head of a deer. The last reported sighting, in Ravenna, stated that their feathers were light-blue. Even more curiously, when it flew on its massive wings the vast shadow was in the shape of a human, its prey. Once a Peryton had killed a human and soaked its body in the half-consumed victim, its shadow returned to its own shape, and it was unable to kill humans again. Although they cannot be killed by any known human weapon, when Scipio and his army invaded Carthage and were attacked by Perytons, they managed to succeed, since the Perytons could kill only one man each and soon departed, leaving some of the army intact.
References 18, 63, 89
See also Griffin, Roc

PEY

These are a class of Ghoul in the Tamil mythology of India and are also known in female forms as the Alakai, Iruci, and Picacu. They are the attendants of Yama and are depicted as a type of monstrous humanoid with shaggy hair. The Pey are cannibalistic vampires that seek out human conflicts and battles to feed on the bodies of the wounded and drink the blood from their open wounds, ensuring their death.
References 95, 125
See also cannibal, Ghoul, vampire

PHAEA

This is the name of a gigantic female pig in the classical mythology of Greece and Rome. Phaea was sent to ravage the countryside of Crommyon in Greece. It was killed by the hero Theseus.
References 139, 178
See also Ætolian Boar, Beigad, Boar of Beann-Gulbain, Buata, Cafre/Kafre, Calydonian Boar, Erymanthean Boar, Hildesuin, Pugot/Pugut, Sachrimnir, Twrch Trwyth, Ysgithyrwyn

PHAETHON

This is the name of a horse in the classical mythology of Greece and Rome. Phaethon, whose name means the "Shining One," is one of the team of Horses of the Sun that pulled the golden chariot that Hephaestus had made for the sun god Helios. Phaethon, like the other horses, is described as the purest white with flaring, fire-breathing nostrils. Each morning the nymphs of time, the Horae, harnessed Phaethon along with the other Horses of the Sun to the chariot for their journey across the sky, and when their journey across the heavens was finished at dusk, they browsed on magical herbs in the Islands of the Blessed until they were harnessed for the next day.
References 139
See also Horses of the Sun

PHANTOM CAT

This is the name of a monstrous cat in the legends and folklore of Japan. It was said to be so huge that it devoured a sacrificed young maid every year in its lair on the island of Oki. It was eventually torn to bits and utterly destroyed by a heroic knight and his dog, Shippeitaro.
References 113
See also Chapalu, Írusán

PHANTOM OF THE LAKE

This is the name of a water monster in the traditions and folklore of Estonia. It mostly is said to resemble the shape of a horse or a gigantic pig as it surfaces in the swamps and wetlands.

References 134
See also monster

PHENG

This is the name of a fabulous bird in the traditions and folklore of the people of Japan. It was described as being so huge that it could take up and consume a camel at one go. Its feathers were so big that when they dropped to the earth humans made water casks from the quills. Its wingspan blocked out the sun from the earth like the Roc in the *Tales of the Thousand and One Nights*.

References 7
See also Roc

PHILAMALOO BIRD, PHILLYLOO BIRD

This is a creature from the folklore of lumberjacks and forest workers, especially in Wisconsin and Minnesota during the nineteenth and early twentieth centuries. It is also known as the Filla-ma-loo Bird and Phillyloo Bird and reputedly sought to remedy its dislike of the cold and damp, which gave it rheumatism, by flying upside-down. The Philamaloo Bird belongs to a group of beings affectionately known as the Fearsome Critters, whose exaggerated proportions and activities not only explained the weird noises of the lonely landscape but also provided some amusement at camps.

References 7, 24
See also Fearsome Critters

PHIOBE

This is an alternative spelling of the name of the Titan Phoebe in the classical mythology of Greece and Rome.

References 20, 47, 78, 94, 125, 139, 166, 178
See also Phoebe

PHLEGON

This is the name of a fabulous celestial horse in the classical mythology of Greece and Rome. Phlegon, whose name means the "Burning One," is one of the four horses that pulled the chariot of the sun god daily across the sky. The others mentioned by the classical poet Ovid (43 B.C.–A.D. 17) are Acthon, Eous, and Pyrois.

References 89
See also Horses of the Sun

PHOEBE, PHŒBE

This is the name of a female Titan in the classical mythology of Greece and Rome. Her name, which means "Brightness," may also be spelled Phiobe. She was the daughter of Uranus and Gaia and, by her sibling Coeus, the mother of Latona, Asteria, and Leto, the latter becoming the mother of the god Apollo.

References 20, 38, 61, 166, 169, 178
See also Coeus, giantess, Titan

PHOENIX

This is the name of a fabulous bird in the ancient legends of Europe and the Middle East that may have its origins in the Egyptian Bennu bird. The Phoenix, also spelled Fenix, is described as looking somewhat like a pheasant in shape but larger than an eagle. Its plumage was mostly a reddish-purple, "Phoenix" being derived from the Greek for purple, with gold around it neck. Other accounts say that it was purple, gold, red, and blue. This magnificent bird was said to be unique, no other bird being alive at the same time. It was said variously to inhabit the regions of Persia, India, Arabia, or Ethiopia where it existed on the finest of aromas. The first accounts of the Phoenix come from the Greek writer Herodotus (485–425 B.C.), who related that as one bird died after 500 years of life another took it to the temple of the sun at Heliopolis for burial. However, Ovid (43 B.C.–A.D. 17) and Pliny the Elder in his *Historia Naturalis* (A.D. 77) suggested that the living Phoenix constructed a nest of spices, upon which it incinerated itself. From this a sort of maggot emerged, which then developed into the progeny that took the ashes of the former bird in the nest to Heliopolis. A later version stated that the Phoenix constructed its nest of spices and sang to the sun god, who filled it with fire, consuming the bird. From the ashes an entirely mature Phoenix emerged, taking the ashes to the altar at Heliopolis. Within the legends and traditions of Greece and Rome, the Phoenix was the symbol of immortality and was portrayed on funerary furnishings.

From these traditions, current with the emergence of Christianity, the Phoenix was adopted ecclesiastically as the symbol of the resurrection of Christ. It was included in the *Physiologus* written in Alexandria reputedly in the second century B.C. Pope Clement of Rome (c. A.D. 96) suggested that it was the evidence for the resurrection of the righteous. From that time the Phoenix was well established in the ecclesiastical repertoire, and commentaries were made by Tacitus (c. A.D. 100) and Aelian (c. A.D. 200). The bird had now achieved a vast size and much more luxurious coloring, together with an estimated lifespan of 1,461 days, equaling four solar years.

The Phoenix was very widely depicted in the medieval Books of Hours, psalters, and bestiaries, where its Christian symbolism was emphasized. It was, however, frequently confused with other birds, such as the eagle, and sometimes with the Salamander. It was also utilized as decoration on church vestments, ecclesiastical furniture, and the structures themselves. The Phoenix also appeared in the *Travels of Sir John Mandeville* written about A.D. 1360, where the description follows closely the one given by Pliny. It has since featured frequently in the arts all over Europe and especially in the literature of Edmund Spenser (c. 1552–1599), William Shakespeare (1564–1616), W. B. Yeats (1865–1939), and D. H. Lawrence (1885–1930).

As a potent image, its symbolism was utilized in the heraldic repertoire of Europe and may still be seen in the coats of arms of families and institutions, especially those concerned with fire insurance.
References 5, 7, 10, 14, 18, 20, 24, 61, 78, 81, 89, 91, 148, 168, 169, 178, 180, 185
See also Bennu, dragon, Feng-Hwang, fung, Heliodromos, Hwa Yih, Ki-Lin, Kirin, Lwan, Salamander, Shui Ying, Simurgh, To Fu, unicorn, Yin Chu, Yoh Shoh, Yu Siang

PHOETUS
This is the name of a giant in the classical mythology of Greece and Rome. Phoetus is one of the Gigantes and, like his brothers, was said to have been engendered from the blood that fell on the earth from the castrated Uranus. These giants were born fully mature and clad in full battle armor. They waged war on the Olympian gods after the defeat of the Titans and were defeated. In that battle Phoetus was not defeated until the final attack. He was buried, like the others, in deep chasms within the earth, upon which mountains and volcanoes were piled.
References 24, 133, 169, 178
See also Aloadae, Cyclopes, giant, Gigantes

PHOLUS
This is the name of a centaur in the classical mythology of Greece and Rome. Pholus, the progeny of a Melian nymph by the Satyr Silenus, was, like Cheiron, a wise and gentle centaur. Because of his sagacity, he was entrusted with the wine store in his cavern home, as centaurs became intoxicated too quickly if it were not controlled. During Hercules/Heracles's hunt for the Erymanthian Boar, he called at the cavern of Pholus, who opened a cask in his honor. The other centaurs

soon smelled the wine, and the party soon became violently rowdy. In the melée that ensued, a centaur named Eleatus was wounded by one of Hercules/Heracles's poisoned arrows and went to Cheiron to have it taken out. As Cheiron did this, he stabbed himself with it accidentally; knowing he would be in eternal pain, he gave his immortality to Prometheus. Pholus received the poisoned arrow and accidentally dropped it on his foot and was also killed.
References 24, 133, 139, 166, 169, 178
See also centaur, Cheiron, Erymanthian Boar, Prometheus, satyr, Silenus

PHOOKA
This is an alternative spelling of Pooka, a monstrous water-horse in the folklore of Ireland.
References 21, 24, 25, 64, 160
See also Pooka

PHORCIDES, PHORCYDES, PHORCYNES, PHORCYNIS
This is an alternative name for the monstrous hags called the Grææ, sisters to the Gorgons, in the classical mythology of Greece and Rome.
References 178
See also Grææ

PHORCYS
This is the name of a giant sometimes depicted as a sea monster in the classical mythology of Greece and Rome. Phorcys, also known as Porcus and Orcus, was the progeny of Gaia and the sibling of the monster Typhon, or the progeny of Pontus and Terra, and consort of Ceto, the grandmother of Polyphemus and the Dragon of Ladon. In some versions the monstrous Gorgons were said to be his daughters. He is depicted as having the body of a gigantic fish and the head and tusks of a wild boar. In some versions Phorcys is considered to be a sea deity; in others he is the gigantic sea monster responsible for death in the ocean depths.
References 134, 178
See also Dragon of Ladon, giant, monster, Paia, Polyphemus, Typhon

PHYNNODDEREE
This is an alternative spelling of the Manx semisupernatural giant known as the Fenodyree in the legends and folklore of the Isle of Man in the British Isles.
References 24, 25, 64, 111, 152
See also Fenodyree

PI NERESKƏ

This is a group of evil humanoid monsters in the folk beliefs of the Cheremis/Mari people of the former Soviet Republic. The name Pi Nereskə means "Dog Nose," and they are described as being the shape of humans with only one foot and hand each and having the nose of a dog. Their prey are human beings, and they use their keen sense of smell to track down humans who travel through the Siberian forests. Because these creatures hunt in pairs, a human may be deceived into thinking that the tracks he has seen are those of a man and not the Pi Nereskə, until it is too late and the human has become their victim.
References 165
See also Fachan, Fuaths

PIASA

This is the name of a water monster in the folk beliefs of the Algonquian Native American people of Mississippi in the United States. A portrayal of this terrifying being was described in 1675 by a French traveler called Marquette. The image painted on the rocks over a massive water fall at Alton, Illinois, showed a being about the size of a deer; the head had the face of a man with a beard but had red eyes; the green body was covered in scales and from it extended a long tail on the end of which was a poisonous barb. It was later considered to be the fish-man of a whirlpool.
References 7, 89, 134, 160
See also monster

PIAST/S

This is the name given to a class of monster in the beliefs and folklore of Ireland. This creature, which is also known by various other names—Biast, Dragon of the Apocalypse, and the Apocalyptic Beast—is described as being part serpent and part salmon, breathing fire like a dragon. A Piast is said to inhabit the murky depths of Loch-Bél-Dracon, which is the Irish name meaning "Lake of the Dragon's Mouth." It has been identified with the dragon of the Apocalyptic Beasts, which will arise to signal the destruction of the earth and the Second Coming of the Lord before the Day of Judgment. However, Saint Patrick has controlled all the serpents of Ireland, and the Piasts are held in check by him until Judgment Day.
References 134
See also Apocalyptic Beast, monster

PICACU

These are the female equivalent of the Ghouls in the Tamil mythology of India.
References 139, 178
See also Ghoul

PIHUECHENYI

This is the name of a monster in the traditions and beliefs of the Araucanian people of Chile. The Pihuechenyi are described as vast, winged snakes that swoop down in the night on humans sleeping in the forests and drink their blood. The Pihuechenyi are a type of vampire.
References 139
See also monster, vampire

PING FENG

This is the name of a monster in the traditions and legends of China. The Ping Feng is described as having the body of a black boar but with the head of a human or with a head at both ends of its body. The Ping Feng appears in the volumes known as the *T'ai P'ing Kuang Chi*, which may be translated as the Great Records Made in the Period of Peace and Prosperity, which was completed ca. A.D. 978 and published in A.D. 981.
References 7, 18
See also Amphisbaena, monster

PINNACLE GROUSE

This is a creature from the folklore of the lumberjacks and forest workers, especially in Wisconsin and Minnesota in the United States, during the nineteenth and early twentieth centuries. This is a curious bird, for it had only one wing, which made it a very lopsided being when it attempted to fly. The Pinnacle Grouse had therefore developed the ability to fly, but only in one direction, with its wingless side stabilized against the side of the conical mountain where it nested. The Pinnacle Grouse belongs to a group of beings affectionately known as the Fearsome Critters, whose exaggerated proportions and activities not only explained the weird noises of the lonely landscape but also provided some amusement at camps.
References 7
See also Fearsome Critters

PIRANU

This is the name of a monstrous fish in the folklore of Argentina. The Piranau is described as a huge black fish but with the head of a horse with huge eyes that inhabits the depths of the rivers. It is particularly aggressive toward any humans that enter its domain and will ram their boats and drown them.
References 134
See also Loch Ness Monster, monster, Monster of Brompton, Sea Horse

PISINÖE

This is the name of one of the Sirens in classical Greek and Roman mythology.

References 178
See also Aglaopheme, Siren

PISUHÄND
This is the name of a household dragon in the folklore of Estonia. The Pisuhänd, also known as the Puuk or Tulihänd, is described as being a serpentine–bodied, four-footed dragon about two feet in length.
References 7
See also Puk

PLAT-EYE
This is the name of an evil monster in the folk beliefs of the people of the West Indies and the state of Georgia in the United States of America. The Plat-eye is described as a large black dog with huge glowing eyes that patrols dark and lonely roads at night. Sometimes only the eyes may appear, seemingly growing larger by the minute. The Plat-eye will grow to immense proportions until it entirely covers the human it encounters and envelopes its victim, who disappears inside it, never to be seen again.
References 24, 119, 160
See also Barguest, Oschaert, Padfoot, Shuck

PODARGE
This is the name of one of the Harpies in the classical mythology of Greece and Rome. Podarge, whose name may be translated as "Swift Foot" or the "Racer," was a monstrous female human-bird hybrid. Together with her sisters, she tortured the blinded King Phineus at Salmydessus in eastern Thrace until driven away by Jason and the Argonauts.
References 89, 139, 178
See also Alkonost, Angka, Garuda, Harpy, Ocypete, Parthenope, Ptitsy-Siriny, Siren, Sirin, Solovei Rakhmatich, Unnati, Zägh

POH
This is an alternative name for the Oriental Unicorn of China.
References 81
See also unicorn

POLYBUTES, POLYBOTES
The name of one of the Gigantes in the classical mythology of Greece and Rome. They were engendered from the blood of Uranus's castration when it fell upon the earth. Alcyoneus, with Porphyrion, was one of their leaders. They were described as being of enormous humanoid proportions but having serpents for legs with the serpents' heads for feet. At their first appearance they were already fully formed adult warriors, complete with spears and in shining armor, ready to do battle. And they attacked the Olympian gods immediately. However, by subterfuge, supernatural powers, and the strength of the hero Hercules/Heracles, one by one they were defeated. Polybutes, whose name means "Cattle Lord," in his turn was vanquished after being pursued by the sea god Poseidon/Neptune and finally buried under the island of Nysirus, which was previously rock torn by the god from the island of Cos.
References 7, 139, 169, 178
See also Alcyoneus, Clytius, Enceladus, Eurytus, giant, Gigantes, Hecatonchieres, Hundred-Handed Giants, Mimas, Pallas, Pelorus, Porphyrion, Rhaetos, Typhon

POLYPEMON
This is an alternative name for the giant Procrustes in the classical mythology of Greece and Rome. Polypemon, whose name may be translated as the "Injurious," also known as Damastes, meaning the "Tamer," was a monstrous giant of Eleusis who offered a bed for the night to belated travelers in a mountainous region. What his victims did not know was that this evil being would make each person fit the bed exactly by cutting off whatever overlapped, whether it be head or feet, if they were too tall. For those who were too small, they would be "racked" and stretched until all their bones were dislocated enough to stretch them to its dimensions. Whichever way, the malicious giant tortured his victims to death, until the hero Theseus dispatched the giant by doing the same to him.
References 78, 133, 139, 178
See also giant, Sinis

POLYPHEMUS, POLYPHEM, POLYPHEMOS
This is the name of a giant in the classical mythology of Greece and Rome. Polyphemus was a member of the gigantic beings known as the Cyclopes. He and his siblings were in some versions the progeny of the sea god Poseidon/Neptune and the nymph Thoosa. Polyphemus was of gigantic humanoid proportions but had, like his brothers, a single eye in the middle of his forehead. He inhabited a cavern in the side of Mount Etna on the island of Sicily, where he herded his sheep. When he fell in love with the nymph Galatea and found her one day with her lover, Acis, he slew him by smashing his skull with a rock. The gods changed the weeping Galatea into a stream, taking her far from Polyphemus to the sea. The enraged giant from that time became a monstrous

The giant is deceived. Odysseus/Ulysses and his men escape the Cyclops. (Rose Photo Archive, UK)

cannibal and trapped all humans that came into his territory.

When the hero Odysseus/Ulysses landed with his men to get water on their journey from the Trojan Wars, they found Polyphemus's cave and made a meal there. When the giant came back, he blocked the entrance to trap his human meal and promptly consumed two of the sailors. The terrified men hid deep in the cave, but when morning came, before he left with his sheep, Polyphemus devoured two more men. While he was absent, the hero took wooden shafts and made spears of them and brought out several goatskins of wine that they had brought from the ship. When Polyphemus returned, devouring yet more of Odysseus/Ulysses's men, the hero went to the giant and offered him some wine. Polyphemus was impressed with the "sang froid" of this man and asked his name, to which the hero replied, "Nobody." Now, the Cyclopes had never tasted wine, and soon the giant was hooked and had drunk the lot dry, sinking rapidly into a drunken stupor. Then the remaining sailors and the hero heated the spears to furnace-white and stabbed them into Polyphemus's one eye, blinding him. When the other Cyclopes heard the screams, they asked who was attacking their brother. When Polyphemus said "Nobody," they left him without knowing the real situation. During the night each of the remaining men strapped themselves under a sheep, and when at dawn the giant felt his sheep as they left, he did not realize that his prisoners had left also. In a violent rage at having been so duped, the giant prayed to his father, the god Poseidon/Neptune, that if the gods forbade the hero's death, at least the men should have the most dangerous voyage possible.
References 20, 61, 125, 133, 166, 169, 174, 178
See also Cyclopes, giant

PONGO

This is the name of a monster in the traditions and legends of the Italian island of Sicily. Pongo was described as a sea monster that constantly raided the island, destroying anything but especially taking unwary humans and devouring them in the sea. The monster was eventually destroyed by the three sons of the dragon-slaying Saint George.
References 20
See also dragon, monster

PONIK

This is the name of a lake monster in the folklore of the region of Lake Pohénégamook in Quebec, Canada. Ponik, said to be a condensed version of the name "Pohénégamook," is described as looking something like a large upturned canoe or jagged log about forty feet long, with jutting, saw-toothed protrusions the length of the dorsal ridge. In some reports, the head resembles that of a horse or cow without ears, but whatever the description, Ponik's arrival is preceeded by frothing of the waters, but it is not considered predatory. Sightings of this monster have been reported in much the same manner as that of the Loch Ness Monster since the nineteenth century. Several were reported in 1873, 1914, and in the 1950s. By 1977 Ponik had become so widely renowned that a camera team from CBS televised a team of divers from Toronto that searched the depths of the lake. Since then, many sightings have been recorded, and a popular Ponik festival has been instituted in the town of Saint-Élenthère by the lake each year.
References 134
See also Loch Ness Monster, monster

PONTARF

This is the name of a fish in the medieval folklore of Europe. It was described as being so huge that it could drag away any unwary child alone on the shore. It is very likely that the Pontarf was used by fishing communities of the North Sea as a type of Nursery bogie to keep wandering children from the dangers of the shorelines.
References 7
See also Nursery bogie

PONTIANAK

This is the name of a terrifying being in the folk beliefs of the Malay people of West Malaysia. The Pontianak is described as appearing in the form of a hideous head with entrails attached and dangling down from it and able to fly through the forests into houses. The Pontianak is a type of vampire that sucks the blood of babies and infants, ensuring that they weaken and die.
References 167
See also Flying Head, Namorodo, vampire

POOKA, POUKA

This is the name of a monstrous water-horse in the folklore of Ireland. This supernatural is also known as Phooka, Pwca, and Púca. The Pooka is described as a horse or a shaggy-haired colt that may be hung about with chains or water-weed. He is said to haunt wild places, the edge of lakes, and streams, where he will try to entice small children to mount his back; if they do, he will race off with them straight into the water or even over a precipice. Curiously, there is an account of a Pooka doing work as a horse in the fields for a poor farmer. On the Celtic feast of Samhain (1 November),

the Pooka, in the shape of a horse, was said to trample the remaining blackberries and to give prophetic answers to those humans who might consult him.
References 7, 21, 24, 25, 64, 93, 119, 128, 160
See also Kelpy

POPE ASS
This is the name of a hybrid monster in the medieval accounts of Italy. The Pope Ass was a derisory alternative name for the Papstesel.
References 7, 89
See also Papstesel

POPE, GIANT POPE
This is the name of a giant in the classical literature of England. He appears in the classic allegorical work *Pilgrim's Progress,* written by John Bunyan and published in 1682. Giant Pope, with Giant Pagan, is considered to be responsible for the slaughter of many people whose bones fill a cave that the pilgrims must pass.

References 20, 31
See also Despair (Giant), giant, Maul, Pagan, Slaygood

POQHIRĀJ
This is the name of a celestial horse in the Hindu mythology of Bengal, India. The Poqhirāj is described as a supernatural flying horse in very much the same traditions as Pegasus in the classical mythology of Greece and Rome.
References 89
See also Pegasus

PORCUS TROIT, PORCUS TROYNT
This is an alternative name for the Twrch Trwyth in the legends and folklore of Wales. The legend of the hunt for this gigantic boar forms part of the list of the *Mirabilia,* or special tasks, in Nennius's *Historia Brittonum* of the eighth or ninth century.
References 54, 105
See also Twrch Trwyth

Giant Pope, a giant in the classical literature of England (Rose Photo Archive, UK)

PORPHYRION

The name of one of the Gigantes in the classical mythology of Greece and Rome. They were engendered from the blood of Uranus's castration when it fell upon the earth. Alcyoneus, with Porphyrion, was one of their leaders. They were described as being of enormous humanoid proportions but having serpents for legs with the serpents' heads for feet. At their first appearance they were already fully formed adult warriors, complete with spears and in shining armor, ready to do battle. And they attacked the Olympian gods immediately. However, by subterfuge, supernatural powers, and the strength of the hero Hercules/Heracles, one by one they were defeated. Porphyrion, whose name means the "Purple One," in his turn was vanquished when he attempted to avenge his brothers. However, he was diverted by Zeus/Jupiter, who compelled the giant with lust for the goddess Hera. While he was thus distracted, Porphyrion was stricken by one of Zeus/Jupiter's thunderbolts and shot by the hero Hercules/Heracles with a poisoned arrow.
References 7, 139, 169, 178
See also Alcyoneus, Clytius, Enceladus, Eurytus, giant, Gigantes, Hecatonchieres, Hundred-Handed Giants, Mimas, Pallas, Pelorus, Polybutes, Rhaetos, Typhon

PORUS

This is the name of a giant in the classic literature of France. Porus appears in the satirical writing of the author François Rabelais (ca. 1494–ca. 1553), in his work *Pantagruel* (1532) and later in *Gargantua* (1534), as ancestors of Pantagruel.
References 174
See also Gargantua, giant, Pantagruel

POSTHON

This is the name of an individual satyr in the classical mythology of Greece of Rome. They are described as having human faces, pointed ears, and horns, but hairy male bodies, below the waist having the body and legs of a goat. They were the attendants of their drunken leader, Silenus, and the god of wine, Dionysus/Bacchus. They inhabited the woods, mountains, and countryside, where they pursued the nymphs and were renowned for aggressive drunken sexuality, lechery, rudeness, and love of playing pranks. This is reflected in some of their names; here, Posthon means "Prick."
References 7, 14, 24, 89, 125, 160
See also satyr

POT-TILTER

This is the name of an ogress in the traditions and folklore of the Crow, Gros Ventre, and Hidatsa Native American peoples of the United States. The Pot-Tilter is described as a hideous old hag who constantly has a cauldron boiling over a fire. If this cauldron is tilted toward someone, they are drawn into it, to be boiled to death. She is, of course, a Nursery bogie used by parents to control the exuberance of their children.
References 24
See also Nursery bogie, ogress

POUAKAI

This is the name of a monstrous bird in the mythology of the Maori people of New Zealand. The Pouakai was so vast that it could take any human or livestock easily in its enormous claws. This bird hunted the local population of the villages for its prey and, when raising its young, would swoop down, screeching, and seize even the fastest people running in terror from its clutches. Then one day the hero Hau-o-Tawera came to the villages and offered to help defeat the Pouakai. He told the men to make the strongest ropes they could from plaiting saplings together. When these were made, they were fashioned into the strongest net possible and strung between the trees at a height and length of sixty feet. Then Hau-o-Tawera told the men to take their strongest spears and hide in the shrubbery beside the net while he walked in front of it as bait. Soon the massive wings of the Pouakai were heard, and as the monster began its screeching descent, Hau-o-Tawera ducked beneath the net before the massive talons could close on him. Then all the men released the vast rope net onto the struggling monster and stabbed it until it was dead.
References 113
See also Poukai, Roc

POUKAI

This is the name of a monstrous bird in the mythology of the Maori people of New Zealand. The Poukai was a monstrous cannibal bird with an enormous beak and huge talons that inhabited the distant caverns of some islands. It existed by taking the local fishermen for its prey. It would swoop down on humans while they fished at the shore or in the rivers, grab them in its enormous beak, and take them back to its cave, where it would smash their skulls and devour them. The terrified people fished in fear until a hero named Pungarehu came with his friend to the local village. Hearing of the plight, the heroes decided to trap and kill the monstrous bird. So Pungarehu asked his friend to stand in the river as though he was fishing. When the Poukai swooped down, Pungarehu rose up from his hiding place and smashed the bird's wing with a massive axe. Then he chopped the other wing off and attacked the body of the Poukai until it was dead. When the heroes climbed into the cave of the bird, the floor was littered with the remains of all the villagers of the past. Then, when they returned home expecting

a hero's welcome, they found that their wives had become old and had other husbands. They had been lost in time so long that everything had changed. But their wives welcomed their husbands of their youth and were reunited, and the others went away.
References 113
See also Pouakai, Roc

PRISCA
This is one of the giants named in the genealogy created by the Italian monk Annius of Viterbo (Giovanni Nanni, c. 1432–1502) to justify the noble descent of the Gauls from a giant biblical race.
References 139, 174
See also giant, Noah

PRISCARAXE
This is the name of a monstrous humanoid serpent said to be from the mythology of ancient Greece. Priscaraxe, according to a "discovered" fragment of ancient Greek script, was the mother of Alector. The name and character was then incorporated by the Italian monk Annius of Viterbo (Giovanni Nanni, c. 1432–1502) as Araxa Prisca, when he re-created a whole genealogy of giants to justify the noble ancestry of the French nobility of the period. This was later supplemented by the humanist and poet Lemaire (1473–1524) and the name changed to Araxa Junior whom he compared as an ancestor, with Melusine.
References 174
See also Melusine, serpent

PRISCUS
This is one of the giants named in the genealogy created by the Italian monk Annius of Viterbo (Giovanni Nanni, c. 1432–1502) to justify the noble descent of the Gauls from a giant biblical race.
References 139, 174
See also giant, Noah

PROCK GWINTER
This is a creature from the folklore of lumberjacks and forest workers, especially in Wisconsin and Minnesota in the United States, during the nineteenth and early twentieth centuries. The Prock Gwinter belongs to a group of beings affectionately known as the Fearsome Critters, whose exaggerated proportions and activities not only explained the weird noises of the lonely landscape but also provided some amusement at camps. It is also known as the Side Hill Dodger.
References 7, 24
See also Fearsome Critters, Guyascutus

PROCRUSTES
This is an alternative name for the giant Polypemon in the classical mythology of Greece and Rome. The name Procrustes may be translated as the "Stretcher." He was a monstrous giant of Eleusis who offered a bed for the night to belated travelers, with murderous intent.
References 78, 139, 178
See also Polypemon

PROMETHEUS
1. This is the name of one of the Titans in the classical mythology of Greece and Rome. Prometheus, whose name means "Forethought," was the progeny of Japetos and Themis or the nymph Clymene. His siblings were Menoetus, Epimetheus, and Atlas. As one of the Titans, he surprisingly defended the Olympian gods against his brethren in the war of the Titans and for this was rewarded. He was also favored by the goddess Athene for having released her from the head of Zeus. Prometheus was then privileged by being able to mold humans from the clay of the earth. Zeus declared that these beings, although given the breath of life, must make sacrifice to the gods. So Prometheus made Zeus choose between a skin of bones and the raw flesh for the sacrifice. He chose the skin and condemned humans to eat raw flesh. Prometheus pitied them and stole fire from the forge of Hephaestos, and for this Zeus punished him. He was condemned to be chained to the Caucasus Mountains, where each day a vulture would feast on his liver. Being an immortal, this torture was endless, for his liver renewed itself each night. After 30,000 years, the Centaur Chiron consented to take his place and break the curse, but he was transformed into a heavenly constellation. But Prometheus knew that Thetis was to produce a child who would be greater than his father, and this secret saved Prometheus, for the grateful god Poseidon was then able to reject her and marry her to Peleus instead.

2. This is one of the giants named in the genealogy created by the Italian monk Annius of Viterbo (Giovanni Nanni, c. 1432–1502) to justify the noble descent of the Gauls from a giant biblical race.
References 20, 38, 125, 133, 139, 166, 169, 174, 178
See also Atlas, centaur, Chiron, Epimetheus, giant, Japetos, Menoetius, Noah

PROPER CONDUCT DRAGON
This is an alternative name for Ying Lung, a winged dragon in the traditions and legends of China.
References 81, 89
See also Ying Lung

PROTEUS
This is the name of a primordial sea giant in the classical mythology of Greece and Rome. Proteus, also referred to as the Old Man of the Sea, was a type of gigantic merman and guardian of the sea creatures. He was subject to the sea god Poseidon/Neptune and

was given the gift of unerring prophecy by the god. However, anyone who wanted to hear these prophesies first had to catch the elusive Proteus, who would change his form to something even more monstrous to escape. It was only when his daughter Eldothea told favored mortals that they were able to trap him as he slumbered on the island of Pharos and gain the information they needed.
References 61, 78, 89, 133, 178
See also giant

PTITSY-SIRINY

This is the name of a class of humanoid monsters in the legends and folklore of Russia. The Ptitsy-Siriny are described as having the body of a bird and the torso and head of a young woman. They bear a close semblance to the Harpy and Siren of classical Greek and Roman legend, from which they may be derived.
References 55
See also Alkonost, Angka, Garuda, Harpy, Parthenope, Podarge, Siren, Sirin, Solovei Rakhmatich, Unnati, Zägh

PTOOPHAGOS

This is the name of one of the great hunting dogs of the giant Orion in the classical mythology of Greece and Rome. Ptoophagos was reputed to have the most enormous appetite in the whole of Boetia (Greece). Orion's other gigantic semisupernatural dog was Arctophonos.
References 20
See also Arctophonos, giant, Orion

PÚCA

This is an alternative name for the Pooka, a monstrous water-horse in the folklore of Ireland.
References 24, 25, 119, 160
See also Pooka

PUGOT, PUGUT

This is the name of a monstrous creature in the folklore of the people of the Philippine Islands. The Pugot, also known as the Cafre or Kafar, is described as a terrifying creature, having a huge black body about the size of a bull with a head resembling that of a wild boar, complete with enormous tusks. This monster travels on its hind legs as it tracks down humans, which it can easily overtake and devour.
References 113
See also Cafre

PUK, PUKIS, PŪKYS, PUUK

This is the name of a household dragon in the folklore of Germany. The Puk is described as being a serpentine–bodied, four-footed dragon about two feet in length that steals and guards treasure for its master.

In some regions it also has wings and can fly through the skies with a fiery tail. The Puk is also known as the Pukis in Latvia, Pūkys or Aitvaras or Kaukas in Lithuania, and Puuk or Tulihänd or Pisuhänd in Estonia.
References 89
See also Aitvaras, Pukis

PUKIS

This is the name of a household supernatural in the folklore of the Latvian people. The Pukis is also known as Pukys to the Lithuanians, and Pukje or Puuk to the Estonians, and may be derived from the German regional names of Puk, Pûks, and Pück. This creature travels through the air as a dragon with a fiery tail but on the ground resembles a huge cat. It is a tricky, treasure-hoarding creature that enriches its master, usually to the detriment of neighbors.
References 119, 120, 125
See also Aitvaras, Kaukas

PUNDARIKA

This is the name of one of the Lokapala Elephants in the Hindu mythology of India. Pundarika stands as the guardian of the southeast quadrant of the world with the god Agni on his back.
References 7, 24, 112
See also Lokapala Elephants

PUNTAN

This is the name of a vast primodial cosmic being in the legends of Micronesia. Puntan eventually died, and from his body all the universe and earthly beings were created.
References 38
See also Ymir

PURUSHA

This is the name of a primordial giant in the Vedic creation mythology of India. Purusha was said to have emerged from a cosmic egg and is described as three-quarters immortal and one-quarter mortal from which Viraj, his consort, emerged. Together they were responsible for all the inhabitants of the earth, and then Purusha was dismembered by the gods to form all the necessary parts of the universe. His head became the sky, his eye became the sun, his breath became the winds, and his limbs became the different people of India. It is said that should the parts of Purusha be reassembled, then the universe would end.
References 24, 78, 125, 133, 166
See also Pangu, Puntan, Ymir

PUSHPADANTA, PUSHPA-DANTA

This is the name of one of the Lokapala Elephants in the Hindu mythology of India. Pushpadanta

(sometimes Anja, according to different legends) stands as the guardian of the northwest quadrant of the world with the god Vāyu on his back.
References 7, 24, 112
See also Lokapala Elephants

PUTEREI SEMBARAN GUNUNG
This is the name of a giantess in the tradtions and legends of the Malay people of West Malaysia. Puterei Sembaran Gunung is so vast that her breasts look like two huge mountains and nourish all the people of the region. This giantess lives on the tops of the mountains, above which she spends her time spinning.
References 113
See also giantess

PWCA
This is an alternative name for the Pooka, a monstrous water-horse in the folklore of Ireland.
References 24, 25, 119, 160
See also Pooka

PYONG
This is the name of a gigantic bird in the legends and folklore of China. The Pyong closely resembles the Roc of the *Tales of the Thousand and One Nights*.
References 7
See also Roc

PYRACMON
This is the name of one of the Cyclopes of classical Greek mythology. He is also known as Arges,

The Pyrassoupi, or Unicorn of Africa (On Monsters and Marvels by Ambroise Paré, trans. by Janis L. Pallister, University of Chicago Press, 1982)

Pyracmon
301

according to whichever poet is describing his role in the myth.
References 169, 178
See also Cyclopes

PYRASSOUPI

This is the name given for the Arabian unicorn in *On Monsters and Marvels*, written by Ambroise Paré (1517–1590). The creature is described as having the size and shape of a mule, shaggy yellow-brown fur like that of a bear, and cloven hooves. However, unlike the usual unicorn, this creature possessed two long twisted horns on its forehead, which, when soaked in water, provided the antidote drink for humans bitten by venomous snakes.
References 147
See also Camphurchii, unicorn

PYROIS, PYROEIS

This is the name of one of the great winged horses of the sun in classical Greek and Roman mythology. Ovid describes how Acthon, with Eous, Phlegon, and Pyrois, were harnessed to the sun's chariot to be driven daily across the heavens.

References 89, 133, 139
See also Horses of the Sun, Phlegon

PYTHON, PYTHO

This is the name of a monstrous serpent or dragon in the classical mythology of Greece and Rome. Python was said to have been engendered in the mud left from the deluge of Deucalion that covered the region near Delphi. When Python grew, it was so vast that its coils surrounded the entire region of the oracle it guarded. When the goddess Hera realized that Leto was her rival for the god Zeus, she sent Python to destroy her. But the god Poseidon hid Leto in the waves, and when Python returned the young god Apollo was waiting for the monster in the Gorge of Parnassus. Apollo shot the monster with the arrows forged by Hephaestus, and eventually Python writhed to its final death throes. Where the stinking corpse of the beast rotted became the oracle of Delphi, and the god Apollo instituted the Pythian Games in honor of his victory.
References 5, 20, 24, 61, 78, 89, 125, 139, 166, 169, 178
See also dragon, serpent

Q

QANEKELAK
This is the name of a gigantic cosmic whale in the traditions and beliefs of the Bela Bela Native American people of the northwestern coastal region of Canada. Qanekelak is described as having the body of a whale with the torso of a human until he metamorphosed entirely into a human shape and became the ancestor of the killer-whale clan.
References 77

QAXDASCIDI
This is the name of a gigantic malicious monster in the traditions and beliefs of the Tanaina Native American people of the subarctic regions of Alaska in the United States. The Qaxdascidi is rarely seen, for it inhabits the depths of the frozen waters, but it can be heard as it roars under the ice.
References 77

QIQION, QIQIRN
This is the name of a monster in the folk beliefs of the Inuit people of Baffin Island, Hudson Bay, and the north-central region of Canada. It is described as having a shape resembling that of a gigantic dog, but it has hair only around its mouth, feet, ears, and tail; the rest of it is a bald skin. The Qiqirn is considered to be responsible for causing the affliction of convulsions in humans when they see it. But it will not otherwise attack humans, choosing to flee from them instead.
References 24, 77, 89, 120, 160
See also Black dogs

QUARESMEPRENANT
This is the name of a giant in the classical literature of France. Quaresmeprenant is one of the characters described by the author François Rabelais (ca. 1494–ca. 1553) in his work *Pantagruel* (1532) and later in *Gargantua* (1534). Quaresmeprenant is not a particularly menacing giant so much as a vast, ungainly, dull-witted being in the same manner as an ogre of folklore.

References 174
See also Bringuenarilles, Gargantua, giant, Pantagruel

QUEEN OF THE FISHES
This is the title, almost all over the world, of the monstrous fish that in legend and folklore herds and guards the fish in large inland stretches of water. In the Fino-Ugric–speaking nations of Finland and the Balkan states, this being is known as the King or Queen of the Fishes. In Teutonic and Gallic areas, it may be the Mother or the Guardian of the Fishes. In the New World, the fish has become a water serpent with the same qualities. These are all ancient semisupernatural beings whose bodies are often covered in mosses and may have fully mature trees growing on their backs. The Queen of the Waters in Alsace is said to be easily visible, for this monstrous trout has a mature pine tree growing from its back.
References 134
See also King of the Fishes

QUEEN OF THE WATERS
The Queen of the Waters, in the folklore of Alsace in France, is said to be easily visible in the lake of Ballon, for this monstrous trout has a mature pine tree growing from its back.
References 134
See also Queen of the Fishes

QUESTING BEAST
This is the name of a hybrid monster in the Arthurian legends of Europe. The Questing Beast, also known as the Blatant Beast, appears in the work the *Morte d'Arthur* (printed by Caxton in 1485), by the English author and poet Sir Thomas Malory (died 1471). The Questing Beast is described as having the body of a lion, the head of a serpent, and the legs and feet of a deer. Its name came from the din made within its belly, which sounded like forty baying or "questing" hounds after the scent of their quarry. However, a previous version of the beast in a thirteenth-century French romance of the Holy Grail (*Perlesvais*, by Gerbert) tells

of its beautiful white body and head with brilliant green eyes. The Questing Beast was said to have been engendered from the union of a princess and the devil, but the image may have been derived from the monstrous Scylla of classical mythology. In *The Once and Future King,* by T. H. White, the monster is hunted by the elderly Sir Pellinore, and later by Palamede, the King of Provence, or, in other versions, Palomides, a Saracen knight who finally vanquished the monster.

References 7, 48, 54, 78, 89
See also Blatant Beast, monster, Scylla

QUTRUB
This is the name of a male Ghoul in pre-Islamic traditions and beliefs. In later times they were identified as a species of Djinn.
References 64, 74, 78, 94, 120, 146
See also Baba Yaga, Djinn, Pey

R

RACUMON
This is the name of a gigantic serpent in the beliefs of the Carib people of the island of Dominica in the West Indies. The Racumon was considered to be responsible for the hurricanes.
References 169
See also serpent

RAGER
This is the name of a monster in the Hebraic scriptures and the Old Testament of the Christian Bible. Rager is envisaged as sea serpent of enormous length and great power, the serpent or dragon of primeval chaos. Rager is the alternative name for Rahab in the Book of Isaiah (30:7, 11) and in the Psalms (89:9–10) and in the Book of Job (9:13; 26:12–13).
References 24, 125
See also Rahab

RAHAB
This is the name of a monster in the Hebraic scriptures and the Old Testament of the Christian Bible. Rahab is envisaged as a sea serpent of enormous length and great power and as the serpent or dragon of primeval chaos. Rahab, also known as Rager in the Book of Isaiah (30:7, 11) and in the Psalms (89: 9–10) and in the Book of Job (9:13; 26:12–13), may be a counterpart of the biblical Leviathan and Tannin.
References 24, 125
See also dragon, Leviathan, serpent, Tannin

RAHU, RÂHU
This is the name of a monster in the Hindu mythology of India. Rahu was a Daitya, or humanoid monster, with a dragon's head and long tail. After the Churning of the Waters at the time of creation, Rahu gate-crashed a festival at which the gods were drinking their sacred Amrita, the draft of immortality. Rahu was discovered by the sun and moon, who reported the interloper to the god Vishnu. The god threw one of his discuses and severed Rahu's head from his body, but he had already drank enough for his head to become immortal. When the monster's head was flung up into the heavens, it chased the moon and devoured it every month, but it infrequently ate the sun, causing eclipses, in revenge for his demise.
References 24, 112
See also Alicha, dragon

RAICHO
This is the name of a fabulous bird in the legends and folklore of Japan. The Raicho is described as resembling a gigantic rook that inhabits the pine trees. It is the terrifying Thunder Bird whose calls bring the fear of the storms to all who hear them.
References 113
See also Thunderbird, Xexeu

RAIJU
This is the name of a creature that was the familiar of the thunder god in the mythology of Japan. Raiju, also known as the Thunder Beast, was depicted as an enormous sort of badger or type of weasel that raced about the earth during storms and created havoc and terror among humans.
References 113, 133

RAINBIRD
This is an alternative name for the Shang Yung in the legends of China.
References 78
See also Shang Yung

RAINBOW SERPENT, RAINBOW SNAKE, RAINBOW MONSTER
This is the name of a class of serpent in many different cultures where the association with the phenomenon of the rainbow is linked to some semisupernatural creature. There is a form of the Rainbow Serpent in the mythologies of the people of the Congo region of central West Africa, in Dahomey and Nigeria in West Africa, on the Caribbean island of Haiti, as well as in

the cultures of the people of Melanesia, Polynesia, Papua New Guinea, and Australia. The Rainbow Serpent is most prevalent in the Dreamtime mythology of the Native Australian people. It is generally described as a vast, python-like serpent whose skin is brilliantly multicolored, or having red and yellow stripes the length of its body, or is a celestial blue. The Rainbow Serpent is associated with all types of freshwater and is said to inhabit deep pools, lakes, and billabongs. In the Dreamtime, they were responsible for forming the deep channels, gullies, and riverbeds when they writhed across the surface of the earth. Rainbow Serpents will sleep in the depths of the mud during the dry season, but during the wet season they rise into the air and may be seen shining in the sky. They are benign toward humans unless disturbed during the dry season, when they may cause a flood to devastate a village and engulf the humans, or may directly swallow the offender. Rainbow Serpents hate blood but enjoy all things iridescent, such as pearls and shells.

In some myths from northern Australia the Rainbow Serpent was said to have concealed inside him all the creatures and vegetation of the earth because he was greedy and the humans were without the necessities of life. They tried everything to get the Rainbow Serpent to release the vegetation and waters that they needed, but to no avail. At last one of their shamans turned himself into the brilliantly colored kukaburra and flew enchantingly around the Rainbow Serpent. While the serpent was transfixed, others slew him and released all the creatures from inside him to populate the earth.

Another myth concerning the Rainbow Serpent from northern Australia tells how when the Rainbow Snake was seen high in the sky some huge white balls rained down on the earth and then burrowed into it. One of the elders of the village, who had been watching, took a digging stick and dug some holes where these "eggs" had fallen. There, in each hole, was a worm. So the elder told the village that the Rainbow Serpent had laid eggs and that they had hatched, producing these progeny. The phenomenon was a shower of monstrous hailstones that entered local folklore.

Local names for the Rainbow Serpent in Native Australian mythology are: Dhakhan of the Kabi Native Australian people; Kaleru, also known as Galeru, in the legends of the Kimberley region of Australia; Wanambi in the legends of the Australian Western Desert region; and Wollunquain in the myths of the Warramunga people. Other names are: Bobi-Bobi, Julunggul, Karia, Kunmanggur, Langal, Mindi, Muit, Ngalbjod, Taipan, Ungur, Woinunggur, Wollunqua, Wonambi, Worombi, Wulungu, Yero, and Yulunggu/r.

The Rainbow Serpent is known as Degei in the mythology and culture of the islands of Fiji in the Pacific.

In West African culture of Dahomey, the Rainbow Serpent, Aido Hwedo, was the first creature to be created. He took the supreme god, Mawu, all across the earth on his back so that the god could fill the world. As they traveled, the serpent's tracks became the rivers and the chasms, and where he defecated he produced mountains. However, the Rainbow Serpent of the Congo is a malevolent being who resides in lakes and rivers, where his reflection may be seen in the waterfalls. Other Rainbow Serpents are named Da in the legends of the Fon people of Dahomey, and Oshumare in the legends of the Yoruba people of Nigeria. From the African Rainbow Serpent was derived the serpent Ayida in the voodoo cults of the island of Haiti in the Carribean.
References 38, 89, 133, 153, 159
See also Aido Hwedo, Ayida, Bobi-Bobi, Da, Degei, Dhakhan, Galeru, Julunggul, Karia, Kun Manggur, Langal, Mindi, Muit, Ngalbjod, Oshumare, Taipan, Ungud, Wanambi, Woinunggur, Wollunquain, Wonungur, Worombi, Wulungu, Yero, Yulunggu, Yurlunggur

RAITARO

This is the name of a dragon in the Buddhist traditions and legends of Japan. The legend tells how a poor farmer named Bimbo desperately prayed to Buddha for rain to save his crops. Soon the rains came, and during the height of the storm he found a tiny child. He carefully took the child home; no parents could be located, so he adopted the child, and he and his wife called him Raitaro, meaning "Thunder Child." Years later, after helping whenever the farmer needed rain or other help with his fields, Bimbo was well off and the couple well provided for. It was then that Raitaro decided to thank them for rescuing him and taking care of him and depart, but before he did they saw him change into a magnificent White Dragon.
References 113
See also Oriental Dragon

RAJA NAGA

This is the name of a gigantic serpent in the legends and beliefs of the Malay people of West Malaysia. The name means "King of the Serpents," thus this vast being is described as the biggest of all the water dragons in the seas. The Raja Naga is said to live in a splendid palace under the ocean called the Pusat Tasik.
References 113
See also Muchalinda, Naga/s

RAKSHASA/S, RAKSHASI

These are the evil monsters in the Vedic myths of India. The Rakshasas, also known as Rakahasa or Rashas, are described as having humanoid shape, often as giants, but are shown hideously deformed with huge arms, multiple heads or eyes, red hair and beards, and enormous, bloated bellies. They have vicious fangs and talons on their hands, which they use to tear at any human victim and then devour them. The females are known as the Rakshasi. While the males indulge in killing and devouring humans, their females may intermarry with humans and be transformed into beautiful damsels. They are strong and very powerful, their strength increasing with the fall of night. During the hours of darkness they defile humans and their food, causing sickness and death. In the *Ramayana*, their king is Ravana, the monstrous king of Lanka. The Rakshasas display every form of vice that is deplored, such as greed, lechery, and violence toward humans and the gods. Toward each other, however, they are loyal, even loving. As Rakshasas are not responsible for the malevolent role they are obliged to perform, the gods allowed them to have a wonderful, jewelled palace as their abode.
References 7, 24, 38, 74, 78, 112, 113, 120, 125, 160, 161, 169
See also Reksoso

RAVAGIO

This is the name of an ogre in the seventeenth-century French story "L' Orangier et l' Abeille" (The Orange Tree and the Bee, 1698), by Marie-Catherine Jumelle de Berneville, Comtesse d' Aulnoy (1650–1705). Ravagio, together with a fellow ogre named Tourmentine, spends his time abducting and either fattening up or devouring human children. Whilst the dialogue between the cannibal ogres may seem gross and bloodthirsty, in the best traditions of fairy tale there is a certain black humor in the stories. It was through the translations of her work into English that the word "ogre" became familiar in the English repertoire of folktale.
References 182
See also cannibal, ogre

RAVENNA MONSTER

This is a monster described by various authors in Europe from medieval times in Italy, France, and Germany. The Ravenna Monster of Italy—for that is where it is supposed to have been seen—first appeared in "De Conceptu et Generatione Hominis," published in 1554 by Jacob Rueff in Zurich (now in Switzerland). It was depicted as having the torso and head of a human with either bat-like or eagle-like wings from the shoulders instead of arms. It had either one leg covered in scales, upon which was a third eye and ending in one enormous eagle's talon, or one leg like this and one like that of a human. The description of this monster circulated for something like five hundred years before finally being consigned to the fabulous.
References 147

RAW GUMS

This is the name of a monstrous cannibal infant in the traditions and legends of the Arapaho Native American people of the United States. The legend tells how when Raw Gums was born the child was never seen to eat but slept all day. While its parents slept, the child stealthily left the home each night and attacked and eventually devoured all the chiefs of the region. One morning the parents noticed human flesh on their child's mouth and realized to their horror why it had not died of starvation. The father prepared a great meal and invited everyone to attend. When all were assembled, he told them what he had discovered about his son. The assembled people said he must decide what to do. Then he suggested that the child be drenched in fat and given to the dogs to devour. But as soon as the child was thrown out to the dogs, he assumed the shape of a young man, who called to the skeletons of his victims to attend him. Horrified, all the people struck camp, including his parents, and left the cannibal Raw Gums behind. With his powers at their height, Raw Gums accepted the challenge of White Owl Woman, and when he succeeded in every way he celebrated by smashing open her skull and spilling her brains on the ground. This is apparently a metaphor for a type of slow-melting snow.
References 77
See also cannibal, Nulayuuiniq

RED DRAGON OF WALES

This is the alternative English name for y Ddraig Goch in the Celtic legend that was substantially rewritten by Geoffrey of Monmouth (1100–1154) in his "Historia Regnum Britanniae" (c. 1147). In this, the Gwiber, or white dragon, represented the invading forces of Vortigern and his Saxons; y Ddraig Goch, the red dragon, was the guardian of the Welsh; and the cavern was Britain, from which the invaders would be completely driven, and ultimately returned to the rightful Celtic peoples.
References 89
See also Ddraig Goch (y), dragon

RED ETIN

Red Etin is the name of an Irish giant in the folktale of Scotland retold in the "Popular Rhymes of Scotland" (1826) by Robert Chambers. The giant is described as being a vast, three-headed cannibal who has captured and beats the daughter of Malcolm, king of Scotland.

*Three versions of the Ravenna Monster (*On Monsters and Marvels *by Ambroise Paré, trans. by Janis L. Pallister, University of Chicago Press, 1982)*

Three-headed giant. Red Etin is described as being a vast, three-headed cannibal. (Scottish Folk Tales and Legends by B. K. Wilson, Oxford University Press, UK, 1954)

However, this ogre can smell humans who might come to rescue her and declares upon sensing a human, "Snouk butt and snouk ben, I find the smell of an earthly man,/Be he living or be he dead, his heart this night will kitchen my bread."

The traditional tale tells how a widow who has two sons sends them in turn to seek their fortune. They fall to the wiles of Red Etin, who finds them in his castle and turns them into pillars of stone. The neighbor's son goes to find what has happened to them. He leaves home with a piece of cake, which he gives to a beggar woman on the way. She in turn gives him a wand and tells him how to answer the riddles that the giant will ask. On his way he meets a shepherd, a swineherd, and a goatherd, who predict that this young man will defeat Red Etin. The young man reaches the castle of Red Etin, where an old woman warns him of the fate of his neighbor's sons. Then Red Etin appears and asks him the riddles, which he can now answer. Thus, the giant's power is broken and the young man chops off his heads. The old woman takes him to the upper floors where all the young women he has captured, including the king's daughter, can be released. Then he touched the two stone pillars, and they become the neighbor's sons again. The whole band makes its way to the king's court, where the youth gains the king's daughter for his bride.

This story was established certainly by the late fifteenth century, when it was supposedly told to the future King James V of Scotland by David Lindsay (ca. 1486–1555), and in 1548 it was quoted in the "Complaynt of Scotland." The rhyme by which Red Etin declared his scent of a victim was adapted and used in "King Lear" (III, iv, 180–181) by William Shakespeare (1554–1616). The name "Red Etin" is said to be derived from the Old English word *eoten*, which may be rendered as "giant."
References 183
See also giant, Gruagach, ogre

REDJAL EL MARJA
This is the name of a class of Djinn in the traditions and folklore of the people of Morocco. Redjal el Marja, which may be translated as the "Men of the Marshes," are described as looking like enormous humans but inhabiting the marshes, like mermen, outside the town of Marrakech. When the marshes were drained, these vast, malevolent Djinns transferred to the canals and fountains supplying Marrakech. People were terrified of the threat that they often made to stop the water supply or even worse to pollute it, so they are propitiated by candles left near the water sources.
References 82, 122, 160
See also Djinn, merman, Triton

RED-LEGGED SCISSOR-MAN
This is the name of a giant Nursery bogie in the nineteenth-century children's stories of England and Germany. The Red-Legged Scissor-man, also known as the The Great, Long-Legged Scissor-man or the Great Tall Tailor, features in the *English Strewwelpeter, or Pretty Stories and Funny Pictures*, by Heinrich Hoffman, published in 1847. The story relates in verse how a child named Conrad habitually sucked his thumb. His mother warned him that if he continued, the Red-Legged Scissor-man would come with his huge pair of scissors and cut off his thumb. Of course, the child did not believe her and, as soon as she was gone, started to suck his thumb. The story goes on:

> The door flew open, in he ran,
> The great long Red-Legged Scissor-man. . . .
> Snip! Snap! Snip! the scissors go;
> And Conrad cries out Oh! oh! oh!
> Snip! Snap! Snip! They go so fast,
> That both his thumbs are off at last.

The Red-Legged Scissor-man belongs to the class of terrifying Nursery bogie that was used by Victorian parents to frighten their children into good behavior.
References 97, 182
See also Agrippa, Nursery bogie

RE'EM, REEM
This is the name of a monstrous beast that resembled an ox in the traditional beliefs associated with the Hebraic scriptures and the Old Testament of the Christian Bible. There was said to be only one pair, a male and a female, in existence at one time. They were described as vast beasts that were as huge as the mountains they inhabited, at the far east and far west of the known world. The male and female existed for about seventy years apart and came together only when they mated. The female produced twin offspring, one male and one female, and soon after their independence from the mother both parents died. The Re'em was frequently depicted in the bestiaries of medieval Europe and was conjectured to have been a distortion of the now-extinct auroch.
References 89

REGINA
This is one of the giants named in the genealogy created by the Italian monk Annius of Viterbo (Giovanni Nanni, c. 1432–1502) to justify the noble descent of the Gauls from a giant biblical race.
References 139, 174
See also giant, Noah

REKSOSO, REKSASI
This is the name for monstrous giants in the traditions and legends of Indonesia. The Reksoso are the counterparts of the Rakshasas in the Vedic mythology of India; Reksasi is the name of their females. These vicious cannibal giants inhabit the jungles, where they will entrap and devour any unwary humans who venture into their territory.
References 113
See also cannibal, giant, Rakshasa

REMORA
This is an alternative name for the Mora or Echeneis, a monstrous fish described by Roman historians.
References 18, 89
See also Echeneis, Murex

REPHAIM
This is the name of a race of giants that appears in the Hebraic scriptures and Genesis, the first book of the Old Testament. Og of Bashan was said to be the last of this race.
References 13
See also giant, Og

RHAETOS, RHATOS
This is the name of a giant in the classical mythology of Greece and Rome. He is also known as Eurytus.
References 139
See also Eurytus

RHEA, RHEIA

This is the name of a female Titan in the classical mythology of Greece and Rome. Rhea was the daughter of Gaia and Uranos and a sibling of Chronos, by whom she bore the future Olympic gods. However, as Chronos knew that one of his progeny would ultimately overthrow him in the heavens, he devoured each of her children as it was born. When the next child was due, Rhea went to Lyctus in Crete, where she secretly brought Zeus into being and hid him until he was strong enough to stand up to Chronos, whom he castrated.
References 20, 47, 61, 125, 133, 166, 178, 182
See also giant, Titan

RHINOCÉROS

This is the name of an ogre in the folklore of France. The story of Rhinocéros is related in the eighteenth-century work "Bearskin," by Madame de Murat, which is similar in motif to that of the Beauty and the Beast.
References 182
See also Beast, Loathly Lady, Odz-Manouk, Riquet à la Houppe

RHITA GAWR, RHITTA GAWR, RHITTA CAWR, RHICCA, RHICCA CAWR

This is the name of a giant in the legends and folklore of Wales. Rhita Gawr was a monstrous, aggressive giant who features in the legends of King Arthur in the region. The giant terrorized the countryside of Yr Wyddfa Fawr, the Snowdon Mountain range, and challenged chieftains and kings to do battle with him. After he had slain each one, he took their beards from their chins and attached them to his cloak as trophies. Rhita Gawr sent a message to King Arthur to send his beard to the giant as tribute; if refused, he would challenge and beat the king anyway. This so enraged King Arthur that he slew the giant and rolled him down the track, now called Rhiw Barfe, "The Way of the Bearded One," to the bottom. Here a cairn was erected over the body that bore his name, Gwyddfa Rhita, "Rhita's Cairn," an ancient tumulus on the summit of Mount Snowdon. This was described by Geoffrey of Monmouth during the twelfth century. And this was how it was later told in the poem by Rhys Goch Eyri (d. 1420):

> *Ar y drum oer dramaur,*
> *Yno gorwedd Ricca Gawr.*
>
> On the ridge cold and vast,
> There the giant Ricca lies.

Unfortunately, the cairn was flattened some time ago to make way for a hotel on the summit of the mountain.

References 54, 128, 183
See also giant

RHŒCUS

This is the name of a centaur in the classical mythology of Greece and Rome. Rhœcus was shot and killed by an arrow from Atalanta when he tried to rape her.
References 169
See also centaur

RHŒTUS

There are two characters that go by this name.

1. This is the name of a centaur in the classical mythology of Greece and Rome. During the riot that followed the insult to the bride at the marriage of Pirithous, Rhœtus was wounded by Dryas and fled. It is possible that he and Rhœcus are the same, but it is not established.

2. This is the name of a giant in the classical mythology of Greece and Rome. Rhœtus, also known as Eurytus, attempted during the wars with the gods to scale Mount Olympus, the home of the gods, but was repelled and slain by Dionysus/Bacchus.
References 169, 178
See also centaur, Eurytus

RI

This is the name of a monster in the traditions and beliefs of the people of New Ireland in Papua New Guinea. The Ri was described as having the body of an enormous sea creature but the torso and head of a woman and inhabited the margins of the mangroves and beaches, making a melodious sound. It was regarded by European travelers during the early centuries as equating with the Siren of the classical mythology of Greece and Rome.
References 134
See also monster, Siren

RICA, RICA CAWR, RICCA, RICCA CAWR

These are alternative names for the giant in the legends of Wales known as Rhita Gawr.
References 54, 128
See also giant, Rhita Gawr

RICKABOO RACKER

This is an alternative name for the Guyascutus in the folklore of lumberjacks and forest workers (and later fraudsters) during the eighteenth and nineteenth centuries, especially in Wisconsin and Minnesota in the United States. This version of the creature was so highly adaptable that if it were being pursued, like the Hunkus, it was able to roll around itself to turn inside-out and escape the opposite way. It belongs to

a group of monsters affectionately known as the Fearsome Critters.
References 7
See also Fearsome Critters, Guyascutus

RIGI

This is the name of a primordial creature in the creation legends of Micronesia. Rigi, like Riiki, was a vast being who was set the task of raising the sky from off the earth. The task was completed but with such an effort that Riiki was completely drained of strength and died. However, his torso and head remained in the heavens, where they became the Milky Way, while his legs, which had remained with the earth, became the worms inside the earth of the world.
References 38
See also Riiki, Ymir

RIIKI

This is the name of a primordial creature created by Nareau in the legends of Micronesia. Riiki, like Rigi, was a vast being who was set the task of raising the sky from off the earth. The task was completed but with such an effort that Riiki was completely drained of strength and died. However, his torso and head remained in the heavens, where they became the Milky Way, while his legs, which had remained with the earth, became the serpents of the world.
References 38
See also Rigi, Ymir

RINJIN

This is the alternative name for Ryujin, a Dragon King in the legends of Japan. Rinjin is a dragon of the sea, where he inhabits a magnificent palace.
References 7
See also dragon, Dragon king, Oriental Dragon, Ryujin

RIQUET À LA HOUPPE

This is the name of a monster or beast in French folktales written by Charles Perrault (1628–1703). Riquet à la Houppe, whose name means "Ricky with the Tuft," was the beast-hero of a tale in the volume "Histoires ou Contes du temps Passé" (1697), in which, in the classic motif of the Beauty and the Beast, he persuades the young woman to love him for himself despite his grotesque appearance.
References 182
See also Beast, Loathly Lady, Odz-Manouk, Rhinocéros

RITHO, RITHO CAWR

This is an alternative name for the giant in the legends of Wales known as Rhita Gawr.
References 54, 128
See also giant, Rhita Gawr

RIZOS

This is the name of a monster of the roads in the folklore of modern Greece. The Rizos is described as being in the shape of a massive dog with enormous claws that may be encountered by travelers on the highways at night. It is a frightening creature that may attack any who attempt to touch it, but more frequently it disappears, leaving the human in a state of terror.
References 17
See also Black dogs

ROC

This is the name of an enormous bird, also known as the Rukh, in the legends of Arabia and Middle Eastern countries around the Persian Gulf. The Roc is described as a vast bird that resembled an enormous eagle or vulture, although some accounts say that it is part lion. It was said to have horns on its head and to have such a huge wingspan and talons that it could grasp an elephant easily and transport it back as food for its young. Accounts of the Roc abound, but the most notable are from the traveler Marco Polo (1254–1324), who claimed that he had seen one of its massive feathers at the court of the Kublai Khan. He suggested that it was an inhabitant of the island of Madagascar. The most famous literary account comes from the story of Sindbad the sailor in the *Tales of the Thousand and One Nights* (1885–1888), translated by Richard Burton (1829–1890). Sindbad was shipwrecked on an island where there was a huge, spherical dome and nothing else but brushwood. Then the sky above grows dark, and he realizes that the dome is a vast egg and that he is in the nest of a gigantic bird. However, he manages to escape by clinging to the foot of the bird, which doesn't notice, and land in a place less dangerous.

Other gigantic birds that closely resemble the description of the Roc are the Anka of Islamic Arabia, the Pyong of China, and the Kreutzet of Russian folklore.

There was anciently a bird of some eight or nine feet in height, the aepyornis of Madagascar, that laid eggs some thirteen inches in diameter, which has been suggested as the basis for the legends.
References 7, 20, 61, 78, 89
See also Angka, Garuda, Griffin, Kreutzet, Pyong

ROCKABORE

This is an alternative name for the Guyascutus in the folklore of lumberjacks and forest workers (and later fraudsters), especially in Wisconsin and Minnesota in the United States.
References 7
See also Fearsome Critters, Guyascutus

Roc's nest. The Roc was said to be a vast bird that resembled an enormous eagle or vulture. (Rose Photo Archive, UK)

RONGEUR D'OS

This is the name of an evil monstrous being in the folklore of Normandy in northern France. The Rongeur d'Os, whose name means the "Gnawer of Bones," is described as having the form of an enormous dog. It is said to waylay and terrify night-bound travelers on lonely roads, in much the same manner as the Gytrash of English folklore.

References 21, 24, 25, 37, 160
See also Barguest, Black dogs, Black Shuck, Mauthe Doog, Padfoot, Skriker, Trash

ROPERITE

This is a creature from the folklore of lumberjacks and forest workers, especially in Wisconsin and Minnesota during the nineteenth and early twentieth centuries. The Roperite is described as being about the size of a horse but having a long prehensile snout that could extend like a lasso. Although it caught mainly rabbits for its prey, it was not above taking a naive young lumberjack if he got caught in the snout extension. The Roperite belongs to a group of beings affectionately known as the Fearsome Critters, whose exaggerated proportions and activities not only explained the weird noises of the lonely landscape but also provided some amusement at camps.

References 7
See also Fearsome Critters

ROSHWALR

This is the name of a sea monster in the folklore of Norway known as a horse-whale. This aquatic beast was described as a vast, smooth body, like that of a whale, but having the head of a huge horse. The Roshwalr was first mentioned in the annals of the papacy, after a severed head was sent to Pope Leo X at the Vatican in 1520. When Bishop Walkendorf sent this head, it was drawn and described later in the works of Father Louis Nicholas and thence by the naturalist Ambroise Paré (1517–1590), during the same period, in his work *On Monsters and Marvels*. By then it had also been named as the Ruszor, or Cetus dentatus. It was a gross exaggeration for what is now recognized as the walrus.

References 134
See also monster

ROSMARINE

This is the name of a sea giant in the English literature of the sixteenth century. It is described as a gigantic humanoid torso with the hindquarters of a walrus or whale, human arms, and a head resembling that of a gigantic walrus with huge ears, all clothed in sealskins. This is how the Rosmarine was envisaged by the Elizabethan poet Edmund Spenser (c. 1552–1599) in his work *The Faerie Queene* (1590).
References 134
See also giant, Rosmer, Tursus

ROSMARUS

This is the name of a sea monster in the popular literature and folklore of the eighteenth century in Norway. The Rosmarus was said to be a gigantic marine creature with a smooth body and a vast head resembling that of a horse. It was perhaps a gross exaggeration of the walrus.
References 134
See also Roshwalr, Rosmarine, Rosmer, Ruszor

ROSMER

This is the name of a vast giant of the sea in the traditions and folklore of sixteenth-century Norway. This vast giant was said to inhabit the seas, where he was protected from the environment by wearing copious sealskins. It is possible that this being was the basis for the Rosmarine in the works of Edmund Spenser, the English Elizabethan poet.
References 134
See also giant, Rosmarine, Tursus

ROSUALT

This is an alternative name for the Murrisk, a monstrous deadly fish in the folklore and legends of Ireland.
References 7
See also Murrisk

ROU SHOU

In Chinese mythology, this is a dragon that always associated with the dragon form of Gou Mang. They are always associated as the messengers of the sky-god and share the form of the double dragon. Rou Shou pressages disaster and the onset of autumn. He is associated with western directions.
References 125, 160
See also Dragon, Gou Mang, Lung, Oriental Dragon

RTA-MGIN

This is the Tibetan name for the giant Daitya of Indian mythology known there as Hayagriva. In Tibetan Buddhism, this monstrous giant, known as rTa-mgin, became, after his conversion, the Lord of Wrath.

References 24, 47, 64, 125, 133, 160
See also Hayagriva

RUAHINE-MATA-MAORI

This is the name of a cannibal ogress in the legends and folklore of the Maori people of New Zealand. Ruahine-mata-maori used to disguise herself by magic to look like the humans upon whom she preyed. In reality she was a vast, hideous cannibal who attracted her victims by pretending to offer hospitality to them. She offered to share her meal with Paowa when he landed on her island, but he became suspicious and escaped. However, Ruahine-mata-maori smeered herself with the magic red ochre and followed him through the waves as fast as he could paddle his canoe. He took refuge in a cliff cave and quickly barricaded himself in with huge boulders and then calmly made a fire and prepared some delicious food. The ogress, thinking she had him trapped, accepted some of the food he stuck through the cracks in the rocks. She liked it so much that when he offered to fill her mouth, she closed her eyes and waited for him to take down the boulders between them. Then he filled her gaping mouth with the red-hot coals that killed her.
References 155
See also cannibal, ogress, Ruuruhi-kerepoo

RUBBERADO

This is a creature from the folklore of lumberjacks and forest workers, especially in Wisconsin and Minnesota in the United States, during the nineteenth and early twentieth centuries. The Rubberado belongs to a group of beings affectionately known as the Fearsome Critters, whose exaggerated proportions and activities not only explained the weird noises of the lonely landscape but also provided some amusement at camps. The Rubberado was described as a porcupine that had rubbery spines and flesh; thus it bounced on land and once cooked, the teeth shot back from the bite and were unable to get enough grip to consume it as food.
References 7, 24
See also Fearsome Critters

RUKH

This is an alternative spelling for Roc, an enormous bird that features in the mythology of Arabia and in the European translation of the *Tales of the Thousand and One Nights*.
References 78, 89
See also Roc

RUKI

This is the name of a sea serpent in the mythology of the people of Kiribati in the Gilbert and Ellice Islands of Micronesia.

References 113
See also serpent

RUMPTIFUSEL

This is a creature from the folklore of lumberjacks and forest workers, especially in Wisconsin and Minnesota during the nineteenth and early twentieth centuries. The Rumptifusel is described as being a long, thin, aggressive creature covered in dense fur. As it had the ability to sleep whilst wound around the trunk of a tree, it was often mistaken by lumberjacks for a fur coat, which, when they attempted to lift it, came alive and swallowed them. The Rumptifusel belongs to a group of beings affectionately known as the Fearsome Critters, whose exaggerated proportions and activities not only explained the weird noises of the lonely landscape but also provided some amusement at camps.

References 7
See also Fearsome Critters

RUSZOR

This is an alternative name for the sea monster known as the Roshwalr in the folklore of Norway.
References 134
See also Roshwalr

RUURUHI-KEREPOO

This is the name of a grotesque cannibal ogress in the legends and folklore of the Maori people of New Zealand. Ruuruhi-kerepoo is described as looking like an ugly old hag but having sharp bones protruding from her skin like spines all over her body. She had huge, hairy hands with talon-like claws on her strong fingers; her mouth was so vast that her fang-like teeth showed as she talked. Ruuruhi-kerepoo was blind and attracted her human victims by her apparent harmlessness. Her demise came when she trapped, beheaded, and swallowed some of the girls from the neighboring village. A party of warriors was sent to see what had happened to them, and as one of them asked Ruuruhi-kerepoo if they had been there, she grabbed him, bit off his head, and devoured him. However, being blind, she had not realized that his companions had seen it all. When they tried to kill her with their clubs, the bones of her victims that protruded from her skin protected her. So the warriors took their spears and stuck them into the cannibal until she was destroyed

References 155
See also Baba Yaga, cannibal, ogress, Ruahine-mata-maori

RYUJIN

This is the name of one of the Dragon Kings in the legends and traditions of Japan. Ryujin is described as an enormous being with a vast mouth that inhabits a magical jewelled palace beneath the seas. He is the controller of the sea tides and the father of a beautiful daughter who was won by the hero Fire Fade, or Prince Hoori, thus becoming the legendary ancestor of the emperors of Japan.

References 113
See also Dragon King, Oriental Dragon

S

SACHRIMNIR, SAEHRIMNIR

This is the name of a massive wild boar in the Norse mythology of Scandinavia. Sachrimnir, whose name may be translated as the "Blackened," was an eternal creature of such vast proportions that when it was roasted each night it fed all the assembled Aesir and warriors of Valhalla. Furthermore, this beast self-generated the following dawn to repeat the process of its being hunted, caught, and roasted once more each evening.

References 7, 89
See also Hildsuin, Totoima

SADHUZAG

This is the name of a fabulous hybrid creature in the bestiaries and travelers' tales of medieval Europe. It was described as very similar to the Leucrotta, or the Yale, having the body of a deer with the head resembling that of a goat but the size of a large bull. Its most unusual feature was that it had seventy-four horns on its head and body, and a bellow to terrify the bravest, or a call to make all listen and admire it.

References 63
See also Leucrotta, Yale

SAFAT

This is the name of a type of dragon in the bestiaries and travelers' tales of medieval Europe. It was said to resemble a winged serpent with the head of a dragon. The Safat was said to inhabit the upper heavens above the clouds and was rarely seen on the ground.

References 7, 89
See also dragon, serpent

SA-GEMPAR 'ALAM

This is the name of a Jinn in the beliefs of the Malay people of West Malaysia. Sa-Lakun Darah, whose name means "Universe Terrifier," is one of the offspring of the king of the Jinns, known as Sang Gala Raja.

References 167
See also Sang Gala Raja

SA-GERTAK RANG BUMI

This is the name of a Jinn in the beliefs of the Malay people of West Malaysia. Sa-Gertak Rang Bumi, whose name means "World Pricker," is one of the offspring of the king of the Jinns, known as Sang Gala Raja.

References 167
See also Sang Gala Raja

SAGITTARIUS

Sagittarius, which in Latin means the "Archer," was the name of a centaur in the classical mythology of Greece and Rome. When Cheiron was killed accidentally, Zeus/Jupiter, the king of the gods, gave him immortality in the heavens. Like many of the dead or metamorphosed characters of mythology, he was transformed into a constellation. The astrological symbol of the archer on horseback of the Babylonians became the centaur of the Greek and Roman astrology that was emblematic also of the astronomical configuration at the center of the Milky Way.

References 24, 61, 78
See also Capricornus, centaur, Cheiron

SA-GUNCHANG RANG BUMI

This is the name of a Jinn in the beliefs of the Malay people of West Malaysia. Sa-Gunchang Rang Bumi, whose name means "World Shaker," is one of the offspring of the king of the Jinns, known as Sang Gala Raja.

References 167
See also Sang Gala Raja

SAHAB

The Sahab was a sea monster said to inhabit the North Sea and the beaches around the coasts of Norway. It was described as having a huge body with a long, extended foot by which it fed itself; the other feet were like those of a cow. The Sahab was reported in the works of Olaus Magnus in the sixteenth century from an apparent sighting of one found beached on the Norwegian shores.

References 7
See also monster

SA-HALILINTAR

This is the name of a Jinn in the beliefs of the Malay people of West Malaysia. Sa-Halilintar, whose name means "He of the Thunderbolt," is one of the offspring of the king of the Jinns, known as Sang Gala Raja.
References 167
See also Sang Gala Raja

SAIDTHE SUARAIGHE

This is the name of a monstrous dog in the legends of Ireland. Saidthe Suaraighe, meaning the "Bitch of Evil," was one of the pack of hounds that belonged to Crom Dubh, a great and legendary chieftain of the Celtic pre-Christian era.
References 128
See also Coinn Iotair

SAINT ATTRACTA'S MONSTER

This is the name of a monster in the legends and folklore of Ireland. It is described as having a large, bulbous body with a tail resembling that of a whale, a head with a single globular eye in the middle of the forehead, a mane like that of a horse, and iron talons on its legs that drew sparks as it moved. This fire-breathing monster inhabited the island of Inis Cathaig (Scattery Island) in the estuary of the River Shannon, but it was vanquished and banished by Saint Senan, a sixth-century bishop, when he founded a monastery there. Saint Attracta, or Saint Araght, was a nun who founded a safehouse for travelers in the same area.
References 7
See also monster

SAINT CHRISTOPHER

See Christopher, Saint

SAIVO-NEITA

This is the name for a mermaid in the folk beliefs of the Lapp people of northern Norway and Finland. Saivo-Neita means the "Sea Maiden."
References 120, 160
See also mermaid

SA-LAKUN DARAH

This is the name of a Jinn in the beliefs of the Malay people of West Malaysia. Sa-Lakun Darah, whose name means "He of the Blood Pool," is one of the offspring of the king of the Jinns, known as Sang Gala Raja.
References 167
See also Sang Gala Raja

SALAMANDER, SALAMANDRA, SALAMANDRAL

This is the name of a monstrous creature in the ancient texts of Greece and Rome and the medieval bestiaries of Europe. The Salamander is mentioned by Pliny the Elder in his *Historia Naturalis* (A.D. 77), in which it is described as a type of monstrous lizard. It was reputed to have secretions that rendered its bite and the consumption of anything that it had touched as fatal. It was also reputed to live on the slopes of volcanoes and to be able to live in the middle of the hottest fire. By the Middle Ages, the Salamander, also known as the Dea and Stellio, was commonly featured in the bestiaries of the period. In a Latin bestiary of the twelfth century, the Salamander is reported to entwine around fruit trees to poison the fruit and that should these fruit fall into a well all who drink there will be poisoned. It was also reputed to put out fires as it crawled through them. An Anglo-Saxon English bestiary of 1220, now in the Bodleian Library at Oxford, relates how the Salamander may stop up the mouths of lions. Within this text is also explained how this creature demonstrates that the faithful will be delivered from the fires of Gehenna on the Day of Judgment.

Like the Phoenix, the Salamander has passed into the repertoire of European heraldry and may be depicted on coats of arms of noble families as well as institutions such as those for fire insurance.
References 5, 10, 14, 18, 20, 24, 89, 124, 132, 146, 148, 160, 185
See also Dea, Stellio

SAMEBITO

This is the name of a monster in the legends of Japan. Samebito, whose name is derived from the Japanese word *same*, meaning "shark," is described as half shark and half human with a black body, a thin, pointed beard on his face, and big, gleaming green eyes. Samebito normally inhabited the seas, but the legend tells how one night, whilst walking on the Long Bridge near his castle, the hero Totaro met the monster. Terrified, the young hero stood his ground, but the monster surprisingly requested food and shelter, because he had been exiled from the seas by the Sea King. Without hesitation, Totaro's breeding and hospitality encouraged him to take Samebito to a lake near the castle in which he lived. There the monster was happily fed without causing threat or alarm to anyone. This lasted until the time that Samebito's benefactor fell deeply in love with Tamana, whose greedy father had set a price for the match as ten thousand jewels. Totaro languished in grave despair, and Samebito, no longer looked after and distraught for his benefactor's imminent death, wept near the castle. However, one of the castle servants discovered that the tears of the monster had

turned into emeralds, pearls, and rubies. All was saved, and the happy couple were married—thanks to Samebito.
References 113
See also dragon, monster

SAMHGHUBHA
This is an alternative name for the Merrow in the folklore of Ireland.
References 21, 24, 25
See also mermaid, Merrow

SAMPATI
This is the name of a huge, fabulous, human-headed bird in the Hindu mythology of India. Sampati is the progeny of Garuda, the steed of the god Vishnu, and the sibling of a similar bird called Jataya. His brother, Jataya, had been destroyed by the demon king of Sri Lanka, called Ravana. So when Hanuman, the monkey god, asked Sampati for help in locating Sita, whom they believed had been abducted by Ravana, Sampati flew to Sri Lanka. There he discovered that Sita was the prisoner of Ravana and was able to fly back to tell Hanuman to take his armies there and destroy the demon king and rescue Sita. When this took place, the death of Jataya had been avenged.
References 112
See also Garuda

SAMVARTA
This is the name of a gigantic horse in the mythology of India. This vast creature is in the form of a great mare that is said to have churning fires in her belly. In some versions there are seven of these horses, all of which inhabit the oceans. The myths relate that with the coming of doomsday Samvarta and her ilk will come up out of the waters and all the fires will be spread over the world, consuming everything.
References 112
See also Horses of the Sun

SANDMAN
This is the name of a fearsome Nursery bogie in the late eighteenth and early nineteenth centuries in England. The Sandman was a vicious and terrifying ogre who came during the night to throw handfuls of coarse sand into the eyes of children who would not go to sleep. When the eyes of the screaming child were rubbed, they dropped out all bloody on the floor. The Sandman gathered these eyes to take in his sack as food for his long-beaked progeny nesting in the crook of the crescent moon. This was the image of the Sandman Nursery bogie in the fairy tale written by E. T. A. Hoffmann in 1817. By the late nineteenth century and into the twentieth century, this image had

changed dramatically to a charming spirit bringing pleasant dreams to children.
References 24, 160, 182
See also Nursery bogie, ogre

SANG GADIN
This is the name of a Jinn in the beliefs of the Malay people of West Malaysia. Sang Gadin is the consort of the king of the Jinns, known as Sang Gala Raja.
References 167
See also Sang Gala Raja

SANG GALA RAJA
This is the name of a king of the Jinns in the beliefs of the Malay people of West Malaysia. Sang Gala Raja, also known as Sa-Raja Jin, is portrayed in human shape but having a red chest and black head with enormous fangs for teeth. He dwells in the depths of the earth with his wife, Sang Gadin. Their seven main offspring are: Sa-Lakun Darah, "He of the Blood Pool," Sa-Halilintar, "He of the Thunderbolt," Sa-Rukup Rang Bumi, "World Coverer," Sa-Gertak Rang Bumi, "World Pricker," Sa-Gunchang Rang Bumi, "World Shaker," Sa-Tumbok Rang Bumi, "World Beater," and Sa-Gempar 'Alam, "Universe Terrifier." All these dwell in wild, lonely, and festering places such as the hollows in the hills, in the deep jungle, and in parasitic growths on trees. They are subdivided according to whether they are the "faithful," known as Jin Aslam, or the "infidel," known as the Jin Kafir; the Jin Afrit, also known as Jin Rafit, was supposed to have been the creator of the Europeans. Other Jinns are the guardians of state property, such as the "royal musical instruments" (protected by Jin Nemfiri or Lempiri, Gendang, and Naubat) and the "royal weapons" (protected by Jin Sembuana); these duties associate them with the Jinn of the state known as Jin Karaja'an. Whatever their status, they are all intent on causing harm to humans unless propitiated.
References 167
See also Djinn, Jin

SAN-SHEN KUO YAN
This is the name of a race of monstrous people in the legends and folklore of China. They are described as having one head on three bodies. The San-Shen Kuo Yan appear in the volumes of the Great Imperial Encyclopedia and were no doubt derived from exaggerated travelers' tales in much the same way as those that influenced the medieval bestiaries of Europe.
References 181
See also Cyclopes, I-Mu Kuo Yan, Nieh-Erh Kuo Yan, San-Shou Kuo Yan, Ting Ling Kuo Yan, Yü-Min Kuo Yan

SAN-SHOU KUO YAN

This is the name of a race of monstrous people in the legends and folklore of China. The San-Shou Kuo Yan are described as having three heads on their humanoid bodies. They appear in the volumes of the *Great Imperial Encyclopaedia* and were no doubt derived from exaggerated travelers' tales in much the same way as those that influenced the medieval bestiaries of Europe.

References 181

See also I-Mu Kuo Yan, Nieh-Erh Kuo Yan, San-Shen Kuo Yan, Ting Ling Kuo Yan, Yü-Min Kuo Yan

SARABROTH

This is the name of a giant in the classical literature of France. Sarabroth is one of the giant ancestors of Pantagruel in the famous work *Pantagruel* (1532) by the French author François Rabelais (ca. 1494–ca. 1553). The other three primary ancestors are Charibroth, Hurtaly, and Faribroth. They all appear in the first edition, which was subsequently edited with many more additional giant ancestors.

References 174

See also Bruyer, Chalbroth, Daughters of Cain, Eryx, Gabbara, Galehaut, Gargantua, giant, Happemousche, Hurtaly, Morguan, Noachids, Noah, Pantagruel

SA-RAJA JIN

This is the name of a Jinn in the beliefs of the Malay people of West Malaysia. Sa-Raja Jin is also known as Sang Gala Raja.

References 167

See also Sang Gala Raja

SARKANY

This is the name of an ogre in the ancient beliefs of the Hungarian people. Sarkany was described as appearing like a human but with up to nine heads sprouting from his shoulders. He rode his wild horse through the thunder clouds armed with a sword. If any human was unfortunate enough to encounter Sarkany, the human would instantly be turned to stone. In today's folklore Sarkany is now a winged dragon.

References 125, 160

See also dragon, ogre

SARMATIAN SEA SNAIL

This is the name of a monstrous creature said to inhabit the shoreline around the Baltic Sea in what was once known as the Sarmatian Sea or the Eastern Germanic Sea during the sixteenth century. The Sarmatian Sea Snail was described by Ambroise Paré (1517–1590), during the same period in his work *On Monsters and Marvels*. It was purported to be an amphibious sea creature that resembled a vast snail but having four hook-like legs and a long, multicolored tail. Its head had branching horns with globular terminal points that glistened; its eyes glowed and its vast slit of a bewiskered mouth grazed the shoreline at low tide.

References 147

SA-RUKUP RANG BUMI

This is the name of a Jinn in the beliefs of the Malay people of West Malaysia. Sa-Rukup Rang Bumi, whose name means "World Coverer," is one of the offspring of the king of the Jinns, known as Sang Gala Raja.

References 167

See also Sang Gala Raja

SARVABHAUMA

This is the name of one of the Lokapala Elephants in the Hindu mythology of India. Sarvabhauma stands as the guardian of the north quadrant of the world with the god Kubera on his back.

References 7, 24, 112

See also Lokapala Elephant

SASABONSAM

This is the name of a type of ogre or cannibal in the beliefs of the Tschwi and Ashanti people of West Africa. The Sasabonsam is described as a tall, thin humanoid shape that is colored red, with straight hair and bloodshot eyes. Their incredibly long legs have feet that point in both directions. They inhabit the forests or individual silk-cotton trees, from which they dangle their limbs like the roots of a Banyan tree, and with these feet they hook up unwary travelers who pass beneath. Around the roots of these trees the earth is red, and it is said to be this color because the Sasabonsam wipes the blood of his victims off himself here. Those humans that do not escape in time will have their blood drained from them. The female counterpart of Sasabonsam is his "wife," known as Shamantin.

References 7, 24, 47, 64, 120, 152, 160

See also cannibal, ogre

SASQUATCH

This is the name of a gigantic Wildman of the Salish and other Native American peoples of the Yukon region of Alaska and the regions of British Columbia, Canada. The name "Sasquatch" comes from the Salish word *se'sxac*, meaning "wild men." The Sasquatch is the counterpart of the Bigfoot but has been a feature of Native American beliefs and folklore long before the European settlers arrived. Indeed, there are over 150 different local names for the Sasquatch. This vast creature is described as a humanoid being of up to fifteen feet in height with shaggy brown-black hair

The Sarmatian Sea Snail was purported to be an amphibious sea creature that resembled a vast snail. (On Monsters and Marvels *by Ambroise Paré, trans. by Janis L. Pallister, University of Chicago Press, 1982)*

covering the whole body, loping silently upright on the hind legs and leaving a footprint of over twenty-four inches. The creature has been encountered from the icy wastes of Alaska to the mountain ranges down the Pacific coastline.

References 61, 78, 94, 134
See also Almas, Bigfoot, Yeti

SA-TUMBOK RANG BUMI

This is the name of a Jinn in the beliefs of the Malay people of West Malaysia. Sa-Tumbok Rang Bumi, whose name means "World Beater," is one of the offspring of the king of the Jinns, known as Sang Gala Raja.

References 167
See also Sang Gala Raja

SATYR

Satyrs are hybrid humanoid creatures in the classical mythology of Greece that were equated with the fauns of Roman mythology. There are several descriptions of them through the various time periods. Originally, they were depicted as a human male with the legs of a goat and small horns on the head. These were the representation of fruitfulness of the land. Later, several different types of Satyr were identified, including those with no nose that breathed through a massive hole in their chests. The Satyrs, during the latest periods, are the ones with the most familiar image, with human faces, pointed ears, horns, but with hairy male bodies above and the body and legs of a goat below. They were the attendants of their drunken leader, Silenus, and the god of wine, Dionysus/Bacchus. They inhabited the woods, mountains, and countryside, known for this reason as Silvani, meaning "Forest People" or "Wild People," where they pursued the nymphs and were renowned for aggressive drunken sexuality, lechery, rudeness, and love of playing pranks. This is reflected in some of their names: Hybris, meaning "Insolence," Komos, meaning "Revelry," Posthon, meaning "Prick," and Simos, meaning "Snubnose." Their attitude toward humans was unpredictable and could be harmful. The humorous and often derisory plays in which they were featured, after performances of the Greek tragedies, is the origin of our present word "satire."

During the medieval period they were somewhat demoted to grotesque animal beings, as portrayed in the thirteenth-century Anglo-Saxon bestiary in the Bodleian Library, Oxford. In this manuscript the Satyrs are depicted as hairy creatures with beards and broad tails, having almost pleasant faces with cloven hooves and holding a snake, wine goblet, or discus. They were discussed as being caught easily in their native Ethiopia but difficult to maintain elsewhere. In other manuscripts of the period, they could be shown as naked men with goats' beards and horns with erect phalluses as the symbol of debauchery and lust.

The Satyrs' image and symbolism were taken into the European heraldic repertoire, portrayed as having the face of a man on the head, neck, and torso of a male lion with the hind parts of an antelope.

In modern times they have become the evil Kallicantzari of Greek folklore.
References 5, 7, 14, 18, 20, 24, 28, 61, 78, 89, 91, 120, 124, 125, 133, 139, 148, 160, 161, 169, 178
See also Faun, Kallicantzari, Satyrisci, Sileni, Silenus

SATYRAL

This is the alternative name for the hybrid beast known as the Manticore in medieval European bestiaries. The Satyral was the type of Manticore, or hybrid man-tiger, that was supposed to inhabit India.
References 7, 89
See also Manticore

SATYRE-FISH

This is the name of a hybrid monster in the heraldic repertoire of Europe. The Satyre-Fish is depicted with the body of a fish, the head of a goat-man with horns and beard, and wings emerging from its back.
References 7
See also satyr

SATYRISCI

This is the plural name for the young satyrs of classical Greek and Roman mythology.

References 20, 28, 120, 125, 161, 178
See also satyr, Sileni

SAUGER

This is an alternative name for the Guyascutus in the folklore of lumberjacks and forest workers (and later fraudsters), especially in Wisconsin and Minnesota in the United States.
References 7
See also Fearsome Critters, Guyascutus

SAUMANASA

This is the name of one of the Lokapala Elephants in the Hindu mythology of India. In the *Ramayana* Saumanasa (sometimes Anjana according to different legends) stands as the guardian of the west quadrant of the world with the god Varuna on his back.
References 7, 24, 112
See also Lokapala Elephants

SAVALA

This is an alternative name for Kama-Dhenu, the universal cow in the Hindu mythology of India.
References 24, 112, 133
See also Kama-Dhenu

SA-YIN

This is the name of a lake monster in the traditions and beliefs of the Native American people in the region of the Gran Chaco (Toba-Pilaga). The Sa-Yin is variously described as resembling a man with long, black hair astride a vast horse, as a man-horse like a Centaur, or as a knight riding a charger through the waves. Sa-Yin is also known as the Master of the Fishes.
References 134
See also Lady of Lake Traun, Master of the Fishes, Mistress of the Lakes

SCARDYNG

This is the name of a giant in the legends of England. Scardyng first appears in the work of Robert Mannyng, also known as Robert of Brunne (died c. 1338), a monk in the Gilbertine monastery of Semperinham. The character of Scardyng is derived from the Viking invader and founder of the town of Scarborough in Yorkshire, Dorgils Scardi, meaning "Dorgils with the Harelip."
References 183
See also giant

SCARLET BEAST

This is the name of one of the Apocalyptic Beasts described in the Book of Revelations of Saint John in the Christian New Testament section of the Bible.
References 89
See also Apocalyptic Beasts

SCATHA THE WORM

This is the name of the leader of the Cold-Drakes, a species of dragon in the literary works of the English academic and author J. R. R. Tolkien (1892–1973) in *The Hobbit* (1937) and *The Lord of the Rings* (1955). These monstrous creatures were bred by the evil Morgoth in Angband during the First Age of the Sun. They are described as having vast bodies covered in iron scales but, unlike their legendary counterparts, although they had wings they could not fly. They had enormous fangs and huge claws. Scatha the Worm led his Cold Drake hordes to rob the dwarfs of their gold in the Grey Mountains during the Third Age of the Sun and would have killed them all and taken their gold. Then the heroic Fram, a prince of the men of Éothéod, did battle with Scatha the Worm and, having slain their leader, the Cold-Drakes fled and did not return until the year 2570.
References 51
See also Cold-Drakes, dragon

SCHACHI HOKO

This is the name of a composite fabulous creature in the traditions and legends of Japan. The Schachi Hoko, also known as the Hai Riyo or the Tobi Tatsu, is described as having the body of a bird with birds' claws and wings and with the head of a dragon.
References 81, 89
See also Hai Riyo, Oriental Dragon

SCHILBUNG

This is the name of one of the giants in the legends of Germany. Schilbung is one of the giant kings ruling, with Nigelung, over twelve giants living in the wilderness of the mountains, forests, and gorges. Their story in the *Nibelungenlied* tells how the rockfalls, cavernous sounds, and water torrents were caused by their grumbling and groans.
References 139
See also giant

SCIAPOD/S, SCIOPOD/S, SKIAPOD/S, SKIAPODES

This is the name of a fabulous race of humanoids first mentioned in the work of the Latin naturalist Pliny the Elder in his *Historia Naturalis* (A.D. 77). They were later incorporated into many of the medieval bestiaries of Europe and the fourteenth-century travelers' tales of Sir John Mandeville. The Sciapods, meaning "Shadow-foot," were also known as Monoscelans. They were described as having a normal human shape but only one leg and foot. This foot was so enormous that should the weather of their native Ethiopia prove inclement, then they would lay upon their backs and take shelter by extending their foot over their entire body. Despite this apparent deformity, the Sciapods could hop very fast indeed. But they did not need to hunt, for they existed on the perfume of the fruits they carried. Should these die, then so too did the Sciapods. These beings were variously described in different texts. Some stated that they had four legs, with one having the vast foot; some that they inhabited the deserts of Libya; while a bench-end carving in the Church of Dennington in England erroneously gives the Sciapod two legs and vast feet.
References 7, 47, 63, 91, 168, 178, 180

SCITALIS

This is the name of a monster in the ancient texts and the medieval bestiaries of Europe. The Scitalis, whose name is derived from the word *scitulus*, meaning "elegant," was described as a type of winged dragon with two front legs only and the head and tail of a serpent. This creature was said to have a multicolored skin that was so beautiful that all who saw it stopped to admire it. This was their downfall, for although the Scitalis was extremely slow to travel, while its admirers were standing still it struck and killed its victims without the necessity to hunt them. This creature, according to a twelfth-century Latin bestiary and an Anglo-Saxon bestiary of 1220, glowed with such heat that even during a severe frost it would come out into the open air to slough off its old skin in the manner of serpents.
References 14, 148, 185
See also dragon, monster, serpent

SCOFFIN

This is the name of a monstrous serpent in the legends of Iceland. The Scoffin is described as a crowned, winged, poisonous serpent looking and behaving very much like the medieval European Basilisk.
References 89
See also Basilisk

SCOLOPENDRA

This is the name of a fabulous sea monster in the medieval legends of Europe. The Scolopendra is described as having a vast body like that of a whale but with numerous legs with which it propels itself on the surface of the water. Its head has a large snout, from which extend numerous long bristles. It was said that if this creature were ever caught by a fishing hook that it would throw up its own stomach, release the hook, and swallow its stomach again.
References 7
See also monster

SCORPION MAN

This is an alternative name for Girtablili in the mythology of ancient Babylon.

References 89
See also Girtablili

SCYLLA, SKYLLA

This is the name of a terrible monster who was originally a water nymph in the classical mythology of ancient Greece and Rome. She was, according to different sources, the daughter of Typhon and Echidne, or Phorcys and Hecate Crataeis. Scylla, whose name is derived from *skulle*, meaning "bitch," is portrayed variously as a beautiful female from the waist up but from the waist down had the heads of six ferocious dogs sprouting from her above twelve dogs' legs; or as an amorphous, tentacled mass with as many as six heads each with three sets of teeth and twelve sets of legs and feet. The legend of Scylla is told in the *Odyssey* by the Greek poet Homer. She had been very beautiful, and Glaucus, who was in turn loved by the sorceress Circe, became infatuated with her. There are a number of versions of the manner in which she was turned into a hideous monster. The first is as a result of the insane jealousy of Circe, who cast a poison into the water where Scylla habitually bathed. Another version of her transformation to a sea monster is as a result of her dallying with Poseidon; while yet another version is for devouring the cattle from the herd of Geryon stolen by the hero Hercules/Heracles, who killed her. In this latter version her father Phorcys restored her through fire and ashes, but she was transformed into the monstrous form. This so terrified her that, according to the Roman poet Ovid, she threw herself into the sea and hid in the caves of southern Italy. As the sea monster, Scylla destroyed ships and devoured the crews that passed through the Strait of Messina, including six of Ulysses's companions, before she was transformed into an equally dangerous rock.

During the Middle Ages, Scylla was often portrayed in bestiaries as a marine monster, described as having the tail of a dolphin on the body of a wolf and from the waist up a young woman.

References 18, 20, 28, 89, 91, 125, 133, 139, 160, 166, 169, 178, 182
See also Echidne, Geryon, monster, Typhon

SCYTHIAN ASS, THE

This is a type of early unicorn found in the poetry of ancient Greece. It was described as a creature looking much like a gray ass but with a single horn from its forehead inhabiting the region of Scythia. This horn was much in demand for medicinal purposes, for it was purported to be the antidote to poison or to be able to hold the waters of the Styx. Its image was soon equated entirely with that of the unicorn.

References 7

See also Amduscias, Ass (Three-Legged), Chio-Tuan, Karkadan, Ki Lin, Kirin, Koresck, Mi'raj (Al-), Onyx Monoceros, unicorn

SCYTHIAN LAMB, THE

This is an alternative name for the Barometz, which is a legendary part-animal, part-vegetable creature of medieval Europe.

References 7, 18, 89
See also Barometz

SEA BUDDHIST PRIEST

This is an alternative name for the Hai Ho Shang, a sea monster in the traditions and legends of China.

References 89
See also Hai Ho Shang, merman

SEA HOG

This is the name of a fabulous monster in the mariners' and travelers' folklore of sixteenth-century Europe. The Sea Hog was described as having the body of a huge fish but the foreparts of a boar, complete with tusks.

References 89
See also Marine Boar, Marine Sow

SEA HORSE, SEA-HORSE

This is the name of a sea creature in the legends and folk beliefs of Scandinavia and Britain. The Sea Horse was described by sailors, fishermen, and travelers as being like an enormous fish with the head and mane of a horse, having legs with cloven hooves. It was equally at home on the land as well as the sea but was mostly to be seen floating on ice floes. An example of this monster was described by Ambroise Paré (1517–1590), in his work *On Monsters and Marvels,* as having been presented to the Pope in Rome.

In the repertoire of European heraldry, the Sea Horse has the head and foreparts of a thoroughbred horse, but with webbed feet instead of hooves, and the hindparts of a vast fish with a dorsal fin from head to tail.

References 5, 7, 89, 147
See also Hippocampus, Hydrippus

SEA-DOG

This is the name of a hybrid beast in the heraldic repertoire of Europe. It is portrayed as a type of talbot, or hunting dog, but with scales covering its entire body; instead of paws it has webbed, three-toed feet; its scaly tail has a thick rounded end, and behind its webbed ears it has a long dorsal fin from its head to its tail.

References 5, 68

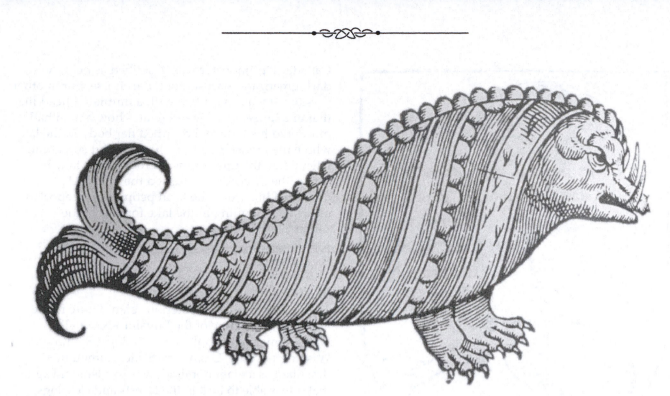

Marine Boar, or Sea Hog (On Monsters and Marvels *by Ambroise Paré, trans. by Janis L. Pallister, University of Chicago Press, 1982)*

The Sea-Horse, a sea creature in the legends and folk beliefs of Scandinavia and Britain (On Monsters and Marvels *by Ambroise Paré, trans. by Janis L. Pallister, University of Chicago Press, 1982)*

Heraldic Sea-Dog (Rose Photo Archive, UK)

SEA-LION

This is the name of a hybrid monster in the repertoire of European heraldry. The Sea-Lion is portrayed as having the head and foreparts of a lion with hindparts like a vast fish's tail.
References 5, 68

SEARBHÁN, SEARBAN, SHARVAN

This is the name of a giant, or Fomorian, in the legends of Ireland. He is also known as Lochlonnach, meaning the "Norseman." Searbhán is described as being extremely skilled in the magic arts and a protector of the magical rowan trees in Dubros, County Sligo. He features in the epic *Tóraigheacht Dhearmada agus Ghráinne* (The Pursuit of Diarmait and Gráinne). Diarmait tried all manner of weapons to vanquish the giant, but this was only achieved when he realized that the only weapon was to be the giant's own club, as his magic was too strong.
References 128
See also Fomor, giant

SEA-SERPENT OF MEMPHRÉMAGOG

This is the name of a lake monster in the folk beliefs of the Abenaki Native American people of Quebec,

Canada. This monster was described as being vast, dark-green, and part serpent, part horse, but in other versions it was a vast fish with a mutilated head like that of a horse. One legend relates how a man had murdered his wife and dumped her body in the lake, where the monster had devoured it. But sometime later, when the husband was crossing the lake by canoe, the monster overturned the boat and devoured him, too. The local people were reported as never swimming in the lake for fear of the serpent.
References 134
See also serpent

SEATCO

This is the name of a mysterious giant figure in the legends and folklore of the Puyallup-Nisqually Native American people of South Puget Sound, Washington State, U.S.A. The Seatco, although described as a giant hominid, was so silent and agile that it was able to lurk in the forests and clearings, usually at night, without being seen. This gigantic being is said to be the enemy of humans and will take their food, break their canoes, and take animals from the traps. If a child wanders into the forest alone, then the Seatco will take the child to become a slave. In this respect the Seatco quite possibly functions as a Nursery bogie to keep adventurous children from harm in the forests.
References 77
See also Bigfoot, Nursery bogie, Sasquatch, Yeti

SECUNDILLA

Secundilla is the name of a giant in the literature of France. He is cited in the genealogy of Pantagruel as an ancestor by the author François Rabelais (ca. 1494–ca. 1553) in his work *Pantagruel* (1532).
References 174
See also Bruyer, Chalbroth, Daughters of Cain, Etion, Gabbara, Galehaut, Gargantua, giant, Happemousche, Hurtaly, Morguan, Noachids, Noah, Pantagruel

SELJORDSORM

This is the name of a lake monster in the traditions and folklore of Norway. It was sighted first in 1750 by Gunleik Andersson, but since then it has been seen more than a hundred times. The Seljordsorm, or Selma, as it is affectionately known, was described in August 1986 as being like a huge black bow when the waters of Lake Seljord were perfectly calm. This neck, or bow, was at least six feet in length and very thick while all around it the water was foaming like the frothing of a wake. However, as the informant, Aasmund Skori, approached to get a better look, it submerged. The rings of this creature have already been compared with those of a similar monster

detailed in the ancient *Hamar Chronicle*. In the English *Guardian* newspaper of Wednesday, 1 September 1999, are the details of a Global Underwater Search team and aerial spotter planes that are currently trying to establish scientific evidence of the existence of the Seljordsorm.
References 134
See also Loch Ness Monster

SEMNAI
This is the name used for the Erinyes in the classical mythology of ancient Greece. The name "Semnai" means the "Venerable Ones" and was used as a euphemism for these monstrous supernatural beings, who were also known as the Dirae, the Eumenides, and the Furies.
References 125, 160
See also Erinyes, Eumenides, Furies

SEMURV, SEMURU
These are alternative names for the Senmurv in the mythology of ancient Mesopotamia and Persia.
References 24, 89, 125
See also Senmurv

SENJEMAND
This is the name of a class of giant in the Norse mythology of Scandinavia. Senjemand is the mountain-dwelling type of Jotunar identified with the island of Senjen. The myth told how when he was rejected by the giantess Juternajesta, he tried to shoot her with a massive arrow of stone. Torge, her lover, deflected it in time with his hat and ran after Senjemand, who leaped on his horse and fled. But Senjemand didn't get very far, for as he galloped through the dawn light the sun rose and bathed him in its glow, turning him instantly to stone. The island of Senjen still has the great stone arrow not far from the hat, with its hole and Senjemand on his horse all petrified forever.
References 24
See also giant, Jotun

SENMURV, SENMURW
This is the name of a fabulous creature or winged monster, also known as the Semurv or the Semuru, in the mythology of the ancient kingdoms of Mesopotamia and Persia. The creature is variously described as having the body of a dog with the head and wings of a bird and, later, as having the head and paws of a dog on the body of a bird, or as having the body of a musk ox, the head of a dog, and the wings of an eagle that roosted like a bat. Whatever the description, this creature was supposed to inhabit the branches of the oldest soma tree, which bore the fruit and seeds of every plant in the world. When the Senmurv descended or alighted from its roost, all the ripened seeds fell to the earth. They were then gathered by the Chamrosh, a similar bird. In the later development of the legends, the Senmurv was transformed and merged with the image of the fabulous bird known as the Simurgh.

The Simyr and Sinam were reportedly similar bird monsters of the same period in that region.
References 7, 24, 89, 125
See also Angka, Bialozar, Chamrosh, Griffin, Kreutzet, Roc, Simargl, Simurgh

SEROU
This is the name of a class of Unicorn mentioned as being in the legends and traditions of Tibet. It was said to be very aggressive.
References 81
See also unicorn

SERPENT, GREAT SERPENT
Serpents have been the subject of myth and folklore from time immemorial and probably link directly to the ancient serpent-worshipping religions of the world. Indeed, many mythologies contain the concept of the great cosmic serpent, such as Ananta Sesha in the Hindu mythology of India; Ahi in the Vedic mythology of India; Aapep, Ka-en-ankh Nereru, Maka, and Mehen in the mythology of ancient Egypt; Falak and Kujata of Islamic countries; Ophion in the ancient Pelagian mythology of Greece; Da in the beliefs of the Fon people of Dahomey; Damballah in the cult of voodoo in the island of Haiti; Hatuibwari of San Cristoval Island in Melanesia; Degei of the people of Fiji; Agunua of San Cristoval Island in Melanesia; in Europe the Midgardsormr of Norse mythology surrounded the universe. Linked with these are also the great Rainbow Serpents of West Africa, Melanesia, and Australian mythologies.

Serpents feature in the mythologies, legends, and folklore of most countries and probably are the foundation upon which the dragon concept was based. There is some basis for this in the fact that the ancient Greek dragon was originally a winged serpent known as the Draco. The serpent may be the guardian of the dead, as with the Lindorm, or of treasure, such as El Cuelebre of Spain. Serpents may be the guardian of cities. One legend from Thailand tells how a convict was sacrificed in a religious ritual at the laying of the foundation stone to the city gate. Before he died he was asked to defend the city when it was required. Years later, when the city was attacked by an army from Burma, a great white serpent emerged from the gate tower, against which none of the enemy's weapons were effective, and the city was saved.

Old woman and serpents. The Great Serpent is one of folklore's legendary serpents. (Rose Photo Archive, UK)]

Serpents in folklore have been said also to have curative powers. One tale from Russia tells of the death of the wife of a faithful *bogatyr'* (knight-hero) who decided to die with her. When he lay in their tomb he was surrounded by serpents, including a massive one, which he beheaded. Then he used the liquids from this serpent on his wife, who was restored to life. They were then brought out of the tomb by rejoicing relatives.

Just as potent are the legendary and folkloric serpents whose malicious attack and poisonous bite will threaten entire communities, such as the Angont of the Huron people of the United States; Kolowisi in the beliefs of the Zuni Native American people of the southwestern United States; Misikinipik in the beliefs of the Cree Native American people of Canada; Vulpangue in the beliefs of the people of the Andes

regions in Chile; Ugrasura in the Hindu mythology of India; Aranda in the folklore of the Native Australians of the Emianga region of Australia; Python in the classical mythology of Greece and Rome; Scoffin in the legends of Iceland; and the Stoorworm in the legends of Britain and Scandinavia.

Serpents are deemed to inhabit virtually every place on earth, and there are serpents in the earth, rivers, lakes, and the seas. There is a wealth of lake serpents in the traditions and beliefs of the Native American people, such as Meshekenabec, just as there is a tradition of sea serpents in the traditions and beliefs of the Europeans, such as the Storsjöodjuret of Sweden.

Many religions have some serpent tradition; in the Judeo-Christian scriptures the Serpent of Eden is the evil deceiver and represents the devil; in the Hindu tradition are the Nagas, who also feature in Buddhism, as their king, Muchalinda, shelters Buddha. In many traditions it is a serpent that will bring about the final destruction of the earth, such as the Midgardsormr in the Norse mythology of Scandinavia.

References 47, 78, 81, 113, 134, 139
See also Angont, Aranda, Draco, Elbst, Great Horned Serpent, Great Lynx, Jormungandr, Julunggul, Kichiknebik, Kinepikwa, Kitchi-at'Husis, Kolowisi, Lindorm, Meshekenabec, Midgardsorm, Mishipzhiw, Misikinipik, Muchalinda, Nagas, Ourobouros, Oyaleroweck, Rainbow Serpent, Serpent of Eden, Sisiutl, Storsjöodjuret, Tcinto-Saktco, Tcipitckaam, Tzeltal, Ugrasura, Vulpangue, Wakandagi, Weewilmekq

SERPENT KING

This is the traditional title given to the monster snake-guardian of the serpent kingdom in the legends and folklore of Sweden. It may be provoked to take revenge for human killings of his subjects or the desecration of a sacred site.

References 134
See also Basilisk, Ch'ang Hao, Dhrana, Dhumavarna, King of the Snakes, Muchalinda, Raja Naga

SERPENT OF EDEN

Traditionally the Serpent of Eden was described in the Hebraic scriptures and the Book of Genesis in the Old Testament of the Christian Bible, as being responsible for the temptation of Adam and Eve, the first people. The depictions of this monster have varied with the artistic conventions of the periods, and whilst it is generally shown as a serpent of such great size that it can entwine around the entire tree of knowledge, it has other distinctive properties. In many early images this serpent has a human face; it has also been given a crown or the plumes and wings of a peacock. In early English art there are many images that give this serpent the horse's profile of the Lindorm of Norse mythology.

References 134
See also Horse-heads, Lindorm

SERPENT OF ISA, FLYING

This is the name of a monstrous serpent in the Christian legends of the medieval period in Europe. This creature is purportedly named in the Old Testament, but later medieval travelers reported that this most venomous of all serpents was hatched from the egg of a Cockatrice in the Ethiopian desert. It was even more deadly than the Cockatrice in that it had the ability to fly at its adversaries.

References 7
See also Basilisk, Cockatrice

SERPENT OF MIDGARD

This is an alternative name for the Great Serpent of Midgard, known as the Midgardsormr, in the Norse mythology of Scandianvia

References 78, 139
See also Midgarsorm

SERPENT OF OMI

This is the name of a monstrous serpent in the legends of Japan. It plagued the region of Omi until it was killed by the hero Yamato Take, the son of King Keiko.

References 113
See also serpent

SERPENT OF SAGARIS

This was a vast serpent in the classical mythology of Greece and Rome. The Serpent of Sagaris was a creature that was terrorizing the country about Sagaris when the hero Hercules/Heracles killed it as he passed through its territory after completing his Twelve Labors.

References 139
See also serpent

SERPENT OF THE REUSS

This is the name of a monstrous serpent in the folklore of Switzerland. The Serpent of the Reuss was reported in 1566 as being a monstrous type of serpent-dragon with four legs and feet with huge claws. It was said to have terrorized the region of Reuss by attacking and devouring the livestock, especially the cattle in the fields.

References 134
See also Elbst

SERPENTIN VERT

This is the name of a heroine in the literature and fairy tales of France. The Serpentin Vert, which means the "Green Serpent," is also known as Laideronette and Uglessa in the tales by the French authoress Marie-Catherine d' Aulnoy (1650–1705). The story follows the traditional motif of the Beauty and the Beast, in which a person of quality has been transformed into a monster by magic and is rescued by unselfish love.

References 182
See also Beast, Loathly Lady, Melusine, Scylla

SERRA

This is the name of a winged sea monster in the medieval travelers' lore of Europe. The Serra was described as being a vast, winged being with the tail of a fish, the wings of a bat or bird, and the head of a lion. It was said that it would pursue any sailing ship for many miles but eventually fold its wings and drop

back into the sea. Although it was reputed to sink the ships, there are no details as to how this was accomplished. In an English Anglo-Saxon bestiary of 1220 in the Bodleian Library, Oxford, the Serra is regarded as symbolic of those who propose good work but fail to carry them through for sinful distractions.
References 7, 10, 14
See also monster

SESHA, SESA

This is the name of the World Serpent, or cosmic serpent, in the Hindu mythology of India. Sesha, also known as Shesha (meaning "All That Is Left") or Ananta or Vasuki, is described as a vast serpent being with up to a thousand heads. Sesha is depicted covered in a purple garment and holding a plough and a vessel in his coils. Sesha exists in the primordial ocean, and his coils support the god Vishnu. As each head yawns, the movement of the vast serpent causes an earthquake somewhere in the world. It is Sesha whose mouths will spew the poison that will consume the earth at the end of time.
References 7, 24, 78, 89, 112, 125, 133, 169
See also Ananta, Midgardsorm, Muchalinda, Vasuki

SEVIENDA

This is the name of the equivalent of the Egyptian Phoenix in the land of India. It was described by the Italian Nicolo d'Conti as having a beak that was full of holes. Like the Phoenix, this bird was consumed by fire but regenerated from a type of caterpillar or worm that was left in the ashes.
References 7
See also Bennu, Phoenix

SGROLMA

This is the name of the primordial giantess in the mythology of Tibet. sGrolma is described as a rock giantess who mated with sPyan-ras-gzigs, the monkey god, from which union all the things of the earth emerged.
References 133
See also giantess

SHAG FOAL

This is the name of a semisupernatural beast in the folklore of Lincolnshire, England. This monster may also be called a Tatter Foal. The Shag Foal is described as a shaggy-haired horse or donkey with huge, fiery eyes. This terrifying creature will appear on dark roads behind lonely travelers but may chase its victims rather than do them actual harm.
References 24, 183
See also Black dogs

SHAGAMAW

This is a creature from the folklore of lumberjacks and forest workers, especially in Wisconsin and Minnesota in the United States, during the nineteenth and early twentieth centuries. The Shagamaw is described as being about the size of a horse but having the foreparts and front paws of a bear but the hindparts and legs of a moose. It habitually walked either on its front legs or just its back legs and then changed to confuse any trackers hunting in its territory. It was particularly prone to eating cloth, and consequently the lumbermen knew that a Shagamaw was nearby when their washing disappeared from the line overnight. The Shagamaw belongs to a group of beings affectionately known as the Fearsome Critters, whose exaggerated proportions and activities not only explained the weird noises of the lonely landscape but also provided some amusement at camps.
References 7
See also Fearsome Critters

SHAITAN/T

In the beliefs of Islam this is a group of evil ogres and monsters that is the third species of Djinn. With the Djinn Iblis they are also known as Sheitan, created from the smokeless fires of hell. They appear in many different forms, such as voluptuous females, sprites, wild animals, or disembodied voices in the desert wind or the whirlwind itself, but the most prominent of these are the ogres and monstrous giants that are detailed in the *Tales of the Thousand and One Nights*. They lurk in the desert, the wastelands, the crossroads, and the marketplaces, where they prey on unwary humans. The Shaitans try to ensnare humans at every possibility with deceits and lead them into sin and everlasting torment.

The name "Shaitan" was a derivation of "Satan," used by Christians as the designation of the Devil.
References 64, 78
See also Djinn

SHANG YUNG

This is the name of a fabulous bird in the traditions and legends of China. The Shang Yung, also known as the Rainbird, is described as a fabulous, huge bird with only one leg. The Shang Yung would be called upon in times of drought but would also appear to warn of coming rains. Legends tell of a particular shaman who had a tame Shang Yung perched on his arm like a parrot wherever he went. Another legend told how it had hopped up to the Prince of Ch'i, who took the advice of Confucius to build canals and drains in the city. This he did, and the city was saved from flooding a little while later.
References 18, 78

Iblis the Djinn, one of the Shaitan (Rose Photo Archive, UK)

SHARAMA

This is the name of a gigantic dog in the Hindu mythology of India. Sharama is the great dog that herds the morning cows of Surya, the sun god, and thus ushers in the dawn each morning. The progeny of Sharama are great dogs with four eyes that are called the Sharameyas.

References 112
See also Sharameyas

SHARAMEYAS

This is the collective name for the great fearsome dogs of the underworld in the Hindu mythology of India. The Sharameyas are the progeny of the great dog of the dawn called Sharama. The Sharameyas are terrifying, great beasts with four eyes each that guard the entrance to the underworld of Yama, the god of death.

References 112
See also Cerberus, Sharama

SHAR-MAR

This is the name of a gigantic serpent in the legends and folklore of Armenia. Shar-Mar, designated the King of the Snakes, was described as a vast serpent, attended by a number of servant snakes, that inhabited a great cavern high in the mountains. The legend tells how a young man called Purto had to take shelter in the cavern from a terrible storm, but while he took refuge courteously just at the entrance Shar-Mar made a sign upon his back. When the storm was over, the young man made a fire and roasted

some of the kill he had made for his family, ate a little, and offered the rest to Shar-Mar for his hospitality. The King of the Snakes was impressed and gave the young man a precious stone. When Purto returned to his family he sold the stone and paid all his debts, then bought a flock of sheep, some of which he took to Shar-Mar and made a great feast of thanks. The King of the Snakes gave Purto a second precious stone, and with this Purto built a lovely house for his family and lived well. But soon his good fortune had become well known, and the ruler of Kilikia (now in Turkey), called Kayen, sent for Purto to attend him at his palace in Adana. Kayen was afflicted with terrible sores and desired Purto to use his influence with Shar-Mar to cure him. Knowing what a risk this would be to the King of the Snakes, Purto refused and was tortured cruelly by the king's men to make him agree. At last Purto consented, and Shar-Mar understood how horribly he had suffered before doing so. The King of the Snakes ordered Purto to eat a particular flower that he gave him, and then the serpent ate a different one. Shar-Mar ordered Purto to give him seven-year-old wine and then decapitate him and bury the body. From the head Purto was to make one infusion from the left of the brain and one from the right. This was then taken to the ruler of Kilikia, who made his doctor test one part of the potion. So Purto gave him the one from the right of Shar-Mar's brain, and the man dropped dead instantly. Purto explained to the king what Shar-Mar had told him to do, and then Kayen drank the remaining potion and was instantly cured. Purto's

fortune was assured in the court of the ruler of Kilikia.
References 55
See also serpent

SHELOB
This is the name of a massive spider, and the daughter of the terrible Ungoliant, in the literary works of the English academic and author J. R. R. Tolkien (1892–1973) in *The Hobbit* (1937) and *The Lord of the Rings* (1955). When the evil spiders covered the greenwood with their disgusting webs, Shelob was more evil and predatory than the rest. Shelob was described as a great black monster covered in poisonous spikes and green slime, with enormous claws on her eight legs and poisonous horns and beak on the fearsome head, upon which only the globular eyes were vulnerable. This vast monster put her web across a pass that later became known as Cirith Ungol, or the Spider's Pass, where anything that approached was devoured. It was her vulnerable eyes that were to prove the method of her destruction, for the little Hobbit Samwise Gamgee managed to spear one. In a blind rage, the injured Shelob fell onto the Hobbit's Elven-blade and was killed.
References 51, 182
See also Ungoliant

SHEM
The Italian monk Annius of Viterbo (Giovanni Nanni, c. 1432–1502) asserted that the biblical Noah was a giant. He re-created a whole genealogy of giants from Noah and Iapetus to justify the constructed line of descent through the giant Dis Samothes to the ancestry of the French nobility of the period. Within this genealogy Annius asserted that the sons of Noah—Shem, Ham, and Japheth—were also giants.
References 174
See also Noah

SHEN LUNG
This is the name of a dragon in the mythology of China. Shen Lung is the master of the rains brought on the wind. The Shen Lung, known also as the Spiritual Dragon, is depicted as the beautiful, multicolored, five-toed Imperial Dragon. Any other person who presumed to wear this image was put to death, as the Shen Lung was assigned only to the emperor of China.
References 89
See also Oriental Dragon

SHEN-NUNG
This is the name of an emperor of China during the period of the mythical third age. Shen-Nung is portrayed as having the head of a bull with horns emerging directly from his forehead but with a human body. He is credited with the introduction of agriculture to the people of China.
References 89
See also Arzshenk, Asterion, Fu-Hsi, Minotaur

SHESHA
This is the alternative spelling for Sesha, the world serpent in the Hindu mythology of India.
References 78
See also Sesha

SHIQQ
These are a type of Djinn in the pre-Islamic mythology of the Yemen. They appeared in the shape of a human that had been divided longitudinally with just one arm and leg. These malevolent beings were the creators of the Nashas by mating with humans.
References 64
See also Biasd Bheulach, Fachan, Paija

SHMOO
This is the name of a fabulous creature in the comic-strip folklore of the United States during the early twentieth century. The Shmoo was described as a sausage-shaped or ham-shaped creature, with a permanent smile on its docile face, that ate nothing yet multiplied continuously. This creature was capable of producing fresh milk, butter, and eggs when needed. If it were observed by a very hungry person, it would die of pleasure and be ready for consumption immediately. It was purported to taste of chicken if boiled but of steak if grilled, and its hide was used for the finest leather, and even its eyes could be used as studs.

The Shmoo was the comic-strip creation of Al Capp in his cartoon "Dogpatch," so called after its main character, Li'l Abner. This all-providing creature came, like many other such beings, as the wish-being of a people who experienced need.
References 7, 24
See also Audumla, Dun Cow of Warwick, Fearsome Critters, Glas Gaibleanir, Kama-Dhenu, Savala

SHOJO
This is the name of a type of Wild Man or being in the legends and folklore of Japan. The Shojo is described as being shaped like a human but with red or pink skin and long, red hair, and they wear seaweed. They are amphibious beings that live on the seabed. They are purported to be masters of the medical and herbal arts and to make a type of *shiro sake,* or brandy, that tastes and behaves as poison to the wicked but as nectar to the good.
References 113
See also mermaid, ningyo

SHOOPILTIE

This is the fearsome water monster in the legends and folklore of the Shetland Islands in the British Isles. The Shoopiltie resembles the Cabyll-Ushtey of the Isle of Man or the Eačh Uisge of the Scottish Highlands. It is more usually seen in the form of a prancing pony on the edge of the sea but can also manifest in the shape of a handsome young man with horses' ears. Its main object is to entice unwary humans to mount its back, whereupon it will dash into the water and devour its prey.

References 24, 25, 60, 160
See also Cabyll-Ushtey, Eačh Uisge, Kelpy, Nix

SHUCK

This is an alternative name for the monstrous Black Shuck in the folklore of England.

References 7, 160
See also Black Shuck

SHUI YING

This is an alternative name for the fabulous Feng Huang, or Phoenix, in the legends of China.

References 81
See also Feng Hwang, Phoenix

SIANACH

This is the name of a monster in the folklore of Scotland. The Sianach, whose name may be translated as "Monster," is described as a huge, ugly, aggresive type of deer. This creature was regarded as particularly predatory and if seen by hunters was left alone.

References 128
See also monster

SIATS

This is the name of a race of monstrous humanoids in the legends and folklore of the Southern Ute Native American people of the Great Basin in the United States. The Siats were described as cannibals that were particularly prone to kidnapping children. The female Siats were called Bapets, and they were even more malevolent. These beings were almost immortal but could be killed with an obsidian arrow. It is possible that in a degraded form these monsters were used by anxious parents to keep their adventurous small children from harm.

References 77
See also Bapet, cannibal, Nursery bogie

SIDEHILL DODGER

This is an alternative name for the Guyascutus in the folklore of lumberjacks and forest workers (and later fraudsters), especially in Wisconsin and Minnesota in the United States.

References 7
See also Fearsome Critters, Guyascutus

SIDEHILL GANGER

This is an alternative name for the Guyascutus in the folklore of lumberjacks and forest workers (and later fraudsters), especially in Wisconsin and Minnesota in the United States.

References 7
See also Fearsome Critters, Guyascutus

SIDESWIPE

This is an alternative name for the Guyascutus in the folklore of lumberjacks and forest workers (and later fraudsters), especially in Wisconsin and Minnesota in the United States.

References 7
See also Fearsome Critters, Guyascutus

SIDEWINDER

This is an alternative name for the Guyascutus in the folklore of lumberjacks and forest workers (and later fraudsters), especially in Wisconsin and Minnesota in the United States.

References 7
See also Fearsome Critters, Guyascutus

SIDI HAMOU

This is the name of one of the leaders of the Djinns in the traditions and folk beliefs of the people of Morocco.

References 82, 122, 160
See also Djinn

SIKULIASUITUQ

This is the name of a giant in the legends and folklore of the Inuit people of eastern Hudson Bay in Canada. Sikuliasuituq, whose name may be translated as the "One Who Does Not Go Ice." This enormous giant lived with his sister, equally huge, on the firm ice over the rocks of the earth. He would not go on the thin ice, where the best catches of fish and seals were made during the long winter months. To survive during these dark months, Sikuliasuituq would steal the catch of any of the Inuit hunters who were unfortunate enough to meet him. But Sikuliasuituq would not take the catch of anyone whose wrists were dirty. Eventually, the people became so annoyed with him that they cleaned their wrists each time and forced Sikuliasuituq to go to the ice floes at night to hunt. There he got too cold and asked the men how they kept warm. They told him to tie his legs and cover himself up, and as soon as he had done this they all stabbed him to death. Without her brother, the giantess died of starvation.

References 77
See also giant

SILENI (pl.), SILENOS (sing.), SILENE (pl.)

This is the name of a race of humanoid creatures in the classical mythology of Greece. The Sileni were a group of beings that instead of being half goat, like the satyrs, had the lower body of a horse with the tail and ears of a horse. Their leader was Silenus, who in some legends was their father. In later Roman mythology they became synonymous with the Satyrs.
References 61, 78, 125, 160, 166, 169, 178
See also Kallicantzari, satyr, Silenus

SILENUS

This is the name of the wisest and oldest of the satyrs in classical Greek mythology. He is possibly derived from the Egyptian guardian spirit Bes. Silenus is portrayed as a drunken, fat old man riding an ass as the attendant of Dionysus/Bacchus. In later myths, the older satyrs were all named Sileni. Silenus, although essentially a comic character, is able to see both the past and the future, and any human who could tie him up long enough could get him to tell them their fate. Silenus and the satyrs were frequently the subjects of Renaissance paintings.
References 20, 28, 78, 120, 124, 125, 139, 166
See also satyr, Sileni

SILVANI

This is an alternative name for the satyrs in the classical mythology of Greece and Rome. They inhabited the woods, mountains, and countryside and were known for this reason as Silvani, meaning "Forest People" or "Wild People," where they pursued the nymphs. They were renowned for aggressive drunken sexuality, lechery, rudeness, and love of playing pranks. The satyrs' most familiar image was with human faces, pointed ears, horns, and hairy male bodies above the waist and the body and legs of a goat below. They were the attendants of their drunken leader, Silenus, and the god of wine, Dionysus/Bacchus.
References 20, 24, 78, 120, 125, 133, 148, 161
See also satyr, Satyrisci, Sileni

SIMARGL

This is the name of a fabulous beast-bird in the folklore of the Slavic people of eastern Europe. It is described as a winged monster resembling a dragon but with the attributes of a bird. As it is the guardian of a tree upon which all the seeds of the world's plants ripen, it is derived from the ancient Persian Simurgh.
References 89, 166
See also dragon, Simorg, Simurgh

SIMORG

This is the name of a fabulous beast-bird in the folklore of Russia and the Ukraine. The Simorg is described as a winged monster resembling a dragon but with the attributes of a bird and the head of a dog. It is portrayed as the guardian of the Tree of Life upon which all the seeds of the world's plants and animals ripen. The tree and its guardian are depicted on an island guarded by voracious fish that will kill anything that tries to reach them. The Simorg was popularly portrayed on jewellery and is derived from the ancient Persian Simurgh.
References 55, 166
See also Angka, Bialozar, Chamrosh, Griffin, Kreutzet, Roc, Simargl, Simurgh

SIMOS

This is the name of an individual satyr in the classical mythology of Greece of Rome. They are described as having human faces, pointed ears, horns, and hairy male bodies above the waist and the body and legs of a goat below. They were the attendants of their drunken leader, Silenus, and the god of wine, Dionysus/Bacchus. They inhabited the woods, mountains, and countryside, where they pursued the nymphs and were renowned for aggressive drunken sexuality, lechery, rudeness, and love of playing pranks. This is reflected in some of their names; here, Simos means "Snubnose."
References 7, 14, 24, 89, 125, 160
See also satyr

SIMURGH, SUMARGH, SIMARGHU, SIMURG

This is the name of a fabulous bird in the legends of Persia, now Iran, and Kashmir in northern India. The Simurgh is considered in some accounts to be the later metamorphosis of the dragon known as the Senmurv. The Simurgh is described as a vast, and sometimes beautifully plumed, bird that inhabits the mountains of Alberz in the north of Persia. Its feathers, which were highly prized, were considered to have healing properties, while the bird itself was considered by other creatures to have wisdom and instill peacefulness. A thirteenth-century poem tells of a journey to find the Simurgh, and another legend tells how a captured Simurgh, thought to sing only with a mate, died when a mirror was placed as a substitute. Other legends credit the bird with a life of 1,700 years and death by fire, like the Phoenix, when its progeny have matured. The Simurgh is known as the Anka in Arabic legends.
References 7, 18, 78, 89, 133
See also Angka, Bialozar, Chamrosh, Griffin, Kreutzet, Roc, Senmurv, Simargl, Simorg

SIN YOU

This is an alternative name for the unicorn in the legends of China.
References 81
See also Kai Tsi, unicorn

SINAA

This is the name of a hybrid humanoid monster in the traditions and legends of the Juruna people of the Xingu River region in Brazil. Sinaa is described as half human and half giant jaguar, as his mother was a human seduced by his giant jaguar father. He was born with an ancient appearance, with his eyes set in the back of his head. Sinaa is said to rejuvenate when he takes off his skin over his head like a shirt and goes to bathe. The end of the world is prophesied to take place when this monster removes the forked pole that holds the heavens apart from the earth.

References 47
See also monster

SÍNACH

This is the alternative name for the Muirdris, a sea monster whose adversary was Fergus mac Léti, in the legends of Ireland.

References 128
See also Caoránach, Muirdris, Oilliphéist

SINAM

The Sinam was reportedly a bird monster similar to the Senmurv of the same period in the regions of ancient Mesopotamia and Persia.

References 89
See also Senmurv

SINHIKA

This is the name of a dragon in the Hindu mythology of India. Sinhika was a female dragon that was the adversary of the monkey god Hanuman. He was eventually able to kill her by leaping into her open mouth and stabbing her from inside her body.

References 78
See also dragon

SINIS

This is the name of a murderous giant in the classical mythology of Greece and Rome. The epithet of Sinis is Pityocamptes, meaning "Pine-bender," from his habit of torturing lonely travelers by attaching their limbs to a bent pine tree and watching them be torn apart. He was the son of the murderous giant Polypemon and was killed by the hero Theseus.

References 78, 133, 139, 178
See also giant, Polypemon

SINURGH

This is an alternative spelling for the Simurgh, a fabulous bird-dragon in the mythology of ancient Persia.

References 78
See also dragon, Simurgh

SIRENA

There are two beings that are known by this name.

1. This is the name of a humanoid monster in the legends and folklore of Spain. In the northwestern Spanish coastal area, "la Sirena" is a type of mermaid that seems to be a derivative of the Siren of classical mythology of Greece and Rome.

2. This is the name of a monstrous serpent in the bestiaries of medieval Europe. The Sirena, also known as the Syren, was described as a winged white serpent that was a highly predatory creature inhabiting the Arabian Peninsula. These creatures were highly dangerous, for they could go faster over the ground than a galloping horse and even faster by flying through the air after their intended victims. The bestiaries considered that their bite was so poisonous that the person was dead before the pain of the injury was felt.

References 10, 14, 139, 169, 182
See also mermaid, serpent, Siren

SIREN/S, SIRENES (pl.), SEIRÉNES (pl.), SIRENAE (pl.)

This is the name of a class of hybrid female humanoid monster in the classical mythology of Greece and Rome. These beings were not described by the Roman poet Homer, but he stated that they were malicious creatures that inhabited the rocks and sang to sailors as they passed in an attempt to lure them to their doom. Their name is variously given as Sireen, Sirene, or Syrene, and they were the offspring of Phorcys or Achelöus. These maidens later appeared, much like the Harpies, as the lower half of a bird and above the waist the torso and head and arms of a woman, on the rocks of Sicily, where they sang melodiously to attract and beguile or devour passing sailors. Their individual names are Aglaopheme, Leucosia, Ligia, Parthenope, Pisinöe, and Thelxiepia. Legend has it that Odysseus/Ulysses was able to pass by their island successfully by stopping up the ears of his men with wax and lashing himself to the mast of his ship. Jason and the Argonauts were said to have caused the demise of the Sirens when they heard Orpheus, Jason's passenger, singing more sweetly than they did.

By the later periods of development and the influence of Christianity, the image of the Siren seems to have been equated with that of the northern mermaid whilst retaining the name Siren and in some cases the original description. The first of these changes may have been in the *Liber Monstrorum* (The book of monsters) that was written possibly during the seventh or eighth century. In one Latin twelfth-century bestiary the Siren is described as having wings and not only lured the sailors into the rocks but pounced upon them and tore them to bits. Whilst in an Anglo-Saxon bestiary of 1220 in the Bodleian Library, Oxford, the Siren is still being described as a bird-human monster. Even later during the thirteenth century three types of Siren were identified: one that sings, one that plays the lute, and one that plays the pipes. Isidore of Seville (c. 560–636) gave them scales and webbed feet, and in some images they had tails with wings. They were often associated in images with the Centaurs.

Whatever the description, during the medieval period there was far more symbolism attached to the image rather than legend, for her attributes were the comb and mirror of vanity; the fish or eel symbols of the entrapped Christian soul ensnared by luxury and vice; the small dragon, the symbol of her liaison with the devil; and her nakedness, taken as a sign of wanton sexuality. Indeed, the name "Meretrix" ("Sea-woman" or "She Who Earns"), which was applied freely during this period, was another name used for a prostitute at the time in canon law.

A Middle English *Physiologus* written probably in Norwich during the fourth century illustrates the confusion and symbolism of the Siren entry as follows:

In ðe se senden selcuðes manie
Ðe mereman is a meiden ilike
On brest & on bodie oc (alðous ze is bunden)
Fro ðe noule niðerward ne is ze (no man like)
Oc fis to ful iwis mið finnes waxen.
Ðis wunder wuneð in wankel stede
ðer ðe water sinkeð.
Sipes ze sinkeð & scaðe ðus werkeð.
Mirie ze singeð ðis mere, & haueð manie stefnes,
Manie & sille, oc it (ben wel ille.
Sipmen here) steringe forzeten for hire stefninge,
Slumeren & slepen & to late waken:
Ðe sipes sinken mitte suk, ne cumen he nummor up
Oc wise men & warre a zen cunen chare,
Ofte arn atbrosten mid here best ouel.
He hauen told of ðis mere, ðat ðus uniemete,
Half man & half fis, sum ðing tokeneð bi ðis.

In the sea are many marvels
The mermaid is like a maiden
On breast and body also (although she is joined)
From her navel downward she is not (no man like)
But fish completely certainly with fins sprouting.
This marvel lives in insecure places
There in the water sinketh
Ships she sinketh and injury thus worked.
Sweetly she singeth this siren, and haveth many voices
Many and resonant, also it (be well dangerous
Sailors they) forget steering for her singing,
Slumber and sleep and too late wake up:
The ships sink sucked down, neither do they come up
  again
But wise men and wary turn back,
Often escaping with all the strength they have.
He has told of this siren that this grotesque

Half human and half fish something is meant by this.
(Middle English Manuscript, British Library Ms Arundel 292, probably from Norwich, dated c. 1300)

From the Middle Ages onward the usual mermaid image and description seem to have become prevalent.
References 7, 10, 14, 18, 20, 24, 28, 60, 78, 89, 120, 124, 125, 133, 134, 139, 147, 148, 161, 166, 169, 178, 182, 185, 186, 188
See also Aglaopheme, Alkonost, Angka, Bahri, centaur, Garuda, Harpy, Parthenope, Podarge, Ptitsy-Siriny, Ri, Siren, Sirena, Sirin, Solovei Rakhmatich, Thelxiepeia, Unnati, Zägh

SIRIN

This is the name of a fabulous bird in the legends and folklore of Russia. The Sirin is described as having the body of a bright-plumaged bird but the head of a beautiful woman. It would come down from the heavens only to sing its sweet melodies to the truly blessed. Those who were rewarded in this way would forget everything as they listened and then died. The Sirin is clearly derived, both in name and the ultimate result of her singing, from the Sirens in the classical mythology of Greece and Rome. The Sirin has a counterpart known as the Alkonost.
References 55
See also Alkonost, Angka, Harpy, Parthenope, Podarge, Ptitsy-Siriny, Siren, Zägh

SIRRUSH

This is an alternative name for the serpent-dragon Mušhuššu in the neo-Babylonian mythology of Mesopotamia. Sirrush is one of the many dragons in the cohorts of Tamat.
References 7, 89, 136
See also dragon, serpent, Tiamat

SISIUTL

This is the name of a monstrous serpent in the traditions and beliefs of the Haidas, Kwakiutl, and Bella Coola Native American people of Canada. Sisiutl is variously described as a salmon-serpent or as a vast, two-horned serpent, or as a two-headed serpent, or as a finned and four-legged part serpent with enormous fangs; however, the traditional image depicted is that of a vast head with hideous fangs forming the gross body from which two serpents emerge at either side. Sisiutl inhabits the coastal waters and estuaries of the British Columbian and northern Pacific regions. Sisiutl can be both benevolent and destructive, and its powers as the assistant to the war god, Winalagilis, are sought by Kwakiutl warriors. However, any unwary people who meet the gaze of Sisiutl will be turned to stone.

References 7, 133, 134, 136
See also Guardian of the Fishes, serpent

SISUPALA

This is the name of a monster in the Hindu mythology of India. Sisupala was said to be the offspring of a human queen and the god Siva. He is described as having been born with a human body but with a third eye in the middle of his forehead and four arms. However, despite his monstrous proportions, the gods prophesied the Sisupala would be fortunate until the day he met the one who would kill him. The sign would be that his extra eye and arms would wither. All went well until he met the god Krishna; the withering took place, and Sisupala lost his good fortune and could only plot how to kill Krishna. But Sisupala's mother extracted a promise from the god to spare his life a hundred times. By the one hundred and first time, Krishna was absolved and called down the sun, which rent Sisupala in half from head to toe, and as his halves fell apart all the anger that boiled out in a flaming torrent was absorbed by the god.
References 133
See also monster

SIVUSHKO

This is the name of a magnificent fabulous horse in the legends of Russia. Sivushko, also known as Barushka Matushka or Kosmatushka, was the wondrous magical steed of the *bogatyr'* (knight-hero)

Il'ya Muromets. Sivushko was described not only as being the most beautiful horse but also capable of taking great strides of about thirty-three miles each time and clearing vast mountain ranges at a leap.
References 55
See also Arion, Balius, Borak (Al), Pegasus

SJØORM

This is the name of a great sea serpent in the legends and folklore of Norway. It was common belief until the end of the nineteenth century that a Sjøorm, or a monstrous Lindorm serpent, were hatched as snakes on land. They were so voracious that as they grew they took larger and larger prey until their size was difficult to manoeuver on land. They eventually found a large body of water where they made their abode on the bed and continued to expand until reaching their monstrous size.
References 134
See also sea serpent

SJÖTROLL

This is the name of a gigantic sea troll in the legends and folk beliefs of Finland. The Sjötroll was said to inhabit the lake bed of Lake Opp in the region of Kökar and to wreak havoc on the fishermen and their catches of fish. Consequently, during some ancient period, two rune stones had been placed, one at each end of the lake, in order to bind the power of the Sjötroll and keep it under the water. However, as

Sea monster. The Sjøorm is a sea monster of Norwegian folklore. (Rose Photo Archive, UK)

Gabriel Olai Hannodius reported in 1680, during times of fog and mist, when the two great stones were obscured, the troll could surface once more to prey upon the inhabitants.

References 134, 160
See also Troll

SKADI, SKAÐI

This is the name of a giantess in the Norse mythology of Scandinavia. Skadi, whose name may be translated as "Winter" or "Shadow," is one of the Hrim-Thursar, or Frost Giants. She is, according to various accounts, the daughter of Kari or Thjazi and a sibling of Bel, Thrym, and Thiassi. When Thjazi was killed for abducting Idun from the Aesir, Skadi went to the Aesir to seek vengeance. She was offered one of their number as a husband in compensation and, as she had fallen madly in love with Balder, accepted. However, she had to choose from the hidden gods with only their feet visible and erroneously selected old Njörd, the god of the seas, or, according to other sources, Ull, the god of frost. Neither would live with the other in their inhospitable palaces. When her main love, Balder,

The giantess Skadi and Niorder (Rose Photo Archive, UK)

was killed by the trickery of Loki, the gods incarcerated Loki in her abode, where she placed a dripping, poisonous serpent permanently above his chained body and head. She had hoped that he would endure poisonous agonies until Ragnarök but reckoned without Loki's faithful wife, who spared him.

References 24, 61, 133, 139
See also Frost Giants, giantess

SKAHNOWA

This is the name of a monstrous turtle in the beliefs and legends of the Seneca Native American people in the northeastern United States. It inhabits the same deep river and lake pools in which the horned serpent Doonongaes is to be found. Skahnowa assists the vast reptile in his hunting of the animal and human victims that he will devour.

References 77
See also Doonongaes

SKATENE

This is the name of a monstrous ogre in the traditions and beliefs of the Choctaw Native American people of the southeastern United States. Skatene is described as being a human that can metamorphose into the shape of a vast owl. She pretends to be a good person to all families, especially those with small children, in order to be invited into the family. Once she has their confidence, Skatene transforms herself at night while they are all asleep and decapitates the father, then makes her escape with the head wrapped in a basket on her arm. The animals of the woodlands have tried to see what is in the basket so that the evidence may bring Skatene to justice. But each time they tried to look they were intimidated into silence, until a tribe of wildcats stopped her. They were bold enough to look and see the head and jumped on her, but she managed to trick them and escape once more to prey on human families.

Skatene appears to have the role both of Vampire and of a type of Nursery bogie to prevent children from talking to strangers, no matter how genial they may appear to be.

References 77
See also Baba Yaga, Nursery bogie, ogre, vampire

SKINFAXI

This is the name of one of the celestial beings in the Norse mythology of Scandinavia. Skinfaxi, whose name means "Shining Mane," together with Hrimfaxi, brought light to the earth. Skinfaxi arose in the morning, and his bright mane spread the light of day and the morning dew.

References 89, 7
See also Horses of the Sun, Hrimfaxi

SKOFFIN

This is the name of a monster in the traditions and folklore of Iceland. The Skoffin is described as looking similar to a bird with dragon qualities. Like its medieval European counterpart, the Basilisk, its stare was deadly to any that it looked upon, including its own race. When two met, they both killed the other simultaneously. In order to rid the island of these malevolent monsters, it was necessary to shoot each one with a silver button on which the cross had been engraved.

References 7, 89
See also Basilisk

SKOLL

This is the name of a monstrous wolf in the Norse mythology of Scandinavia. This gigantic wolf, along with others, pursues the sun on its journey across the heavens; when he catches and swallows it, the whole earth is plunged into darkness.

References 89
See also Aapep, Fenrir

SKRIKER, SHRIKER

This is the local name in Lancashire, England, for the beast that may also be known as Brash, Gytrash, Skriker, or Trash. The name "Trash" is used to describe the squelching noise it may make as it moves along behind someone in the dark. The Shriker has been described as taking the form of a huge dog or a shape with enormous, glowing eyes. It appears in front of lonely travelers, drawing them irresistibly toward it, or pads along beside them, constantly moaning or howling. It may also be heard shrieking in the woods. To try to attack it or beat it off brings disaster or death.

References 21, 24, 25, 37, 160
See also Barguest, Black dogs, Black Shuck, Mauthe Dhoog, Padfoot, Trash

SKRIMSL

This is the name of a sea monster in the traditions and folklore of Iceland. The Skrimsl is described as a giant sea serpent that inhabits the region of Lagarfljöt. It was reported as being seen in the Middle Ages and again during the eighteenth century. But it was firmly believed that it could do no harm, as the saint, Bishop Gudmund, had "bound" its power until Judgment Day; thereafter it would break loose and wreak havoc at Fljötsdal.

References 134
See also Apocalyptic Beast, monster, Sea-Serpent of Memphrémagog

SKRYMIR

This is the name of a giant in the Norse mythology of Scandinavia. Skrymir, also known as Vasty and

The Skriker appears in front of lonely travelers, drawing them irresistibly toward it, or pads along beside them, constantly moaning or howling. (Lancashire Ghosts by K. Eyre, Dalesman Books, UK)

Utgard-Loki, is a Frost Giant who is immense. When Thor, Loki, and Thjalfi were traveling through the woods at night, they mistakenly lay down to sleep in the thumb of one of the giant's gloves because they mistook it for a cave. In the morning the snoring of the giant awoke them with the shaking of the ground like an earthquake. Thor attempted to stop the snoring by hammering the skull of the giant, but he didn't even wake up; he simply rolled over after brushing what he thought was a leaf on his head. Skrymir had, in fact, protected himself during his slumbers by placing an invisible mountain over his head, which resisted anything that might do him harm.

References 139, 166

See also giant, Hymir, Utgard-Loki

SKRYMSLI

This is the name of a giant in the Norse mythology of Scandinavia. The legend most associated with Skrymsli tells of how he won a chess competition with a foolish mortal who bet the life of his son on the game. When Skrymsli came to take the child, his father prayed to the gods to intervene. First the child was changed into a grain in a field of wheat that the giant mowed and ate, but before he got to that particular grain the gods changed the child into a feather on a swan. Then he was changed into an egg in the roe of a deep sea fish after Skrymsli killed and ate the swan. When the fate of the fish was in danger, Loki changed the child back to his normal shape after having laid a trap for the giant. When the giant fell into the trap, Loki chopped off his leg to bring him crashing down. But before he could kill the giant, his leg had regenerated. This time Loki cut the leg and stabbed it with a burning brand to prevent its regrowth, and as Skrymsli bled to death the child was saved.

References 133

See also giant

SLAY-GOOD

This is the name of a giant in the classical literature of England. He appears in the classic allegorical work *Pilgrim's Progress*, written by John Bunyan and published in 1682. The giant Slay-good is a cannibal who traps pilgrims and other travelers on their road past his cavern, then drags them to his lair to be devoured. When the pilgrims' guide, Great-heart, hears of this, he goes to the cavern in his armor, with doughty companions, to do battle. They are just in time to rescue a trapped pilgrim named Feeble-mind, and in the ensuing fight the giant Slay-good is killed and decapitated. The victors take the head back to prove his death.

References 20, 31

See also Despair (Giant), giant, Maul, Pagan, Pope

SLEIPNIR

This is the name of a vast horse in the Norse mythology of Scandinavia. Sleipnir is the eight-legged horse of Odin, the king of the Norse gods. He was said to have been engendered by the god Loki in the guise of a mare when the magic stallion Svadilfari carried its giant master, a Hrimthurse, to the land of the gods. Sleipnir could traverse anything so fast that neither water, nor air, nor land impeded his stride. When Hrungnir challenged Odin to a race, no matter how fast he rode Sleipnir and his master, Odin, were always in front. A similar myth tells of the rescue of the mortal Hadding wrapped in the cloak of Odin astride the pommel of Sleipnir's saddle. Hadding was told not to look but of course did; to his horror he

The giant Skrymir attacked by Thor (Rose Photo Archive, UK)

found that they were galloping across the sea. (Of course, this was a familiar feature of horse races on ice during hard northern winters.) A further journey of this gigantic horse was to take the brother of Balder, called Hermod, to the gates of Hel to ask for the return of the dead Balder. The journey took nine days until Hermod saw the Gates of Hel and the mighty horse charged straight through. When negotiations had taken place, the magic horse returned to Asgard.
References 7, 24, 61, 78, 89, 133, 139, 166, 169
See also Al Borak, Arion, Balius, giant, Hrimthurse, Hrungnir, Pegasus, Sivushko, Svadilfari, Thökk

SLIDRINGTANNI

This is the name of a gigantic wild boar in the Norse mythology of Scandinavia. Slidringtanni, whose name may be translated as "Terrible Tusk," was associated with the goddess Freya. Like Gulinbursti and Hildisiuin, they were frequently the wild, vicious, rapid steeds of the gods running through the underbrush of the forests.
References 7, 78, 89, 105
See also Ætolian Boar, Beigad, Boar of Beann-Gulbain, Buata, Cafre/Kafre, Calydonian Boar, Erymanthean Boar, Gulinbursti, Hildesuin,

Head of giant Slay-Good, who appears in the classic allegorical work Pilgrim's Progress *(Rose Photo Archive, UK)*

Pugot/Pugut, Sachrimnir, Twrch Trwyth, Ysgithyrwyn

SLIMY SLIM
This is the name of a monstrous serpent in the traditions and beliefs of the Native American people and Europeans around Lake Payette in the State of Idaho in the United States. Slimy Slim is described as having a serpentine body of at least thirty-six feet in length and a head resembling that of a crocodile. As the lake has numerous deep chasms within it and is said to be unfathomable, the monster is said to be mostly within the depths and rarely seen on the surface.
References 134
See also serpent

SLIVER CAT
This is a creature from the folklore of lumberjacks and forest workers, especially in Wisconsin and Minnesota in the United States, during the nineteenth and early twentieth centuries. The Sliver Cat is described as having a large body; its head has red eyes that are just vertical slits. Its tail, however, is a weapon of

considerable repute, long and spiked and ending in a hard knob. This predatory creature lurked in the pine trees, awaiting unsuspecting lumberjacks to pass beneath. When one approached, the cat would drop its tail on the man's head, knocking him out with its knob, and then scoop him up with its spikes to be devoured. The Sliver Cat belongs to a group of beings affectionately known as the Fearsome Critters, whose exaggerated proportions and activities not only explained the weird noises of the lonely landscape but also provided some amusement at camps.
References 7
See also Cactus cat, Cheshire Cat, Fearsome Critters

SMAUG THE GOLDEN
This is the name of a dragon in the literary works of the English academic and author J. R. R. Tolkien (1892–1973) in *The Hobbit* (1937) and *The Lord of the Rings* (1955). Smaug the Golden is one of the Fire-Drakes, a species of Urulóki, and was described as a vast dragon with scales of iron and the wings of a giant bat. Smaug was the sworn enemy of the dwarfs and, having smashed down their defenses, raided their stronghold, stole all their treasure, and ruled

their kingdom for two hundred years. Then the Hobbit Bilbo Baggins came with the real king, Thorin Oakenshield, with a band of twelve dwarfs. They knew that the only place of weakness in Smaug's armored body was one small place on his underbelly. When the glowing red beast rose into the air, Bard the Bowman shot one black arrow into this place and felled the mighty Smaug forever.

References 51
See also Ancalagon the Black, dragon, Fire-drake, Urulóki

SNAKE GRIFFON

This is the name of a specific type of Griffin in the medieval travelers' tales of Europe. The Snake Griffon is described as having the head of a snake on the foreparts of a lion but having hind legs like those of an eagle. It appeared in some medieval bestiaries and today occasionally in heraldry.

References 89
See also Griffin

SNARK

This is the name of a monster that appears in the classic work *The Hunting of the Snark* (1876) by the English academic and author Lewis Carroll (Charles Lutwidge Dodgson, 1843–1898). The name "Snark" is a combination of the words "snake" and "shark." The description given in this satirical poem is so nebulous as to confuse the primary characters into trapping the terrible Boojum instead. The Snark was said, by the Bellman, to be slow, have no sense of humor, and sleep late. There were several types, of which the Boojum was a relatively ferocious one, but others were said to be edible despite having skins like sandpaper.

References 7, 20, 40
See also Bandersnatch, Boojum, Jabberwock, Mock Turtle

SNAWFUS

This is the name of a fabulous creature in the traditions and beliefs of the Ozark Native American people of the Ozark mountain region of the United States. The Snawfus was described as a pure white deer of supernatural abilities.

References 94

SNEE-NEE-IQ

This is the name of a malevolent hybrid animal-humanoid, or Narnauk, in the traditions and legends of the Kwakiutl Native American people in the Canadian province of British Columbia. She is a cannibal monster who seeks the children of humans to devour. Snee-Nee-Iq inhabits the high mountainsides but descends secretly to trap wandering children on their own, then carries them off in a pannier on her back up the mountain to be consumed. It is possible that Snee-Nee-Iq had the role of a Nursery bogie for the anxious parents of adventurous children.

References 77
See also Nursery bogie, Skatene

SNOER

This is the name of a giant in the Norse mythology of Scandinavia. Snoer, whose name may be translated as "Snow," is one of the Hrim-Thursar, or Frost Giants. He is the son of Thrym and the sibling of Frosti, Johul, and Drifta.

References 24
See also Frost Giants, giant

SNOW SNAKE

This is a creature from the folklore of lumberjacks and forest workers, especially in Wisconsin and Minnesota in the United States during the nineteenth and early twentieth centuries. The Snow Snake belongs to a group of beings affectionately known as the Fearsome Critters, whose exaggerated proportions and activities not only explained the weird noises of the lonely landscape but also provided some amusement at camps. The Snow Snake was described as a white-bodied serpent with deadly pink eyes that, apart from its eyes, was all but invisible in the snow until it sank its fangs into its prey.

References 7, 24
See also Fearsome Critters, serpent

SO'LA

This is the name of a Jinn in the Islamic beliefs of the people of Saudi Arabia. The So'la is said to be a cannibal Jinn that devours human beings.

References 79

SOLOVEI RAKHMATICH, SOLOVEY RAKHMATICH

This is the name of a monstrous hybrid humanoid in the legends of Russia. Solovei Rakhmatich, whose name means "Nightingale Son of Rakhmat," was described as being half bird with the torso and head of a man. This terrifying creature lived in a perch in a vast tree overlooking the pass between Cheringov and Kiev. From this vantage point Solovei Rakhmatich gave his piercing whistle, which killed all who tried to go through, whom he robbed. Eventually the *bogatyr'* (knight-hero) Il' ya Muromets came on his horse Sivushko; he was attacked and the horse was hit. The hero took his bow and arrows and shot Solovei Rakhmatich from his perch and took the captive robber back to Kiev. After Solovei Rakhmatich had been shown as a prisoner to the whole city, Prince

Vladimir Bright Sun ordered the monster to be beheaded out in the Steppe.
References 55
See also Alkonost, Angka, Harpy, Parthenope, Podarge, Ptitsy-Siriny, Siren, Sirin, Sivushko, Zägh

SPHINX
There are three major types of Sphinx, all in the legends of Europe and North Africa, which are given separately.

Egyptian Sphinx
The first of the Sphinxes were those of ancient Egyptian mythology and art. The most usual depiction is that of a lion's body with the head of a pharaoh, most notably that located at Giza, which was known as Harmachis, dating from about 2500 B.C. There were other depictions and names for these, such as the Androsphinx, with the head of a man, the Criosphinx, with the head of a ram, and the Hieracosphinx, with the head of a falcon, all having different functions. They were almost invariably male and symbolized various aspects or attributes of the gods and the pharaohs.

Middle Eastern Sphinx
The influence of the Egyptian Sphinxes was used in the depiction of this hybrid being in the mythology and art of Babylon in Mesopotamia by 1600 B.C., but the image had become female, although retaining the full lion's body, with the addition of wings. This image was also incorporated into the visual arts of the Greeks via the island of Crete, where Minoan examples of the Sphinx wear a type of hood with flames, which bear no relation to the later mythological development.

Greek Sphinx
This was a monster in the classical mythology of Greece that was said to be the progeny of Orthos and either Typhon or the Chimaera. This Sphinx was described as having the body and legs of a lion, with the wings of an eagle and tail of a serpent, its foreparts being the head and torso of a beautiful young woman. This creature sat upon a rock guarding a pass to the city of Thebes, where if any mortal travelers could not answer her riddle she would immediately tear them apart and devour them. The riddle asked what creature was it that has one voice but is four-footed in the morning, two-footed in the afternoon, but three-footed in the evening. When Oedipus tried to pass, he was challenged by the Sphinx, who was shocked to hear the correct answer—"man." For a man as an infant crawls on all fours, then stands when mature, and may use a cane to walk in his twilight years. With the answer given, the startled Sphinx crashed over the precipice and broke her neck; the people of Thebes were freed of her terror.

The classical Sphinx has entered the repertoire of European heraldry and may be depicted as having the hindquarters of a lion, the torso and head of a maiden, and the wings of an eagle on coats of arms and other heraldic devices.
References 5, 7, 18, 20, 47, 61, 78, 89, 125, 133, 139, 166, 169, 178, 182
See also Androsphinx, Chimaera, Criosphinx, Echidne, Hieracosphinx, monster, Orthos, serpent, Typhon

SPIDER
The Spider is a traditional monster adversary in the traditions and folklore of Japan. The traditional tales have the motif of the weary traveler seeking shelter in an old mansion or castle for the night and being engulfed in the webs of a gigantic Spider. These Spiders are vast, malevolent creatures whose webs are enchanted and unbreakable, except by supernatural means. The victim, if he has no access to these powers, is doomed to be consumed.
References 113
See also Djieien, Spider-Woman, Tsuchi-Gumo, Ungoliant

SPIDER-WOMAN
This is the name of a gigantic evil spider in the legends of Japan. The Spider-Woman inhabited a mountain lair, where she was attended by two decrepit humanoids. The legend tells how Raiko and his retainer, Tsuna, were traveling very late and, as they approached a ruin, saw a skull flying into it. Investigating the mystery, Raiko was soon caught in a glutinous web by what had seemed to be a beautiful woman. As she enclosed him, Raiko stuck his sword, though the mass broke and she fled. Tsuna rescued his master, and together they searched the ruin, at last finding the enormous, grotesque, white spider dying, with the tip of his sword protruding from its belly. As it split open, first the skulls of its victims and then her monstrous progeny spilled out. One by one the heroes slew the spider children, and the region was saved from the plague of gigantic spiders.
References 113
See also spider, Ungoliant

SPLINTER CAT
This is a creature from the folklore of lumberjacks and forest workers, especially in Wisconsin and Minnesota in the United States, during the nineteenth and early twentieth centuries. The Splinter Cat was said to be a huge, hard-headed creature that fed exclusively on racoons and bees. In order to feed itself, it was obliged to break into the tree trunks by charging at

them, splintering them as though struck by lightning. This creature belongs to a group of beings affectionately known as the Fearsome Critters, whose exaggerated proportions and activities not only explained the weird noises of the lonely landscape but also provided some amusement at camps.
References 7, 24
See also Fearsome Critters

SPLIT-FACED BEING

This is the name of a giant in the beliefs and folklore of the Iroquois and Onondaga Native Americans of the northeastern United States. Dehotgohsgayeh may be translated as "Split-faced Being" or "Wry-face," for this giant is reputedly ugly; his body is red on one side and black on the other.
References 77
See also Dehotgohsgayeh

SQUONK

This is a creature from the folklore of lumberjacks and forest workers, especially in the hemlock forests of Pennsylvania in the United States, during the nineteenth and early twentieth centuries. The Squonk is a particularly ugly creature, with a wrinkly skin covered in moles and warts. It is so aware of its ugliness that it weeps continuously and is hardly ever about in daylight. Many people who have tried to trap a Squonk have managed to follow its trail of tears, but rarely has it been caught. On the few occasions that this has taken place, when the sack in which it had been caught was opened, the creature had literally dissolved in tears, leaving only a damp sack with bubbles. For this reason, the epithet *Lacrimacorpus disolvens* has been used for the Squonk. This creature belongs to a group of beings affectionately known as the Fearsome Critters, whose exaggerated proportions and activities not only explained the weird noises of the lonely landscape but also provided some amusement at camps.
References 7, 18, 24
See also Fearsome Critters

STALO

This is the name of a giant in the traditions and legends of the Sami (Lapp) people in the north of Norway, Sweden, and Finland. Stalo is described as exceptionally huge and strong.
References 24
See also giant

STARKADR

This is the name of a giant in the Norse mythology of Scandinavia. Starkadr is described as being a monstrous demonic member of the Jötnar giants but, unlike most of them, having eight heads.

References 24
See also giant, Jötun

STCEMQESTCINT

This is the name of a type of humanoid being in the traditions and folk beliefs of the Coeur d'Alene Native American people of the United States. The name Stcemqestcint, which may be translated as "Tree People," relates to beings that look like humans but wear nothing but buffalo skins over their peculiarly stinking flesh. If they are encountered by humans, they change rapidly into tall trees and await the human's leaving. However, if the human continues to stare at them, they will be prevented from ever looking like a human again.
References 77

STELLIO

This is a type of creature or reptile that is described in an English bestiary of 1220 as a Salamander. The Stellio is the Latin name for the Dea, which is illustrated as a monstrous lizard that consumes and exists within fires.
References 14
See also Dea, Salamander

STEROPES

This is one of the three gigantic Cyclopes in the classical mythology of Greece and Rome. His brothers were Brontes and Arges. Steropes's name may be translated as "Lightning"; like his brothers, he had only one eye, located in the center of his forehead. They were born of Gaia and fathered by Uranos, who threw them into the depths of Tartarus for rebellion. In his work *Theogony* (ca. 750 B.C.), Hesiod describes them both as giants and as Titans, but the Cyclopes were distinct from both.
References 78, 139, 178
See also Cyclopes

STHENO

This is the name of one of the Gorgons in the classical mythology of Greece and Rome. Like her sisters, Euriale and Medusa, she had been very beautiful but was transformed into a snake-haired monster; unlike Medusa, Stheno, whose name means the "Strong One," was immortal.
References 89
See also Gorgons, Medusa, monster

STIHI

This is the name of a dragon in the traditions and folklore of Albania. Stihi is described as a huge dragon that emits flames and fire from its mouth and nostrils. It is the guardian of hoards of treasure.
References 125
See also dragon

STIKINI

This is the name of a class of humanoid monsters in the traditions and beliefs of the Seminole Native American people of Oklahoma and the southeastern United States. The Stikini are transformed humans who, having thrown up their internal organs at night in the forest, are metamorphosed into the part form of the horned owl. In this shape they prey upon sleeping humans, drawing their beating hearts out from their mouths. These they take and devour after cooking them in a special pot. To return unnoticed after their gruesome night's work, all they have to do is relocate and ingest their organs. If a hunter sees or smells such organs whilst in the forest, then special arrows prepared with herbs and owl feathers are used to kill the Stikini.
References 77
See also vampire

STOLLENWURM

This is the name of a terrifying dragon or type of lizard in the traditions and folklore of Switzerland. The Stollenwurm is described as having the face of a cat on the head of a lizard with a long ridge on a dragon's warty body ending in a very long tail, the whole being covered in scales interspersed with red veins and bristles. This gruesome creature presents a terrifying appearance to any humans by standing on its hind legs and raising itself far above them. There have been numerous accounts of this creature in the Alpine passes from France to Austria, where it is called the Tatzelwurm.
References 134
See also Arassas, Dard, dragon, Tatzelwurm

STOMACH-FACES

This is an alternative name for the ancient classical and medieval European monster called the Gryllus.
References 89, 182
See also Gryllus

STONE GIANTS

There are Stone Giants in the mythology of many cultures.

In the legends of the Iroquois and Huron Native American people, they were massive primordial cannibal giants that were finally defeated by Hino, the god of thunder, who pulverized them. In the legends of the Abenaki Native American people, the Stone Giants were a massive primordial race that was defeated by the culture hero Gluscap.

In the legends of the Yahgan people of Tierra del Fuego, on the southernmost tip of South America, a Stone Giant was defeated through the cunning of the hummingbird attacking the vulnerable soles of his feet and making the giant's heart explode.

In European mythology, the Jotuns are giants made of or inhabiting rocks and mountains.
References 24, 38, 133, 139
See also Jotuns, Titans

STONECOATS

This is an alternative name for the winter cannibal giants called the Jokao in the traditions and beliefs of the Iroquois and Seneca Native American people of the United States.
References 77
See also cannibal, Jokao

STOORWORM

This is the name of a monstrous serpent in the legends of Britain and Scandinavia. The Stoorworm, whose name means "Great Serpent," was so vast that its body could have covered the whole of northern Europe. The monster inhabited the great northern seas, but when it emerged it started to flood all the islands of Britain. Soon human sacrifices were made to appease the monster and keep it from doing more damage. However, when the king's daughter was to be the next, he offered half his kingdom to whoever would kill the Stoorworm, and Assipattle volunteered. He devised a stratagem of keeping a fire of slow-burning peat close by, and when the monster opened its mouth he threw in peat after peat, which kept on burning the monster from inside. The writhings and thrashing of the Stoorworm cut Denmark from Sweden and Norway, creating the Skaggerak. As it thrashed its charred jaws, the teeth were spat into the northern seas to form the Orkney, Faroe, and Shetland Islands. The body of the burning Stoorworm shrank until it was a fiery ball, forming an island that still exists—Iceland.
References 78
See also Midgardsorm, Worm

STORSJÖODJURET

This is the name of a monster in the folklore of Sweden. Storsjöodjuret is said to be something like a lake serpent or serpentine monster with horns or ears that inhabits Lake Storsjön in the region of Jämtland. It had been a feature of the local and national folk belief for some considerable time, as a rune stone on the island of the lake had anciently been considered to keep the Storsjöodjuret supernaturally under control. In 1894 a team of people constructed a vast metal cage, lowered it into the lake, and baited it with pigs' carcasses; this construction is on display in the museum at Östersund, along with the harpoons that they had hoped to use but never did.
References 134
See also Loch Ness Monster, Midgardsorm, monster, serpent

STRIGAE, STRIGÆ

These are evil female creatures in the beliefs of the people of ancient Rome. They manifest as birds with female faces that would steal small children left unattended. They were a type of vampire and also used as a very evil Nursery bogie to control the behavior of children. This word now denotes a witch in modern Italian folklore.

References 125
See also Nursery bogie, Stringes, vampire

STRINGES

This is the name of a class of vampire in the folklore of modern Greece. The Stringes are said to descend on the bodies of sleeping humans and suck their blood. They are no doubt derived from the Strigae of ancient Rome.

References 7, 125
See also Nursery bogie, Strigae, vampire

STVKWVNAYA

This is the name of a serpent in the traditions and beliefs of the Seminole Native American people of Oklahoma in the United States. The Stvkwvnaya, also known as the Tie Snake, is described as being a vast serpent with a horn of some length protruding from its head and inhabiting deep waters. This horn is valued as an aphrodisiac and charm ingredient, and Stvkwvnaya is therefore summoned with magical chanting to have the horn scraped for this purpose. Whilever Stvkwvnaya is enchanted by the songs, it offers its precious horn to be pared, but should anyone not know these, then it is very dangerous to encounter this creature.

References 77
See also serpent

STYMPHALIAN BIRDS

This is the name of a vast flock of horrific birds in the classical mythology of Greece and Rome. These birds, described as having beaks, feathers, and claws of either bronze or iron, according to the source, inhabited the marshes of Stymphalus in Arcadia. They were fearsome creatures that ravaged the region by flying over living beings, including humans, and dropping their metal feathers onto the victim. Then they would swoop down and tear and devour their flesh. The hero Hercules/Heracles was given the task of getting rid of these birds as part of his Twelve Labors. At first he could kill only one at a time, being safely protected by the pelt of the Nemean Lion from their feathers. He appealed to the goddess Athena, who had Hephaestus forge a huge, noisy rattle. When the hero crept toward the birds and then shook the rattle, they were so startled that he could empty his quiver into their confusion in the air more rapidly. The birds flew off and settled on the island of Ares in the Euxine Sea, where the only people ever to see them again was Jason and the Argonauts on their way to Colchis.

References 7, 24, 78, 133, 139, 178
See also Nemean Lion

SUEVUS

This is the name of a giant who appeared in the medieval work *Officina* by the erudite Jean Tixier de Ravisy (alias Ravisius Textor, c. 1480–1524), who proposed that Tuyscon Gigas was actually a son of the giant Noah whose progeny were the ancestors of European nobility. He constructed a line of giant descendants, of whom Suevus was one of many legendary figures.

References 174
See also giant, Noah, Tuyscon Gigas

SUHUR-MAS

This is the name of a hybrid monster in the mythology of ancient Sumer. The Suhur-mas, whose name may be translated as "Ram-fish," was described as having the head and body of a ram but the tail parts of a fish. It was associated with the constellation now known as Capricorn.

References 7, 20, 24, 89
See also Capricorn

SUILEACH

This is the name of a monster in the traditions and beliefs of Ireland. The Suileach is described as a vast lake monster with many eyes on its head that inhabited the Lough of Swilly in County Donegal. This creature plagued the area about the waters until it was vanquished, some say, by Saint Colum Cuille (521–595) and was never seen again.

References 78, 89, 134
See also dragon, Loch Ness Monster, monster, Worm

SUIRE

This is an alternative name for the Merrow in the folklore of Ireland.

References 21, 24, 25
See also mermaid, Merrow

SUKUYAN

This is the name for the vampire in the folk beliefs of the people of the islands of Trinidad and Tobago in the Caribbean. The Sukuyan cannot gain entry to a house unless she is invited in and to do so will visit many houses during the day, requesting matches or salt. Should the householder give her these, then the entire household will receive visits from her as her real, monstrous, blood-sucking self.

The Sukuyan will drain them until death and then repeat the process. The only way to be rid of her, once the symptoms have been recognized, is to chant "Thusday, Friday, Saturday, Sunday" three times as one marks a cross over every door and window and hangs a mirror there. Then when the Sukuyan returns for her nightly feed, she will be compelled to see herself in the mirror with the mark of the cross above and will depart, but it doesn't kill her.

References 24
See also Azeman, Legarou, Loup garou, vampire, Werewolf

SUN RAVENS

This is the name of celestial birds in the legends of China. Originally the heat and light of the earth was delivered by ten vast birds whose plumage spread this, one for each hour of the daylight and warmth needed, then darkness fell as they rested. However, one day they mis-timed their arrival and departure so that they all arrived over the earth simultaneously. The consequences of their combined heat and light would have been catastrophic for the world, had not the Excellent Archer, named I, shot down the nine surplus Sun Ravens.

References 139

SUPRATIKA

This is the name of one of the Lokapala Elephants in the Hindu mythology of India. Supratika stands as the guardian of the northeast quadrant of the world with, according to different legends, the gods Prthivi or Siva or Soma on his back.

References 7, 24, 112
See also Lokapala Elephants

SURABHI

This is an alternative name for the universal cow, Kama-Dhenu, in the hindu mythology of India.

References 24, 112, 133
See also Kama-Dhenu

SURMA

This is the name of a monster in the legends of Finland. Surma is described as a pair of vast jaws with rows of huge fangs attached to a voracious, never-ending gullet. This being was the guardian to the gates of the underworld, where the goddess Kalma reigned. Those who were entitled to pass were allowed through the gates, but any imprudent or foolhardy mortals who ventured close were grabbed by Surma, torn to shreds by the fangs, and swallowed into the eternal gullet.

References 133, 139
See also Cerberus, Charybdis, monster

SURYABHAUMA

This is the name of one of the Lokapala Elephants in the Hindu mythology of India. Suryabhauma stands as the guardian of the northern quadrant of the world with the god Kubera on his back.

References 7, 24, 112
See also Lokapala Elephants

SUS LIKA

This is the name of a monstrous dog in the traditions and beliefs of the Tanaina Native American people of the Sub-Arctic regions of Alaska in the United States. The Sus Lika inhabits the mountain passes, awaiting the unwary traveler under the earth. Sometimes it can be heard traveling or barking but never allows anyone to see it.

References 77

SUTEKH

This is an alternative name for Set in the mythology of ancient Egypt.

References 139

SUTR, SURT, SURTR

This is the name of a giant in the Norse mythology of Scandinavia. Sutr, whose name means "Soot," is one of the Fire Giants and the ruler of Muspelheim. He is the possessor of the flaming sword that used to belong to the god Frey. It is Sutr who will bring his hordes of Fire Giants to destroy the world at Ragnarök.

References 24, 47, 125, 133, 139
See also Fire Giant, Gerda, giant, Jotun

SUTTUNG

This is the name of a giant in the Norse mythology of Scandinavia. Suttung was, for a while, the keeper of the draft of inspiration called Kvasir. Two evil dwarfs, Fjalar and Galar, murdered a wise and gentle man called Kvasir and collected his blood to make a magic mead of knowledge and eloquence. Soon the fame of the mead brought many to seek the dwarfs, few realizing how they had come by it. Two such visitors were the giant Gilling and his wife, who came as guests to the table of the dwarfs but were murdered by them. When they did not return from their visit, Suttung, the nephew of Gilling and his wife, went in search of them. When he reached the abode of the dwarfs, he too drank some of the magic mead, and he knew immediately what had befallen Gilling and his wife. Suttung immediately slew the dwarfs and took the mead back to the giants. However, this mead was desired by the gods, especially by Odin, their king, so Suttung made his daughter, Gunnlöd, guard it in the cavern where it was hidden. But Odin knew that Baugi, Suttung's brother, was weak, and the god

persuaded him to let him into Suttung's abode. Once inside, Odin was able to seduce the giant's daughter and gain the mead.
References 64, 127, 133, 139, 160, 166
See also Baugi, giant, Gilling, Gunnlöd

SVADILFARI, SWADILFARI

This is the name of an enormous magical horse in the Norse mythology of Scandinavia. Svadilfari carried its giant master, a Hrimthurse, to the land of the gods, the Aesir, who were trying to surround Asgard with a protective wall and gate. He volunteered to do it in three winters if he could have the goddess Freya as his wife, and the sun and moon. The Aesir were persuaded by Loki to accept if he could do it in one winter. The bargain was struck, if his horse, Svadilfari, was allowed to help. The giant, aided by Svadilfari, was completing the task so quickly that the Aesir became terrified of losing their goddess of joy, and the lost light of day and night would kill the earth. So they went to Loki and threatened him horribly if he did not think of a way in which to stall completion. In the morning when the giant set to work, Svadilfari's attention was taken by the whinnying of a pretty mare on the edge of the forest. Off the stallion raced after her, all day, until their union was accomplished, while the giant was prevented from building, chasing after Svadilfari all day. When night came the magical horse, Sleipnir, was born of the union, and then Loki changed back into his normal shape. The delay had been accomplished, but the giant was bent on revenge, until he was slain when Thor threw his magic hammer, Miölnir, and cleft his head into splinters.
References 61, 127, 139
See also Hrimthurses, Jotun, Sleipnir

SVARA

This is the name of a dragon in the legends and folklore of Armenia. Svara is described as a vast yellow dragon with an enormous horn on its head, huge ears, and fangs as long as a man's arm. This monstrous creature poisoned anything within its reach until the hero Keresapa vanquished it.
References 7
See also dragon, Oriental Dragon, Yellow Dragon

SVYATOGOR, SVIATOGOR

This is the name of a giant in the mythology of the Slavic people of Europe, where his name is spelled Svyatogor, and of the people of Russia, where his name is spelled Sviatogor. The same legend occurs in both cultures. This legend tells how Svyatogor, like most giants and ogres of European folklore, takes on a challenge to his strength. While out on his horse he

saw a bag on the ground and wished to know what was inside. He bent down to pick it up, but it was too heavy, so he dismounted. Try as he might, it did not seem to shift until at last it reached about to his knees. Then he suddenly realized that he had not lifted it at all but instead had gradually pushed himself into the ground. Despite all his strength and best straining and tears, he remained there until he starved to death.

A further Russian legend of the demise of Sviatogor tells how he met the *bogatyr'* (knight-hero) Il' ya Muromets along the road. Both knew of the other's reputation, and the hero swung his club at the giant. However, the giant was unmoved by any of the attacks and lazily lifted the knight by his hair and deposited him in a pouch on his saddle. The horse stumbled with the weight, and Sviatogor, removing Il' ya Muromets, recognized him as a Knight of Holy Russia. The giant thereafter desired the hero's companionship. While they traveled, they saw a vast stone coffin by the roadside, and the hero jumped in. As it was too big, the giant took his companion out and showed what a good fit it was for him and, to prove it, pulled the lid over himself. But when the *bogatyr'* tried to release his companion, the magic coffin only tightened its binding bands of steel. In desperation, the giant told Il' ya Muromets to use his sword, but that made the lid so fast that it was sealed forever. The giant instructed his newfound friend to tie his horse to the tree to die with him and to leave him to his fate, which he did with sadness and departed.
References 133
See also giant

SWAMFISK

This is the name of a fabulous fish in the legends and folklore of Norway. It was a predatory fish that entrapped others by covering itself in a slime or skin that made it appear dead. Then it would snap up any fish attracted to its "carcass."
References 7

SYKRAKEN

This is the name of a vast sea monster in the traditions and legends of Norway and northern Scandinavia. The Sykraken is more usually known as the Kraken.
References 89
See also Kraken

SYMIR

The Symir was reportedly a bird monster similar to the Senmurv of the same period in the regions of ancient Mesopotamia and Persia.
References 89
See also Senmurv

SYREN

This is the name of a monstrous serpent in the bestiaries of medieval Europe. The Syren, also known as the Sirena, was described as a winged white serpent that was a highly predatory creature inhabiting the Arabian Peninsula.

References 185

See also Sirena

SZ

This is the alternative name for the unicorn of Oriental mythology.

See also unicorn

T

TAGES

This is the name of a monstrous child in the mythology of the Etruscans of preclassical Italy. Tages is described as looking like a human boy but with two serpents as legs. He was said to have come from the earth as it was being ploughed and emerged from one of the furrows and then taken to the village. There he started to make prophesies by divining from the entrails of sacrificial creatures in the temple, a system known as Haruspicina.
References 125
See also Fu-Hsi, Nu Kwa

TAIPAN

This is a regional name for the Rainbow Serpent in the Dreamtime mythology of the Native Australian people.
References 133
See also Rainbow Serpent

TAIRBE UISGE, TAIRBH-UISGE

These are alternative spellings of the name of the monstrous water-horse Tarbh Uisge in the legends and folklore of Scotland and Ireland.
References 134
See also Tarbh Uisge

TAKSHAKA

This is the name of a king of the Nagas in the Hindu mythology of India. The legend in the *Mahabharata* relates how a modest hermit was insulted by a boastful and arrogant Raja named Parikshit. The son of the defenseless monk implored the Naga king, Takshaka, renowned for his vicious tenacity, to avenge the wrongs to his father. The Raja was quite sure that when he retreated to his fortress in the middle of a lake that he was beyond the Naga's grasp. However, some monks attended the fortress, laden with gifts of fruit as tribute to the lord. When the final piece of fruit was opened, a strange insect with red eyes emerged then transformed into the Naga, who then strangled the Raja in his coils.

References 139
See also Muchalinda, Naga

TAKUJUI

This is the name of a fabulous creature in the mythology of Japan. The Takujui is portrayed as very similar to the Kudan, with the body of an animal with eyes and spines on it and with the head of a human. It was regarded as a creature of auspicious periods and appeared at a time of justice and good government, as did the Ch'i-Lin of China.
References 7
See also Ch'i-Lin, Kudan

TALL AGRIPPA

This is the alternative name for Agrippa, or Great Agrippa, a character from the popular Victorian children's book *The English Struwwelpeter, or Pretty Stories and Funny Pictures*, written by Dr. Heinrich Hoffmann and published in Britain in 1847.
References 97, 182
See also Agrippa

TALL MAN

This is the alternative name for Fsti capcaki, a giant in the traditions and beliefs of the Native American people of Oklahoma in the U.S.A.
References 77
See also Fsti capcaki

TALOS

This is the name of a giant in the classical mythology of Greece and Rome. Talos was said to be the last of the sons of the primordial giants and the Titans. He was covered in bronze or brass and was invulnerable except for the base of his heel, where a plate covered the vein of *ichor*, which ran the length of his body from the neck to his feet. Talos was the guardian of the island of Crete, being given to Asterius in some accounts by Zeus, the king of the gods, or by Hephaestos/Vulcan, or by Daedalus. Talos's task was to keep strangers away, and this he did by taking each one that landed in his red-hot arms and burning them to death and, in other versions, by casting rocks upon them from the height of the clifftops. His demise came when the hero Jason landed with his Argonauts or at the hands of the heroes of Rome, Castor and Pollux. According to different versions, the witch Medea enchanted the giant as he was pelting the Argonauts with rocks and caught his vulnerable heel on one, releasing the *ichor,* or when Medea removed the bronze pin over the vein and drained the *ichor* and bled him to death.

References 7, 18, 78, 169, 178
See also Be Chasti, Golem

TAMA-O-HOI

This is the name of an ogre in the legends of the Maori people of New Zealand. Tama-o-hoi was said to have been one of the primeval race of giants that first inhabited the islands. When the later humans came to the islands, he would set upon them and devour them if they ventured onto his mountain, Tarawera. Eventually, by powerful incantations, the priest Ngaatoro-i-rangi made a vast chasm open in the mountaintop into which he thrust the ogre and sealed him in. When this volcano erupted in 1886 it was believed that Tama-o-hoi had caused it.

References 155
See also cannibal, ogre

TAMMATUYUQ

This is the name of a cannibal monster in the legends and folk beliefs of the Inuit people of eastern Hudson Bay in Canada. Tammatuyuq existed at the time of the primordial people and preyed upon their infants. First the giant gained the confidence of the new mother and then, when left alone with it, took the child to its lair. There Tammatuyuq sucked out its life forces through a straw or needle that pierced the baby's head.

References 77
See also monster

TANGATA

This is the name of the primordial giants in the mythology of Polynesia. The name "Tangata" equates with the word *kanaka,* meaning "people," for these giants traversed the oceans in the crafts they made without plans or instruments. The Tangata intermarried with human wives, and the progeny became the gods of the Polynesians, and their descendants the Polynesians themselves.

References 113
See also giant

TANGIE

This is the name of a sea horse in the folklore of the Orkney and Shetland Islands in the British Isles.

Tangie is usually described as a rough-haired type of pony with seaweed or shells in its mane, or it may look like a type of merman. It is more in keeping with the Kelpie or the Noggle in its terrorizing the lonely traveler, especially young women on lonely roads at night near the lochs, whom it will abduct and devour under the water. It is recorded that a fearsome sheep rustler named Black Eric rode a Tangie, which gave him supernatural assistance in a fight with a crofter named Sandy Breamer. Although Black Eric finally fell over a coastal cliff known as Fitful Head, the Tangie continued to terrorize the area, particularly the young women he was hoping to abduct.

References 20, 24, 67, 107, 160
See also Eačh Uisge

TANIHWA

This is the name of a class of gigantic monster in the traditions and legends of the Maori people of New Zealand. Tanihwa is described as a vast, lizard-like creature or dragon with huge fangs in its jaws and a long, spiny tail that attacked and devoured any humans that it encountered. The legends tell of the hero Pitaka who, with a band of fearless men and some magic chants, managed to trap and kill three of these Tanihwa, from which the bodies of all the people they had devoured tumbled when the bodies were slit open.

References 113
See also Bingbuffer, Dea, Fillyloo, Golligog, Salamander, Stellio, Stollenwurm

TANNGNIORTR

This is the name of a gigantic celestial goat in the Norse mythology of Scandinavia. Tanngniortr, whose name means "Tooth-gnasher" was, with Tanngrisnir, one of a pair of goats that pulled the chariot of the Norse god Thor across the skies.

References 78
See also Tanngrisnir

TANNGRISNIR

This is the name of a gigantic celestial goat in the Norse mythology of Scandinavia. Tanngrisnir, whose name means "Tooth-grinder" was, with Tanngniortr, one of a pair of goats that pulled the chariot of the Norse god Thor across the skies.

References 78
See also Tanngniortr

TANNIN

This is the name of a monster in the Hebraic scriptures and the Old Testament. Tannin is envisaged as a sea serpent of enormous length and great power, the serpent or dragon of primeval chaos, and may be an alternative for the Leviathan or Rahab.

References 24, 125
See also Leviathan, monster, Rahab, serpent

TANTI-GÁHA
This is the name in the Mágadha language for the Nyan, a monstrous serpentine creature in the traditions and legends of Burma.
References 81
See also Nyan

T'AO-TIEH, T'AO T'IEH
This is the name of a hideous monster in the mythology and legends of China. The T'ao-Tieh, whose name may be translated as the "Glutton," is described as a vast head and cavernous mouth with a neck and the foreparts of the same animal, which may be a dragon, human, or tiger. The hind part of this monster is comprised of two hind bodies with vast stomachs. This monster symbolized greed and sensuality, and its image was frequently painted on dishes to warn diners of the sin of overindulgence.
References 18
See also Kirtimukha

TAPAGÖZ
This is the name of a class of giant in the legends of Armenia. They may have three heads or only one, but each head has a single eye in the middle of the forehead, like the Cyclopes in the classical mythology of Greece and Rome. Each head was so huge that they were said to weigh the equivalent of 1,800 pounds whilst a single tooth was the equivalent of 180 pounds. One of these vast giants stole the daughter of King Zarzand, Smizar, and imprisoned her in his castle. The hero Zurab, later called Aslam, killed the Tapagöz and rescued her.
References 55
See also Cyclopes, giant

TARANDRUS
This is the name of a fabulous beast in the classical literature of Rome. The Tarandrus featured in the work *De Natura Animalium,* written by the Latin author Claudius Aelianus (c. 220) and later in medieval European bestiaries. It was described as a gray, long-haired animal resembling an ox. However, if this creature were disturbed by hunters or other predatory animals, its coat took on the colors of the vegetation around and camouflaged it, much as a chameleon.
References 7

TARANUSHI
In the beliefs and folklore of the Islamic countries of Mediterranean North Africa, Taranushi was the first Djinn created from the Saharan wind, the Simoon. He

was charged with controlling the activities of all the other Djinns.
References 107, 122, 125
See also Djinn

TARASCA
This is the name of a dragon in the legends and folklore of Spain. Originally, this dragon may have had much to do with the Tarasque of southern France and epitomizes the dragons that threaten the community by eating its children. Today the Tarasca is taken in effigy to be vanquished by the population on the feast day of Corpus Christi in Redondela, Pontevedra. The dragon is paraded with small children seated inside its belly.
References 182
See also dragon, Tarasque

TARASQUE
This is the name of a dragon in the medieval legends of France. The Tarasque was said to be the progeny of the monstrous Leviathan and a Bonnacon and was described as having a body like that of an enormous ox, with the legs and feet of a bear. It was the terror of the countryside in the region of Aix la Chapelle until the blessed Saint Martha tamed and vanquished it. Since that time, the Tarasque has been paraded in the town's festivals and has influenced similar names of dragons in Spain known as the Tarasca.
References 7, 20, 57, 89, 128, 134, 174, 182
See also Bonnacon, dragon, Leviathan, Tarasca

TARBH UISGE
This is the name of a monstrous animal in the Celtic folklore of both Scotland and Ireland. Its name in Gaelic may be translated as the "Water Bull." The Tarbh Uisge, also known as the Tairbh-Uisge, was a vast black bull with fiery red nostrils that inhabited the sea and shores. At night it would emerge from the waves and rampaged across the land or mate with the local cows. The progeny were called Corc-chluasask, meaning "Split-ears," for they only had half-ears. Traditionally on the Isle of Skye these were killed instantly to prevent the disaster they could bring.
References 128, 134
See also Taroo Ushtey

TAROO USHTEY
This is the name of the Celtic water bull in the Manx folklore of the Isle of Man in the British Isles. The Taroo Ushtey, also known as the Theroo Ushta, was not so malignant as the Tarbh Uisge, from which it was clearly derived. Neither did it live in the sea; it inhabited the swampy lowlands and inland pools.
References 128
See also Tarbh Uisge

Dragon threatens a child. Tarasca is a dragon in the legends and folklore of Spain. (Rose Photo Archive, UK)

TARTARO

This is the name of a giant in the folklore of the Basque people of southwestern France and northwestern Spain. The Tartaro can also be described as a hideous animal or human, but in the folktales he is usually depicted as a vast giant with one eye in the middle of his forehead. Like most giants or ogres, he is not blessed with intellect and is frequently outwitted by his human foes.

References 24
See also Cyclops, giant, ogre

TATSU

This is the name of a class of dragon in the mythology of Japan. The Tatsu is depicted as having a very serpentine body with only three claws on each foot. This dragon is associated with the sea and is an astrological creature in the Japanese zodiac.

References 7, 89, 113
See also Oriental Dragon

TATTER FOAL

This is the alternative name for the Shag Foal, a semisupernatural beast in the folklore of Lincolnshire, England.

References 24
See also Shag Foal

TATZELWURM

This is the name of a monstrous creature in the folklore of Austria. The Tatzelwurm is described as a huge hybrid lizard-like creature with the head of a cat. Each description is, however, not consistent as to the number of legs or even if it has any; similarly the body may be smooth, lumpy, scaly, or covered in hair. It has, like its counterpart in Switzerland, the Stollenwurm, a fearsome reputation for aggression whenever it meets with a human in the high mountain passes.

References 134
See also Arassas, Dard, Stollenwurm

TAULURD

This is the name of a giant in the Arthurian legends of Britain. According to Geoffrey of Monmouth (1100–1154) in his *Historia Regnum Britanniae* (c. 1147), Taulurd was killed by Marhaus.

References 54
See also Albion, giant

TCINTO-SAKTCO

This is the name of a serpent in the traditions and beliefs of the Cree Native American people of Canada. The Tcinto-Saktco, also known as the "Long-horned Serpent," is described as a vast serpent with horns or antlers like those of a deer. There are different types of Tcinto-Saktco, distinguished by their different body color, which may be blue, white, or yellow.

References 134, 139
See also Angont, Horned Serpent, Kichiknebik, Kinepikwa, Kitchi-at'Husis, Mishipzhiw, Oyaleroweck, serpent, Sisiutl, Tcipitckaam, Tzeltal, Wakandagi, Weewilmekq

TCIPITCKAAM

This is the name of a lake serpent in the traditions and beliefs of the Micmac Native American people. The Tcipitckaam, sometimes called the Unicorn Serpent, is described variously as a horse-head serpent and, at other times, as having the shape of an alligator but with either a long red or yellow spiral horn emerging from the center of its forehead. The Tcipitckaam is reported as inhabiting Lakes Utopia and Ainslie. These monsters are quite dangerous to humans and have been said to transform into young men in order to abduct young women and dive back into the lake with their victim.

References 134
See also Kelpy, Ponik, serpent, Weewilmekq

TE TUNA

This is the name of a sea monster in the traditions and mythology of Tahiti. Te Tuna is described as a vast, eel-like monster of the seas that was briefly the husband of Hina before she mated with Maui.

References 133
See also monster

TEAKETTLER

This is a creature from the folklore of lumberjacks and forest workers, especially in Wisconsin and Minnesota in the United States, during the nineteenth and early twentieth centuries. The Teakettler belongs to a group of beings affectionately known as the Fearsome Critters, whose exaggerated proportions and activities not only explained the weird noises of the lonely landscape but also provided some amusement at camps.

References 7, 24
See also Fearsome Critters

TEEHOOLTSOODI

This is the name of a water monster in the traditions and folk beliefs of the Navajo Native American people of the United States. The Teehooltsoodi is described as looking something like a very large otter with smooth fur but having enormous horns on its head like those of the buffalo. Teehooltsoodi is a powerful being and in one traditional tale, when his child is abducted by the Spider-Woman, in his grief caused a massive flood.

References 77, 134
See also monster

TEELGET

This is the name of a monster in the traditions and beliefs of the Navajo people of the United States. The Teelget was a fearful, predatory being that was killed by an arrow made of chain lightning from the bow of the hero Nayenygami.

References 78
See also monster, Yeitso

TEGID FOEL, TEGYD FOËL, TEGID VOEL

This is the name of a giant in the traditions and legends of Wales. The name is made up of the two Welsh words: *teg* and *foel,* meaning "beautiful" and "bald," respectively. Tegid Foel, who inhabits the region of Pennllyn, is the husband of Ceridwen and features in the *Hanes Taliesin* (Tale of Taliesin). Numerous Welsh heraldic genealogies cite Tegid Foel as an ancestor.

References 128
See also giant, Melusine

TELCHINES

This is a type of merman or sea monster in the classical mythology of ancient Greece and Rome. The Telchines were described as having a thick, dumpy body with flipper-like arms and legs but with the head of a dog with eyes that sent poisonous miasmas over anyone that angered them. They were skilled in the arts of metalworking and magic and forged the tridents for Poseidon/Neptune and the sickle with which Cronus castrated Uranus. They at first inhabited the Mediterranean islands of Crete, Rhodes, and Cyprus, but they interfered with the Olympian gods' domain and tried to abduct Aphrodite, for which they were scattered all over the world.

References 64, 125, 133, 160, 178
See also Cronus, merman, monster, Uranus

TENGU/S, TEN-GU

This is the name of a class of giant humanoid monsters in the traditions and folklore of Japan. The Tengus are described as having the body of a human with glowing eyes, but with the long red beaks and wings of a bird. The female Tengus are described as having a humanoid body but the head of an animal with huge fangs for teeth and enormous ears and noses. There are two other types of Tengu—the Karasa Tengu and the Konoha Tengu. The Tengus are particularly aggressive and skilled in the martial arts. They inhabited a fortress in the dark forests of Mount Kurama north of Kyoto, where warriors hope to meet one and absorb their skills, but any other traveler will be turned mad if they encounter a Tengu.

In modern times these monsters have been demonized to become pranksters and child-stealing beings, something like a Nursery bogie.

References 7, 47, 64, 74, 89, 113, 120, 125, 160, 166
See also Kappa, Karasa Tengu, Konoha Tengu, monster, Nursery bogie

TETHYS

This is the name of a Titan in the classical mythology of Greece and Rome. Tethys is the daughter of Gaia and Uranus and, by Okeanus, the mother of the sea nymphs known as the Oceanides.

References 125, 178
See also Titan

TEUMESSIAN VIXEN

This is the name of a monstrous fox in the classical mythology of Greece and Rome. The Teumessian Vixen was the scourge of the countryside in the land of Cadmeia, but because she was immortal and destined never to be caught, no one could exterminate her to give relief. The beast demanded that a child be given once a year or she would do worse. In terrified anguish, the people turned to Laelaps, who was immortal and destined to catch anything he pursued, to attempt to catch the monstrous vixen. However, such a quarry and hunter provided an insoluble situation, which Zeus/Jupiter settled by petrifying the pair forever in the chase.

References 89

TEUTANES

This is the name of a giant who appeared in the medieval work *Officina* by the erudite Jean Tixier de Ravisy (alias Ravisius Textor, c. 1480–1524), who proposed that Tuyscon Gigas was actually a son of the giant Noah, whose progeny were the ancestors of European nobility. He constructed a line of giant descendants, of whom Teutanes was one of many legendary figures.

References 174
See also giant, Noah, Tuyscon Gigas

THANACTH

This is the name of a strange creature in the travelers' tales of medieval and sixteenth-century Europe. The Thanacth was described as having a completely black body about the same proportions as a tiger; however, it had no tail and its head was like that of a man with frizzled hair. This creature had been seen in the Middle East, where it had been apparently imported by some men traveling from India, as a food source to be killed and eaten. The Thanacth was described by Thevet in his sixteenth-century work *Cosmography* and again included by Ambroise Paré (1517–1590), during the same period, in his work *On Monsters and Marvels.*

References 147

THARDID JIMBO

This is the name of an enormous cannibal giant in the Dreamtime mythology of the Native Australian people. Thardid Jimbo was described as being vast and a tracker of humans, his favorite food. One day he had watched a gentle human, called Mummulbery, skillfully track and kill a kangaroo to take for his two happy wives in their camp. Just as the man flung the beast over his shoulder and was about to depart, Thardid Jimbo loomed up in front of him and demanded to see the beast. As the unsuspecting Mummulbery turned to show it to him, the giant bit the man's head off, then dismembered him and cooked the limbs for his evening meal. When he had finished, Thardid Jimbo took the remains and traced the tracks of the dead man back to his camp, where his two wives were waiting for the kangaroo. To their horror, the giant threw the head and torso of their husband to the ground and demanded that his meal be cooked from it. Mummulbery had always taught them to be resourceful, so they quelled their misery and disgust; while pretending to do as the giant said, they plotted. At last they told him that the body was not good enough for them and that they wanted such a big, brave giant to get them something really special. The flattered Thardid Jimbo took his *nullanulla* (club) and advanced on the cave they had directed him to for a really succulent dingo bitch. They encouraged him to go right to the far end, where she could be found, while they quickly gathered tinder-dry scrub and piled it up to the roof of the entrance and set light to it. Soon the wind took the thick smoke and fire well into the cave, and try as he might, the giant could not get past. At last he tried to jump over the flames but, being a giant, smashed his head against the rock roof and fell unconscious on top of the fire. When the giant had at last expired, the two wives sobbed as they took care of their dear, mutilated husband. Their grief was so great for the loss of such a good man that they could not bear to eat food or leave him. As their father was a *wirinun* (shaman) of great power, they decided to light a smoke message for him to come to them. When he arrived, he listened to them with great sadness and said that no one had the right to ask for a man to be returned to life in such a state when he was now clothed in light. Then he asked if they loved him so much and wished to be united with him and were they willing to cast off their present form. They consented, and in great sorrow he embraced them for the last time before starting his chants. Soon the form of Mummulbery in golden light stood before them and, holding out a blessing to the father of his wives, took each one of them by the hand. As they departed into the golden light, their father turned to the bodily forms of his children and their husband and prepared them for burial.

References 154
See also giant

THEIA

This is the name of a female Titan in the classical mythology of Greece and Rome. Theia was the daughter of Uranus and Gaia and the wife of the Titan Hyperion. By him she was the primordial giant mother of the other new gods Eos, Helios, and Silene.
References 125, 169, 178
See also giant, Titan

THELGETH

This is the name of a group of monsters in the beliefs and folklore of the Navajo peoples of the United States. These monsters manifest as gigantic, grotesque, headless beings covered in shaggy fur. Unlike the Blemmyes of European medieval traditions, the Thelgeth were grotesque torsos that were full of malice toward other creatures, upon whom they preyed. They are related in their birth to the Binaye Ahani and the feathered Tsanahale, with whom they constituted the group of monsters known as the Anaye.
References 7
See also Anaye, Binaye Ahani, Blemmyes, giant, monster, Tsanahale

THELXIEPEIA

This is the name of one of the Sirens in classical Greek and Roman mythology.
References 178
See also Siren

THEMIS

This is the name of a female Titan in the classical mythology of Greece and Rome. Themis was the daughter of Uranus and Gaia and, by Zeus, one of the Olympian gods, the mother of the Parcae and the Horae. She was depicted as the bringer of justice, with her eyes blindfolded and holding scales in one hand and a sword in the other, as on the top of the "Old Bailey," the major criminal court in London.
References 133, 178
See also giant, Titan

THEROO USHTA

This is an alternative name for the Taroo Ushtey, the Celtic water bull in the Manx folklore of the Isle of Man in the British Isles.
References 128
See also Taroo Ushtey

THETIS

This is one of the giants named in the genealogy created by the Italian monk Annius of Viterbo

(Giovanni Nanni, c. 1432–1502) to justify the noble descent of the Gauls from a giant biblical race.
References 139, 174
See also giant, Noah

THIA

This is an alternative spelling of Theia in the classical mythology of Greece and Rome. She was the daughter of Uranus and Gaia and the wife of the Titan Hyperion and the primordial mother of the other Titans, Eos, Helios, and Silene.
References 169, 178
See also Theia, Titan

THIASSI

This is the name of a giant in the Norse mythology of Scandinavia. Thiassi, whose name may be spelled Thjassi, means "Ice." He is one of the Hrim-Thursar, or Frost Giants. He is the son of Kari and the sibling of Skadi (in some accounts his daughter), Bel, and Thrym. Thiassi spent much of his time in the shape of a gigantic eagle and in this shape came upon the Aesir gods Honir, Loki, and Odin trying to roast an ox. The giant tricked them into letting him swallow much of it before Loki stabbed him with a spear. The giant eagle, Thiassi, rose in the air with the god attached. He let Loki down to the earth only after he had promised to bring Idun to the giant. Idun, the wife of Bragi, guarded the apples of immortality for the Aesir gods, and she and they were taken to Thiassi. But the trickster god, Loki, was threatened with the first god's death if he did not get her and the apples of immortality back, which he did by transforming into an eagle. When Thiassi followed as an eagle, the gods built a fire that burned his feathers, and he crashed to earth, where he was then killed by the god Thor. He threw the giant's huge eyes into the heavens, where they remained as stars.
References 24, 61, 125, 133, 139
See also Bel, Brag, Frost Giants, giant, Skadi, Thrym

THINGUT

This is a monster in the legends and folklore of medieval Europe. Also known as the Chichevache, this female monster was portrayed as an undernourished panther with a human face and miserable expression. The name "Thingut" was popular during the sixteenth century.
References 7
See also Chichevache

THOAS

This is the name of a giant in the classical mythology of Greece and Rome. Thoas is one of the Gigantes and, like his brothers, was said to have been engendered from the blood that fell on the earth from the castrated Uranus. These giants were born fully mature and clad in full battle armor. They waged war on the Olympian gods after the defeat of the Titans and were defeated. In that battle, Thoas, whose name means "Fast," was not defeated until the final attack. He was buried, like the others, in deep chasms within the earth, upon which mountains and volcanoes were piled.
References 24, 133, 169, 178
See also Aloadae, Cyclopes, giant, Gigantes

THÖKK

This is the name of a giantess in the Norse mythology of Scandinavia. She is described as vast, old, and inhabiting the most isolated place in the world. When the most beautiful god, Balder, was killed accidentally by the blind Höd with the only thing that could harm him—a stick of mistletoe cunningly provided by Loki—the Aesir gods grieved. His brother, Hermod, immediately undertook the perilous journey on the back of Sleipnir to the underworld to ask Hel to release him for everyone who grieved. The awesome goddess agreed, so long as she could see that all things grieved the loss of Balder. Hermod returned, and the Aesir and all the Jotuns agreed to show their grief, but in a distant, remote cavern Hel could see one giantess, Thökk, who showed no remorse. So Balder was kept in the underworld of the dead, and when this was accomplished the jealous trickster Loki transformed himself from the giantess back to his own shape.
References 139
See also giantess, Jotun

THRYM, THRYMR

This is the name of a giant in the Norse mythology of Scandinavia. Thrym, whose name may be translated as "Frost," is the leader of the Hrim-Thursar, or Frost Giants. He is the son of Kari and the sibling of Bel, Skadi, and Thiassi. His own giant children are Drifta, Frosti, Johul, and Snoer. In the Icelandic epic *Thrymskvida*, written c. A.D. 900, is told the story of how Thrym stole the massive magic hammer Miölnir, depriving the gods of their defense. Thrym told them that they could redeem it by giving him the goddess Freya as his wife. She refused, so Loki persuaded Thor to dress up as Freya and go to Thrymheim to get the hammer back. When they arrived at the marriage feast, Thrym was astonished that such a bride could devour a whole ox, several salmon, and swallow three casks of wine. When Thrym brought out the hammer to display it, Thor grabbed it and slew all that got in the way and several of the giants trying to escape. Then they took the magic hammer Miölnir back to the Aesir.
References 24, 47, 78, 166

THU'BAN

This is the name of a dragon in the mythology of
ancient Persia (now Iran). Thu'ban is described as an
enormous, fire-breathing dragon with numerous
heads. It may be evolved from an earlier serpent-
dragon. It is known in the legends of the Arab world
as Tinnin.
References 89
See also dragon, serpent

THUGINE

This is the name of a class of Rainbow Serpent in the
traditions and beliefs of the Native Australian
people in the northern territories of Australia. One
of the legends tells how two young boys were
allowed to accompany the men on their hunting trip
to the northern shores of the sea. When the party
arrived, the boys were told that they must stay near
the camp during the day. They were very
disappointed, because they had never seen the sea
and wanted to fish there. However, they were told
that it was too dangerous. When the men had gone,
the two became very curious and thought just a look
wouldn't hurt. So they went to the shore and
marvelled at the lapping sea. It was very hot, so
they entered the water. No sooner had they done so
when they saw a black, swirling shape under the
water. Before they knew it, Thugine had coiled
around them and dragged them down into the
swirling depths. When the men returned, they
traced the boys footprints to the shore and suddenly
saw two small rocks that had never been there
before. Then they said to each other that Thugine
had taken and transformed the boys, and as they
said this Thugine arched in all the colors of the
spectrum up out of the sea and over the islets.

Here Thugine is probably being used as a Nursery
bogie in much the same way as Jenny Greenteeth in
England: to keep curious children away from
dangerous waters.
References 153
See also Jenny Greenteeth, Nursery bogie, Rainbow
Serpent, serpent

THUNDEL

This is the name of a giant in the literature of
eighteenth-century and Victorian England. Thundel is
described as a vast ogre with three heads but with
very little intellect in any of them. He belongs to a
tradition of Nursery and light literature giants that
were created as fairy tales for the nursery or as
Nursery bogies.
References 182

THUNDER DRAGON

This is the title of Lei, the father of Lei Chen-Tzu, in
the mythology of China.
References 133, 160, 181
See also Lei Chen-Tzu, Oriental Dragon

THUNDERBIRD

This is the name of a class of fabulous, gigantic bird in
the traditions and beliefs of most Native American
people in North America. There are many different
traditions; some revere the Thunderbird as a deity,
others simply as a semisupernatural being of the
skies. The Thunderbird may be portrayed as a
gigantic type of eagle with either red plumage or a
feathered cape (Crow tradition), sometimes with a
human face (Sioux tradition), or a human face on its
belly (Haida tradition). In some traditions, they claw
down the trunks of trees to find grubs (Algonquian
tradition), and in others they hunt for whales far out
to sea (Haida tradition), while in others it is a
predatory bird that hunts deer, whales, and humans
(Yukon). They may inhabit the high peaks of the
mountains (Dakota tradition), or the tops of the
forests (Algonquian tradition). It is with the beat of
their vast wings that the thunder is made, while the
flashing of their eyes produces lightning. In some
traditions, they are said to shoot arrows of lightning
from their wings or from their beaks. According to the
Algonquian people, the Thunderbirds make constant
war on the horned water serpents. In the Shawnee
tradition, these vast birds are transformed boys who
have gained the power to move great earth features
but still speak in human tongues, but their speech is
reversed. The Thunderbird represents summer in the
Arapaho tradition, when he overcomes the White
Owl of winter. Names for the Thunderbird are also
regional, such as the Tinmiukpuk of the Yukon region
of Alaska and Waukheon of the Sioux in the Dakota
region.
References 24, 61, 77, 89, 94, 113, 134, 136, 139
See also Garuda, Great Horned Serpents, Waukheon

THURSES, THURSIR

1. This is an alternative name for the Hrimthurses,
who are the Frost Giants in the Norse mythology of
Scandinavia. They were the first giants and were
engendered at the same time as Ymir from the
melting ice of the northern world.

2. The Thursir took on a different role in legend
after Christianity entered the Teutonic regions of
northern Europe. They became relegated to malicious,
big-eared, hairy giants or ogres that brought
misfortune in Germanic folklore.

References 125, 127
See also Frost Giants, giant, Hrimthurses, Kiwahkw

TI LUNG

This is the name of a dragon in the traditions and mythology of China. The Ti Lung is the Celestial Water Dragon that is responsible for the control of the waters in the rivers and streams.
References 89
See also Oriental Dragon

TIAMAT

This is the name of the World Dragon, or cosmic dragon, in the mythology of the ancient kingdoms of Sumer and Babylon. Tiamat was a female dragon described in the *Enuma Elish* of Babylon as having a vast, serpentine body impenetrable to weapons, with two forelegs, an immense tail, and huge horns on her head. Together with Apsu they produced the heavens and the earth and then spawned the gods. They in turn fought with Apsu and Tiamat for control, and the pair produced further monsters, the Girtablili, for the battle. But Apsu was destroyed, and the god Marduk/Merodach carried on the fight when Tiamat took Kingu as her second consort. Marduk was too clever for her, and with a huge net he held her mouth open so that he could shoot his arrows directly to her heart. When dead, her dismembered body gave up the earth, the skies, or the Milky Way, and from her blood came the rivers.
References 7, 24, 47, 78, 89, 125, 136, 139, 166, 169
See also Bel, dragon, Girtablili, Lahamu, serpent, Ymir

TI-CHIANG

This is the name of a celestial bird in the traditions and legends of China. It is described as having scarlet plumage and three pairs of feet, but it has neither eyes nor beak on its head.
References 7, 18
See also Feng Hwang

TIEHOLTSODI, TIEHOLTSALI

This is the name of a great water monster in the creation legends of the Navajo Native American people of the United States. Tieholtsodi, also described as the King of the Ocean, had several children who were stolen by the first people. In great anger, he caused a massive flood that threatened to drown every living thing. Ultimately, the rain and fire gods, Tonenili and Hastsegini, rescued the Navajo ancestors and returned Tieholtsodi's children. From then on his aggression has diminished, but he threatens with minor flooding every now and again just to make sure.
References 47, 166
See also monster

T'IEN KOU

This is the name of a malicious and gigantic celestial dog in the traditions and mythology of China. T'ien Kou was a vast being described as a huge dog with a plumed, fiery tail. It lived in the heavens but was sustained by descending to the earth at night and seeking the small children of humans to devour; if none was left alone, then he would kill a human adult and consume his or her liver. If he went hungry and had to return to the heavens without, then he would consume the moon. When this occurred, Hou I, the Celestial Archer, would have to shoot down T'ien Kou to rescue the heavenly light. But another T'ien Kou would be regenerated and the process started all over again. T'ien Kou is mentioned in the legend of the monkey king.
References 89, 181
See also Aapep, Alklha, Toad (Three-Legged)

TIEN LUNG, T'IEN LUNG

This is the name of a dragon in the mythology of China. Tien Lung is a vast celestial dragon that is charged with supporting the foundations of the celestial temples of the gods.
References 89, 94
See also Oriental Dragon

TIGRE CAPIANGO

This is the name of a type of Werewolf in the traditions and folklore of Argentina. It was presumed that some humans were not all that they seemed and that at night they assumed the form of a jaguar to prey upon their neighbors and their livestock. Later, as this belief faded, the Tigre Capiango became more of a frightening figure than a cannibal but still terrifying enough for highway robbers to assume the guise for their purposes. More recently, it was still conjectured that General Facundo Quiroga had a regiment of Tigre Capiangos to terrorize the opposition during the civil war of the nineteenth century.
References 18
See also Werewolf

TING LING KUO YAN

This is the name of a race of monstrous people in the legends and folklore of China. The Ting Ling Kuo Yan are described as having humanoid bodies and heads with very long hair, but they have the legs and hooves of horses. Thus they are credited with both great speed and the length of stride to cover at least one hundred miles each day. They appear in the volumes of the *Great Imperial Encyclopedia* and were no doubt derived from exaggerated travelers' tales in much the same way as those that influenced the medieval bestiaries of Europe.

References 181
See also I-Mu Kuo Yan, Nieh-Erh Kuo Yan, San-Shen
Kuo Yan, San-Shou Kuo Yan, Yü-Min Kuo Yan

TINMIUKPUK

This is the name of the Thunderbird in the traditions and beliefs of the Inuit of the Yukon-Kuskokwin Delta in the state of Alaska in the United States. The Tinmiukpuk is a monstrous, predatory bird that is described as a vast creature but resembling an eagle with huge talons. It preys upon caribou and other animals, which it can swoop down on and lift easily into the air and take back to its mountain haunt. If there are no caribou, then it will prey upon any unwary, isolated humans in its territory.

References 77
See also Roc

TINNIN

This is the name of a multiheaded, fire-breathing dragon in the pre-Islamic Arab legends. Tinnin is also known in the Persian mythology as Thu' Ban.

References 89, 125
See also dragon, Thu'Ban

TIOMAN

This is the name of a princess who became a dragon in the mythology and folklore of the Malay people of West Malaysia. Tioman fell in love with the son of a neighboring king, and, although she was a princess in her own right, the prince did not return her devotion. In the agonies of unrequited love, she brooded and was so consumed with tortured thoughts that her outward appearance metamorphosed into that of a dragon with horns on her head and a vast, swirling tail. Despairing even further in her reptilian form, she swam into the South China Sea and sat in the waters, where she again transformed. Soon her vast bulk became an island called Pulau Tioman, where her horns showed as the two peaks standing high from her back as the mountains of Bali Hai, and the great tail swirled above the waves to Salang. This is now the most beautiful of the Malaysian islands off the eastern coast and was used as the location for the Bali Hai of the film South Pacific.

References 113
See also dragon

TIPAKA

This is the name of a magical horse in the traditions and mythology of Thailand. Tipaka is described as the most beautiful horse, sometimes depicted with wings. He was capable of traveling so fast that the horse was at its destination even as the name was given and was capable of journeying through the heavens. He is the steed of the legendary King Sison.

References 113
See also Arion, Balios, Borak (Al), Haizum, Pegasus, Sivushko, Sleipnir

TISIKH PUK

This is the name of a monstrous humanoid being in the traditions and beliefs of the Inuit people of the Bering Sea coastal region of the state of Alaska in the United States. The Tisikh Puk was a primordial being of mythology that takes the form of a vast caterpillar or worm-like creature that metamorphosed into the shape of a human being.

References 77

TISIPHONE

This is the name of a fearsome supernatural being in the mythology of ancient Greece and Rome. Tisiphone, whose name means "Retaliation," is the means of ultimate revenge. This being is described as a snake-haired woman wearing a bloodied robe who waits by the gates of hell. She is one of the Furies who exact retribution from those whose hideous crimes, especially matricide or patricide, remain unpunished by human law.

References 20, 38, 160, 161, 178
See also Erinyes, Furies

TITAN

This is the name of a class of primordial giants in the classical mythology of Greece and Rome. The Titans were the progeny of Uranus and Gaia and originally were twelve in number: six sons named Coeus/Koios, Crius/Kreios/Creius, Cronus, Hyperion, Japetus/Iapetus, and Okeanus/Oceanus; and six daughters, known as the Titanides, named Mnemosyne, Phoebe/Phiobe, Rhea/Rheia, Tethys, Theia, and Themis. Their names and number varied, including Euribia/Euribie, Clymene/Klymene, and Dione during the classical period, but the Italian poet Boccaccio (1313–1375) mentions others who, in the classical period, were not counted as Titans but as other classes of giant, including Briareus, Typhon, Typheus, Enceladus, Egon, Atlas, Astreus, and Alous. These giants were the siblings of the Furies, the Cyclopes, and the Hundred-Handed Giants. The Titans were so ugly that Uranus, their father, threw them into Tartarus, or the belly of Gaia in some accounts.

The Titans rebelled against their father, Uranus, and Cronus took a sickle and castrated him. Cronus, however, knew that one of his children would also rebel against him and so set out to devour each one as it emerged. However, the last, Zeus, was hidden by his mother, Rhea, who persuaded Cronus to vomit up the other children, the Olympian gods, who waged a long war against the Titans and eventually threw them into Tartarus.

References 20, 24, 47, 61, 78, 94, 125, 136, 139, 166, 169, 174, 178, 182
See also Alous, Astreus, Atlas, Briareus, Clymene/Klymene, Coeus/Koios, Crius/Kreios/Crieus, Cronus, Cyclops, Enceladus, Furies, Gaia, Hundred-Handed Giants, Hyperion, Japetus/Iapetus, Mnemosyne, Okeanus/Oceanus, Phoebe/Phiobe, Rhea/Rheia, Tethys, Theia, Themis, Typhon

TITANIDES
This is the collective name for the female Titans in the classical mythology of Greece and Rome.
References 20, 47, 78, 94, 125, 139, 166, 178
See also Titan

TITYUS
1. This is the name of a giant in the classical mythology of Greece and Rome. Tityus was the son of Zeus and Terra or Gaia or Elara and is described as so vast that his body covered nine acres of ground. He tried to abduct and rape Latona, the daughter of the Titaness Phoebe, but her children, Apollo and Diana, shot him with arrows. For this crime he was placed in the depths of Tartarus, where two vultures were set to devour his liver, which regenerated for the same agonies each day.

2. This is the name of a giant in the classical mythology of Greece and Rome. Tityus is one of the Gigantes and, like his brothers, was said to have been engendered from the blood that fell on the earth from the castrated Uranus. These giants were born fully mature and clad in full battle armor. They waged war on the Olympian gods after the defeat of the Titans and were defeated. In that battle Tityus, whose name means "Risker," was not vanquished until the final attack. He was buried, like the others, in deep chasms within the earth, upon which mountains and volcanoes were piled.
References 20, 24, 133, 139, 169, 178
See also Aloadae, Cyclops, giant, Gigantes, Prometheus, Titan

TLATECUHTLI
This is the name of a gigantic frog in the mythology of the Aztec people of ancient Mexico. Tlatecuhtli is described as a monstrous, frog-shaped being with enormous fangs whose vast mouth often represented the opening to the land of the dead. Tlatecuhtli was usually the companion of Coatlicue, the serpent goddess.
References 47

TO FU
This is the name of a fabulous bird in the traditions and legends of China. It is a form of the Lwan and is described as looking something like a much larger and more beautiful and graceful type of pheasant. However, this bird is capable of changing its body color and is known by different names accordingly. As the To Fu, it is the yellow form of the Lwan.
References 81
See also Fung, Hwa Yih, Lwan, Phoenix, Yu Siang

TO KAS
This is the name of a class of horned water serpent in the traditions and beliefs of the Klamath Native American people of the state of California in the United States. These terrifying serpents are described as vast creatures that have huge white horns and are particularly aggressive toward humans, devouring anyone foolish enough to enter their territory. They inhabit such bodies of water as Crater Lake, where Ge-wus initiates are submerged as part of the ceremony.
References 134
See also horned serpent, serpent

TOAD, THREE-LEGGED
This is the name of a monster in the traditions and mythology of China. This monster was originally Ch'ang O, who had been the wife of the Celestial Archer, Hon I. He was the guardian for the gods of the elixir of immortality, which she stole; to escape her pursuers, she flew to the moon. But her triumph was short-lived; for when she escaped the elixir had the effect of transforming her, and she became the gigantic, hideous, three-legged toad. Now she remains there, unable to show herself, but still immortal; to feed herself, she eats away at the moon and sometimes is so ravenous that she devours it completely.
References 181
See also Aapep, monster, Thiassi, T'ien kou

TOBI TATSU
This is the name of a composite fabulous creature in the traditions and legends of Japan. The Tobi Tatsu, also known as the Hai Riyo or the Schachi Hoko, is described as having the body of a bird with birds' claws and wings but with the head of a dragon.
References 81, 89
See also Hai Riyo

TOM DOCKIN, TOM DONKIN
This is the name of an ogre or fiend in the traditions and folklore of England. Tom Dockin is described as a huge ogre with teeth of iron that devours children who behave badly. He is a nineteenth-century Nursery bogie.
References 24, 160, 182
See also Nursery bogie, ogre

TOMPONDRANO

This is the name of a water monster in the traditions and beliefs of the people of the island of Madagascar. The Tompondrano is described as being a vast, seagoing creature with a body covered in a plated skin, much like that of the crocodile. Its head, however, glows in the dark and can be seen under the water as well as when it surfaces. Few humans would stay in the vicinity of such a glow, which was reported in 1926 by some fishermen off the coast.

References 134
See also monster

TOO JON SHEU

This is an alternative name for the unicorn in the mythology of China.

References 81
See also Ki-lin, unicorn

TORC TRIATH

This is the name of a gigantic boar in the legends of Ireland. Torc Triath was regarded as one of the Kings of the Boars and equivalent to Twrch Trwyth, whose story is told in the *Mabinogion* of Wales.

References 54
See also Twrch Trwyth

TORK

This is the name of a giant in the legends and folklore of Armenia. Tork was so massive that he was equated with the mountain that bears his name. He was described as being very ugly, of evil temperament, and extremely strong. Later, he became the guardian of the mountain and its wildlife.

References 125
See also giant

TORNGARSOAK

This is the name of a gigantic bear in the traditions and beliefs of the Inuit people of the Hudson Strait in Labrador, Canada. Torngarsoak is a giant creature in the form of a white bear. He is considered to be the master of the seals and whales of Ungava Bay, where he has his abode in a deep cavern.

References 77

TORNIT

This is the name of a class of giants in the traditions and beliefs of the Inuit people of Canada. These Tornit were regarded by some as the ancestors of the people.

References 24
See also giant

TOROGS

This is the name of a race of cannibal giants in the literature of the English academic and author J. R. R. Tolkien (1892–1973). The Torogs were as big as they were stupid but nevertheless terrified other beings, and they especially hunted and ate humans who were foolish enough to travel alone through their territory. They offered their strength to the Dark Enemy, known as Morgoth, during the wars of Beleriand.

References 51
See also Dumbeldors, Ents, Fastitocalon, Fire-drake, giants, Mûmarkil, Oliphaunts, Olog-Hai, Onodrim

TORRENT

This is the alternative name for a monster in the folklore of Wales.

References 128
See also Carrog

TORTO

This is the name of a cannibal giant in the folklore of the Basque people of northwestern Spain and southwestern France. Torto is described as a vast humanoid shape but with only one eye in the middle of his forehead, like the Cyclopes in the classical mythology of Greece and Rome. This giant would stalk and trap young humans, then rip them apart to be consumed.

References 125
See also cannibal, giant

TOTOIMA

This is the name of a monstrous supernatural boar in the mythology of the Orokaiva people of the island of Papua New Guinea. Totoima took a human woman as his wife, and during their nights together he came to her in the shape of a human. However, during the day he resumed his monstrous shape, and each time she gave birth to a child his snout would smell it out and devour it. Eventually, the wife gave birth to twins but only managed to grab the girl after he had swallowed the boy. His wife brought a shaman who managed to revitalize the boy child inside his father, where the child grew to adulthood immediately and burst out through the side of Totoima. The joyful mother allowed a wedding ceremony to be prepared for her daughter and the shaman, and for the feast the body of Totoima was cooked and divided amongst all the village. Thus, the supernatural power of the monster boar was shared by all, and this is reenacted each time a pig is shared in ceremonies to this day.

References 133
See also Sachrimnir

TOURMENTINE

This is the name of an ogre in the popular literature and folklore of seventeenth-century France. Together with Ravagio, he appears in the fairy tale *L'Orangier et l'Abeille* (The Orange Tree and the Bee, 1698).

Tourmentine and Ravagio are described as huge with a skin like a pelt that could withstand the ball from a pistol shot. Together they plot the abduction of a child to be fattened and consumed.

References 182
See also giant, ogre, Ravagio

TOWN GIANTS

In Europe the tradition of parading a Town Giant has been established for centuries. The giants, who usually had a mythological or local folkloric origin, were not so much a mascot as a defined representative of control and the domestication of the Otherworld powers. The Town Giant, unlike dragons and other such effigies, is preserved through countless generations, and if by some accident they become destroyed, as during World War II, they are remade as a matter of civic necessity. Two of the most famous are Gog and Magog, the Guildhall Giants of London in England whose first recorded appearance was for the triumphal procession of King Henry V in 1413 and again in 1420 and in 1432, when they greeted King Henry VI. During the sixteenth century they paraded for Emperor Charles V of the Holy Roman Empire, King Philip of Spain, and Queen Elizabeth I. During the seventeenth century they were destroyed by the Great Fire of London 1666 and replaced in 1672. By the eighteenth century they were once more in need of restoration and were replaced in 1710, surviving as representatives until a bomb destroyed them in 1940. They were replaced in time for Queen Elizabeth II's coronation in 1953.

Another famous giant is Goliath. In a curious twist to the story of this biblical giant, the ancient Town Giants (from c. A.D. 1460) of the towns of Anvers (Belgium), Ath (Belgium), Hasselt (Holland), Lierre (Belgium), Malines (Belgium), Nieupoort (Belgium), Nivelles (Belgium), and Troyes (France) were all given the name "Goliath." During the visit of the future King Charles VIII in 1486 to the town of Troyes, their Goliath reenacted the challenge and his defeat by a local "David."

Other Town Giants are paraded for the Feast of Corpus Christi in Catalonia, as well as in Barcelona and Valencia, Spain, where they may be known as Cabezudos; there are also the giants Druon and Antigonus in Antwerp and Gayant in the town of Douai, all in Belgium; there are giants in Lille, France, and Giant Onion in the town of Silchester, England.

From April 29–30, 2000, in the town of Steenvoorde in Belgium, the "Third European Dance of the Giants" is to take place. During this festival some one hundred giants from various European countries will parade along with the local town giant called Jean le Bucheron.

References 13, 174, 182

See also Antigonus, Cabezudo, Corineus, Druon, gayant, Giant Onion, Gigantes, Gog and Magog, Goliath, Tarasque

TOYOTAMA, TOYO-TAMA,

This is the name of a monstrous princess in the mythology and traditions of Japan. Toyotama, whose name means "Luminous Jewel" or "Rich Jewel," is also known as Otohime. When Yamasachi (in some versions Hoori) the son of the god Ninigi, lost his brother's best fishing hook, he had to retrieve it. So he searched the depths of the ocean and enlisted the aid of Owatatsumi, the sea god. During that timespan of three human years, Yamasachi had fallen in love with Toyotama, the daughter of Owatatsumi, and taken her as his wife. But when the fishing hook was eventually found, he had to return to the surface and the earth. Toyotama agreed to follow, so long as he promised not to be present when their child was born. They went back to earth, and when the time came Yamasachi could not resist a look to see his child emerge. To his horror, what had been his wife now lay on the couch as a vast, monstrous creature resembling a crocodile or a dragon. His shout alerted others, and she slid away quickly back to the sea. But as he raised their child, the part monster, part god never forgot his origins and eventually married his mother's sister, Tamayori. Their child, Jimmu, was said to be the ancestor of the Japanese Imperial family.

References 113, 133
See also dragon, Melusine, monster

TRAGOPAN

This is the name of a fabulous bird in the ancient and medieval travelers' tales of Europe. The Tragopan was described as a huge bird with a brown body and wing feathers, purple head feathers, and two enormous horns like those of a ram on its head. In an account by the Roman writer Pliny, it was supposed to exist in Ethiopia.

References 7

TRAPANI

See Giant of Trapani

TRASH

This is an alternative name for the monster known as the Skriker in the folklore of Lancashire in northern England.

References 21, 24, 25, 37, 160
See also Skriker

TRECHEND

This is an alternative name for the monster Aillén Trechenn of Ireland.

See also Aillén Trechenn

TRELQUEHUECUVE

This is the name of a giant water monster in the folklore of the Araucanian people of Chile. The Trelquehuecuve is described as a flat, extended skin like a huge, rounded cow's hide with eyes and claws around the perimeter; its color was brown with blotches of white. This creature lures and sucks unwary humans down into the whirlpools in the water, where it folds around their bodies and devours them. The creature has been known to climb out onto the land, where it lies in the sun, but its return was said to be the cause of whirlwinds. The Trelquehuecuve is said to be the minion of the Invunche, which never leaves its lair. The Trelquehuecuve lures young girls swimming or getting water from the edge of the water, who are then abducted and taken under the lake to the Invunche, who drains them of their blood like a vampire. There has been some speculation that it could have been some form of giant squid.
References 134, 189
See also Cuero, Hide, Invunche, Manta, vampire

TRIPODEROO

This is a creature from the folklore of lumberjacks and forest workers, especially in California in the United States, during the nineteenth and early twentieth centuries. The Tripoderoo is described as being a relatively small creature but having a long prehensile snout that could extend like its legs, which were telescopic. It would stalk its prey deftly through the shrubbery until it was within aiming distance. Then it would extend its legs to get a good sighting and shoot a quid of clay through its snout. The Tripoderoo belongs to a group of beings affectionately known as the Fearsome Critters, whose exaggerated proportions and activities not only explained the weird noises of the lonely landscape but also provided some amusement at camps.
References 7
See also Fearsome Critters

TRITON, TRITONS

This is the name of a merman and, later, a class of mermen in the classical mythology of Greece and Rome. The original Triton was said to have been female, but most images from ancient times are those of a male. The Tritons are the sons of Neptune/Poseidon and Amphitrite and are described as having humanoid bodies covered in fishes' scales with tails like those of a dolphin. Their heads have matted green or yellow hair, with gills behind their pointed ears, and their wide mouths have huge, fang-like teeth. They are the escorts of the Nereid sea nymphs and the attendants of the sea deities. They precede the sea god Poseidon/Neptune and his consort, Amphitrite, and announce their arrival by blowing on a conch-shell horn. This conch-shell instrument is also used for causing great waves on the ocean or for calming storms. The Greek poet Hesiod stated that they inhabited golden palaces under the sea. During the medieval period, the Tritons were regarded as the male counterparts of the Sirens and equally symbolic of deceit and lasciviousness. Ambroise Paré (1517–1590), in his work *On Monsters and Marvels,* mentions that a male and a female Triton had been seen emerging from the waves on the shores of the Nile River in Egypt. The Tritons were frequently portrayed in Italian art of the Renaissance period and have become part of the repertoire of heraldic coats of arms throughout Europe, especially of maritime cities.
References 7, 20, 24, 61, 87, 89, 91, 139, 147, 161, 169, 178, 186
See also Centauro-triton, Ichthyocentaur, merman

A Triton, a class of mermen in the classical mythology of Greece and Rome (Rose Photo Archive, UK)

TROLL

This being is essentially Scandinavian, but variations in description and characteristics are apparent between Trolls in Scandinavia and the other countries that have Trolls in their folklore. In Scandinavia the Troll may also be referred to as "Trold" or "Trolld." They were originally described as vast, ugly, hairy giants or ogres with a malignant character, but in some regions they are degraded to a smaller and often dwarf-like size. In Ebletoft, Denmark, the Trolls were ogres who had humps on their backs, large hooked noses, and wore gray jackets and pointed red caps; but in Gudmanstrup, Denmark, the Trolls were giants in long black clothes.

The Trolls in Norway are described as malicious, hairy ogres, but their women were said to be beautiful, with long red hair. They lived in communities under the hills in long barrows and ancient earthworks. Their homes were said to be wonderful palaces full of treasure that may glow at night. The Trolls hate noise and have been driven away from places with church bells. Their attitude toward humans is sometimes ambivalent; they will endow a family they like with riches and good fortune, while at other times they will be malicious, often being destructive of crops and woodlands. They will also steal women, children, and property and have been said to be the worst of cannibals at times. A branch of mistletoe is used to protect humans and animals from being taken. The Trolls are considered to be expert metalworkers, expert healers with herbs and magic, but will only ever be seen between dusk and dawn, as they will turn to stone if the sun shines on them. The standing stones of the north are said to be what is left of petrified Trolls.

In the Faroe Islands the Trolls are known as Fodden Skemaend; they are the Hollow Men or the Underground People who were known for abducting humans and keeping them for many years as slaves.

In Iceland the Trolls are malicious, one-eyed giants.

In Finland there was an evil lake-dwelling Troll known as the Sjötroll. It was said to be confined to the depths of the water by way of two runic stones placed at each end of the lake it inhabited at Kökar. When there was a fog or a storm and the magic of the stones was obscured, the people stayed inside and would not fish, because the Troll was released and would drown them.

The Trolls of the Shetland and Orkney Islands in the British Isles were known as Trows or Drows, of which there were three distinct groups: the Land Trows, the Peerie Trows, and the Sea Trows, but these have very little of the grotesque characteristics of their Scandinavian ancestors.

The Trolls of Greenland and Canada in the folklore of the Inuit/Ihalmiut people resemble the more ancient concept of the giant hairy Scandinavian Troll.

These are described as malignant giants having an enormous, hairless belly that drags along the ground and talons on the fingers so sharp that they are like knives. These Trolls inhabit the hills, where they lurk, waiting for the opportunity to attack humans and rip the flesh from their victims.

In the more recent literature of the English academic and author J. R. R. Tolkien (1892–1973), *The Hobbit* (1937) and *The Lord of the Rings* (1955), the Trolls, derived from this ancient folklore and legend, are described as black-blooded giant cannibals with green, scaly skin, enormous strength, and little intellect. Like their folkloric predecessors, they were derived from darkness and could be destroyed and turned to stone in the light. They were created during the First Age by the Enemy, known as Melkor, in the depths of Angband and were sent with the Orcs to rampage through the universe. After being defeated they were hidden, but during the Second Age the servant of Melkor, Sauron, imbued them with a dangerous, deceitful mind, and a more evil race was created. By the time the Third Age came, there were many different classes of Troll, known as the Cave-trolls, the Hill-trolls, the Mountain-trolls, the Snow-trolls, and the Stone-trolls. These were evil cannibals that descended on the village people of each region and slaughtered them like cattle for the table. Soon there was a new breed, known as the Olog-Hai, that could withstand the rays of the sun, but they also were ultimately defeated.

References 7, 18, 20, 24, 25, 26, 51, 61, 67, 78, 94, 107, 120, 124, 125, 134, 138, 139, 152, 160, 161, 182, 183
See also cannibal, Ent, Henkies, Olog-Hai

TROLL FISK

According to the Norwegian priest and folklorist of the eighteenth century, Bishop Pontoppidan of Bergen, this is a general term for sea monsters in Scandinavia.
References 134
See also monster

TROYNT

This is an alternative name for the Twrch Trwyth in the legends and folklore of Wales. The legend of the hunt for this gigantic boar forms part of the list of the *Mirabilia*, special tasks undertaken by the hero, in Nennius's *Historia Brittonum* of the eighth or ninth century.
References 54, 105
See also Twrch Trwyth

TSANAHALE

This is the name of a group of monsters in the beliefs and folklore of the Navajo people of the United States.

These monsters manifest as grotesque, gigantic, feathered beings that resembled, in many features, the Harpies of European classical mythology. Tsanahale were full of malice toward other creatures, upon whom they preyed. They are related in their birth to the limbless Binaye Ahani and the headless, furry Thelgeth, with whom they constituted the group of monsters known as the Anaye.

References 7

See also Anaye, Binaye Ahani, Harpy, monster, Thelgeth

TSAVOOJOK

This is the name of a giant in the traditions and legends of the Paviotso Native American people of the Great Basin of the United States. Tsavoojok was a cunning giant who in his great age still yearned after the young wives of humans. So he caused quarrels between the husbands, and while they fought each other he abducted their wives. But like most giants and ogres, Tsavoojok was cunning but not intelligent; consequently, when a trap was laid for him by angry husbands, he fell right into the ambush and was killed.

References 77

See also giant, ogre

TSEMAUS

This is the name of a maritime monster in the traditions of the Native American people of British Columbia, Canada. The Tsemaus is described as being a gigantic fish-monster with an vast dorsal fin that is so sharp that it can cut a human in the water entirely in two. The Tsemaus was said to inhabit the waters of the Skeena River estuary.

References 134

See also monster

TSENAHALE

This is the name of a monstrous bird in the traditions and legends of the Navajo Native American people of the southwestern United States. The Tsenahale was described as a vast bird resembling an eagle that was destroyed by Nayenezgami with an arrow of lightning. As the dying bird descended to the earth, its feathers turned into other small birds, whose own progeny were the mountain eagles.

References 78

See also Roc, Yeitso

TSOPO

This is the name of a class of unicorn mentioned as being in the legends and traditions of Tibet. It was said to be very aggressive.

References 81

See also unicorn

TSUCHI-GUMO

This is the name of a gigantic spider in the traditions and beliefs of Japan. Tsuchi-Gumo is described as a vast spider that was almost immortal, as no metal could harm it. It preyed upon the region's population and destroyed everything in its way. Ultimately, it was killed by trapping it in its cave with a huge mesh of steel wire and building such great fires that it was smoked and roasted to death.

References 7

See also Djieien, spider, Spider-Woman, Ungoliant

TUBAL

This is the name of a giant who was conjectured by the Italian monk Annius of Viterbo (Giovanni Nanni, c. 1432–1502) to be the founder of the culture and peoples of Spain.

References 174

See also Dis Samothes, giant, Noah

TUGARIN

This is the name of a monstrous giant in the traditions and folklore of Russia. Tugarin is described as being so enormous that his eyes were at least two feet apart and his ears almost eight inches in length. His vast belly was so big that it resembled two tree trunks side by side. Tugarin was renowned for being very aggressive, but he excelled himself one day at the Kiev court of Prince Vladimir by trying to throw a dagger at Alesha for a supposed insult. Luckily, Alesha's squire, Ekin, caught the dagger before it could penetrate its intended victim. But the argument did not end there, for Tugarin challenged Alesha to a duel on the Steppe. When Alesha arrived, he saw that Tugarin was not only astride his powerful stallion but had also gained magical wings. Alesha prayed for the very thing that could ruin the magic wings, a torrent of rain, and when a storm arrived the giant's wings melted and he fell to the earth. As the giant spurred his horse to charge Alesha, the hero grabbed the powerful horse by the mane and crawled high enough to swing his stave at the giant's neck, severing his head. The triumphant hero rode back on Tugarin's stallion to Kiev with the giant's head on his stave.

References 55

See also giant

TUI DELAI GAU

This is the name of a giant in the traditions and beliefs of the people of Gau Island in the Pacific islands of Fiji. Tui Delai Gau is so huge and so magical that he can send his hands off by themselves, walking on their fingers, to the shore to fish for him. Whenever he needs to see further than where he rests, he will remove his head and hold it in whichever direction he needs to observe. He is well disposed toward humans

and taught them how to use a spade to dig for their food and how to cook it.
References 113
See also giant, Polyphemus

TUISCO GIGAS

This is an alternative name for the giant of European antiquity known as Tuyscon Gigas.
References 174
See also Tuyscon Gigas

TUISTO, TUISTO GIGAS

This is the name of a giant in the ancient writing of Rome. Tuisto was mentioned in the work *Germania* by the Roman historian Publius Tacitus (c. 55–120) as being the ancestor of the first human named Mannus according to the Germanic tribes of the period.
References 139
See also giant, Tuyscon Gigas

TULIHÄND

This is the name of a household dragon in the folklore of Estonia. The Tulihänd is also known as the Puuk or Pisuhänd and is described as being a serpentine-bodied, four-footed dragon about two feet in length that steals and guards treasure for its master. In some regions it also has wings and can fly through the skies with a fiery tail.
References 7
See also Puk

TUMBURU

This is the name of one of the leaders of the Gandharvas in the Hindu mythology of India.
References 7, 24, 112, 125
See also Gandharvas

TUMU-RA'I-FUENA

This is the name of a sea monster in the traditions and beliefs of the people of Tahiti. Tumu-Ra'i-Fuena is described as a vast octopus with a spotted skin. This creature had a grip with every tentacle on the earth and the heavens, and although the god Rua tried to make it release its grip through chanting and magic, it was to no avail.
References 38
See also monster

TUNIQ

This is an alternative name for the Tuurnngaq, a class of giant in the traditions and beliefs of the Inuit people of eastern Hudson Bay in Canada.
References 77
See also Tuurnngaq

TUNNITUAQRUK

This is the name of a class of monsters in the traditions and beliefs of the Inuit of eastern Hudson Bay in Canada. The males are described as having a humanoid body but with an enormous head covered in tatoos, from which Tunnituaqruk gets his name (the word *tunnit* means "tattoo"). He and his female counterpart, known as Katyutayuuq, follow the humans or seek out their recently abandoned snow houses to search for discarded scraps. They have a nasty habit of hiding in abandoned bedding and terrifying anyone who might happen on them.
References 77
See also Katyutayuuq, monster

TUNTABAH

This is an alternative name for the Bunyip, a water monster in the traditions and beliefs of the Native Australian people.
References 89
See also Bunyip

TURSUS

This is the name of a marine monster in the literature and folklore of Finland. It is variously described as a gigantic humanoid torso with the hindquarters of a walrus or whale, human arms, and a head resembling that of a gigantic walrus with huge ears, clothed in sealskins. It has been considered by many to be the same as the Rosmer of Norwegian folktale and derived from the Thursir of Norse mythology. It is conjectured that it is the basis upon which the Rosmarine was envisaged by the Elizabethan poet Edmund Spenser (c. 1552–1599) in his work *The Faerie Queene* (1590).
References 125, 134
See also monster, Rosmarine, Rosmer, Thursir

TU-TE-WEHIWEHI

This is the name of a monster in the traditions and beliefs of the Mangaian people of the Cook Islands of the Pacific. Tu-Te-Wehiwehi is also known as Moko.
References 113
See also Moko, monster

TUURNNGAQ

This is the name of a class of giant in the traditions and beliefs of the Inuit people of eastern Hudson Bay in Canada. They were renowned for constructing habitations out of the living rock. The Tuurnngaq, also known as the Tuniq, were particularly aggressive toward human beings, and wherever their paths crossed the human would never be seen again.
References 77
See also giant

Marine monster, like the Tursus of Finnish folklore (On Monsters and Marvels by Ambroise Paré, trans. by Janis L. Pallister, University of Chicago Press, 1982)

TUYSCON GIGAS

This is the name of a giant first mentioned in antiquity by the Roman historian Publius Tacitus (c. 55–120) in his work *Germania*. Tuyscon Gigas, whose name may also be rendered as Tuisco Gigas or Tuisto Gigas, was said to have been the giant hereditary leader of the Tuyscones, a tribe of Germanic peoples in a region that stretched from the Rhine at present-day Frankfurt to the coast at Hamburg and Arnhem in Belgium. Through a historical misreading of the name Tuyscones, the Babylonian priest and writer Berosus and, later, the medieval Italian monk Annius of Viterbo (Giovanni Nanni, c. 1432–1502) conjectured that the giant Tuyscon Gigas had ruled the Tuscans of ancient Italy and used him in a genealogy to justify the noble descent of the Gauls and their medieval rulers from a giant biblical race. The name and character appeared later in the medieval work *Officina* by the erudite Jean Tixier de Ravisy (alias Ravisius Textor, c. 1480–1524), who proposed that Tuyscon Gigas was actually a son of the giant Noah whose grandson, Mannus, ruled the Germanic region. He in turn constructed a line of giant descendants who were named as Gambrivius, Hercules, Herminon, Hunnus, Ingaevon, Istaevon, Masus, Suevus, Teutanes, and Vandaluus.

References 174
See also giant, Noah

TWISTED FACE

This is an alternative name for the giant known as Haduigona in the traditions and beliefs of the Iroquois Native American people of the United States.
References 136
See also giant, Haduigona

TWRCH TRWYTH

This is the name of a gigantic boar in the Celtic legends and folklore of Ireland and Wales. Twrch Trwyth features in the *Mabinogion* legend of Culhwch and Olwen, in which the hero must undertake many supernatural feats in order to win the hand of Olwen, the daughter of the giant Ysbaddaden.

Twrch Trwyth, also known as Porcus Troit or Porcus Troyn, was originally said to have been a king who was turned into a gigantic boar as a punishment for his wickedness. Together with his sons, Grugyn Silver Bristles and Llwydawg the Hewer, and with other siblings, they ravaged the whole of Ireland. Then the heroic King Arthur was called upon to rid the land of these monstrous beasts, and three ferocious battles took place before the brood was

Twrch Trwyth, a gigantic boar in the Celtic legends and folklore of Ireland and Wales (Scottish Folk Tales and Legends *by B. K. Wilson, Oxford University Press, UK, 1954*)

driven from Ireland. Undaunted, the tribe of gigantic boars swam the Irish Sea to the coast of Wales, where they were once more bent on destruction. Arthur and his heroic knights pursued the beasts from the Wye River across the land. One by one the boars were killed, with many warriors gored and slain, until only Twrch Trwyth and his sons, Grugyn Silver Bristles and Llwydawg the Hewer, were left. A vicious battle ensued, but Grugyn Silver Bristles, by then exhausted, was hacked down. Llwydawg the Hewer carried on as far as Ystrad Yw, goring and savaging as many pursuers as possible until his demise.

This left the sire Twrch Trwyth, who was pursued by Culhwch, since Ysbaddaden had demanded that only the comb, shears, and razor from behind the ears of this dangerous enemy could be used for his shave before the wedding. At last the beast was cornered by King Arthur and Culhwch in the River Severn, where Mabon grabbed the razor and Cyledyr took the shears, but the great boar broke loose again and bolted into the county of Cornwall. Then when they got the beast up on the tops of the cliffs, they managed to grab the comb as it leapt over the cliffs and swam from sight; it was never seen again.
References 7, 54, 78, 105
See also Ætolian Boar, Beigad, Boar of Beann-Gulbain, Buata, Cafre/Kafre, Calydonian Boar, Erymanthean Boar, giant, Grugyn Silverbristles, Hildesuin,

Llwydawg the Hewer, Pugot/Pugut, Sachrimnir, Ysbaddaden, Ysgithyrwyn

TYGER
This is the name of a hybrid beast in the heraldic repertoire of Europe. The Tyger is portrayed as having the body and tail of a lion but a head resembling that of a wolf.
References 68

TYPHON
There are two beings by this name.

1. This is the name of a monster in the classical mythology of Greece and Rome. Typhon, also known as Typhoeus, Typheus, Typhaon, and Typhois, is variously described as a giant or nebulous form with over a hundred dreadful dragons' heads and arms and legs that were serpents. From his searing eyes came scorching flames, and lava poured from his mouths. Typhon was said to have been created by Gaia after the defeat of the Gigantes so that he could assail the Olympian fortress of the gods. In one version, the Olympian gods fled to Egypt until Athene, the goddess of wisdom, persuaded them to return. Typhon was made drunk by the three Fates, and then Zeus attacked him. Typhon could throw vast mountains and was far stronger than the god, but Zeus's strategy was to shoot his thunderbolts and

blast the rocks before Typhon had thrown them, and the shattered splinters tore into Typhon himself. Before long, the monster was defeated and buried beneath Mount Etna, where he still causes eruptions.

2. This is one of the giants named in the genealogy created by the Italian monk Annius of Viterbo (Giovanni Nanni, c. 1432–1502) to justify the noble descent of the Gauls from a giant biblical race.
References 7, 20, 24, 47, 61, 78, 125, 133, 139, 174, 178, 182
See also Cerberus, Chimera, Cronus, Cyclopes, Delphyne, Dragon of Ladon, Echidna, giant, Hydra, Nemean Lion, Noah, Orthos, Prometheus, Sphinx, Uranus

TYTAN/S
This is the spelling that the Italian poet Boccaccio (1313–1375) gave in his literary works for the Titans in the classical mythology of Greece and Rome. His fourth book is entirely concerned with the "sons of Tytan," engendered with terra, the Titan Earth Mother, who equates with Gaia. Boccaccio numbers among their progeny Atlas, Astreus, Alous and the Aliods, Ceus, Enceladus, Egeon, Ephialtes, Japetus, Otus, Pallenes, and Typhon/Typheus.

References 174
See also Aloids, Alous, Astreus, Atlas, Ceus, Egeon, Enceladus, Ephialtes, giant, Japetus, Otus, Pallenes, Titan, Typhon

TYTEA MAGNA, TITEA MAGNA
This is the name of a giantess in the literature of medieval Europe. She was purported to be the wife of the giant Noah in a work by the Italian monk Annius of Viterbo (Giovanni Nanni ca. 1432 –1502). Tytea Magna, whose name means "Tytea the Great," was said to be a god-fearing person of integrity who was also said to have instituted a guarded, eternal, sacred flame.
References 174
See also giantess, Noah

TZELTAL
This is the name of a Great Serpent in the traditions and beliefs of the Chiapas Native American people of the United States. The Tzeltal is described as a vast horned serpent.
References 134
See also Horned Serpent, Tcinto-Saktco, Weewilmekq

U

UATH

This is the name of a giant in the traditions and legends of Ireland. The legend tells how the giant Uath challenged the heroes of the court of Conchobar by stating that anyone brave enough could smite his head from his shoulders so long as they presented themselves the following day for the same treatment. Believing that they would have nothing to fear from the death of the giant, Conall of the Victories and then Leary the Triumphant smote the giant's head from his shoulders. To their horror, he simply bent down and picked it up again. Then Cuchulainn took his club and smashed Uath's head into the ground. Again the giant gathered up the head, and then departed. The following night, Conall and Leary did not answer the giant's call to come for the next part of the bargain. But Cuchulainn stepped forward, and Uath raised his mighty axe, then smashed it down into the ground next to the hero. He declared that Cuchulainn was the only hero with honor, then transformed from being a giant into his state as the magical king of Munster. This legend motif is thought to be the derivative for the very well known Arthurian legend of Sir Gawain and the Green Knight.
References 78
See also giant

UFFINGTON DRAGON
See Dragon at Uffington

UGJUKNARPAK

This is the name of a gigantic rodent in the traditions and beliefs of the Inuit people of Alaska in the United States. The Ugjuknarpak is described as looking like a huge mouse with an extremely long prehensile tail that it uses to pull over the *umiaks* (a type of kayak) and grab its victims from within. It has a pelt that is impenetrable by any known weapon that a hunter might use and has exceptional hearing and speed. The Ugjuknarpak is therefore a particularly dangerous creature, and no hunter or fisherman will go near the island that it inhabits.
References 77

UGLESSA

This is an alternative name for the Serpentin Vert in the tales by the French authoress Marie-Catherine d' Aulnoy (1650–1705).
References 182
See also Serpentin Vert

UGRASURA

This is the name of a demonic serpent in the Hindu mythology of India. When Krishna was in his youthful stage, Ugrasura swallowed him whole, hoping to extinguish the progress of the god. But Krishna suddenly advanced his growth to his fullest size; as the serpent's body could no longer hold him, it exploded, and the god was released.
References 133
See also serpent

UHEPONO

This is the name of a giant in the traditions and beliefs of the Zuñi Native American people of the southwestern United States. Uhepono is described as a vast humanoid giant with enormous round eyes and with woolly fur entirely covering his skin.
References 24
See also giant

UILE BHÉISD A' CHUAIN, UILEBHEIST

This is an alternative name for the Cìrein Cròin, a gigantic sea serpent in the beliefs and folklore of the Highlands of Scotland. The name may be translated from the Scottish Gaelic as the "Monster of the Ocean."
References 7, 128
See also Cìrein Cròin, Oilliphéist

ULLIKUMMI

This is the name of a giant in the Hurrian mythology of ancient Syria. His story is told in the *Song of Ullikummi*, which was found on Hittite tables in Hathusa during an archeological survey. Ullikummi is described as a giant formed from green quartz that continuously expanded, forcing the earth back into the primordial oceans and the heavens up too high. He had been created by Kumarbi, the father of the gods, in response to the young gods' battle to usurp his powers. Everything that the new gods did to destroy Ullikummi failed until the massive feet of the giant were cut from his ankles and he toppled into the ocean and was swallowed up forever.

References 47, 133
See also Atlas, giant, Titan

UMAI-HULHLYA-WIT

This is the name of a water monster in the traditions and beliefs of the Diegueño Native American people of California. Umai-Hulhlya-wit is said to have existed since time began as a vast primordial serpent in the cosmos. Then when the earth was peopled by Chacopá and Chacomát, curiosity got the better of Umai-Hulhlya-wit, who descended to see more. But the serpent monster was far too big and terrified everyone. However, Chacopá and Chacomát encouraged everyone to make a place of brushwood for Umai-Hulhlya-wit to join them. This they did, and the vast serpent wound his coils until he was in place. Then the people set the brushwood alight, and Umai-Hulhlya-wit, who could not escape, heated to boiling and exploded, sending out into the world, with his parts, all the cultural elements such as the arts, languages, music, rituals, and legends that were needed by the people.

References 133
See also monster, serpent

UNCEGILA

This is the name of a giant water snake in the traditions and beliefs of the Sioux Native American people of the United States. Uncegila is described as a vast female whose great serpentine body is covered with flint scales; her heart is a rock crystal, and her eyes shot flames. Uncegila dwelled in the oceans but several times a year swam up into Nebraska, where she took great tidal waves with her and turned all the waters brackish and unfit for the humans who relied on it. So armed with the knowledge of her most vulnerable spot and the magic to dull her reactions, two young men set out to kill Uncegila. When she saw these puny humans she raised her great bulk out of the water, and while one recited the charms to hold her there, the other shot her through the seventh point below her head and killed her. The sun was so grateful for her death that it dried up everything in sight and turned the land completely dry. Then the two who had taken the crystal heart gained the power of prophecy until the crystal was despoiled by the uninitiated and then disintegrated.

References 133
See also serpent

UNDERGROUND PANTHER, UNDERWATER PANTHER

These are alternative names for the Mishipizhiw in the traditions and beliefs of the Native American people of the United States.

References 134
See also Mishipizhiw

UNGOLIANT

This is the name of a gigantic spider being in the literary works of the English academic and author J. R. R. Tolkien (1892–1973) in *The Hobbit* (1937) and *The Lord of the Rings* (1955). Ungoliant was a vast female spider that wove her vicious web of Unlight, killing the light of the trees of Valar. When she bred with her kind in the Nan Dungotheb, or "Valley of Dreadful Death," she produced Shelob among many of the other monstrous spiders. They were eventually killed in the raging floods after the War of Wrath, and she was said to have consumed herself with hunger.

References 51
See also Djieien, Shelob, spider, Spider-Woman, Tsuchi-Gumo

UNGUD, UNGUR

This is an alternative name for the great Rainbow Snake in the Dreamtime mythology of the Native Australian people. It is also a name for the Dreamtime itself.

References 125, 166
See also Kaleru, Rainbow Serpent, Wanambi

UNHCEGILA

This is the name of a monster in the traditions and legends of the Lakota Sioux people of the United States. Unhcegila is described as resembling a massive dragon that is aggressive and predatory toward humans and deemed to be responsible for their disappearances.

References 77
See also dragon, monster

UNICORN, UNICORNIS

This is the name of a fabulous beast in the mythology and legends of many cultures. Owing to the differences in characteristics, this will be divided into the categories of Occidental and Oriental Unicorns.

Occidental Unicorns

The Unicorn was reported in ancient times under various descriptions. Accounts such as that of Ctesias, the Greek historian, writing in Persia during the fifth century B.C., suggest that it was a white-bodied creature like an ass but with a purple head with blue eyes and in the forehead a horn of red, black, and white. He termed this the "Monoceros." It was also

The Unicorn gained royal, popular, and ecclesiastical recognition and was assimilated readily into the heraldic repertoire of Europe. (Rose Photo Archive, UK)

mentioned by Herodotus (485–425 B.C.), and Pliny the Elder in his *Historia Naturalis* (A.D. 77) described it as having the body like that of a horse with the legs and feet like an elephant, the tail like that of a boar, and the head of a deer which had a single long black horn. Aelian (c. A.D. 200) mentions a beast that he says is called the Cartazonon of India that was like a horse colored yellowish-red with a black horn and long mane. All suggest that it is very aggressive and that it inhabits the deserts and wastes of the mountains, where it was said to be the enemy of the lion. It was asserted that it may be killed but never taken alive.

The Judeo-Christian scriptures mention a beast known as the Re'em, which was earlier translated as Unicorn. It was subsequently corrected; however the association remained and the Unicorn was adopted into the repertoire of Christian emblematic beasts. The Unicorn was depicted in the *Etymologies* of Isidore of Seville (c. 560–636), where it was said to be able to kill an elephant with one stab of its massive horn. When the *Physiologus* of Alexandria became widely available and the compilation of bestiaries took place within medieval Europe, the Unicorn had been assured its religious symbolism. In a Latin bestiary dating from the twelfth century is related the stratagem of entrapping the Unicorn by taking a virgin girl to the woods and leaving her until the Unicorn arrives. The beast is said to be so enchanted with her purity that it lays its head in her lap and is caught by the waiting hunters. An English Anglo-Saxon bestiary of 1220, now in the Bodleian Library at Oxford, describes also how the Unicorn sleeps in the maiden's lap and is then taken to be displayed in the king's palace. It also goes on to explain the symbolism of its capture as the betrayal of Christ, His subsequent capture, and crucifixion. From that time, the Unicorn seems to have acquired a graceful piety that the earlier descriptions had lacked.

The more ferocious variety was still reported in such as the accounts of the travels of Marco Polo (1254–1324) and the later *Travels of Sir John Mandeville*, written about 1360. Later travelers mentioned the Persian Koresk, which was revered as a royal beast; a Unicorn with a forked end to its horn was described in Russia; while other versions of the Congo in Africa indentified the Abada and in South Africa the Ndzoodzoo, and in the Arabian Peninsula it was called Pyrassoupi.

It was the subject not only of legend but also incorporated into the literature of the period. In his work *The Faerie Queene*, the English Elizabethan poet Edmund Spenser (c. 1552–1599) suggested that the Unicorn was the bitter enemy of the lion and that they met in a duel. This theme of the Lion and the Unicorn was further related in popular verse and English

chapbooks from the early eighteenth century onward after the union of England and Scotland (see below). It was later incorporated into the work *Through the Looking Glass* (1851/1852) by Lewis Carroll (Charles Lutwidge Dodgson, 1832–1898), the eminent Victorian English author of *Alice in Wonderland.*

Meanwhile the inventories of the nobility and wealthy ecclesiastics boasted the purchase of Unicorn horns for the detection of poisons in their food and wines. The Unicorn had gained royal, popular, and ecclesiastical recognition and was assimilated readily into the heraldic repertoire of Europe. Two Unicorns were the emblem of James VI of Scotland, and when he assumed the throne of England as James I in 1603, the red Dragon of the Tudor Dynasty was replaced with a Unicorn as supporter opposite the Lion of England. The Unicorn still features in many of the coats of arms of Europe.

Oriental Unicorn

The Unicorns of the Far East have quite a different character from those of the West. There are several types, the main one being the Ki Lin, or Ch'i Lin. It is variously described in the ancient texts of China as being the male Ki and the female Lin, which are spoken of as a unit. They are depicted as having the body of a deer with the hooves of horses with a fine head and a single horn. The body may be multicolored in blue, black, red, white, and yellow, and the creature is described in one text as being about twelve feet high. The Ki Lin was said to be one of the celestial beings with the dragon, the tortoise, and the Feng Hwang. Its appearance was auspicious, and many dignitaries such as Confucius were honored by its presence.

The King is described as a single-horned type of stag with a tail more like that of the water buffalo.

Another Unicorn was the Kioh Twan, which was described much as the Ki Lin but it was green and had a thick tail like that of a horse, but its horn was on its muzzle. It was extremely fast and could stride great distances.

In the plains of Mongolia was said to live a beast called the Poh, which was like a beautiful white horse. It was said to have a huge black tail but had claws on its feet like a tiger and great fangs for teeth and a horn from the center of its forehead. This aggressive being hunted the tigers and leopards of the region.

The Hai Chai, also known as the Kai Tsu, is described as having a body like a horse but is a reddish-yellow color with a single black horn. It is said to be able to detect the guilty and tell who is innocent.

A further different Chinese Unicorn, the Too Jou Shen, was more like a lion in appearance, but it had the legs and cloven hooves of a deer and a much shorter rounded horn. They were regarded as guardian figures and depicted at the entrance to tomb complexes.

Other words for different Unicorns were the Lu, similar to an ass, the Sz, similar to an ox, and the Chiai Tung, similar to a lamb or small ewe.

In the legends of Japan the Unicorn was transferred from the Ki Lin of China, and the name became "Kirin." Although similar in image, the Kirin was covered in scales. Another Unicorn, the Kai Tsi or the Sin You, was described as being similar to a lion or a sheep with a single horn. This being was said to be able to make judgments concerning the guilt or innocence of an accused person.

Other Unicorn creatures mentioned as being in the legends and traditions of Tibet were the Kere, the Serou, and the Tsopo, all of which were said to be very aggressive.
References 5, 7, 10, 14, 18, 20, 61, 68, 78, 81, 89, 91, 134, 147, 148, 168, 185
See also Abath, Afanc, Alicorn, Amduscias, Ass (Three-Legged), Biasd Na Srognig, Cartazonon, Chiai Tung, Chio-Tuan, dragon, Feng Hwang, Hai Chiai, Kai Tsi, Kai Tsu, Karkadan, Kere, Ki-Lin, King, Kioh Twan, Kirin, Koresck, Licorn, Lu, Mi'raj (Al-), Monoceros, Ndzoodzoo, Onyx Monoceros, Oriental Dragon, Poh, Pyrassoupi, Re'em, Scythian Ass, Serou, Sz, Too Jon Sheu, Tsopo

UNIVERSAL EYE

This is an alternative name for the Bunyip, a monstrous being in the legends of the Native Australian people. The Bunyip is called the Universal Eye in Tasmania, where it is depicted with a serpentine shape.
References 89
See also Bunyip

UNKTEHI

This is an alternative name for the Uncegila, a gigantic water serpent in the traditions and beliefs of the Sioux Native American people in the United States. They inhabit the waterfalls and other deep-flowing waters. They are aggressive and constantly at war with the Thunderbirds.
References 77, 133
See also Thunderbirds, Uncegila, Wakinyan

UNNATI

This is the name of a celestial bird in the Hindu mythology of Nepal in India. Unnati is described as having the body of a beautiful bird and the head of a woman. She is the consort of Garuda.

References 7
See also Alkonost, Angka, Garuda, Harpy, Parthenope, Podarge, Ptitsy-Siriny, Siren, Sirin, Solovei Rakhmatich, Zägh

UNTEKHI

This is the name of a water guardian in the traditions and beliefs of the Native American people of the United States. The Untekhi inhabits and is the guardian of the Missouri River.
References 133

UPELLERU

This is the name of a giant in the ancient Hurrian beliefs of the place now known as Anatolia in the Middle East. Upelleru is described as a primordial giant who stands waist-deep in the oceans holding the earth and heavens apart with his outstretched arms.
References 125
See also Atlas, Ceus, giant, Manzaširi, Ymir

UPIR

This is the name of a monster in the traditions and folklore of Russia. The Upir may be described as either a Werewolf or a vampire.
References 55
See also monster, vampire, Werewolf.

URAEUS

This is the name of a serpent in the mythology of ancient Egypt. The Uraeus was described as a huge, poison-spitting serpent that was coiled around the solar disc of the god Ra. One legend tells how when Ra had left the Ureus with some of his hair and staff in a casket, the casket was opened by Geb and his followers. The resulting powerful spray of poison from the Ureus killed all the company and seriously affected the god's father, Geb. In another version Ureus is the guardian of the goddess Hathor.
References 89, 139
See also Basilisk, serpent

URANUS, URANOS

This is the name of one of the primordial giants in the classical mythology of Greece and Rome. Uranus, also spelled Ouranos or Ouranus, was the progeny of Gaia, with whom he produced the Titans, the Hundred-Handed Giants, and the monstrous Cyclopes. He so detested these beings that he enforced their stay in Gaia or, according to some versions, in the depths of Tartarus. However, Gaia conspired with Cronus to overthrow Uranus, and while he lay with Gaia, Cronus castrated his father with a sickle. The blood from this act engendered the Furies, and when it dropped over the sea, Aphrodite/Venus was born from the foam.

References 78, 125, 166, 178
See also Arges, Briareus, Brontes, Cottus, Cronus, Cyclops, Furies, Gaia, giant, Gyges, Hundred-Handed Giants, Steropes, Titan

URGAN

This is the name of a giant in the ancient and medieval legends of Europe. Urgan possessed Petitcrien, a fairy dog of wonderful ability. In the Arthurian legend *Tristan and Iseult,* Tristan desired the dog to give to Iseult, but the giant would not part with it. So Tristan fought Urgan for the dog, and the giant was slain.
References 54
See also giant

URISK, ÙRUISG

The Uruisg is a type of supernatural monster belonging to the class known as Fuath in the folklore of Scotland. The Urisk, whose name in Scottish Gaelic means "Water Man," is described as having the upper half of a human and the lower half of a goat, like the faun or Satyr of classical Greek mythology. They inhabited the wild places of the Highlands and particularly congregated at Loch Katrine in the Trossachs. Individuals inhabited Glen Lyon, a waterfall near Tyndrum and Beinn Dorain. Although usually solitary beings, the Urisks were also of a frolicsome nature, prone to chasing a woman of their fancy, and accused of killing sheep. Their ugly shape made them unwelcome companions on lonely roads when they suddenly appeared ambling beside terrified travelers at night.
References 21, 24, 25, 96, 111, 128, 160, 170
See also Fenodyree, Fuath, Peallaidh, satyr

UROBOROS

This is an alternative spelling of Ouroboros, the monstrous dragon-serpent in the mythology of ancient Egypt.
References 18
See also dragon, Ouroboros, serpent

URUKS, URUK-HAI

This is the name of a type of giant in the literature of the English academic and writer J. R. R. Tolkien (1892–1973) in *The Hobbit* (1937) and *The Lord of the Rings* (1955). The Uruk-hai, the name being shortened in the narrative to Uruks, were a class of the terrible Orcs but, unlike them, were unafraid of the light. The Uruks are described as being about the size of men but incredibly strong and evil and descending on the population from out of Mordor during the Third Age of the Sun.
References 51
See also giant, Orc

URULÓKI

This is the name of a class of dragon in the literary works of the English academic and author J. R. R. Tolkien (1892–1973) in *The Hobbit* (1937) and *The Lord of the Rings* (1955). The monstrous creatures are bred by the evil Morgoth in the Pits of Angband during the period of the First Sun. Like their legendary and folkloric counterparts the Fire-Drakes, they flew across the sky on bat-like wings, breathing destructive fire on all beneath. They were as feared as they were hideous, and all the other beings shared the same dread of their arrival. The most dreadful of these were Ancalagon the Black, the Dragon of Erebor, named Smaug, and Glaurung.
References 51
See also Ancalagon the Black, dragon, Fire-drake, Glaurung, Smaug

URUS

This is the name of a creature mentioned in the bestiaries written in medieval Europe. The Urus is described as a huge beast about the size of a very large bull but having two extremely long horns with jagged or sawed edges that it apparently used for cutting into the surrounding trees. The Urus could be captured when it drank seawater and became so disoriented that it stabbed at the ground with its horns or became entangled in the trees it was trying to cut. It is believed that this is an exaggerated description of the ancient oxen called the auroch that inhabited the Middle East.
References 7

UTGARD-LOKI, UTGARDLOKI

This is the name of an enormous giant in the Norse mythology of Scandinavia. In one of the many adventures of the god Thor, he, Loki, and Thialfi traveled to his castle at Utgard, where as part of the evening's entertainments the three gods were asked by Utgard-Loki to demonstrate their power before qualifying for their hospitality as gods. Each was given a task: Loki was to have an eating contest with the giant Logi, Thjalfi was to outrun Hugi, and Thor was to wrestle with both the giant's cat and his aged mother Elli and to drink a draft from Utgard-Loki's drinking horn. All of the gods to their astonishment were defeated. Then Utgard-Loki explained that all had been an illusion that even the gods could not control. They had been in contest with elements that the gods themselves could not defeat, for the giant Logi was "fire," the giant Hugi was "thought," the giant's drinking horn was filled constantly by the seas, the giant's cat was the formidable Midgardsormr, and his giantess mother was "old age."
References 125, 139, 166, 169
See also giant, Hugi, Logi, Midgardsorm

UTUKKU

These were originally evil devils and demons in the beliefs and mythology of the ancient Assyrians and Babylonians of the Middle East. There were two types of Utukku, the souls of the dead that could not rest until they could be appeased, and the truly evil spirits that were said to emanate from the bile of an Ea, or deity. Later, as the mythology was denigrated by time and invasions, these beings were no longer regarded in the same category and became a type of folkloric monster. These Utukku were described as looking like men with animal heads, claws, and horns. They inhabited caverns in cliffs and lonely ruins but still were malicious and evil toward humans.

References 125, 139, 160
See also monster

UWABAMI

This is the name of a monstrous serpent in the traditions and legends of Japan. The Uwabami is described as being like a vast serpent sometimes with wings, sometimes without, but flying through the air. It was particularly predatory toward humans and would descend to scoop them up in its huge jaws. Even a knight on horseback was not safe from the Uwabami until it was despatched by the hero Yegara-no-Heida.
References 113
See also serpent

V

VAIROCHANA
This is an alternative name for the monstrous Bali in the Hindu mythology of India.
References 78, 112
See also Bali

VAJRAVINA
This is the name by which the Hindu giantess Viraj is known in Buddhist Tibet.
References 78
See also giantess, Purusha, Viraj

VALEDJÁD
This is the name of a primordial giant in the beliefs of the Tupari people of Brazil. Valedjád is a Stone Giant and was engendered when a vast crack rent the mother earth. He was no sooner independent than he wished to destroy all about him and tore into the gates holding back the seas from the land. His mother the earth called to the sun for assistance and he evaporated the escaping waters and sent Arkoayó, a supernatural, to "bind" the power of Valedjád. While the giant was asleep Arkoayó carefully poured beeswax into his ears, eyes, and nose and then sealed his fingers together. When the giant was stuck and unable to help himself the supernatural used the powerful magic of the holly plant to seal the giant's predicament, knowing that no Stone Giant can break the spell of holly. When this was done Arkoayó called to the flocks of birds to take Valedjád's vast body to the far north of the world. There he struggles with his bonds to this day, causing earthquakes as he struggles, thunder as he roars in his frustration, and lighting up the sky with the fierce red anger of his face.
References 133
See also giant

VAMANA
This is the name of one of the Lokapala Elephants in the Hindu mythology of India. Vamana (sometimes Mahapadma, according to different legends) stands as the guardian of the south quadrant of the world with the god Yama on his back.
References 7, 24, 112
See also Lokapala Elephants

VAMPIRE
This is the name of a monstrous humanoid being that has been transformed from a wicked unrepentant mortal human into an immortal creature that must suck the blood of another in order to survive. These beings are to be found in most cultures around the world but do not necessarily take the form of a human when they hunt their prey. In many European traditions they are the development from the dead Werewolf. They may take the form of a monstrous bat, a fox, or a cat to mesmerize and drain the blood of their victim. The only ways in which they may be defeated is by the use of holy water, the use of a silver cross, pinning through the heart with a wooden stake, and allowing the sunlight to fall on them. Hawthorn and garlic were said to repel them, and they could be recognized from throwing no shadow, or a reflection in a mirror. During the Middle Ages and for sometime after, whole graveyards were exhumed when a catastrophe set the people looking for the Vampire that was to blame.

The European concept was developed from an eastern European tradition of the Balkan states where the Slavic word *vampir* exists with variants in the Czech, Hungarian, Polish, and Russian languages. The legends of the Vampire were current long before the Greek scholar Leone Allaeci made his study in the middle 1600s. By 1734 some of the legends had been translated into English, and in 1746 the French Benedictine monk Augustin Calmet (1672–1757) published a study of the phenomenon. By the end of the nineteenth century Europe had become fascinated by the horror story of the Vampire, with both eminent authors such as Goethe and Baudelaire responding to the public demand that spawned horror comics such as "Varney the Vampire" (1847). The major development of the theme came with the publication

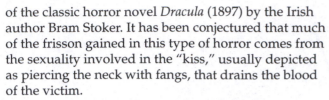

of the classic horror novel *Dracula* (1897) by the Irish author Bram Stoker. It has been conjectured that much of the frisson gained in this type of horror comes from the sexuality involved in the "kiss," usually depicted as piercing the neck with fangs, that drains the blood of the victim.

In other countries the tradition of El Broosha has devolved into the traditions of Spain from the early Jewish settlers. This Vampire was derived from the legend of Lilith, the first wife of Adam in the Book of Genesis. In Japan the Vampire is the Cat of Nabeshima, which takes the form of the princess who was its first victim and then tries to kill the royal prince but is destroyed. In China the Vampires inhabit abandoned temples and castles and attack travelers at night. In the beliefs of the Araucanian people of Chile there are the Colo-Colo, the Invunche, and the Pihuechenyi; in Surinam the Azeman; in the Islands of Trinidad and Tobago in the Caribbean it is a Sukuyan. In the United States the Skatene is the Vampire in the beliefs of the Choctaw Native American people of the southeastern United States and the Stikini in the beliefs of the Seminole Native American people of Oklahoma. In Scotland the Vampire is Lammikin. In ancient Rome it was Lamia and the Strigae, which was the source of the modern Greek Vampire, the Stringes. The Vulkodlac is a Vampire in modern Slavic folklore and the Upir in modern Russia. In India the Pey is the Vampire in Tamil mythology; in West Malaysia the Pontianak is the Vampire of the Malay people; while the Vis is a Vampire in the beliefs of the Lakalai people of central New Britain in Melanesia.
References 20, 24, 49, 51, 61, 69, 78, 94, 113, 125, 133, 181, 182
See also Azeman, Colo-Colo, Dracula, Flying Heads, Invunche, Lamia, Lammikin, Namorodo, Pey, Pihuechenyi, Pontianak, Skatene, Stikini, Strigae, Stringes, Sukuyan, Upir, Vis, Vulkodlac, Werewolf

VANAPAGAN
This is the name for a giant in the traditions and folklore of Estonia.
References 24
See also giant

VANDALUUS
This is the name of a giant who appeared in the medieval work *Officina* by the erudite Jean Tixier de Ravisy (alias Ravisius Textor, c. 1480–1524), who proposed that Tuyscon Gigas was actually a son of the giant Noah whose progeny were the ancestors of European nobility. He constructed a line of giant descendants, of whom Vandaluus was one of many legendary figures.

References 174
See also giant, Noah, Tuyscon Gigas

VASTY
This is the nickname of Skrymir, a Frost Giant in the Norse mythology of Scandinavia.
References 47, 89
See also Skrymir, Utgard-Loki

VASUKI
This is the name of the son of Sesha the World Serpent in the Hindu mythology of India. During the Churning of the Ocean at the creation, Vasuki was used as the rope and became so weary that he tried to poison the waters with his venom. All the time Garuda was taking the other serpents and making off with them. So Vasuki made a pact with Vishnu that Garuda could take only one each day. During the great Flood when Manu had to rescue a pair of every living thing, he had used Vasuki as the rope to hold the vessel from being swept away, so the legend relates that humans survived because of Vasuki.
References 24, 112, 125, 133, 139
See also Garuda, Naga, serpent, Sesha

VEGETABLE LAMB OF TARTARY
This is an alternative name for the Barometz, a legendary part-animal, part-vegetable creature of medieval Europe.
References 20, 89, 189
See also Barometz

VELI JOZE
This is the name of a giant in the traditions and folklore of Croatia. Veli Joze, whose name literally means "Big Joe," was described as a vast being that was a warrior in the Istra Peninsula town of Motovun. When he became incensed at the tyranny of the local ruler, Veli Joze went to the town where the lord lived and, as the gates were shut, took hold of the vast gate tower and shook it. The gate tower cracked and started to topple at an angle, similar to that of the Leaning Tower of Pisa, and then held, as it stands today. But the feudal lord was so furious at the destruction of his tower that Veli Joze was taken to the nearest ravine and his two arms were tied to rings at either side and he was suspended there above the torrent.
References 55
See also giant

VERETHRAGHNA
This is the name of a terrible boar in the Hindu mythology of India. Verethraghna is described as a vast creature with enormous tusks and a raging temperament that no one dares approach. This vast creature is the instrument of destruction used by the

Sleeping giant Skrymir, nicknamed Vasty (Rose Photo Archive, UK)

god Mithra to wreak havoc and destruction on humans and their property when they have angered him.
References 47
See also Ætolian Boar, Beigad, Boar of Beann-Gulbain, Buata, Cafre/Kafre, Calydonian Boar, Erymanthean Boar, Hildesuin, Pugot/Pugut, Sachrimnir, Twrch Trwyth, Ysgithyrwyn

VILKACIS
This is the name of a Werewolf in the traditions and folklore of Latvia. Although the Vilkacis is usually an object of terror, there are also tales of his having a treasure hoard to share.
References 125
See also Werewolf

VILKATAS
This is the name of a Werewolf in the traditions and folklore of Lithuania. The Vilkatas may also be called a Vilkolakis and, although a terrifying monster, may hoard treasure to share with a favored few.
References 24, 125
See also Vilkacis, Werewolf

VILKOLAKIS
This is an alternative name for the Werewolf of Lithuania that is usually also known as Vilkatas.

References 24, 125
See also Vilkatas, Werewolf

VIRABANDRA
This is the name of a monster in the Hindu mythology of India. The god Shiva had been insulted by the arrangement for a massive sacrificial ceremony that excluded him, so he created the monstrous Virabandra. This humanoid being was vast and had a thousand eyes, feet, and arms. His face had enormous fangs and his sides had horns protruding from them. Virabandra rampaged through the gods, dwarfing them and wreaking havoc. In different versions the god Vishnu made Shiva destroy Virabandra; in another version Daksha apologized and Shiva withdrew the monster.
References 112
See also monster

VIRADHA
This is the name of a grotesque, monstrous giant in the Hindu mythology of India. Viradha is one of the Rakshasas, a vast humanoid shape whose garments were tiger skins. His face was equally grotesque, for he had enormous yellow eyes and a huge mouth with fangs continuously dripping blood from the humans that he devoured. One day three gods met this

monster in the forest and he attacked them, but they got the better of him. They smashed his frame to the ground, and though he would not die they were determined to control him and so threw him into a pit and covered him. To their surprise a Gandharva emerged from the earth and thanked them for breaking the curse that had been placed on him by Kubera.

References 112
See also giant

VIRAJ

This is the name of the first gigantic female made by the subdivision of the primordial giant Purusha. Viraj, also known in Tibet as Vajravina, is variously described as dressed in red, holding a musical instrument seated on a swan, or a fearsome figure with three faces and six limbs. It is she who was responsible for giving humans the things they needed to survive.

References 78, 133
See also Purusha

VIRCOLAC

This is a name for the Werewolf to be found in the Balkan states of eastern Europe.

References 89
See also Werewolf

VIRUPAKSHA

This is the name of one of the Lokapala Elephants in the Hindu mythology of India. In the *Ramayana*, Virupaksha (in some legends it is Airāvata) stands as the guardian of the eastern quadrant of the world with the god Indra on his back.

References 7, 24, 112
See also Lokapala Elephants

VIS

This is the name of a vampire in the traditions and beliefs of the Lakalai people of central New Britain in Melanesia. The Vis is described as a flying monster with long talons that shines brightly in the night sky. It is not only a predatory creature but also tears out the eyes of its victims with its long talons.

References 133, 136
See also vampire

VISHAP

This is the name of a dragon in the legends of Armenia. Vishap was a fearsome, terrifying dragon that was said to inhabit the tops of Mount Ararat. However, many warriors sought to kill this dragon, not for its ravaging of the countryside but for the legend that its blood would render any weapon it touched so poisonous that the slightest wound would be fatal.

References 7
See also dragon

VISVAVASU

This is the name of one of the Gandharvas in the Hindu mythology of India. The Gandharvas are described as being shaggy, part-animal hybrids very similar in form to the centaurs of classical Greek mythology, with the head of a human and a horse's body. Visvavasu is one of their three leaders.

References 7, 24, 38, 112, 125, 133, 139, 156, 160, 161
See also centaur, Chitra-ratha, Gandharvas, Kinnara

VITHAFNIR

This is the name of a gigantic cockerel in the Norse mythology of Scandinavia. Vithafnir, also known as Gollinkambi, is the watch-bird that stays alert on the top of Yggdrasil, the Ash Tree of the World, to warn the gods of any threat. Vithafnir is described as having radiantly brilliant golden plumage.

References 7

VITRA

This is an alternative spelling of Vritra, a vast, monstrous creature in the Hindu mythology of India.

References 139
See also Vritra

VODIANOI, VODYANOI, VODYANOY

This is the name of a dangerous water being in the folklore and traditions of Russia. The Vodianoi, also called Vodyanoi, Vodyanoy, or Vodnik, is variously described as a floating, moss-covered log with wings; an old man with a blue face, white beard, and green hair; an old man covered in scales or fur with huge paws, glowing eyes, horns, and a tail; or entirely as an enormous, grotesque fish. In their humanoid form they would seem younger or older with the phases of the moon. The Vodyanoi was said to dwell in the very depths of the water, where it had either a beautiful illuminated palace that glowed on certain nights of the year, or to live in the very slime of the bottom with which it was sometimes covered. It was to be seen lurking in rivers, mill pools, and ponds, where it would lure any unwary humans to a horrible death in the water. This monster was a threat to all humans except the millers and fishermen. It would appear at night very frequently in the mill race, and to keep the Vodyanoi from doing harm, the millers would propitiate him with a cockerel. Often in the past a drunken stranger passing the water mills would also have been sent tumbling into the mill pool in place of

the cockerel—and then was devoured by the waiting Vodyanoi.
References 38, 103, 125, 134, 139, 166
See also monster, Näkk, Nix

VODNIK
This is an alternative name for the Vodianoi in the traditions and folklore of Russia.
References 38, 103, 134, 166
See also Vodianoi

VÖRYS-MORT, VÖRYS-MURT
This is the name of a giant in the traditions and folklore of the Russian states in the regions bordering the River Volga. Vörys-mort is described as being so enormous that he can look down on the tops of the trees. But unlike most tall beings he is not slow; he races along so fast that anything in the way, human or animal, gets caught up and carried along with him. Vörys-mort was regarded, however, as useful when he helped trap animals for the hunters by driving them ahead into their traps.
References 7
See also giant

VOUGH
This is a type of monster known as a Fuath in the folklore of Scotland. The Vough are water beings that materialize in a humanoid form, but they are afraid of the light. They are usually said to be female and described as having no nose on their faces, yellow hair extending as manes down their backs to an emergent tail, with webbed feet and hands. They have usually been seen dressed in green. Occasionally, they have been known to intermarry with humans. One of the Vough of Beann na Caltuinn was said to be the ancestor of the Munroes, whose earlier progeny showed signs of a caudal appendage and a mane of hair on the spine.
References 128, 160, 170
See also Melusine

VOUIVRE
This is the French version of the English Wyvern; the Vouivre is also known as the Wyvre in the region around Nevers. This monster is portrayed as a type of dragon with the foreparts of a well-endowed woman who has a ruby or diamond between her eyes. This jewel is the means by which the Vouivre can see, and if she is asleep it may be stolen and she could be killed. Many sorcerers required this ruby for their magic purposes. The Vouivre inhabited abandoned chateaux and monasteries, where she was said to guard hoards of treasure.
References 89, 134
See also Wyvern

VRIKODARA
This is the name of a giant in the Hindu mythology of India. Vrikodara is an epithet, which may be translated as "Wolf's Belly," by which the giant Bhima was known. He was famous for his ravenous appetite that frequently left others without food. Vrikodara was of enormous proportions and extremely strong; he could also fly as the legacy of his father, the wind god Vayu.
References 112
See also Bhima, giant

VRITRA, VRTRA, VITRA
This is the name of a vast dragon or serpent in the Hindu mythology of India. The name means the "Encloser," and he is visualized variously as a gigantic spider or, more usually, as a three-headed serpent that encircles the whole world and is often identified with Ahi. As the destructive element of nature, Vritra was the main cause of drought. Vritra, as one of the evil Asuras, was the enemy of Indra. After many battles between the two the god Vishnu declared that they should leave each other alone and that neither should attack the other with any iron, stone, or wood that was wet or dry during night or day. The truce seemed sealed until one evening when the sun was setting and it was neither night nor day, Indra saw Vritra on the shore where the surf was breaking. Quickly the god entered the foam on the surf and flew at his enemy in an element that was neither wet nor dry nor composed of any of the other forbidden elements. Thus Indra finally slew the sky serpent and released the cloud-cattle (rains) that had been held captive in the mountains.
References 7, 47, 78, 89, 112, 125, 133, 139, 160, 166
See also Aapep, serpent

VSESLAV
This is the name of a Werewolf in the traditions and folklore of Russia and Belorussia. Vseslav was considered to be the offspring of a princess, who had been violated by a serpent, and born during an eclipse of the sun. His legend appears in the *Lay of Igor's Campaign,* written in the twelfth century about the historical eleventh-century Prince of Polotsk. Vseslav was trained as a mighty warrior and was capable of using the magic arts to achieve his aims, especially as a wolf at night.
References 55
See also Werewolf

VUKUB-CAKIX
This is the name of a giant in the ancient mythology of the Quiché-Maya of Central America. Vukub-cakix is mentioned as an Earth Giant in the Popul-Vuh sacred texts as being of inflated arrogance and trying

to assume his position as sun, moon, and light. The gods Xmucane and Xpiyacoc, together with their divine sons Hun-Ahpu and Xbalanque, dealt with and overthrew Vukub-cakix.

References 169

See also giant

VULKODLAC

This is the name for a transforming Werewolf in the traditions and folklore of the Slavic people of eastern Europe. In the traditions of this region the Werewolf and vampire were interrelated in that when a Werewolf was killed it would transform into a vampire. This vampire would then also be able to reassume the shape of a wolf from time to time during its predations. This particularly terrifying monster was known as the Vulkodlac, which may be translated as "Wolf's Hair."

References 55, 89

See also vampire, Werewolf

VULPANGUE

This is the name of a monstrous serpent in the traditions and beliefs of the people of the Andes regions in Chile. The Vulpangue is variously described as a vast serpent with a head resembling that of a fox, or as a type of Hide or Cuero with a huge, circular, flat or inflated body with eyes around the edge. This creature is so predatory and dangerous to humans that no one will wash or bathe in any waters where a Vulpangue is suspected to exist.

References 134

See also Cuero, Hide, serpent

VUOKHO

This is the name of a monstrous bird in the legends of the Sami (Lapp) people of northern Scandinavia and Finland. The Vuokho is described as a vast bird with enormous wings that make a thunderous noise. It is a malicious and predatory creature that is said to inflict misery on humans. The Vuokho is the subject of a poem by the English poet Samuel Taylor Coleridge (1772–1834).

References 7

See also Roc, Thunderbird

VURM

This is an alternative spelling of the words "orm" and "worm" in the northern legends and folklore of Europe. It indicates a vast, serpent-like being that is not necessarily a reptile, but it usually has those characteristics.

References 89

See also Lambton Worm, Midgardsorm

W

WADE

This is the name of a giant in the traditions and ancient legends of England. Wade was said to live in the north of the county of Yorkshire, where he built the castles of Pickering and Mulgrave with the help of his wife, Bel. As they had only one hammer between them they had to keep throwing it from one to the other across the valleys. Sometimes the stones that she carried fell from her apron and remained piled between the two. A causeway that runs between the two was traditionally built so that she could milk her cows on the other side of the hills; however, it is a Roman road. During the eighteenth century some ancient bones, probably those of a whale, were displayed as "evidence" of the burial of the giants in the local Iron Age tomb.
References 54, 183
See also giant

WAKANDAGI

This is the name of a water monster in the traditions and beliefs of the Omaha and Mohawk Native American people of the United States. This massive being has a long serpentine body with horns on its head and legs with hooves, all of which resemble those of a deer. However, it is observed only infrequently and even then only through a mist, but it will attract and dispose of anyone who is foolish enough to travel in his region alone. The Wakandagi was said to inhabit vast lakes and stretches of the Missouri River, where it would challenge those who ventured on its waters by throwing spheres of water at them. If these were not returned they would explode, killing the occupants of the boat. On one occasion a Mohawk who thought he had encountered the Wakandagi emerging from a frozen lake was thrown from his boat and saw a fireball flying through the sky. Only initiates were said to be safe in his territory.
References 89, 134
See also monster, Wakandagi Pezi

WAKANDAGI PEZI

This is the name of a water monster in the traditions and beliefs of the Omaha Native American people of the United States. This massive being reputedly has horns on its head, but it is observed only infrequently and even then only through a mist. The Wakandagi was said to inhabit vast lakes and stretches of the Missouri River and have the respect of the people. But when the Christian missionaries came to the area there was little room for competition, and Wakandagi was renamed Wakandagi Pezi, thus demonizing the existing beliefs and subordinating them to the new religion.
References 77, 134
See also monster, Wakandagi

WAKINYAN

This is the name of a class of Thunderbird in the traditions and beliefs of the Dakota Native American people of the United States. The Wakinyan, also known as the Waukkeon, are vast beings whose enormous wings carry them far above the clouds where humans cannot view them. There are four types of Wakandagi: those with no eyes or ears that have bright blue feathers; those that have bright red feathers; those that have an enormous beak and black feathers; and those that have no beak at all but have brilliant yellow feathers. These are protective rather than predatory beings, but their calling is the sound of thunder over the horizon when they fight with the Unktehi or against the north winds.
References 77
See also Thunderbird

WALUTAHANGA

This is a water monster in the mythology and folklore of Melanesia. Walutahanga means "Eight Fathoms." The legend tells how this creature was born to a mortal woman as a female snake. Her mother hid her, fearing the father's reaction. When another child was born, Walutahanga was sent to look after the child, but the father saw the serpent and chopped up the being watching his other child, not knowing it was his daughter. After eight days of rain Walutahanga became whole again but in revenge devoured the people. Once again she was caught and chopped up. To complete her destruction Walutahanga was cooked in a stew for food. Everyone except one woman and her child ate the stew. Walutahanga reemerged and became the guardian of the two who refused to eat and brought them both good fortune.

References 38, 160

See also serpent

WANAMBI

This is an alternative name for the great Rainbow Snake in the traditions and beliefs of the Native Australian people of the Western Desert region.

References 166

See also Rainbow Serpent, Yurlunggul

WANDIL

This is the name of a giant in the folklore of the county of Wiltshire in England. The giant was described not only as immense but also as immortal and extremely malicious. He persecuted the humans viciously with his tyranny. But the gods reacted to his final act of evil on the land. Wandil had stolen the spring season and left the land in the grip of winter, so the gods ejected him from the earth and out into the heavens. There, in the constellation of Gemini, on deep winter nights when humans can see the glowing hatred of his eyes brightly staring at the earth, he will once more send the grip of freezing weather.

References 13

See also giant

WANDLEBURY GIANT

This is the name of a giant in the folklore of the county of Cambridgeshire in England. The Wandlebury Giant, also known as All Paunch, meaning "Having a Huge Belly," was described during the seventeenth century as a vast being and so huge that even his teeth were each as big as a man's head. There was an ancient chalk hill carving of the giant at Wandlebury outside the county town of Cambridge, located by an ancient earthworks and rampart of the Iron Age that had ceased to be occupied. In some legends this was called Gogmagog, after the Gogmagog Hills on which it was carved. It was still extant during the eighteenth century, as was the eleventh-century legend of the giant knight or warrior who would take on any challenge called in the earth ramparts on a moonlit night and inflict supernatural injuries on his opponent.

References 13

See also giant, Gogmagog

WANDLIMB THE LIGHTFOOTED

This is the name of an Entwife in the literary works of the English academic and author J. R. R. Tolkien (1892–1973) in The Hobbit (1937) and The Lord of the Rings (1955). The Entwives were skilled in the arts of horticulture and agriculture and inhabited the plains and valleys while their husbands were guardians of the forest trees. Wandlimb the Lightfooted was the wife of the Ent called Fimbrethil. She was killed by the Orcs when the Entwives' gardens were destroyed during the War of the Ring.

References 51

See also Ents, Fimbrethil

WANTLEY, THE DRAGON OF

This is the name of a monstrous dragon in the legends and folklore of Yorkshire in northern England. Wantley, as mentioned in the manuscript known as Percy's Reliques containing the details of the story, is conjectured as being the present-day Wharncliffe. The tale relates how the local hero, More of Mere's Hall, to combat this dragon, had a special suit of armor made that was covered in spikes. When he attacked the dragon by kicking it in its vulnerable rear, it impaled itself on the spikes trying to attack him and was vanquished.

References 20

See also dragon

WARRIOR-OF-THE-WORLD

This is an alternative name for the giant Winalagilis in the beliefs of the Kwakiutl Native American people of the northwestern coast of Canada.

References 77

See also Winalagilis

WAS

This is the name of a monster in the traditions and beliefs of the Tsimshian Native American people of the northwestern coast of the United States. The Was is said to be a monstrous being that affords his protection to the shamans, and his image is said to be located on the prow and stern of the otherworld canoes.

References 77

See also monster

WATER-BULL

This is the name of a monstrous creature in the traditions and folklore of Scotland. The Water-bull was described as a being that had the shape of a bull but was black all over its slimy, loathsome body. It inhabited isolated lochs, where it might engender split-eared progeny by ordinary cattle.

References 7

See also Corc-chluasask, Huallepén, monster, Tairbe-Uisge

WAUKHEON

This is the name of the Thunderbird in the traditions and beliefs of the Sioux Native American people of the Black Hills in the United States.
References 89
See also Thunderbird

WAUKKEON

The Waukkeon, also known as the Wakinyan, are vast Thunderbirds in the traditions and beliefs of the Dakota Native American people. Their enormous wings carry them far above the clouds, where humans cannot view them.
References 77
See also Thunderbird, Wakinyan

WAYLAND SMITH

This is the name of a giant in the traditions and folklore of England. He is derived from the Germanic and Norse Völund, of whom the same legend is told in the Waldere Manuscript dated to c. A.D. 1000. Before this period Wayland's Smithies were of great importance to local populations, who believed that the great supernatural giant was associated with the Bronze Age and Iron Age stone burial monuments. This is demonstrated by the inclusion in a charter of Berkshire dated A.D. 855 of "Weandes Smidde." On the ancient Ridgeway of Berkshire (now in Oxfordshire), to this day is the same megalithic tomb referred to, now called Wayland's Smithy. Wayland, also known as Weiland Smith and Weland Smith, is variously described as a giant or an invisible giant. It is his skills that are more clearly described. King Alfred the Great (d. A.D. 899) referred to him as "that famous and wise goldsmith Welund."

Wayland is renowned as a swordsmith and armorer, especially in the saga of *Beowulf* and the twelfth-century French chronicles of the Counts of Angoulême. In later centuries in Britain this giant was supposed to inhabit lonely ancient hill forts, cromlechs, and sacred sites, where his prowess as a blacksmith drew wary travelers. It was said that a horse left with a piece of money outside a Wayland Smithy would be found newly shod the following day. Francis Wise in his letter to Dr. Mead gives an account of this in 1738. Sir Walter Scott introduced the legend of Wayland Smith in his novel *Kenilworth* (1821), and Rudyard Kipling retold the tradition of him in *Puck of Pook's Hill* (1906). Numerous sites are credited with being the workplace of this giant, including Wayland's Pool. This is a stretch of water near Shevage Wood in Somerset, where he was said to cool the metal he forged into horseshoes for the spectral Wild Hunt. It is reported by locals that any horse will remain quietly there, even if the rider were to dismount and walk away.

References 20, 54, 64, 78, 160, 161, 183, 187
See also giant

WAZIYA

This is the name of a giant in the traditions and beliefs of the Lakota Sioux Native American people of the United States. The name "Waziya" is derived from the three words *wa*, *zi*, and *ya*, meaning "snow," "green" and "doing something with the mouth"; this giant is described as a huge being clothed in great furs. He is the guardian of the dance through the sky of the Aurora Borealis, or Northern Lights, and lives in the far north during the summer. But during the winter he travels south through the country and is said to be responsible for blowing the cold winds of winter that bring the frosts and blizzards.
References 77
See also giant

WEEWILMEKQ

This is the name of a giant water worm in the traditions and beliefs of the Algonquian Native American people of the United States. The Weewilmekq is variously described as a horned water serpent, or a sturgeon-serpent with spines, or a serpent with the horns resembling a deer's antlers. It resides in deep rushing waters such as the base of a waterfall or in the whirlpool or rapids. Its horns were greatly prized by evil sorcerers.
References 134
See also serpent, Great Horned Serpent

WEILAND SMITH, WELAND SMITH

These are alternative names for the supernatural giant Wayland Smith of English folklore and legends.
References 20, 64, 78, 161, 183
See also giant, Wayland Smith

WENDIGO

This is the name of a monster in the traditions of the Native American people of the United States. There are three different descriptions of the Wendigo, which may also be known as the Wiendigo or Windigo, according to the region of belief as follows:

1. In the beliefs of the Algonquin people the Wendigo is a transformed lost hunter who, having been lost without food, preyed upon human flesh and metamorphosed into a cannibal ogre.

2. This is the name of an amphibious monster with the body shape resembling that of an alligator but having tracks left by feet resembling those of a bear and/or cloven hooves. It was said to inhabit the Berens Lake in the region of Ontario, Canada, where it did considerable damage to the fishing nets of the community.

3. The Windigo is the name of an ogre in the traditions of the Ojibwa people that has been used as a form of Nursery bogie to control their children's behavior.
References 24, 134
See also cannibal, giant, monster, Nursery bogie, ogre

WERE-BEAR

This is the name of a variation of the Werewolf motif in the folk beliefs of various peoples in North America and in the Russian Federation.
References 24, 94
See also Werewolf

WERE-BOAR

This is the name of a variation of the Werewolf motif in the folk beliefs of various peoples in the countries of Greece and Turkey.
References 24, 94
See also Werewolf

WERE-CROCODILE

This is the name of a transformed human in the folklore of the people of Indonesia. Some evil men have the power of the *tiang maleh rupa*, a charm that will cause their metamorphosis to the form of a crocodile if they wish to do harm. They will await their human prey on the banks of a river or lake, where they will attack and devour them.

Were-crocodiles are also known in the folklore of various peoples on the continent of Africa, especially Egypt and Zambia.
References 113
See also Werewolf

WERE-DOG

This is the name of a malicious variant on the Werewolf motif in the folklore of the peoples of the island of Timor near Papua New Guinea. This is a human that has the power not only to transform himself into a dog but also to transform unsuspecting people into other animals while they sleep. The Were-dog will transform at night, leaving his bodily shell supposedly asleep while he seeks a victim. The victim's *sumangat*, or soul, will be transformed into some animal for the table such as a cow or goat. But as the head of a normal human will remain on the animal body, the Were-dog will cut this off before taking his booty back to be consumed. The following day the carcass will be prepared by the unsuspecting family for the next meals, while the grieving family of the victim will find the soul of their loved one has gone and they will die very quickly. They might even be invited to take part in the meal from the transformed soul-carcass. Should the Were-dog ever be discovered on his night prowls, then the penalty is instant death.

Were-dogs are also known in the folklore of both France and Russia but follow more strictly the Werewolf motif.
References 113
See also Macan Gadungan, Werewolf

WERE-FOX

This is the name of a variation of the Werewolf motif in the folk beliefs of various peoples in the countries of China and Japan.
References 24, 94
See also Werewolf

WERE-HARE

This is the name of a variation of the Werewolf motif in the folk beliefs of various peoples in the southern states of the United States.
References 24, 94
See also Werewolf

WERE-HYENA

This is the name of a variation of the Werewolf motif in the folk beliefs of various peoples on the continent of Africa.
References 94
See also Werewolf

WERE-JACKAL

This is the name of a variation of the Werewolf motif in the folk beliefs of various peoples on the continent of Africa.
References 94
See also Werewolf

WERE-JAGUAR

This is the variant on the Werewolf motif in the folklore of the peoples of South America.
References 7, 94
See also Jaguar-Man, Werewolf

WERE-LEOPARD

This is the name of a variation of the Werewolf motif in the folk beliefs of various peoples on the continent of Africa.
References 94
See also Werewolf

WERE-TIGER

This is the name of a variation of the Werewolf motif in the folk beliefs of various peoples on the sub-continent of India, in Malaysia, Borneo, China, and Japan.

In the folk beliefs of Java, Indonesia, certain men are deemed to possess a tiny *sarong* (waist skirt/wrap) no bigger than their big toe, which when put about their waist at night transforms to a huge yellow and black covering over their whole body. In this manner they transform into the Were-tiger and prowl their region for unwary traveling victims. This process is perpetuated because the soul of the victim, in turn, must lure another to be devoured before his soul is released.

In the folk beliefs of West Malaysia the Were-tiger preys upon livestock, especially chickens, and should a person be suspected of being a Were-tiger, he is given an emetic. If he vomits feathers, then his fate is sealed at the hands of his neighbors.

References 24, 89, 94, 113, 181
See also Macan Gaduagan, Werewolf

WEREWOLF

This is the name of a transformation of a human into a monstrous cannibal wolf. This tradition exists throughout Europe; the name "Werewolf" is derived from the Old English wer, meaning "man," added to "wolf." The phenomenon exists, however, throughout the world where the metamorphosis is into some other animal that is prevalent in the region.

The Werewolf is essentially a human form during the day but transforms, according to different versions, either at the height of the full moon, or by donning a special wolf skin, or permanently by some curse. A person may have become a Werewolf by being cursed, or being conceived under a new moon, or by having eaten certain herbs, by sleeping under the full moon on a Friday, or by drinking water that has been touched by a wolf, or by eating the brain of the wolf itself (which was practiced by sorcerers), but a person who has lived a life of bestiality may also become a Werewolf at death. Recognition of the Werewolf follows some of the traditions of the vampire. They may have eyebrows that meet between their eyes, they may have different-colored eyes or have fangs instead of canine teeth in their mouths, their fingers may be short with claw-like nails, they may have the ruddy birthmark known as the "mark of Cain," and above all they may have a very hirsute skin.

The Werewolf was dreaded for its ravenous hunger, as it would devour herds of livestock and steal children sleeping in the home; it would attack travelers at night and destroy what it could not devour. And as it was practically indestructible, there was little that could be done to guard against its predations except to find the person and deal with him through special means.

Those who transform through the skin of an animal must remove the skin at daybreak and hide it in order to resume the human guise. These kinds of Werewolves can be killed if the pelt is found and destroyed. If, however, they are seriously injured as a wolf, they may be recognized in their human shape, because the injury will be visible on their skin later,

and may die from it but be released from the curse. However, it was not easy to do any of these things, since the pelt of the monster was impervious to normal weapons and immortal in that state. Special dedications of silver in a church sacred to Saint Hubert were suggested as being efficacious.

European belief in Werewolves may be traced to the ancient times in Greece and Rome, where it was known as the versipellis, "turnskin" in Latin, during Roman times. In ancient Greece it was believed that a person could be transformed by eating the meat of a wolf that had been mixed with that of a human and that the condition was irreversible. The Greek traditional origin was from the overzealous worship of Zeus by Lycaeon, who sacrificed his child, some say by cannibalism. For this the god turned him into a wolf. A cult of wolf worshippers was established that would wear wolf masks and hunt the sacrificial being, sometimes human, through the forests, to be destroyed by them. Herodotus (485–425 B.C.) suggested that the Neuri, a tribe of sorcerers, were capable of this transformation automatically on certain feasts of the year. Later Pliny the Elder in his Historia Naturalis (A.D 77) stated that a member of the prestigious family of Antaeus remained as a Werewolf, or Lycanthrope, for nine years after having been selected by drawing lots.

During the medieval period in England after the demise of the native wolf, it was thought that witchcraft was the source of Werewolves, and numerous people were accused and put to death. In France more than 30,000 people were executed between 1520 and 1630 as suspected Werewolves. A very well documented case in Germany, published in England in 1590, was that of Peter Stubbs of Bedburg, who in the guise of a wolf raped, murdered, and ate humans, including his own family, as well as terrorizing the region for some twenty-five years until caught, tortured, and executed. After the eighteenth century the belief passed into relative decline, but many parts of Europe still retained the folklore, and a resurgence of a case appeared from time to time well into the twentieth century.

The many different names for the Werewolf in Europe are: Wer-wolf in Germany, Loup Garou in France, Vlkodlaks or Vookodlaks in Slovakia, Vircolak in other Balkan states, Vulkodlak in Russia, Lob Omem in Portugal, Lob Ombre in Spain, and Lupo Manaro in Italy. But the wolf is not the only beast that has this transformation; in France, Germany, Scandinavia, and Russia there exist tales of Were-bears, Were-cats, Were-dogs, and Were-foxes.

In the rest of the world the Werewolf may manifest as another animal, such as the Were-crocodile, Were-jackal, Were-hyena, and Were-leopard of African countries, the Were-tiger of Borneo, India, China, and

The Werewolf, a monstrous cannibal wolf (Rose Photo Archive, UK)

Japan, the Were-fox of China and Japan, the Were-boar of Greece and Turkey, the Were-mountain cat and Were-bear of the United States, and the Were-jaguar of South America.

The names of Were-beings around the world are: Bisclaveret and Bleiz-Garv and Den-Bleiz in Brittany in France, but Loup-Garou is the more usual word; Anjing Ajak and Macan Gadungan in the folklore of Java in Indonesia; Azeman in the folklore of Surinam; Legarou in the island of Haiti in the Caribbean; Sukuyan in the islands of Trinidad and Tobago in the Caribbean; Jaguar-Man in the foklore of Paraguay; Lobíson in the folk beliefs of southern Brazil and Uruguay; Tigre Capiango in the folklore of Argentina; Upir in the folklore of Russia and Vseslav in both Russia and Belorussia; Vilkatas and Vilkolakis in the folklore of Lithuania; and Zmag Ognjeni Vuk in the folklore of Bosnia and Serbia.

The basis of such prevalent traditional and folkloric beliefs may be the folk memory of prehistoric northern invaders, or the mounted, fur-clad raiders of warring tribes. The actual enmity between humans and wolves, born of the competition for food in times of famine or freezing conditions, may have given rise to the accusation of this beast being able even to infiltrate the human psyche.

There is also a recognized mental condition, Lycanthropy, in which the sufferer believes himself to be an animal and will crave uncooked food and even emulate the gait of that animal.
References 7, 20, 24, 51, 55, 61, 89, 94, 113, 133, 134, 139, 174, 181, 182
See also Anjing Ajak, Azeman, Bisclaveret, Bleiz-Garv, Den-Bleiz, Jaguar-Man, Legarou, Lob Omem, Lobíson, Loup garou, Lycanthrope, Macan Gadungan, Sukuyan, Tigre Capiango, Upir, Vilkacis, Vilkatas, Vilkolakis, Vseslav, Zmag Ognjeni Vuk

WHAPPERNOCKER
This is a creature from the folklore of lumberjacks and forest workers in the United States during the nineteenth and early twentieth centuries. The Whappernocker belongs to a group of beings affectionately known as the Fearsome Critters, whose exaggerated proportions and activities not only explained the weird noises of the lonely landscape but also provided some amusement at camps. It was originally featured in the *General History of Connecticut,* written by the Reverand Samuel Peters (1781).
References 7, 24
See also Fearsome Critters

WHIMPUS
This is a creature from the folklore of lumberjacks and forest workers in the United States during the nineteenth and early twentieth centuries. The Whimpus is described as a monster having a long, rigid snout and curious legs that were telescopic. It would stalk its human victims while they slept in the woods until it was within aiming distance, then it would extend its legs to get a good sighting and shoot a quid of clay through its snout. The Whimpus belongs to a group of beings affectionately known as the Fearsome Critters, whose exaggerated proportions and activities not only explained the weird noises of the lonely landscape but also provided some amusement at camps.
References 7, 134
See also Fearsome Critters, Hodag, Tripoderoo

WHITE CHEST
This is the name of a monstrous water serpent in the traditions and beliefs of the Araucanian people of Chile. The White Chest belongs to a class of monster known as Fox Serpents that are said to inhabit Lake Aluminé. White Chest was considered to be of enormous strength and, like the others in its class, would take and devour the livestock that went to the water's edge to drink.
References 134
See also Glyryvilu, monster, serpent

WHITE PANTHER
This is the name of a lake monster in the traditions and beliefs of the Wyandot Native American people of the United States. The White Panther was a creature that inspired a whole cult system from an event that took place on the banks of the River Huron by Lake Erie. After seeing a luminous effect on the waters followed by turbulence on the surface and simultaneous thunder and lightning strikes, the group of Wyandot hunters made offerings, and a pure white panther emerged from the waters. The hunters shot at the creature; from the wound that the arrow had made, they gathered the precious magical blood that was to become the focus of the brotherhood that they formed. With the dried blood of the White Panther in medicine bundles, the brotherhood worked a particular type of charm on the prey they hunted, both animal and human. By the eighteenth century this was described by the Europeans as witchcraft, and the brotherhood was condemned as devil worshippers. The situation was exacerbated by the slaughter of two women and an alliance with the Seneca people, and a wholesale persecution was undertaken. Eventually, any person found with the particular medicine bundle was executed, and the cult of the White Panther declined rapidly.
References 134
See also monster

WHOWHIE

This is the name of a monster in the traditions and legends of the Native Australian people in the region of the Murray River in Australia. Whowhie was described as a gigantic type of lizard that was so huge that a meal of up to thirty humans was usual. Wherever it went, great gullies and tunnels were formed by its great bulk. This monster terrorized the region at first only sporadically, then his raids became more frequent. Whowhie soon learned to evade the sentries and raid the camps for the children. Then he started to eat the sentries and the children until one night he devoured an entire village except for one small child, who escaped to tell his relatives. All the people gathered together to decide what to do. Eventually they all went to the huge cave complex where Whowhie was sleeping off his meal. They collected brushwood and lit fires that burned just in the entrance fanned by the winds for seven days until the charred, coughing, blinded Whowhie emerged through the smoke and flames. Then all the people rushed on the monster and hacked and clubbed and speared Whowhie until the monster fell and not a muscle moved ever again.

References 154
See also monster

WIENDIGO

This is an alternative name for the monster known as the Wendigo in the traditions of Native American people.

References 24, 134
See also Wendigo

WIHWIN

This is the name of a sea monster in the traditions and beliefs of the Mosquitoes subgroup of the Caraibes people of Honduras in Central America. The Wiwhin is described as resembling the shape of a horse but with enormous fangs. During the hot months the creature leaves the sea and prowls the hills, hunting its human prey, but it returns to the sea when the rains come.

References 134
See also Kelpy, monster

WIKATCHA, WI KATCHA

This is the name of a creature that is a type of underwater cat in the traditions and beliefs of the Creek Native American people of the southern United States. This water monster inhabited a stretch of water near the town of Coosa and mated with one of the women from the town. When she had the child, her family was intent upon killing it and so she went to Wikatcha, who raised a flood so devastating that the entire place and most of its inhabitants were engulfed.

Those who escaped founded the new town of Tulsa, while the monstrous Wikatcha took the woman and child, who were never seen again.

References 77
See also Michi-Pichoux, monster

WIKRAMADATTA

This is the name of a giant in the traditions and legends of Java, Indonesia. Wikramadatta, who was the king of all the giants in the region, was regarded as a wise being. He demanded from the king of the island that he should make tribute by sending all the weapons of battle to him. When King Jamajaya complied and sent the instruments of battle to Wikramadatta, the result was that no one could threaten anyone on the island, and peace was thus restored.

References 113
See also giant

WILD BEAST OF GÉVAUDAN

This is the name of a monster in the folklore of eighteenth-century France. The Wild Beast of Gévaudan was described as looking something like a hyena with long legs, a shaggy coat, and glaring eyes, but it was widely believed to be a Werewolf. It roamed the countryside reportedly during the period 1764–1765, when it was said to have killed and consumed over a hundred people in the region.

References 94
See also monster, Werewolf

WILD BOAR OF ERYMANTHUS

See Erymanthean Boar

WILDMAN, WILD MAN OF THE WOODS

This is the name of a humanoid being in the legends and traditions from the thirteenth to the sixteenth centuries in Europe, especially England. The Wildman, also known as the Woodwose, Woodhouse, Wooser, and Ooser in English texts, was described as a gigantic, hairy, club-wielding, skin-clad humanoid, often with green hair, inhabiting the forests. But the Wildman was not a giant in the traditional sense. In the medieval culture he represented the antithesis of the Christian establishment. He was the untamed nature that had existed before the advent of Christianity, and to the Christians was representative of the "Other" that came to be associated with noble savagery. In this guise Charles VI of France and five of his nobles performed a masque for the court in 1392. Unfortunately, their costumes caught alight from a torch, and four of the noble performers died in their costumes.

In some traditions the Wildmen were bestial cannibals who abducted children to be devoured,

A wild man on coat of arms, portrayed as a noble guardian (Rose Photo Archive, UK)

such as the one depicted in *The Faerie Queene,* by the English Elizabethan poet Edmund Spenser (1552?–1599). During this period of the great European explorations, much of this imagery of the Wildman was conflated with the descriptions of the new cultures visited. Consequently, such beings as Caliban in the English playwright William Shakespeare's (1554–1616) *The Tempest* (1611), and the Yahoos, featured in the work *Gulliver's Travels* (1726) by the politician and author Jonathan Swift (1667–1745), were a parody of this new culture based on the European concept of the Wildman.

The Wildman appeared in literature and art for a considerable time, gradually resuming a folkloric role. However, the Wildman and his counterpart, the Wildwoman, are still a recognized feature in the heraldic repertoire of Britain, where their status as noble guardians is portrayed on coats of arms.
References 5, 7, 26, 128, 174
See also Caliban, Faun, Gruagach, Sasquatch, satyr, Yeti

WINALAGILIS
This is the name of a giant in the traditions and beliefs of the Kwakiutl Native American people of Canada. Winalagilis, also known as Warrior-of-the-World, travels forever in a mighty canoe. He is associated with spirits that return the dead to the world of the living.
References 77
See also giant

WINDIGO
There are two creatures that are known by this name.

1. This is a creature from the folklore of lumberjacks and forest workers, especially in Wisconsin and Minnesota in the United States, during the nineteenth and early twentieth centuries. The Windigo belongs to a group of beings affectionately known as the Fearsome Critters, whose exaggerated proportions and activities not only explained the weird noises of the lonely landscape but also provided some amusement at camps.

2. This is an alternative name for the monster known as the Wendigo in the traditions of Native American people.
References 7, 24, 134
See also Fearsome Critters, Wendigo

WISHPOOSH
This is the name of a monster in the traditions and beliefs of the Nez Perce Native American people of Washington State. Wishpoosh is described as a gigantic beaver with enormous claws that inhabited a vast lake. The monster wanted to be the sole being that fished there and repelled or devoured any other creature that came. Eventually, the Nez Perce people were so desperate that they asked the trickster culture-hero Coyote for help. The trickster went to the lake to fish, armed with a massive spear tied to him and a sharp knife. Sure enough, the monster emerged, and there ensued a great battle between Wishpoosh and Coyote. As they thrashed in the water, the lake was churned and widened, then as the monster tried to shake him off Coyote speared and attached himself to Wishpoosh. The monster raced off down the river that drained the lake but to no avail; Coyote was firmly attached. As the pair sped to the sea, great chasms and gorges were created. In the sea the exhausted monster swallowed whales to revitalize himself and swallowed Coyote, who had turned himself into a floating log. Once inside the monster, Coyote returned to his own shape and stabbed at the heart of Wishpoosh from the inside until it was dead. Then the trickster created out of the vast body the new races of people—the Chinook, the Klickitat, the Nez Perce, and the Yakima—to populate the western region.
References 47, 133
See also monster

WITICO
This is the name of giant cannibal beings in the traditions and folk beliefs of the Native American people of North Dakota, Michigan, and Wisconsin in the United States and from Manitoba, Ontario, Saskatchewan, Canada, as well as the Naskapi and Montagnais. The diaries of the Hudson Bay Company give an interesting account of this phenomenon dating from the early eighteenth century.

There are two classes of Witico:

1. The first are human beings who have transformed by having eaten human flesh in times of hardship or through isolation in the subzero temperatures of the wilderness. They could also have transformed through having dreamed of the evil spirits North and the Ice. These people, whose metamorphosis is not so apparent, may request their relatives to put them to death sooner than continue as a monster evicted by their people.

2. Witico are also predatory giants whose filthy bodies and malicious countenance cover an interior of solid ice. They hunt down humans in the wilderness and devour them.

Both types of Witico are dangerous in the extreme. They are a threat to the communities' survival in the harsh conditions, and all must be on their guard. The manner in which a Witico may be defeated is by magic ritual, by the smearing of human excreta, which will disorient them and even take away their sight, but the best means is to avoid the places that they inhabit.
References 77
See also cannibal, giant, monster

WIVERN

This is an alternative spelling for the Wyvern, a class of dragon in European legends and heraldry.
References 20, 5
See also dragon, Wyvern

WIVRE

This is the name of a monstrous reptile in the traditions and legends of France. The Wivre, also known as the Guivre, is very similar to the Vouivre, the French form of the Wyvern. The Wivre was described as being like a dragon that did not have wings, but unlike others it would only attack something that was wearing clothing. Consequently, the way in which to avoid attack was to disrobe, and the Wivre would flee.
References 7, 89
See also dragon, Gargouille, Vouivre, Wyvern

WIWILEMEKW

This is the name of a sea monster in the traditions and beliefs of the Maliseet-Passamaquoddy Native American people of southeastern Canada and northeastern United States. The Wiwilemekw is described as having a shape resembling that of a crocodile but is said to have enormous horns. It is these horns that hold all the power of the creature, and the scrapings of these would endow the brave person who managed to take the parings with their strength and powers.
References 77
See also monster

WIZARD'S SHACKLE

This is an alternative name for a grotesque, leech-like creature known as the Burach Bhadi in the folklore of Scotland.
References 7, 89
See also Burach Bhadi

WODE WORM OF LINTON

This is the name of a monstrous creature in the legends of the North of England. The hero managed to stave its rampaging of the region by attacking it and, while its mouth was open, thrusting a burning block of peat down its gullet. Once lit, peat is very difficult to extinguish, and the monster was burned to death from the inside out.
References 89
See also Worm, monster

WODEHOUSE

This is an alternative name for the Wildman of European traditions and legends.
References 7, 128, 174
See also Wildman

WOGLOG

This is the name of a giant in the traditions and folklore of England. Woglog was described as an enormous giant that spent much of his time rampaging around the countryside, terrorizing the inhabitants, and destroying anything that got in his way, such as Westbridge Pier. The story told in the publication *The Tale of Tommy Trip* (1767), probably by John Newbery, tells how this malicious giant was eventually tamed by Tommy Trip aided by his dog, Jouler. When Woglog was subdued, he then became the epitome of the gracious neighbor, taking upon his shoulders, like a latter-day Saint Christopher, those who would cross swollen streams, becoming so moral that he even chastised gamblers. This is a moralizing tale and may have been used in much the same way as the giants who were Nursery bogies.
References 182
See also Christopher (Saint), giant, Nursery bogie

WOINUNGGUR

This is a regional name for the Rainbow Serpent in the Dreamtime mythology of Native Australian people.
References 133
See also Rainbow Serpent

WOLLUNQUA, WALLUNQUAIN

This is the name for the Great Rainbow Snake in the traditions and beliefs of the Warramunga people of Australia. Wollunqua was so vast that he was able to emerge from his waterhole and travel many miles without his tail leaving the place he had emerged from. However, one legend tells how on such an occasion the being known as Mumumanugara came out of the extended body of Wollunqua and demanded that they return, laying into Wollunqua as he did so. The serpent complied after coiling around and retrieving Mumumanugara. This has since become integral in the art and ceremonies for the initiation of the Warramunga people.
References 38
See also Rainbow Serpent

WONUNGUR

This is a regional name for the Rainbow Serpent in the Dreamtime mythology of Native Australian people.
References 133
See also Rainbow Serpent

WOODWOSE

This is an alternative name for the Wildman of European traditions and legends.
References 7, 128, 174
See also Wildman

WOOSER

This is an alternative name for the Wildman of European traditions and legends.
References 7, 128, 174
See also Wildman

WORM

This word is used in the traditions and legends of the British Isles for a class of dragon. The name is derived from the Norse word for "dragon," which is usually rendered as *worm, orm,* or *vurm,* and is found mostly in the northern and eastern regions that were invaded by the Vikings over a thousand years ago. The Worm is generally described as having a vast, serpentine body with a head shaped somewhere between that of a horse and a dragon, sometimes with horns, always with huge, protruding eyes and fangs. It may breathe fire or stinking fumes. Whatever the description, a Worm is always malicious and of totally evil intent, unlike the dragon, which may have redeeming features, even in Western legends. The Worm had less supernatural attributes and was more easily dispatched by a hero than was a dragon, despite its ability to move amazingly fast. This monster inhabited the most foul of swamps and dank places, sometimes the lakes and wells (as with the Lambton Worm), or even the sea.
References 89
See also dragon, Kitchi-at'Husis, Laidley Worm, Lambton Worm, Lindorm, Loathly Worm, Midgardsorm, Orm, Peiste, Stoorworm, Vurm, Weewilmekq, Wode Worm of Linton

WOROMBI

This is a regional name for the Rainbow Serpent in the Dreamtime mythology of Native Australian people.
References 133
See also Rainbow Serpent

WRNACH

This is the name of a giant in the traditions and legends of Wales. Wrnach features in the legend of Culhwch and Olwen in the Welsh *Mabinogion* and is the one who possesses a mighty sword that Culhwch has been set the task of obtaining before he can marry Olwen. Culhwch manages to trick the mighty giant and kill him and thus gained his sword.
References 54, 128, 139
See also giant, Ysbaddaden

WRY FACE

This is the name of a giant in the beliefs and folklore of the Iroquois and Onondaga Native Americans of the northeastern United States. His name, Dehotgohsgayeh, may be translated as "Split-faced

Being" or "Wry-face," for this giant is reputedly ugly; his body is red on one side and black on the other.
References 77
See also Dehotgohsgayeh

WUCHOWSEN

This is the name of a gigantic bird in the traditions and beliefs of the Maliseet-Passamaquoddy Native American people of Maine in the northeastern United States. The Wuchowsen is an enormous creature that, even though he stays still most of the time on his rock at the furthest most northerly point of the world, the slightest movement of his feathers causes winds across the world. He caused so much distress that ultimately Glooscap, the culture-hero, had to bring Wuchowsen under control.
References 77
See also Roc

WULGARU

This is the name of a gigantic artificial humanoid being in the traditions and beliefs of the Native Australian people. The legend tells how a man called Djarapa took living wood directly from a tree and made the shape of a gigantic human. By carving it to resemble human characteristics, such as giving it ball and socket joints of stone and wood, a large mouth with shards of flint for teeth, with pebble eyes and human hair, he hoped his magic would bring his Wulgaru to life to do his work. All day and night he chanted his ritual magic, but on the second day, when nothing happened, he kicked the gigantic thing and walked away in disgust. But as he walked back to the village, he heard strange thumping noises that mimicked his own footsteps and the noise of wood grating against stones. He went along the path through the high grasses and, when he reached the end, turned on his heel to see what followed him so closely. There was the Wulgaru, with such an evil look on its face that suddenly Djarapa was terrified of the thing he had made from a tree not long before. He ran as fast as he could, but wherever he went he could not get away until he came to the river. He went back to a clump of trees carefully, making sure that the only visible tracks left were those to the river. As he hid, he saw the pursuing Wulgaru go straight into the river and keep on walking until it was totally submerged. He breathed a sigh of relief, but as he did so a ripple started at the other side and the giant emerged, having walked across the bottom of the riverbed unscathed and continued straight on. The horrified Djarapa ran to tell the villagers, who became terrified of the Wulgaru. And that is how the people came to have the giant who can never be disposed of by any means, who comes at night to punish and devour

those who break the tribal laws but leaves those who are good unharmed.
References 153
See also giant, Golem, Talos

WULUNGU, WULUNGEN
These are alternative names for the Rainbow Snake in the Native Australian Dreamtime legends.
References 89
See also Rainbow Serpent, Yulunggur

WYVERN
This is the name of a fabulous creature in the legends and folklore of Europe. Images of the Wyvern were frequently to be seen in the bestiaries of medieval Europe, especially in England and France. The creature is described as having the body of a serpent, the head of a dragon, the wings of a bat, and just two legs, while its long serpent's tail was usually barbed. This monster was said to be predatory and to destroy whatever it came upon. Today its image is mostly seen in the coats of arms as a part of the heraldic repertoire of Europe.
References 5, 7, 20, 68, 78, 89
See also dragon, serpent

Today the Wyvern is mostly seen as a part of the heraldic repertoire of Europe. (Rose Photo Archive, UK)

X

XAN

This is the name of a fabulous monster or beast in the mythology of the Kicher people of Guatemala. The Xan is mentioned in the sacred texts of the *Popul Vuh*.
References 169
See also monster

XANTHOS, XANTHUS

This is the name of a horse in the classical mythology of Greece and Rome. Xanthos is one of a pair of horses, the other being Balios, which were the offspring of Podarge, one of the Harpies, from her union with Aeolus or Zephyrus, the spirit of the winds. Xanthos and Balios were given by the sea god Poseidon/Neptune to Pelops to draw his chariot through the skies. The two horses later pulled the chariot of the Greek hero Achilles during the Trojan Wars. When the hero Patroclus was killed and Achilles considered that Xanthos and Balios could have saved him, Xanthos chided Achilles for questioning the decisions of the gods and prophesied that Achilles would also be slain soon by a god. When the otherwise immortal Achilles was hit by an arrow in his one mortal place, the heel, the Erinyes struck dumb Xanthos to prevent further tragic prophesies.
References 7, 24, 89, 133, 139, 178
See also Balios, Erinyes, Harpy, Horses of the Sun, Podarge

XELHUA

This is the name of a giant in the Aztec mythology of Mexico. He is said to be one of a group of six giants who, after climbing the mountain of Tlaloc, survived the primordial flood. In reverence for this event, Xelhua set about constructing the great pyramid of Cholula.
References 169
See also giant

XEXEU

This is the name of a class of gigantic bird in the traditions and mythology of the Cashmawa people of South America. The Xexeu are said to be responsible for assembling great billowing black clouds in the heavens, sometimes so violently that massive storms are created.
References 24
See also Ngani-vatu, Raicho, Thunderbird

XIANG YAO

This is the name of a hideous monster in the traditions and folklore of China. Xiang Yao is described as having the body of a serpent and nine human heads and, wherever he goes in the company of the black dragon, Gong-Gong, their excrement makes lakes and rivers into fetid swamps.
References 125, 160
See also Gong-Gong, monster

XÓLOTL

This is the name of a monstrous dog in the Aztec mythology of Mexico. Xólotl is described as a celestial gigantic creature whose head faced in the opposite direction from its legs and feet; its ears pointed in all directions according to whim. This hideous being chased and set its fangs into the sun each day and dragged it down into the underworld, leaving the earth in darkness. Some accounts tell of Xólotl giving fire to humans, but his ambivalence toward them was more likely to bring disaster than benefits.
References 133
See also Aapep

401

Y

YAGIM

This is the name of a sea monster in the traditions and beliefs of the Kwakiutl Native American people in northwestern Canada. The Yagim, also known as the Iak Im, is described as a creature that resembles a vast shark, but in the ceremonies of the Tsetseka, it is represented by a huge, red-fringed mask. The Yagim is deemed to be responsible for all manner of malicious acts against fishermen and will capsize their boats and devour the occupants.

References 77
See also monster

YAHOO

The Yahoos, featured in the work *Gulliver's Travels* (1726) by the politician and author Jonathan Swift (1667–1745), were degraded, humanlike creatures that served as the slaves of the Houyhnhnms. They are described as having bare skin and thick, rough hair on the tops of their heads, beards like that of a goat, and shaggy fur on their chests, the ridge of their back, and on their legs, which ended in huge claws. They were agile creatures that generally walked on all fours but could stand on their hind legs and could also climb trees like squirrels, and the rocks of the mountains where they lived.

References 63, 177
See also centaur, Houyhnhnms

YALE, YALI

This is the name of a fabulous beast of European legend, also known as the Centicore, Eale, or Jall, said to inhabit the Middle East and India. It was originally mentioned by Pliny the Elder in his *Historia Naturalis* (A.D. 77), then in the Alexandrian *Physiologus,* and later copied copiously in the bestiaries of medieval Europe. The Yale, whose name may have been derived from the Hebrew *ya-el,* meaning "mountain goat," was described variously as having the black or brown body of a goat but was the size of a horse, covered in multicolored spots, with the tail and jaws of a wild boar with huge horns. Other versions credit it with the feet of a unicorn, or the head of a goat and the tail of an elephant. Whatever the description, it is its horns that distinguish it, for these were said to be not only exceptionally long but able to be adjusted in direction from front to back facing according to the defense of itself in battle. The Yale became a symbol of proud defense and was taken into the heraldic repertoire of Europe, where it appears as one of the heraldic beasts of the Queen of England and other ancient noble families. There is some conjecture that the Yale could have been derived from the Indian water buffalo, which has the ability to move its horns forward one after the other when threatened.

References 7, 10, 14, 89, 148, 185
See also unicorn

YANNIG, YANNIG AN OD

This is the name of a sea monster in the traditions and folklore of the Breton people of Brittany in northwestern France. The Yannig spends the daylight hours in the sea, but after dark it comes to the shore to track down its human prey. It may be heard to call like an owl, and anyone answering it will give away their location, whereupon the Yannig will be immediately behind them and will devour them instantly.

References 128
See also monster

YAQUARU

This is the name of a monster in the traditions and folklore of Argentina. The Yaquaru is a water monster that inhabits the freshwater and rivers.

References 134
See also monster

YARA-MA-YHA-WHO

This is the name of a monstrous humanoid in the folklore of the Native Australian people. The Yara-ma-yha-who are described as having an enormous belly on an otherwise small body with legs. The head is vast with huge glowing eyes but is taken up mostly by the huge jaws that are so wide that they can accommodate swallowing a child whole. These horrifying beings have long, tentacle-like fingers with suckers on the end, which they attach to their prey to haul them to their gaping mouths. The Yara-ma-yha-who can be seen quite easily, for they are red from head to toe, but they hide in the trees during the day looking for disobedient children. Once the child has been sucked of its blood through the vile tentacles, it is swallowed into the stomach through the enormous mouth. However, there is still a possibility for escape, for the Yara-ma-yha-who will then go and drink vast quantities of water, and the contents of its stomach will flow out of its mouth onto the ground. Then when it goes to sleep, any clever being that has "played possum" (simulated death) will be left on the ground while the Yara-ma-yha-who sleeps. Then they can make their escape. However, any child that is not so clever will immediately be swallowed again and be regurgitated in the growing shape of a Yara-ma-yha-who. The Yara-ma-yha-who is, of course, a Nursery bogie with which parents threaten their children into good behavior.

References 153

See also monster, Nursery bogie

YATA GARASU

This is the name of a gigantic bird in the traditions and mythology of Japan. The Yata Garasu is described as an enormous black bird resembling a crow but having three legs. This massive bird is the messenger for all the deities in the heavens.

References 7

See also Hugin, Muninn

YEHWE ZOGBANU

This is the name of a giant in the mythology of the people of the West African state of Dahomey. Yehwe Zogbanu is described as an enormous humanoid having thirty horns on his head and body. He is a highly predatory giant who tracks down and kills human hunters foolish enough to enter his territory.

References 24

See also giant, Sasabonsam

YEITSO

This is the name of a terrifying giant in the traditions and legends of the Hopi and Navajo Native American peoples of the United States. Yeitso was a fearful, predatory giant whose body was covered in scales. He was one of the primordial giants who hunted the humans as their prey. The primordial twins Nayenygami and Tobadzistsini went to the sun god for help in dealing with the monstrous Yeitso and two others named Teelget and Tsenahale. The sun god gave them magic arrows of rainbow,

sunbeams, sheet, and chain lightning, and when they returned to the earth through the sky-hole they were able to use these to kill Yeitso and the other monsters.

References 78, 166

See also monster, Teelget, Tsenahale

YELLOW CEDAR BARK OGRE

This is the name of an ogre in the traditions and beliefs of the Nootka Native American people. The traditional tale tells how a young man gives his wife some yellow cedar bark, instructing her to make a robe for him out of it. Then he lazily wanders into the mountains, where, to his horror as well as amusement, he is stalked by a green, slimy ogre that calls his name. When his life is spared, he remains in the mountains to make a traditional fast and pray. On his return the yellow cedar bark robe that his wife has made takes on a new significance and at the coming Wolf Ritual he wears this and a mask he has fashioned in the image of the ogre.

References 77

See also ogre

YELLOW DRAGON

This is the name of a class of dragon in the traditions and mythology of China. There are two notable Yellow Dragons in the Chinese mythology, the first is revered for bringing the eight trigrams of the I Ching; the second was a monstrous predatory being that was dispatched by one of the Eight Immortal Holy Ones named Lu Tung-pin.

References 89, 139

See also Oriental Dragon, Svara

YENRISH

This is the name of a water monster in the traditions and beliefs of the Huron-Wyandot Native American people in the northeastern United States. The Yenrish is described as a type of water lion that inhabited the depths of Lake Erie.

References 134

See also monster

YERO

This is a regional name for the Rainbow Serpent in the Dreamtime mythology of the Native Australian people.

References 133

See also Rainbow Serpent

YETI

This is the condensed name from the Sherpa word *yeh-teh*, an anthropoid monster in the traditions and beliefs of the people of Tibet and Nepal. The concept of this elusive, giant, hairy humanoid existing in the mountains was first recorded in 1938 and made popular in Europe by Eric Shipton's Everest expedition on the Menlung glacier in 1951, and the later Hillary-Tensing conquest party also reported evidence in 1953. The name "Abominable Snowman" was given by the European explorers and mountaineers to the creature. However, in the region there is more than one type, and they are known by three separate names: Dzu-teh, Meh-Teh, and Yeh-Teh, the latter being the one most commonly used. These names are used according to size and description, the Yeh-teh being described as smaller, even though gigantic, and more bear-like in appearance than the other two. There has been considerable evidence for the existence of these beings from photographs of enormous footprints in the upper Everest reaches, to actual rust-colored, hairy skins purporting to be the cranium of such a creature. Much discussion has taken place as to their origins and possible form of existence, but nothing has ever been conclusive.

References 78, 94

See also Abominable Snowman, Bigfoot, Chorti, Dzu-teh, Fsti capcaki, Hairy-Man, Meh-Teh, Mountain Man, Nee-gued, Wildman, Yeh-Teh

YFRIT

This is an alternative spelling for Afrit, which is one classification of the five types of the powerful Jinns of Muslim and Arabic mythology and folklore.

References 20, 38, 63, 64, 74, 89, 124, 146, 160, 161

See also Afrit

YIN CHU

This is the name of a fabulous bird in the traditions and legends of China. It is a form of the Lwan and is described as looking something like a much larger and more beautiful and graceful type of pheasant. However, this bird is capable of changing its body color and is known by different names accordingly. As the Yin Chu, it is the black form of the Lwan.

References 81

See also Fung, Hwa Yih, Lwan, Phoenix, To Fu, Yu Siang

YING LUNG

This is the name of a dragon in the traditions and legends of China. It is also known as the Proper Conduct Dragon. This dragon differs from the usual Chinese dragons in that it is the only one portrayed with wings. This dragon, in keeping with the others, is a guardian of the waters of the earth and associated with the clouds of heaven.

References 81, 89

See also Hai Riyo

YMIR

This is the name of the primordial giant in the Norse mythology of Scandinavia. Ymir, also known as Aurgelmir, was engendered from the ice of the far north when the flames of the fire kingdom Muspelheim melted the ice in the frozen kingdom of Niflheim. At the same time, the great cosmic cow Audhumla emerged from the ice and started to lick the melt waters from the giant, and another giant emerged, called Buri. Ymir was nourished by the milk that came from her four vast udders, and as he grew in strength he produced the Frost Giants from where his own limbs touched. A male and female emerged from his armpit, and his legs produced his six-headed son. All of these mated and the son of Buri, named Bor, took Ymir's daughter, Bestla. Together these two produced the Aesir gods Odin, Vili, and Ve. These three were discontent and immediately started to wage war on the giants. They killed Ymir and put his body in the abyss called Ginnungagap. There, as his blood flowed, it became the rivers and seas and then a great flood in which all but one of the giants, Bergelmir, drowned. Then the gods made the earth from Ymir's flesh, mountains from his bones, rocks from his teeth, heavens from his skull, trees and vegetation from his hair, and clouds from his brain. Then the gods created their new home, called Asgard, and Midgard for mortals, which they fenced with Ymir's eyelashes or eyebrows.

References 20, 24, 61, 78, 125, 127, 133, 139, 166, 169

See also Audhumla, Aurgelmir, Bergelmir, Bestla, Frost Giants, giant, Purush

YN FOLDYR GASTEY

This is an alternative name for the Manx semisupernatural giant, known as the Fenodyree, in the legends and folklore of the Isle of Man in the British Isles. Yn Foldyr Gastey, which means the "Nimble Mower," is described as a huge hairy being that is amazingly strong and very ugly who does farmwork, especially reaping, through the night.

References 24, 25, 64, 111, 152

See also Fenodyree

YOFUNE-NUSHI

This is the name of a sea serpent in the traditions and beliefs of Japan. This gigantic, monstrous creature was both predatory and destructive, preying upon the fishermen and the inhabitants of the islands remorselessly. The Yofune-Nushi was placated by the local fishing population by sacrificing a maiden on the thirteenth of every June to its lair under the island of Oki. Eventually, the turn came of the heroine Tokoyo, who took with her a dagger with which she stabbed out the eyes of the monster, and while it was thrashing in agony she was able to kill it.

References 113
See also serpent

YOH SHOH

This is a name given for a fabulous bird in the traditions and mythology of China. The Yoh Shoh are the chicks of the fabulous bird known as the Feng Hwang.
References 81
See also Feng Hwang, Phoenix

YOUDIC DOGS

This is a class of monstrous dogs in the traditions and folklore of the Breton people of Britanny in northwestern France. These dogs are described as enormous beasts that inhabit the swamps known as the Youdic in that region. They rampage over the countryside and terrify any belated lonely travelers.
References 128
See also Black dogs

YOWIE

This is the name of a monster in the Dreamtime mythology of the Native Australian people. The Yowie is described as a gigantic, hairy, predatory being.
References 78
See also Bigfoot

YPOTAMIS

This is the name of a fabulous animal in the travelers' folklore of medieval Europe. The Ypotamis is described as an amphibious being that is part horse and part human, hunting humans as its prey. It is almost certainly a distortion of the hippopotamus.
References 7

YSBADDADEN, YSBADDADEN BENCAW, YSPADDADEN PENKAWR

This is the name of the king of the giants in the traditions and Celtic legends of Britain. Ysbaddaden, also known as Isbaddaden, appears in the legend of Culhwch and Olwen in the Welsh *Mabinogion,* in which the hero Culhwch wants to marry Ysbaddaden's daughter, Olwen. First they have to get to see the giant who is in his mighty castle guarded by nine gates and guards with mastiffs. Culhwch and his companions manage to get past them, and when they meet the chief giant, Ysbaddaden, he is so vast that he has to have his eyelids raised on pitchforks by servants so that he can see them. However, the giant is loath to let him marry Olwen and therefore sets him many *anoethu* (impossible tasks) to complete. Culhwch calls upon his cousin, King Arthur, to help him. The tasks include gaining the shears, razor, and comb from between the ears of the gigantic boar Twrch Trwyth for grooming the giant's hair, and gaining the tusk from the mighty boar Ysgithyrwyn with which to give him a shave. The accounts of these hunts, which take place across southern Ireland, Wales, and England, are savage, with many knights and heroes killed before the implements are taken from the boars. When Culhwch and the hunters return, the giant is shaved and slaughtered by Culhwch and Goreu, whose brothers were slain by the giant.
References 54, 78, 128, 139, 166, 183
See also giant, Twrch Trwyth

YSGITHYRWYN

This is the name of gigantic boar in the traditions and Celtic legends of Britain. Ysgithyrwyn appears in the legend of Culhwch and Olwen in the Welsh *Mabinogion,* in which the hero Culhwch wants to marry Ysbaddaden's daughter, Olwen. The giant Ysbaddaden sets him many *anoethu* (impossible tasks) to complete. The tasks include gaining the tusk from the mighty boar Ysgithyrwyn with which to give Ysbaddaden a shave, and gaining the shears, razor, and comb from between the ears of the gigantic boar Twrch Trwyth for grooming the giant's hair. Culhwch calls upon his cousin, King Arthur, to help him, and it is King Arthur's own dog, Cafall, that brings the monster to bay and thus gains the tusk.
References 7, 139
See also Twrch Trywth, Ysbaddaden

YU LUNG, YÜ LUNG

This is the name of a monstrous fish in the traditions and legends of China. The Yu Lung is described as a dragon but having the head and fins of a gigantic fish. It had been a celestial carp, but when it leapt the Dragon's Gate waterfall it was transformed into the dragon that became the emblem of examination success.
References 89
See also Oriental dragon

YU SIANG

This is the name of a fabulous bird in the traditions and legends of China. It is a form of the Lwan and is described as looking something like a much larger and more beautiful and graceful type of pheasant. However, this bird is capable of changing its body color and is known by different names accordingly. As the Yu Siang, it is the blue form of the Lwan.
References 81
See also Fung, Hwa Yih, Lwan, Phoenix, To Fu

YULU YULARA

This is the name of a giant in the Dreamtime mythology of the Native Australian people. The

Ysbaddaden the giant is so vast that he has to have his eyelids raised on pitchforks so that he can see. (Rose Photo Archive, UK)

legend of Yulu Yulara explains the Native Australian knowledge of coal long before the arrival of the Europeans to their land. Yulu Yulara was an ancestral giant who was rather flamboyant in every way. When he decided to attend a ceremony on the far side of Australia, he also thought he would signal his coming to his hosts. So at every stop that he made he lit a huge fire until he arrived. But behind him Yulu Yulara had left too many fires of too many trees that continued to burn and denuded the whole of the region beyond the Flinders Range. These burnt trees became the charred deposits and coal under the ground. When mining took place in this area, the legend proved an indication that fires had taken place, for vast deposits of charred, fossilized wood and coals were found.

References 159

See also giant

YULUNGGU, YURLUNGUR, YURLUNGGUR

This is the name of the Rainbow Snake or Rainbow Serpent in the Dreamtime mythology of the Yolngu

Native Australian people of Arnhem Land in northern Australia. Yulunggu, also known as Julunggul, Julungsul, and Wulungu, was a vast being that inhabited deep water pools. A legend tells how the Wawalug/Wawilak sisters, named Boalere and Misilgoe, came from the south, naming plants and camping by the pool of Yulunggu without realizing he was there. They tried to cook on their fire to give food to their girl and boy, but everything jumped away and into the pool. Then the Rainbow Serpent caused a great flood, and they realized what was wrong and started to chant and dance to keep Yulunggu from their children. But soon they were exhausted, and when they slept the Rainbow Serpent swallowed up all four of them. Then he rose in the heavens and boasted to his brethren assembled there what he had done. But swallowing humans was not approved, and he descended to the earth and regurgitated them. This is reenacted as part of the traditional rites of puberty for boys and girls.

References 38, 78, 89, 125, 133, 153, 166
See also Rainbow Serpent

YÜ-MIN KUO YAN

This is the name of a race of monstrous people in the legends and folklore of China. The Yü-Min Kuo Yan are described as hatching from eggs and having their humanoid bodies completely covered in feathers like the bodies of birds with wings instead of arms. They are supposed to be very shy and retreat when anyone approaches. The Yü-Min Kuo Yan appear in the volumes of the *Great Imperial Encyclopedia* and were no doubt derived from exaggerated travelers' tales in much the same way as those that influenced the medieval bestiaries of Europe.

References 181
See also I-Mu Kuo Yan, Nieh-Erh Kuo Yan, San-Shen Kuo Yan, San-Shou Kuo Yan, Ting Ling Kuo Yan

YURLUNGGUR, YURLUNGGUL

These are alternative spellings for Yulunggu, the great Rainbow Snake in the Dreamtime mythology of the Native Australian people.

References 78
See also Bulaing

YURUPARI

This is the name of a class of monstrous being in the traditions and beliefs of the Tupinamba people of Brazil. They are mostly described as a type of ogre that inhabits deserted places and the forests. They are to be avoided by humans, as they are particularly malicious.

References 139
See also ogre

Z

ZÄGH

This is the name of a fabulous bird in the legends of Islamic countries. The Zägh is described as a gigantic bird, somewhat similar in appearance to the Roc, but having a human face and the ability to speak human languages. It is mentioned in Islamic literature and poetry.
References 89
See also Alkonost, Angka, Bahri, Garuda, Harpy, Parthenope, Podarge, Ptitsy-Siriny, Roc, Siren, Sirin, Solovei Rakhmatich, Unnati, Zägh

ZAMZUMIN

This is the name of a race of giants mentioned in the Hebrew texts that now comprise the Old Testament of the Christian Bible.
References 13
See also Anakim, Enim, giant, Noah, Zamzumin, Zuzim

ZANGARRÓN, EL

This is the name of a giant in the traditions and folklore of Spain. El Zangarrón is described as a vast humanoid giant with a huge head and wearing a pointed, floppy cap and rough peasant garb. His face is rough with warts and he has a thick, black beard, protruding hooked nose, deep, dark eye sockets, and piercing eyes under thick eyebrows. His mouth lolls open, ready to bite or swallow the unwary. The tradition relates how in the town of Sanjoles del Vino, in Zamora, the inhabitants who had prayed to Saint Esteban did not have their request fulfilled. So they gathered in the town square in front of the saint's statue and pelted it with stones. Suddenly, El Zangarrón appeared and terrified them from their abuse and chased them away. In celebration of this, a Cabezudo effigy of the giant with a vast pig's bladder chases the young people of the town in the parades for the feast of Saint Stephen every 26 December.
References 182
See also Cabezudo, giant, Town giant

ZARATAN

This is an alternative name for the Aspidochelone of European medieval travelers' lore; this name is used mostly in the Middle East, especially in the *Physiologus*, a manuscript said to have been written in Alexandria, Egypt, about 200 B.C. Since that time the Zaratan has entered Arab and Islamic legends through the work of the ninth-century zoologist Al-Jahiz, later refuted by the Spanish naturalist and author Miguel Palacios in his version of the *Book of Animals*, and thence copied into a ninth-century Anglo-Saxon bestiary in England as a symbol of the devil. This was followed by a further mention in the thirteenth-century *Wonders of Creation* by the Al Qaswini in Persia (now Iran) and later used as a metaphor for Satan in the work *Paradise Lost* by the English Puritan John Milton (1608–1674). The descriptions of the Zaratan have been equally diverse, ranging from fairly close to that of the whale, or of a vast seagoing turtle, or as a sea monster with huge spines on its dorsal ridge. But whatever the general shape, the creature is festooned with rocks, crevices, and valleys where greenery and trees grow. Consequently, it was mistaken for an island by the sailors who landed there and lit a fire for their food, who were then drowned when the monster submerged, often, so the tales relate, taking the entire ship with it. The most famous mention of the Zaratan must be in the first voyage of Sindbad the Sailor, whose encounter with the creature is told in the *Tales of the Thousand and One Nights*.
References 18, 53, 78, 89
See also Aspidochelone, Imap Umassoursa, monster

ZIMBARDO

This is the name of a giant in the literature of Italy that features in the work *Orlando Innamorato*, written by Matteo, Maria Boiardo, Count of Scandiano (1434–1494).
References 174
See also giant

ZIPACNA

This is the name of a giant in the mythology of the Quiché people of Guatemala. Zipacna, whose name may be translated as "Earth-heaper," is described in the text of the *Popul Vuh* as a member of the enormous earth giants whose activities terrified all those inhabiting the earth. Soon everyone tired of him, and a conspiracy was made to rid the earth of him. Then celestial heroes laid a trap into which he fell, and they put a building over the place hoping to keep him entombed. But the pit was not deep enough, and soon Zipacna rose up through the building and turned it into a pile of rubble. Then the heroes Hun-Ahpu and Xbalanque dug a great series of tunnels under a mountain and enticed the giant to the base of it with a curious mechanical crab. Once the giant was there, the supernatural heroes threw down the mountain over the top of Zipacna, where he remains to cause the earthquakes of the region.

References 169
See also giant, Jotun

ZIPHIUS

This is the name of a fabulous fish in the travelers' lore of medieval Europe. The Ziphius was said to have the body of an enormous fish. However, its head, which had grotesque eyes and a wedge-shaped beak over a vast, gaping mouth, was supposed to resemble that of an owl. This monstrous creature was said to attack ships in the northern seas it inhabited.

References 7, 89
See also Aspidochelone, monster, Zaratan

ZIZ

This is the name of an fabulous bird in the Hebraic mythology of the Middle East. The Ziz was described as a vast bird whose body stretched the distance between the earth and the heavens, similar to the Roc of Islamic legends.

References 7, 61
See also Roc

ZLATOROG

This is the name of a fabulous animal in the traditions and legends of Slovenia. The Zlatorog was described as a pure-white goat like a chamois but with horns of pure gold. Naturally, it was a great prize and was hunted right up into the topmost crags of Mount Triglav, where it browsed. It was, however, an intelligent creature, and the Zlatorog was known to lure the hunters and mislead them to the edge of precipices, where their lack of footing would cause them to tumble to their deaths. One hunter who had survived such a ploy managed to wound the Zlatorog, but where its blood spilled on the earth a beautiful red flower emerged, which it ate, and from this its wounds disappeared. It is said that this flower is now the emblem of Slovenia.

References 55
See also Alicanto

ZMAG OGNJENI VUK

This is the name of a monster in the legends and folklore of Bosnia and Serbia. The Zmag Ognjeni Vuk, whose name may be translated as "Fiery Dragon Wolf," is described as a Werewolf that was identified with the legendary fifteenth-century lord named Despot Vuk. This overlord was deemed to be the fire-breathing Werewolf by the blood-red birthmark with tufts of red hair on his forearm. Zmag Ognjeni Vuk was supposedly the son of a dragon and grew at astonishing speed into a fearsome warrior destined to vanquish this dragon, according to local folk songs. At night, and sometimes during overcast days when the sun was obscured, he would transform into the Werewolf and terrorize the region.

References 55
See also dragon, Werewolf

ZMEI GORYNICH

This is the name of a monster in the legends and folklore of the people of Slovenia and Russia. Zmei Gorynich is described as a monstrous hybrid serpent that has the body of the reptile but a human head, sometimes a human torso and head with the lower half of a serpent. This monster is associated with the activities of Baba Yaga and is a threat to the humans of the region, especially any vulnerable, lonely women, whom Zmei Gorynich may trap and abduct.

References 166
See also Baba Yaga, monster, serpent

ZÛ

This is the name of a huge dragon or storm bird in the mythology of ancient Mesopotamia, Sumer, and Babylon. Zû, also known as Anzu, was variously described as having a lion's body and the head of an eagle, or having the body of an eagle and the torso of a man with a beard. This monster was the attendant of the monstrous Tiamat. Zû stole the sacred tablets, the *Tupsimati*, from the god Enlil, who ruled the universe with the aid of their power. Zû flew high up into the top of the Sabu Mountains and stored the tablets like eggs in his nest, little knowing their power. Enlil sent his son Ninurta to get them back, and the storm god took his storm birds to the mountains to threaten Zû. But all the threats were to no avail, so he surrounded the monster with the clouds and grabbed him, tore off his wings, and

decapitated him. Thus, the tablets of destiny were returned to Enlil.
References 7, 47, 89, 125, 133, 166
See also dragon

ZUZECA
This is the name of a monstrous snake in the traditions and beliefs of the Lakota Sioux Native American people of the United States. The Zuzeca is more monstrous in its activities, since it is deemed to be responsible for inciting deceit.
References 77
See also serpent

ZUZIM
This is the name of a race of giants mentioned in the Hebrew texts that now comprise the Old Testament of the Christian Bible.
References 13
See also Annakim, Enim, giant, Noah, Zamzumin, Zuzim

ZYPHOEUS
This is the name of a monstrous being in the mythology of the Arimi people of ancient Asia Minor.
References 169
See also monster

SELECTED BIBLIOGRAPHY

1. Allardice, P. *Myths, Gods, and Fantasy: A Source Book.* Bridport, U.K: Prism Press, 1991.
2. Anderson, Hans Christian. *Danish Fairy Legends and Tales.* London: George Bell and Sons, 1891.
3. *The Anglo-Saxon Chronicles.* Translated and collated by Anne Savage. Guild Publishing, 1983. Heinemann ed., 1985.
4. Ashton, J. *Chapbooks of the Eighteenth Century.* 1882. Reprint, London: Skoob Books, 1992.
5. Aveling, T. *Heraldry: Ancient and Modern, Including Boutell's Heraldry.* London: Frederick Warne, 1891.
6. Bamberg, R. W. *Haunted Dartmoor: A Ghost-hunter's Guide.* Devon, England: Peninsular Press, 1993.
7. Barber, R., and A. Riches. *A Dictionary of Fabulous Beasts.* Ipswich: Boydell Press, 1971.
8. Barclay, Revd. James. *Barclay's Universal Dictionary.* London: James Virtue, 1848.
9. Baring-Gould, S. *A Book of Folklore.* London: Collins, 1890.
10. Baxter, R. *Bestiaries and Their Users in the Middle Ages.* Courtauld Institute. London: Sutton Publishing, 1998.
11. Bayley, H. *Archaic England.* London: Chapman and Hall, 1919.
12. Beare, B. *Ireland, Myths, and Legends.* Bristol, U.K.: Sienna Print of Paragon Books, 1996.
13. *Beowulf.* Edited by J. Glover from translations by M. Alexander and E. Morgan. Gloucester, England: Alan Sutton, 1988.
14. *Bestiary (1220–1250): Being and English Version of the Bodleian Library Oxford Ms. Bodley 764.* Translated by R. Barber. Woodbridge, U.K.: Boydell Press, 1993.
15. Bett, Henry. *English Legends.*London: Batsford, 1950.
16. *The Big Foot Mystery.* U.K. television program, April 13, 1997.
17. Blum, R., and E. Blum. *The Dangerous Hour: The Lore of Crisis and Mystery in Rural Greece.* London: Chatto and Windus, 1970.
18. Borges, J. L., and M. Guerro. *The Book of Imaginary Beings.* Translated by M. T. di Giovanni. London: Jonathan Cape, 1969 (republ. from old manuscript).
19. Bozic, S., and A. Marshall. *Aboriginal Myths.* Melbourne: Gold Star Publications, 1972.
20. *Brewer's Dictionary of Phrase and Fable.* Centenary Edition. Edited by Ivor Evans. London: Cassell, 1978.
21. Briggs, K. *The Anatomy of Puck.* Routledge and Keegan Paul, 1959.
22. Briggs, K. *British Folktales and Legends—A Sampler.* London: Paladin, 1977.
23. Briggs, K., and R. L. Tongue (eds). *Folktales of England.* London: Routledge and Kegan Paul, 1965.
24. Briggs, Katherine. *An Encyclopaedia of Fairies (Hobgoblins, Brownies, Bogies, and Other Supernatural Creatures).* New York: Pantheon Books, 1976.
25. Briggs, Katherine. *The Vanishing People.* London: Batsford, 1978.
26. Brown, M. E., and B. A. Rosenberg. *Encyclopedia of Folklore and Literature.* Santa Barbara, Calif.: ABC-CLIO, 1998.
27. Brown, Theo. *Devon Ghosts.* Norfolk, England: Norwich, Jarrold, 1982.
28. Bullfinch, Thomas. *The Age of Fable.* London: Everyman.
29. *Bullfinch's Complete Mythology.* London: Hamlyn, 1964.
30. Bullock, M. *Easter Island.* London: Scientific Book Club, 1957.
31. Bunyan, J. *The Pilgrim's Progress.* Glasgow: Wm. MacKenzie, UK ed., 1861.
32. Burland, C. *Myths of Life and Death.* London: MacMillan, 1972.
33. Burland, C. *North American Indian Mythology.* London: Hamlyn, 1965.
34. Burland, C., I. Nicholson, and H. Osborne. *Mythology of the Americas.* London: Hamlyn, 1970.
35. Burland, C., I. Nicholson, and H. Osborne. *Mythology of the North Americans.* London: Hamlyn, 1970.
36. Burne, C. S. *The Handbook of Folklore.* London: Sidgwick and Jackson, 1914.
37. Carew-Hazlitt, W. *Faiths and Folklore: A Dictionary.* London: Reeves and Turner, 1905.
38. Carlyon, Richard. *A Guide to the Gods.* London: Heinemann/Quixote, 1981.
39. Carrington, R. *Mermaids and Mastodons: A Book of Natural and Unnatural History.* London: Chatto and Windus, 1957.
40. Carroll, L. *Alice's Adventures Through the Looking Glass and What Alice Found There.* Orig. publ. 1872. Oxford: Oxford University Press, 1985.
41. Cavendish, R., ed. *Legends of the World.* London: Orbis Publishing, 1982.
42. Chisholm, L., and A. Steedman. *A Staircase of Stories.* London: Thomas Nelson and Sons, ca. 1945.
43. Clairvaux, Bernard of. *Apologia XII: 29.* Trans C. Rudolph. In *Things of Greater Importance, Bernard of*

Clairvaux, Apologia, and The Medieval Attitude Towards Art. Philadelphia: University of Pensylvania, 1990.

44. Cliffe, S. *Shadows: A Northern Investigation of the Unknown.* Cheshire, U.K.: Sigma Press, 1993.

45. Cohen, J. J. "Of Giants: Sex, Monsters, and the Middle Ages." *Medieval Cultures* 17 (1999).

46. *The Complete Works of William Shakespeare.* London: Collins Cleartype Press (no date; reprint ca. 1930).

47. Cotterell, A. *A Dictionary of World Mythology.* London: Windward, 1979.

48. Coughlan, R. *The Illustrated Encyclopaedia of Arthurian Legends.* Shaftesbury and Dorset, U.K.: Element Books, 1993.

49. Dale-Green, P. *The Cult of the Cat.* London: Heinemann, 1973.

50. Dame Kiri Te Kanawa, ed. *Land of the Long White Cloud: Maori Myths, Tales, and Legends.* London: Puffin Books, 1989.

51. Day, D. *A Tolkien Bestiary.* London: Chancellor Press, 1979 (1997 ed.).

52. Dickson, M. *The Saga of the Sea Swallow.* London: H. D. Innes, 1896.

53. Dixon, E., ed. *Fairy Tales from the Arabian Nights.* London: Dent, 1893.

54. Dixon-Kennedy, M. *Arthurian Myth and Legend: An A–Z of People and Places.* London: Blandford Press, 1995.

55. Dixon-Kennedy, M. *Encyclopedia of Russian and Slavic Myth and Legend.* Santa Barbara, Calif.: ABC-CLIO, 1998.

56. *The Economist* (November 6–15, 1996): 115–121.

57. Edwards, W. *A Mediaeval Scrap Heap.* London: Rivingtons, 1930.

58. The Enchanted World Series. *Night Creatures.* Amsterdam: Time Life Books, 1985.

59. The Enchanted World Series. *Spells and Bindings.* Amsterdam: Time Life Books, 1985.

60. The Enchanted World Series. *Water Spirits.* Amsterdam: Time Life Books, 1985.

61. *Encyclopaedia Britannica.* CD-ROM Version, 1994.

62. *The Encyclopaedia of Comparative Religion.* London: Everyman, 1965.

63. Epstein, P. *Monsters: Their Histories, Homes, and Habits.* New York: Doubleday, 1973.

64. *Everyman's Dictionary of Non-Classical Mythology.* London: Everyman Reference, 1965.

65. Eyre, K. *Lancashire Ghosts.* Yorkshire: Dalesman Books, 1979.

66. Fewkes, J. W. *Designs on Hopi Pottery.* New York: Dover Publications, 1973.

67. *Folklore Myths and Legends of Britain.* London: Reader's Digest, 1973.

68. Fox-Davies, A. C. *Heraldry Explained.* London: T. C. and E. C. Jack, 1907.

69. Frayling, C. *Vampires: From Lord Byron to Dracula.* London: Faber and Faber, 1991.

70. Frazer, J. G. *The Golden Bough.* London: Papermac, 1987.

71. Gainsford, J., ed. *The Atlas of Man.* Omega Books, 1987.

72. Gaselee, Stephen. *Stories from the Christian East.* London: Sidgwick and Jackson, 1918.

73. Gaskell, D. S. *Dictionary of Scripture and Myth.* New York: Dorset Press, 1883.

74. Gaynor, F., ed. *Dictionary of Mysticism.* London: Wildwood House, 1974.

75. Gerritsen, W. P., and A. G. van Melle. *A Dictionary of Medieval Heroes.* Translated by T. Guest. Woodbridge, England: Boydell Press, 1998.

76. Gheerbrant, A. *The Amazon Past, Present, and Future.* New York: Thames and Hudson, 1992.

77. Gill, S. D., and I. F. Sullivan. *Dictionary of Native American Mythology.* Santa Barbara, Calif.: ABC-CLIO, 1992.

78. Gordon, Stuart. *The Encyclopaedia of Myths and Legends.* London: Headline, 1993.

79. Gouda, Y. "Jinns." Saudi Arabia: *Saudi Gazette* (March 31, 1995).

80. Gouda, Y. "Jinns." Saudi Arabia: *Saudi Gazette* (April 14, 1995).

81. Gould, C. *Mythical Monsters.* 1886, Senate Imprint Studio Editions, 1995.

82. Greenwood, J. *Savage Habits and Customs.* London: S. O. Beeton, 1865.

83. Guerber, H. *Myths and Legends of the Middle Ages.* London: Harrap, 1948.

84. Gwynn Jones, T. *Welsh Folklore and Folk Custom.* London: Methuen, 1930.

85. Hall, S. C. *The Book of British Ballads.* London: Jeremiah How, 1847.

86. Hall, S. C., ed. *The Book of British Ballads.* Rev. ed. London: J. How, 1848.

87. *Hall's Dictionary of Subjects and Symbols in Art.* London: Murray, 1979.

88. Hanson, A., and L. Hanson. *Counterpoint in Maori Culture.* London: Routledge and Kegan Paul, 1983.

89. Hargreaves, J. *Hargreaves New Illustrated Bestiary.* Glastonbury, England: Gothic Image Publications, 1990.

90. Harner, M. J. *The Jívaro: People of the Sacred Waterfalls.* London: Robert Hale, 1973.

91. Hassig, D. *Mediaeval Bestiaries: Text, Image, Ideology.* Cambridge, U.K: Cambridge University Press, 1995.

92. Hawthorne, N. *A Wonder Book for Boys and Girls and Tanglewood Tales.* London: Dent, 1910.

93. Henderson, W. *Folklore of the Northern Counties of England and the Borders.* London: Longmans Green, 1866.

94. Hill, D., and P. Williams. *The Supernatural.* London: Aldus Books, 1965.

95. Hiltebeitel, A., ed. *Criminal Gods and Demon Devotees.* Albany: State University of New York, 1989.

96. Hippisley-Coxe, Anthony D., *Haunted Britain,* Pan Books Ltd, 1973.

97. Hoffman, Dr. Heinrich. *The English Strewwelpeter, or Pretty Stories and Funny Pictures.* London: George Routledge and Sons, 1847.

98. Hole, C. *A Dictionary of British Folk Custom.* London: Paladin/Collins, 1986.

99. *The Holy Bible.* With notes by the Revd. H. Stebbing, Alan Bell and Co. London: Simpkin and Marshall, 1837.

100. Housman, L. *All-Fellows.* London: Kegan Paul Trench Trübner, 1896.

101. Housman, L. *The Field of Clover.* London: Kegan Paul Trench Trübner, 1898.

102. Hyslop, Robert, ed. *Echoes from the Border Hills.* Pentland Press, 1992.

103. Ivanits, Linda J. *Russian Folk Belief.* New York: M. E. Sharpe, 1989.

104. Jacobs, Joseph, ed. *Celtic Fairy Tales.* London: David Nutt, 1895.

105. Jones, G. *Kings, Beasts, and Heroes.* Oxford: Oxford University Press, 1972.

106. Jones, Rev. Henry, and Lewis Kropp. *The Folk Tales of the Magyars.* London: The Folklore Society, 1889.

107. Keightley, Thomas. *The Fairy Mythology.* Whittacker-Treacher, 1833.

108. Kendall, L. *Shamans, Housewives, and Other Restless Spirits.* Honolulu: University of Hawaii Press, 1985.

109. Ker Wilson, B. *Scottish Folktales and Legends.* Oxford: Oxford University Press, 1954.

110. Kerven, R. *The Mythical Quest: In Search of Adventure, Romance, and Enlightenment.* Orig. publ. by the British Library for exhibition, 1996. Pomegranite Artbooks, 1996.

111. Killip, M. *Folklore of the Isle of Man.* London: Batsford, 1975.

112. Knappert, J. *Indian Mythology: An Encyclopaedia of Myth and Legend.* London: Diamond Books, 1995.

113. Knappert, J. *Pacific Mythology: An Encyclopaedia of Myth and Legend.* London: Diamond Books, 1995.

114. Knatchbull-Huggeson, E. *River Legends.* London: Daldy Ibister, 1875.

115. Lang, A. *Custom and Myth.* London: Longmans Green, 1898.

116. Lang, A., ed. *The Elf Maiden and Other Stories.* London: Longmans Green, 1906.

117. Lang, A., ed. *The Snow Queen and Other Stories.* London: Longmans Green, 1906.

118. Langer, William L., ed. *The Encyclopaedia of World History.* London: Harrap/Galley Press, 1987.

119. Leach, M., ed. *The Dictionary of Folklore.* Chicago: Funk and Wagnall, 1985.

120. Leach, M., ed. *The Standard Dictionary of Folklore.* Funk and Wagnall, 1972.

121. Leacock, S., and R. Leacock. *Spirits of the Deep.* New York: Doubleday, 1972.

122. Legey, F. *The Folklore of Morocco.* French ed., 1926. Translated by L. Hotz. London: Allen and Unwin, 1935.

123. Litvinoff, Sarah, ed. *The Illustrated Guide to the Supernatural.* London: Marshall-Cavendish, 1990.

124. *Lloyd's Encyclopaedic Dictionary.* London: Edward Lloyd, 1895.

125. Lurker, Manfred. *Dictionary of Gods and Goddesses, Devils and Demons.* Translated by Campbell. London: Routledge, 1989.

126. Lyon, P. J. *Native South Americans.* Boston: Little Brown, 1974.

127. Macdowall, M. W. *Asgard and the Gods—Tales and Traditions of Our Northern Ancestors.* Adapted from the work of Dr. W. Wägner. London: Swan Sonnenschein, 1902.

128. MacKillop, J. *Dictionary of Celtic Mythology.* Oxford: Oxford University Press, 1998.

129. MacKinnon, J. *Scottish Folk Tales in Gaelic and English.* Edinburgh: JMK Consultancy Publishing, 1991.

130. Maple, Eric. *Superstition and the Superstitious.* London: W. H. Allen.

131. *Mars Landing Transmission Direct from Pasadena U.S.A.* U.K.: BBC, July 4, 1997.

132. Martin, B. W. *The Dictionary of the Occult.* London: Rider, 1979.

133. McLeish, K. *Myths and Legends of the World Explored.* London: Bloomsbury Press, 1996.

134. Menger, M., and C. Gagnon. *Lake Monster Traditions: A Cross-Cultural Analysis* London: Fortean Tomes, 1988.

135. Mollet, J. W. *An Illustrated Dictionary of Antique Art and Archaeology.* Omega, 1927.

136. Moon, B., ed. *An Encyclopaedia of Archetypal Symbolism.* Boston and London: Archive for Research on Archetypal Symbolism, Shambhala Publications, 1991.

137. orrisson, S., ed. *Wm. Cashen's Manx Folklore.* Douglas Isle of Man: G. L. Johnson, 1912.

138. Mowat, F. *People of the Deer.* London: Readers' Union, Michael Joseph, 1954.

139. *New Larousse Encyclopaedia of Mythology.* London: Book Club Associates, 1973.

140. Newman, P. *Gods and Graven Images.* London: Robert Hale, 1987.

141. Notes from the Library of the Vladimir Pedagogical Institute. Vladimir University, Russia.

142. O'Hogain, Dr. D. *Myth Legend and Romance: An Encyclopaedia of the Irish Folk Tradition.* New York: Prentice Hall, 1991.

143. Opie, P., and I. Opie. *The Oxford Dictionary of Nursery Rhymes.* Oxford: Oxford University Press, 1977 ed.

144. Owen, D. D. R. *The Legend of Roland: A Pageant of the Middle Ages.* Phaidon Press, 1973.

145. Owen, W. *Strange Scottish Stories.* Norwich: Jarrold Press, 1983.

146. *The Oxford English Dictionary.* Compact ed. Oxford: Oxford University Press, 1971.

147. Paré, Ambroise. *On Monsters and Marvels.* Trans. J. Pallister. Chicago: University of Chicago Press, 1983.

148. Parry-Jones, D. *Welsh Legends and Fairy Folk Lore.* London: B. T. Batsford, 1953.

149. Payne, A. *Medieval Beasts.* London: British Library, 1990.

150. Piggott, J. *Japanese Mythology.* London: Chancellor Press, 1969 (1997 ed.).

151. Poignant, R. *Myths and Legends of the South Seas.* London: Hamlyn, 1970.

152. Porteous, A. *Forest Folklore.* London: G. Allen and Unwin, 1928.

153. Reed, A. W. *Aboriginal Fables and Legendary Tales.* Sydney, Australia: New Reed Holland, 1965 (1998 rep.).

154. Reed, A. W. *Aboriginal Tales from Australia.* Sydney, Australia: New Reed Holland, 1980 (1998 rep.).

155. Reed, A. W. *Maori Myth and Legend.* Auckland, New Zealand: Reed Books, 1983 (repr. 1996).

156. *The Rider Encyclopaedia of Eastern Philosophy and Religion.* London: Rider, 1986.

157. Risdon, J., A. Stevens, and B. Whitworth. *A Glympse of Dartmoor—Villages, Folklore, Tors, and Place Names.* Devon, England: Peninsular Press, 1992.

158. Robbins, R. H. *The Encyclopaedia of Witchcraft and Demonology.* London: Bookplan/Hamlyn, 1959.

159. Roberts, A., and D. Roberts. *Shadows in the Mist.* S. Australia: Art Australia, 1989.

160. Rose, C. *Spirits, Fairies, Gnomes, and Goblins: An Encyclopedia of the Little People.* Santa Barbara, Calif.: ABC-CLIO, 1996.

161. Rose-Benét, W., ed. *The Reader's Encyclopaedia.* London: Book Club, 1974.

162. *Royal Pageantry, Customs, and Festivals of Great Britain and Northern Ireland.* London: Purnell and Sons, 1967.

163. Ryan, J. and G. Bardon. *Mythscapes: Aboriginal Art of the Desert.* Melbourne: National Heart Foundation, National Gallery, 1989.

164. Saggs, H. W. F. *Civilization Before Greece and Rome.* London: Batsford, 1989.

165. Seebok, T. A., and F. J. Ingemann. "Studies in Cheremis: The Supernatural." *Fund Publications in Anthropology,* No. 22. Werner-Gren Foundation for Anthropological Research Inc, New York: Viking, 1956.

166. Senior, Michael. *The Illustrated Who's Who in Mythology.* Edited by G. Paminder. MacDonald Illustrated, 1985.

167. Skeat, W. W. *Malay Magic.* Oxford: Oxford University Press, 1889 (Rep., Singapore, 1984).

168. Smith, J. C. D. *A Guide to Church Wood Carvings, Misericords, and Benchends.* Newton Abbot, U.K.: David Charles, 1974.

169. Spence, L. *A Dictionary of Mythology.* London: Cassell, 1910.

170. Spence, Lewis. *The Minor Traditions of British Mythology.* London: Rider, 1948.

171. Spence, Lewis. *North American Indians, Myths, and Legends.* Studio Editions. London: Bracken Books, 1985.

172. Squire, C. *Celtic Myth and Legend.* London: Gresham, 1889.

173. Squire, Charles. *Celtic Myth and Legend, Poetry and Romance.* Gresham, 1910. Reprint, Hollywood, Calif.: Newcastle, 1975.

174. Stevens, W. *Giants in Those Days.* Lincoln: University of Nebraska Press, 1989.

175. Stow, John. *Stow's Annales.* London: John Stow, 1600.

176. Summers, Montague. *The History of Witchcraft.* Mystic, Conn.: Mystic Press, 1925.

177. Swift, J. *Gulliver's Travels.* Orig. publ. 1726. New York: Minster Classics, Lancer Books, 1968.

178. Swinburne-Carr, T. *A New Classical Lexicon of Biography, Mythology and Geography.* London: Simpkins Marshall, 1858.

179. Thornton, Robert of. *Morte Arthure: An Alliterative Poem of the 14th Century.* Edited by Mary Macleod Banks. London: Longmans Green, 1900.

180. *The Travels of Sir John Mandeville,* ca. 1390 A.D. (abridged version). Commentary by N. Denny and A. Filmer-Sankey. London: Collins, 1973.

181. Walters, D. *Chinese Mythology, An Encyclopaedia of Myth and Legend.* London: Aquarian/Thorsons (Harper Collins), 1992.

182. Warner, M. *No Go the Bogeyman: Scaring, Lulling, and Making Mock.* London: Chatto and Windus, 1998.

183. Westwood, J. *Albion: A Guide to Legendary Britain.* London: Grafton, 1992.

184. Westwood, J., ed. *The Atlas of Mysterious Places.* London: Guild Publishing, 1987.

185. White, T. H. *The Book of Beasts, Being a Translation from a Latin Bestiary of the 12th Century.* London: Jonathan Cape, 1954 (1956 rep.).

186. Wier, A., and Jerman, J. *Images of Lust: Sexual Carvings on Medieval Churches.* 1986. Reprint, London: Routledge, 1999.

187. Williams-Ellis, A. *Fairies and Enchanters.* London: Nelson, 1933.

188. Wirtjes, Henneke, ed. *The Middle English Physiologus.* From British Library Ms. Arundel 292 ca. 1300 A.D. Oxford: Early English Text Society, Oxford University Press, 1991.

189. Yeats, W. B., ed. *Fairy and Folk Tales of the Irish Peasantry.* W. Scott. Reprint, Dover: 1992

APPENDIXES

1. BEINGS ASSOCIATED WITH APOCALYPSE OR WORLD'S END

Antichrist, Apocalyptic Beast, Apocalyptic Beasts, Arzshenk, Dabbat, Dahak, Dragon of the Apocalypse, Elbst, Fenrir, Fire Giants, Frost Giants, Garm, Gog, Gridr, Hrimthurses, Hrym, Hydra, Jormungandr, Midgardsorm/r, Piast/s, Samvarta, Scarlet Beast, Sinaa, Skrimsl, Sutr

2. BEINGS ASSOCIATED WITH CATASTROPHE

Afanc, Ahi, Aido Hwedo, Anaye, Ao Chin, Ao Kuang, Ao Shun, Aries, Bergelmir, Bochica, Bunyip, Chang Lung, Cheeroonear, Daitya, Dea, Dragon (Ethiopian), Enceladus, Flaming Teeth, Giant of Wales, Gibborim, Gigantes, Gong-gong, Hapalit, Hayicanako, Hiintcabiit, Hurtaly, Jinshin Uwo, Jishin-Mushi, Jokao, Kalevanpojat, Kamapua'a, Kami, Kulshedra, La Velue, Moshiriikkwechep, Naga Pahoda, Nephilim, Noah, Nulayuuiniq, O Goncho, Og, One-Standing-and-Moving, Oriental Dragon, Oshädagea, Palet, Palulukon, Rainbow Serpent, Rou Shou, Salamander, Samvarta, Sesha, Shang Yung, Stellio, Stoorworm, Teehooltsoodi, Tieholtsodi, Valedjád, Vasuki, Vritra, Werewolf, Wikatcha, Xelhua, Ymir, Yulu Yulara, Yulunggu, Zipacna

3. BEINGS ASSOCIATED WITH LAKES AND RIVERS

Lakes

Afanc, Amhuluk, Ancient One, Ancient Serpent, Antukai, Apocalyptic Beast, Ashuaps, Butatsch-ah-Ilgs, Champ, Elbst, Emogoalekc, Great Horned Serpent, Hînqûmemen, Hoga, Horned Serpent, Invunche, Kitchi-at'Husis, Lenapizka, Loch Ness Monster, Lockski Nesski Monsterovich, Manetuwi-Rusi-Pissi, Manipogo, Mashernomak, Meshekenabec, Mhorag, Mishipizhiw, Misiganebic, Miskena, Monoceros Marinus, Monster of Brompton, Monster of Lake Fagua, Msi-Kinepikwa, Mystery of the Waters, Naitaka, Nykkjen, Ogopogo, Oilliphéist, Oniares, Oyaleroweck, Pamba, Phantom of the Lake, Piast/s, Ponik, Queen of the Waters, Sa-yin, Sea-Serpent of Memphrémagog, Seljordsorm, Sjötroll, Skahnowa, Slimy Slim, Storsjöodjuret, Suileach, Tcipitckaam, To Kas, Trelquehuecuve, Wakandagi, Wendigo, Were-Crocodile, White Chest, White Panther, Wishpoosh, Yenrish

Rivers

Afanc, Aicha Kandida, Ambize, Angont, Angulo, Apalala, Aranda, Ashuaps, Bäckahäst, Burach Bhadi, Cheval Bayard,

Cutty Dyer, Doonongaes, Dracs, Fuath, Gaasyendietha, Gargouille, Glashtin, Great Serpent of Lorette, Guirivulu, Gurangatch, Hiintcabiit, Hogfish, Horned Serpent, Hydrus, Kaliya, Kappa, Kiau, La Velue, Lik, Llamhigyn y Dwr, Master of the Water, Michi-Pichoux, Migas, Mi-Ni-Wa-Tu, Mother of the Fishes, Nicker, Nyan, Odontotyrannus, Opkən, Oriental Dragon, Pal-rai-yuk, Papstesel, Peg Powler, Piranu, Rainbow Serpent, Serpent, Skahnowa, Ti Lung, Tiamat, Tsemaus, Untekhi, Vodianoi, Vörys-mort, Wakandagi, Wakandagi Pezi, Xiang Yao, Yaquaru, Ymir

4. BEINGS ASSOCIATED WITH THE MOON OR SUN

Moon

Alklha, Alsvid, Balam, Disemboweller (the), Dragon (Occidental), Iqi-Balam, Manzaširi, Pangu, Rahu, Sandman, T'ien Kou, Toad (Three-Legged), Vodianoi, Vukub-cakix, Werewolf

Sun

Aapep, Actaeon, Acthon, Æthon, Alklha, Alsvid, Ananta, Arrak, Arusha and Arushi, Arvaak, Astrope, Bennu, Big Owl, Bronte, Cailleach Bheur, Dadhikra, Dragon (Occidental), Eous, Epirotes, Etasa, Gandarva, Gong-gong, Horses of the Sun, Hrimfaxi, Hyperion, Ka-en-ankh Nereru, Kama-Dhenu, Kua Fu, Lampon, Maka, Manzaširi, Mehen, Merwer, Mnevis, Namtar, Pangu, Phaethon, Phlegon, Phoenix, Purusha, Pyrois, Rahu, Sharama, Sisupala, Skinfaxi, Skoll, Sun Ravens, Vseslav, Vukub-cakix, Xólotl

5. BEINGS ASSOCIATED WITH WEATHER

Frost, Ice, and Snow

Ahi, Antero Vipunen, Audumla, Bel (2), Bergelmir, Cailleach Bheur, Drifta, Frost Giants, Frosti, Hrimthurses, Hrym, Ice Giants, Johul, Jokao, Joukahainen, Kari, Kiwahkw, Logi, Louhi, Mi-Ni-Wa-Tu, Miqqiayuuq, Paija, Sikuliasuituq, Skadi, Skrymir, Snoer, Snow Snake, Stonecoats, Thiassi, Thrym, Thurses, Vasty, Wandil, Waziya, Witico, Ymir

Rain or Storm

Ahuizotl, Airāvata, Big heads, Blue Men of the Minch, Caillagh ny Groamagh, Ccoa, Dinny Mara, Elbst, Flying Heads, Fomor/s, Great Horned Serpent, Halfway People, Harpy, Havfinë, Havfrue, Imdugud, Jurawadbad, Kari, Lei, Lightning Monsters, Lightning Serpent, Lung, Muchalinda, Naga/s, Oriental Dragon, Raicho, Raiju, Raitaro, Sa-

Halilintar, Thunder Dragon, Thunderbird, Tinmiukpuk, Valedjád, Wakinyan, Waukheon, Xexeu, Zû

Rainbow

Aido Hwedo, Ayida, Bobi-Bobi, Da, Damballah, Dhakhan, Jormungandr, Joukahainen, Julunggul, Kaleru, Karia, Kun Manggur, Langal, Midgardsorm/r, Mindi, Muit, Ngalbjod, Oshumare, Rainbow Serpent, Taipan, Thugine, Ungud, Wanambi, Woinunggur, Wollunqua, Wonungur, Worombi, Wulungu, Yero, Yulunggu, Yurlunggur

Wind

Alcyoneus, Bmola, Djin/n, Fei Lian, Harpy, Shaitan/t, Shen Lung, Taranushi

6. BEINGS FROM LITERATURE

Achlis, Agrippa, Albion, Alifanfaron, Alous, Amermait, Anakim, Ancalagon the Black, Anthropophagus, Antichrist, Apocalyptic Beasts, Apotharni, Ass (Three-Legged), Astreus, Balan, Bandersnatch, Barometz, Barong, Basilisk, Bayard, Beigad, Bel, Bellerus, Blemmyes, Bloody-man, Borogove, Bringuenarilles, Brobdingnagians, Bruyer, Caligorante, Callitrice, cannibal, Capaneus, Celtes, Chalbroth, Chan, Chiang-Liang, Ch'ou-T'i, Ch'uan-T'ou (People of), Cichol, Cold-Drakes, Corineus, Daughters of Cain, Dercynus, Despair (Giant), Dossenus, Draco, Dragon (Occidental), Dumbeldors, Enay, Ents, Entwives, Eryx, Etion, Fama, Fangorn, Faribroth, Farracutus, Fastitocalon, Ferragut, Fimbrethil, Finglas, Fire-drake, Flandrif, Foawr, Fomor/s, Fracassus, Frankenstein's Monster, Gabbara, Galatea, Galathes, Galehaut, Galemelle, Gargamelle, Gargantua, Gayoffe, Gemmagog, Giant, Giant Onion, Gibborim, Glaurung, Glumdalclitch, Glyryvilu, Gog, Goliath, Gos et Magos, Grandgousier, Grant-Gosier, Griffin, Grim, Hai Ho Shang, Haizum, Happemousche, Hercules Libyus, Hippocentaur, Houyhnhms, Hsiao, Hsing-T'ien, Hui, Hurtaly, Hydra, Ichthyocentaur, Idrus, I-Mu Kuo Yan, Ingcél Caech, Inhabitants of Islands near Dondun, Jabberwock, Jaculus, Kami, King Kong, Kraken, Kw' Ên, Lady of the Land, Leviathan, Loathly Worm, Loup garou, Lycaon, Manducus, Manticore, Maul, Micromégas, Monocentaur, monster, Morgante, Morguan, Mûmarkil, Nephilim, Nieh-Erh Kuo Yan, Nimrod, Nyan, Nymbrotus, Offotus, Ogre, Oliphaunt, Olog-Hai, Onocentaur, Onodrim, Orc, Otus, Pagan, Pai Lung, Pallenes, Pantagruel, Papillon, Parandus, Peryton, Phoenix, Ping Feng, Pope, Porus, Quaresmeprenant, Rager, Rahab, Rephaim, Riquet à la Houppe, Roc, Roshwalr, Rosmarine, Rosmarus, Rosmer, Sahab, Salamander, Sandman, San-Shen Kuo Yan, Sarabroth, satyr, Scardyng, Scarlet Beast, Scatha the Worm, Sciapod/s, Scitalis, Secundilla, Serpent of Eden, Serpentin Vert, Serra, Shelob, Siren/s, Slay-good, Smaug the Golden, Tarandrus, Thundel, Ting Ling Kuo Yan, Torogs, Tourmentine, Troll, Tursus, Tytan/s, Tytea Magna, Ungoliant, unicorn, Uruks, Urulóki, vampire, Wandlimb the Lightfooted, Whappernocker, Wildman, Yahoo, Yü-Min Kuo Yan, Zägh, Zaratan, Zimbardo

7. BEINGS THAT ARE BIRD OR PART BIRD

Ai Tojon, Alan, Alicanto, Alkonost, Aloés, Angka, Asipatra, Ass-Bittern, Bahri, Bakbakwalanooksiwae, Bar Yachre, Bennu, Bialozar, Bird-Man, Bmola, Boobrie, Borak (Al), Borogove, Boroka, Chamrosh, Ch'uan-T'ou (People of), Cornu, Dragon (Occidental), Estas, Firebird, Fung, Galon, Garuda, Gillygaloo, Goofus, Griffin, Griffin Vulture, Gwagwakhwalanooksiwey, Hai Riyo, Heliodromos, Hraesvelg, Hsiao, Humility, Hwa Yih, Jataya, Kaneakeluh, Kargas, Kerkes, Khrut, Khyung, Kirni, Konoha Tengu, Kreutzet, Lion-Griffon, Luan, Lwan, Makara, Naul, Ngani-vatu, Ngutu-Lei, Nunyenunc, O Goncho, Ocypete, Opinicus, Owner-of-a-Bag, P' Êng, Parandus, Parthenope, Peryton, Pheng, Philamaloo Bird, Phoenix, Pinnacle Grouse, Podarge, Pouakai, Poukai, Ptitsy-Siriny, Pyong, Raicho, Roc, Rukh, Sampati, Schachi Hoko, Senmurv, Serra, Sevienda, Shang Yung, Simargl, Simorg, Simurgh, Sinam, Siren/s, Sirin, Skoffin, Solovei Rakhmatich, Symir, Tengu/s, Thunderbird, Ti-Chiang, Tinmiukpuk, To Fu, Tobi Tatsu, Tragopan, Tsenahale, Unnati, Vuokho, Wakinyan, Waukkeon, Wuchowsen, Xexeu, Yata Garasu, Yin Chu, Yoh Shoh, Yu Siang, Yü-Min Kuo Yan, Zägh, Ziz

8. BEINGS THAT ARE BOARS OR PIGS

Ætolian Boar, Ambize, Aunyainá, Battleswine, Beast, Beigad, Boar of Beann-Gulbain, Buata, Cafre, Calydonian Boar, Catoblepas, Elbst, Erymanthean Boar, Glawackus, Goldbristles, Grugyn Silver Bristles, Gryllus, Gulinbursti, Hildesuin, Hog (Sea), Hoga, Hwch Ddu Gota, Kamapua'a, Llwydawg the Hewer, Lobíson, Lustucru (Le Grand), Marine Boar, Marine Sow, Monoceros (1), Nependis, Phaea, Phantom of the Lake, Phorcys, Ping Feng, Porcus Troit, Pugot, Sachrimnir, Sea Hog, Slidringtanni, Torc Triath, Totoima, Troynt, Twrch Trwyth, Verethraghna, Yale, Ysgithyrwyn

9. BEINGS THAT ARE CANNIBALS AND HUNTERS OF HUMANS

Abere, Ahuizotl, Aicha Kandida, Anaye, Anthropophagus, Antiphates, Asin, Asterion, Atcen, Aunyainá, Baba Yaga, Bakbakwakanooksiwae, Big Man-eater, Big Owl, Black Annis, Black Devil, Black Tamanous, Boraro, Boroka, Bungisngis, Buso, Caliban, cannibal, Ce Sith, Cheeroonear, Child Guzzler, Chivato, Crooked Beak of Heaven, Cutty Dyer, Cynocephali, Deadoendjadases, Dracula, Drake, Dzoavits, Dzoo-noo-qua, Encerrados, Fastitocalon, Flaming Teeth, Ganiagwaihegowa, Ga-oh, Gather-on-the-Water, Gergasi, Giant Dingo, Giant Holdfast, Gougou, Gwagwakhwalanooksiwey, Haakapainizi, Hagondes, Hariti, Harpy, He-Li-Di, Hidebehind, Hidimba, Hokhoku, Horomatangi, Hotu-puku, Huru-kareao, Ihu-maataotao, Irraq, Jaguar-Man, Jokao, Karitei-mo, Kewanambo, Kinderschrecker, King Kong, Kirata, Kiwahkw, Kraken, Laestrygonians, Lamus, Loha-Mukha, Long Nose, Lustucru (Le Grand), Lycaon, Macan Gadungan, Manticore, Mares of Diomedes, Maul, Minotaur, Näkki, Ngutu-Lei, Nulayuuiniq, Ogre, Olog-Hai, Ongwe Ias, Paiyuk, Pey, Polyphemus, Poukai, Ravagio, Raw Gums, Red Etin, Reksoso, Ruahine-mata-maori, Ruuruhi-kerepoo, Sasabonsam, Siats, Slay-good, Snee-Nee-Iq, So'la, Stone Giants, Stonecoats, Tama-o-hoi, Tammatuyuq, Thardid Jimbo, Tigre Capiango, Torogs, Torto, Wendigo, Were-bear, Were-boar, Were-crocodile, Were-dog, Were-fox, Were-hare,

Were-hyena, Were-jackal, Were-jaguar, Were-leopard, Were-tiger, Were-wolf, Wihwin, Witico, Yannig

10. BEINGS THAT ARE CAT OR PART CAT
Cat
Aitvaras, Arassas, Barguest, Big Ears, Cactus Cat, Capalus, Cat Sith, Cat-Fish, Cath Paluc, Chapalu, Cheshire Cat, Dard, Fearsome Critters, Írusán, Kludde, Palug's Cat, Phantom Cat, Pukis, Sliver Cat, Splinter Cat, Stollenwurm, Tatzelwurm, vampire, Wikatcha

Leopard
Apocalyptic Beasts, Camel-Leopard, Fei Lian

Lion
Amermait, Androsphinx, Baku, Centycore, Chimera, Cigouave, Corocotta, Criosphinx, Dogs of Fo, Dragon (Occidental), Enfield, Glawackus, Griffin, Gryps, Gulon, Har-machis, Hieracosphinx, Hippogryph, Humbaba, Ichthyocentaur, Imdugud, Kirtimukha, Leucrotta, Lion-Griffon, Lyon-Poisson, Mafedet Manticore, Marine Lion, Mušhuššu, Nemean Lion, Opinicus, Questing Beast, Roc, satyr, Sea-Lion, Serra, Snake Griffon, Sphinx, Tyger, Yenrish, Zû

Lynx
Great Lynx, Lynx, Mishipizhiw, Missipissy

Panther
Bicorne, Bulchin, Chiang-Liang, Glawackus, Lynx, Thingut, Underground Panther, White Panther

11. BEINGS THAT ARE DOG OR PART DOG, WOLF OR PART WOLF
Dog
Ahuizotl, Alecto, Arctophonos, Aufhocker, Axehandle Hound, Az-i-wû-gûm-ki-mukh-'ti, Barguest, Black dogs, Black Shuck, Brash, Buggane, Calchona, Ce Sith, Cerberus, Cetus, Chamrosh, Cheeroonear, Christopher (Saint), Cir Sith, Coinchenn, Coinn Iotair, Cwn Annwn, Cynocephali, Cynoprosopi, Devil's Dandy Dogs, Dirae, Dogs (Sea), Dogs of Fo, Druggen Hill Boggle, Empusa, Ereshigal, Erinyes, Falcon-fish, Freybug, Furies, Gaborchend, Galley-trot, Gargittios, Garm, Geri and Freki, Geryon's Dogs, Grant, Gwyllgi, Gytrash, Hemicynes, Hounds of Rage, Hsiao, Hui, Hydra, Jin, Kalkes, Kallicantzari, Keelut, Ki Du, Kludde, Koerakoonlased, Lobíson, Loup garou, Lynx, Mauthe Dhoog, Mimick Dog, Orthos, Oschaert, Padfoot, Pi Nereskə, Plat-eye, Ptoophagos, Qiqion, Questing Beast, Rizos, Rongeur d' Os, Saidthe Suaraighe, Scylla, Sea-Dog, Senmurv, Sharama, Sharameyas, Simorg, Skriker, Sus Lika, Telchines, T'ien Kou, Were-Dog, Xólotl, Youdic Dogs

Wolf
Akhlut, Amarok, Anjing Ajak, Beast, Calopus, Corocotta, Dragon-wolf, Enfield, Fenrir, Freki, Hrodvitnir, Hvcko Capko, Kisihohkew, Loup garou, Lucive, Lycanthrope, Lycaon, Scylla, Skoll, Tyger, Vilkacis, Vseslav, Vulkodlac, Werewolf

12. BEINGS THAT ARE FISH OR PART FISH OR WHALE
Fish
Abaia, Abgal, Acipenser, Adaro, Aloés, Ambize, Ancient One, Aspidochelone, Az-i-wû-gûm-ki-mukh-'ti, Bahamut, Big Fish of Iliamna, Bishop Fish, Capricornus, Cat-Fish, Cock-fish, Dhakhan, Dogs (Sea), Elbst, Equus bipes, Ereshigal, Falcon-fish, Flying Fish, Giddy Fish, Glyryvilu, Goofang, Guardian of the Fishes, Gurangatch, Hai Ho Shang, Hakenmann, Halfway People, Hare (Sea), Havfinë, Havhest, Havstrambe, Hippocamp, Hog (Sea), Hoga, Hogfish, Hydrippus, Igpupiara, Ikalu Nappa, Jasconius, Jinshin Uwo, Jishin-Mushi, Kaia, Kami, Kar-Fish, King of the Fishes, Kujata, Kul, Kulili, Kw' Ên, Liban, Lung Wang, Lyon-Poisson, Makara, Marine Boar, Master of the Fishes, Mermaid/e, Merman, Merrow, Miskena, Missipissy, Monk Fish, Monoceros (2), Monoceros Marinus, Monster of Brompton, Mora, Moshiriikkwechep, Mother of the Fishes, Murex, Murrisk, Mystery of the Waters, Näkineiu, Näkinneito, Ningyo, Nix, Orobon, P' Êng, Parthenope, Phorcys, Piasa, Piranu, Pontarf, Queen of the Fishes, Queen of the Waters, Remora, Rosualt, Satyre-Fish, Sea Hog, Sea Horse, Sea-Serpent of Memphrémagog, Serra, Siren/s, Suhur-mas, Swamfisk, Te Tuna, Tsemaus, Vodianoi, Yu Lung, Ziphius

Whale
Akhlut, Cetus, Derketo, Fastitocalon, Galemelle, Orc, Qanekelak, Roshwalr, Rosmarine, Saint Attracta's Monster, Scolopendra, Tursus, Zaratan

13. BEINGS THAT ARE HORSES OR PART HORSE
Aavak, Actaeon, Aethon, Alsvid, Aonbárr, Apotharni, Arion, Arrak, Arusha and Arushi, Astrope, Aufhocker, Baku, Balios, Barushka Matushka, Bayard, Biasd na Srognig, Black Devil, Borak (Al), Boroka, Brag, Bronte, Buckland Shag, Camahueto, Cartazonon, Ceffyll-dŵr, centaur, Centycore, Champ, Cheiron, Cheval Bayard, Cichol, Conopenii, Dadhikra, Dragon-Horse, Eačh Uisge, Énbarr, Endrop, Eous, Equus bipes, Fomor/s, Gaki, Gandarva, Glashtin, Goborchinu, Gryps, Gytrash, Haietlik, Haizum, Havhest, Hayagriva, Hippocamp, Hippocentaur, Hippocerf, Hippogryph, Horse (Oriental), Horse of Neptune, Houyhnhms, Hrimfaxi, Hydrippus, Ichthyocentaur, Inhabitants of Islands near Dondun, Ipopodes, Karkadan, Kelpy, Keshi, Ki-lin, Kimpurushas, Kinnara, Kludde, Koresck, Kosmatushka, Lampon, Loup garou, Ma Mien, Mares of Diomedes, Misiganebic, Monoceros (1), Monster of Brompton, Nara, Neugle, Nicker, Nix, Nogle, Ogopogo, Oschaert, Papillon, Pegasi, Pegasus, Phaethon, Phantom of the Lake, Phlegon, Piranu, Ponik, Pooka, Poqhirāj, Pyrois, Roshwalr, Rosmarus, Samvarta, Sa-yin, Sea Horse, Sea-Serpent of Memphrémagog, Shag Foal, Sileni (pl), Sivushko, Skinfaxi, Sleipnir, Svadilfari, Tairbe Uisge, Tangie, Tcipitckaam, Ting Ling Kuo Yan, Tipaka, unicorn, Visvavasu, Wihwin, Xanthos, Ypotamis

14. BEINGS THAT ARE HUMANOID OR PART HUMAN
Abominable Snowman, Adaro, Alcyoneus, Almas, Amduscias, A-mi-kuk, Anakim, Androsphinx, Angka,

Apotamkin, Apotharni, Araxa Junior, Arion, Arzshenk, Asin, Asterion, Aunyainá, Azi Dahaka, Bahri, Bali, Baphomet, Basilisk, Beast of Lettir Dallan, Betikhân, Bicha, Bicorne, Bigfoot, Bird-Man, Black Devil, Blemmyes, Bobalicón, Bockman, Bogyman, Boraro, Boroka, Bulchin, Bulugu, Buso, Cacus, Caliban, Callitrice, Capricornus, Cecrops, Celphie, Ch'uan-T'ou (People of), Cheeroonear, Cheiron, Cheval Bayard, Chiang-Liang, Chichevache, Chonchonyi, Chorti, Cichol, Cigouave, Circhos, Ciudach, Clytius, Cockatrice, Coinchenn, Crom Crumh Chomnaill, Cyclopedes, Deadoendjadases, Dhumavarna, Dirae, Direach, Djin/n, Doonongaes, Dossenus, Dracula, Drake, Ents, Ereshigal, Erichthonius, Erinyes, Eurytus (1), Faun, Fer Caille, Fomor/s, Frankenstein's Monster, Fsti capcaki, Fuath, Fu-Hsi, Gaborchend, Gandharvas, Garuda, Geryon, Girtablili, Glashtin, Goborchinu, Golem, Gougou, Grindylow, Gryllus, Haduigona, Hairy-Man, Hai-uri, Har-machis, Havman, Hemicynes, Hippocentaur, Hirguan, Hsiao, Hsing-T'ien, Human Snakes, Humbaba, Hybris, Ichthyophagi, Igpupiara, Ipopodes, Jabberwock, Jaguar-Man, Jarapiri, Jidra, Kabanda, Kaia, Kallicantzari, Kashehotapolo, Katyutayuuq, Keen Keengs, Keinnara, Kelpy, Keyeme, Kimpurushas, Kinnara, Kirata, Koerakoonlased, Kojin, Komos, Konoha Tengu, Kudan, Kul, Lailoken, Lama, Lamassu, Lamya, Leshii, Liban, Lioumere, Loathly Lady, Lobíson, Lung Wang, Lycanthrope, Ma Mien, Manducus, Manticore, mermaid/e, merman, Minotaur, Monk Fish, Monocoli, Mountain Man, Murghi-i-Ādami, Naga/s, Näkinneito, Näkki, Nalusa Falaya, Namorodo, Nashas, Nee-gued, Nehebkau, Nellie Long Arms, Niu T'ou, Nu Kwa, Ocypete, ogre, ogress, Old Man of the Sea, Omo Nero, Onditachiae, Paija, Palesmurt, Papstesel, Peg Powler, Pelorus, Pey, Pi Nereskə, Ping Feng, Podarge, Polybutes, Porphyrion, Posthon, Priscaraxe, Ptitsy-Siriny, Qanekelak, Rahu, Rakshasa/s, Ravenna Monster, Rosmarine, Samebito, Sang Gala Raja, San-Shou Kuo Yan, Sarkany, Sasabonsam, Sasquatch, satyr, Sciapod/s, Serpent of Eden, Shen-Nung, Shiqq, Shojo, Sileni, Silenus, Silvani, Simos, Sinaa, Sirena (1), Siren/s, Sisupala, Skatene, Solovei Rakhmatich, Stcemqestcint, Stikini, Tages, Takujui, T'ao-Tieh, Tengu/s, Thingut, Thunderbird, Ting Ling Kuo Yan, Tisikh puk, Torto, Triton, Tunnituaqruk, Tursus, Uhepono, Urisk, Vampire, Virabandra, Viradha, Visvavasu, Vodianoi, Vough, Were-Crocodile, Were-Dog, Werewolf, Wildman, Witico, Wulgaru, Xiang Yao, Yahoo, Yara-ma-yha-who, Yehwe Zogbanu, Yeti, Ypotamis, Yü-Min Kuo Yan, Zägh, Zangarrón, Zmei Gorynich

15. BEINGS THAT ARE LAND SERPENTS, SNAKES, AND WORMS OR PART SERPENT

Land Serpents
Äi, Aiatar, Äijätär, Äijo, Ajatar, Akhekhu, Angont, Azi Dahaka, Beast, Beithir, Boa, Bolla, Bullar, Camoodi, Cerastes, Cuelebre, Dabbat, Dhakhan, Dhrana, Dhumavarna, Doonongaes, Draco, Draconcopedes, Dragon of Saint Leonard's Forest, Drake, Eight-Forked Serpent of Koshi, Epirotes, Falak, Glycon, Great Serpent of Hell, Horned Serpent, Hornworm, Jaculus, Jin, Jormungandr, Kichiknebik, King of the Snakes, Kitzinackas, Lightning Serpent, Lindorm, Make, Manitoukinebic, Midgardsorm/r, Misikinipik, Misikinubick, Msi-Kinepikwa, Muchalinda,

Naga Pahoda, Naga/s, Namtar, On Niont, Python, Racumon, Raja Naga, Scoffin, serpent, Serpent King, Serpent of Eden, Serpent of Isa (Flying), Serpent of Omi, Serpent of Sagaris, Serpent of the Reuss, Shar-Mar, Sirena (2), Sisiutl, Slimy Slim, Snow Snake, Stoorworm, Stvkwvnaya, Syren, Tcinto-Saktco, Tzeltal, Ugrasura, Uraeus, Uwabami, Vasuki, Vritra, Vulpangue

Land Snakes
Bobi-Bobi, Bolla, Ch'ang Hao, Dhrana, Great Horned Serpent, Herensugue, Hoop Snake, Kaia, King of the Snakes, Odz-Manouk, Pihuechenyi, Snow Snake, Zuzeca

Part Serpent or Snake
Alcyoneus, Amphiptere, Amphisbaena, Apocalyptic Beast, Chimera, Clytius, Cockatrice, Echidne, Enceladus, Erichthonius, Eurale, Eurytus (1), Fei Lian, Fu-Hsi, Gegeneis, Gigantes, Gorgon (3), Gratium, Groot Slang, Guivre, Hippolytus, Humbaba, Iémisch, Iriz Ima, Jarapiri, La Velue, Lamia, Lamya, Mafedet, Medusa, Mimas, Mušhuššu, Nehebkau, Nu Kwa, Otus, Papstesel, Pelorus, Phoetus, Piast/s, Polybutes, Porphyrion, Questing Beast, Scitalis, Snake Griffon, Sphinx, Tages, Thoas, Tityus, Wyvern, Xiang Yao, Zmei Gorynich

Worms and Orms
Burach Bhadi, Kitchi-at'Husis, Laidley Worm, Lambton Worm, Lindorm, Loathly Worm, Midgardsorm/r, Orm, Peiste, Scatha the Worm, Stoorworm, Vurm, Weewilmekq, Wode Worm of Linton, Worm

16. BEINGS THAT ARE WINGED OR FLYING
Airāvata, Alan, Alecto, Alicanto, Alklha, Amphiptere, Aries, Arion, Asipatra, Aspis, Baba Yaga, Basilisk, Bird-Man, Bmola, Boa, Borak (Al), Borogove, Boroka, Catoblepas, Ceffyll-dŵr, Chamrosh, Chonchonyi, Ch'uan-T'ou (People of), Cockatrice, Cold-Drakes, Cuelebre, Cynoprosopi, Dadhikra, Dirae, Dogs of Fo, Draco, Dracula, Dragon (Ethiopian), Dragon (Occidental), Dumbeldors, Eous, Erinyes, Eurale, Fire-drake, Flying Fish, Flying Heads, Fung, Furies, Garuda, Goofus, Gorgon, Griffin, Hai Riyo, Harpy, Hatuibwari, Herensugue, Hippocamp, Hofafa, Hraesvelg, Hua-Hu-Tiao, Humility, Imdugud, Jabberwock, Jaculus, Jurik, Kaukas, Keen Keengs, Konoha Tengu, Kuçedrë, Lama, Llamhigyn y Dwr, Medusa, Melusine, Monster of Lake Fagua, Mountain Woman, Nara, Nashas, Ngani-vatu, Nix, Opinicus, Oshädagea, P' Êng, Papillon, Pegasus, Peryton, Philamaloo Bird, Pinnacle Grouse, Pontianak, Poqhirāj, Pouakai, Puk, Ravenna Monster, Sampati, Satyre-Fish, Scatha the Worm, Schachi Hoko, Senmurv, Serpent of Eden, Serpent of Isa (Flying), Serra, Sirena (2), Siren/s, Smaug the Golden, Sphinx, Stymphalian Birds, Tengu/s, Thunderbird, Tipaka, Tobi Tatsu, Tugarin, Tulihänd, Urulóki, Uwabami, vampire, Vis, Vodianoi, Vrikodara, Vuokho, Wakinyan, Waukkeon, Wyvern, Ying Lung, Yü-Min Kuo Yan

17. DRAGONS—OCCIDENTAL
Ahi, Äi, Aiatar, Äijätär, Äijo, Aitvaras, Ajatar, Alicha, Alklha, Amphisbaena, Anantaboga, Ancalagon the Black,

Anzu, Apalala, Arakho, Asdeev, Aspis, Azi Dahaka, Basilic, Beast, Beithir, Bel, Bistern Dragon, Brobinyak, Campacti, Catoblepas, Chudo-Yudo, Coca, Cockatrice, Cold-Drakes, Cynoprosopi, Dahak, Ddraig Goch (Y), Derketo, Draco, Dracontides, Dragon (Epidaurian), Dragon (Ethiopian), Dragon (Occidental), Dragon at Uffington, Dragon Maid, Dragon of Ladon, Dragon of Saint Leonard's Forest, Dragon of the Apocalypse, Dragonmaid, Dragon-Tygre, Dragon-wolf, Drake, Elbst, Epirotes, Fafnir, Fire Dragon, Fire-drake, Gaasyendietha, Gandareva, Ganj, Gargouille, Girtablili, Glaurung, Glyryvilu, Gorgon (2), Gorynich, Goryshche, Gowrow, Grendel, Guita, Guivre, Guyascutus, Gwiber, Herensugue, Hippocamp, Hog (Sea), Hordeshyrde, Hydra, Hydrus, Illuyankas, Jabberwock, Kashchei, Kaukas, King of the Snakes, Koshchei, Kuçedrë, Kulili, Kulshedra, Lady of the Land, Loathly Worm, Loch Ness Monster, Lotan, Melusine, Mušhuššu, Naul, Nidhogg, Odz-Manouk, Oilliphéist, Orm, Ouroboros, Peiste, Piast/s, Pisuhänd, Puk, Pukis, Python, Rager, Rahab, Red Dragon of Wales, Safat, Sarkany, Scatha the Worm, Scitalis, Simargl, Simorg, Simurgh, Sinhika, Sirrush, Skoffin, Smaug the Golden, Stihi, Stollenwurm, Svara, Tanihwa, Tannin, Tarasca, Tarasque, Thu'ban, Tiamat, Tinnin, Tulihänd, Unhcegila, Urulóki, Vishap, Vouivre, Vritra, Wantley (the Dragon of), Wivre, Worm, Wyvern, Zmag Ognjeni Vuk, Zû

18. DRAGONS—ORIENTAL
Anantaboga, Ao Chin, Ao Jun, Ao Kuang, Ao Ping, Ao Shun, Apalala, Azure Dragon, Barong, Blue Dragon, Bujanga, Chang Lung, Chi Lung Wang, Dragon Kings, Dragon of Izumo, Dragon-Carp, Dragon-Horse, Fu-ts'ang, Golden Dragon Naga Mas, Gong-gong, Gou Mang, Hai Riyo, Jishin-Mushi, Jurik, Kih Tiau, Kiyo, K'uei, Lei, Lei Chen-Tzu, Li No Zha, Lung, Lung Wang, Naga Mas, O Goncho, Oriental Dragon, Pai Lung, Proper Conduct Dragon, Raitaro, Rinjin, Rou Shou, Ryujin, Samebito, Schachi Hoko, Shen Lung, Sinhika, T'ao-Tieh, Tatsu, Thunder Dragon, Ti Lung, Tien Lung, Tioman, Tobi Tatsu, Toyotama, Xiang Yao, Yellow Dragon, Ying Lung, Yu Lung

19. GIANTS AND GIANTESSES—BIBLICAL
Anakim, Antichrist, Christopher (Saint), Daughters of Cain, Enim, Gibborim, Gog, Goliath, Ham, Japheth, Nebrod, Nephilim, Nimrod, Noachids, Noah, Og, Palet, Rephaim, Zamzumin, Zuzim

20. GIANTS AND GIANTESSES IN FOLKLORE AND TRADITIONAL TALES
Albastor, Antero Vipunen, Antigonus, Arimbi, Ascapard, Azrail, Balan, Balor, Begdu San, Bell, Berrey Dhone, Bevis, Big Man-eater, Bigfoot, Binaye Ahani, Bishop Fish, Blunderbore, Bobalicón, Bombomachides, Boo-bagger, Bran, Brandamour, Brobinyak, Buggane, Bungisngis, Bunyan (Paul), Caillagh ny Groamagh, Cailleach Beinne Bric, Cailleach Bheur, Caravinaigre, Carl of Carlisle, Carn Galver, Cawr, Cerne Abbas Giant, Chahnameed, Child Guzzler, Chorti, Cichol, Cliff-Ogre, Coco, Colbrand, Cormeilian, Cormelian, Cormoran, Cymidei Cymeinfoll, Dehotgohsgayeh, Dev, Dillus Farfog, Direach, Diwrnach Wyddel, Drake, Druon, Fachan, Fachtna Fáthach,

Fenodyree, Fir Chreig, Flaming Teeth, Foawr, Gayant, Geldegwsets, Gergasi, Ghaddar, Giant Holdfast, Giant of Smeeth, Giant of Wales, Giant Onion, Giants of Callanish, Gogmagog, Gorm, Gourmaillon, Hairy-Man, Idris, Inugpasugssuk, Jokao, Kalevanpojat, Kallicantzari, Kinderschrecker, King Auriaria, Konoha Tengu, Labasta, Llassar Llaes Gyfnewid, Long Man of Wilmington, Louhi, Loup garou, Lustucru (Le Grand), Matau, Mauleon, Metal Old Man, Milžinas, Nahgane, Näkki, Nalmuqtse, Nickneven, Red Etin, Rhita Gawr, Rosmer, Sikuliasuituq, Skrimsl, Split-Faced Being, Tartaro, Thelgeth, Tork, Torto, Troll, Tugarin, Vanapagan, Veli Joze, Vörys-mort, Wandil, Wandlebury Giant, Wayland Smith, Woglog, Wry Face, Yn Foldyr Gastey, Zangarrón

21. GIANTS AND GIANTESSES—LEGENDARY
Alchendic, Arimbi, Ascapard, Azrail, Begdu San, Belagog, Bendigeifran, Bevis, Bran, Bunyan (Paul), Carl of Carlisle, Chahnameed, Charlemagne, Chernubles de Munigre, Cichol, Colbrand, Cormelian, Cymidei Cymeinfoll, Dillus Farfog, Direach, Dis Samothes, Diwrnach Wyddel, Druon, Dzoo-noo-qua, Fachtna Fáthach, Flaming Teeth, Foawr, Fomor/s, Gambier, Gargam, Gayant, Giant of Mont Saint Michel, Giantess of Loch Ness, Giantesses of Putney and Fulham, Gog and Magog, Gogmagog, Gowrow, Ice Giants, Idris, Kalevanpojat, Kallicantzari, King Auriaria, Kiwahkw, Li No Zha, Llassar Llaes Gyfnewid, Lochlonnach, Lumakaka, Midchaín, Miodhchaoin, Moll Walbee, Morholt, Mountain Woman, Nabon, Nigelung, Nulayuuiniq, Orribes, Pangu, Puterei Sembaran Gunung, Reksoso, Rhita Gawr, Scardyng, Schilbung, Searbhán, Seatco, Sikuliasuituq, Sinaa, Stalo, Stone Giants, Tammatuyuq, Tapagöz, Taulurd, Tegid Foel, Tork, Tsavoojok, Uath, Urgan, Wade, Wikramadatta, Wildman, Wrnach, Wulgaru, Yeitso, Ysbaddaden

22. GIANTS AND GIANTESSES—LITERARY
Agrippa, Albion, Alifanfaron, Alous, Anthropophagus, Araxa, Astreus, Balan, Bellerus, Bloody-man, Bran, Bringuenarilles, Brobdingnagians, Bruyer, Capaneus, Celtes, Chalbroth, Christopher (Saint), Cichol, Corineus, Crana, Cranus, Cymidei Cymeinfoll, Dercynus, Despair (Giant), Dhoya, Dis Samothes, Druon, Egeon, Enay, Ents, Entwives, Eryx, Etion, Faribroth, Farracutus, Ferragut, Fierabras, Fimbrethil, Finglas, Flandrif, Fracassus, Gabbara, Galatea, Galathes, Galehaut, Galemelle, Gambrivius, Gargamelle, Gargantua, Gayoffe, Gemmagog, Glumdalclitch, Goemagot, Gos et Magos, Granaus, Grandgousier, Grim, Ham, Happemousche, Herminon, Hunnus, Hurtaly, Ingaevon, Ingcél Caech, Inhabitants of Islands near Dondun, Istaevon, Japetus Junior, Japheth, Jovis Bellus, Jovis Saga, Loup garou, Macrus, Masus, Maul, Micromégas, Morgante, Morguan, Nembrotus, Noachids, Noah, Nymbrotus, Oceanus (2), Offotus, Ogre, Ogyges, Olog-Hai, Onodrim, Pagan, Pallenes, Pandora Junior, Pantagruel, Pope, Porus, Prisca, Priscus, Prometheus, Quaresmeprenant, Red-Legged Scissor-man, Regina, Rosmarine, Sarabroth, Secundilla, Shem, Slay-good, Suevus, Taulurd, Teutanes, Thetis, Thundel, Torogs, Tourmentine, Tubal, Tuisto, Tuyscon Gigas, Typhon, Tytan/s, Tytea Magna, Uruks, Vandaluus, Woglog, Zimbardo

23. GIANTS AND GIANTESSES—MYTHOLOGICAL

Aegir, Agrius, Albion, Alcyoneus, Aloadae, Angboda, Antaeus, Antero Vipunen, Arges, Argus, Atlas, Aurgelmir, Bali, Balor, Baugi, Be Chasti, Bébinn, Bel (2), Bergbui, Bergelmir, Bergjarl, Bergriser, Bestia, Bhima, Bochica, Bolthorn, Borr, Briareus, Brontes, Cannibal-at-the-North-End-of-the-World, Ceus, Ch'os-skyon, Clymene, Clytius, Coeus, Cottus, Cratos, Crius, Cyclops, Damastes, Dehotgohsgayeh, Dercynus, Dharmapālas, Dione, Drifta, Dzoavits, Eggther, Enceladus, Ephialtes, Epimetheus, Eurymedon, Eurytion, Eurytus (1), Fárbauti, Fiorgyn, Fire Giants, Fornjotr, Frost Giants, Frosti, Fsti capcaki, Gaia, Ga-oh, Geirröd, Gerd, Geryon, Gigantes, Gilling, Gougou, Grandfather, Gratium, Gridr, Guhyaka, Gunnlod, Gwrgwnt, Gyes, Gyges, Gymir, Haduigona, Hayagriva, Hayicanako, Hecate, Hecatoncheires, Hippolytus, Hok Braz, Hrimthurses, Hrungnir, Hrym, Hugi, Humbaba, Hundred-Handed Giants, Huwawa, Hymir, Hyperion, Iapetus, Iarnsaxa, Iya, Japetidæ, Johul, Jokao, Jörd, Jotun, Joukahainen, Juternajesta, Juternsaxa, Kabanda, Kaitabha, Kari, Keen Keengs, Khumbaba, Kois, Kronos, Kua Fu, Kumbaba, Kumbhakarna, Læstrygones, Lamus, Logi, Loha-Mukha, Louhi, Lycaon, Magni, Manzaširi, Margygr (1), Másaw, Menoetius, Mikula, Mimas, Mimir, Modi, Muchukunda, Muircartach, Muspel, Oceanus (1), One-Standing-and-Moving, Ongwe Ias, Ophion (2), Orion, Oshädagea, Otus, Pallas, Pelagon, Pelorus, Perses, Phoebe, Phoetus, Phorcys, Polybutes, Polypemon, Polyphemus, Porphyrion, Procrustes, Prometheus, Proteus, Purusha, Rhaetos, Rhea, Rhœtus (2), rTa-mgin, Senjemand, sGrolma, Sinis, Skadi, Skrymir, Skrymsli, Snoer, Starkadr, Stone Giants, Sutr, Suttung, Svyatogor, Tall Man, Talos, Tangata, Tethys, Thardid Jimbo, Theia, Themis, Thiassi, Thoas, Thökk, Thrym, Thurses, Titan, Titanides, Tityus, Tornit, Tui Delai Gau, Twisted face, Typhon, Uhepono, Ullikummi, Upelleru, Uranus, Utgard-Loki, Vajravina, Valedjád, Vasty, Viradha, Viraj, Vrikodara, Vukub-cakix, Warrior-of-the-World, Waziya, Winalagilis, Xelhua, Yehwe Zogbanu, Yeitso, Ymir, Yulu Yulara, Zipacna

24. HERALDIC BEASTS

Allocamelus, Amphiptere, Amphisbaena, Amphisien, Ass-Bittern, Bagwyn, Baphomet, Basilisk, Calopus, Calygreyhound, Camel-Leopard, Cat-Fish, centaur, Centicore, Cockatrice, Cock-fish, Dogs (Sea), Dragon (Occidental), Dragon-Tygre, Dragon-wolf, Enfield, Epimacus, Falcon-fish, Garuda, Giant, Griffin, Guivre, Harpy, Hippocamp, Hippocerf, Hydra, Lion-Griffon, Lyon-Poisson, Man-Tiger, Melusine, Mermaid/e, Merman, Nependis, Opinicus, Parandus, Phoenix, Salamander, satyr, Satyre-Fish, Sea Horse, Sea-Dog, Sea-Lion, Snake Griffon, Sphinx, Triton, Tyger, unicorn, Wildman, Wyvern, Yale

25. PRIMORDIAL BEINGS

Antero Vipunen, Aurgelmir, Azi Dahaka, Bestia, Bolthorn, Borr, Campacti, Ceus, Da, Delgeth, Emusha, Fire Dragon, Fornjotr, Frost Giants, Gēush Urvan, Gaia, Giant, Giant of Cardiff (N.Y.), Gigantes, Girtablili, Gosh, Hadhayōsh, Hatuibwari, Hundred-Handed Giants, Itherther, Jotun, Joukahainen, Kaitabha, Kamapua'a, Keen Keengs, Kholomodumo, Kua Fu, Kujata, Lakhamu, Leviathan, Logi, Lotan, Madhu, Manzaširi, Mikula, Misikinipik, Naga

Pahoda, Ophion (1), Pallas, Pangu, Proteus, Puntan, Purusha, Rager, Rahab, Rahu, Rigi, Riiki, Sesha, sGrolma, Stone Giants, Talos, Tammatuyuq, Tangata, Tannin, Theia, Thia, Tieholtsodi, Tisikh puk, Titan, Ullikummi, Umai-Hulhlya-wit, Upelleru, Uranus, Valedjád, Vasuki, Viraj, Yeitso, Ymir

26. SATIRICAL OR COMICAL MONSTERS

Alicanto, Argopelter, Augerino, Axehandle Hound, Bandersnatch, Bildad, Bunyan (Paul), Cactus Cat, Cuba, Dew-Mink, Ding Ball, Dossenus, Fearsome Critters, Fracassus, Giant, Giddy Fish, Gillygaloo, Glawackus, Godaphro, Goofang, Goofus, Gouger, Gumberoo, Guyanoosa, Guyascutus, Gwinter, Hidebehind, Hodag, Hoop Snake, Humility, Jabberwock, Kickle Snifter, Leprocaun, Lucive, Lunkus, Manducus, Moskitto, Mountain Stem-Winder, Mugwump, Philamaloo Bird, Pinnacle Grouse, Porus, Prock Gwinter, Rickaboo Racker, Rockabore, Roperite, Rubberado, Rumptifusel, Sauger, Shagamaw, Shmoo, Sidehill Dodger, Sidehill Ganger, Sideswipe, Sidewinder, Silenus, Sliver Cat, Snark, Snow Snake, Splinter Cat, Squonk, Teakettler, Tripoderoo, Whappernocker, Whimpus, Windigo (1)

27. SEA MONSTERS AND SEA SERPENTS
Sea Monsters

Auvekoejak, Balena, Beisht Kione, Camahueto, Chan, Derketo, Fastitocalon, Flying Fish, Golden Dragon Naga Mas, Hafgygr, Hai Ho Shang, Hare (Sea), Havstrambe, Imap Umassoursa, Keto, Kih Tiau, Kraken, Margygr, Marine Boar, Marine Sow, Mokêle-Mbêmbe, Monoceros (2), Monoceros Marinus, Naga Mas, Nuckalevee, Orc, Parata, Phorcys, Pongo, Roshwalr, Rosmarus, Ruszor, Sahab, Scolopendra, Scylla, Sea Buddhist Priest, Serra, Sínach, Skrimsl, Sykraken, Te Tuna, Telchines, Tumu-Ra'i-Fuena, Tursus, Wihwin, Wiwilemekw, Yagim, Yannig, Zaratan

Sea Serpents

Cìrein Cròin, Curtag Mhòr a' Chuain, Dhumavarna, Echeneis, Hedammu, Kih Tiau, Lindorm, Mial Mhòr a' Huain, Rager, Rahab, Ruki, Sjøorm, Skrimsl, Tannin, Uile Bhéisd a' Chuain, Yofune-Nushi

28. WORLD SERPENT AND COSMIC SERPENTS AND BEINGS
Cosmic Serpents

Aapep, Agunua, Ahi, Ananta, Ayida, Da, Damballah, Degei, Falak, Hatuibwari, Jormungandr, Ka-en-ankh Nereru, Kujata, Maka, Mehen, Midgardsorm/r, Ophion (1), Palulukon, serpent, Sesha, Umai-Hulhlya-wit

Other Cosmic Beings

Akūpāra, Amala, Anjana, Audhumla, Bahamut, Behemoth, Dhaul, Dhol, Gēush Urvan, Great Galactic Ghoul, Hayicanako, Himapandara, Kama-Dhenu, Khara, Kujata, Kumuda, Kurma, Leviathan, Lokapala Elephants, Mahapadma, Moshiriikkwechep, Mušhuššu, Nidhogg, Oceanus (1), Ouroboros, Palulukon, Pangu, Pundarika, Puntan, Purusha, Pushpadanta, Qanekelak, Rigi, Riiki, Sarvabhauma, Saumanasa, Supratika, Suryabhauma, Tiamat, Ullikummi, Upelleru, Vamana, Virupaksha

29. BEINGS BY COUNTRY, REALM, OR PEOPLE
Ancient Realms (and Countries Whose Boundaries No Longer Exist)

Anatolia: Ullikummi, Upelleru

Assyria: Dragon, Lama, Lamassu, Lion-Griffon, Utukku

Babylon: Anzu, Bel, Celtes, Derketo, Galathes, Girtablili, Hercules Libyus, Kingu, Lamassu, Mušhuššu, Scorpion man, Sphinx, Tiamat, Tuyscon Gigas, Zû

Classical Mythology of Greece and Rome: Acamas, Actoridæ, Æthon, Agrius, Alcyoneus, Alecto, Aloadae, Antaeus, Aper Calydonius, Arctophonos, Arges, Argus, Aries, Arion, Asterion, Astreus, Astrope, Atlas, Balius, Briareus, Brontes, Calydonian Boar, Campe, Capricornus, Capri-pedes, Celaeno, Centaur, Centauro-triton, Centimanes, Cerberus, Cercopes, Cerynean Hind, Cetus, Ceus, Charybdis, Cheiron, Chimera, Chrysaor, Chrysomallus, Clytius, Coeus, Cottus, Cratos, Cretan Bull, Crieus, Crius, Cronus, Cteatus, Cyclops, Cyllarus, Damastes, Deino, Delphyne, Dione, Dracontides, Dragon of Ladon, Echidne, Enceladus, Enyo, Eous, Ephialtes, Epimetheus, Epirotes, Erichthonius, Erymanthean Boar, Eurale, Eurymedon, Eurytion, Eurytus (1), Eurytus (2), Exedra, Gaia, Gargittios, Gegeneis, Geryon, Geryon's Dogs, Gigantes, Gorgon, Græ æ, Gratium, Griffin Vulture, Gryps, Gyes, Hecate, Hippocamp, Hippolytus, Horse of Neptune, Hundred-Handed Giants, Hylæus, Hyperion, Iapetionidæ, Iapetus, Ipopodes, Japetidæ, Japetus, Kentaure, Kérberos, Keto, Klymene, Koios, Kois, Kreios, Kronos, Kyklopes, Laestrygonians, Lamia, Lampon, Lamus, Lernean Hydra, Leucosia, Lycidas, Mares of Diomedes, Medusa, Menoetius, Mimas, Minotaur, Mnemosyne, Molionids, Monychus, Nemean Lion, Nessus, Oceanus (1), Ocypete, Ophion (2), Ophion (3), Orion, Orthos, Otus, Oxen of Geryon, Pallas, Pallenes, Parthenope, Pegasus, Pelagon, Pelorus, Pemphredo, Perses, Phaea, Phaethon, Phlegon, Phoebe, Phoetus, Pholus, Phorcides, Phorcys, Podarge, Polybutes, Polypemon, Polyphemus, Porphyrion, Procrustes, Prometheus, Proteus, Ptoophagos, Python, Rhaetos, Rhea, Rhœcus, Rhœtus (1), Rhœtus (2), Saggitarius, Serpent of Sagaris, Silvani, Sinis, Siren/s, Steropes, Stheno, Stymphalian Birds, Talos, Tethys, Teumessian Vixen, Theia, Themis, Thoas, Titan, Titanides, Tityus, Triton, Typhon, Uranus, Xanthos

Egypt, Ancient: Aapep, Akhekhu, Amam, Amermait, Ammit, Androsphinx, Apis, Bennu, Buchis, Bukhe See, Bull of Meroe, Criosphinx, Epaphus, Griffin, Gryllus, Hap, Harmachis, Hieracosphinx, Hor-em-akhen, Hydrus, Ka-en-ankh Nereru, Mafedet, Maka, Mehen, Menuis, Merwer, Mnevis, Namtar, Nehebkau, Ouroboros, Sutekh, Uraeus

Mesopotamia: Abgal, Anzu, Capricornus, Chamrosh, Derketo, Gandareva, Girtablili, Griffin, Hedammu, Hippocamp, Humbaba, Huwawa, Illuyankas, Imdugud, Khumbaba, Kingu, Labbu, Lakhamu, Lakhmu, Lotan, Manticore, Mušhuššu, Semurv, Senmurv, Sinam, Sirrush, Sphinx, Symir, Zû

Persia (now Iran): Asdeev, Ass (Three-Legged), Chamrosh, Conopenii, Cynocephali, Dahak, Ganj, Gēush Urvan, Glycon, Gosh, Hadhayōsh, Kar-Fish, Karkadan, Khara, Koresck, Onyx Monoceros, Phoenix, Senmurv, Simurgh, Sinam, Symir, Thu'ban, Unicorn, Zaratan

Sumer: Abgal, Amphitrites, Anzu, Apkallu, Bull of Heaven, Capricornus, Dragon (Occidental), Ereshigal, Gandareva, Goat (Sea), Gudanna, Humbaba, Kulili, Kundrav, Lama, Suhur-mas, Tiamat, Zû

Modern Boundaries and Cultures
Africa

East Africa—Zambia: Were-Crocodile

North Africa—Libya: Al

South Africa—General: Beast; **Khoisin people:** Aigamuchas, Aigamuxa, Ga-gorib, Hai-uri, Ndzoodzoo

Southeast Africa—Sotho people: Kholomodumo; **Tanzania:** Pamba; **Zambia:** Lightning Monsters, Were-Crocodile; **General:** Were-Hyena, Were-Jackal, Were-Leopard

West Africa—Dahomey: Aido Hwedo, Da, Dan Ayido Hwedo, Groot Slang, Iriz Ima; **Congo Region:** Abada, Migas, Rainbow Serpent; **Yoruba People of Nigeria:** Oshumare; **Tschwi and Ashanti People:** Sasabonsam

Armenia
Agog-Magog, Azrail, Basilisk, Beast, Cockatrice, Dev, Horses of the Sun (Enik, Menik and Senik), Odz-Manouk, Shar-Mar, Svara, Tapagöz, Tork, Vishap

Australia
Aranda, Bobi-Bobi, Bulaing, Bulugu, Bunyip, Cheeroonear, Dhakhan, Dheeyabery, Dhinnabarrada, Eer-Moonan, Galeru, Gambier, Giant Dingo, Good Hoop, Gunapipi, Gurangatch, Hobyah, Jarapiri, Julunggul, Jurawadbad, Kaleru, Kalseru, Karia, Keen Keengs, Keleru, King Pratie, Kun Manggur, Kunapipi, Kurrea, Langal, Lightning Serpent, Maldape, Mindi, Muit, Munga Munga, Namorodo, Ngalbjod, Rainbow Serpent, Taipan, Thardid Jimbo, Thugine, Tuntabah, Ungud, Universal Eye, Wanambi, Whowhie, Woinunggur, Wollunqua, Worombi, Wulgaru, Wulungu, Yara-ma-yha-who, Yero, Yowie, Yulu Yulara, Yulunggu, Yurlunggur

Austria
Dard, Lady of Lake Traun, Mistress of the Lake, Monoceros Marinus, Tatzelwurm

Belgium
Antigonus, Bullebak, Druon, Gayant, Goliath, Kludde, Town Giants

Burma
Avagráh, Gráha, Keinnara, Nagini Besandi, Nyan, Tanti-gáha

Canada
Amarok, Ashuaps, Auvekoejak, Bakbakwakanooksiwae, Bigfoot, Cannibal-at-the-North-End-of-the-World, Champ, Crooked Beak of Heaven, Engulfer, Erqigdlit, Estas, Galokwudzuwis, Great Serpent of Hell, Gwagwakhwalanooksiwey, Haietlik, Halfway People, Hînûmemen, Hokhoku, Horned Serpent, Ikuutayuuq, Inugpasugssuk, Kaneakeluh, Katyn Tayuuq, Katyutayuuq, Keelut, Kisihohkew, Loup garou, Manipogo, Mashernomak, Matchi-Manitou, Michipichi,

Michi-Pichoux, Miqqiayuuq, Misikinipik, Miskena, Missipissy, Mystery of the Waters, Nahgane, Naitaka, Nogle, No-Kos-Ma, Nulayuuiniq, Ogopogo, One Who Drills, One-Standing-and-Moving, Oniares, Oyaleroweck, Paija, Ponik, Qanekelak, Qiqion, Sasquatch, Sea-Serpent of Memphrémagog, Serpent, Sikuliasuituq, Sisiutl, Tammatuyuq, Tcinto-Saktco, Torngarsoak, Tornit, Troll, Tsemaus, Tuniq, Tunnituaqruk, Tuurnngaq, Warrior-of-the-World, Wendigo, Winalagilis, Witico, Wiwilemekw, Yagim

Caribbean Islands
Ayida, Cigouave, Damballah, Legarou, Plat-eye, Racumon, Rainbow Serpent, Sukuyan

Central and South America
Argentina: Cherufe, Piranu, Tigre Capiango, Yaquaru
Brazil: Aunyainá, Igpupiara, Lobíson, Minata-Karaia, Sinaa, Valedjád, Yurupari
Chile: Alicanto, Calchona, Camahueto, Cherufe, Chivato, Chonchonyi, Colo-Colo, Cuero, Encerrados, Glyryvilu, Guirivulu, Hide, Huallepén, Invunche, Lampalugua, Manta, Monster of Lake Fagua, Pihuechenyi, Serpent, Trelquehuecuve, vampire, Vulpangue, White Chest
Colombia: Bochica
Ecuador: Iwančï
Guatemala: Chorti
Guyana: People of Caora
Honduras: Wihwin
Mexico: Ahuizotl, Balam, Balam-Agab, Balam-Quitzé, Campacti, Chorti, Hoga, Iqi-Balam, Mahu-Catah, Tlatecuhtli, Xelhua, Xólotl
Paraguay: Jaguar-Man
Peru: Ccoa
Surinam: Azeman
Venezuela: Ewaipanoma

China
Ao Chin, Ao Jun, Ao Kuang, Ao Ping, Ao Shun, Azure Dragon, Begdu San, Blue Dragon, Celestial Stag, Chan, Ch'ang Hao, Chang Lung, Ch'i Lin, Chi Lung Wang, Chiai Tung, Chiang-Liang, Chi'i-Lin, Chinese Dragon, Chio-Tuan, Ch'ou-T'i, Ch'uan-T'ou (People of), Dogs of Fo, Dragon Kings, Dragon-Horse, Fei Lian, Feng Hwang, Fu-Hsi, Fum Hwang, Fung, Fu-ts'ang, Gong-gong, Gou Mang, Hai Chiai, Hai Ho Shang, He-Li-Di, Hsiao, Hsing-T'ien, Hua-Hu-Tiao, Hui, Hwa Yih, Hwang, I-Mu Kuo Yan, Kai Tsi, Kiau, Kih Tiau, Ki-lin, King, Kioh Twan, Kishi-Mojin, Kua Fu, K'uei, Kw' Ên, Kylin, Lei, Lei Chen-Tzu, Li No Zha, Lu, Luan, Lung, Lung Wang, Lwan, Ma Mien, Nieh-Erh Kuo Yan, Niu T'ou, Nu Kwa, Oriental Dragon, P' Êng, Pai Lung, Pangu, Ping Feng, Poh, Proper Conduct Dragon, Pyong, Rainbird, Rou Shou, San-Shen Kuo Yan, San-Shou Kuo Yan, Sea Buddhist Priest, Shang Yung, Shen Lung, Shen-Nung, Shui Ying, Sin You, Sun Ravens, Takujui, T'ao-Tieh, Thunder Dragon, Ti Lung, Ti-Chiang, T'ien Kou, Ting Ling Kuo Yan, To Fu, Toad (Three-Legged), Too Jon Sheu, Unicorn, Were-Fox, Were-Tiger, Xiang Yao, Yellow Dragon, Yin Chu, Ying Lung, Yoh Shoh, Yu Lung, Yu Siang, Yü-Min Kuo Yan

Czech
Baba Yaga, Golem, Jazi Baba, Jezi Baba, vampire

Denmark
See Scandinavia

Eastern Europe, Including Croatian, Slav, Serbian, Bosnian, and Rumanian Peoples
Djin/n, Endrop (R), Laskowice, Leschia, Ljeschi, Nix, Ohyns, Simargl, Svyatogor, vampire, Veli Joze (C), Vircolac, Vulkodlac (S), Werewolf, Zmag Ognjeni Vuk (B, S)

Egypt
See Islamic countries

England
Agrippa, Albion, Allocamelus, Ancalagon the Black, Anthropophagus, Ascapard, Bandersnatch, Barghest, Basilisk, Bell (1), Bell (2), Bellerus, Bevis, Bistern Dragon, Black Agnes, Black dogs, Black Shuck, Blatant Beast, Bloody-man, Blunderbore, Boguest, Bombomachides, Boo-bagger, Boojum, Borogove, Brag, Brandamour, Brash, Brobdingnagians, Brobinyak, Buckland Shag, Bugbear/e, Caliban, Calygreyhound, Carl of Carlisle, Carn Galver, Cerne Abbas Giant, Cheshire Cat, Child Guzzler, Cockatrice, Colbrand, Cormeilian, Cormoran, Cutty Dyer, Dea, Despair (Giant), Devil's Dandy Dogs, Dogs (Sea), Dracs, Dragon at Uffington, Dragon of Saint Leonard's Forest, Druggen Hill Boggle, Dumbeldors, Dun Cow of Warwick, Dunnie, Ents, Entwives, Fangorn, Fastitocalon, Father Flog and Madam Flog, Fimbrethil, Finglas, Fire-drake, Flandrif, Frankenstein's Monster, Freybug, Galley-trot, giant, Giant Holdfast, Giant of Smeeth, Giant of Wales, Giant Onion, Giantesses of Putney and Fulham, Gilitrutt, Glaurung, Glumdalclitch, Gourmaillon, Great Tall Tailor, Grendel, Grendel's Mother, Grim, Grindylow, Guildhall Giants, Gytrash, Hobyah, Hordeshyrde, Houyhnhms, Inhabitants of Islands near Dondun, Jabberwock, Jenny Greenteeth, Jumar, Laidly Worm, Lambton Worm, Loathly Worm, Long Man of Wilmington, Maul, Mermaid/e, Mock Turtle, Moll Walbee, Monoceros (2), Morholt, Mûmarkil, Nellie Long Arms, Ogre, Oliphaunt, Olog-Hai, Onodrim, Padfoot, Pagan, Peg Powler, Pope, Questing Beast, Red-Legged Scissor-man, Rosmarine, Sandman, Scardyng, Scatha the Worm, Sciapod/s, Shag Foal, Shelob, Shuck, Skriker, Slay-good, Smaug the Golden, Snark, Stellio, Tall Agrippa, Tatter Foal, Thundel, Tom Dockin, Torogs, Town Giants, Trash, Troll, Ungoliant, Unicorn, Uruks, Urulóki, Wade, Wandil, Wandlebury Giant, Wandlimb the Lightfooted, Wantley (The Dragon of), Wayland Smith, Werewolf, Wildman, Wode Worm of Linton, Woglog, Wyvern, Yahoo, Yale, Zaratan
Britain—General: Amphiptere, Belagog, Bogyman, Bran, Corineus, Cormelian, Goemagot, Gog and Magog, Gogmagog, Gorm, Morholt, Nabon, Sea Horse, Stoorworm, Taulurd

Estonia
Äi, Äijätär, Äijo, Ajatar, Ancient One, Cows of Näkki, Guardian of the Fishes, Koerakoonlased, Näkineitsi, Näkineiu, Näkki, Nökk, Phantom of the Lake, Pisuhänd, Tulihänd, Vanapagan

Europe, Including Medieval Europe
Abath, Abominable Snowman, Achlis, Acipenser, Akhekhu, Alchendic, Alicorn, Aloés, Ambize, Amphiptere, Amphisbaena, Amphisien, Amphivena, Aspidochelone, Aspis, Baba Iaga, Bagwyn, Balena, Baphomet, Barometz, Basilcoc, Basilisk, Behemoth, Bicorne, Bishop Fish, Bonnacon, Borametz, Bulchin, Busse, Callitrice, Calopus, Camel-Leopard, cannibal, Carbuncle, Cat-Fish, Cath Paluc, Catoblepas, Celphie, centaur, Centycore, Cerastes, Chapalu, Chichevache, Christopher (Saint), Cockatrice, Cock-fish, Corocotta, Cynocephali, Draconcopedes, Dragon (Ethiopian), Dragon (Occidental), Dragon-Tygre, Dragon-wolf, Drake, Eale, Echeneis, Epimacus, Falcon-fish, Fastitocalon, Fenix, Fierabras, Fire-drake, Forneus, Gambrivius, Giant, Golem, Griffin, Grumbo, Grylio, Haiit, Hare (Sea), Heliodromos, Hemicynes, Hercules, Hercules Libyus, Herminon, Hippocamp, Hippocerf, Hippogryph, Hornworm, Hunnus, Huspalim, Hydrippus, Hydrus, Ichthyocentaur, Ichthyophagi, Idrus, Ingaevon, Istaevon, Jaculus, Jall, Jeduah, Jidra, Lamie, Leucrotta, Licorn, Lion-Griffon, Loathly Lady, Lycanthrope, Lycopodium, Lynx, Lyon-Poisson, Mancomorion, Manticore, Man-Tiger, Mantiserra, Marine Boar, Masus, Memecoleous, Mermaid/e, Merman, Mimick Dog, Monk Fish, Monoceros (2), Monocoli, Monoscelans, Murex, Nependis, ogre, ogress, Ooser, Opinicus, Palug's Cat, Parandus, Phoenix, Pontarf, Questing Beast, Ravenna Monster, Re'em, Sadhuzag, Safat, Salamander, Satyral, Satyre-Fish, Sciapod/s, Scitalis, Scolopendra, Scythian Lamb, Sea Hog, Sea-Dog, Sea-Lion, Serpent of Isa (Flying), Serra, Sirena (2), Snake Griffon, Sphinx, Stomach-Faces, Suevus, Syren, Tarandrus, Teutanes, Thanacth, Thingut, Town Giants, Tragopan, Triton, Tyger, Tytea Magna, unicorn, Urgan, Urus, vampire, Vandaluus, Vegetable Lamb of Tartary, Vurm, Werewolf, Wildman, Wodehouse, Woodwose, Wooser, Wyvern, Yale, Ypotamis, Ziphius

Faroe Islands
See Scandinavia

Finland
Aiatar, Antero Vipunen, Joukahainen, Kalevanpojat, King of the Fishes, Louhi, Näkinneito, Näkki, Nøkke, Queen of the Fishes, Saivo-Neita, Sjötroll, Stalo, Surma, Tursus, Vuokho

France
Ænotherus, Amduscias, Arassas, Balan, Basilic, Bayard, Beast, Bisclaveret, Bleiz-garv, Bringuenarilles, Bruyer, Capalus, Centicore, Chalbroth, Chernubles de Munigre, Cheval Bayard, Cocqcigrues, Croquemitaine, Cyclopedes, Den-Bleiz, Dis Samothes, Dragon (Occidental), Enay, Eryx, Etion, Faribroth, Ferragut, Fierabras, Gabbara, Galatea, Galehaut, Galemelle, Gargam, Gargamelle, Gargantua, Gargouille, Gayoffe, Gemmagog, Giant, Giant of Mont Saint Michel, Goliath, Gos et Magos, Grandgousier, Guivre, Happemousche, Hercules, Herensugue, Hok Braz, Hurtaly, Ki Du, La Velue, Laideronette, Lamia, Lou Carcolh, Loup garou, Lustucru (Le Grand), Mélisande, Melusine, Micromégas, Morguan, Offotus, Ogre, Pantagruel, Peluda, Père Fouettard, Porus,

Quaresmeprenant, Queen of the Waters, Ravenna Monster, Rhinocéros, Riquet à la Houppe, Rongeur d' Os, Sarabroth, Secundilla, Serpentin Vert, Tarasque, Tartaro, Torto, Tourmentine, Town Giants, Uglessa, Vouivre, Were-Dog, Werewolf, Wild Beast of Gévaudan, Wildman, Wivre, Wyvern, Yannig, Youdic Dogs

Germany
Old Teutonic: Aavak, Alsvid, Alswider, Arrak, Audumla, Fafnir, Fire-drake, Fornjotr, Giant, Hakenmann, Hrimfaxi, Jotun, Logi, Midgardsorm/r, Skinfaxi, Sleipnir, Svadilfari, Thurses

Modern: Aufhocker, Bockman, Golem, Great Tall Tailor, Hakenmann, Kinder-fresser, Kinderschrecker, Monoceros Marinus, Nigelung, Nix, Papstesel, Puk, Red-Legged Scissor-man, Schilbung, Werewolf

Greece, Modern
Alous, Amphisbaena, Aspidochelone, Basilisk, Busse, Callicantzari, Cynocephali, Dragon (Epidaurian), Griffin, Kalkes, Lamia, Lycanthrope, Manticore, Rizos, Stringes, Were-Boar, Werewolf. *See also* Classical mythology

Greenland
Adlet, Auvekoejak, Az-i-wû-gûm-ki-mukh-'ti, Disemboweller, Erqigdlit, Havstrambe, Imap Umassoursa, Margygr (2)

Hungary
Beast, Sarkany, vampire

Iceland
See Scandinavia

Indian Subcontinent
India: Aeternae, Ahi, Airavana, Airāvata, Akūpāra, Ananta, Anjana, Apalala, Arusha and Arushi, Asipatra, Bali, Betikhân, Bhainsāsura, Bhima, Bull of Inde, Cartazonon, Chitra-ratha, Dadhikra, Daitya, Danavas, Dharmapālas, Dhol, Dhrana, Dhumavarna, Dragon (Occidental), Emusha, Etasa, Face of Glory, Gandarva, Gandhabbas, Gandharvas, Gara, Garuda, Ghoul/e, Goat (Sea), Guhyaka, Hariti, Hayagriva, Hidimba, Himapandara, Horses of the Sun, Jala-Turga, Jataya, Kabanda, Kaitabha, Kaliya, Kama-Dhenu, Karkadan, Keinnara, Keshi, Kimpurushas, Kinnara, Kirata, Kumbhakarna, Kumuda, Kurma, Loha-Mukha, Lokapala Elephants, Mada, Madhu, Mahapadma, Mahisha, Makara, Muchalinda, Muchukunda, Naga/s, Nagini Besandi, Nagini/s, Nandi, Nandini, Nara, Nee-gued, Nyan, Pey, Poqhirāj, Pundarika, Purusha, Pushpadanta, Rahu, Rakshasa/s, Sampati, Samvarta, Sarvabhauma, Saumanasa, Savala, Sesha, Sevienda, Sharama, Sharameyas, Simurgh, Sinhika, Sisupala, Supratika, Surabhi, Suryabhauma, Takshaka, Tumburu, Ugrasura, Unnati, Vairochana, Vamana, Vasuki, Verethraghna, Virabandra, Viradha, Virupaksha, Visvavasu, Vritra, Were-Tiger

Nepal: Abominable Snowman, Meh-Teh, Unnati, Yeti
Pakistan: Apalala
Sri Lanka: Jataya

Tibet: Abominable Snowman, Ch'os-skyon, Dharmapālas, Dzu-teh, Hayagriva, Kere, Khyung, rTa-mgin, Serou, sGrolma, Tsopo, Vajravina, Yeti

Indonesia
Anantaboga, Anjing Ajak, Arimbi, Barong, Garuda, Gergasi, Jurik, Keinnara, Kinnara, Macan Gadungan, Makara, Naga Pahoda, Naga/s, Reksoso, Were-Crocodile, Were-Tiger, Wikramadatta

Iran (Persia)
See Ancient realms

Ireland
Aillén Trechenn, Aonbárr, Apocalyptic Beast, Balor, Beast of Lettir Dallan, Bébinn, Biast, Bledlochtana, Bledmall, Boar of Beann-Gulbain, Bocanách, Bruckee, Cailleach Beinne Bric, Cailleach bera, Caoránach, Cichol, Ciudach, Coinchenn, Coinn Iotair, Corc-chluasask, Cornu, Crom Crumh Chomnaill, Dhoya, Dillus Farfog, Diwrnach Wyddel, Dobharchú, Donn of Cuálgne, Dorraghow, Dragon (Occidental), Dragon of the Apocalypse, Duineach, Énbarr, Fachan, Fachtna Fáthach, Fer Caille, Fomor/s, Gaborchend, Giant, Glas Gaibleanir, Goborchinu, Goll Mac Carbada, Gruagach, Grugyn Silver Bristles, Hounds of Rage, Ingcél Caech, Írusán, Jasconius, Keeronagh, Leprocaun, Liban, Llwydawg the Hewer, Lochlonnach, Merrow, Mhorag, Midcháin, Miodhchaoin, Mochaen, Moruadh, Muircartach, Muirdris, Muir-Gheilt, Murdhuacha, Murrisk, Nuckalevee, Oilliphéist, Ox of Dil, Peiste, Phooka, Piast/s, Pooka, Rosualt, Saidthe Suaraighe, Saint Attracta's Monster, Samhghubha, Searbhán, Sínach, Suileach, Suire, Tarbh Uisge, Torc Triath, Trechend, Twrch Trwyth, Uath

Islamic Countries
General to Most: Afreet, Borak (Al), Dalham, Djin/n, Efreet, Ghawwas, Ghoul/e, Gulah, Hofafa, Jin, Kujata, Mi'raj (Al-), Murghi-i-Ādami, Nun, Qutrub, Roc, So'la, Taranushi, Zägh, Zaratan

Egypt: Akhekhu, Chaarmarouch, Diff Errebi, Djin/n, Fastitocalon, Ghaddar, Hamou Ukaiou, Khadem Quemquoma, Lalla Mira, Maezt-Dar l' Oudou, Moulay Abdelkader Djilani, Redjal el Marja, Sidi Hamou. *See also* Ancient Egypt

Morocco: Aicha Kandida
Saudi Arabia: Angka, Ghawwas, Hofafa, Jin, So'la
Syria: Kul
Turkey: Kargas, Shar-Mar, Were-Boar
Yemen: Ghaddar, Nashas, Shiqq

Isle of Man (United Kingdom)
Beisht Kione, Ben Varrey, Berrey Dhone, Buggane, Cabyll-Uisge, Cabyll-Ushtey, Caillagh ny Groamagh, Dinny Mara, Eačh Uisge, Fenodyree, Foawr, Glashtin, Goayr Heddagh, Mauthe Dhoog, Nikyr, Phynnodderee, Taroo Ushtey, Theroo Ushta, Yn Foldyr Gastey

Israel, Including Jewish and Hebrew Traditions
Anakim, Bar Yachre, Basilisk, Behemoth, Daughters of Cain, Dragon (Occidental), Enim, Gibborim, Gog, Golem, Goliath, Hapalit, Leviathan, Livjatan, Nephilim, Nimrod, Noah, Og, Palet, Rager, Rahab, Re'em, Rephaim, Serpent of Eden, Tannin, Zamzumin, Ziz, Zuzim

Italy
Alous, Araxa, Araxa Junior, Astreus, Bayard, Caligorante, Capaneus, Crana, Cranus, Egeon, Flying Fish, Giant, Giant of Trapani, Granaus, Griffin, Hippogryph, Japetus Junior, Jovis Bellus, Jovis Saga, Lupo Manaro, Macrus, Morgante, Nembrotus, Noachids, Nymbrotus, Oceanus (2), ogre, Ogyges, Omo Nero, Orc, Papillon, Papstesel, Pongo, Pope Ass, Prisca, Priscaraxe, Priscus, Prometheus, Ravenna Monster, Regina, Sevienda, Strigae, Tages, Thetis, Tubal, Tuyscon Gigas, Tytan/s, Tytea Magna, Werewolf, Zimbardo

Japan
Baku, Bird-Man, cannibal, Centipede, Dragon Kings, Dragon of Izumo, Eight-Forked Serpent of Koshi, Gaki, Giant, Hai Riyo, Ho-o, Jinshin Uwo, Jishin-Mushi, Kami, Kappa, Karasa Tengu, Karitei-mo, Kijo, Kirin, Kirni, Kiyo, Kojin, Konoha Tengu, Kudan, Kurdan, Moshiriikkwechep, Mountain Man, Mountain Woman, Ningyo, O Goncho, ogre, Oriental Dragon, Otohime, Phantom Cat, Pheng, Raicho, Raiju, Raitaro, Rinjin, Ryujin, Samebito, Schachi Hoko, Serpent of Omi, Shojo, Spider, Spider-Woman, Takujui, Tatsu, Tengu/s, Tobi Tatsu, Toyotama, Tsuchi-Gumo, unicorn, Uwabami, vampire, Were-Fox, Were-Tiger, Yata Garasu, Yofune-Nushi

Korea
Dragon-Carp

Lapp/Sami Peoples
See Scandinavia

Latvia
Koerakoonlased, Pukis, Vilkacis

Lithuania
Beast, Kaukas, Koerakoonlased, Milžinas, Vilkatas, Vilkolakis, Werewolf

Malaysia (East and West)
Bujanga, Gerjis, Golden Dragon Naga Mas, Jin, Jin Gendang, Jin Karaja'an, Jin Naubat, Jin Nemfiri, Jin Sembuana, Naga Mas, Naga/s, Nagini/s, Pontianak, Puterei Sembaran Gunung, Raja Naga, Sa-Gempar 'Alam, Sa-Gertak Rang Bumi, Sa-Gunchang Rang Bumi, Sa-Halilintar, Sa-Lakun Darah, Sang Gadin, Sang Gala Raja, Sa-Raja Jin, Sa-Rukup Rang Bumi, Sa-Tumbok Rang Bumi, Tioman, vampire, Were-Tiger

Melanesia
Abaia, Abere, Agunua, Buata, cannibal, Hatuibwari, Kaia, Nevinbimbaau, Rainbow Serpent, Ri, serpent, vampire, Vis, Walutahanga

Micronesia, Including Caroline Islands and Gilbert and Ellice Islands
Giant, King Auriaria, Lioumere, Puntan, Rigi, Riiki, Ruki

Morocco
See Islamic countries

Netherlands (Holland)
Giant/s, Goliath, Town Giants

New Zealand
Horomatangi, Hotu-puku, Huru-kareao, Ihu-maataotao, Kurangai Tuku, Lumakaka, Matau, Parata, Pouakai, Poukai, Ruahine-mata-maori, Ruuruhi-kerepoo, Tama-o-hoi, Tanihwa

North Africa and Middle East
See Islamic countries

Norway
See Scandinavia

Peru
See Central and South America

Philippine Islands
Boroka, Bungisngis, Buso, Cafre, cannibal, Kafre, Mauleon, Pugot

Poland
Bialozar, Golem, Ienzababa, Jezda, Monk Fish, vampire

Polynesia, Including Cook Islands, Fiji, Hawaii, Tahiti
cannibal (F), Degei (F), Flaming Teeth (F), Kamapua'a (H), Moko (CI), Ngani-vatu (F), Ngutu-Lei (F), Rainbow Serpent (F), serpent (F), Tangata, Te Tuna (T), Tui Delai Gau (F), Tumu-Ra'i-Fuena (T), Tu-Te-Wehiwehi (CI)

Portugal
See Spain

Russia and Russian Federated States, Including Siberia and Ukraine
Ai Tojon (S), Alicha (S), Alklha (S), Alkonost, Almas (S), Arakho (S), Baba Iaga, Barushka Matushka, cannibal, Chudo-Yudo, Firebird, Giant, Gorynich, Goryshche, Kashchei, Koshchei, Kosmatushka, Kreutzet, Leshak, Leshii, Lesnoi, Lisun, Lockski Nesski Monsterovich, Mikula, Naul, Palesmurt, Ptitsy-Siriny, serpent, Simorg (R and U), Sirin, Sivushko, Solovei Rakhmatich, Svyatogor, Tugarin, Unicorn, Upir, vampire, Vodianoi, Vodnik, Vörysmort, Vseslav, Were-Bear, Were-Dog, Werewolf, Zmei Gorynich

Scandinavia
Denmark: Havfrue, Havman, Monk Fish, Nickel, Nøkke
Faroe Islands: Nickar
Iceland: Beigad, Haikur, Nickur, Ninnir, Nix, Nykur, Scoffin, Skrimsl, Troll
Lapp/Sami Peoples (northern regions of Scandinavia): Saivo-Neita, Stalo, Vuokho
Modern, General to All: Circhos, Dragon (Occidental), Giant, Havhest, Huld, Kraken, Lindorm, Mermaid/e, Nicker, Nicor, Nikke, Nix, Sea Horse, Stoorworm, Sykraken, Troll

Norse Legends: Aavak, Aegir, Alsvid, Alswider, Angboda, Arrak, Arvaak, Audumla, Aurgelmir, Battleswine, Baugi, Bel (2), Bergbui, Bergelmir, Bergjarl, Bergriser, Bestia, Bolthorn, Borr, Dragon (Occidental), Drifta, Eggther, Fafnir, Fárbauti, Fenrir, Fiorgyn, Fire Giants, Fornjotr, Freki, Frost Giants, Frosti, Garm, Geirröd, Gerd, Geri and Freki, Giant, Giantess, Gilling, Goldbristles, Gollinkambi, Gridr, Gulinbursti, Gunnlod, Gygr, Gymir, Hafgygr, Hildesuin, Hordeshyrde, Hraesvelg, Hrimfaxi, Hrimthurses, Hrodvitnir, Hrungnir, Hrym, Hugi, Hugin, Hymir, Iarnsaxa, Iörmungandr, Jarnsaxa, Johul, Jörd, Jormungandr, Jotun, Juternajesta, Juternsaxa, Kari, Logi, Magni, Margygr (1), Midgardsorm/r, Mimir, Modi, Muninn, Muspel, Nidhogg, Orm, Sachrimnir, Senjemand, Serpent of Midgard, Skadi, Skinfaxi, Skoll, Skrymir, Skrymsli, Sleipnir, Slidringtanni, Snoer, Starkadr, Sutr, Suttung, Svadilfari, Tanngniortr, Tanngrisnir, Thiassi, Thökk , Thrym, Thurses, Utgard-Loki, Vasty, Vithafnir, Ymir

Norway: Havfinë, Havhest, Huld, Kraken, Marine Sow, Nykkjen, Roshwalr, Rosmarus, Rosmer, Ruszor, Sahab, Seljordsorm, Sjøorm, Swamfisk, Sykraken, Troll, Troll Fisk, Vuokho

Sweden: Drake, Gulon, Jerff, Lindorm, Näcken, Nix, Serpent King, Stoorworm, Storsjöodjuret

Scotland, Including Hebrides, Orkney and Shetland Islands
Arachd, Arrach, Athach, Aughisky, Beannach-nimhe, Beithir, Biasd Bheulach, Biasd na Srognig, Big Ears, Black dog, Blue Men of the Minch, Boobrie, Burach Bhadi, Cailleach Beinne Bric, Cailleach Bheur, Cailleach Uragaig, Cat Sith, Ce Sith, Cìrein Cròin, Ciudach, Coluinn Gun Cheann, Corc-chluasask, Curtag Mhòr a' Chuain, Direach, Eač Uisge, Ech-Uskya, Fir Chreig, Fuath, Giant, Giantess of Loch Ness, Giants of Callanish, Glaistig, Glas Gaibleanir, Gruagach, Henkies, Kelpy, Lailoken, Lammikin, Loch Ness Monster, Long Lankin, Maighdean uaine, Mermaid/e, Mhorag, Mial Mhòr a' Huain, Monster of Loch Awe, Muilearteach, Neugle, Nickneven, Peallaidh, Red Etin, Shoopiltie, Sianach, Tarbh Uisge, Uile Bhéisd a' Chuain, Unicorn, Urisk, Vough, Water-bull, Wizard's Shackle

Spain, Portugal, Including Basque Region and Canary Islands
Alifanfaron, Basajaun, Basilisk, Beast, Bicha, Bobalicón, Cabezudo, Caravinaigre, Carneros, Coca, Coco, Cuelebre, Giant, Guita, Herensugue, Lamia, Lob Ombre, Lob Omem, Manticore, Mermaid/e, Ogre, Orribes, Sirena (1), Tarasca, Tartaro, Torto, Zangarrón

Sweden
See Scandinavia

Switzerland
Apotharni, Butatsch-ah-Ilgs, Elbst, Nix, Serpent of the Reuss, Stollenwurm

Tanzania
See Africa

Thailand

Con Trăm Nu' ó' c , Elephant-tiger, Galon, Giant, Keinnara, Khrut, Kinnara, Makara, Naga/s, Nagini/s, serpent, Tipaka

Turkey

Busse, Cercopes, Chimera, Kargas, Were-Boar, Werewolf

United States

Native American Peoples: Amala, Amarok, Anaye, Ancient Serpent, Angont, Aniwye, Antukai, Apotamkin, Asin, Bapets, Be Chasti, Big Fish of Iliamna, Big heads, Big Man-eater, Big Owl, Bigfoot, Binaye Ahani, Bingbuffer, Black Devil, Bmola, Bogey, Chahnameed, Dahdahwat, Deadoendjadases, Dehotgohsgayeh, Delgeth, Djieien, Doonongaes, Dzoavits, Emogoalekc, Fillyloo, Fire Dragon, Flying Heads, Fsti capcaki, Gaasyendietha, Ganiagwaihegowa, Ga-oh, Gather-on-the-water, Geldegwsets, Golligog, Gougou, Gowrow, Grandfather, Great Horned Serpent, Great Lynx, Great Tiger, Gugu, Gugwe, Haakapainizi, Haduigona, Hagondes, Hairy-Man, Hakulaq, Hayicanako, Horned Alligator, Horned Serpent, Horned Water Serpent, Human Snakes, Hvcko Capko, Ice Giants, Indacinga, Irraq, Iya, Jokao, Kashehotapolo, Keelut, Kichiknebik, Kinepikwa, Kitchi-at'Husis, Kitzinackas, Kiwahkw, Kogukhpuk, Kolowisi, Kukuweaq, Lenapizka, Little Manitou, Long Ears, Long Nose, Manetuwi-Rusi-Pissi, Manitou Kinebik, Másaw, Master of the Fishes, Meshekenabec, Metal Old Man, Mi-Ni-Wa-Tu, Mishipizhiw, Misiganebic, Misikinubick, Missipissy, Mitchipissy, Moogie, Msi-Kinepikwa, Nalmuqtse, Nihniknoovi, Nunyenunc, On Niont, Onditachiae, Ongwe Ias, Oshädagea, Owner-of-a-Bag, Paiyuk, Pal-rai-yuk, Pot-Tilter, Qaxdascidi, Sasquatch, Seatco, serpent, Siats, Skahnowa, Skatene, Slimy Slim, Snawfus, Split-Faced Being, Stcemqestcint, Stikini, Stonecoats, Sus Lika, Tall Man, Teehooltsoodi, Teelget, Thelgeth, Tieholtsodi, Tinmiukpuk, Tisikh puk, To Kas, Tsanahale, Tsavoojok, Twisted face, Tzeltal, Ugjuknarpak, Uhepono, Umai-Hulhlya-wit, Uncegila, Underground Panther, Unhcegila, Unktehi, vampire, Wakandagi, Wakandagi Pezi, Wakinyan, Was, Waukheon, Waziya, Weewilmekq, Wendigo, White Panther, Wikatcha, Wishpoosh, Witico, Wiwilemekw, Wry Face, Wuchowsen, Yeitso, Yenrish, Zuzeca

Other American Peoples: Argopelter, Augerino, Axehandle Hound, Babe the Blue Ox, Bigfoot, Bildad, Bunyan (Paul), Cactus Cat, Champ, Cuba, Cuter-Cuss, Dew-Mink, Ding Ball, Fearsome Critters, Giddy Fish, Gillygaloo, Glawackus, Godaphro, Goofang, Goofus, Gouger, Great Galactic Ghoul, Gumberoo, Guyanoosa, Guyascutus, Gwinter, Hidebehind, Hodag, Hoop Snake, Humility, Hunkus, Kickle Snifter, King Kong, Leprocaun, Lucive, Lunkus, Monster of Brompton, Moskitto, Mountain Stem-Winder, Mugwump, Philamaloo Bird, Pinnacle Grouse, Prock Gwinter, Rickaboo Racker, Rockabore, Roperite, Rubberado, Rumptifusel, Sauger, Shagamaw, Shmoo, Sidehill Dodger, Sidehill Ganger, Sideswipe, Sidewinder, Slimy Slim, Sliver Cat, Snow Snake, Splinter Cat, Squonk, Teakettler, Tripoderoo, vampire, Were-Hare, Werewolf, Whappernocker, Whimpus, Windigo (1)

Venezuela

See Central and South America

West Indies

See Caribbean

Zambia

See Central and South Africa

CPSIA information can be obtained
at www.ICGtesting.com
Printed in the USA
LVOW03*1538211016
509748LV00019B/240/P